Delphi 2 Multimedia Adventure Set

Delphi 2 Multimedia Adventure Set

Scott Jarol

Dan Haygood

Chris D. Coppola

CORIOLIS GROUP BOOKS

Publisher	Keith Weiskamp
Project Editor	Scott Palmer
Copy Editor	Maggy Miskell
Interior Design	Brad Grannis
Layout Production	Rob Mauhar
Proofreader	Michael Stabler
Indexer	Caroline Parks

Trademarks: Microsoft is a trademark and Windows is a registered trademark of Microsoft Corporation. All other brand names and product names included in this book are trademarks, registered trademarks, or trade names of their respective holders.

Copyright © 1996 by The Coriolis Group, Inc.

All rights reserved.

Reproduction or translation of any part of this work beyond that permitted by section 107 or 108 of the 1976 United States Copyright Act without the written permission of the copyright owner is unlawful. Requests for permission or further information should be addressed to The Coriolis Group, 7339 E. Acoma Drive, Suite 7, Scottsdale, Arizona 85260.

The Coriolis Group, Inc.
7339 E. Acoma Drive, Suite 7
Scottsdale, AZ 85260
Phone: (602) 483-0192
Fax: (602) 483-0193
Web address: http://www.coriolis.com

ISBN 1-883577-64-0 : $44.99
Printed in the United States of America

10 9 8 7 6 5 4 3 2 1

Contents

Introduction   xiii

Chapter 1   The Delphi-Multimedia Connection   1

Go Interactive   2
Exploring the Windows 95 Multimedia System   2
Windows Programming—A Black Art?   6
The Visual Difference   7
The Essential Delphi   12
Intrinsic Multimedia   17
The MediaPlayer Control   22
Missing Links   25
What's Next?   25

Chapter 2   Foundations of Hypermedia Display   27

The Explosion of Hypermedia   28
Organized Chaos—The Magic of Hyperlinking   29
Hyperlinking on the Information Superhighway   33
Creating Text Links   36
Before Hypertext, Text   41

Chapter 3   Building a Hypermedia Engine   65

Handling Hypertext   66
Creating the Form   70
   Creating the MiscLib Unit   71
   Units: A Classic Encapsulation   73

Basic Font Support   76
Relating an HTML Font to a Windows Font   78
Measuring Text   78
Formatted Text   82
Segments of Formatted Hypertext   82
Overriding Destroy   89
Dissecting HTML   90
Parsing HTML   94
HTML, At Last   101
Breaking Formatted Text into Lines   108
The Line-Breaking Mechanism   112
Starting a New Line   118
Displaying HTML Text on the Control   120
The Event Response Code for Hyper I   124
One Giant Step for Us, One Small Step Towards Hypertext   129

The Building Blocks of Life   129

A Basic HTML Vocabulary   130
Running Hyper II   132
A Parsing Class to Make Life Easier   132
Hyperlinking Data Structures   138
A Place for HTML   144
HTML Special Characters   150
Parsing HTML Tags   155
Modifications to the Units Font and FmtText   160
Modifications to DispBuf   161
Mods to Main   168
A Stopping Place?   168

Finishing the Hypertext Engine   169

Running Hyper III   170
Adding More Font Capability   174
Supporting Preformatted Text   185
Named Destinations in Preformatted Text   201
Hyperlinking in the User Interface   201
Hyperjumps and URLs   206

A Firm Foundation for Nimble Navigation   209

Chapter 4 Introducing the Windows 95 Multimedia System 211

A Look at the High-Level 212
Adding Multimedia to the HTML Hypertext Engine 213
   Setting Up for Multimedia 214
Exploring the Windows Multimedia System 219
   A Tour of the Multimedia API 219
   Using High-Level Multimedia Functions: MessageBeep and PlaySound 220
   Creating the MCIPlay I Project 223
   Running the Updated MCIPlay I Project 225
Scratching the Surface 229

Chapter 5 Inside the Windows Multimedia System 231

Using the MCI 231
   Making WAVes with mciSendString and mciSendCommand 233
   Creating the MCIPlay2 Project 237
   A Closer Look at mciSendString and mciGetErrorString 240
   Expanding the MCIPlay2 Project 243
Combing the Depths of the Low-Level Audio Functions 248
   The Mysteries of RIFF Files 248
   The WAV File Structure 251
   A Peek at the Multimedia I/O Functions 252
   Wrapping up the API 255
   Reading and Processing a WAV File 256
   Playing the WAV File 272
The View from the Cellar 281

Chapter 6 Exploring Imaging—From Pixels to Palettes 283

The Graphics Device interface 283
   Display Contexts 284
   Understanding Bitmaps 284

    Windows Color   285
    The Magic of Color Palettes   285
    Inside the Palette Manager   287

Exploring Colors with Delphi   290
    Selecting Colors the Easy Way   291
    Creating the RGB() Program   291
    Using More Colors—Loading a Palette   294
    A Closer Look at Colors   295
    Creating the Palette Program   296
    Using the API to Access Colors   299
    Creating the Palette Edit Program   302
    Modifying the Code   311
    Building the Palette   315
    Plugging in AnimatePalette   317

A Practical Example   318

Chapter 7   Palette Animation and ROPs   321

The Magic of Color Palette Animations   322
    Creating the Marquee Project   322
    Adding the Event Handler Code   322

Pixels and Raster Operations   330
    Creating the NotPen Project   331
    Adding the event handler code   331
    Mixing Pixels   333
    ROPs and the Split System Palette   334
    Processing Bitmaps—Using BitBlt Functions   335
    Creating the BitBltex Project   337
    Adding the Event Handler Code   338
    Creating the ROPs Project   338
    Adding the Event Handler Code   341

Chapter 8   Advanced Imaging— Special Visual Effects   345

Introducing the Dissolve   346
ROPs Revisited   346
    Creating the Rops2 Project   347

Adding the Code   349
Combining Bitmaps   360
   Hunting through Raster Operations   361
Creating the Basic Digital Dissolve   364
   Creating the First Dissolve   364
   Adding the Code   365
   A Closer Look at the First Dissolve   373
   Creating the Palette Aware Dissolve   374
More About the Palettized Dissolve   392

Chapter 9   The Art of Hyperimaging   393

Windows Is Hypermedia!   394
   Using Controls as Pictures   394
   Using Controls as Hotspot Buttons   395
   Uncovering the BitBtn   398
Using Rectangular Window Regions   403
   How the Hotspot Editor Works   405
   Designing the Hotspot Editor   406
   Hotspots   407
   Creating and Closing the Main Form   410
   Setting the Bait—Outlining Hot Regions   412
   Adding the Menu System   416
   Starting and Stopping, as a User   417
   Drawing or Testing?   420
   Saving Hotspots—A Simple Filing System   423
   Retrieving Hotspot Records   425
   Defining the Other Menu Options   432
What's Next?   443

Chapter 10   Hyperimaging: The Next Dimension   445

Mastering Irregular Hotspots   446
   Running the Program—Testing the Polygon Hotspots   447
   Creating the Form   448
   Drawing Polygons   453
   Redrawing Polygons   457

Initialization and Clean-up Code   457
Starting a New Polygon   459
Adding Polygon Hotspots to Images   459
Running the Hotspot Editor   461
Representing and Storing Polygonal Hotspots   462
Drawing Polygonal Hotspots   473
User Interaction With The Editor   476
The Hot Irregular-Spot Editor   479
Hotspots: The Next Generation   488

Chapter 11   Expanding the VB Multimedia Engine   491

Modifying the Form   493
Supporting Referenced Images   494
Loading the Documents' Images   498
Refining the Hypermedia Engine   517
Running the Magic Hypermedia Engine   519
Proportionally-sized Images and their Panels   520
Hotspots and their Region Lists   525
Putting it All Together   532
Extending the Multimedia Engine   540

Chapter 12   The Hypermedia Engine at Work—Building a Web Browser   541

User Interface Issues   542
Repackaging the Hypermedia Engine   543
Modifying the Form   544
Handling In-Line Images with Text   546
Supporting the <IMG> Tag   546
A Picture-Perfect Memory   551
Bringing Pictures In-Line   552
No Time To Reload!   556
Improving the Interface   565
It's a Great Big World (Wide Web) Out There   571

The Internet Connection   571
    Opening the Door: A Brief Introduction to Sockets   573
    Getting Files from the Internet   574
    Using Our Internet Support   579
    A Sense of History   583
    Upgrading the HTML Browser   588

Chapter 13   The Magic of Animation   593

Exploring Cell Animation   594
    Creating the CellAnim Project   594
    Adventures with Sprite Animation   602
    Creating the Sprite1 Project   603
    Animating Sprites with Block Transfer Routines   607
    Creating the Sprite2 Project   608
    Transparent Bitmaps—Sprites and Masks   614
    Developing the Sprite2 program   615
    Making Masks and Sprites Automatically   619
    Creating the MakeMask Project   620

Chapter 14   Better Animation   625

Creating Flicker-Free Animation   625
    Creating the Sprite4 Project   627
    The Sprite Class   638
    The Mechanics of the Sprite4 Project   641
    Running the Program   650
    Improving the Sprite Engine   650
    Creating the Sprite5 Project   651
    Running the Program   672
Enhancing the Sprite Animation   673

Chapter 15   Exploring Waveform Audio   675

Audio: A Potent Medium   676
Checking Out the Options   676

Redbook Audio   676
MIDI   677
Waveform Audio   678
Digital Audio Basics   678
Creating the Wave2 Project   681
Real-Time Audio Effects   704
Introducing WaveMix   705
Cutting Edge Audio Technology   705
Recording Wave Audio   728

Chapter 16   Using the Musical Instrument Digital Interface   733

Everything You Need to Know about MIDI   734
The Musical Connection   734
A Look at MIDI Messages   735
The MIDI Offspring   741
MIDI and Windows   743
MIDI Connections   743
The Windows MIDI Mapper   744
Sending MIDI Messages   749
Receiving MIDI Messages   766
Windows Callbacks   766
Beyond MIDI Basics   785

Appendix A   32-Bit Application Development   787

Appendix B   HTML 3 Reference Guide   793

Appendix C   Using the CD-ROM   823

Introduction

Dan Haygood

Multimedia is everywhere—and not just on CD-ROM. The fastest growing segment of the Internet is the World Wide Web, a global hyperlinked multimedia system. The Web, which is based on a standard document format known as Hypertext Markup Language (HTML), enables anyone with access to the Internet to publish his or her own online multimedia documents, with links to any number of other Web pages or Internet resources.

Besides the revolution in multimedia, there's also been a revolution in the tools we use. Windows 95 rushed us all into the brave new world of 32-bit applications, while Borland International's Delphi 2 made 32-bit programming power faster and easier than ever before.

If you're new to Windows multimedia programming, Delphi 2, or both, don't worry! We'll make learning the Windows Multimedia System as easy as possible. We will, however, assume that you have at least a basic knowledge of Windows and Delphi programming. Since several existing books introduce and thoroughly explain the concepts of programming in Delphi, we won't rehash them here. We will, however, discuss why we've chosen Delphi 2 as a multimedia development system, and review concepts that pertain directly to the projects in this book. We'll work our way up from basic principles to working systems, so even if you're just getting started, you'll pick up quite a bit along the way.

You'll learn the basics of animation, sound effects, and music. You'll learn how to use Delphi 2 with HTML. You'll learn how to use components and OLE in your multimedia programs. You'll learn about API calls that put the full power of Windows 95's Multimedia System at your fingertips. And you'll learn the secrets of special effects, raster operations, and waveform audio in a way that you won't find anywhere else.

What You Will Need

To complete most of the projects in this book, all you need is Windows 95, Delphi 2, and a multimedia-capable PC. To produce commercial multimedia titles, however, you'll need to invest in all kinds of stuff: a scanner, one or more image editing and drawing programs, an animation program, a WAV audio editing program, and a video digitizer and a video source, such as a VCR, camcorder, or both.

If your PC system isn't already equipped for multimedia—although most new PCs are—we recommend that you buy one of the many upgrade kits, now available through almost all PC vendors. We've done it both from individual components and from kits, and the upgrade kits can really save you from a configuration nightmare.

How This Book Is Structured

The most logical way to organize this book would be in sections—sound, images, video, and so on. But that would be too dull. Instead, we've mixed up the material a little, working through all the topics, and gradually adding features to the multimedia engine along the way.

We'll begin, in Chapter 1, with a basic introduction to using Delphi 2 for multimedia programming. Chapters 2 through 5 get you started building a Windows 95 multimedia engine, and introduce more of the basic concepts you'll need for the rest of your multimedia adventure.

Chapters 6 through 10 start you off with basic techniques for animation and imaging, then guide you step by step as you master techniques of increasing power and sophistication. Chapters 11 and 12 show you how to expand your hypermedia engine and create a basic Web browser that incorporates the ideas you've learned.

Chapters 13 through 16 take you all the way up to professional-level techniques for animation and sound, including waveform audio and MIDI. Finally, the book's appendices give you more in-depth general background on 32-bit programming and HTML, the core language of the World Wide Web.

It's going to be a rip-roaring good time, with lots of surprises along the way. So buckle up! Your multimedia adventure is about to begin!

Acknowledgments

So many people have contributed to this project that it's hard to remember everyone, but a few names stand out. We offer our deepest gratitude to Keith Weiskamp, Jeff Duntemann, and Scott Palmer, who shepherded this project from conception to completion. Several artists have contributed to this book, including Susan Haygood, who drew the moth sprites for the animation programs; Kane Clevenger of Tier 3 Productions, who drew the dictionary pages for the FLIPBOOK programs; and James Cowlin, whose gorgeous landscape photos appear in several program examples.

We also wish to thank Nels Johnson of The San Francisco Canyon Company, who contributed his knowledge and insight into the profoundly technical world of digital video, and Arthur Edstrom of Arctic Software, Inc., whose VB MIDI Piano program was modified for Chapter 16. Many thanks also to The Coriolis Group book production team, including Michelle Stroup, Brad Grannis, Rob Mauhar, and Kim Eoff.

We are all indebted to the companies that contributed clip art for the companion CD-ROM. These include Adobe Systems, AJS Publishing, Inc., Andover Advanced Technologies, Cambium Development Corp., Crisp Technology, Inc., Data Techniques, Inc., First Byte, Interactive Publishing Corp., Media-Pedia Video Clips, Inc., Media Architects, Microsoft Corp., Rainbow Imaging, Software Interphase, and Ulead Systems, Inc.

Scott Jarol

I want to thank Scott Jarol for allowing me the opportunity to write this book, and co-author Chris Coppola for his generous efforts writing the book's graphics chapters and later MCI chapters. Special thanks go to Dr. George Wood of GetNet International for sharing his expertise in technical review of the hypermedia engine chapters and his concise explanation of sockets in Chapter 12. My brother, Hal, kindly lent his editorial skill and copy-editing ability to some of the same chapters. Finally, without the support of my wife, Susan (a.k.a. "Rocky") and daughter Kari, who turned one year old when the manuscript was complete, this book could never have been written.

Dan Haygood

Sara, without your support, I could not have done this. You put as much work into supporting me as I did completing the book. Thanks.

Chris Coppola

Chapter 1

Delphi and Windows 95 make perfect partners for developing all types of multimedia applications.

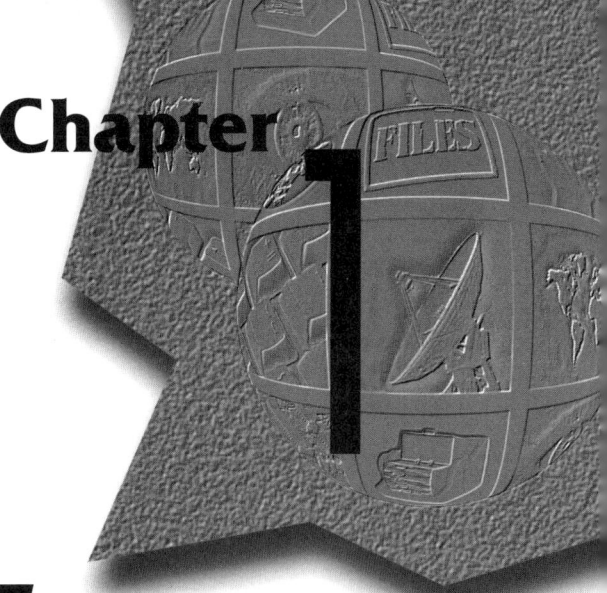

The Delphi-Multimedia Connection

Dan Haygood

Ah, multimedia! Sit back, throw your feet up on your desk, fire up your computer, and get lost in a world of adventure and fun—a world where you can explore historical events and fascinating places by watching videos and participating in interactive stories. Or journey into the Grand Canyon and raft down the awesome rapids of the Colorado river. That's multimedia as it should be. But when you try to create apps like this, you'll discover multimedia development is practically a black art, and you'll need all the help you can get.

Gone are the days when a program required only a few algorithms, a database, and some interface code in order to come to life. As multimedia takes PCs into the twenty-first century, traditional programming languages and development tools alone simply won't cut it anymore. With sound, music, video, 3D animation, scrolling images, hypertext, and online services to support, you'll need a visual development environment that provides the right multimedia connections.

And that's where Delphi comes in. If you used a non-visual (and I mean that in a very specific sense of the word) language like plain old C++ to develop multimedia apps, you could drown in the low-level technical minutiae of Windows, event-driven, message-passing architecture. And using any dedicated multimedia authoring system locks you into its own way of doing things (but, you certainly have your pick of the many packages competing for the spotlight). With Delphi, you have the best of both worlds—let your creativity soar!

Go Interactive

The multimedia we'll be exploring in this book isn't the boring "slide show" stuff that first emerged when the multimedia world arrived at the PC's doorstep. Because the demand for multimedia products has been high, the temptation for just throwing "shovel ware" software together on a CD-ROM has been unavoidable. Such products still permeate the market. Our interest is in creating adventurous, interactive multimedia that brings new worlds to the user, not just filmstrip presentations with sound.

Imagine being able to watch any part of a basketball game from any player's position. Put yourself in Hakeem Alajuwon's shoes as he spins around Shaq for a graceful dunk, follow the official as he breaks up a fight. If you want to replay a shot, click your mouse and step back in time for a moment. Images, sounds, motion—experience the action, rather than just watching from the sidelines. Now *that's* interactive.

Creating quality interactive multimedia takes a lot of knowledge and the right tools. You must know how to present your information and how to manipulate it in realtime. Of course, you won't become an instant content expert from reading this book, but you will learn how to create the tools to process your multimedia images, sound files, music, animation, video, and hypertext. We'll start by exploring some of the tools that Windows 95 provides for manipulating these components, and then we'll create our own. You'll be amazed by the multimedia power and flexibility that Delphi brings to the table.

Exploring the Windows 95 Multimedia System

The Windows Multimedia System, which is built into Windows 95, provides a set of services that you can use in your programs to manipulate sound, graphics, and video. Windows 95 (or Windows 3.1, or Windows 3.0 with Multimedia Extensions) also includes some multimedia utilities that give you instant access to these capabilities. However, Windows 95 offers some major advantages over the previous versions. The Sound Recorder, for instance, will let you add digitized sounds, such as oral annotations, to Word documents, Excel spreadsheets, or other apps that support Windows Object Linking and Embedding (OLE). The Windows Media Player utility will play back WAV files, MIDI sequencer files, or AVI video files (that's video as in television video, not PC display video) right from your hard disk or CD-ROM drive. Media Player can also play standard audio CDs on your CD-ROM drive, and if you load the right drivers, it can operate video laser disks, video tape decks, and other external devices equipped with serial or SCSI interfaces.

Windows 95 uses the same programs as previous versions; the big difference is that they have been upgraded to 32 bits. That means twice the bandwidth, and therefore, twice the resolution. In audio terms, you may not notice a big change, but with video clips, you will see a tremendous improvement. This is because video takes so much more processing power than audio does. Look at it this way: a thirty-second compact disc quality WAV file takes up almost five megabytes. If you think that's a lot, a thirty-second full-screen AVI file compressed with a 32-bit CODEC (*c*ompression/*dec*ompression algorithm) can take up a whopping 30 megabytes of disk space!

Multimedia Extensions and Abbreviations

As we get into multimedia, we're going to run into a myriad of different file types and mysterious abbreviations. Table 1.1 shows a list of some of the most common extensions and abbreviations. We'll be using these abbreviations throughout this book. You can expect this list to grow!

So you can see how it would be helpful to be able to pass that information through as fast as possible. Even in a 32-bit environment, you must be careful how and where you use video. If you must have full-screen animation, then forget AVI files altogether; look to MPEG, a CODEC that can improve the performance of your product by reducing the amount of data that must be transferred to your computer from, say, a four-year-old single-spin CD ROM drive. (Oh yes. It will happen. Even years from now.) As this book was being written, software-based MPEG was difficult at best, so we did not cover it. However, by the time this book gets on the shelves, there should be a new set of standards for software-based MPEG CODECs that will make it much easier for the average programmer to use, mostly because you do not have to worry about any proprietary hardware standards. Now, back to what we will teach you.

Table 1.1 Common Multimedia Abbreviations and Extensions.

Abbreviaton/Extension	Description
WAV	Audio Waveform files
MIDI, MID	Musical Instrument Digital Interface
AVI	Audio/Video Interleave
MPEG, MPG	Motion Picture Experts Group video
JPEG, JPG	Joint Picture Experts Group still image
GIF	Graphics Interchange Format
BMP	Windows Bitmap
TIFF, TIF	Tagged Image Format
SCSI	Small Computer Serial Interface[?]
OLE	Object Linking and Embedding
DLL	Dynamic Link Library
DDE	Dynamic Data Exchange
API	Application Programming Interface (usually, but not necessarily, for Microsoft Windows)
GUI	Graphical User Interface
OOP	Object-Oriented Programming
HTML, HTM	Hypertext Markup Language

No Programming Necessary

Not everyone aspires to multimedia fame. Some of us just want to use sound and pictures to make a point or to assist with day to day tasks, or just to play music. Fortunately, you can use Windows 95 Multimedia features without ever touching a programming language or an authoring system. Let's explore a simple example.

Start up any Windows app that supports Object Linking and Embedding (OLE), such as Microsoft Word or Excel. Create or load any file. Then, locate the option that enables you to insert a Windows object into a document. In Word, choose Insert | Object. Word will display the dialog box shown in Figure 1.1.

Choose the Sound option from the *Object Type* list box to open the Sound Recorder utility. You can record from a microphone plugged into your sound card or you can record from a CD playing in your CD-ROM drive. Press the Record Button (the little red button), and say something. Try to be as profound as Alexander Graham Bell when he tested his first

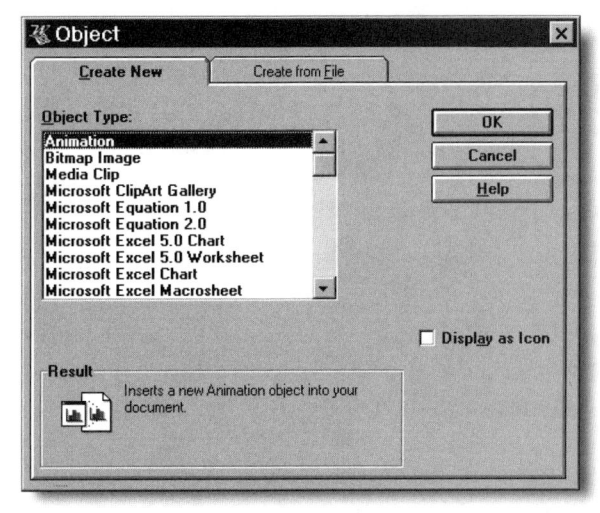

Figure 1.1 *The Microsoft Word Insert Object dialog box allows you to insert Windows objects into a document.*

telephone ("Watson, come here. I need you!"). But keep it brief; digital audio recordings gobble disk space if you are recording at a high-quality level!

When you're done, close the Recorder. Word will display a microphone icon in your document, as shown in Figure 1.2.

You may insert text as you please before or after this *embedded object*. To replay your recording, just double click on the microphone icon. If you transmit your document by email to other people who use Word for Windows, they too will see the Recorder icon and can replay your message.

By the way, you can embed existing recordings just as easily as new ones by selecting the Media Clip option from the *Object Type* list box. When the Media Player appears, choose *Device|Sound* from the menu. Then open and play any WAV file. When you're done, close Media Player.

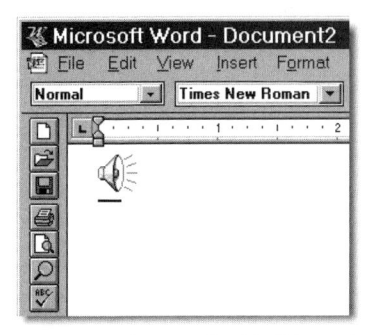

Figure 1.2 *Microsoft Word document with an embedded Recorder object.*

> In this case, Word will display the Media Player icon rather than the Sound Recorder's microphone. Double click on the icon to replay the sound.
>
> If you want a little more flexibility but are truly wary of programming, you can use an authoring system to build presentations. Without programming, you can get to all the same *kinds* of services (sound, graphics, animation, and video) as you can with programming; you just won't have as much flexibility in how you present them.

These handy utilities perform some amazing operations behind the scenes. And Microsoft gives us the functions we need to build our own programs to manipulate the devices and data that comprise the Multimedia System. They're contained in a Windows DLL called WINMM.DLL. Delphi wraps these calls in a unit named MMSystem. Just like with any other Windows API functions, we can call these functions from our own apps.

Windows Programming—A Black Art?

Windows programming resembles no other type of programming that most of us have ever encountered. The Windows GUI is designed to make programs look similar. Obviously, you can only go so far in this direction, or all programs would look exactly the same. But many apps, especially productivity programs like word processors and spreadsheets, share dozens of common operations. For example, all word processors offer cursor movement, printing, rulers, cut and paste operations, and a variety of other features. And all programs need navigation tools so you can get from one option or data field to another.

Windows provides functions that perform many of these common operations. In fact, the Windows 95 API offers almost 2,000 functions! Some do spectacular things, like playing back a video file with a single call; others perform small, specialized operations like reporting the position of the cursor. To program a Windows app, all you have to do is stack up a series of calls to the appropriate Windows functions.

Right!

A Windows app carries on an intimate relationship with the operating system. Like young lovers, they exchange messages at a frantic rate. Almost any time something happens in Windows, whether it's in your app or another one running at the same time, Windows sends your app a message, offering it an opportunity to respond. Often the response triggers a flurry of exchanges. You may already be familiar with the infamous **WinProc**, the often gargantuan procedure familiar to Borland Pascal and C/C++ Windows programmers, consisting primarily of a lengthy **case** statement piled high with procedures that respond to messages. This is where the work of a Windows app happens.

To write a Windows app—at least one that works reliably—you have to anticipate all the messages your app might receive and need to act upon.

Unless you write your application in Delphi.

The Visual Difference

A few of you (bless your souls) have come from the dark world where the first routine of any program tells Windows where to find the second: a giant **case** statement that handles each message Windows sends to your application, no matter how seemingly insignificant. Messages telling you this, telling you that—things that you really didn't want to worry about.

Some of you didn't even have the advantage of a development environment that integrated your code editor and your compiler. Others of you had impressive tools that would allow you to drop controls onto a window box, and would then write the (rather generic) framework code for you, leaving only a few empty places to fill. Those of you from these worlds will have a difficult time accepting the idea of a truly visual environment.

If, however, you've never programmed "traditionally," your ideas will express themselves so naturally that you may not even realize what you just did. A truly visual environment does this. In a visual environment, you "program" with pictures. You draw your application by dropping components—Buttons, Labels, Edit Boxes—onto a "form" that represents the window of your running program. Without having added any code, you have created a working Windows program. The Buttons click, the Labels appear, and are repainted after being covered up temporarily, and you can type away to your heart's content in the edit boxes.

This doesn't appear to be anything too special. The magic happens when you look at your program's code. In a truly visual environment, there isn't any! All right, we're telling a white lie. You *will* see a little code in your Delphi application, but it's only the little bit of code required to make the shell of a Pascal program. Unlike the framework built by a "visually-aided" tool, consisting of hundreds of lines of support code (the only virtue of which is that you didn't need to write it, even though you do need to fill it in and worry about whether or not it compiles), the most "active" piece of your Delphi program will be a call to a method named **Run**. You will never need to worry about, or even look at, **Run.** (But you could, if you wanted—as long as you have Delphi's *VCL Source Code*. Delphi is written in *itself*.)

Of course, now that you've built a program out of all those components (whose names you'll see when you look through your code, but whose source code you'll probably never have to worry about), you'll want your program to *do* something. Each of the components you use will have certain *events* associated with them. These are important actions that the component can be involved in, that the component's designer thought you might want to have a hand in yourself. A Delphi Button's **OnClick** event is the basic example: The Button's events, as you'll see, are enumerated on the screen. By double clicking the **OnClick** event, you open up a code window, where you can put in the actions you'd like to see happen then the Button is clicked.

In a truly visual environment, the only code you'll ever see will be code that you wrote specifically to solve the problem at hand. You'll never need see any of the support code that, for instance, draws the image of a raised Button on the screen and changes it to the image of a depressed Button when the user clicks the mouse on it. This is the true power of Delphi's visual development environment.

Delphi as a Windows Development System

Prepare yourself for a suspicious claim:

You can accomplish a lot more in a lot less time with Delphi than you can with one of the traditional languages like C, C++, or Pascal.

Languages like the non-visual Borland Pascal, C/C++, and even Assembler were once necessary for writing tight, fast code that dealt directly with the lower-level capabilities of the hardware and operating system—and for some projects, like device drivers and communication programs, these languages may still be the most appropriate choice for some tasks. In fact, because the computer user doesn't need to interact with the low-level services of the Windows Multimedia System, this code lends itself to a non-visual implementation.

Most of us want to write applications and utilities that solve higher-level, day-to-day problems like amortizing loans or storing information about clients and patients. Delphi reaches down and grabs hold of those basic services and brings them to life without a ton of code. Borland has a marketing buzzword: *RAD*. But it's more than marketing—for *Rapid Application Development*, Delphi is your ticket.

Delphi Takes Care of Windows Housekeeping Chores for You

Huge sections of the Windows API perform routine functions like opening and closing windows, managing memory, formatting text, and displaying scroll bars. Because most Windows apps use these features, they tend to call the same functions and respond to the same messages over and over. Delphi takes care of many of these basic Windows housekeeping chores for you. Delphi calls hundreds of API functions and responds to all the appropriate messages behind the scenes. You only need to fill in the blanks.

It's Event-Driven

To program in Windows, you have to think in Windows, and Windows is a world of events. Almost anything an app does in Windows is a response to an event. Windows notifies your program of each event by sending it a message.

Delphi is designed around this event-driven model. If you click on a Command Button in a typical Windows program, some program code would need to be called to perform an operation. Delphi provides you with built-in event handlers for standard events, such as mouse clicks, so that you can easily create truly event-driven programs. Delphi even goes one step further and incorporates the event-driven nature of Windows into the Delphi development environment. For example, you can click on a Command Button to open a window and display your code as you are designing your programs.

Interactive Development Puts the User First

Delphi offers the most interactive way to develop interactive programs. The ease with which you can add controls helps you to design and modify your programs so that they work and feel just right for your users.

When you create a program with a traditional language, the initial focus is on the task you want to automate. Once you think you know how to solve the tough problems, you begin to grind out the code. Along the way, you build the user interface: menus, windows, interactive controls, data entry fields, and so on.

But with Delphi, you begin with the most important component—the user.

Visual Programming Power

Visual design is a handy feature for creating many types of Windows apps. For interactive multimedia, it's essential. Interactive multimedia is a new medium—a visual medium. The success of a project depends on how the user can interact with it. A movie director would never hand over a script to his crew and wait in his office for the final film footage. Much of what ends up on the screen is discovered on the set. When you design your multimedia title, you need feedback every step of the way. Are the Buttons too big? Too small? Too many? Does the picture get lost among the controls? Can you read the text without covering the images?

With Delphi, you can fine-tune your apps as you work. And when (not *if*) you find you still need low-level horsepower, Delphi can take you clear down to the hardware with its built-in Assembly language and inline machine language to harness the true 32-bit architecture of the post-386 CPUs. And Delphi has complete support for the Windows API. This book is your map to guide you as you machete your trail through the API jungle.

Easy-to-Use Support of the API

A huge number of Windows API functions deliver their goods to us through Delphi's *Visual Class Library* (*VCL*). Even so, some of them must be called directly, which, thankfully, is easy. (Actually, it isn't so much that the API functions are difficult to understand individually. The tricky part is finding the right combinations to successfully complete the task at hand.) To prove just how easy it is, let's try one.

Playing Multimedia with a Few Lines of Code

Our first Delphi multimedia project shows you how to use the **mciExecute** multimedia API call to play a WAV file.

Start up Delphi and create a new application by selecting *File|New Application* from the menu. Place a Button on the form Delphi gives you, and set the Button's **Caption** to "&Execute MCI Command". Next, double click on the Button. Delphi displays the framework for the **TForm1.Button1Click** event shown in Figure 1.3. We're going to call upon the services of the simplest function in the multimedia API—**mciExecute**. This function executes MCI commands.

This project, project1.dpr, is saved on the accompanying CD-ROM in the directory \PROGRAMS\CHAP01\MCI.

The function **mciExecute** takes a single argument, a string, which contains a plain English command as shown in Listing 1.1. In this simple example, all we want to do is play a WAV file. The MCI **play** command will automatically open and close the WAV device for us.

Add the call to **mciExecute** to the **TForm1.Button1Click** framework. Then, use the arrow keys to move above the procedure, and insert the **uses** clause. Listing 1.1 shows the entire unit after these modifications.

The Delphi-Multimedia Connection

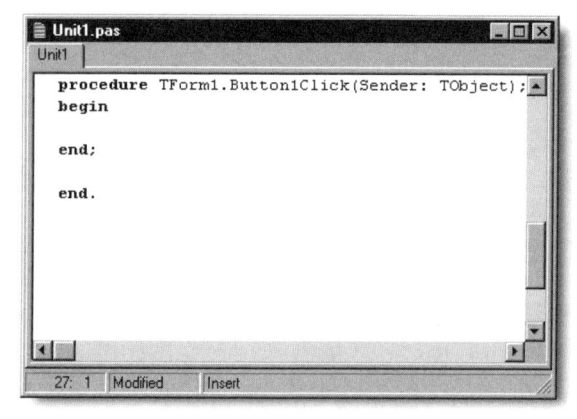

Figure 1.3 The Delphi Editor window with the **TForm1.Button1Click** event procedure framework displayed.

Listing 1.1   mciExecute Called from the TForm1.Button1Click Event Procedure

```
unit Unit1;

interface

uses
  SysUtils, Windows, Messages, Classes, Graphics, Controls, Forms, Dialogs,
  StdCtrls;

type
  TForm1 = class(TForm)
    Button1: TButton;
    procedure Button1Click(Sender: TObject);
  private
    { Private declarations }
  public
    { Public declarations }
  end;

var
  Form1: TForm1;

implementation

   uses
      MMSystem;

{$R *.DFM}

procedure TForm1.Button1Click(Sender: TObject);
begin
```

```
    mciExecute('play c:\Windows\Media\Tada.Wav');
end;

end.
```

mciExecute is actually a **function**, not a **procedure**, but Delphi's syntax (introduced in Borland Pascal version 6.0) allows functions to be called as procedures, discarding their result. The result, in this case, is actually of type **BOOL**, defined by Delphi as a **LongBool**, a new native representation of a four-byte boolean value. This **BOOL** indicates success or failure, but because we don't plan to act upon that result, we're just discarding it.

Of course, if Windows 95 is installed on a drive other than *C:*, make the appropriate change to the command string argument. Then, run the program and click on the Button. You can insert the name of any WAV file into this command. Try it out and give it a listen!

Actually, you can insert the name of any MCI-supported data file into the **play** command. Windows 95 comes with a sample MIDI sequencer file called *Canyon.MID*. In the code below, replace the WAV file name with the name of this MIDI file and run the program again.

```
mciExecute('play c:\Windows\Media\Tada.Wav');
```

Unlike the brief WAV files, Canyon will play for a couple of minutes.

I would be misleading you if I told you that all the Windows multimedia API calls were this easy to use, even with the aid of the VCL. Many functions take several arguments. Occasionally, you'll need to deal directly with the Windows API, where you have to follow arcane rules to pass arguments from Delphi to Windows functions. Some functions work only in combination with other functions. Other functions that were present in Windows 3.1 have been taken out of Windows 95 and, of course, all the new 32-bit functions are new to Windows programming (though the VCL will shield you, to some degree). In Chapter 4, we'll begin to look at the multimedia capabilities provided by the Windows Multimedia System API. By the time we've finished with the presentation system we'll start building in the next chapter, you'll know how to use many of the key functions that will propel our programs into the multimedia age.

The Essential Delphi

Before we begin programming in earnest, let's rummage around in the Delphi closet and figure out what we can use. We'll start by sorting the components we'll be needing into their proper compartments.

A Delphi program usually consists of a least one *form* on which we find one or more objects, in the form of *controls*. Controls have *properties*, which define their appearance and general behavior, and *event procedures*, which determine what will happen when the control is activated by one or several operator actions, or *events*.

Forms Present

Forms are actually objects themselves, and like control objects, they offer some event procedures. For most purposes, we generally think of a form as a frame within which to place controls. In general, we'll abide by that convention, although we'll also see that plain unpopulated forms can perform some useful functions in screen presentation, as well.

Objects Behave

Most of the real action takes place within controls. Much of the activity on the screen requires the services of more than one control. A Command Button, for example, might load a bitmap image into an Image control. Each type of control offers its own selection of event procedures. Some overlap, but many do not.

Properties Define

Properties determine states, such as background color or the name by which we'll reference the control elsewhere within our program.

Events Happen

Events *should* trigger everything that happens in Delphi programs. Events form the core of the Delphi programming model. As the user takes various actions in the GUI, for instance, moving the mouse or touching a key, Windows sends of a flurry of messages. These messages may affect your program, or any of the others running. Those programs may respond to those messages, and ask Windows to perform actions that may require it to send out even more messages. Events are Delphi's way of making sense of this overwhelming web of messages.

As messages are sent to your program, the most important become events. Events, as we'll see, are directly supported in the way you write Delphi code, and give you a way to easily respond to the messages most important to you, while ignoring the constant background noise.

The concept of events extends beyond Windows programming, into many multimedia systems. As you'll see when we discuss MIDI (the Musical Instrument

Digital Interface) in Chapter 16, events are useful in handling many types of user interaction, from clicking Command Buttons to playing piano.

Loops... Well, Loops Happen

Should you happen to write a program that loops away on its own, without regard to events—which you *can* do—you'll effectively disable Windows 3.x, and cripple the performance of other applications running under Windows 95. (Under Windows 3.x, you may even be forced to reboot the computer.) An infinite loop in a Windows 3.x program will hang your system just as well as an infinite loop in a DOS program. But thanks to multitasking, there's more to crash. An infinite loop in a Windows 95 program, fortunately, only hangs the program.

Even though you'll be working in an environment that supports event-driven code, writing event-driven programs, it's surprising how easy it is to forget about this, and start writing processor-intensive procedural code that can practically hang you computer while you respond to a single event. In Windows 3.x, programs usually display an hourglass, and the system can't respond to any other events until the processing is over. Have you ever wondered if the program you were running was *ever* going to "come back" to you?

Windows 95 provides several services to avoid this problem. *Multi-threading* is a technique used in truly pre-emptive multitasking systems, like Windows 95. Because this is an advanced topic unto itself, we'll only touch on multi-threading, but the concept is simple: If a process will take a lot of time for itself, it can spawn its own *thread*, or line of processing, and leave the other threads, that might be handling the user interface and other processes, alone. The operating system lets each thread operate for a short period of time, and then switches threads. In this way, even if one thread goes into an infinite loop, other threads continue their processing. Windows 95, itself, uses these techniques to isolate 16-bit programs running in the environment. That's why some crashes that used to bring your system to its knees now just pop up a simple warning explaining that Windows must now terminate your rouge program.

Functions, Procedures, and Methods Work

Functions and *procedures* contain program statements that manipulate data. When we want something done, we call a procedure; when we want something back, we call a function. Event procedures are special procedures that Delphi calls when something happens in Windows that might affect a particular form or control. Delphi also includes dozens of other built-in functions that perform common operations like converting strings of digits to numbers, or calculating the cosine of an angle. Of course, we can also write our own procedures and functions.

Forms and controls offer special types of procedures and functions that perform work under program control rather than in response to user events. These routines are defined as integral components of their host objects. In OOP, such routines are called *methods*. (Delphi, by the way, is object-oriented in its design, and is, as a matter of fact, written in Delphi—yes, it's written in itself. Later, we'll define our own objects and methods—sometimes from scratch, and sometimes derived from existing objects. Unlike its most popular rival, Microsoft's Visual Basic, this capability makes Delphi *in*ternally *ex*tensible. (How's that for colliding jargon?)

The difference between a method and any other procedure or function built into the language is that a method belongs to its host object and usually modifies a property of that object, whereas a general-purpose routine accepts and modifies conventional data elements, such as variables, constants, and arrays—most of the time. You *can* write procedures that modify an object's properties. The difference between these two entities will just continue to get fuzzier, and I promised a brief review, so we'll move on.

Units Organize

Considering the way we scatter code around in a Delphi program, you have to wonder whether we're still entitled to call it "structured." The Delphi programming system—and it is a system, not just a language—dictates not only syntax, but architecture. In fact, the apparently chaotic organization of a Delphi program reflects a purer form of the structured ideal than the linear listings required by traditional programming languages. Like protein molecules, procedures perform distinct operations. They offer a single entry point and a single exit. (Well, as long as you don't use the built-in procedure **exit**.) The order in which we create them matters only to the extent that one procedure cannot call another unless the one being called already exists.

Yet, within any given program, procedures tend to cluster. So-called low-level procedures perform minute repetitive tasks and tend to call built-in language or operating system features. Higher-level procedures call on low-level procedures, so much so that the low-level procedures sometimes obscure the identity of the host language. Several procedures may perform related tasks, like disk and file management. And Delphi puts all of our event procedures for each form in one place.

As we write event procedures for our Delphi programs, we find that we want to write procedures we can call upon over and over again without duplicating their code. We may even want to bag some of these tools to tote them from one program to another. So we place them in *units*. Just as we gather our related code together, Delphi keeps all of the event procedures for each form in its own unit.

You can add your own general procedures and functions to a form's unit, also, but if you create a separate unit to store those items, they can be called by procedures in other forms as well. And if you add that unit to another project, the same code can be called from units or forms in both projects. Throughout this book we'll bundle code into units that you can incorporate into your own projects.

Code Style Clarifies

The most overlooked component of any language is overlooked because it isn't a component, but a philosophy. Some would say, even, a religion. *Code style* illuminates a program's rails and switches. A digital computer runs a program in a particular order. That order is determined by a set of critical statements that divert the processor into loops and branches. You can weave as many loops and branches into your program as you wish, and as long as you obey the language's rules of syntax, the compiler doesn't care how your code looks. But *you* should care, because if *you* can't follow it, it probably doesn't work the way you think. Even if it does work, you can be sure no one else will be able to follow it.

The most obvious element of code style is *indentation*. This apparently trivial technique has fanned some hot debates. Everyone has personal views on indentation, and because none of the mainstream languages impose indentation style, we all stick to our own guidelines. This discussion won't shed any light on multimedia, so we'll just say that we'll try to indent our code in order to clarify its structure. We never write code without indentation—not even tiny programs—but we are not purists and our style may not satisfy your needs. We recommend two things: Develop or adopt a style, and *apply it consistently.* Inconsistent indentation can hang you as surely as no indentation, maybe worse—we don't expect any help from unformatted code, but randomly formatted code plays pranks on us.

The second key element of code style is *scoping*. Delphi uses the same static scoping rules as basic Pascal, described in any of the introductory texts on the language. We won't waste your time by repeating the same technical discussion. Think of scoping as containment, like a nest of Chinese boxes. When you're done with a program, nothing should show outside those boxes, except what you need to run that program. And at each layer within, the same rule pertains: nothing more or less than you need should appear outside that level of scope. Each time you declare a variable, consider where you'll use it, then put it in the smallest box you can. By eliminating global variables, passing information around as arguments instead, you'll write more reusable code that is more readable by those that follow after you. Remember, structured programming is the *artful* hiding of details. This rule too, we will try to follow as closely as possible.

Intrinsic Multimedia

You'll find yourself using a large assortment of Delphi's features to write any serious application. Thus, any Delphi feature could be considered useful for multimedia projects. But some of Delphi's features turn out to be particularly useful. Let's take a closer look.

The most exciting feature of Delphi is its **MediaPlayer** component. This ready-to-use encapsulation of the Windows *MCI (Media Control Interface)* API makes adding bits of multimedia to your application nearly trivial.

Forms, Images, and their Canvases, representing their graphical information, are essential multimedia tools, both in obvious and—as we'll learn in Chapter 2—surprising ways. These two components (and in fact, all visual components) share several useful capabilities, like the **Canvas** property and its graphical methods.

Forms are the platforms on which we'll stage our productions. To make effective presentations, we need to think carefully about forms, how many to display, how to size them, and how to move them.

Graphics methods provide essential graphic capabilities to our programs at runtime; say, the ability to draw a portion of an arc in a window. Delphi also provides the **Shape** control, which can take on one of several predefined shapes. We can use this control to decorate our forms at design-time.

Delphi also lets us add pictures to our applications either at design-time or at runtime. We can move them, resize them, and remove them. With a simple technique based on arrays, we can even animate them. We'll use Images, Edit controls, and Forms themselves extensively in our applications. And we'll end up using many of their properties and methods. By layering these elements and manipulating their properties at runtime, we can really get the show moving. Let's try a simple example.

Moving Pictures

This project shows you how to use a few Delphi programming tricks to move a picture around in a window. Follow the directions below to build this project. Table 1.2 indicates the property settings and Figure 1.4 shows the completed form. (The table doesn't give

Chapter 1

position or dimension information unless it is critical. File names are given relative to CD-ROM drive *X:*, so you'll probably want to change that to its designation on your system.)

> *This project, Project1.DPR, is saved on the accompanying CD-ROM in the directory \PROGRAMS\CHAP01\IMAGE.*

Start a new application. We won't need to reference the default form's **Name** property, so you can name the form anything you wish. On the Form, place a Panel control and stretch it to proportions shown in Figure 1.4.

Next, click on the Image control icon on the palette's *Additional* page. The Image is represented by a picture of a desert vista. Click and drag a "rubberbanded" Image inside the Panel control. *Make sure you start drawing the Image rectangle inside the Panel, not over the bare Form.* We need to align the upper-left corners of the Image and Panel controls so that the Panel disappears underneath. The easiest way to clean up the edges is to set the **Top** and **Left** properties of the Image to 0 in the Delphi Object Inspector. **Top** and **Left** determine the position of the Image relative to its container, in this case, the Panel.

The accompanying CD-ROM contains a subdirectory called *\MEDIA\IMAGES*. In it you will find a file called *YakiDawn.BMP*. We want to assign this file to the **Picture** property of the Image.

Table 1.2 Properties for the Moving Pictures Project.

Class	Property	Value
TForm	Name	Form1 (default)
TPanel	Name	Panel1 (default)
TImage	Name	Image1 (default)
	Top	0
	Left	0
	Picture	x:\Media\Images\YakiDawn.BMP
	AutoSize	True
TTimer	Name	Timer1
	Interval	56
	OnTimer	Timer1Timer
TTimer	Name	Timer2
	Interval	60000
	OnTimer	Timer2Timer

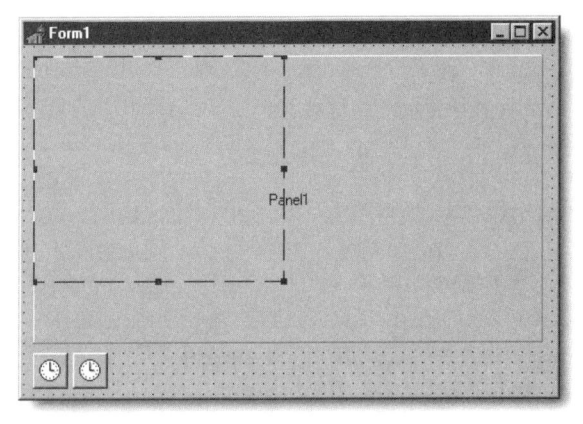

Figure 1.4 *The Moving Pictures form with the Image highlighted and aligned to the top-left-corner of the Panel.*

We need to change one other property of the Image, **AutoSize**. Set this property to "True". The **AutoSize** property causes the Image to match its size to the height and width of the currently active picture—the image assigned to its **Picture** property. The picture is much larger than what we can see on the screen. To see the entire picture as shown in Figure 1.5, open the file in

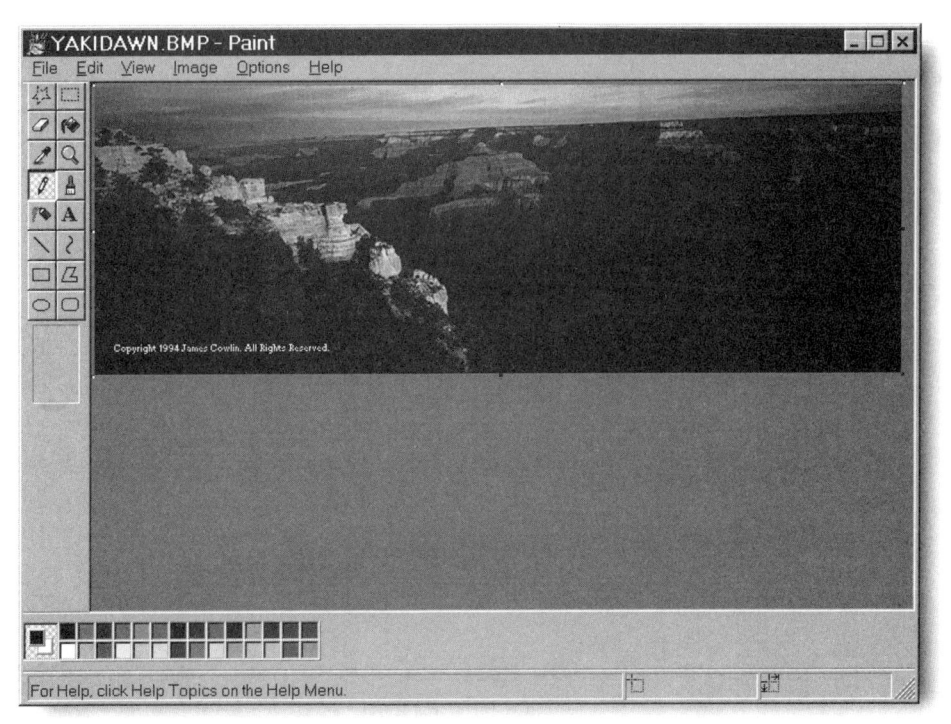

Figure 1.5 *The entire YakiDawn.BMP image.*

Windows 95 Paint. (You can switch a **Boolean** property between its two values, **True** and **False**, by double clicking on its value in the *Properties* list.)

The Panel masks the Image so we can only see the portion of the picture that is visible through the Panel.

Place two Timer controls anywhere on the form. The Timers will disappear at runtime so it doesn't matter where they go. Generally, if you put more than one Timer on a form, you may want to locate them on or near the other controls to which they're most closely related. Timers service only one event, **OnTimer**, and have only four design-time properties.

The only Timer properties that affect us are **Enabled**, which must be "**True**", and **Interval**. The **Interval**, measured in milliseconds, determines how often the **OnTimer** event occurs. Actually, the Timer control can't tick any more often than the system timer, which ticks 18 times per second, so the shortest meaningful interval is one eighteenth of a second, or about 56 milliseconds. We are going to make use of the Timers to animate our image, and we want the smoothest motion we can coax from it, so set the **Interval** of the first one (automatically named **Timer1** by Delphi) to "56". For now, set the **Interval** of the other Timer, **Timer2**, to "60000".

We're going to use the **OnTimer** event to slide the Image from right to left behind the Panel (even though we had to design the form with the Image *over* the Panel), creating the illusion that we're panning the landscape. Listing 1.2 shows the code needed for the **TForm1.Timer1Timer** event procedure.

Listing 1.2   TForm1.Timer1Timer Event Procedure

```
procedure TForm1.Timer1Timer(Sender: TObject);
begin
    Image1.Left := Image1.Left - 5;
end;
```

The **Left** property indicates the position of the Image control relative to the left edge of its *parent window* in pixels. Because we made such a big deal about putting the Image down, originally, on top of the Panel, not on top of the Form, we should tell you why: The Panel is a member of a special group of controls that can act as *parent controls*. To make a control, like our Image, into a *child* of a control, like our Panel, you must create the child inside the *parent*. (Funny, how life works, eh?) The benefit of this is that the parent can control the child (How unlike real life...); in our case, the display of the Image is clipped by the Panel.

As we subtract pixels from **Image1.Left**, increasing its negative magnitude, the whole Image control slides further and further left of the left edge of the Panel. The negative value indicates how many pixels the control's left edge rests from position zero, the Panel's left edge. Run the program to see what happens.

Don't forget to stop the program after the Image disappears. To prevent the Image from sliding right on past us, let's add some "bumpers", and a terminating condition. The entire new unit is shown in Listing 1.3.

Listing 1.3 The New **Timer1** and **Timer2** Event Procedures

```
unit Unit1;

interface

uses
  SysUtils, Windows, Messages, Classes, Graphics, Controls, Forms, Dialogs,
  ExtCtrls;

type
  TForm1 = class(TForm)
    Panel1: TPanel;
    Image1: TImage;
    Timer1: TTimer;
    Timer2: TTimer;
    procedure Timer1Timer(Sender: TObject);
    procedure Timer2Timer(Sender: TObject);
  private
    { Private declarations }
  public
    { Public declarations }
  end;

var
  Form1: TForm1;

implementation

{$R *.DFM}

var
    Delta : integer;

procedure TForm1.Timer1Timer(Sender: TObject);
begin
    if -Image1.Left >= (Image1.Width - Panel1.Width) then
        Delta := 5
      else
          if Image1.Left >= 0 then
              Delta := -5;
    Image1.Left := Image1.Left + Delta;
end;

procedure TForm1.Timer2Timer(Sender: TObject);
begin
```

```
    Timer1.Enabled := false;
    Timer2.Enabled := false;
end;

end.
```

With the **Width** property, we can stop the motion of the image either by diverting around the **subtraction** statement, or, as we've done here, by reversing the direction of movement. We added the declaration for the variable **Delta**, which now, rather than "5", tells us how many pixels to move per step.

The difference between the Image width and the Panel width tells us how much of the Image will be hanging out to the left of the Panel when that happens. **Image1.Left** will contain a negative value, so we negate it before comparing it to the difference of the object widths.

Finally, we use that mysterious **Timer2** to stop the show. We set its Interval property to "60000" milliseconds previously, which is 60 whole seconds. When **Timer2** fires for the first time, after the program has run for one minute, its **OnTimer** handler disables both timers by setting their **Enabled** properties to **false**. Neither Timer will fire again, since we never re-enable either one.

That's animation with ten lines of code, no function calls, and one bitmap. Now *that's* intrinsic multimedia.

We'll look at some more animation techniques in Chapters 8, 13, and 14.

The MediaPlayer Control

Delphi comes with a control called the MediaPlayer. You can operate all kinds of devices with this control, including the system's sound card, Microsoft's AVI (Audio/Video Interleave) files, CD-Audio, and external VCRs and video disc players. But you don't need the MediaPlayer to operate many of these devices. In fact, the MediaPlayer can be cumbersome when all you want to do is play back a WAV file or a MIDI sequence. Yet, as an interface to external devices, the MediaPlayer control can come in handy.

Multimedia the Delphi Way

We're going to drop a few stock controls on a form, and end up with a powerful media player. All in six lines of code. Table 1.3 shows the property settings for the project and Figure 1.6 shows the completed form.

This project, project1.dpr, is saved on the accompanying CD-ROM in the directory \PROGRAMS\CHAP01\MEDIA.

Table 1.3 Properties for the Media Project.

Class	Property	Value
TForm	Name	Form1 (default)
TButton	Name	Button1 (Default)
	Caption	"&Open"
	OnClick	Button1Click
TOpenDialog	Name	OpenDialog1 (default)
TLabel	Name	Label1 (default)
	Caption	<blank>
TPanel	Name	Panel1 (default)
	Caption	"(No media loaded.)"
TMediaPlayer	Name	MediaPlayer1
	AutoEnable	True
	AutoOpen	False
	FileName	<blank>
	Display	Panel1

Start a new application, and drop the following controls onto the form: a **Button**, an **OpenDialog** (from the *Dialogs* page of the palette), a **Label**, a **Panel**, and a **MediaPlayer** (from the *System* page). Your life will be easier if you don't try to set the MediaPlayer's properties until the Panel has been added to the Form.

Set the Button's **Caption** to "&Open". By now you might be wondering what that ampersand is doing there. This symbol is used to underline the letter following the symbol, making that letter the "hotkey" for the control. So, when the program is running, pressing "O" will click **Button1**.

The Label defaults to *autosizing*, so after you blank out its **Caption**, the control won't be visible at design-time, except when it's selected. Set the Panel's **Caption** to "(No media loaded.)".

Select the MediaPlayer, and make sure its **AutoEnable** property is set to **True**, its **AutoOpen** property is set to **False**, and its **FileName** property is blank. Set the **Display** property by choosing **Panel1** off the drop-down list provided when you click on the property in the *Object Inspector*. The form, with **Label1** selected, should look something like Figure 1.6 when you're finished.

Because the MediaPlayer takes care of itself, we only need to write the code to set things up when the user clicks on the Open Button. Listing 1.4 shows the entire unit.

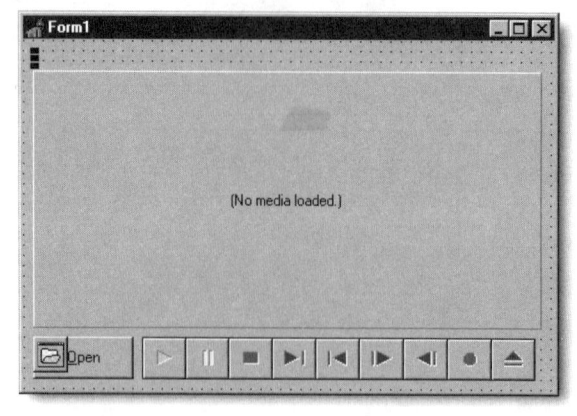

Figure 1.6 *The Media Player form, with the non-visual **OpenDialog** control overlapping the Open **Button**.*

Listing 1.4 The Media Player Unit

```
unit Unit1;

interface

uses
  SysUtils, Windows, Messages, Classes, Graphics, Controls, Forms, Dialogs,
  StdCtrls, ExtCtrls, MPlayer;

type
  TForm1 = class(TForm)
    MediaPlayer1: TMediaPlayer;
    Button1: TButton;
    OpenDialog1: TOpenDialog;
    Label1: TLabel;
    Panel1: TPanel;
    procedure Button1Click(Sender: TObject);
  private
    { Private declarations }
  public
    { Public declarations }
  end;

var
  Form1: TForm1;

implementation

{$R *.DFM}

procedure TForm1.Button1Click(Sender: TObject);
begin
    if OpenDialog1.Execute then begin
```

```
            Label1.Caption := OpenDialog1.FileName;
            Panel1.Caption := 'Playing ' + OpenDialog1.FileName;
            MediaPlayer1.FileName := OpenDialog1.FileName;
            MediaPlayer1.Open;
            end;
end;

end.
```

Run the program, and see how it handles your favorite media files. Some places to look, if you don't think you have any, are *C:\WINDOWS\MEDIA* (WAVs and MIDs), and *C:\WINDOWS\HELP* (there are some AVIs there).

Missing Links

As good as Delphi is at displaying screens with text, still images, and controls, plus its ability in responding to user activity, it provides only limited intrinsic support for the most exciting multimedia elements: sound, animation, and video.

In many cases, Delphi will serve us well as an application framework, tending to the menial tasks of Windows management. For much of what we'll do, we'll rely on Delphi's numerous features, especially when it comes to the user interface. With its assortment of ScrollBar, ListBox, Image, and various Button-type controls, we can assemble some attractive, functional forms.

Where Delphi leaves off, we'll look to the Windows API. Sometimes we'll have to sneak past Delphi, intentionally avoiding its zealous attempts to protect us from the fearsome machinery below.

What's Next?

We'll start our multimedia presentation kit in the next chapter by building a hypertext system based on Hypertext Markup Language (HTML), which we'll create entirely with plain vanilla Delphi. HTML is the language used to create Web pages for the World Wide Web. By using HTML, we'll be able to create an especially powerful and flexible engine that can be used to present multimedia from your own PC or it can be extended to build multimedia applications that work across the World Wide Web. As the multimedia industry is quickly moving from delivery engines that work on a single platform to integrated systems that can work transparently across client/server networks, you'll be ahead of the pack by learning how to build your own powerful development tools.

Chapter 2

In this chapter, we'll lay the groundwork for understanding the art of hypermedia. On our way to building a powerful hypermedia engine, we'll also cover the basics of hypertext and its display.

Foundations of Hypermedia Display

Dan Haygood

If you've been watching the computer industry explode over the past few years, you've probably witnessed the growth of CD-ROM and online information networks that support multimedia, like the World Wide Web. From 3D games to dinosaur adventures to interactive encyclopedias, CD-ROM has ushered in a new age of desktop computing. And little wonder. A CD-ROM holding thousands of images and millions of words can bring the magical world of multimedia to your PC. However, to make good use of all the interesting data forms that can be stored on a CD-ROM, you'll need a way to organize, process, and link together your stunning images, intriguing sounds, dazzling video, and important text.

Which is exactly where *hypermedia* comes in. Hypermedia isn't a new miracle cure, though. It's simply a way of organizing information—text, graphics, pictures, video, and so on—so that you can create powerful, interactive interfaces. If you've used multimedia products on the World Wide Web, you're already aware of the benefits of hypermedia. For example, when you click on the name of a street in an electronically displayed street atlas and a document window pops up to give you directions, you're experiencing the power of hypermedia at work. Or when you surf the Web with a browser like Netscape and click on a hyperlink, it is through the magic of hypermedia that you are quickly transported to another online location to experience new sights and sounds.

Because hypermedia is the foundation of interactive multimedia, this is the best place to start. We'll introduce you to some of the hypermedia key concepts, such as hyperlinks and hypertext. We'll then show you how to write the Delphi code to support the fundamental medium: text. In Chapter 3, we'll implement hyperlinking; and by Chapter 4, we'll be able to include links to other media so easily it might surprise you. From there, because hypermedia systems tend to resemble each other in many ways, we'll be creating a hypermedia system that you can adapt to a variety of multimedia projects.

For our major project in this chapter, we'll create a very useful text display engine that uses HTML or Hypertext Markup Language—the hypertext language for the World-Wide Web. HTML is a great foundation for building a multimedia engine because it provides everything needed to link documents with text, images, video, sound, and animation. Instead of creating our own specialized language, we can benefit by using a language like HTML that has been tested extensively in the field and has become a global standard. As a bonus, the multimedia engine that we develop can be adapted for use as an interactive Web browser. How's that for power?

The Explosion of Hypermedia

Just a few years ago, hypermedia-based systems were regarded as lab experiments. Apple Computer brought hypermedia into the mainstream when they released the innovative HyperCard for the Mac. Since that time, a number of unique applications have emerged that incorporate hypermedia capabilities. Even the help systems of most major DOS software products now use hypermedia techniques that are inherent in the Windows Help system. Over the past year, the Internet (and especially the World Wide Web) has brought the power of hypermedia to the masses. With a simple Web browser, a user can access a dazzling multimedia world of everything from music samples of popular rock bands to interactive encyclopedias. As the Web continues to grow, more and more people are experiencing the power of hypermedia; while software developers are scrambling to develop tools and applications to help users take advantage of a world that is dynamically connected.

In a hypermedia presentation, you can navigate by jumping from topic to topic, or topic to media element—picture, sound, video, and so on. You can also locate information by clicking on keywords and icons in specially-prepared documents. Such a document could consist of text or graphics, or a combination of both. For example, you could click on a particular spot in a world map and *voilà!*— an article about the history of Portugal appears on your screen. In the middle of your history lesson, you could click on the word "currency," and guess what? Up comes an article about Portuguese currency, along with pictures of various bank notes and coins.

Some visionaries like Ted Nelson, who came up with the idea of hypertext, claim that soon all information—magazine articles, books, newspapers, scientific papers, stock quotes, network news stories, movies, music, everything—will be available as hypermedia. This information could be available online and accessible by satellite from your personal computer. Of course, someone will need to convert all of this stuff into an electronic form. The raw data will undergo *information renewal*, transforming into entirely new works at the hands of skilled multimedia producers.

Organized Chaos—The Magic of Hyperlinking

Hypermedia systems are designed so that you can explore information in a variety of formats by activating *hyperlinks*. A hyperlink operates like an underground tunnel to connect points of data. These pieces of data may appear in an application as "highlighted" text, a picture with a "hot" spot, a graphic embellishment, or an icon. (Since the field of hypermedia is still relatively new, many creative techniques for representing hyperlinks are just starting to emerge.)

In more traditional or document-based systems, the term *hypertext* refers to text-based information that is connected with hyperlinks. Some hypertext documents mix two or more kinds of markers, each one performing a different function. Figure 2.1 shows how Delphi utilizes the hyperlinking capability provided by Windows in its hypertext-based help system.

Hyperlinking can serve many purposes. Sometimes you may want to look up a term and then return to what you were doing. At other times you may discover a subtopic that you want to explore more thoroughly, so you jump to another topic, completely leaving your previous work. Occasionally, you may want to refresh your knowledge on a subject or acquire some background information, then return to your point of departure. Good hypermedia browsers, like Netscape, provide a *history* feature so that you can keep track of the links you've previously explored and easily return to them later. If you get lost as you are exploring, you can also backtrack.

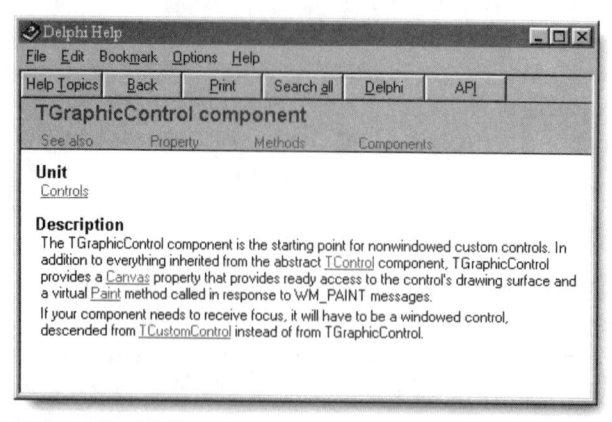

Figure 2.1   A typical hypertext Help screen.

The manner in which hyperlinks are placed in a multimedia application can determine how useful the application will be. If too few links are used, users may feel constrained. (After all, a multimedia application is supposed to be more fun and interesting than flipping pages in a book.) On the other hand, if too many links are used, users might feel as if they are trapped in a maze. Figure 2.2 shows how an organized hypermedia system stacks up against more disorganized systems.

If you add links (hotspots) to images, it's important to make sure that your users can locate them. Otherwise, users might not even realize that hotspots are provided and they'll end up skipping over something important. If you've spent much time surfing the Web, you've probably already experienced this type of situation. Many Web pages use graphics images with *mappable* links, in which clicking on certain parts of an image can take you to different destinations. However, the links are often so difficult to detect that typically a user will not even realize that they can click on the image to access additional information. We'll implement such links and discuss related user-interface issues later in this book.

The network of linked pathways provides the first and most-used layer of interactivity. And this is where the relationship between content and interface begins. In the publishing world, authors and editors have to choose and stick to a single structure for each publication they create. Sometimes the material will dictate the structure. But sometimes the structure that at first seems most natural ends up being the least effective—and the most boring!

Fortunately, most topics become fascinating—almost magical—when they are examined from a variety of angles. On paper, one word follows another, paragraph after paragraph, chapter after chapter. With hyperlinks, on the other hand, you can connect thoughts and ideas in much more creative ways, which is the main benefit of the hyperlinking approach.

Foundations of Hypermedia Display

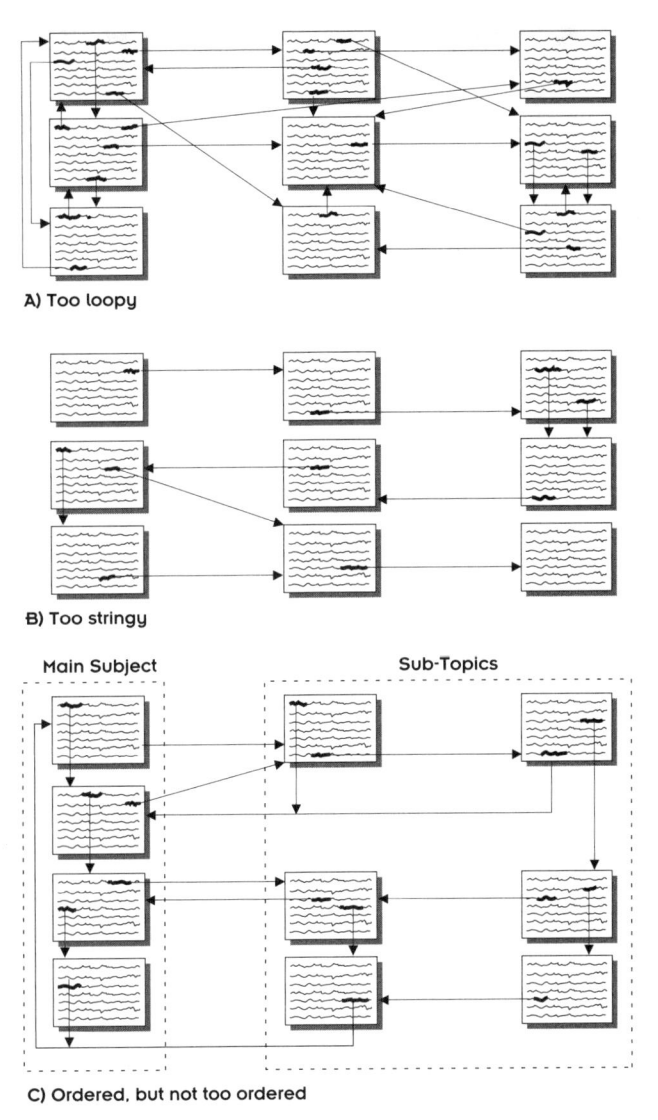

A) Too loopy

B) Too stringy

Main Subject | Sub-Topics

C) Ordered, but not too ordered

Figure 2.2 *Disorganized hypertext systems versus a well-organized system.*

Before we started the first edition of this book for Visual Basic users, we created a working outline. We used Microsoft Word's Outline View feature so we could move freely through our material, expanding and collapsing headings, jumping from section to section, adding and removing topics as new ideas emerged. As you can guess, the finished outline—a portion of which is shown in Figure 2.3—defined a book organized by subject categories—a section for images, one for sound, another for text, and so on.

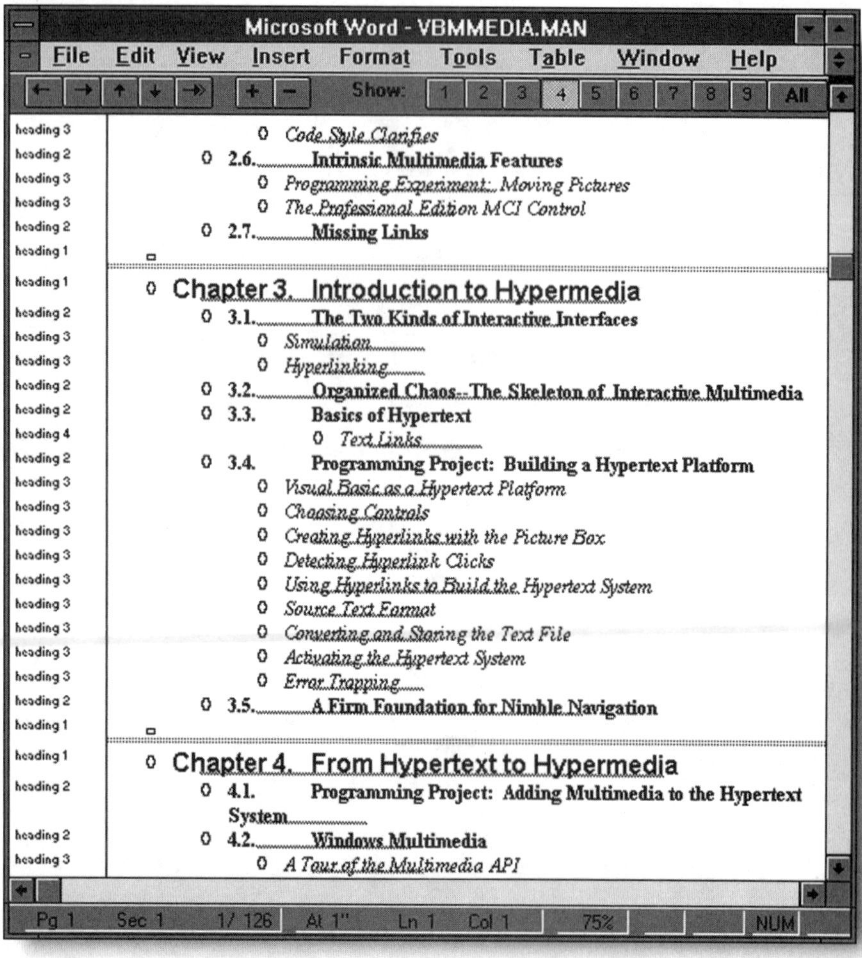

Chapter 2

Figure 2.3   Part of an early outline for this book, as it appears in Microsoft Word.

When the outline was finished, we realized that the book really needed a more creative approach. So we reorganized the material into chapters that began with basic concepts, then built upon those concepts, intertwining ideas, techniques, and fun projects to complete the multimedia adventure set. We actually needed to maintain two outlines—one that organized the book by subject, and another that split subjects into smaller chunks spread across multiple chapters. At one point, we even began to contemplate creating a third structure that would be organized by technical issues, so we could sort through the programming projects more easily! If we had created this book as a hypermedia document, we could have offered the different views of the outline as interfaces. Hypermedia provides the option of using any number of different interfaces, and can even display them all at the same time!

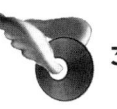

Many of the hyperlinks you incorporate into your productions will be utilitarian—digressions on subtopics or simple glossary lookups. But hyperlinking is also an editorial lantern that enables you to illuminate secret passages through your ideas and concepts.

> ### Using Hyperlinks with *Explore the Grand Canyon*
>
> When we created the *Explore the Grand Canyon* multimedia adventure, we wanted to give users the experience of playing an adventure game. To accomplish this, we included thousands of links that access all types of content—video, text, photos, music, voice narration, sound effects, and so on. The "surprise" element comes from the fact that users don't always know what they'll get when a hotspot is selected.
>
> As shown in Figure 2.4, hotspots are placed in the terrain of both an explorer-style map and a 3D Virtual Landscape. When a hotspot is selected from the map, a pop-up window presents a list of near-by topics. Selection of one of the topics, or a more precisely located hotspot in the *3DVL*, presents users with multimedia content. The goal is to encourage users to explore in order to find interesting material. When the users find something of interest, they can interact with the material presented by clicking on additional links.
>
> Another technique used to enhance the "explorer" nature of the multimedia experience involves adding different types of hotspots to pictures. When a picture is displayed in the multimedia viewer, the user can move the mouse pointer around within the image and the pointer will change. For example, one type of pointer looks like a plant icon as shown in Figure 2.5. When a user clicks on a hotspot referenced by this icon, information about plant life in the Grand Canyon is displayed. Overall, we found this to be a very effective way to link different types of contextual information into a picture.
>
> In the *3DVL*, we took this technique further and actually used the position of the cursor within the window to allow repositioning of the vantage point. As the user moves the cursor to different areas of the window—to the top, to move forward, or the right side to look to the right—the cursor changes to indicate what will happen when the mouse is clicked.

Hyperlinking on the Information Superhighway

Hypertext and hyperlinking have been receiving a tremendous amount of press recently due to their use in *Hypertext Markup Language* (*HTML*), the grammatical foundation of the World-Wide Web. This standardized protocol

34 Chapter 2

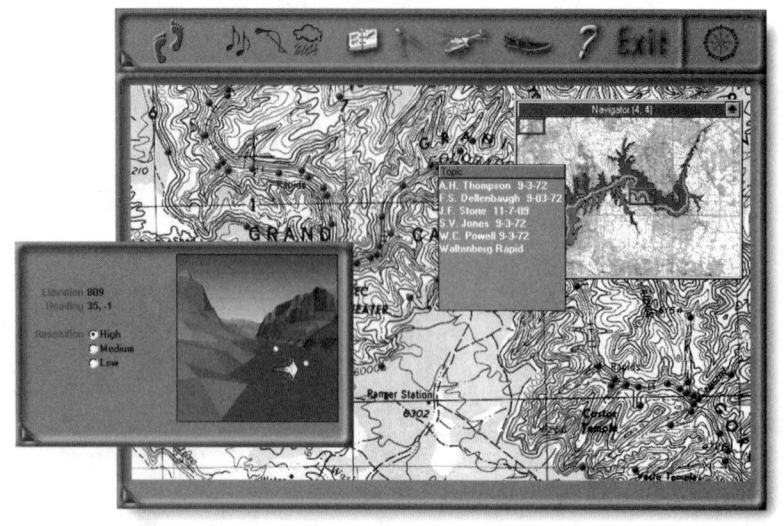

Figure 2.4 Implementing links in Explore the Grand Canyon.

Figure 2.5 A cursor used to indicate different types of hotspots.

allows users to create hypertext documents and share them with the world, regardless of what type of hardware is used to view them. Through HTML, a Windows user with a Web browser can get on the Internet and travel to Web sites created by people all over the world, using different kinds of hardware and operating systems. A person working within Windows 95, for example, can download pages from documents created by people using platforms as varied as Unix, DOS, Windows 3.1, NeXTStep, *ad infinitum*. The point here is that HTML provides a standardized notation for presenting documents.

Hypertext Markup *Language*?

The word "language" shows up again and again in this book. For example, even though we'll use "Delphi" and "Pascal" interchangeably, it sometimes helps to make the distinction between *Delphi*, the visual application development system, and *Pascal*, the language.

To some people, *Language* is a very precise term, and a very foreboding one at that. It conjures up images of shelves of reference manuals, compilers that *just stop* at the first misplaced character, and a learning curve approaching the hike up from the bottom of the Grand Canyon with an 85-pound pack.

That's one reason why we like to think of HTML as a set of simple, easy-to-use formatting codes that can be dropped into a document with any editor that's handy. Of course, syntax *is* important—after all, we're dealing with a computer, here—but a brief skimming of the HTML Reference in the appendix will give you an ample overview of HTML's capabilities and make this "language" a lot less intimidating.

HTML's standardization and its graphical nature are directly responsible for the popularity of the Web. Web page creators, potentially anyone with a modem and terminal, can easily add images, sounds, video—in fact, *any* type of multimedia—to documents that will be seen throughout the world.

The only problem right now with the Web is that its multimedia features demand phenomenal bandwidth. A typical Windows user working with a modem can receive about 28,000 bits per second at best. Downloading an average video file of two or three megabytes can take half an hour! Needless to say, not too many people are willing to sit at their computers for that long each time they click on a video link, waiting for files to download.

If we could ignore physics for a while, we could say the answer would be to simply speed up our connection. Unfortunately, phone companies must follow physical laws, and the current phone technology will not allow data transfer much over the current best of 28.8 Kb/s without special connections and dedicated lines. Thus, from a PC user's point of view, the answer is to use multimedia wisely and sparingly within an online document. This can be said of all multimedia presentations, not just HTML documents. If you create a program that tries to display too many videos, or plays too many simultaneous sounds, things tend to get bogged down. Not everyone who uses your software will have a 300 MHz Pentium and 128 MB of RAM anyway, so you'll need to decide what the lowest common denominator will be for your software and design for that. (Or, if you can't entirely give up the slick effects, you could have separate versions for different systems.)

Regardless of multimedia's technical bottlenecks, HTML has rapidly emerged as the standard for online interactive publishing. And for that reason we decided to completely rewrite the hypermedia engine introduced in the first edition of this book, turning it into an HTML-driven engine that eventually serves, not only as an interactive multimedia engine, but also as the heart of a Web browser.

Creating Text Links

To set up a hypertext system, you'll need to link up text-based information using *anchors*. An *anchor* is simply a designated word or phrase in your text that links up to other information. When a user selects a *reference anchor* by clicking the mouse or pressing a key on the keyboard, a specified *target*, often referred to as a *destination*, is triggered. A target in a hypertext-only system will be yet another item of text; triggering it may simply replace the text currently being displayed with the target text. In a more sophisticated system, targets might display a graphic image, run a video clip, play a sound, or even execute another program. The actual form a hyperlink takes will depend on the format of the source documents you adapt or create for your hypertext system.

Sometimes, it's handy to be able to go to a particular part of a larger work—to go to a particular paragraph of a book chapter, or a particular frame of a video. A *name anchor* can be used to name a particular place or position in a target. This is a subtlety not often explored in traditional PC-based applications, like *WinHelp.Exe* (the Windows Help System program). However, it's one of the basic capabilities of HTML as seen on the Web, allowing users to easily move around in a document without going back out to the Web. One thing is important to remember: while anchors are usually the start of a link, and usually *refer* to general targets (*reference anchor*), they can also be used to indicate the destination of a *named* target (hence *name anchor*). Anchors work both ends of a link.

A hyperlink may advance the user to the beginning of a topic (a simple target) or to a particular line within a lengthy passage (using a name anchor). For documents composed of many brief topics that are short enough to fit entirely on the screen, either type of link would produce the same result. In lengthy documents that remain essentially linear, you could link from word to word or from phrase to phrase. In a presentation that incorporates two or more separate but whole documents, a hyperlink might take the user directly to the top of a document, or to any point within another document. Figure 2.6 shows some examples of hyperlinks in a hypertext system.

Creating a Hypertext System

Now that we've explored the basics of hyperlinking and hypertext, let's embark upon our journey to hypertext. We'll start by simply displaying text with Delphi's event-driven interface. Then, we'll build on this project, adding text formatting and basic hyperlinking. In Chapter 3, we'll build a full-fledged hypertext system with support for features such as pop-up message windows and more-advanced document handling. In Chapter 4, we'll create a full-blown hypermedia system, using Windows API calls to attach multimedia events to our hypertext screens, linking them directly to the "hot" words embedded in the text. By the time we're finished, we'll be making calls to an OCX that hooks us into the Internet—and we'll have ourselves a basic World-Wide Web browser!

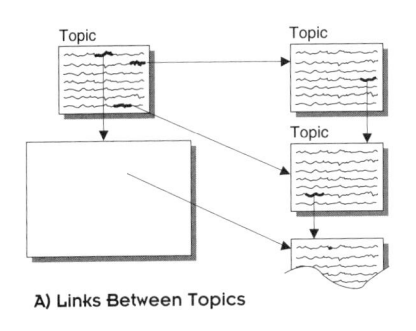

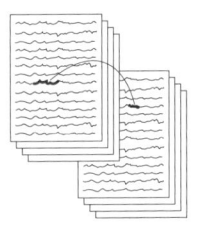

A) Links Between Topics

B) Links between two points in lengthy, contiguous documents.

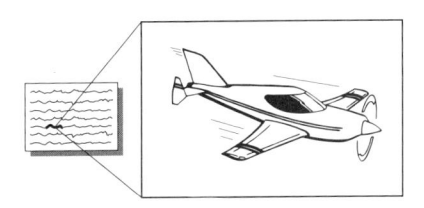

C) Play a multimedia sound, animation, or video, and return.

Figure 2.6 *Types of hyperlinks used in a hypertext system.*

Delphi as a Hypertext Platform

Delphi practically jumps up and screams to become a multimedia development platform. With its powerful built-in and third-party controls (with more appearing every day), direct support for bitmapped graphics, and a remarkable event-driven interface, Delphi gives you more flexibility than you'll find with other multimedia development environments. Delphi also provides easy-to-use encapsulations of most of the Windows API, and the bits left over are still easy to access.

Unfortunately, Delphi doesn't provide a control for hypertext linking; so we have to roll our own. We'll need to display text that contains highlighted "hotlinks." Clicking on these causes the system to display a text page (known as a *topic* or *subject*) that elaborates on or defines the highlighted word. If all this seems like too much work for you, take heart; custom controls are available to perform these operations. However, custom controls require extra resources, and by creating our own system, we can customize it without any limitations or restraints imposed on us by someone else's code. Besides, we're going to hold your hand as we walk you through the process of building this system; so you won't feel all alone.

Searching for the Right Control

Of all the controls included with Delphi, there are three possible options for our hypertext system:

- The Edit control; its brother, the Memo; and their younger 32-bit cousin, the Rich Edit control
- Combinations of Labels and Buttons
- Images and Paint Boxes

Let's examine each of these approaches with a critical eye.

- **Edit, Memo, and Rich Edit controls** These controls are designed to display and edit text. They support the standard Windows mouse techniques for selecting text and performing clipboard operations (and in the case of the RTF Memo, even text formatting such as bolding, font size, and so forth is supported). Unfortunately, they don't provide many mouse events for external programmed responses, because they offer their own internal mouse-dependent editing functions. As user-operable editing boxes, they represent an overkill. Our main problem with these controls lies in the fact that we have no way to determine exactly where certain text—say, our hotlinks—is displayed. And if we don't know where our hotlinks are displayed, we can't find out if a user has clicked on one. It looks as if we'll have to scrap these controls for now.

- **Labels and Buttons** A combination of labels and buttons can be used to implement our hypertext system (for a garish example, see Figure 2.7). All *plain* text (text that isn't hotlinked) could appear on the form as Labels. To display a hotlink, we could place a Button between Labels and set the button's caption to the word or phrase to which we wanted to link. Then all we would need to do is respond to the **OnMouseClick** event for the Buttons.

  Displaying text dynamically this way requires some fancy footwork. If our hypertext document has multiple screens, we'd need to place controls at runtime and neatly align them into well-formatted text. Although this approach might work, we'd find ourselves buried in the mechanics of formatting text. Of course, if we just wanted to compose a simple title screen menu with clickable text—this might be a simple way to do it. Let's forget it, though; it's too much work and not very attractive!

- **Images and Paint Boxes** Images and Paint Boxes are the most general display controls available in Delphi. It may seem like a lot of power to harness, but this generality encompasses a range of Delphi and Windows API features that facilitate text formatting. Within a single control, we can mix *typefaces, type size, character attributes*, and even *color*. Now we're talking! We can easily highlight the hotlinks by boldfacing, underlining, or using color contrast. Adding images to our text comes naturally with these graphic controls.

  But there's a dark cloud: words displayed in Images and Paint Boxes are stored as bitmapped images—no longer words, but just pictures of words. On top of that, we have to specify the exact pixel position of the words to be displayed. On the other hand, here is the silver lining. Fortunately,

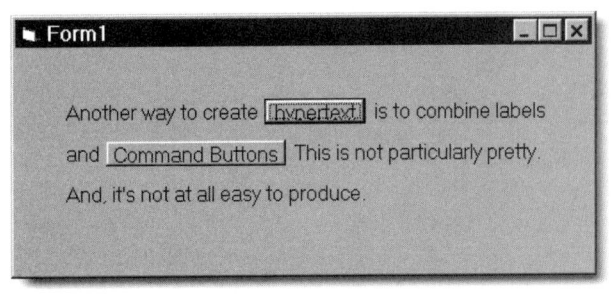

Figure 2.7 *A patchwork of Label and Button controls.*

we don't really need to know the actual word on which the user has clicked—just its location on the screen—so a bitmapped image is OK. To achieve a "hyper jump," knowledge of only three things is required:

- *When* the user clicks on a hotlink
- *Which* link the user clicks on
- The *destination subject*, or *target*

The controls' **OnMouseDown** event can tell us when and where a click has occurred, and we can keep a table that correlates screen coordinates (actually, relative to the Image or Paint Box itself) with destination subjects. Figure 2.8 shows an example of how the Paint Box control can be used to implement our hypertext system.

Images or Paint Boxes?

The only thing left to decide is whether to use an Image control or a Paint Box control. While they both function the same way—that is, display a picture of some sort—there are a couple of subtle differences between them. If you look through the design-time property list for these two components, notice that the Image has a **Picture** property, and that the Paint Box has a **Font** property. On the other hand, the Image doesn't have a **Font**, and the Paint Box doesn't have a **Picture**.

This suggests that the designers of these components had specific purposes in mind for these controls: Images work well with existing pictures, and don't support nice design-time properties for easy drawing (like the Paint Box's **Color** and **Font**); Paint Boxes provide this basic support for

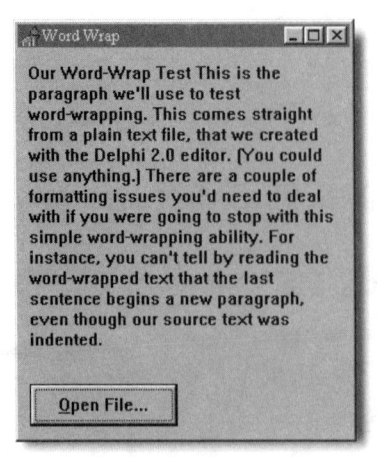

Figure 2.8 Text in a Paint Box, from Word Wrap.

drawing, but don't provide easy-to-use properties for dealing with display of existing images (like **Picture** and **AutoSize**).

Since we'll be creating our own picture in the control by drawing text in it, we'll use the Paint Box for now.

Before Hypertext, Text

So far, we've been singing the praises of hypermedia and, in particular, hyperlinks. Throughout the rest of this chapter and the next, we'll focus on the very basic techniques for creating a hypertext system with Delphi. After that, we'll expand the code presented here to create more powerful hypermedia support tools. We'll also take a look at the Windows 95 Multimedia API.

For the remainder of this chapter, we'll be exploring the world of "ordinary" text display. As mundane as that might sound, we're going to show you the power of Delphi's encapsulation of the elegant Windows GDI text functions, taking advantage of Delphi's **TCanvas** class to make our lives easier. Remember, the root word of *hypertext* is "text"; hypertext presentations, then, are rooted in the simple written word.

You mean, I have to be able to read?!

Yup—that's just the way it is. Okay, perhaps that isn't a very creative way to look at things, but we've stumbled onto the bandwidth "thing." Of the four tractable multimedia elements available today—text, still images, sound, and video—the most responsive medium is text. Let's face it: It's *really* hard to click on a spoken word for a definition. It could be done. You could make your users click the mouse button during (or just after) a word, and give them fast-forward and rewind buttons for the passage to time things just right. When they finally hit the button at the right instant, you could, say, insert a spoken definition of the word, or jump to another passage. Personally, this strikes us as putting an unnecessary burden on your users. Why not just let your users talk into a microphone, and use speech recognition technology to handle the vocal input: "Wait. Define that term, and spell it for me!" The answer is simple: This isn't the bridge of the starship *Enterprise*. You simply can't do that stuff in 1996—at least not economically.

Interaction with video is a little less demanding: There are now techniques that can tie animated hotspots to moving frames of a video. When we talk about *hit detection* in still images, though (in Chapter 11); you'll have a good idea of the work involved in processing this interaction. You may wonder if a 486/33 could handle moving images. Games offer a more

> attainable interaction with a *dynamic environment*, where the media presentation changes through time. We'll discuss some of the basic techniques in Chapters 13 and 14.
>
> Of course, interaction with a *static* environment—fixed in time and position, like a still image, or text— isn't difficult at all. And, if you look around at products on the market, you'll find this is how virtually all of the products today work. Our own *Explore the Grand Canyon* just begins to push the envelope of what will be possible given the more powerful machines of the future, with static maps containing hundreds of hotspots, and its dynamic 3D Virtual Landscape containing hotspots embedded within an interactive 3D model of the Grand Canyon.
>
> The simple written word—or, perhaps, hyperword—is not only the most condensed form of information available to us as multimedia developers; it's also the most powerful conveyance of information we can use, simply because we can put so much in front of a user so quickly and effectively. The simple written word is as close to pure information as human beings can grasp.

Text is the most powerful graphic primitive available to us. It's quite a juxtaposition: Words, with all of their inherent meaning, coupled with their emotional graphic representation, present information that carries an impact from the sublime to the supreme. But, you already know this if you've ever picked up a newspaper. Our job here is to embody this potential in a package that supports hypertext through our chosen hypertext language, HTML.

The Windows API provides us with one key routine for displaying text: **TextOut**. Several other routines are available, and techniques other than those we'll use here are supported. They are fine for the simple text display seen in message boxes and labels; unfortunately, none of them are geared for general formatted text display. **TextOut** takes only two important pieces of information: the location at which the text should be displayed, and the text itself.

Our first project, *Word Wrap*, covers a lot of ground for an applet that handles only four events with two support procedures. TextOut is only one of many key issues in the display of text. As you'll see shortly, it's by no means simple to harness the power and flexibility of text display in Windows. There are no great mysteries, either.

Word Wrap: Basic Text Handling in a Paint Box

For our first real project, this one is pretty substantial. From **pchar** to **PenPos**, from **TOpenDialog** to **FormResize**, we're going to cover a lot of basics. We're even going to play an object game called "I know you're there, but I can't see you!"

However, the most important issues we'll cover are going to deal with text processing. One of the simplest and most important machinations required in working with text is *word-wrapping*. Everywhere we interact dynamically with text, from our word processor to our Web browser, we are constantly seeing text reformatted to fit within our margins or within our window or frame. The technique is simple: break the text into words and start a new line in the display when we can't fit the next word to display on the current line.

1. Create a project directory, *WordWrap*, and a subdirectory to hold our compiler by-products, *WordWrap\Bin*.

2. Start a new project (*File | New Project*). If you are presented with the *Browse Gallery* dialog box, choose "Blank form." On the *Project Options* dialog box (*Options | Project*), on tab...
   - **Application** Set the **Title** to "Text I."
   - **Directories/Conditionals** Set the Output Directory to "Bin."

3. Save the Project (*File | Save Project As*). Save **Unit1** as "Main.Pas" in directory *WordWrap*. Save **Project1** as "Text1.Dpr" in the same directory. The relative path reference, "Bin," from step 2, will now be relative to the project's directory (*WordWrap*).

4. Unit **Main** (originally **Unit1**) brought with it the project's default form, called **Form1**. We won't bother to rename it now. Add controls to **Form1** as described in the section below, *Creating the Form*. A table of important design-time properties and their settings is shown in Table 2.1.

5. Add the text-handling support code to unit **Main**. This form requires the routines
   - Function **Able_to_get_word_from** (Listing 2.1), and
   - Procedure **Display** (Listing 2.2).

6. Add the event handling code (Listing 2.3, the entire unit **Main**) for
   - The Button's **OnClick** event,
   - The PaintBox's **OnPaint** event,

- The Form's **OnCreate** event, and
- The Form's **OnResize** event.

This project, WordWrap.DPR and its support files can be found on the accompanying CD ROM in the directory \Programs\Chap02\WordWrap.

Running Word Wrap

If you run the program and click the **Open File...** button, you will be able to select a file to display in the Paint Box. We chose *\Media\HyperTxt\Sample.Txt* from the CD-ROM in Figure 2.8, above, and our own *Main.Pas* in Figure 2.9. *Word Wrap* will then display the word-wrapped text. Keep in mind that we are skipping a whole bunch of important decisions you'd need to make in order to make this usable in a real application. These problems will gradually be addressed as we progress, but many of the solutions will bring along another set of problems as well.

Creating the Form

Our new form requires three controls: a Button (from the Component Palette's *Standard* page) to open a file for display, an OpenDialog (from the *Dialogs* page) to actually select the file, and a PaintBox (from the *System* page) that occupies most of the form area. Figure 2.10 shows our layout.

On **Form1** itself, we only need to set its **Caption** property to "Word Wrap." Table 2.1 summarizes properties for "Word Wrap'. Set the Button's **Name**

Table 2.1 Properties for Word Wrap.

Class	Property	Value
TForm	Name	Form1 (default)
	Caption	'Word Wrap'
	OnCreate	FormCreate
	OnResize	FormResize
TButton	Name	Open_button
	Caption	'&Open File...'
	OnClick	Open_buttonClick
TOpenDialog	Name	OpenDialog1 (default)
TPaintBox	Name	PaintBox1 (default)
	OnPaint	PaintBox1Paint

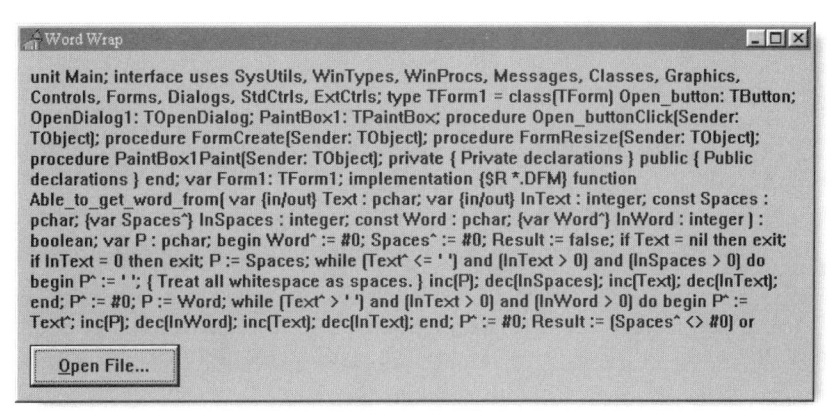

Figure 2.9 Main.Pas, as displayed by Word Wrap.

property to "Open_button" and its **Caption** property to "&Open File..." We'll use the default control names of "OpenDialog1" and "PaintBox1." These controls' default properties are just fine as they are.

Adding the Support Code

We haven't completed the visual part because we haven't written our event handlers. But, as a matter of practice we'll try to start now; we'll first build the support code required to handle the event handling code. This will keep our project compilable. (Though design should be done in a "top-down" manner, smaller module implementation is often made easier through "tool-building": write the code to be called by higher-level routines first, even if it means writing short stubs, and then write the calling routines. This "bottom-up" approach simplifies compilation, because you can stop at any point along the

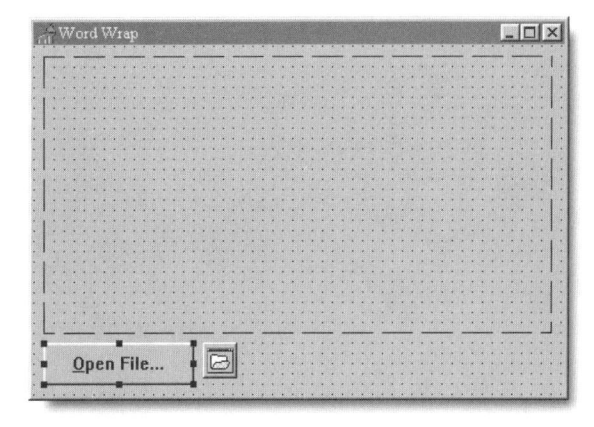

Figure 2.10 Setting up *Form1* (unit *Main*) in Word Wrap.

way to compile and check your syntax. Instead of a real application, you can even write and run brief test routines to make sure your underlying logic is sound.)

To add code to the main form, **Form1**, bring its associated unit, **Main**, to the front. Scroll down past the **implementation**, just after the resource file inclusion directive, **{$R *.DFM}**. Here, we can just drop in our own code. Since Delphi puts its event-response procedure headers just before the unit's final **end**, our own code will be fairly obvious. We'll also use our own indentation, which, hopefully, will distinguish it from the code Delphi writes for us. Later, when we have larger bodies of code not directly related to event responses, we'll move these to their own units.

Dividing Text into Words

In order to do our own word-wrapping, we need a way to get words from our input data. We'll get our text word by word, measuring what we intend to display against the boundaries of our display control. We'll do a "word-wrap" when a word crosses the right side.

Able_to_get_word_from, shown in Listing 2.1, is our most-basic parsing routine. It strips any leading whitespace from a string, returns it in **Spaces**, and then strips a word (a consecutive sequence of non-whitespace characters) and returns it in **Word**. The function value itself is returned as **true**—if indeed, we were able to get either some spaces or a word from the **Text**. This implies that we will return **false** if our **Text** is null (because if it isn't null, either spaces and/or a word must be present).

Listing 2.1   Function **Able_to_get_word_from** from *Main.Pas*

```
function Able_to_get_word_from(
  var {in/out} Text    : pchar;
  var {in/out} lnText  : integer;
  const        Spaces  : pchar;    {var Spaces^}
               lnSpaces : integer;
  const        Word    : pchar;    {var Word^}
               lnWord  : integer
) : boolean;
  var
     P : pchar;
  begin
     Word^   := #0;
     Spaces^ := #0;
     Result := false;
     if Text = nil then exit;
     if lnText = 0 then exit;
```

Foundations of Hypermedia Display

```
        P := Spaces;
        while (Text^ <= ' ') and (lnText > 0) and (lnSpaces > 0) do begin
            P^ := ' '; { Treat all whitespace as spaces. }
            inc(P);
            dec(lnSpaces);
            inc(Text);
            dec(lnText);
            end;
        P^ := #0;

        P := Word;
        while (Text^ > ' ') and (lnText > 0) and (lnWord > 0) do begin
            P^ := Text^;
            inc(P);
            dec(lnWord);
            inc(Text);
            dec(lnText);
            end;
        P^ := #0;

        result := (Spaces^ <> #0) or (Word^ <> #0);
        end;
```

This routine deals with **pchar**s (pointers to characters, defined by Delphi as **type pchar = ^char**). Pchars are usually used to point to *null-terminated strings*, sometimes referred to as *z-strings* (zero-terminated strings). Z-strings live in memory as a sequence of characters, ending with a null, **char(0)**. The main advantage of pchars over Delphi's built-in **ShortString** type is the lack of arbitrary length limit on z-strings pointed to by pchars. This is important to us, because with proportionately-spaced variable-size fonts, and 21-inch displays with 2048 pixels across the screen, it's not unrealistic that we'll have to display more than 255 characters on a line. Heck, some World Wide Web URLs (addresses on the Web) are more than 255 characters! We could (and will, eventually) use Delphi's new **ANSIString**; but, unless we cover the basics of using pchar-based strings, we might end up bewildered!

Able_to_get_word_from is passed the string from which to remove the word via a pointer to its characters, **Text**. Although we could assume **Text** to be a z-string, we'll be interested in its length, passed in as **lnText.** (The prefix "ln" stands for "length"—the length of the string, not including the trailing null.) Why not use the **length** function? Well, with type cohesion, **length** does tell us the length of a z-string pointed to by a **pchar**; it boils down to a routine in the Delphi standard unit **SysUtils**: **StrLen**. Since z-strings don't have a built-in length specifier, like **ShortString**s, **StrLen** is really inefficient; it must actually scan the entire string, comparing each character on the way to a null. So, we pass in the length of the **Text**, measured only once, and decrement it as we remove spaces and words from the **Text**.

We're also going to use another **pchar** technique. Notice that **Text** is passed by reference (using **var**). As we remove characters from the **Text**, we'll increment **Text**, the pointer to the characters. Delphi's extended syntax supporting pchars allows us to actually add offsets to pointers, as long as the pointers are **pchars**. (If you wrote this routine for **string**s, you'd have to delete the removed words with the **delete** routine; delete actually has to copy the remainder of a string to become the start of a string each time it's used—which rivals **StrLen**'s inefficiency.) By simply incrementing **Text** by one, we effectively delete the first character of **Text**.

Beware! Novice programmers can get into trouble here! You may well have dynamically allocated the string you pass in as **Text** (say, with **new**). Since **Able_to_get_word_from** *changes* the value of the pointer, **Text**, you won't be able to free your string (say, with **dispose**), *Unless You Keep an Unchanged Copy of the Pointer to the Start of the String*. In this program, that is the responsibility of the calling routine.

How does **Able_to_get_word_from** work? We've discussed how **Text** is passed. We also passed places in which to store the spaces and word that will be removed, with the pointers **Spaces** and **Word**. To make sure we don't put characters where they don't belong, we also pass the allowable maximum length of the spaces and word, **lnSpaces** and **lnWord**.

Initially, we set the **Word** and **Spaces** to null, by putting a null character (ending the z-string) at the place they point. We then set result to **false**, so we fail when we **exit** if either the **Text** pointer is nil, or the **Text** pointer points to the end of the text string:

```
Word^   := #0;
Spaces^ := #0;
result := false;
if Text = nil then exit;
if lnText = 0 then exit;
```

Then we loop through the **Spaces**. First, we set **P** to point at the first character of the **Spaces** we'll return. Then we loop while (a) the start of the **Text** is whitespace (a space, or any control character); (b) there is some **Text** left, determined by making sure its length is greater than zero; and (c) there is still room to add more spaces to **Spaces**, determined by checking that the allowable length is still greater than zero.

```
P := Spaces;
while (Text^ <= ' ') and (lnText > 0) and (lnSpaces > 0) do begin
    P^ := ' '; { Treat all whitespace as spaces. }
    inc(P);
```

```
        dec(lnSpaces);
        inc(Text);
        dec(lnText);
        end;
P^ := #0;
```

At each whitespace character, if it's truly a space, we put a space into our current place in **Spaces** (held by **P**), move **P** to the next place for a space, and decrement **lnSpaces**, the maximum allowable **Spaces** length (That's why **lnSpaces** is passed by value, and not **const**'ed). Whether or not the whitespace was really a space, we increment **Text**, effectively deleting the whitespace from the front of the string, and decrement the **Text**'s length, **lnText**. When we stop looping (ordinarily, because we hit a letter), we terminate the **Space**s' string by putting a null at the place we would have put the next space.

The same loop structure serves for the **Word** also, except that we always add non-whitespace characters to the **Word**.

```
P := Word;
while (Text^ > ' ') and (lnText > 0) and (lnWord > 0) do begin
    P^ := Text^;
    inc(P);
    dec(lnWord);
    inc(Text);
    dec(lnText);
    end;
P^ := #0;
```

Finally, we return our result as **true** if either **Spaces** or **Words** is not null. If the document ends with a period, followed by a carriage-return/linefeed, the final call to **Able_to_get_word_from** will handle the whitespace (CR/LF) properly, but will still return no **Spaces** and no **Word**. Therefore, we return **false** because we weren't able to get anything printable from the **Text**:

```
result := (Spaces^ <> #0) or (Word^ <> #0);
```

Word-Wrapping

Basic word-wrapping is pretty simple, really. The support routine **Display** does this. It expresses itself well in code; with a couple of **pchar** tricks, it becomes almost elegant in its implementation. We're going to have some explaining to do; let's start with the code shown in Listing 2.2. This code follows **Able_to_get_word_from**.

Listing 2.2   Procedure **Display** from *Main.Pas*

```
type
    tGraphicControlWithCanvas = class(TGraphicControl)
        property Canvas;
        end;

procedure Display(
  const Control      : tGraphicControlWithCanvas;
  const Document     : pchar;
  const lnDocument   : integer
  );
    const
        lnSpaces = 255;
        lnWord   = 254;
    var
        Client_width       : integer;
        lnText             : integer;
        Text,
        Spaces,
        Word_with_space,
        Word_without_space,
        The_word           : pchar;

    begin
        with Control do begin
            with ClientRect do
                Client_width := Right - Left;
            with Canvas do begin
                Brush.Color := Color;
                FillRect(ClientRect);
                MoveTo(Client_width,0{-TextHeight('Xy')});
                SetTextAlign(Handle,TA_BASELINE + TA_UPDATECP);
                end;
            end;

        Spaces             := strAlloc(lnSpaces+1);
        Word_with_space    := strAlloc(lnWord+1+1);
        Word_with_space^   := ' ';
        Word_without_space := Word_with_space+1;

        Text   := Document;
        lnText := lnDocument;
        while
            Able_to_get_word_from(
              Text,lnText,Spaces,lnSpaces,Word_without_space,lnWord
              )
          do begin
            if Spaces^ <> #0 then
                The_word := Word_with_space
              else
                The_word := Word_without_space;
            with Control.Canvas do begin
```

```
            if (PenPos.X + TextWidth(The_word)) > Client_width then begin
               MoveTo(0,PenPos.Y + TextHeight('Xy'));
               The_word := Word_without_space;
               end;
            TextOut(PenPos.X,PenPos.Y,The_word);
            end;
      end;

   strDispose(Word_with_space);
   strDispose(Spaces);
   end;
```

We promised the wrapping itself would be straight-forward, so let's review it first. We begin by looping while we are able to get a word from the text. We'll take a closer look later, but for now, we just need to know that the variable holding the text is **Text**, and the spaces and words we get each time, in **Spaces** and **Word_without_space**. Through some hocus-pocus, we can also refer to the same word, only with a leading space for display, through **Word_with_space**.

```
while
   Able_to_get_word_from(
     Text,lnText,Spaces,lnSpaces,Word_without_space,lnWord
      )
  do begin
    if Spaces^ <> #0 then
       The_word := Word_with_space
      else
       The_word := Word_without_space;
    with Control.Canvas do begin
       if (PenPos.X + TextWidth(The_word)) > Client_width then begin
          MoveTo(0,PenPos.Y + TextHeight('Xy'));
          The_word := Word_without_space;
          end;
       TextOut(PenPos.X,PenPos.Y,The_word);
       end;
    end;
```

As long as we can get a word from the text, we need to measure it against the width of our control. If there are any **Spaces**, **The_word** we want to measure is set to the **Word_with_space**; otherwise, it's set to **Word_without_space**. To measure the word, we call our **Control**'s **Canvas** method, **TextWidth**. If the **TextWidth**, starting from the current *pen position* (where we just finished drawing, before now—presumably the end of the previous word) is greater than the **Control**'s **Client_width** (which we need to calculate ourselves, by the way); then we need to break the line. The pen position is retrieved through the **Canvas** property **PenPos**, and has both an **X** and **Y** component.

To break the line, we **MoveTo** the left margin, an x-coordinate of 0, and add the height of a line to the y-coordinate. To get the height of a line, we call the **Canvas** method **TextHeight**, receiving what is traditionally known as a font's *X-height* (so we pass in "X") plus the depth of a descender (thus, "y"). We also drop the leading space (if it's there), and switch **The_word** to **Word_without_space**. That way, we don't display leading spaces on our word-wrapped lines.

People toss around time-honored typographical terms these days with abandon—can you pronounce "leading"?—but "X-height" typically refers to the height of the tallest capital letters of a font. We can afford to be loose with our terms, though. It seems Windows almost always returns the height of a general character cell in the font, regardless of whether the actual letters have ascenders or descenders. Also added in is the minimal whitespace between lines specified by the font itself, called *internal leading*. By the way, that's *lead*, as in the metal—specifically, the strips of metal used to space out lines of type in olden days.

Finally, starting from the current pen position, (where our last word ended) we call the **Canvas** method **TextOut** to draw **The_word**. This moves the pen to the end of the current word so the process can start again.

Hocus-Pocus

We were pretty sneaky using **The_word**, **Word_with_space**, and **Word_without_space** before. All three of these variables are **pchar**s. **Word_with_space** is the only one we specifically allocate. This is a buffer in which we will always have a leading space.

```
Word_with_space     := strAlloc(lnWord+1+1);
Word_with_space^    := ' ';
Word_without_space  := Word_with_space+1;
```

When we **strAlloc** the word, we receive room for the maximum length of the word (**lnWord**), plus room for a terminating null (**+1**), plus room for a leading space (**+1**). **Word_without_space** is then pointed at the buffer, after the space we forcibly set. Now, whenever we deal with whole words, all we need to do is look at **Word_without_space**. If we want to see the leading space, we look at **Word_with_space** instead. That's what we did above. By assigning whichever of these values was appropriate to **The_word**, we could change whether or not we were considering a leading space.

Foundations of Hypermedia Display

I know you're there, but I can't see you!

In order to keep **Display** as re-usable as possible, we want to be able to pass it any kind of graphical control. In this project, we used a Paint Box—but who's to say we won't want to pass an Image control later?

```
type
    tGraphicControlWithCanvas = class(TGraphicControl)
        property Canvas;
        end;

procedure Display(
  const Control    : tGraphicControlWithCanvas;
  const Document   : pchar;
  const lnDocument : integer
  );
```

With a little research in Delphi's *Help*, we discover that Paint Boxes and Images both descend from the same parent class, **TGraphicControl**. We can cast an object to be any of its ancestors safely in Delphi's Object Pascal; so now, we can display text on any **TGraphicControl**. Problem is, even though *Help* tells us **TGraphicControl** has a **Canvas** property, you'll discover if you try to reference it that you'll get a compile-time error. If you look through the properties of a **TGraphicControl** with *the Object Browser*, you'll discover why: it's a **protected** property. You can only access it in the unit in which it is defined, which means you'd have to rewrite Delphi's own *Controls.Pas* unit to get to it!

Fortunately, there's a back-door that let's you re-visible-ize **protected** elements of an object to other units. For a **property**, like Canvas, you just announce it without a **read** or **write** clause. That's what we've done in declaring our own **tGraphicControlWithCanvas**. Since this is equivalent to **TGraphicControl**, we can safely cross-cast **TImage** and **TPaintBox** to this class, also.

Once we can see the Canvas, we can manipulate it by referring to its methods and properties as we did above. We jump right into it when we initialize **Display**, too.

```
with Control do begin
    with ClientRect do
        Client_width := Right - Left;
    with Canvas do begin
        Brush.Color := Color;
        FillRect(ClientRect);
        MoveTo(Client_width,0);
```

```
        SetTextAlign(Handle,TA_BASELINE + TA_UPDATECP);
      end;
end;
```

To get the **Client_width**, we examine the *client rectangle* (the usable area of the **Control** we were sent to **Display** upon). Subtracting **Control.ClientRect.Left** from **Right** gives us the width of the rectangle. Shouldn't there be a "+1" somewhere there? Yes, except Windows defines **Right** (and **Bottom**) as already being one pixel further (thus, "+1") than the actual pixels involved in a control. This is called a *bounding rectangle* and is discussed a little more in Chapter 9, as well as shown in Figure 9.4.

Before we draw, we set the **Canvas.Brush.Color** to the **Control**'s **Color**, and blank the **Canvas** with **FillRect**. By moving to an x-coordinate of **Client_width**, we will force the first word we display to move us to the start of the first valid line of the display. As you can see from the call to **SetTextAlign**, we are specifying the *baseline* of the text with these coordinates. Don't confuse this with the *top* (where the position of the tops of the character cells is specified), or *bottom* (where the position of the bottoms of the character cells is specified).

SetTextAlign is a somewhat different call that represents a direct call to Windows. In order to let Windows know which of the many graphic environments (called *device contexts*) we're working in, we need to pass in a *handle*. A handle is just a unique integer identifier that Windows uses to refer to "things." The thing we're concerned with here is a device context. A device context is what Windows uses to store all of the information about the current graphic set-up of a particular window. Delphi shelters us from this with its **Canvas** property. However, if we ever do need to go straight to Windows (as we do now), Delphi's **Canvas** has a property, **Handle**, that Windows is perfectly happy to use.

The text alignment we want to use allows us to specify the left baseline as the starting point of the text we draw with **TextOut**. The constant used to represent this setting is **TA_BASELINE**. By default, Delphi makes us specify the *top* left corner of the text we wish to draw. For the work we'll be doing, this is a little more difficult. The other setting we specify is **TA_UPDATECP**, or *update current position*. Neither Windows text drawing or Delphi maintains the current pen position for text by default, so we need to explicitly turn on position tracking for text.

Adding the Event Handlers

Here's where we are finally able to make things happen! Here's the strategy: We want to be able to load a file into memory and keep it around; and whenever we need to repaint the screen, we'll be able to re-**Display** the file. Our **OpenDialog1** will spring into action if the user clicks the **Open_button**. as soon as we know what file to load, we'll load the file, referred to as a *document*, into a structure called a **TMemoryStream**. We're going to let the Paint Box's own **OnPaint** handler actually call **Display**; since any time **PaintBox1** is painted, we want to redisplay our document. If we want to force the document to be displayed—for instance, when it's loaded—we can force the **OnPaint** event to happen with a call to the Paint Box's **Refresh** method.

We're also going to handle resizing the form and its controls right from the start. A great deal of code is needed to support this, and in some cases, it can get tricky. In this case, fortunately, it's not too bad.

Listing 2.3 shows the entire unit **Main**, with all of the code in place.

Listing 2.3 The Entire Unit **Main** for *Word Wrap*

```
unit Main;

interface

uses
  SysUtils, WinTypes, WinProcs, Messages, Classes, Graphics, Controls,
  Forms, Dialogs, StdCtrls, ExtCtrls;

type
  TForm1 = class(TForm)
    Open_button: TButton;
    OpenDialog1: TOpenDialog;
    PaintBox1: TPaintBox;
    procedure Open_buttonClick(Sender: TObject);
    procedure FormCreate(Sender: TObject);
    procedure FormResize(Sender: TObject);
    procedure PaintBox1Paint(Sender: TObject);
  private
    { Private declarations }
  public
    { Public declarations }
  end;

var
  Form1: TForm1;

implementation

{$R *.DFM}

function Able_to_get_word_from(
    var {in/out} Text     : pchar;
    var {in/out} lnText   : integer;
    const        Spaces   : pchar;   {var Spaces^}
                 lnSpaces : integer;
```

```
        const     Word       : pchar;    {var Word^}
                  lnWord     : integer
        ) : boolean;
          var
              P : pchar;
          begin
              Word^   := #0;
              Spaces^ := #0;
              Result := false;
              if Text = nil then exit;
              if lnText = 0 then exit;

              P := Spaces;
              while (Text^ <= ' ') and (lnText > 0) and (lnSpaces > 0) do begin
                  P^ := ' '; { Treat all whitespace as spaces. }
                  inc(P);
                  dec(lnSpaces);
                  inc(Text);
                  dec(lnText);
                  end;
              P^ := #0;

              P := Word;
              while (Text^ > ' ') and (lnText > 0) and (lnWord > 0) do begin
                  P^ := Text^;
                  inc(P);
                  dec(lnWord);
                  inc(Text);
                  dec(lnText);
                  end;
              P^ := #0;

              Result := (Spaces^ <> #0) or (Word^ <> #0);
              end;

type
    tGraphicControlWithCanvas = class(TGraphicControl)
        property Canvas;
        end;

procedure Display(
    const Control     : tGraphicControlWithCanvas;
    const Document    : pchar;
    const lnDocument  : integer
    );
      const
          lnSpaces = 255;
          lnWord   = 254;
      var
          Client_width        : integer;
          lnText              : integer;
          Text,
          Spaces,
          Word_with_space,
```

Foundations of Hypermedia Display

```
            Word_without_space,
            The_word           : pchar;

    begin
        with Control do begin
            with ClientRect do
                Client_width := Right - Left;
            with Canvas do begin
                Brush.Color := Color;
                FillRect(ClientRect);
                MoveTo(Client_width,0{-TextHeight('Xy')});
                SetTextAlign(Handle,TA_BASELINE + TA_UPDATECP);
                end;
            end;

        Spaces             := strAlloc(lnSpaces+1);
        Word_with_space    := strAlloc(lnWord+1+1);
        Word_with_space^   := ' ';
        Word_without_space := Word_with_space+1;

        Text   := Document;
        lnText := lnDocument;
        while
            Able_to_get_word_from(
              Text,lnText,Spaces,lnSpaces,Word_without_space,lnWord
              )
          do begin
            if Spaces^ <> #0 then
                The_word := Word_with_space
              else
                The_word := Word_without_space;
            with Control.Canvas do begin
                if (PenPos.X + TextWidth(The_word)) > Client_width then begin
                    MoveTo(0,PenPos.Y + TextHeight('Xy'));
                    The_word := Word_without_space;
                    end;
                TextOut(PenPos.X,PenPos.Y,The_word);
                end;
            end;

        strDispose(Word_with_space);
        strDispose(Spaces);
        end;

var
    The_document : TMemoryStream;

procedure TForm1.Open_buttonClick(Sender: TObject);
    begin
        if OpenDialog1.Execute then begin
            The_document.LoadFromFile(OpenDialog1.FileName);
            PaintBox1.Refresh;
            end;
        end;
```

```
var
    Resizing_ourselves : boolean;
    Form1s_old_width,
    Form1s_old_height  : integer;

procedure TForm1.FormCreate(Sender: TObject);
    begin
        The_document := TMemoryStream.Create;
        Resizing_ourselves := false;
        Form1s_old_width   := Width;
        Form1s_old_height  := Height;
        end;

procedure TForm1.FormResize(Sender: TObject);
    var
        PaintBox1s_new_width,
        PaintBox1s_new_height,
        Catchup_width,
        Catchup_height     : integer;
    begin
        if Resizing_ourselves then exit;
        Resizing_ourselves := true;
        PaintBox1s_new_width  := PaintBox1.Width  + (Width  - Form1s_old_width);
        PaintBox1s_new_height := PaintBox1.Height + (Height - Form1s_old_height);

        Catchup_width := 0;
        Catchup_height := 0;
        if PaintBox1s_new_width < Open_button.Width then
            Catchup_width := Open_button.Width - PaintBox1s_new_width;
        if PaintBox1s_new_height < 20 then
            Catchup_height := 20 - PaintBox1s_new_height;
        inc(PaintBox1s_new_width, Catchup_width);
        inc(PaintBox1s_new_height,Catchup_height);

        if Catchup_width <> 0 then
            Width  := Width  + Catchup_width;
        if Catchup_height <> 0 then
            Height := Height + Catchup_height;
        with PaintBox1 do begin
            Width  := PaintBox1s_new_width;
            Height := PaintBox1s_new_height;
            end;
        Open_button.Top := Open_button.Top + (Height - Form1s_old_height);
        Resizing_ourselves := false;
        Form1.Refresh;

        Form1s_old_width   := Form1.Width;
        Form1s_old_height  := Form1.Height;
        end;

procedure TForm1.PaintBox1Paint(Sender: TObject);
    begin
        if Resizing_ourselves then exit;
```

```
      Display(
        tGraphicControlWithCanvas(PaintBox1),
        The_document.Memory,The_document.Size
        );
      end;

end.
```

Opening a Document

When we click the **Open_button**, we want to bring up the **OpenDialog1** dialog box, then load the selected document. To insert the framework for the **Open_buttonClick** event handler at design time, double-click on the button itself, or double-click on the **OnClick** line of the *Events* page of *the Object Inspector* dialog box. Flesh out the framework with the code shown.

```
var
    The_document : TMemoryStream;

procedure TForm1.Open_buttonClick(Sender: TObject);
    begin
        if OpenDialog1.Execute then begin
            The_document.LoadFromFile(OpenDialog1.FileName);
            PaintBox1.Refresh;
            end;
        end;
```

The_document is a global variable that holds the document in memory. It is a member of the **TMemoryStream** class. A Memory Stream is Delphi's encapsulation of a chunk of memory that can be accessed much like a file. We really aren't interested in these capabilities, though. We are going to take advantage of the fact that Delphi streams like **TMemoryStream** themselves support actual file I/O for purposes of initialization and storage. We don't want to **Write** to a **TMemoryStream**, but we do want to use its **LoadFromFile** method to get it from the disk.

Evaluating the **Execute** method puts up the **OpenDialog1** dialog box and lets the user select a file. If no file is selected, **Execute** returns **false**. If a file is selected, we call **The_document.LoadFromFile** to load the document; and then we **Refresh** the Paint Box. This causes **PaintBox1**'s **OnPaint** handler to be invoked.

Painting the Paint Box—Displaying the Document

We have only one chore when the Paint Box is repainted, whether we forced it to repaint by calling **Refresh**, or Windows caused the repainting by uncovering it.

```
procedure TForm1.PaintBox1Paint(Sender: TObject);
   begin
      if Resizing_ourselves then exit;
      Display(
        tGraphicControlWithCanvas(PaintBox1),
        The_document.Memory,The_document.Size
        );
      end;
```

Before we take care of our chore, we first make sure we aren't in the process of resizing the main form. We're about to look at those gyrations; for now, we just need to realize that the Paint Box could be painted many times during a form resizing, and we don't want to respond to any of those events. **Resizing_ourselves** is the flag we use to indicate that we're in the middle of those gyrations. If we are, we **exit**.

Otherwise, we call **Display**, passing **PaintBox1**, appropriately type-cast to its ancestor-equivalent, **tGraphicControlWithCanvas**, as the destination for the display. We then need to pass a **pchar** pointing to the first character of **The_document**, and the length of **The_document**. We use **TMemoryStream**'s properties **Memory**, which points to the first byte of the data in the Memory Stream, and **Size**, which stores the number of bytes in the stream. Remember, since **Able_to_get_word_from** works by comparing the length remaining to zero, we don't need to worry about whether or not **The_document** is null-terminated.

Resizing the Form

To handle form resizing, we need three global variables. **Resizing_ourselves** indicates that we are currently resizing ourselves and not responding to a user's resizing request. This would be necessary if the user tried to make the form too small, and we wanted to resize it ourselves, backing out to some comfortable minimum size.

```
var
    Resizing_ourselves : boolean;
    Form1s_old_width,
    Form1s_old_height  : integer;

procedure TForm1.FormCreate(Sender: TObject);
   begin
      The_document := TMemoryStream.Create;
      Resizing_ourselves := false;
      Form1s_old_width   := Width;
      Form1s_old_height  := Height;
      end;
```

Foundations of Hypermedia Display

In order to determine how much the form has changed in size, we'll record the form's width and height in **Form1s_old_width** and **Form1s_old_height**. We initialize these variables upon form creation. We also create **The_document**, so that we'll have something (even if it's blank) to **Display** other than an uninstantiated object.

Handling the **OnResize** event is tedious, but not difficult. One of the keys to understanding what is really going on here is realizing that we're interested in our component's relative positions and amounts of movement as opposed to specific positioning.

Before we do anything, we check to see if the resizing event is happening, because we set **Form1**'s size ourselves. If it is, we simply **exit**. If not, we go ahead and announce that we are resizing. At this point, other code, like **PaintBox1Paint**, will recognize that we're handling resizing right now.

```
procedure TForm1.FormResize(Sender: TObject);
    var
        PaintBox1s_new_width,
        PaintBox1s_new_height,
        Catchup_width,
        Catchup_height      : integer;
    begin
        if Resizing_ourselves then exit;
        Resizing_ourselves := true;
        PaintBox1s_new_width  := PaintBox1.Width  + (Width  - Form1s_old_width);
        PaintBox1s_new_height := PaintBox1.Height + (Height - Form1s_old_height);

        Catchup_width := 0;
        Catchup_height := 0;
        if PaintBox1s_new_width < Open_button.Width then
            Catchup_width := Open_button.Width - PaintBox1s_new_width;
        if PaintBox1s_new_height < 20 then
            Catchup_height := 20 - PaintBox1s_new_height;
        inc(PaintBox1s_new_width, Catchup_width);
        inc(PaintBox1s_new_height,Catchup_height);
```

The first thing we do is calculate a new size for our Paint Box, **PaintBox1s_new_width** and **...height**, by changing its size by the amount **Form1** itself has changed size. We then calculate a **Catchup_width** and **...height**, which is how much larger we'll need to make the Paint Box to get it up to its minimum comfortable size. In our case, we've decided it must be at least as wide as the **Open_button**, and at least twenty pixels high.

The catch-up factor is used to increase the new size of our Paint Box, and also used to resize our form. This is the point at which our **OnResize** handler could cause an **OnResize** event, thus causing an endless, recursive loop. Without the **Resizing_ourselves** flag, this would surely happen.

```
    if Catchup_width <> 0 then
        Width  := Width  + Catchup_width;
    if Catchup_height <> 0 then
        Height := Height + Catchup_height;
    with PaintBox1 do begin
        Width  := PaintBox1s_new_width;
        Height := PaintBox1s_new_height;
        end;
    Open_button.Top := Open_button.Top + (Height - Form1s_old_height);
    Resizing_ourselves := false;
    Form1.Refresh;

    Form1s_old_width   := Form1.Width;
    Form1s_old_height  := Form1.Height;
    end;
```

After we've resized the Form (if it needed to be enlarged), we resize the Paint Box and move the Button down by the amount of the Form's final size change. Once everything is moved, we set **Resizing_ourselves** to **false**, and call **Form1.Refresh** to make sure all of our sizing changes are displayed. This **Refresh** will invoke the **OnPaint** event for all of the Form's child controls, so we'll now call **PaintBox1Paint** to **Display The_document** in the resized window. Finally, we record the Form's **Width** and **Height**, so we can do this all over again.

Wrapping up Word Wrap

This digression to ordinary text display has been a big first step, hasn't it? But it's one we had to take to implement professional text display. First and foremost, we covered the basic ideas of breaking text down into its components, words and whitespace, and the display of this text in an orderly fashion. We also covered several of Delphi's key VCL routines for working with text, **TextOut**, **TextWidth**, **TextHeight**, and the **PenPos**. We didn't leave out the raw Windows API, either, with our call to **SetTextAlign**. To go a little further, you could make more efficient use of Windows than the VCL by using **GetTextExtentPoint**. With some research, you could even determine how the property **PenPos** works and make direct API calls to replace the property use. Look into it.

Along with a little hand-waving about objects, we discussed getting to a **TGraphicComponent**'s **Canvas**. Along the way, we also covered some powerful techniques for working with **pchar**s and null-terminated strings.

In the next project, we'll work on encapsulation, the division of software components into packages of related parts. The packages are often referred to as *black boxes*—after a piece of code is embodied in one of these "black boxes," programmers using the box no longer need to know anything (in theory, at least) about how the box does its work, just what it does. We'll add our first *support units*, units without related forms; and we'll create our first *class*.

Use of the class model is one of the cleanest encapsulation techniques available to programmers today. Without it, virtually all moderately large software systems could never be written. Word processors such as Microsoft's *Word*, IBM's *Lotus 1-2-3*, and even *Delphi* itself would not have been possible without this technology, based on *object-oriented methodologies*.

An *object* represents a combination of a data structure and routines to manipulate it. In Delphi, an object is a variable declared in a **var** section. Of course, you must declare the variable to be of a certain type. An object's type is referred to as a *class*, and is defined in a **type** section. In the same way that we say, "X and Y are numbers of type integer," we can say "My_steely and Your_catseye are objects, that are members of the class Marble." But that takes us too far ahead of ourselves, and we have a lot more ground to cover.

Chapter 3

To create powerful multimedia applications with Delphi, you'll want your own custom multimedia engine. In this chapter we'll create a flexible engine that uses HTML as its hypermedia language.

Building a Hypermedia Engine

Dan Haygood

Before we can display hypertext with highlighted hotlinks, we need to define a format for our *source text*, and we need to decide how it should behave. As we mentioned earlier, we eventually want to add Web browsing functions to this application, so we should start using HTML right from the beginning. Since we're battling with simple text output right now, we only need to know how HTML hypertext (or simply "HTML") acts when it is displayed.

Since HTML was created as a device-independent textual/graphic communication medium, its designers couldn't set a fixed screen size or page size. As a result, HTML simply adapts to whatever display it is given, which means that we'll have to draw upon our word-wrapping experience from Chapter 2.

Actually, word wrapping is the least of our problems. HTML utilizes notations (or *tags*) to support everything from underlining to hotlink anchor specification. Many of these features deal only with simple character attributes: underlining, italics, boldface. Others, however, are particularly challenging. In our *Word Wrap* project from Chapter 2, we were able to advance from line to line simply by moving down by the height consisting of a capital letter and a small letter with a descender. HTML supports a varying font size; so to move down from one baseline to the next, we'll need to advance by the depth of our current line's ascenders, and then by the height of the next line's ascenders. As you can see, supporting some of these features will cut straight and quickly to the heart of our deepest mechanism.

Handling Hypertext

The first thing we need to do is plan a strategy for handling our hypertext. This problem has three facets. First, we need to be able to parse HTML tags. Secondly, we must be able to identify sections of text that share the same formatting specified by HTML tags. Finally, we must be able to display the text, breaking it into lines based on the dimensions of the output device and the text we want it to display.

Basic HTML

What is HTML, and how does it format text? Simply defined, it's a notation for device-independent, formatted hypertext. Since it is device-independent, many of the techniques we typically use to format text are useless. For instance, in a simple text file, you might format your text using tabs to establish a margin, spaces to separate words, and indentation to signal the start of a new paragraph to the reader. This would be fine if everybody had the same-sized screen.

Since that is definitely not the case, we need to treat the text more like the text in a modern word-processing document. In a typical word processor, if you type past the right margin, the word you are typing will be dropped to the start of the next line. When you are finished with a paragraph, you press the [enter] key, and the next line will start at the left margin. If you insert text that causes a word near the right margin to cross it, the word-processor will automatically re-word-wrap the entire paragraph.

Unfortunately, HTML documents are just plain ASCII text files. They don't contain those magic formatting characters such as paragraph breaks. When you put a carriage return in an HTML document by pressing [enter] in your favorite plain-text editor, it just starts a new line. So instead of relying on ethereal "codes," HTML relies on tags—simple embedded format specifications—typed into a document along with the text, as shown in the snippet below:

```
This is a paragraph.  Since this is the beginning of the
document, it doesn't need a tag to indicate that it's a new
paragraph.  <P> But inside the document, adding the
```

```
tag "<P>" indicates to a <i>browser</i> that a new paragraph
should be started.
```

This sample illustrates just one of the many tags available in HTML, demonstrating how they are simply notations in the text. By the way, if you had a browser that indicated the start of a new paragraph by skipping a line and indenting (most don't—they just start the next paragraph on the next line at the left margin), you'd get something that looks like the snippet below:

```
     This is a paragraph.  Since this
is the beginning of the document, it
doesn't need a tag to indicate that
it's a new paragraph.
     But inside the document, adding
the tag "
     " indicates to a browser that a
new paragraph should be started.
```

Oops. That second **<P>**, even though it was in quotes, is still a paragraph break. Don't worry; we have ways to get around this. Just keep in mind that HTML can take you very literally.

With just the simple paragraph tag, **<P>**, we've already solved one of the problems with our simple *Word Wrap* text from Chapter 2. We have paragraphs again.

Parsing HTML

Finding tags in an HTML document is really as easy as it looks. Find an opening angle-bracket, <, and grab all of the text up to the closing angle-bracket, >. Then you can look at the tag and assume that the text after the tag will have the format specified by the tag. Here's the rub: **<U>** (underline) is pretty easy to read and act on. But try the code line shown below:

```
<IMG ALIGN=LEFT BORDER=5 HSPACE=10 VSPACE=5 WIDTH=150 HEIGHT=200 SRC="FACE.GIF">
```

This thing practically has a language of its own!

Formatted Text

Each tag we encounter is going to change the format of all the text we display subsequently. This naturally specifies the first level of device-independent organization of an HTML document. As you'll see, the first level of our hypertext processing will consist of a simple cycle: Process a tag; set the current format. Get some text. Process a tag. Get some text. And so on.

Displaying the Text

The chunks of formatted text will be easy to track, but the format changes will virtually never line up with the margins of a typical browser. We need to impose another layer of organization on the formatted text. Once we have a list of chunks of text, we'll need to go through the list, indicating at which points we should advance our display position to the left side of the next line.

This is where our word-wrapping skills go to work. The process for breaking up the formatted text into lines remains the same: Measure a word. If it fits on the current line, add it. If not, start a new line, and place it there. Do the next word, and the next, and the next, until all of the current format's words are exhausted—then go on to the next format's words.

Once the formatted text is broken into lines, displaying the lines is just a matter of looping through the list and drawing the text on a Paint Box with **TextOut**.

Hyper I: Basic Formatted Text Display

This project demonstrates the method outlined above for displaying formatted text. We're going to implement the fundamental paragraph tag, **<P>**, and the italic, **<I>**, and underline, **<U>**, tags also. Along the way, we'll talk about units and objects.

1. Create a new project directory, *Hyper1*, and an output subdirectory, *Bin*.

2. Open a new application, and in the *Project Options* dialog box, set its Application Title to "Hyper1" and its Output Directory to "Bin."

3. You might want to take this opportunity to save the project in the *Hyper1* project directory. Save the project as *Hyper1.DPR*, and the default form's (**Form1**) associated unit as *Main.Pas*.

4. Do the visual work on the main form, **Form1**. We need a Panel with a PaintBox on top of it (to make an attractive presentation area), an OpenDialog, a Button to run the OpenDialog, an Edit control in which to show the filename, and finally, a close Button. The form at design-time is shown in Figure 3.2; the important properties of the controls are given in Table 3.1.

5. Add the support unit *MiscLib.Pas* (Listing 3.1) by choosing *File | New Form* from Delphi's menu. To name the unit something other than Delphi's default name, **Unit1**, choose *File | Save As* and

specify the name **MiscLib**. The ".pas" extension will be assumed. This is just one of four units we'll be adding to the project in addition to **Form1**'s associated unit, *Main.Pas*.

6. Add the support unit *Font.Pas* (Listing 3.2). This defines some of the basic data types with which we'll be working.
7. Add the support unit *FmtText.Pas* (Listing 3.3). This declares the list of formatted text that we'll be building, line-breaking, and displaying in unit **DispBuf**, below.
8. Add the support unit *DispBuf.Pas* (Listings 3.4, 3.5, 3.6, and 3.7). This unit implements our parse-break-display HTML engine. There's a lot of meat on this bone.
9. Finally, add the event handlers to unit **Main** (Listing 3.8).

This project, Hyper1.DPR, and all of its support files, can be found on the accompanying CD-ROM, in the directory \Programs\Chap03\Hyper1. Sample data can be found in the directory \Media\HyperTxt.

Running Hyper I

To see the basic rendition of our sample hypertext, click the **Open File...** button, and choose *Sample.HTM* from the *\Media\HyperTxt* directory. You can also simply enter the filename directly into the Edit control and press [enter] to load the file. *Hyper I*, running with the sample loaded and the window resized, is shown in Figure 3.1.

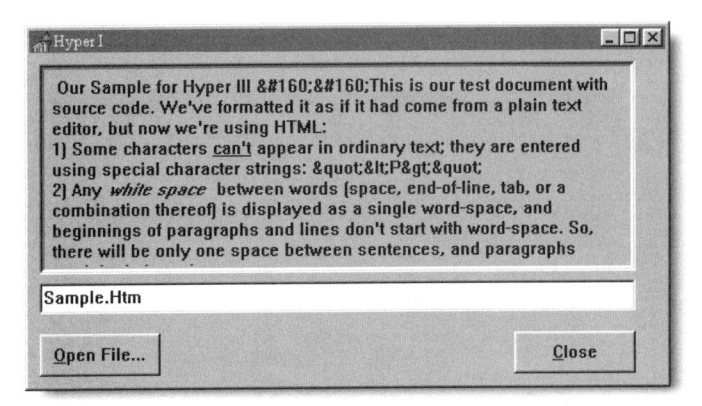

Figure 3.1 *Basic formatted text display with Hyper I.*

Creating the Form

The placement of the controls on the form is shown in Figure 3.2. Before we begin placing controls, set **Form1**'s **Caption** to "Hyper I." First, we need a stage for our presentation. From the *Standard* page of the *Component Palette*, select a Panel and click-and-drag a panel over most of the top half of **Form1**. Blank its **Caption**, set its **BevelOuter** to Lowered, its **BevelWidth** to 2, **BorderStyle** to Single, and **BorderWidth** to 2. We'll use its default **Name** of **Panel1**. Then, from the *System* page, select a PaintBox, and click-and-drag it over most of the Panel. Make sure you start and stop on top of the Panel. We achieve the effect of margins by making the PaintBox slightly smaller than the Panel. We'll use its default properties, including its **Name**, **PaintBox1**.

Now it's time to add support for loading files. Drop a Button from the *Standard* page in the lower-left corner of **Form1**. Set its **Caption** to "&Open File..." and its **Name** to **Open_button**. We'll use the **Open_button** to start an OpenDialog from the *Dialogs* page. Its **Name**, **OpenDialog1** is fine, but we'll want to set it up nicely. Set its **DefaultExt** to "htm," and its **InitialDir** to the location of the *\Media\HyperTxt* files on your machine. You may even want to set its **Filename** property to "Sample." Double-click on the **Filter** property's value area, and the *Filter Editor* will appear. Add one line with a Filter Name of "Hypertext," and a Filter of "*.Htm," and a second line, "Plain Text," with "*.Txt," then "OK" the editor. Add an Edit control from the *Standard* page, in which we'll display the name of the currently loaded file, allowing users to directly enter the names of files they'd like to load. Set the control's **Name** to **Filename**. Blank its **Text**.

Finally, add a Button to the lower-right corner. **Name** it **Close_button** and set its **Caption** to "&Close." The important properties for all of these control are shown in Table 3.1.

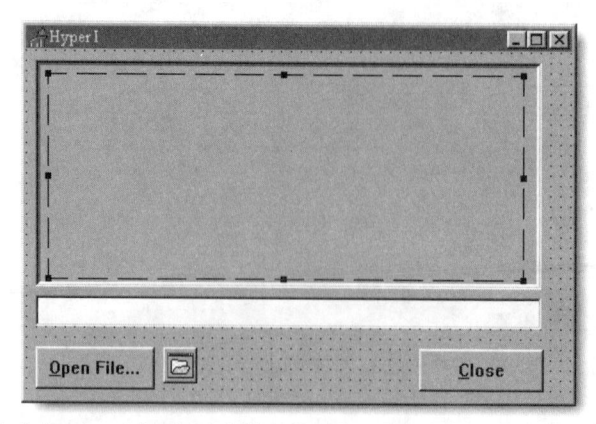

Figure 3.2 *Control placement for Hyper I. Note the placement of the PaintBox on top of the Panel.*

Table 3.1 Properties for **Form1** in Hyper 1.

Class	Property	Value
TForm	Name	Form1 (default)
TPanel	Name	Panel1 (default)
	Caption	blank
	BevelOuter	bvLowered
	BevelWidth	2
	BorderStyle	bsSingle
	BorderWidth	2
TPaintBox	Name	PaintBox1 (default)
TButton	Name	Open_button
	Caption	'&Open File...'
	OnClick	Open_buttonClick
TOpenDialog	Name	OpenDialog1 (default)
	DefaultExt	'htm'
	InitialDir	your choice
	Filename	'Sample'
	Filter	'Hypertext|*.Htm|Plain Text|*.Txt'
TEdit	Name	Filename
	Text	blank
	OnKeyPress	FilenameKeyPress
TButton	Name	Close_button
	Caption	'&Close'
	OnClick	Close_buttonClick

Creating the MiscLib Unit

If you followed the steps above, you have a unit that looks something like the code shown below:

```
unit Misclib;

interface

implementation

end.
```

Simply fill in the blanks with the **Int_max**, **Int_min**, and **StrXlate** functions shown in Listing 3.1, indenting as you prefer.

Listing 3.1 The *MiscLib.Pas* support unit

```pascal
unit MiscLib;

interface

function Int_max(
  const A, B : integer
  ) : integer;

function Int_min(
  const A, B : integer
  ) : integer;

function StrXlate(
        S      : pchar;
  const C_from,
        C_to   : char
  ) : integer;

implementation

uses
     SysUtils;

function Int_max(
  const A, B : integer
  ) : integer;
    begin
        if A > B then result := A else result := B;
        end;

function Int_min(
  const A, B : integer
  ) : integer;
    begin
        if A < B then result := A else result := B;
        end;

function StrXlate(
        S      : pchar;
  const C_from,
        C_to   : char
  ) : integer;
    begin
        result := 0;
        S := strScan(S,C_from);
        while S <> nil do begin
            inc(result);
            S^ := C_to;
            S := strScan(S+1,C_from);
            end;
        end;
```

```
{initialization}
end.
```

Units: A Classic Encapsulation

Those readers coming from a Borland Pascal background (well, at least since the introduction of *Turbo Pascal 4.0*) should already be familiar with the concept of dividing programs into manageable chunks with *units*—they might skip ahead. For those of you who are new to units, read on.

A unit has two major sections: the *interface* and the *implementation*. These form a classic black box—the **interface** describing what the black box can do to the outside world, and the **implementation** telling the compiler exactly what must be done to accomplish the tasks at hand. The third section, **initialization**, is used only when some program load-time initialization needs to be performed.

The Interface Section

The **interface** section contains declarations for constants, types, variables, and routines that a unit will make available to other units, programs, or libraries that use it in a **uses** clause. Delphi itself uses units whenever you write a program. Here is the default **uses** clause from the **interface** section of a Delphi 2.0 unit with an associated form:

```
uses
  Windows, Messages, SysUtils, Classes, Graphics, Controls, Forms, Dialogs;
```

All of the declarations made in the interface sections of the units listed here can be used in the form's unit from this point on. Which is good, because the next thing that Delphi automatically generates in the form's unit is the declaration of the form shown in the code snippet below:

```
type
  TForm1 = class(TForm)
  private
    { Private declarations }
  public
    { Public declarations }
  end;
```

The **TForm** base class is defined in the interface section of the VCL unit **Forms** (*VCL* stands for Visual Class Library, the name of the Object Pascal framework used by Delphi and application developers using Delphi).

By the way, our basic **MiscLib** unit doesn't have the "default" **uses** list because we asked Delphi to give us a new **unit**, not a new *form*. A new form would have come up along with a unit that contains the **uses** list shown above.

We aren't defining basic Windows functionality in **MiscLib**, so we don't want to go too far afield. All we're trying to do is put a couple of simple routines out of the way. Since we want to make these routines available to other code, we'll put them in the interface, shown in the code snippet below:

```
interface

function Int_max(
  const A, B : integer
  ) : integer;

function Int_min(
  const A, B : integer
  ) : integer;

function StrXlate(
        S       : pchar;
  const C_from,
        C_to    : char
  ) : integer;
```

We only declare the three functions we'll be using elsewhere. If a declaration has no associated code, the entire declaration goes in the interface. This unit doesn't have any declarations without code—**const**s, **type**s, **var**s—but you'll see these later. When declarations do have associated code—**procedure**s, **function**s, **class** methods—only the declaration of the routine is specified in the interface. This gives the compiler enough information to know how to call the routine, but doesn't bog it down with implementation details. For that, we have an **implementation** section.

The Implementation Section

The body of the code for interfaced routines is put in the **implementation** section. In **MiscLib**'s **implementation** section, we use **SysUtils** to utilize its **pchar**-string routines; then we show the bodies of the routines declared in the **interface** section, as in the code snippet below:

```
implementation

uses
    SysUtils;
```

```
function Int_max(
  const A, B : integer
  ) : integer;
    begin
        if A > B then result := A else result := B;
        end;

function Int_min(
  const A, B : integer
  ) : integer;
    begin
        if A < B then result := A else result := B;
        end;

function StrXlate(
         S        : pchar;
  const C_from,
        C_to     : char
  ) : integer;
    begin
        result := 0;
        S := strScan(S,C_from);
        while S <> nil do begin
            inc(result);
            S^ := C_to;
            S := strScan(S+1,C_from);
            end;
        end;
```

Another interesting aspect of Delphi's declaration scheme is that the bodies in the **implementation** section don't *have* to be restated. Delphi gives you a choice of either re-declaring a routine in the **implementation**, or simply introducing it solely by its name (so the compiler can distinguish the body of one routine from another). If you choose to re-declare the routine, it must be declared exactly as it was in the **interface** section. If you choose to introduce it, the only re-declaration needed is the routine's name. For instance, consider the following code snippet:

```
function Int_max(
  const A, B : integer
  ) : integer;
    begin
        if A > B then result := A else result := B;
        end;
```

Instead of that, we could use the code shown in the snippet below:

```
function Int_max;
    begin
```

```
        if A > B then result := A else result := B;
    end;
```

In this book (and, we sincerely hope, for the rest of your work), we'll always completely re-declare the routines in the **implementation** section. That way, we won't ever need to look back to the **interface** section to find out what parameters were passed to us. If it worries you to have two separate declarations of the same routine, rest assured that the compiler will check to see that they are identical.

Basic Font Support

We're going to be building quite a structure on this basic program. We will be adding support for all sorts of text display goodies; even though we aren't going to take advantage of many features at all in our first program, *Hyper I*, we'll still build a framework for full-blown font support. We'll fill out this framework in project *Hyper III*, later in this chapter, where we'll add a lot of features to make our engine good-looking and easy to use.

Right now, the only aspect of Windows' many text-related features we'll worry about is the font style and the measurement of the text we'd like to display. In unit **Font**, we will declare a type that represents our basic font display information, **tHTML_font_spec**. This is just a repository for the information we'll need to display text in an HTML environment. Right now, the record has only one field: **specStyle**. This is a set of values representing Windows' basic character formatting: **fsBold**, **fsItalic**, **fsUnderline**, and **fsStrikeOut**. (These values are declared in Delphi's standard unit, **Graphics**.) Listing 3.2 shows the declaration of this type and the rest of the unit **Font**.

Listing 3.2   The *Font.Pas* support unit

```
unit Font;

interface

uses
    Windows, Graphics;

type
    tHTML_font_spec = record
        specStyle : TFontStyles;
        end;

    tHTML_format = record
        Serial_number    : integer;
        Leading_newlines : integer;
```

```
          Font              : tHTML_font_spec;
        end;

procedure Set_font_from_spec(
  const Font : TFont;  { var .properties }
        Spec : tHTML_font_spec
  );

type
    tText_measurement = record
        case boolean of
          false : (
            Width,
            Height,
            Ascent,
            Descent : integer;
            );
          true : (
            Extent : TSize
            );
        end;

function Measurement_of(
  const Text     : pchar;
  const lnText   : integer;
  const Canvas : TCanvas;  { var .Font }
  const Font     : tHTML_font_spec
  ) : tText_measurement;
```

implementation

```
uses
    SysUtils;

procedure Set_font_from_spec(
  const Font : TFont;  { var .properties }
        Spec : tHTML_font_spec
  );
    begin with Font, Spec do begin
        Style := specStyle;
        end; end;

function Measurement_of(
  const Text     : pchar;
  const lnText   : integer;
  const Canvas : TCanvas;  { var .Font }
  const Font     : tHTML_font_spec
  ) : tText_measurement;
    var
        DC : HDC;
        TM : TTextMetric;
    begin with result do begin
        Set_font_from_spec(Canvas.Font,Font);
```

```
      DC := Canvas.Handle;
      GetTextExtentPoint(DC,
        Text,lnText,
        Extent
        );
      GetTextMetrics(DC,TM);
      Ascent  := TM.tmAscent;
      Descent := TM.tmDescent;
    end; end;

{initialization}
   end.
```

Relating an HTML Font to a Windows Font

Our application will be tracking only HTML-specific information about fonts in **tHTML_font**. Otherwise, we could simply use Delphi's built-in **TFont** object. The major difference we'll encounter is in the representation of font size. HTML has seven fixed sizes, 1 through 7, that browsers are free to interpret as they wish. Windows uses a *point* size, where a point is 1/72nd of an inch. We'll cover this in more detail in our work on *Hyper III*. For now, we just need to know that because of subtle differences like this, we should make a distinction between our own HTML font support and Delphi's built-in Windows font support.

If we're going to differentiate between the types of fonts, we'll need a way to go back and forth between them. As it turns out, text display is a one-way road for us, so all we need to do is provide a way to set **Delphi's TFont** from our **tHTML_font**. The routine is pretty simple at this point, as shown in the code snippet below:

```
procedure Set_font_from_spec(
  const Font : TFont;   { var .properties }
        Spec : tHTML_font_spec
  );
    begin with Font, Spec do begin
        Style := specStyle;
        end; end;
```

Measuring Text

This is the other major text-related function we'll need to use when displaying our text. In *Word Wrap*, from Chapter 2, we used a **Canvas**'s **TextWidth** and **TextHeight** methods. Here, we'll need to know a little bit more about the size of a font because we want to accurately advance from one line to the next, passing the proper amount of space for the lines' ascenders and descenders. Although we could, in theory, take these measurements just once at the start of *Hyper I*, we must look to the future when we will be supporting multiple font sizes within the same line, or even the same word.

To measure text, we must use two Windows GDI functions, **GetTextExtentPoint** and **GetTextMetrics**. At the end of Chapter 2, we encouraged you to look at **GetTextExtentPoint**. As it turns out, it's one of the gears behind the machinations of **TextWidth** and **TextHeight**. We'll use this function to measure each little bit of text we display. **GetTextMetrics** returns information that only changes when the current font changes, but we'll still call it every time we measure a chunk of text. This will simplify our code a little bit, at the expense of many unnecessary calls to the GDI. Once you understand this code, you could try to avoid those extra calls.

GetTextMetrics and the Measurement of Fonts' Characteristics

As seen in Figure 3.3, many different measurements describe a font. We need to know some of these characteristics now that we are going to handle different font sizes. At this point, we have only one goal: to align the baseline of text in different fonts on the same line. We'll only need one key measurement to do this, but the only way to get it is to ask Windows for the whole set of a font's text metrics. For this, we use the Windows GDI function **GetTextMetrics**, as shown in the code snippet below. Like many API functions, it returns 0 if it fails. Since failure is rare, we'll discard the result and use it as a procedure.

```
var
    DC : HDC;
    TM : TTextMetric;

GetTextMetrics(DC,TM);
```

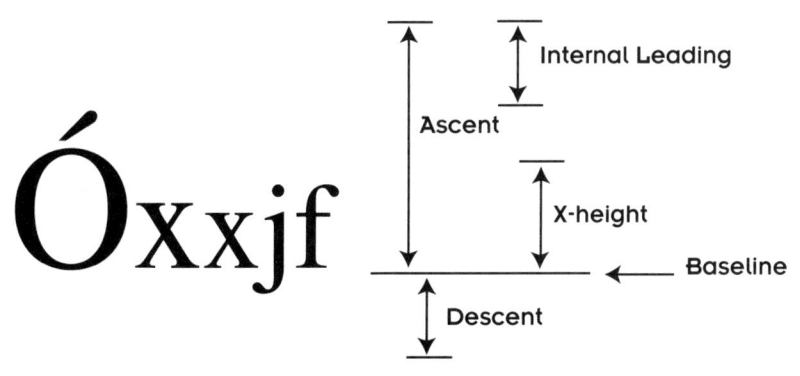

Figure 3.3 *Just some of the important measurements of a character in Windows.*

Rather than measuring a font directly, the font must be *selected* into a *device context*, or DC. This is because other aspects of the DC can affect the font's display size. A DC encapsulates all of the information that Windows will use when drawing to a particular window (device), and is identified by a unique *handle*, sometimes known as an HDC, or *handle to a device context.* By selecting drawing tools (such as a font or a pen) into a DC, you gain the ability to use them. Delphi wraps all of this functionality into its **TCanvas** object.

By having all of the DC's information, **GetTextMetrics** can supply accurate results. Up in Delphi, we don't have DCs; we need to use a **Canvas**'s **Handle** property when we call these GDI functions. The metrics are returned in the **TTextMetric** record that is passed to it. Its structure is shown in the snippet below:

```
TTextMetricA = packed record
    tmHeight                : Longint;
    tmAscent                : Longint;
    tmDescent               : Longint;
    tmInternalLeading       : Longint;
    tmExternalLeading       : Longint;
    tmAveCharWidth          : Longint;
    tmMaxCharWidth          : Longint;
    tmWeight                : Longint;
    tmOverhang              : Longint;
    tmDigitizedAspectX      : Longint;
    tmDigitizedAspectY      : Longint;
    tmFirstChar             : AnsiChar;
    tmLastChar              : AnsiChar;
    tmDefaultChar           : AnsiChar;
    tmBreakChar             : AnsiChar;
    tmItalic                : Byte;
    tmUnderlined            : Byte;
    tmStruckOut             : Byte;
    tmPitchAndFamily        : Byte;
    tmCharSet               : Byte;
    end;
TTextMetric = TTextMetricA;
```

As you can see, quite a bit can be learned about the font currently selected into a DC. We are only interested in two measurements: **tmAscent** and **tmDescent**. By the way, **TTextMetricA** is a structure that uses **ANSIChar** (normal one-byte Windows characters). There is also a **TTextMetricW** that uses "wide" two-byte characters. Since Microsoft started using **WideChar** late in the game, the "generic" **TTextMetric** is redefined as the **TTextMetricA**, as shown in the following code snippet:

```
type
    tText_measurement = record
```

```
            case boolean of
              false : (
                Width,
                Height,
                Ascent,
                Descent : integer;
                );
              true : (
                Extent : TSize
                );
            end;

:

function Measurement_of(
  const Text   : pchar;
  const lnText : integer;
  const Canvas : TCanvas;  { var .Font }
  const Font   : tHTML_font_spec
  ) : tText_measurement;
    var
        DC : HDC;
        TM : TTextMetric;
    begin with result do begin
        Set_font_from_spec(Canvas.Font,Font);
        DC := Canvas.Handle;
        GetTextExtentPoint(DC,
          Text,lnText,
          Extent
          );
        GetTextMetrics(DC,TM);
        Ascent  := TM.tmAscent;
        Descent := TM.tmDescent;
        end; end;
```

Function **Measurement_of** handles all of the text measurement for us when passed a string (specified by a pointer and length), a **Canvas** on which it should be measured, and the **tHTML_Font** in which it will finally appear. The measurement is returned as a **tText_measurement;** and this may be viewed in detail as a **Width**, **Height**, and character **Ascent** and **Descent**, or simply as an **Extent**, by using Pascal's variant **case** record structure.

To measure the text, we set the **Canvas**'s **Font** property from our **Font** specification, and then measure it with **GetTextExtentPoint**. In order to get the **Ascent** and **Descent** of the **Font**'s characters, we call **GetTextMetrics**. It may strike you as odd that we actually change the **Canvas**'s **Font** to do the measurement, but we don't return it to what it was originally. It would actually be a good idea from a maintenance point of view, since this is a *destructive* procedure as written. However, because of the way we'll be using this routine in this project and the ones to come, it's OK as is. It also avoids a whole parade of unneeded (in our case) font-setting gyrations.

Formatted Text

We have one more structure of interest declared in unit **Font** that is related to font handling. **tHTML_format** is the structure that will grow to represent all of the HTML information about a formatted segment of text, including its **Font** (of type **tHTML_font_spec**).

The text's **Font** alone doesn't entirely describe the HTML information needed to implement hypertext. Later, we'll add other attributes here such as hyperlink jump information, and whether or not the text is *preformatted* (and thus, should not be word-wrapped). For now, all we need is one piece of information that tells us if a particular segment of text should begin on a new line. We store this information as a count of the number of new lines we should output before the text itself is displayed. A zero in **Leading_newlines** would indicate that this text just follows the text previously output on the same line, as shown in the code snippet below:

```
type
    tHTML_format = record
        Serial_number    : integer;
        Leading_newlines : integer;
        Font             : tHTML_font_spec;
        end;
```

The **Serial_number** is exactly that: a number that increments each time we encounter a tag that could change our current format. This is used in a pretty subtle way when handling the format of spaces in our hypertext source document.

Segments of Formatted Hypertext

As we parse a hypertext document, we will build a list of segments of formatted hypertext. Each element of the list will contain text and a format for the text, including font characteristic information. We'll look at the creation of this list in detail in our discussion of unit **DispBuf**. Right now, we're going to examine how this list is maintained in unit **FmtText**, shown in Listing 3.3.

Listing 3.3 The *FmtText.Pas* support unit

```
unit FmtText;

interface
```

Building a Hypermedia Engine 83

```pascal
uses
    Windows, Classes,
    Font;

type
    tFormatted_text = class
      private
        Direct           : boolean;
      public
        Text             : pchar;
        Format           : tHTML_format;
        Meas             : tText_measurement;
        Base_left_corner : TPoint;
      public
        constructor Create_direct(
          const _Format : tHTML_format;
          const _Text   : pchar
          );
        constructor Create(
          const _Format : tHTML_format;
          const _Text   : pchar
          );
        destructor Destroy; override;
        end;

    tFormatted_text_list = class(TList)
      public
        procedure Break_at(
          const I : integer;  { Index of item to break }
                P : pchar     { Pointer to space to break at }
          );
        destructor Destroy; override;
        end;

implementation

uses
    SysUtils;

constructor tFormatted_text.Create_direct(
  const _Format : tHTML_format;
  const _Text   : pchar
  );
    begin
        inherited Create;
        Text   := _Text;
        Format := _Format;
        Direct := true;
        end;

constructor tFormatted_text.Create(
  const _Format : tHTML_format;
  const _Text   : pchar
  );
```

```
    begin
        inherited Create;
        Text   := strNew(_Text);
        Format := _Format;
        Direct := false;
        end;

destructor tFormatted_text.Destroy;
    begin
        if not Direct then StrDispose(Text);
        inherited Destroy;
        end;

procedure tFormatted_text_list.Break_at(
   const I : integer;  { Index of item to break }
         P : pchar     { Pointer to space to break at }
   );
    begin
        { Break the string.  We don't need to remeasure
          the portion we broke from, because the Height,
          Ascent, and Descent will remain the same, and
          the Width is not used, since it is now the last
          item on the line. }
        P^ := #0; inc(P);
        { Insert the new Formatted_text_element. }
        Insert(
          I + 1,
          tFormatted_text.Create_direct(
            tFormatted_text(Items[I]).Format,
            P
            )
          );
          { Copy format info from the Item we broke; use P,
            the remainder of the string we broke.
        end;

destructor tFormatted_text_list.Destroy;
    var
        I : integer;
    begin
        for I := 0 to Count-1 do
            tFormatted_text(Items[I]).Free;
        inherited Destroy;
        end;

{initialization}
    end.
```

TList: Dynamic Structures for the Rest of Us

If you have come from a formal or standard Pascal background, or if you can remember Borland's *Turbo Pascal*, you've no doubt worked a little with *dynamic data structures*. For those of you new to Delphi, a dynamic data structure contains information of indeterminate size, as opposed to a *static data structure* that holds only a certain amount of information. Let's take a simple example. Say you're developing a "typical" multimedia encyclopedia that offers a keyword search through all of its text, returning a list of each occurrence of the search word. Using the static data structure approach, each occurrence could be recorded in an array that was declared to be as large as the largest manageable list, such as that shown in the code snippet below:

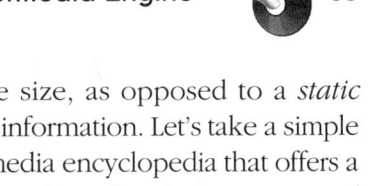

```
var
    Occurrence = array[1..200] of tWord_reference;
```

It would be a bad thing if the user searched for "the" in your encyclopedia. You'd finally have to give up after 200 matches, and explain with some sort of dialog that you couldn't list all of the occurrences. With pointers and dynamic memory allocation, it is possible to build *linked lists* that can handle these kinds of problems—and many times, this may be a simple solution.

To implement a linked list, you basically declare a data record that includes, along with the elements data, a pointer to the next data record. To build the list, you dynamically allocate a data record, set its fields, and then set a previous record's "Next element" pointer to point at the record, and set the record's "Next element" pointer to point to whatever the next data element may be. Of course, there are special cases at the beginning and the end of the list. With pointers to this and pointers to that, this type of code can get very complex; however, you can keep allocating space for data as needed until you exhaust the entire system's memory.

To simplify things for those who are unfamiliar with pointers and their use (and those of us who get their pointers all tied up in knots when they try to use them), Delphi provides the **TList** class. **TList** hides much of the implementation of the simple list, one of the most-often used dynamic structures. It's not as simple as you might imagine, though, because Delphi's **TList** is actually a list of pointers. This is convenient for lists of objects; as you may recall, they are stored as pointers. You still need to reference other data by a pointer, too; so generally, you must dynamically allocate data records and set them up before recording them in a **TList**.

That's what we'll do with our **tFormatted_text_list** class. We'll be storing simple records, so we'll need to dynamically allocate them and then record their pointer in the list. **tFormatted_text_list** is a descendant of **TList**, to which we've added a couple of custom methods: **Break_at** and **Destroy**. **Break_at** splits a list entry into two pieces. We'll do this when we break up our **tFormatted_text_list** for display in unit **DispBuf**. **Destroy** is a replacement for **TList.Destroy**; we need to define this in order to **Free** our element objects.

Formatted Text List Elements

This not-quite-so-simple object represents a segment of formatted text. Its public data tells us all we need to know about the segment. **Text** points to a null-terminated string, and **Format** contains all of the HTML formatting information for the **Text**. **Meas** and **Base_Left_Corner** are used in the hypertext Display method we'll cover in unit **DispBuf**; they represent the size and location of the displayed text on the screen, as shown in the code snippet below:

```
type
    tFormatted_text = class
      private
        Direct           : boolean;
      public
        Text             : pchar;
        Format           : tHTML_format;
        Meas             : tText_measurement;
        Base_left_corner : TPoint;
      public
        constructor Create_direct(
          const _Format : tHTML_format;
          const _Text   : pchar
          );
        constructor Create(
          const _Format : tHTML_format;
          const _Text   : pchar
          );
        destructor Destroy; override;
        end;
```

The private value, Direct, is a flag indicating whether or not this object's Text really belongs to this object. We'll need to look at the code before this statement makes sense, as shown in the snippet below:

```
constructor tFormatted_text.Create(
  const _Format : tHTML_format;
  const _Text   : pchar
  );
    begin
      inherited Create;
      Text   := StrNew(_Text);
      Format := _Format;
      Direct := false;
      end;
```

```
destructor tFormatted_text.Destroy;
    begin
        if not Direct then StrDispose(Text);
        inherited Destroy;
        end;
```

Create makes a new copy of the text that is passed to it, so the calling application can do its own string management without worrying if we are currently pointing to some portion of a hypertext document. Of course, if we make a new copy, **Text**, of the **_Text** with **StrNew**, we must dispose of our copy with **StrDispose**, in **Destroy**.

In **Destroy**, however, there are times when we won't want to **StrDispose** our string. This seems pretty peculiar, until you understand how we will break these list elements up to fit on display lines. In **Break_at**, we will use the method **Create_direct** to insert a new element after an element to be broken. **Break_at** will always be called with a pointer to a space in an element's **Text**. The character after that space becomes the character at the start of a new line, so a new element is added to the list, with a pointer back into the original element's **Text**. Even though we place a null where the space used to be (to end the original **Text**), **StrDispose**-ing the original text will still dispose the entire number of bytes originally **StrNew**-ed.

When we break the original element's **Text**, we need to create the new element with **Create_direct**, which just records the position of the remaining text in the original string instead of making a copy of the string. To ensure that we don't try to dispose our **Text** (or, actually, the remaining portion) twice, the **Direct** field is set to **true**, rather than **false**, as shown in the snippet below:

```
constructor tFormatted_text.Create_direct(
  const _Format : tHTML_format;
  const _Text   : pchar
  );
    begin
        inherited Create;
        Text   := _Text;
        Format := _Format;
        Direct := true;
        end;
```

With that said, the actual code for **tFormatted_text_list.Break_at** isn't so intimidating, as shown in the code snippet below:

```
procedure tFormatted_text_list.Break_at(
  const I : integer;  { Index of item to break }
```

```
          P : pchar     { Pointer to space to break at }
    );
    begin
        { Break the string.  We don't need to remeasure
          the portion we broke from, because the Height,
          Ascent, and Descent will remain the same, and
          the Width is not used, since it is now the last
          item on the line. }
        P^ := #0; inc(P);
        { Insert the new Formatted_text_element. }
        Insert(
          I + 1,
          tFormatted_text.Create_direct(
            tFormatted_text(Items[I]).Format,
            P
            )
          );
        { Copy format info from the Item we broke; use P,
            the remainder of the string we broke. }
        end;
```

Since we assume we're called with a pointer to a space on which we should break a line (**P**), we don't need to worry about the space, and can replace it with a null to effectively end the current element's **Text**. We could go looking through the entire list to find the element with **Text** that contains **P**; however, to keep track of the element we're dealing with, we'll also have the caller pass in an element index, **I**.

Now we can just **Insert** a new element after element **I**. Instead of calling create, though, with our break-pointer **P** incremented to point to the character after the space, we call **Create_direct**. We pass in the current element's **Format** to **Create_direct** because, by and large, it won't change. (In the calling code, we will change the **Leading_newlines** value to 1, which causes the line break to happen. But we're getting ahead of ourselves.)

Destroying the **tFormatted_text_list** takes the form typical for **TList** use. Since the **TList** can't possibly know the "right" way to dispose of the elements you've placed in the list, you are responsible for *overriding* the **TList**'s **Destroy** method with one that can destroy all of the list's elements as well. Next, we'll discuss what we're really doing when we override **Destroy**.

```
destructor tFormatted_text_list.Destroy;
    var
        I : integer;
    begin
        for I := 0 to Count-1 do
            tFormatted_text(Items[I]).Free;
        inherited Destroy;
        end;
```

Overriding Destroy

The methods of an ancestor class can be *overridden* or *replaced*. Replacing an ancestor's method is simple: You just declare a method in your descendant with the same name as the ancestor's method you wish to replace. When the compiler sees references to the name of the method in other methods of the descendant, or when called from an object that belongs to the descendant class, it will use the most recently declared routine. Overrides are a special form of replacement: Even ancestor's methods will call the overriding descendant method.

All Delphi classes descend from the class **TObject**, shown in the code snippet below:

```
TObject = class
    constructor Create;
    { Other less interesting methods }
    procedure Free;
    destructor Destroy; virtual;
    end;
```

TObject declares a **Free** method that is quite straight-forward, as shown in the code snippet below:

```
procedure TObject.Free;
    asm
        TEST    EAX,EAX
        JE      @@exit
        MOV     EDX,[EAX]
        CALL    dword ptr [EDX].vtDestroy
@@exit:
        end;
```

Well, okay, it's not *that* straight-forward when viewed that way. Delphi's runtime library writes the routine in assembler, but it's still pretty simple. The object is specified in register EAX. The TEST checks to see if EAX is zero (or **nil**, as we'd recognize it). If an object is **nil**, then it hasn't been created yet and the routine jumps to @@exit and doesn't do anything. If the object is not **nil**, the *virtual* routine **Destroy** is called, as shown in the code snippet below:

```
procedure TObject.Free;
    begin
        if Self <> nil then Destroy;
        end;
```

Free simply saves you from accidentally trying to **Destroy** an object that hasn't yet been created, or one that's already been **Free**d and set back to **nil**. If you thought **Free** was simple, you'll really appreciate **TObject.Destroy**, shown in the code snippet below:

```
destructor TObject.Destroy;
    begin
        end;
```

Destroy is declared in the class as a *virtual* method. Without the **virtual** declaration (or the **dynamic** declaration, which has the same effect but a different implementation), methods are *static*. The virtue of a virtual method is that it can be overridden, not just replaced. For us, this means that we don't have to rewrite **Free** when we declare our **tFormatted_text_list**. **TObject**'s **Free** will call our overriding **Destroy**. If **Destroy** were static, not virtual, then **TObject**'s **Free** could only call **TObject**'s **Destroy**, not the "youngest" descendant **Destroy**.

Dissecting HTML

We've laid a lot of groundwork. It's time to put it all to good use on real HTML documents. Unit **DispBuf**, for **Display Buffer**, will actually take HTML all the way from its simple, quiet life as a file to its ultimate destination: the user's screen. Before we look at the code in Listings 3.4, 3.5, 3.6, and 3.7, let's look at what we expect this code to accomplish.

We tried to design an easy-to-use, control-like object with some simple properties and methods. We named the object, rather diminutively, **tDisplay_buffer**. It has a constructor, destructor, two real methods, and a couple of properties we'll find handy to have exposed later.

- **Create** The constructor of a **Display Buffer** takes any Control descended from **TGraphicControl** to be used as the destination of the hypertext.
- **Destroy** The destructor takes care of all of the housekeeping we'll need to do when we have finished using the **Display Buffer**. We won't call this, of course; we'll just call its inherited **Free** method.
- **Load_HTML_file** This method loads and processes an HTML file. Its responsibilities include everything from finding tags in the hypertext by looking for open angle-brackets, to building a list of formatted text, to actually word-wrapping the text for display.
- **Display** This method displays the loaded file in the **Control** specified at creation-time.

- **Display_top** This property (actually just a field) can be set before calling **Display** to indicate how far down (in pixels from the start of the document) the **Display** should begin. The pixel-row specified here will be displayed in the top of the **Control**'s window and continue down from there.
- **Display_bottom** This property (also really a field) is set by **Load_HTML_file** to let the calling application know the total height of the document, in pixels.

We should make a couple of notes about the implementation as seen by the calling application. First, you may remember from Chapter 2 that we need to typecast the **Control** we pass to **Create** to a special descendant of **TGraphicControl**, called **tGraphicControlWithCanvas**. Secondly, although we wouldn't do something as simple as try to hold the entire document's display in a giant bitmap; we *do* save the entire document text, as well as its formatting information, in memory at once. With extremely large individual files, this could become cumbersome.

This first listing, Listing 3.4, can act as a guide map through the deep reaches of what is required to process HTML.

Listing 3.4 The interface and infrastructure of the *DispBuf.Pas* unit

```
unit DispBuf;

interface

uses
    Classes, Graphics, Controls,
    Font, FmtText;

type
    tGraphicControlWithCanvas = class(TGraphicControl)
        property Canvas;
        end;

    tDisplay_buffer = class
      private
        { Formatted Text Storage }
        Formatted_text_list : tFormatted_text_list;
        { "Breaker" Data -- Line Breaking list }
        Line_list : TList; {of integer}
        { "Displayer" Data }
        Control : tGraphicControlWithCanvas;
      public
        { Display Positioning and Height, calc'd by "Breaker" }
        Display_top,
        Display_bottom : integer;
```

```
    public
      constructor Create(
        const _Control : tGraphicControlWithCanvas
        );
      destructor Destroy; override;
      procedure Load_HTML_file(
        const Filename : string
        );
      procedure Display;
      end;

implementation

uses
    SysUtils, Windows, Dialogs,
    MiscLib;

const
    Length_of_buffer = 1024-1;

constructor tDisplay_buffer.Create(
  const _Control : tGraphicControlWithCanvas
  );
    begin
        inherited Create;
        Formatted_text_list := tFormatted_text_list.Create;
        Line_list := TList.Create;
        Control := _Control;
        Display_top := 0;
        Display_bottom := 0;
        end;

destructor tDisplay_buffer.Destroy;
    begin
        Line_list.Free;
        Formatted_text_list.Free;
        inherited Destroy;
        end;

procedure tDisplay_buffer.Load_HTML_file(
  const Filename : string
  );

    procedure Process_HTML_string(
      const Text : pchar
      );

        procedure Parse_HTML(
          Text   : pchar;
          Format : tHTML_format
          );

            procedure Reset_buffer;
```

```
      procedure Add_buffer_to_list;

      procedure Set_format(
        var F : tHTML_format
        );

      procedure New_line;

      procedure Emit(
        S   : pchar;
        lnS : integer
        );

      function Is_whitespace(const C : char) : boolean;

      function Is_word(const C : char) : boolean;

    procedure Break_into_lines;

      procedure Start_new_line(
        const Line_count : integer
        );

procedure tDisplay_buffer.Display;

    function Line_after(
      const Pixel_row : integer
      ) : integer;

    function Line_before(
      const Pixel_row : integer
      ) : integer;

{initialization}
    end.
```

The first thing declared in this unit is a new class descending from **TGraphicControl** that exposes the **Control**'s **Canvas**, as we discussed in Chapter 2 and is further illustrated by the code snippet below. From there, it is straight on to the declaration of **tDisplay_buffer.**

```
type
    tGraphicControlWithCanvas = class(TGraphicControl)
        property Canvas;
        end;
```

tDisplay_buffer maintains two lists. The first list, **Formatted_text_list**, is a list of segments of HTML-formatted text supported by the unit **FmtText**, above. The second list, **Line_list**, is a list of integers that reference the elements of **Formatted_text_list**. The elements in **Line_list** are actually **pointer**s;

but as you'll see, we treat them as **integer**s. The "integer" of the first element of the **Line_list** references the element of the **Formatted_text_list** that begins the first line of the display. The second element, likewise, points to whichever element of the **Formatted_text_list** starts the second line of the display, and so forth.

Privately, as shown in the code snippet below, we store a reference to the **Control**. Publicly, we keep a couple of fields we'll use when formatting and displaying the hypertext file, **Display_top** and **Display_bottom**. In this project, we won't rely on these fields too heavily. They do come in handy when we're dealing with scroll bars, though.

```
tDisplay_buffer = class
  private
    { Formatted Text Storage }
    Formatted_text_list : tFormatted_text_list;
    { "Breaker" Data -- Line Breaking list }
    Line_list : TList; {of integer}
    { "Displayer" Data }
    Control : tGraphicControlWithCanvas;
  public
    { Display Positioning and Height, calc'd by "Breaker" }
    Display_top,
    Display_bottom : integer;
  public
    constructor Create(
      const _Control : tGraphicControlWithCanvas
      );
    destructor Destroy; override;
    procedure Load_HTML_file(
      const Filename : string
      );
    procedure Display;
    end;
```

Finally, we declare our methods, as advertised above. Before we get into the meat of this project, note that in the implementation section, **Create** and **Destroy** do exactly what we'd expect them to do with our fields; and in both cases, we call our inherited **Create** (before we start messing) and **Destroy** (after we're really, *really* finished).

Parsing HTML

As you can see from our roadmap, **Load_HTML_file** has one sub-procedure to handle an HTML document, **Process_HTML_string**. We'll shortly see that **Load_HTML_file** handles only the pesky chore of reading in the HTML document from the specified **Filename**. **Process_HTML_string** has two subprocedures, **Parse_HTML** and **Break_into_lines**. **Break_into_lines** deals more with the mechanical manipulation of the hypertext once it's been parsed, so we'll save it for later. The code for the HTML parsing process is shown in Listing 3.5.

Listing 3.5   The **Load_HTML_file** method and its parsing code from unit **DispBuf**

```
procedure tDisplay_buffer.Load_HTML_file(
  const Filename : string
  );

    procedure Process_HTML_string(
      const Text : pchar
      );

        procedure Parse_HTML(
          Text   : pchar;
          Format : tHTML_format
          );

            { Format state variables}
            var
                Current_format       : tHTML_format;
                Pending_newlines     : integer;

            { Buffer Data Structure }
            var
                Buffer,
                End_of_buffer           : pchar;
                Remaining_buffer_length : integer;

            procedure Reset_buffer;
                begin
                    Buffer^ := #0;
                    End_of_Buffer := Buffer;
                    Remaining_buffer_length := Length_of_buffer;
                end;

            procedure Add_buffer_to_list;
                var
                    S : pchar;
                begin
                    S := Buffer;
                    if Pending_newlines > 0 then
                        while (S^ <> #0) and (S^ <= ' ') do inc(S);
                    if S^ <> #0 then begin
                        Current_format.Leading_newlines :=
                            Pending_newlines;
                        Formatted_text_list.Add(
                            tFormatted_text.Create(Current_format,S)
                            );
```

```
                Pending_newlines := 0;
            end;
        Reset_buffer;
        end;

{ Buffer building }

procedure Set_format(
  var F : tHTML_format
  );
    var
        S : pchar;
    begin
        Add_buffer_to_list;
        Current_format := F;
        end;

procedure New_line;
    begin
        Add_buffer_to_list;
        Pending_newlines := 1;
        end;

procedure Emit(
  S   : pchar;
  lnS : integer
  );
    var
        Chars_to_take     : integer;
    begin
        while lnS > 0 do begin
            Chars_to_take :=
              Int_min(Remaining_buffer_length,lnS);
            strLCopy(End_of_Buffer,S,Chars_to_take);
            inc(End_of_buffer,Chars_to_take);
            End_of_buffer^ := #0;
            dec(Remaining_buffer_length,Chars_to_take);
            dec(lnS,Chars_to_take);
            inc(S,Chars_to_take);
            if Remaining_buffer_length = 0 then
                Add_buffer_to_list;
            end;
        end;

function Is_whitespace(const C : char) : boolean;
    begin
        result := (C <> #0) and (C <= ' ');
        end;

function Is_word(const C : char) : boolean;
    begin
        result := (C <> #0) and (C > ' ') and (C <> '<');
        end;
```

```
var
    Need_a_newline,
    Preceeding_newline,
    Preceeding_space   : boolean;
    Space_format       : tHTML_format;
    The_end : pchar;
    Saved   : char;
    EOL     : pchar;
    Word    : pchar;

begin
    Buffer := strAlloc(Length_of_buffer+1);

    Current_format.Serial_number := -1;
    Pending_newlines             := 0;
    Reset_buffer;

    Preceeding_newline := false;
    Preceeding_space := false;
    while Text^ <> #0 do

        if Text^ = '<' then begin

            { Process a Tag }

            The_end := strPos(Text,'>');
            if The_end = nil then begin
                { Oops, there was no closing ">" on the tag. }
                { We'll handle this here, trivially.         }
                Text := strEnd(Text);
                exit;
                end;

            inc(Text);
            The_end^ := #0;
            strUpper(Text);

            Need_a_newline := false;
            inc(Format.Serial_number);
            if Text = 'P' then
                Need_a_newline := true
              else if Text = 'I' then
                include(Format.Font.specStyle,fsItalic)
              else if Text = '/I' then
                exclude(Format.Font.specStyle,fsItalic)
              else if Text = 'U' then
                include(Format.Font.specStyle,fsUnderline)
              else if Text = '/U' then
                exclude(Format.Font.specStyle,fsUnderline);

            Text := The_end + 1;
            Preceeding_newline :=
              Preceeding_newline or Need_a_newline;
```

```
            if Preceeding_newline then
                Preceeding_space := false;
            Set_format(Format);
            end

        else if Text^ <= ' ' then begin

            { Process Whitespace }

            if not Preceeding_newline then begin
                Preceeding_space := true;
                Space_format := Format;
                end;
            while Is_whitespace(Text^) do inc(Text);
            end

        else begin

            { Process Words }

            Word := Text;
            while Is_word(Text^) do inc(Text);
            The_end := Text;
            Saved := The_end^;
            The_end^ := #0;
            if Preceeding_newline then
                New_line
              else if Preceeding_space then
                if  Space_format.Serial_number
                   =
                    Format.Serial_number
                  then
                    Emit(' ',1)
                  else begin
                    {Re-} Set_format(Space_format);
                    Emit(' ',1);
                    {Re-} Set_format(Format);
                    end;
            Emit(Word,The_end-Word);
            The_end^ := Saved;
            Preceeding_newline := false;
            Preceeding_space   := false;
            end;

        Add_buffer_to_list; { Last little bit. }

        strDispose(Buffer);
        end;

  procedure Break_into_lines;
  { See Listing 3.6. }

    var
        Format     : tHTML_format;
```

```
        The_Text   : pchar;
        lnThe_Text : integer;
    begin
        with Format, Font do begin
            Leading_newlines := 0;
            Serial_number    := 0;
            specStyle        := [];
            end;
        Parse_HTML(Text,Format);
        Break_into_lines;
        end;

    var
        C : char;
    begin
        if Filename = '' then exit;
        with TMemoryStream.Create do
            try
                try
                    { Load Document. }
                    LoadFromFile(Filename);
                    Seek(-1,soFromEnd); { Last character }
                    Read(C,sizeof(C));
                    { Add a CR if necessary. }
                    if C <> #13 then begin
                        C := #13;
                        Write(C,sizeof(C));
                        end;
                    { Null termination }
                    C := #0;
                    Write(C,sizeof(C));
                    { Do it. }
                    Process_HTML_string(Memory);
                except on E : EInOutError do
                    MessageDlg(E.Message,mtWarning,[mbOk],0);
                end;
            finally
                Free;
            end;
    end;
```

Let's start at the outside, and go in. **Load_HTML_file** loads an HTML file into a **TMemoryStream** object that is created on the stack with a **with** statement. We need to be careful when we do this; if the **with** statement's scope should end from an exception (or some other reason) before the stacked object's **Free** method is called, the object and its resources can never be freed, since the only reference to the object was on the stack. That's why just inside the **with** we've added a *resource-protection block*.

This resource-protection block is implemented with Delphi's **try...finally** statement. If any unhandled exceptions should occur within the statements being **try**-ed, Delphi will do its darndest to see to it that the statements in the **finally** block are executed. Without this "catch-all," an exception will percolate up through the stack, looking for a handler—until, perhaps, it hits Delphi's default exception handler. Exception processing will never return back down to your previously-executing code; the **try...finally** just makes sure something is done before it leaves, as shown in the code snippet below:

```
procedure tDisplay_buffer.Load_HTML_file(
  const Filename : string
  );
:
:
    var
        C : char;
    begin
        if Filename = '' then exit;
        with TMemoryStream.Create do
            try
                try
                    { Load Document. }
                    LoadFromFile(Filename);
                    Seek(-1,soFromEnd); { Last character }
                    Read(C,sizeof(C));
                    { Add a CR if necessary. }
                    if C <> #13 then begin
                        C := #13;
                        Write(C,sizeof(C));
                        end;
                    { Null termination }
                    C := #0;
                    Write(C,sizeof(C));
                    { Do it. }
                    Process_HTML_string(Memory);
                except on E : EInOutError do
                    MessageDlg(E.Message,mtWarning,[mbOk],0);
                end;
            finally
                Free;
            end;
    end;
```

Inside the block, we use a simple exception handler to catch I/O errors like "File not Found." If we *are* able to load a document, we need to prepare it. **Process_HTML_string** takes a null-terminated string, unlike the process in *Word Wrap* from Chapter 2 (which depended on a length, instead). Before we null-terminate the string, we add a carriage-return onto it, if one is needed. That's just a rule we're making—all documents end with a final carriage-return. We check for this by **Seek**-ing in the memory stream one character back from the end of the stream and **Read**-ing the character we find.

Once everything is prepared, we call our local procedure **Process_HTML_string**, shown in the code snippet below:

```
procedure Process_HTML_string(
  const Text : pchar
  );
:
:
  var
       Format     : tHTML_format;
       The_Text   : pchar;
       InThe_Text : integer;
  begin
       with Format, Font do begin
           Leading_newlines := 0;
           Serial_number    := 0;
           specStyle        := [];
           end;
       Parse_HTML(Text,Format);
       Break_into_lines;
       end;
```

This routine illustrates the three tasks necessary to get HTML into a displayable structure in this program. We set up a default initial **Format** with no **Leading_newlines** (we'll already be at the start of a new line when we start), a **Serial_number** of zero (we have to start counting someplace), and no special character formatting in **Format.Font.specStyle**. Then all we do is **Parse_HTML**, and **Break_into_lines**.

HTML, At Last

Now we're into the meat. We went through two layers of routines that didn't do much of anything except indent our source code a couple of levels, but we're finally here. This routine is pretty lengthy, so we'll tackle it in sections.

Buffering Text in the Current Format

Our basic control structure will require us to read and save all of the text between tags. We'll eventually put the text and its format onto the **Formatted_text_list**; but before we do that, we need a temporary structure to hold the text. We do this with a simple null-terminated string, **Buffer**, shown in the code snippet below:

```
{ Buffer Data Structure }
var
    Buffer,
    End_of_buffer            : pchar;
    Remaining_buffer_length : integer;
```

We use **End_of_buffer** as a quick way to get to the end of the **Buffer** when we need to append more text to it. We are going to have to allocate some fixed amount of space for the **Buffer**—actually, **Length_of_buffer** bytes, plus 1 for the terminating null—which in our case, works out to 1024 bytes that hold a string of 1023 characters. This will hold a pretty long paragraph of identically-formatted HTML text. **Remaining_buffer_length** tells us how much space is left in our **Buffer**. If it fills up, we'll have to empty it out into the **Formatted_text_list**, in spite of the fact that the format didn't change.

When we start, and after we've emptied the **Buffer** for any reason, we'll need to effectively empty the **Buffer** with **Reset_buffer**.

```
procedure Reset_buffer;
    begin
        Buffer^ := #0;
        End_of_Buffer := Buffer;
        Remaining_buffer_length := Length_of_buffer;
    end;
```

To actually empty the **Buffer**, we use the procedure **Add_buffer_to_list**; this does some clean-up on the text and then calls **Formatted_text_list.Add**, passing a newly **Create**d segment of **tFormatted_text**. The clean-up is reasonable: If **Pending_newlines**, which indicates how many times we should start a new line before outputting the buffered text, is not zero, then the text in the **Buffer** will start a new line. Since we don't want leading spaces on our word-wrapped lines, we'll strip the leading spaces. Note that we only add the buffered text if any exists there to add. When we're finished, we reset the **Buffer**, as shown in the code snippet below:

```
procedure Add_buffer_to_list;
    var
        S : pchar;
    begin
        S := Buffer;
        if Pending_newlines > 0 then
            while (S^ <> #0) and (S^ <= ' ') do inc(S);
        if S^ <> #0 then begin
            Current_format.Leading_newlines :=
                Pending_newlines;
            Formatted_text_list.Add(
                tFormatted_text.Create(Current_format,S)
                );
            Pending_newlines := 0;
            end;
        Reset_buffer;
    end;
```

In the main body of **Parse_HTML**, we allocate and reset the **Buffer**, starting with no **Pending_newlines**. When we're finished, we flush the last bit of text out with **Add_buffer_to_list** and **StrDispose** the **Buffer**, as shown in the code snippet below:

```
begin
    Buffer := strAlloc(Length_of_buffer+1);
    Reset_buffer;
    Pending_newlines := 0;
    Current_format.Serial_number := -1;
:
:
    Add_buffer_to_list; { Last little bit. }
    strDispose(Buffer);
    end;
```

Placing Text in the Buffer

We'll find it easier to work with the **Buffer** with three routines, shown in the code snippet below. **Set_format** is used to flush the **Buffer** to the **Formatted_text_list** when a new format is encountered. **New_line** is used to force a line break, as we'll need to do when we handle a tag that requires a line break, like **<P>**. **Emit** is used to put a string onto the **Buffer**, and goes through the gyrations to make sure the **Buffer** doesn't overflow with an extra-long string.

```
{ Buffer building }

procedure Set_format(
  var F : tHTML_format
  );
    var
        S : pchar;
    begin
        Add_buffer_to_list;
        Current_format := F;
        end;

procedure New_line;
    begin
        Add_buffer_to_list;
        Pending_newlines := 1;
        end;

procedure Emit(
  S   : pchar;
  lnS : integer
  );
    var
        Chars_to_take       : integer;
```

```
begin
   while lnS > 0 do begin
      Chars_to_take :=
         Int_min(Remaining_buffer_length,lnS);
      strLCopy(End_of_Buffer,S,Chars_to_take);
      inc(End_of_buffer,Chars_to_take);
      End_of_buffer^ := #0;
      dec(Remaining_buffer_length,Chars_to_take);
      dec(lnS,Chars_to_take);
      inc(S,Chars_to_take);
      if Remaining_buffer_length = 0 then
         Add_buffer_to_list;
      end;
   end;
```

Note that **Emit** doesn't require null termination; it just needs to know how many characters to put on the **Buffer**.

Scanning through the HTML String

Now we're ready to go scanning through the HTML **Text**. We do this with a simple loop that has three main parts. The code snippet below shows the short version:

```
Preceeding_newline := false;
Preceeding_space := false;
while Text^ <> #0 do
   if Text^ = '<' then begin
      { Process a Tag }
      end
   else if Text^ <= ' ' then begin
      { Process Whitespace }
      end
   else begin
      { Process Words }
      end
```

In the **while** loop, we just look at the next character and decide what action to take with it. Each of the three sections is responsible for moving the **Text** pointer to the character after whatever-it-was they handled. **Preceeding_newline** and **Preceeding_space** are flags used in the individual sections to ensure that important whitespace information isn't lost.

Processing a Tag

There are three parts to this process. First, we must find the closing angle-bracket of the tag and then turn it into an uppercase null-terminated string for easy comparison work with Delphi's string-type cohersion. When we're done,

Text points to our tag which is ready for identification, and the remainder of the document lies just after the **The_end** of the tag, as shown in the code snippet below:

```
{ Process a Tag }

The_end := strPos(Text,'>');
if The_end = nil then begin
    { Oops, there was no closing ">" on the tag. }
    { We'll handle this here, trivially.        }
    Text := strEnd(Text);
    exit;
    end;

inc(Text);
The_end^ := #0;
strUpper(Text);
```

It's now time to identify the tag. We'll be working with five tags: Paragraph, which causes a paragraph break in the output; Italics On and Off; and Underline On and Off. These are just barely enough tags to indicate that we know what we're doing. We start by knowing that most tags don't require the start of a new line in their output, and we increment the **Format.Serial_number**, as shown in the code snippet below:

```
Need_a_newline := false;
inc(Format.Serial_number);
if Text = 'P' then
    Need_a_newline := true
  else if Text = 'I' then
    include(Format.Font.specStyle,fsItalic)
  else if Text = '/I' then
    exclude(Format.Font.specStyle,fsItalic)
  else if Text = 'U' then
    include(Format.Font.specStyle,fsUnderline)
  else if Text = '/U' then
    exclude(Format.Font.specStyle,fsUnderline);
```

We now have a modified **Format**, or perhaps a **Need_a_newline** flag. As shown in the code snippet below, **Need_a_newline** is factored in with the flag **Preceeding_newline**, used back in **Add_buffer_to_list**. This boolean mechanism ensures that multiple paragraph tags will result in only one start of a new paragraph. This seems a little strange, now; but when we start handling tags like the end of a heading, which should naturally start a new paragraph, we don't want a user's overzealous use of paragraph tags to result in strange-looking vertical space.

```
Text := The_end + 1;
Preceeding_newline :=
  Preceeding_newline or Need_a_newline;
if Preceeding_newline then
    Preceeding_space := false;
Set_format(Format);
end
```

Text is advanced to the character after the null at **The_end** of the tag. Finally, **Set_format** is called.

Processing Whitespace

Whitespace is pretty easy to ignore in the source text. There are situations, though, where it can get tricky. Let's look at an example:

```
Hello_<I> _<U>_There</U></I>
```

Let's treat the underscores as spaces, and then ask ourselves a question. We know there should be a word-space between "Hello" and "There" in the output. But will it be a plain space, an italicized space (which may be a little wider than normal), or an underlined, italic space? In our case, we use the flag **Preceeding_space** to remember that we should do a word-space in the output and we save the latest whitespace's format in **Space_format**. In our case (always remembering the latest format), we'll get an underlined, italic space. Of course, if some previous tag has already requested a new line before the text, we will ignore the request for a **Preceeding_space**. This is illustrated in the code snippet below:

```
{ Process Whitespace }

if not Preceeding_newline then begin
    Preceeding_space := true;
    Space_format := Format;
    end;
while Is_whitespace(Text^) do inc(Text);
end
```

Processing a Word

This is where we do all of the output of fresh text to the **Buffer**, with **Emit**. The processing of tags and whitespace just set the flags **Preceeding_newline** and **Preceeding_space**. (Well, tag processing *did* keep track of our current format, and space processing *did* remember the format to be used on and preceding word-space.) By delaying the application of this information to the text we want to display, we'll have an easier job of making things look good.

Before this, though, we need to get our **Word**. (**Is_word;** which, by the way, stops at whitespace or open angle-brackets.)

```
{ Process Words }

Word := Text;
while Is_word(Text^) do inc(Text);
The_end := Text;
Saved := The_end^;
The_end^ := #0;
```

If we need a new line, we call **New_line**, flushing the old **Buffer**. As you recall, **New_lines** also sets the **Pending_newlines** that will be used when the **Buffer** (which will shortly contain the **Word**) is later added to the **Formatted_text_list** with **Add_buffer_to_list**.

```
if Preceeding_newline then
    New_line
  else if Preceeding_space then
    if  Space_format.Serial_number
      =
        Format.Serial_number
      then
        Emit(' ',1)
      else begin
        {Re-} Set_format(Space_format);
        Emit(' ',1);
        {Re-} Set_format(Format);
        end;
Emit(Word,The_end-Word);
The_end^ := Saved;
Preceeding_newline := false;
Preceeding_space    := false;
end;
```

We have to do a dance with whitespace. We use the **Serial_number** to determine if the whitespace we need to display (if **Preceeding_space** is **true**) is in the same format as the **Word**'s **Format**. If the format has changed, and the most recent whitespace was in another, previous format, we need to make sure we emit that space in the previous format.

Once we've sent the **Word** to the **Buffer** with **Emit**, we know we can't have a **Preceeding_newline** or **Preceeding_space**. We'll have to set these again, after examining the next character in the HTML string with another turn of the **while** loop.

When we're all finished, we'll have a **Formatted_text_list** like the one shown in Figure 3.4.

Text:	This could be a paragraph with an
Format:	
Leading-newlines	●
Style	[ ]

↓

Text:	italic
Format:	
Leading-newlines	●
Style	[fs italic]

↓

Text:	word.
Format:	
Leading-newlines	●
Style	[ ]

↓

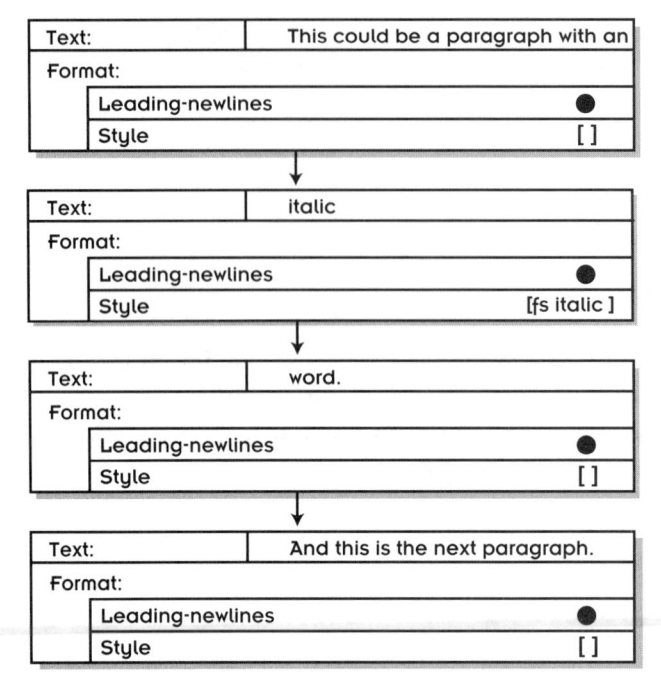

Text:	And this is the next paragraph.
Format:	
Leading-newlines	●
Style	[ ]

Figure 3.4 *The structure of the **Formatted_text_list** field for some sample text.*

Breaking Formatted Text into Lines

Up to this point, we have done nothing but break our text up into simple segments where all of the text within a segment share the same HTML format. We have not measured the text, nor have we done anything with line-breaking, aside from indicating in the individual elements of **Formatted_text_list** if the text therein should start on a new line.

We have two choices at this point. We can either transfer the existing **Formatted_text_list** structure into another **tFormatted_text_list** structure (in which all of the text of an element is on the same line), or we can impose this structure on the **Formatted_text_list** we already have built. You can guess what we're going to do if you remember the implementation of **tFormatted_text_list.Break_at**, but we'll discuss both of these alternatives.

Our **Formatted_text_list** is a pure representation of the HTML structure of the document at this point. If we were to line-break it into another structure, copying the data instead of re-arranging it, we could always refer back to the pure formatted text if we wanted to change our line breaking. If the user resized the display, we would only have to re-break the existing **Formatted_text_list** rather than re-read and re-parse the entire file again.

On the other hand, if we break the existing **Formatted_text_list**, we don't incur the resource overhead of a second complete copy of the file in memory. We do, indeed, need to reload and re-parse the file from scratch, though.

This is a classic Speed *versus* Resource problem. In these projects, we're going to opt for the low-memory-use version, even if we need to redo everything when the user resizes the display area. Don't worry—by the time this project becomes a Web browser, it will be double-buffering the document so it doesn't need to hit the 'net on every resize event. Sometimes it's just nice to see how things can be made to behave nicely—with a small appetite—in a world hallmarked by the unbounded greed of today's sloppy applications.

The code for line-breaking our Formatted_text_list in place is shown in Listing 3.6.

Listing 3.6 The **Break_into_lines** procedure from unit **DispBuf**

```
procedure Break_into_lines;

    var
        Current_item_index    : integer;
        EOW                   : pchar;
        Last_EOW              : pchar;
        Last_EOW_item_index   : integer;
        Line_pos              : TPoint;
        Last_line_meas,
        Current_line_meas     : tText_measurement;

    procedure Start_new_line(
      const Line_count : integer
      );
        var
            L, I : integer;
        begin
            for L := 1 to Line_count do begin
                Line_pos.Y :=
                    Display_bottom + Current_line_meas.Ascent;

                if L = 1 then begin
                    Line_pos.X := 0;
                    for I :=
                        integer(Line_list.Items[Line_list.Count-1])
                      to
                        Current_item_index-1
                      do
                        with tFormatted_text(
                            Formatted_text_list.Items[I]
                            )
                          do begin
                            Base_Left_Corner := Line_pos;
                            inc(Line_pos.X,Meas.Width);
```

```
                    end;
            end;

        Display_bottom :=
            Line_pos.Y + Current_line_meas.Descent;
        end;

    with Current_line_Meas do begin
        Width   := 0;
        Height  := 0;
        Ascent  := 0;
        Descent := 0;
        end;
    Line_list.Add(pointer(Current_item_index));
    Last_EOW  := nil;
    end;

var
    P, BOW       : pchar;
    Real_EOW     : boolean;
    Saved        : char;
    Broken       : boolean;
    Start_width  : integer;
    Canvas_width : integer;
begin
    with Control.ClientRect do
        Canvas_width := Right - Left;
    with Last_line_meas do begin
        Width   := 0;
        Height  := 0;
        Ascent  := 0;
        Descent := 0;
        end;
    Current_line_meas := Last_line_meas;
    Line_pos.Y := 0;
    Display_bottom := Line_pos.Y;
    Current_item_index := 0;
    Line_list.Add(pointer(Current_item_index));
    with Formatted_text_list do begin
        while Current_item_index < Count do
            with tFormatted_text(
                    Items[Current_item_index]
                    ),
                 Format
            do begin
              if Current_item_index = 0 then
                  Leading_newlines := 0;
              if Leading_newlines > 0 then
                  Start_new_line(Leading_newlines);
              P := Text;
              Broken := false;
              Start_width := Current_line_meas.Width;
              while (not Broken) and (P <> nil) do begin
```

```
                    { Get to Space or Null at end of next
                      word, advance P. }
                    BOW := P;
                    EOW := strScan(P,' ');
                    Real_EOW := EOW <> nil;
                    if Real_EOW then
                        P := EOW + 1
                      else begin
                        EOW := strEnd(P);
                        P := nil;
                        end;
                    Saved := EOW^;
                    EOW^ := #0;
                    StrXlate(BOW,#160,' ');
                    EOW^ := Saved;

                    { Measure word; if adding it passes
                      right edge, then break line. }
                    Meas := Measurement_of(Text,EOW-Text,
                            Control.Canvas,
                            Font
                            );
                    if  (Start_width + Meas.Width)
                      >
                         Canvas_width
                      then
                        if Last_EOW <> nil then begin
                          Break_at(
                            Last_EOW_item_index,
                            Last_EOW
                            );
                          Current_item_index :=
                            Last_EOW_item_index;
                          tFormatted_text(
                            Items[Current_item_index + 1]
                            ).Format.Leading_newlines := 1;
                          Broken := true;
                          end;
                    if not Broken then begin
                      if Real_EOW then begin
                        { Track previous space to break on. }
                        Last_EOW := EOW;
                        Last_EOW_item_index := Current_item_index;
                        end;
                      with Current_line_meas do begin
                        Height  := Int_max(Height, Meas.Height);
                        Width   := Start_width + Meas.Width;
                        Ascent  := Int_max(Ascent, Meas.Ascent);
                        Descent := Int_max(Descent, Meas.Descent);
                        end;
                      end;
                    end;
              inc(Current_item_index);
              end;
```

```
            Start_new_line(1);
            Line_list.Delete(Line_list.Count-1);
          end;
     end;
```

As with any large piece of code, we'll look at this from the outside, going in.

The Line-Breaking Mechanism

We must obviously traverse the **Formatted_text_list** and determine where the line breaks should go. The outer loop is simple. (We've taken some liberties with the actual code, here.)

```
procedure Break_into_lines;
    begin
        { Initialize a bunch of positions and sizes. }
        Current_item_index := 0;
        with Formatted_text_list do begin
            while Current_item_index < Count do
                with tFormatted_text(
                        Items[Current_item_index]
                        ),
                     Format
                    do begin
                       {Break the element if it causes the line we're
                        working with to become wider than the Canvas. }
                    end;
                inc(Current_item_index);
            end;
        { Clean up }
    end;
```

Going through the **Formatted_text_list** isn't difficult. We do need to remember that when we break the elements and **Insert** new elements into **Formatted_text_list**, we will be increasing **Formatted_text_list.Count**. This means we won't be able to use a **for** loop.

Since we always add new elements after the current one, we will always get a chance to re-examine their fit on the next time through the loop. For instance, let's say we have one segment—a paragraph without any font changes—that will end up as four lines on the display. When we encounter this element, we will break it so that its **Text** becomes the first line. We insert the remainder of the text as a new element after this one. The next time through the loop, we won't be finished, since our **Count** increased by one when we inserted the second element. We will look at our new, second element and break it so that it contains the text for the second line, inserting the remaining text as a third element. This continues until we look at the fourth line and find that it doesn't need to be broken. Finally, we fall out of our **while** loop, having modified the first element to be one line, and having added three more elements for the remaining lines.

When we break the lines, we'll call the local procedure **Start_new_line**. This calls the **Formatted_text_list.Break_at** method to actually split the element, inserting the remaining text using the **Create_direct** method of **tFormatted_text**. The first element we started with will still "own" all of the **Text** in the paragraph. We will just be breaking that **Text** into separate null-terminated strings by replacing the spaces at the line breaks with nulls. Figure 3.5 illustrates this hypothetical situation.

Measurement and Positioning

We will enlist the aid of several data structures to help us break the **Formatted_text_list** elements into lines. Most important are the **Last_line_meas** and **Current_line_meas** records, containing the overall dimension of the previous and current lines that begin output, along with their ascent and descent. These will track important dimensions of our lines, allowing us to determine if adding another word from our element's **Text** to the line would force it past the right edge of the **Control**. If adding the next word will overflow the line, we need to break the element and start a new line. Our lines start out with no size at all, as shown in the code snippet below:

```
with Control.ClientRect do
    Canvas_width := Right - Left;
with Last_line_meas do begin
    Width   := 0;
    Height  := 0;
    Ascent  := 0;
    Descent := 0;
    end;
Current_line_meas := Last_line_meas;
```

Next, as shown in the code snippet below, we use some trial values to track our space projections. The **Line_pos** holds the running location across the

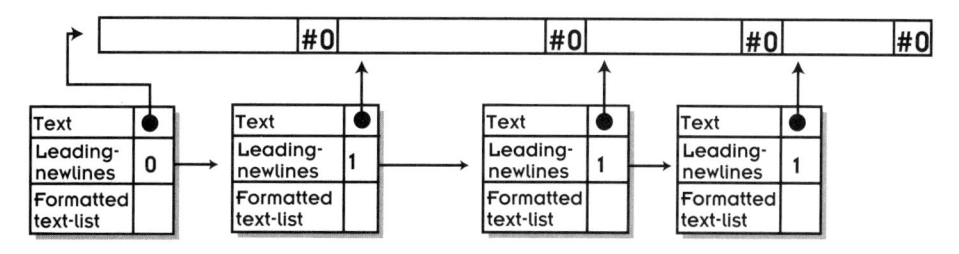

Figure 3.5 *The structure of a **Formatted_text_list** and its text after line-breaking.*

line of text that we will actually place in a particular position when we **Start_new_line**. We set its vertical position to zero, leaving the baseline of a "previous" line at the top of the **Control**. The first thing this algorithm will do is move the **Line_pos** down by the ascent of the first line of text, once it has been accumulated.

```
Line_pos.Y := 0;
Display_bottom := Line_pos.Y;
Current_item_index := 0;
Line_list.Add(pointer(Current_item_index));
with Formatted_text_list do begin
    while Current_item_index < Count do
        :
        { Measure the item and add it to the current line's
          measurement, or break it onto a new line. }
        :
    Start_new_line(1);
    Line_list.Delete(Line_list.Count-1);
    end;
```

The **Line_list** structure is an ordinary **TList** of pointers. By treating the pointers as **integer**s, we can create a dynamic array of integers. Even though **TList.Destroy** doesn't know how to destroy objects or strings that might be pointed to by the list elements, it does know how to destroy the elements (the pointers) themselves. So if we use the pointer elements as integers, instead of objects or pointers, **TList** can take care of our cleanup automatically.

Line_list is a list of indexes into the **Formatted_text_list**. We do this so we can located where in the **Formatted_text_list** we would find the start of, for example, display line 15. We start **Line_list** by adding the index of the first element of the **Formatted_text_list**, 0, as the first element (and hence, first line) of our **Line_list**. Once this is accomplished, we're set to process the text.

When we're finished, we call **Start_new_line**, which has the effect of dumping out the last line. This starts a new line in **Line_list** that points to a **Current_item_index,** for which there is no real element in **Formatted_text_list**; so we **Delete** that last element from the **Line_list**.

Handling a Formatted Text Segment

Given the framework of current positions and measurements, all we need to do with an individual element is see if it crosses the right edge of the **Control**. If it does, we need to break it at the space nearest and before the edge; if it doesn't, we just increase the size of the current line. Since we would need to loop through the line, space by space, if we *did* need to break the line; we'll just do this in all cases. This is illustrated in the code snippet below:

```
while Current_item_index < Count do
    with tFormatted_text(
            Items[Current_item_index]
            ),
        Format
    do begin
        if Current_item_index = 0 then
            Leading_newlines := 0;
        if Leading_newlines > 0 then
            Start_new_line(Leading_newlines);
        P := Text;
        Broken := false;
        Start_width := Current_line_meas.Width;
        while (not Broken) and (P <> nil) do begin
            :
            { Loop through the words now pointed to by P. }
            :
            end;
        inc(Current_item_index);
        end;
```

First, we make sure we don't display any leading new lines before the first line we'll display. Secondly, we call **Start_new_line**, passing in the count of lines we need to output before starting this section of formatted text. **Start_new_line** will go ahead and do the screen positioning of the last measured line when passed a count of one; for higher values, it will then advance the **Line_pos** by a line's height the required number of times. In this project, we've only been assigning 1 to the number of **Leading_newlines** through the processes of **Parse_HTML**, above. We've allowed for the possibility of multiple line advancement so that we can support preformatted text (wherein we must display all of the line breaks, as given) in the future.

We will move the pointer **P** through the **Text**, word by word—or more precisely, space by space. We need to break the line when the display width of the string from **Text** to **P**, when added to our current position along the line, becomes greater than the width of the **Control**. Our current position along the line, before we start adding words from this element, is held in **Start_width**. Of course, we can stop looping after our first break, because the new element inserted by breaking will be visited the next time through the outside element loop. **Broken** indicates this condition.

Processing Individual Words

First, we must advance **P** by one word, as shown in the code snippet below:

```
{ Get to Space or Null at end of next
  word, advance P. }
BOW := P;
EOW := strScan(P,' ');
Real_EOW := EOW <> nil;
if Real_EOW then
    P := EOW + 1
  else begin
    EOW := strEnd(P);
    P := nil;
    end;
```

We save a pointer to the beginning of the word in **BOW**, and point **EOW** to the next space after **P**. If **EOW** is **nil**, then we're dealing with the last word in the element. **Real_EOW** tells us whether or not we have a real, breakable space between words with which to work. If this is the case, then **P** can continue to advance, starting after the word. Otherwise, **EOW** is set to the null that ends the text, and then **P** is set to **nil**, effectively ending the looping, as shown in the code snippet below:

```
Saved := EOW^;
EOW^ := #0;
StrXlate(BOW,#160,' ');
EOW^ := Saved;
```

Before continuing, we force a null into the character at the end of the word, making **BOW** the pointer to the word as a null-terminated string. We do this so that we can translate all of the **#160** characters in the string to spaces with our **MiscLib** routine **StrXlate**. This is an interesting kludge implemented in a few browsers (including this one) to support *non-breaking*, or *hard* spaces. Once we have finished, we restore the proper character—be it a space or a null—from **Saved** (it must be one of those).

Now we can measure the entire string from the beginning of the **Text** to the end of the new word we're trying to include on the line, as shown in the code snippet below. The text is still pointed to by **Text**, and the length of the string with the new word, not including the terminating space or null, is **EOW-Text**. We pass this information about the string, as well as the **Control**'s **Canvas** and **Format**'s **Font** information to **Measurement_of**, in the unit **Font**.

```
{ Measure word; if adding it passes
  right edge, then break line. }
```

```
Meas := Measurement_of(Text,EOW-Text,
         Control.Canvas,
         Font
         );
if  (Start_width + Meas.Width)
  >
    Canvas_width
  then
    if Last_EOW <> nil then begin
        Break_at(
          Last_EOW_item_index,
          Last_EOW
          );
        Current_item_index :=
          Last_EOW_item_index;
        tFormatted_text(
          Items[Current_item_index + 1]
          ).Format.Leading_newlines := 1;
        Broken := true;
        end;
```

If the new word causes the line to be wider than the **Canvas_width**, then we can *try* to break the line. Sometimes a single word will be too long for the display. When this happens, we won't have a space to break it on, so we'll not even make the attempt. When we draw text too wide for the display, Windows will clip it for us, so it won't be a problem.

Last_EOW points to the last valid space on the line we are building. It may well be that the last valid space was in a previous segment with another format and a different item index. Thus, we also need to use **Last_EOW_item_index**. We'll reset these variables later. Here, we just call **Break_at** to break the line.

Here's an important action to notice. Since we may have broken an earlier element, we must go back to that element and remeasure everything up to where we are. We do this by setting our **Current_item_index** to the **Last_EOW_item_index**. At the end of the loop body, **Current_item_index** will be incremented to point to the newly-inserted remainder element.

If the line was broken by adding the word, we set the newly-inserted element's **Leading_newlines** to 1, so that we'll know to advance a line before positioning this element. If the line wasn't broken by adding the word, we need to record the end of the word (if it was a real space, not a null) in **Last_EOW** for breaking purposes. We also save the **Current_item_index** in **Last_EOW_item_index** to point to the proper element containing the **Last_EOW**, as shown in the code snippet below:

```
if not Broken then begin
  if Real_EOW then begin
```

```
        { Track previous space to break on. }
        Last_EOW := EOW;
        Last_EOW_item_index := Current_item_index;
        end;
    with Current_line_meas do begin
        Height  := Int_max(Height, Meas.Height);
        Width   := Start_width + Meas.Width;
        Ascent  := Int_max(Ascent, Meas.Ascent);
        Descent := Int_max(Descent, Meas.Descent);
        end;
    end;
```

Finally, we also need to adjust the **Current_line_meas** to reflect the new size. (Remember, we are breaking on width alone; even though we're tracking the line width word-by-word, we still have the original line width, before we started adding words from this element, saved in **Start_width**.)

Starting a New Line

We've mentioned the routine **Start_new_line** several times now, as the routine that positions formatted text elements. This is going to be a little tricky, since many elements can appear on a single line. Our work is aided by our **Line_list**, and the fact that, since we initialized it, its last element will point to the formatted element that should start the current line. The current line's size has been diligently maintained in **Current_line_meas**. Again, let's shorten the code for easy digestion, as shown in the snippet below:

```
procedure Start_new_line(
  const Line_count : integer
  );
    var
        L : integer;
    begin
        for L := 1 to Line_count do begin
            { Move the baseline marker down from the
              previous location by the ascent of our
              current line. }
            if L = 1 then begin
                :
                { "Output" the current line. }
                :
                end;
            { Move the baseline marker to the base
              of our descender. }
            end;
        { Reset the current line measurement. }
        { Add a new line pointer to Line_list,
          pointing to the next formatted text element. }
```

```
    { Invalidate the pointer to the previous
      breakable space. }
  end;
```

The main loop is pretty simple. **Line_count** specifies the number of lines to advance before the calling code starts a new line. The first time through this loop, the current line that has been built already will be "output." Advancing the baseline marker is not too difficult.

```
Line_pos.Y :=
  Display_bottom + Current_line_meas.Ascent;

if L = 1 then { "Output" the current line. }

Display_bottom :=
  Line_pos.Y + Current_line_meas.Descent;
```

We use the interplay of **Display_bottom** and **Line_pos.Y** to move down a line. On the first line, we stop at what will be the baseline and position some text. **Display_bottom** really is the bottom of the text displayed; it's not just the baseline of the last line positioned. When we're finished, **Line_pos.Y** does happen to hold the last baseline's vertical position.

Positioning the Formatted Elements of a Line

The last item of the **Line_list** contains the index into the **Formatted_text_list** of the element that starts this line. (When we're finished, we keep it that way.) By the time **Start_new_line** is called, the **Current_item_index** points to the first element of the next line, past the current line that has been measured. We can use a simple **for** loop to traverse the formatted text elements between these indices, as shown in the code snippet below:

```
Line_pos.X := 0;
for I :=
    integer(Line_list.Items[Line_list.Count-1])
  to
    Current_item_index-1
  do
    with tFormatted_text(
         Formatted_text_list.Items[I]
         )
      do begin
        Base_Left_Corner := Line_pos;
        inc(Line_pos.X,Meas.Width);
        end;
```

Along the way, we track the horizontal placement of each element with **Line_pos.X**. This starts out at the left edge of the **Control**, which we assume to be 0. **Line_pos.Y** was already advanced to the baseline of our text. For each element, all we need to do is set its **Base_Left_Corner** to **Line_pos**, and then move **Line_pos** by the measured width of the element, **Meas.Width**.

Setting Up for the Next Line

Once we've positioned the formatted text elements that make up the line, we need to do some housekeeping to prepare for the next line. First, we clear the current line's measurements. We add the **Current_item_index**, which references the formatted text element that starts the next line, to the **Line_list**. Finally, as shown in the code snippet below, we set **Last_EOW**, the position of the last valid breaking space, to **nil** because we have not yet started processing the next line, and thus have no space on which to break it.

```
with Current_line_Meas do begin
    Width   := 0;
    Height  := 0;
    Ascent  := 0;
    Descent := 0;
    end;
Line_list.Add(pointer(Current_item_index));
Last_EOW  := nil;
```

Displaying HTML Text on the Control

Once we have virtually-positioned, line-broken, formatted text, created by the **tDisplay_buffer** method **Load_HTML_file**, all that's left to do is display it. The **Display** method is relatively simple, thanks to all the work that has gone before it. It is shown in Listing 3.7.

Listing 3.7   The **Display** method of the **tDisplay_buffer** class in unit **DispBuf**

```
procedure tDisplay_buffer.Display;

    function Line_after(
      const Pixel_row : integer
      ) : integer;
        begin with Formatted_text_list do begin
            result := 0;
            while
                (result < Line_list.Count)
              and (then)
                (
                    tFormatted_text(Items[integer(Line_list.Items[result])])
                      .Base_left_corner.Y
```

Building a Hypermedia Engine

```
                    <
                      Pixel_row
                    )
                do
                    inc(result);
            end; end;

function Line_before(
    const Pixel_row : integer
    ) : integer;
        begin with Formatted_text_list do begin
            result := 0;
            while
                (result < Line_list.Count)
                and {then}
                (
                    tFormatted_text(Items[integer(Line_list.Items[result])])
                        .Base_left_corner.Y
                    <=
                      Pixel_row
                )
                do
                    inc(result);
            if result > 0 then dec(result);
        end; end;

var
    First_line,
    Last_line,
    First_elem,
    Last_elem    : integer;
    I            : integer;

begin with Formatted_text_list do begin
    if Count = 0 then exit;
    First_line := Line_before(Display_top);
    First_elem := integer(Line_list.Items[First_line]);
    Last_line  := Line_after(Display_top +
                                Control.ClientRect.Bottom);
    if Last_line >= (Line_list.Count-1) then
        Last_elem := Count - 1
      else
        Last_elem := integer(Line_list.Items[Last_line+1]) - 1;

    with Control.Canvas do begin
        Brush.Color := Color;
        FillRect(ClientRect);
        SetTextAlign(Handle,TA_BASELINE);
        end;
    for I := First_elem to Last_elem do
        with tFormatted_text(Items[I]), Format do
            if Text <> nil then begin
                Set_font_from_spec(Control.Canvas.Font,Format.Font);
```

```
            Control.Canvas.TextOut(
              Base_left_corner.X, Base_left_corner.Y - Display_top,
              Text
              );
            end;

      end; end;
```

This is basically a big **for** loop that traverses the **Formatted_text_list**, using the font information built by **Parse_HTML** and the positioning information built by **Break_into_lines**, to display text on the **Control** with the **TextOut** method.

We could just loop through the entire document and let Windows clip the text that is too far down in the window to appear in the display. But we can do a little better than this. We can easily determine the height of the **Control**, and by looking at the **Base_Left_Corner** of the formatted list elements referred to by the **Line_list**, we can determine which lines are actually visible (or partially visible), displaying only the elements that appear on the display. The code snippet below shows how we find our **First_elem** index:

```
First_line := Line_before(Display_top);
First_elem := integer(Line_list.Items[First_line]);
```

Line_before is a local function that scans the **Line_list**, looking for the line that lies vertically, completely before the given pixel row. We use the field **Display_top** for this value. We won't use a **Display_top** value other than zero until *Hyper III*, but we threw this in here just in case you would like to try your hand at adding a scroll bar to this project. (If you want to do that, you'll need to use **Display_bottom** as well, which will tell you the total height of the text.) Finding the last element is a little trickier, as shown in the code snippet below:

```
Last_line   := Line_after(Display_top +
                          Control.ClientRect.Bottom);
if Last_line >= (Line_list.Count-1) then
   Last_elem  := Count - 1
  else
   Last_elem  := integer(Line_list.Items[Last_line+1]) - 1;
```

Last_line is the **Line_after** the bottom of the display, when laid over the text. The bottom is just the **Display_top** plus the height of the **Control** (which is really **Bottom - Top** in the **Control.ClientRect**; but since we haven't done anything to change the Control's local coordinate system, **Top** will always be zero).

If the **Last_line** points past the lines that we actually have, the last element we want to bother with is the last element of the **Formatted_text_list**, referenced by **Count - 1**, since the **Items** property array is zero-based. Otherwise, we want to use the last element of the **Last_line**, which is the element *before* the element that starts the *next* line.

Once we have the **First_elem** and **Last_elem**, we can loop through the **Formatted_text_list Items**. Before we do that, we need to set up the **Control.Canvas** for drawing our text, as shown in the code snippet below:

```
with Control.Canvas do begin
          Brush.Color := Color;
          FillRect(ClientRect);
          SetTextAlign(Handle,TA_BASELINE);
          end;
```

First, we clear the area upon which we are going to paint. In our case, this is the whole client area—you could make the modification to repaint just the current clipping rectangle so you don't waste time on the **OnPaint** event. Before drawing baseline-aligned text, we need to call **SetTextAlign**. We don't need to track the current pen position the way we did in *Word Wrap*, because we've already pre-positioned all of our text. Now we can loop through the elements, as shown in the code snippet below:

```
for I := First_elem to Last_elem do
    with tFormatted_text(Items[I]), Format do
        if Text <> nil then begin
            Set_font_from_spec(Control.Canvas.Font,Format.Font);
            Control.Canvas.TextOut(
              Base_left_corner.X, Base_left_corner.Y - Display_top,
              Text
              );
            end;
```

This becomes a pretty trivial task. We simply loop from **First_elem** to **Last_elem**, calling **Set_font_from_spec** to change our display attributes, and **TextOut** to draw our text on the **Control**'s **Canvas**. Of course, we translate the **Base_Left_Corner** vertically to handle the **Display_top** field.

Line_before and Line_after

These two routines are pretty similar. In the code snippet below, we look at **Line_after**, since **Line_before** only gives trivial results in this project as it stands now.

```
function Line_after(
  const Pixel_row : integer
  ) : integer;
    begin with Formatted_text_list do begin
        result := 0;
        while
            (result < Line_list.Count)
          and {then}
            (
                tFormatted_text(Items[integer(Line_list.Items[result])])
                  .Base_left_corner.Y
              <
                Pixel_row
              )
        do
          inc(result);
      end; end;
```

All this simple function does is loop through the **Line_list** until it finds a line that has its baseline after the specified **Pixel_row**. Back in the main code, we still want to display this line because even though the line's baseline falls after the **Pixel_row**, the tops of the letters on that baseline should still show on the display.

The Event Response Code for Hyper I

We now have several hundred lines of support code behind us, and now we're ready to use the **tDisplay_buffer** we've built. In unit **Main**, we've capped off some of the calls to **Load_HTML_file** with the local procedures **Load_HTML** and **Load_new_HTML_file**. **Display** is called only from the **OnPaint** handler of **PaintBox1**. Another thing we're supporting right from the start is the ability to resize the form. The entire unit is shown in Listing 3.8.

Listing 3.8   The event handling code for *Hyper I* in unit *Main.Pas*

```
unit Main;

interface

uses
  SysUtils, WinTypes, WinProcs, Messages, Classes, Graphics, Controls,
  Forms, Dialogs, StdCtrls, ExtCtrls;

type
  TForm1 = class(TForm)
    Filename: TEdit;
    Panel1: TPanel;
    Open_button: TButton;
    Close_button: TButton;
```

```
    OpenDialog1: TOpenDialog;
    PaintBox1: TPaintBox;

    procedure FormCreate(Sender: TObject);
    procedure FormResize(Sender: TObject);
    procedure FilenameKeyPress(Sender: TObject; var Key: Char);
    procedure Open_buttonClick(Sender: TObject);
    procedure Close_buttonClick(Sender: TObject);
    procedure PaintBox1Paint(Sender: TObject);
  private
    { Private declarations }
  public
    { Public declarations }
  end;

var
  Form1: TForm1;

implementation

uses
    MiscLib, DispBuf;

{$R *.DFM}

var
    Output : tDisplay_buffer;

procedure Load_HTML;
    begin
        Output.Free;
        Output := tDisplay_buffer.Create(
                    tGraphicControlWithCanvas(Form1.PaintBox1)
                    );
        Output.Load_HTML_file(Form1.Filename.Text);
        end;

procedure Load_new_HTML_file;
    begin
        Load_HTML;
        Form1.PaintBox1.Refresh;
        end;

procedure TForm1.FilenameKeyPress(Sender: TObject; var Key: Char);
    begin
        if Key = #13 then begin
            Load_new_HTML_file;
            Key := #0;
            end;
        end;

procedure TForm1.Open_buttonClick(Sender: TObject);
    begin
        if OpenDialog1.Execute then begin
```

```
            Filename.Text := OpenDialog1.Filename;
            Load_new_HTML_file;
            end;
        end;

procedure TForm1.Close_buttonClick(Sender: TObject);
    begin
        Close;
        end;

procedure TForm1.PaintBox1Paint(Sender: TObject);
    begin
        Output.Display;
        end;

var
    Resizing_ourselves : boolean;
    Form1s_old_width,
    Form1s_old_height  : integer;

procedure TForm1.FormCreate(Sender: TObject);
    begin
        Resizing_ourselves := false;
        Form1s_old_width   := Form1.Width;
        Form1s_old_height  := Form1.Height;
        Output := nil;
        end;

procedure TForm1.FormResize(Sender: TObject);
    var
        Minimum_width,
        Panel1s_new_width,
        Panel1s_new_height,
        Catchup_width,
        Catchup_height      : integer;
    begin
        if Resizing_ourselves then exit;

        Panel1s_new_width  := Panel1.Width  + (Width  - Form1s_old_width);
        Panel1s_new_height := Panel1.Height + (Height - Form1s_old_height);

        Minimum_width := Open_button.Width + Close_button.Width + 30;
          { 30 pixels between &O and &C}

        Catchup_width  := 0;
        Catchup_height := 0;
        if Panel1s_new_width < Minimum_width then
            Catchup_width := Minimum_width - Panel1s_new_width;
        if Panel1s_new_height < 30 then
            Catchup_height := 30 - Panel1s_new_height;
        inc(Panel1s_new_width, Catchup_width);
        inc(Panel1s_new_height,Catchup_height);
```

```
        Resizing_ourselves := true;
        with Form1 do begin
            if Catchup_width <> 0 then
                Width  := Width  + Catchup_width;
            if Catchup_height <> 0 then
                Height := Height + Catchup_height;
            end;
        with PaintBox1 do begin
            Width  := Panel1s_new_width  - (Panel1.Width  - Width);
            Height := Panel1s_new_height - (Panel1.Height - Height);
            end;
        with Panel1 do begin
            Width  := Panel1s_new_width;
            Height := Panel1s_new_height;
            end;
        with Filename do begin
            Width := Panel1.Width;
            Top   := Top + Form1.Height - Form1s_old_height;
            end;
        with Open_button do
            Top := Top + Form1.Height - Form1s_old_height;
        with Close_button do begin
            Top  := Open_button.Top;
            Left := Panel1.Left + Panel1.Width - Close_button.Width;
            end;
        Resizing_ourselves := false;

        Form1s_old_width  := Form1.Width;
        Form1s_old_height := Form1.Height;

        Load_new_HTML_file;

        Form1.Refresh;
        end;

end.
```

Loading and Displaying Hypertext

The routine **Load_HTML** is used to **Free** and re-**Create** our **Output** display buffer, and then load the file specified in the **Filename** control. One of the features we haven't added to our **tDisplay_buffer** is the ability to clear it and re-use it without this free/re-create cycle. It's not a difficult thing to do; as shown in the code snippet below, it just means a few more lines of code in unit **DispBuf**, if you'd like to tackle that.

```
var
    Output : tDisplay_buffer;

procedure Load_HTML;
    begin
```

```
        Output.Free;
        Output := tDisplay_buffer.Create(
                    tGraphicControlWithCanvas(Form1.PaintBox1)
                    );
        Output.Load_HTML_file(Form1.Filename.Text);
        end;
```

Load_new_HTML_file calls **Load_HTML** to do the free/re-create cycle, and then calls **PaintBox1**'s **Refresh** to cause the **OnPaint** handler to trigger, thus calling **Output.Display**, as shown in the code snippet below:

```
procedure Load_new_HTML_file;
    begin
        Load_HTML;
        Form1.PaintBox1.Refresh;
        end;

procedure TForm1.PaintBox1Paint(Sender: TObject);
    begin
        Output.Display;
        end;
```

To allow the user to type a filename directly on the form and load a new file by pressing enter, we've added support for the **Filename**'s **OnKeyPress** event. This also demonstrates the call to **Load_new_HTML_file**, as shown in the code snippet below:

```
procedure TForm1.FilenameKeyPress(Sender: TObject; var Key: Char);
    begin
        if Key = #13 then begin
            Load_new_HTML_file;
            Key := #0;
            end;
        end;
```

Of course, we can still use the **Open_button** to use the Windows common control, the *Open* dialog box. Since **Load_new_HTML_file** uses **Filename.Text** as the file to load, we need to set the chosen filename into **Filename**, as shown in the code snippet below:

```
procedure TForm1.Open_buttonClick(Sender: TObject);
    begin
        if OpenDialog1.Execute then begin
            Filename.Text := OpenDialog1.Filename;
            Load_new_HTML_file;
            end;
        end;
```

This leaves us with only the form creation and form resize code, as shown in the code snippet below. **TForm1.FormCreate** has only one task apart from initializing variable for the resizing handler. It must set the **Output** display buffer to **nil**, so that **Load_HTML** can call **Free** with an initialized, but uninstanciated, **Output** object. The rest of the resizing code in **TForm1.FormResize** falls along the same lines as the code in *Word Wrap* in Chapter 2, so we'll avoid re-hashing that discussion.

```
procedure TForm1.FormCreate(Sender: TObject);
   begin
      Resizing_ourselves := false;
      Form1s_old_width   := Form1.Width;
      Form1s_old_height  := Form1.Height;
      Output := nil;
      end;
```

One Giant Step for Us, One Small Step Towards Hypertext

Text, until it's hyperlinked, is just text. And that's all we have at this point, even for all of our hard work in *Hyper I*. Hyperlinking brings text to life. With just a little more code built on top of this foundation, the text we display will gain a life of its own. The text will be an interactive interface to itself, not just a static lump of information to be peered at through a window with arrow keys and scroll bars to raise and lower the shades.

The Building Blocks of Life

When we place hypertext under the microscope, we see that its component parts are simple. The careful assemblage of these basic ingredients create a system much more powerful than the sum of the parts. We need only a few capabilities:

- **Recognize words in the text that are important.** HTML includes a number of tags that indicate hypertext references. The most important hypertext tag is the anchor tag, **<A>**, which indicates a direct hypertext link. **<A>** takes some parameters, the most important of which is the *reference* of the link, also called a *destination* or a *target*, indicated by the keyword **HREF** (for Hypertext REFerence). We'll need to be able to parse the **<A>** tag to identify our hyper-words (or *anchor text*) and to determine what action to take if the user activates the *link* (a hypernavigation tag).
- **Remember where we displayed our words.** We went to a lot of trouble in the last chapter to calculate precisely where we should display our

text. When we run across an anchor, we can take advantage of our earlier work and store the screen location of the anchor. We need to do this, because we'll need to be able to tell if the user clicks the anchor.

- **Know where the user clicks the mouse.** As we'll see, this is a trivial but very important task. With the click location in hand, we can look through the screen's anchor location list and determine which anchor was clicked.
- **Know what to do if the user clicked on an important word.** This is the most difficult part of hypertext. It will tie back to parsing hyperlink tags; but more importantly, it requires the implementation of *some* sort of action. The action could be as simple as moving the point of text display to another part of a document, as mundane as opening a window to compose mail for a Web page's author, or as complex as interpreting a program written in a language developed for the Web, like Sun's *Java*. We won't go that far; still, we will want to be able to activate sounds, play music, display pictures, and show video.

A Basic HTML Vocabulary

We've already mentioned the tag we'll need to support hyperlinking, **<A>**. Along with our trivial subset from *Hyper I*, our next project will support a set of basic text formatting tags and will be able to recognize the anchor tag. Table 3.2 shows the tags we'll support with *Hyper II*.

Table 3.2 *The HTML tags implemented in Hyper II.*

Tag		Description
<!text>		Comment. This syntax is not standard HTML.
<HTML>	</HTML>	Tells browser that following text is HTML. Ignored by our program.
<B>	</B>	Displays text in bold-face.
<I>	</I>	Displays text in italics.
<U>	</U>	Displays underlined text.
<STRONG>	</STRONG>	Displays text in "Strong" format.
<EM>	</EM>	Displays text in "Emphasized" format.
<CITE>	</CITE>	Displays text as a citation.
<HR SIZE=height>		Displays a horizontal rule.
<H1>	</H1>	Displays text as a top-level heading.

Continued

Table 3.2 The HTML tags implemented in Hyper II (Continued).

Tag		Description
<H6>	</H6>	Displays text as the lowest-level heading
<P>	</P>	Starts and Ends a paragraph. </P> is optional and ignored.
 		Forces a line break.
<A HREF="url"> text </A>		Defines a reference anchor, highlighting the text between the tags.

Hyper II: Bringing HTML to Life

This project will add a richer subset of HTML support to our hypertext engine. We're going to make three important enhancements to the engine: we will add support for the **<A>** tag, so we will be able to detect hotlinks clicks; we will add the capability to place a simple graphic, a horizontal rule, to our text; and behind the scenes, we'll add a simple string parser with which we can dissect tags.

This builds on the existing source code of *Hyper I*, so we'll be able to use everything we've done so far.

1. We're going on to version two; so let's make a new project directory, *Hyper2*, and an output subdirectory beneath this, *Bin*. With the *Explorer*, copy the project files from your *Hyper1* directory to your *Hyper2* directory. Rename your "Hyper1" files to "Hyper2." You'll need the *.DPR*, *.PAS*, and *.DFM* files.

2. Open your **Hyper2** Project file in Delphi. The compiler will complain that its name is wrong ("Module header is missing or incorrect."). Change its program name from **Hyper1** to **Hyper2**. In the *Project Options* dialog box (from *Project | Options*), set the Application Title to "Hyper II," and its output directory to "Bin."

3. View **Form1** from unit **Main**. In the *Object Inspector*, change its **Caption** from "Hyper I" to "Hyper II."

4. While you have **Form1** up, highlight **PaintBox1** and double-click on its **Font** property. Delphi will open the *Font* dialog box. Change the font to something other than the default bold System font. For our examples, we used Times New Roman, regular, 10pt.

5. Add the new support units **Parser** (Listing 3.9), **HyperLnk** (Listing 3.10), and **HTML** (Listing 3.11), as described in the sections that follow. Refer back to the instructions for project *Hyper I* if you need more detail.
6. Make the required minor modifications to the existing units **Font** and **FmtText** (Listing 3.12).
7. Make the required modifications to **DispBuf** (Listing 3.13).
8. Finally, add an **OnMouseDown** handler to **PaintBox1** on the main form and make *Hyper II* squeak like a mouse, or at least pop up a message box (Listing 3.14). If you really want to make the program squeak, all you need is a WAV file and the simple techniques shown in Chapter 4!

This project, Hyper2.DPR, and all of its support files can be found on the accompanying CD-ROM in the directory \Programs\ Chap03\Hyper2. Sample data can be found in the directory \Media\HyperTxt.

Running Hyper II

To see the improved rendition of our sample hypertext, click the **Open File...** button and choose *Sample.Htm* from the *\Media\HyperTxt* directory once again. You can also simply enter the filename directly into the Edit control and press [enter] to load the file. *Hyper II*, running with the sample loaded and the window resized, is shown in Figure 3.6.

Hotlinks appear as underlined text in *Hyper II*. In our next project, we'll color them blue, too. If you click on the hyperlink, *Hyper II* will pop up a message box showing you the *URL* (Uniform Reference Locator) of the file being referenced by the hotlink. If you only wanted to pop up definitions over words, you could stop here!

A Parsing Class to Make Life Easier

Parsing is one of the most important chores in multimedia. It's a chore...because most of the time, we simply don't want to think about it. As developers, we want to write HTML or play video. Parsing, in one form or another, is at the heart of every medium's presentation; since every medium we use lives in a file and must be made to come to life.

Later, we'll explore the parsing of a few different files types, including the *RIFF* (*Resource Interchange File Format*), which defines the basic structure of

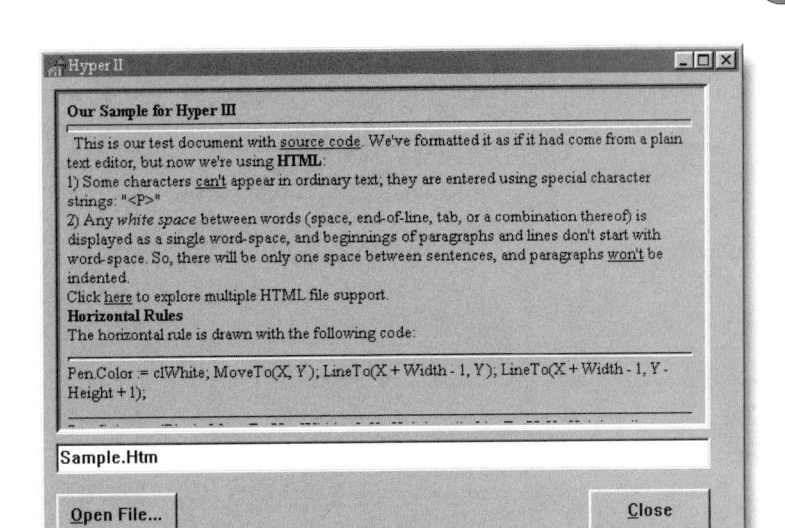

Figure 3.6 *Improved text display with Hyper II. Note the underlined hyperlink near the top of the text.*

a WAV sound file (among others). This type of parsing isn't quite as demanding as what we need to do here. Most of the media files an invariant format, and we'll just need to wade through them. Our HTML tags, however, are more challenging: HTML authors have some degree of freedom in what they write, and even in how they format their tags. For instance, they'll drop in an extra space or will use a strange capitalization scheme.

To this end, we're going to write a parser class, **TParser**, to aid us in the dissection of the text with which we'll be working. Its design is straightforward. If we look at the expression to parse (in this case, an HTML tag) as a stream, we know what to *expect* verbatim (like keywords) and where we should be able to *find* other variant elements, such as a link name, that will be different from one tag to the next. This is why we need **Expect** and **Find**. When we find some text, we need to return it. We'll do this in such a way that the calling routine can use the identifier **Last_found**. It will also be handy to get the remainder of the expression to parse; we'll use **Remainder**. For cleaning up those extra spaces that authors are so wont to use, we need **Skip_whitespace**. Of course, we also need the ability to create and destroy a **TParser**. We'll pass in the string to parse to the constructor; it reads better to use **Parse** as the constructor's name. You'll see we need to do some housecleaning at the end, so we'll write our own overriding **Destroy**. Finally, we'll use Delphi's exception handling to resolve our parsing problems, as well. The class **TParser** implemented in unit **Parser** is shown in Listing 3.9.

Listing 3.9 The **TParser** class in unit *Parser.Pas*

```pascal
unit Parser;

interface

uses
    SysUtils;

type
    EParseError = class(Exception);
    TParser = class
      private
        Expression,
        UC_Expression,
        Orig_UC_Expr   : pchar;
        Raising_errors,
        Parse_error    : boolean;
      public
        Last_found     : pchar;
      private
        procedure Do_error(const S : string);
        procedure Skip_whitespace;
      public
        constructor Parse(const _Expression : pchar);
        destructor Destroy; override;
        procedure Expect(
          const Target : pchar
          );
        function Expect_one_of(
          const Target : array of pchar
          ) : integer;
        procedure Find(
          const Target : pchar
          );
        function Remainder : pchar;
        procedure No_errors;
        procedure Raise_errors;
        function Error : boolean;
      end;

implementation

uses
    MiscLib;

constructor TParser.Parse(
  const _Expression : pchar
  );
    begin
        inherited Create;
        Expression    := _Expression;
        UC_Expression := strUpper(strNew(_Expression));
```

```
            Orig_UC_Expr   := UC_Expression;
            Last_found     := strNew('');
            Raising_errors := true;
            Parse_error    := false;
            end;

destructor TParser.Destroy;
    begin
        strDispose(Last_found);
        strDispose(Orig_UC_Expr);
        inherited Destroy;
        end;

procedure TParser.Do_error(
  const S : string
  );
    begin
        if Raising_errors then
            raise EParseError.Create(S)
          else
            Parse_error := true;
        end;

procedure TParser.Skip_whitespace;
    begin
        while (Expression^ <> #0) and (Expression^ <= ' ') do begin
            inc(Expression);
            inc(UC_Expression);
            end;
        end;

procedure TParser.Expect(
  const Target : pchar
  );
    begin
        Skip_whitespace;
        if Target = '' then
            if Expression = '' then
                {OK}
              else
                Do_error('Expected <end-of-expression>')
          else
            if strLIComp(Expression,Target,length(Target)) = 0 then begin
                inc(Expression,length(Target));
                inc(UC_Expression,length(Target));
                end
              else
                Do_error('Expected "'+Target+'"');
        end;

function TParser.Expect_one_of(
  const Target : array of pchar
  ) : integer;
```

```
    var
        Found : boolean;
        I     : integer;
    begin
        Result:= 0;
        Skip_whitespace;
        Found := false;
        I := 0 { = low(Target) for open arrays };
        while (I <= high(Target)) and not Found do begin
            if Target[I] = '' then
                Found := Expression = ''
            else
                if strLIComp(Expression,Target[I],length(Target[I])) = 0 then
                    begin
                        inc(Expression,length(Target[I]));
                        inc(UC_Expression,length(Target[I]));
                        Found := true;
                    end;
            inc(I);
            end;
        if not Found then
            Do_error('Expected one of several tokens')
          else
            Result := I; { = 1, if Found on I=0. }
        end;

procedure TParser.Find(
  const Target : pchar
  );
    var
        UC_Target,
        P             : pchar;
        I             : integer;
    begin
        Skip_whitespace;
        UC_Target := strUpper(StrNew(Target));
        P := strPos(UC_Expression,UC_Target);
        if P <> nil then begin
            P := Expression + (P - UC_Expression);
            P^ := #0;
            strDispose(Last_found);
            Last_found := strNew(Expression);
            P^ := Target^;
            inc(Expression,length(Last_found)+length(Target));
            inc(UC_Expression,length(Last_found)+length(Target));
            end
          else
            Do_error('Couldn''t find "'+Target+'"');
        end;

function TParser.Remainder : pchar;
    begin
        Skip_whitespace;
```

```
            Remainder := Expression;
        end;

procedure TParser.No_errors;
    begin
        Raising_errors := false;
        end;

procedure TParser.Raise_errors;
    begin
        Raising_errors := true;
        end;

function TParser.Error : boolean;
    begin
        Error := Parse_error;
        Parse_error := false;
        end;

{initialization}
    end.
```

We should cover some interesting points of this class. First, witness how case insensitivity is achieved. Although **Expect** can use a case-insensitive comparison, **Find** must use the **strPos** function, which has no case-insensitive corollary. Upon construction in **Parse**, we make ourselves an uppercase *copy* of the **Expression**:

```
UC_Expression := strUpper(strNew(_Expression));
```

There is a drawback here: We can't (well, we *shouldn't*) use this to parse very long expressions. Although the space is all on the heap, memory is still a limited resource on most machines, and the copying takes some time.

Expect provides us with a way to make sure the entire **Expression** has been consumed. By calling **Expect('')**, we will raise an exception if the **Expression** still contains characters.

Expect_one_of gives us a simple way to find optional keyword switches. It returns the *cardinal* index of the token actually found. If we are sent an array of three tokens, regardless of the actual array's index range, we will return 2 if the second token is found. The tokens are passed in as an *open array* of **pchar**-based strings. Open array parameters may be passed an array of any size (of the specified type). Delphi sends the routine being called (in this case, **Expect_one_of**) the information necessary to find the low bound (always zero for open arrays) and high bound of the array passed to it.

Find has some tricky pointer math. The section of code shown below is the culprit.

```
if P <> nil then begin
    P := Expression + (P - UC_Expression);
    P^ := #0;
    strDispose(Last_found);
    Last_found := strNew(Expression);
    P^ := Target^;
    inc(Expression,length(Last_found)+length(Target));
    inc(UC_Expression,length(Last_found)+length(Target));
    end
  else
    Do_error('Couldn''t find "'+Target+'"');
```

This code locates the uppercase **UC_Target** in the uppercase **UC_Expression**, and then "moves" the pointer from **UC_Expression** to **Expression** itself so that the **Last_found** text can be set to the real text of the **Expression**, not the uppercased version. (This happens in the third line.) While we're here, note that **Expression** and **UC_Expression** are both moved up through the text as it is parsed; hopefully, the calling code still has a pointer to the beginning of the **Expression** when parsing is done.

Finally, **Last_found** is simply a field; but the function **Remainder** takes the useful step of removing leading whitespace from the **Expression**.

Exception Handling

TParser provides two modes for handling errors. Ordinarily, the parser will raise an **EParseError** exception when an error occurs. Calling **No_errors** disables this, and you must query the **Error** function to determine if an error occurred. Calling **Error** resets the error state. To re-enable exception raising, call **Raise_errors**.

Hyperlinking Data Structures

In order to support hyperlinking, we need some way to record our document's "hot" screen locations, and to what URLs the locations point. In unit HTML, coming up next, we are going to add a field to the **tHTML_format** record that specifies the URL associated with a particular section of text. Not all sections of text will have associated URLs; in fact, only the text between Anchor tags, **<A>** and **</A>** will.

Complicating this structure is the fact that different formatting can be used within Anchor tags' text. For this reason, the anchor's referenced URL is really an attribute that can persist through many elements of formatted text. Each of

Building a Hypermedia Engine

these elements, as we saw in *Hyper I*, is individually placed and has its own individual hot rectangle associated with it.

The anchor is a data structure with two parts to support it. In our case, the first substructure is a list of referenced URLs; but generically, we'll call the string that might be associated with several rectangles a "name." The second substructure is a list of records containing an ID and a rectangle. The ID simply identifies to which name the rectangle belongs—so it could either be a literal name, stored in each record, or simply the index of the name in the list of names. We'll choose the index.

Using this scheme, we can store an ID in the **tHTML_format**, setting it when we record a URL from an **<A>** tag with the position of the URL in the name list, and resetting it to an initial, invalid list index of, say, –1. When we actually position elements for display, we can add the text's surrounding rectangle, using the stored name list index as the ID for the rectangle.

In *Hyper III*, we'll add support for "named" destination anchors that are specified by the **<A NAME>** tag, so the term "name" might be a little confusing. On the other hand, it makes for an obvious, if not entirely clear, name for our descendant class: **tNamed_rectangle_list**. As a viable object definition, it looks like this.

```
tNamed_rectangle_list = class
  private
    Names : TStringList;
    Rects : TList;
  public
    constructor Create;
    destructor Destroy; override;
    function Add_name(
      const Name : string
      ) : integer;
    function Add_rect(
      const _ID   : integer;
      const _Rect : TRect
      ) : integer;
    function Name_of_point(
      const X, Y : integer
      ) : string;
    function First_rect_of_name(
      const Name : string
      ) : TRect;
  end;
```

The rectangles are stored in Delphi's **TList** structure, which holds elements of the generic type **pointer**. In the implementation, as shown in the code snippet below, we declare a record containing IDs and rectangles; we'll save dynamically-allocated pointers to these records in the **Rects** list.

```
Rect_with_ID_ptr = ^Rect_with_ID;
Rect_with_ID = record
    ID   : integer;
    Rect : TRect;
    end;
```

The methods are the ones we'd expect to see. **Create** and an overriding **Destroy** handle the chores of creating and freeing our **Names** and **Rects** lists. **Add_name** puts a name on the **Names** list, and returns the position at which it was placed. This will become the ID for its rectangles. **Add_rect** takes an ID and a rectangle, placing it on the **Rects** list. **Name_of_point** and **First_rect_of_name** are used to get information out of the structure for hyperlinking, as discussed below. The unit **HyperLnk** is shown in its entirety in Listing 3.10.

Listing 3.10   The tNamed_rectangle_list class in unit *HyperLnk.Pas*

```
unit HyperLnk;

interface

uses
    Windows, Classes;

type
    tNamed_rectangle_list = class
      private
        Names : TStringList;
        Rects : TList;
      public
        constructor Create;
        destructor Destroy; override;
        function Add_name(
          const Name : string
          ) : integer;
        function Add_rect(
          const _ID   : integer;
          const _Rect : TRect
          ) : integer;
        function Name_of_point(
          const X, Y : integer
          ) : string;
        function First_rect_of_name(
          const Name : string
          ) : TRect;
        end;

implementation

type
```

```
    Rect_with_ID_ptr = ^Rect_with_ID;
    Rect_with_ID = record
        ID   : integer;
        Rect : TRect;
        end;

constructor tNamed_rectangle_list.Create;
    begin
        inherited Create;
        Names := tStringList.Create;
        Rects := tList.Create;
        end;

destructor tNamed_rectangle_list.Destroy;
    var
        I : integer;
    begin
        Names.Free;
        for I := 0 to Rects.Count-1 do
            dispose(Rect_with_ID_ptr(Rects.Items[I]));
        Rects.Free;
        inherited Destroy;
        end;

function tNamed_rectangle_list.Add_name(
  const Name : string
  ) : integer;
    begin
        result := Names.Add(Name);
        end;

function tNamed_rectangle_list.Add_rect(
  const _ID   : integer;
  const _Rect : TRect
  ) : integer;
    var
        R : Rect_with_ID_ptr;
    begin
        new(R);
        with R^ do begin
            ID := _ID;
            Rect := _Rect;
            end;
        result := Rects.Add(R);
        end;

function tNamed_rectangle_list.Name_of_point(
  const X, Y : integer
  ) : string;
    var
        Found : boolean;
        I     : integer;
    begin
        result := '';
```

```
            Found := false;
            I := 0;
            while (I < Rects.Count) and not Found do begin
                with Rect_with_ID_ptr(Rects.Items[I])^ do begin
                    with Rect do
                        Found :=
                            (X>=Left) and (X<=Right) and (Y>=Top) and (Y<=Bottom);
                    if Found then result := Names.Strings[ID]
                    end;
                inc(I);
                end;
        end;

function tNamed_rectangle_list.First_rect_of_name(
    const Name : string
    ) : TRect;
    var
        Target_ID : integer;
        Found     : boolean;
        I         : integer;
    begin
        result := Rect(-1,-1,-1,-1);
        Target_ID := Names.IndexOf(Name);
        if Target_ID <> -1 then begin
            Found := false;
            I := 0;
            while (I < Rects.Count) and not Found do begin
                with Rect_with_ID_ptr(Rects.Items[I])^ do begin
                    Found := ID = Target_ID;
                    if Found then result := Rect;
                    end;
                inc(I);
                end;
            end;
        end;

{initialization}
    end.
```

Associating Locations with Names

Since we get a mouse click in our display control (still **PaintBox1**, by the way), we have to be able to tell if the click was in one of our hot rectangles. **Name_of_point** retrieves the name of the first rectangle in the **Rects** list (which will be uppermost on the screen) that contains the specified point.

```
function tNamed_rectangle_list.Name_of_point(
    const X, Y : integer
    ) : string;
    var
        Found : boolean;
        I     : integer;
```

```
begin
    result := '';
    Found := false;
    I := 0;
    while (I < Rects.Count) and not Found do begin
        with Rect_with_ID_ptr(Rects.Items[I])^ do begin
            with Rect do
                Found :=
                    (X>=Left) and (X<=Right) and (Y>=Top) and (Y<=Bottom);
            if Found then result := Names.Strings[ID]
            end;
        inc(I);
        end;
    end;
```

This code just goes looping through our **Rects** list, looking for a good fit and stopping when it finds one. Before we inspect an item, we need to cast it from a generic **pointer** to a **Rect_with_ID_ptr**. When we do, we use its **ID** field to index into our **Names** and return the rectangle's name. If we should fail to find a containing rectangle, we return a null string as our error indicator.

First_rect_of_name uses the same looping technique on the **Rects** list; but instead of looking for a point fit in the **Items**' **Rects** fields, it looks for the first rectangle with an **ID** that matches the position of the given **Name** in the **Names** list, as shown in the code snippet below:

```
function tNamed_rectangle_list.First_rect_of_name(
  const Name : string
  ) : TRect;
    var
        Target_ID : integer;
        Found     : boolean;
        I         : integer;
    begin
        result := Rect(-1,-1,-1,-1);
        Target_ID := Names.IndexOf(Name);
        if Target_ID <> -1 then begin
            Found := false;
            I := 0;
            while (I < Rects.Count) and not Found do begin
                with Rect_with_ID_ptr(Rects.Items[I])^ do begin
                    Found := ID = Target_ID;
                    if Found then result := Rect;
                    end;
                inc(I);
                end;
            end;
    end;
```

If no rectangle is found, this routine returns a (–1,–1)-(–1,–1) rectangle. This indicates some sort of internal error: It would mean a name was added to the **tNamed_rectangle_list**, but no rectangles were added.

A Place for HTML

You may remember from *Hyper I* a little piece of code, buried deep inside layers of local procedures. It's really the heart of the system. It is within this code that the program acts upon the tags that it has found, as shown in the code snippet below:

```
Need_a_newline := false;
inc(Format.Serial_number);
if Text = 'P' then
    Need_a_newline := true
  else if Text = 'I' then
    include(Format.Font.specStyle,fsItalic)
  else if Text = '/I' then
    exclude(Format.Font.specStyle,fsItalic)
  else if Text = 'U' then
    include(Format.Font.specStyle,fsUnderline)
  else if Text = '/U' then
    exclude(Format.Font.specStyle,fsUnderline);
```

This code is going to grow much longer in *Hyper II*, as we add support for several more tags. This new unit, **HTML**, moves this decision tree and other **tHTML_format**-specific code out of **DispBuf** and into a smaller, more maintainable unit that contains code specifically related to HTML basics.

A new feature introduced in *Hyper II* is *special character* handling, which provides a way to introduce special characters into a document that might otherwise be impossible to add, or have some other meaning in HTML. For instance, an open angle-bracket, "<", *always* introduces a tag in HTML. So how can you write a document that includes angle-brackets as part of its text—say, an HTML primer? Using special characters, you can tell a browser to display a certain character without actually having it present in the file where it might be treated as HTML. Special characters allow us to write:

```
A paragraph mark, &lt;P&gt;, is
used to introduce a new
paragraph. <P> In fact, that
was one just now!
```

and see:

```
    A paragraph mark, <P> is
used to introduce a new
paragraph.
    In fact, that was one
just now!
```

tHTML_format, special characters—and of course, tag recognition—are all handled in unit **HTML**, shown in Listing 3.11.

Listing 3.11 HTML support routines in unit *HTML.Pas*

```
unit HTML;

interface

uses
    Classes,
    Font, HyperLnk;

procedure Process_special_characters(
  S : pchar { var S^ }
  );

type
    tHTML_format = record
        Serial_number      : integer;
        Leading_newlines   : integer;
        Font               : tHTML_font_spec;
        Rule_height        : integer;
        Anchor_reference   : integer;
        end;

procedure Parse_tag(
  const       The_tag         : pchar;
  var (in/out) Format          : tHTML_format;
  const       HRef_anchors    : tNamed_rectangle_list;
  var         Do_a_newline    : boolean;
  var         Rule_height     : integer
  );

implementation

uses
    SysUtils, Graphics,
    MiscLib, Parser;

function Special_character_of(
  S : pchar
  ) : char;
    const
        Err_char = '*';
        SC_table : array[1..4] of
                    record
                        Name      : pchar;
                        Character : char;
                        end = (
        (Name : 'lt';   Character : '<'),
        (Name : 'gt';   Character : '>'),
```

```
            (Name : 'amp';  Character : '&'),
            (Name : 'quot'; Character : '"')
            );
    var
        Found : boolean;
        I     : integer;
    begin
        result := Err_char;
        if S^ = '#' then
            try
                {$R+}
                { Delphi32 did not yet actually raise Range
                  Check errors when this code was written. }
                result := char(StrToInt(S+1));
                {$R-}
            except
                on EConvertError do {nothing};
                on ERangeError   do {nothing};
            end
        else begin
            Found := false;
            I := low(SC_table);
            while not Found and (I <= high(SC_table)) do
                with SC_table[I] do begin
                    Found := strComp(Name,S) = 0;
                    if Found then
                        result := Character
                      else
                        inc(I);
                end;
        end;
    end;

procedure Process_special_characters(
  S : pchar { var S^ }
  );

    function Special_character_from(
      var P : pchar
      ) : char;
        var
            B     : pchar;
            Found : boolean;
        begin
            inc(P);
            B := P;
            Found := false;
            while (P^ <> #0) and (P^ <> ';') do inc(P);
            if P^ = ';' then begin
                P^ := #0;
                inc(P);
                result := Special_character_of(B);
            end
```

Building a Hypermedia Engine   147

```
                else
                    result := #0;
                end;

        var
            P : pchar;
        begin
            P := S;
            while P^ <> #0 do
                case P^ of
                    '&' : begin
                        S^ := Special_character_from(P);
                        inc(S)
                        end;
                    #10 :
                        inc(P);
                    else begin
                        S^ := P^;
                        inc(P);
                        inc(S);
                        end;
                    end;
            S^ := #0;
            end;

    var
        Font_before_Hn    : tHTML_font_spec;
        Font_before_A     : tHTML_font_spec;

    procedure Parse_tag(
        const           The_tag         : pchar;
        var {in/out}    Format          : tHTML_format;
        const           HRef_anchors    : tNamed_rectangle_list;
        var             Do_a_newline    : boolean;
        var             Rule_height     : integer
        );

        var
            The_parser : TParser;

        procedure Parse_HR_tag;
            var
                Trial_rule_height : integer;
            begin with The_parser do begin
                try
                    Expect('SIZE');
                    Expect('=');
                    Trial_rule_height := StrToInt(Remainder);
                        {Could raise errors}
                    if Trial_rule_height <= 0 then exit;
                    Rule_height := Trial_rule_height;
                except
                    on EConvertError do {nothing};
                    on ERangeError   do {nothing};
```

```
                    end;
                end; end;

procedure Parse_Heading_tag(
  const Word : pchar
  );
    begin with Format, Font do begin
        if strLen(Word) <> 2 then exit;
        if not (Word[1] in ['1'..'6']) then exit;
        Font_before_Hn := Font;
        include(specStyle,fsBold);
        Do_a_newline := true;
        end; end;

procedure Parse_end_Heading_tag(
  const Word : pchar
  );
    var
        Prev_format : tHTML_format;
    begin with Format, Font do begin
        if strLen(Word) <> 3 then exit;
        if not (Word[2] in ['1'..'6']) then exit;
        specStyle := Font_before_Hn.specStyle;
        Do_a_newline := true;
        end; end;

procedure Parse_A_tag;
    var
        Token : integer;
    begin with The_parser do begin
        Expect('HREF');
        Expect('=');
        Expect('"');
        Find('"');
        Expect('');
        with Format,Font do begin
            Font_before_A := Format.Font;
            include(specStyle,fsUnderline);
            Anchor_reference := HRef_anchors.Add_name(Last_found);
            end;
        end; end;

procedure Parse_end_A_tag;
    begin with Format do begin
        Anchor_reference := -1;
        with Font do begin
            specStyle := Font_before_A.specStyle;
            end;
        end; end;

procedure Process_tag(
  const Word : pchar
  );
```

Building a Hypermedia Engine

```
begin with Format do begin
    if Word[0] = '!' then
        { Comment -- Do nothing. NOT STANDARD HTML! }
    else if StrComp(Word,'HTML') = 0 then
        { Nothing special to do. }
    else if StrComp(Word,'/HTML') = 0 then
        { Nothing special to do. }
    else if StrComp(Word,'B') = 0 then
        include(Font.specStyle,fsBold)
    else if StrComp(Word,'/B') = 0 then
        exclude(Font.specStyle,fsBold)
    else if StrComp(Word,'I') = 0 then
        include(Font.specStyle,fsItalic)
    else if StrComp(Word,'/I') = 0 then
        exclude(Font.specStyle,fsItalic)
    else if StrComp(Word,'U') = 0 then
        include(Font.specStyle,fsUnderline)
    else if StrComp(Word,'/U') = 0 then
        exclude(Font.specStyle,fsUnderline)
    else if StrComp(Word,'STRONG') = 0 then
        include(Font.specStyle,fsBold)
    else if StrComp(Word,'/STRONG') = 0 then
        exclude(Font.specStyle,fsBold)
    else if StrComp(Word,'EM') = 0 then begin
        include(Font.specStyle,fsItalic);
        include(Font.specStyle,fsBold);
        end
    else if StrComp(Word,'/EM') = 0 then begin
        exclude(Font.specStyle,fsItalic);
        exclude(Font.specStyle,fsBold);
        end
    else if StrComp(Word,'CITE') = 0 then
        include(Font.specStyle,fsItalic)
    else if StrComp(Word,'/CITE') = 0 then
        exclude(Font.specStyle,fsItalic)
    else if StrComp(Word,'HR') = 0 then
        Parse_HR_tag
    else if StrLComp(Word,'H',1) = 0 then
        Parse_Heading_tag(Word)
    else if StrLComp(Word,'/H',2) = 0 then
        Parse_end_Heading_tag(Word)
    else if StrComp(Word,'P') = 0 then
        Do_a_newline := true
    else if StrComp(Word,'/P') = 0 then
        { No action to take }
    else if StrComp(Word,'BR') = 0 then
        Do_a_newline := true
    else if StrComp(Word,'A') = 0 then
        Parse_A_tag
    else if StrComp(Word,'/A') = 0 then
        Parse_end_A_tag
    else
        { It's a currently unsupported tag. }
        ;
    end; end;
```

```
var
    Word : pchar;

begin
    Do_a_newline := false;
    Rule_height  := 0;
    inc(Format.Serial_number);
    if The_tag^ = #0 then exit;    { Null tag. }

    The_parser := TParser.Parse(The_tag);
    with The_parser do begin

        { Get main keyword. }
        No_errors;
        Find(' ');
        if Error then
            Word := strNew(Remainder)
          else
            Word := strNew(Last_found);
        Raise_errors;

        { Process, based on the Word. }
        try
            Process_tag(strUpper(Word));
          except
            on EParseError do {nothing};
          end;

        strDispose(Word);
        Free;
        end;
    end;

{initialization}
    end.
```

HTML Special Characters

HTML supports *special characters*, i.e., characters that aren't in the lower 128 ASCII characters, and characters that would otherwise have a special meaning in HTML. There are two types of special characters: numerically-based characters and name-based characters.

The need for special characters arose for two reasons. Although most computers (for the last 20 years, at least) support an eight-bit character set (allowing for 256 characters), early internet connections often only supported the transmission of seven-bit textual data. If an operator tried to send data with a significant high bit, the internet would usually strip the high bit and send garbage to the destination. Hence, many ways of dealing with this problem have been developed. The Unix-world programs used **uuencode** and

uudecode to format true binary data safe seven-bit transmission and reconstruct it at its destination. Email systems often support MIME encoding, a similar system. HTML, even though it is primarily text-based, allows transmission of an eight-bit character as a decimal number. Thus, to display character 214 on a viewer's screen, you can write "Ö".

Even this is not really device independent: Character 178 in one viewer's font may not be the same as character 178 in another. (Although viewers are all supposed to use the standard ISO 8859-1 character set, not all do.) To provide true device independence, HTML also supports name-based specification: Character 214 should be "Ö" (capital-O, umlaut). To guarantee this (if the user's viewer supports named characters), you can write "Ö". Note that this must be case-sensitive; otherwise, how could you write "ö"?

We aren't going to go for full foreign character set support here, but you'll see how it can be done. We are more interested in using name-based special characters to display characters that otherwise might have a special meaning to an HTML interpreter, like "<".

A special character always opens with an ampersand (&), and closes with a semicolon (;). If the first character within is a pound-sign (#), the remaining characters are taken to be the decimal ordinate of the character to be displayed. If not, the remaining characters are taken to be the device-independent name of a special character.

Interpreting Special Characters

The local routine **Special_character_of** is used to interpret the basic special character format. Given a string representing the special character, it returns that special character. Its first notable feature is a table of device-independent special characters, **SC_table**, as shown in the code snippet below:

```
SC_table : array[1..4] of
            record
                Name      : pchar;
                Character : char;
            end = (
  (Name : 'lt';   Character : '<'),
  (Name : 'gt';   Character : '>'),
  (Name : 'amp';  Character : '&'),
  (Name : 'quot'; Character : '"')
  );
```

When **Special_character_of** gets hold of a string, it looks for a leading pound-sign, indicating a following decimal code, as shown in the following code snippet:

```
if S^ = '#' then
    try
        result := char(StrToInt(S+1));
    except
        on EConvertError do {nothing};
        on ERangeError   do {nothing};
    end
```

The numeric processing is embedded in a **try...except** block. Two things can happen: If **StrToInt** encounters a conversion error—a character in the middle of digits, for example—it will raise the exception **EConvertError**. If **StrToInt** is successful, but the number is outside the valid range of ordinal character values, the assignment will cause an **ERangeError**. We explicitly turn on the *Range checking* compiler option here, since it is necessary for this exception to be generated. If **StrToInt** returns a value within the range of **char**, the character is returned.

If the string doesn't look like a numeric special character, it scans the **SC_table**, as shown in the code snippet below:

```
Found := false;
I := low(SC_table);
while not Found and (I <= high(SC_table)) do
    with SC_table[I] do begin
        Found := strComp(Name,S) = 0;
        if Found then
            result := Character
          else
            inc(I);
        end;
```

The table processing isn't very interesting, except that we use the **Low** and **High** functions to get the low and high array indexes for the **SC_table**. This makes it easy to add mode special characters later—we won't need to change any code outside of **SC_table**'s declaration.

Pulling a Special Character out of a String

This routine is used to pull a special character, at a particular index, out of a string, and advance the index to the character after the special character string. It's declared local to **Process_special_characters**, as shown in the code snippet below:

```
function Special_character_from(
      var P : pchar
      ) : char;
```

```
var
    B     : pchar;
    Found : boolean;
begin
    inc(P);
    B := P;
    Found := false;
    while (P^ <> #0) and (P^ <> ';') do inc(P);
    if P^ = ';' then begin
        P^ := #0;
        inc(P);
        result := Special_character_of(B);
        end
      else
        result := #0;
    end;
```

This routine returns a null if it can't find the end of the special character string. If you were to drop this character into the middle of a **PChar**-based string or **ANSIString** (as we *will* do), the string would end right there. Other than that, this is a pretty straight-forward routine.

Processing Special Characters in a String

This is the interfaced routine for which we've been doing all this work. Eventually, we're going to have to display HTML strings that contain special characters. Before we actually display that text, we'll send it to this routine to convert the special characters' notation to characters that **TextOut** can display.

Process_special_characters takes a pointer to a null-terminated string and replaces the special character substrings with single displayable characters, as shown in the code snippet below:

```
procedure Process_special_characters(
  S : pchar { var S^ }
  );

    { function Special_character_from }

    var
        P : pchar;
    begin
        P := S;
        while P^ <> #0 do
            case P^ of
              '&' : begin
                S^ := Special_character_from(P);
                inc(S)
                end;
              #10 :
```

```
            inc(P);
        else begin
            S^ := P^;
            inc(P);
            inc(S);
            end;
        end;
    S^ := #0;
    end;
```

Two pointers to the same string, **S** and **P**, are used to translate the string "in place," that is, without making a copy of the string. **S** is passed by value, so we can manipulate within the routine, here; but the calling code won't see the change in the pointer. The calling code will only see that the characters pointed to will have been modified, if special characters or linefeeds were present.

S represents a pointer to the "destination" version of the string; **P** is used to look at the "source" of our string. If we don't encounter anything odd, the loop becomes essentially as shown in the code snippet below:

```
while P^ <> #0 do begin
    S^ := P^;
    inc(P);
    inc(S);
    end;
S^ := #0;
```

This merely copies the string onto itself, character by character. The character pointed to by **P** (the same character pointed to by **S**) is put back to its own place, for every character up to the terminating null. Then we reassign a null to the end of the finished string, which is all the while pointed to by **S**.

We eliminate linefeeds (**#10**) by only incrementing **P** so that it points one character in front of **S**. From this point on, **P** is now pointing to the character ahead of **S**; the next time through, since we didn't adjust **S**, the character after the linefeed will be written over the linefeed.

When we encounter an ampersand, "&", we do something very similar. **Special_character_from** will advance the pointer **P** past the special character's representation and return the character itself. Rather than ignoring it, as we did the linefeed, we will save it back at our current **S** position.

P always stays back with **S**, or moves ahead. It will move ahead by one, in the case of a linefeed, or by the length of the special character string. There is no chance that it will fall behind and break this mechanism.

Linefeed Handling

We went to a couple of lines of trouble in **Process_special_characters** to eliminate linefeeds. This is because DOS-world text typically uses a carriage-return/linefeed combination to end a line in a text file. This linefeed is essentially a garbage character, because the carriage-return is already used to identify the line-break in the source text to treat as whitespace. So, we just kill it.

In the Unix world, linefeeds aren't used. Instead, they utilize the concept of a "newline" character. Since they use the carriage-return to represent "newline," our code still works on Unix-style files. Our ignoring of linefeeds doesn't break anything, since they aren't used.

Parsing HTML Tags

The routine **Parse_tag** is now responsible for the parsing of tags. It will call upon the resources of unit **Parser** to accomplish its chores. The main body simply sets up the tag for parsing and gets the first word from the tag. This word is then passed to the local routine **Process_tag**, which in turn calls specialized subroutines like **Parse_A_tag**, to process more complicated tags.

Before we discuss **Parse_tag**, we should look at the expanded **tHTML_format** we'll be using in *Hyper II*. We've moved this out of the unit **Font**, so that **Font** handles *only* font issues. It's shown in the code snippet below.

```
tHTML_format = record
    Serial_number      : integer;
    Leading_newlines   : integer;
    Font               : tHTML_font_spec;
    Rule_height        : integer;
    Anchor_reference   : integer;
    end;
```

We've added a **Rule_height** and an **Anchor_reference**. The **Rule_height**, if not zero, specifies that a horizontal rule should be drawn across the display that is **Rule_height** pixels deep. The **Anchor_reference** is used to index a **tNamed_rectangle_list**'s **Names** property, and acts as a unique identifier for a name when adding rectangles later. We'll see how this works when we discuss the parsing of the <A HREF> tag in a local procedure of **Parse_tag**.

Parse_tag takes a tag, **The_tag**, as a null-terminated string with both brackets removed. It modifies a **tHTML_format**, **Format**, based on the tag. If the tag specifies a reference anchor (<A HREF>), it records the referenced URL in the **HREF_anchors** list. Finally, it returns a couple of pieces of state information, **Do_a_newline** and **Rule_height**. The calling code will be responsible for using these values, and putting them into the **Format**. This is because the handling of this information is more complex, as shown in the code snippet below:

```
procedure Parse_tag(
   const         The_tag        : pchar;
   var {in/out}  Format         : tHTML_format;
   const         HRef_anchors   : tNamed_rectangle_list;
   var           Do_a_newline   : boolean;
   var           Rule_height    : integer
   );
```

The procedure itself sets up **Do_a_newline** and **Rule_height** to false and zero, respectively. The Paragraph tag, **<P>**, and others that require a new line to be started in the output will set **Do_a_newline**; the Horizontal Rule tag, **<HR>**, will set the **Rule_height**. The **Format**'s **Serial_number** is incremented; then the procedure exits in the case of the null tag, <>, as shown in the code snippet below:

```
Do_a_newline := false;
Rule_height  := 0;
inc(Format.Serial_number);
if The_tag^ = #0 then exit;  { Null tag. }
```

Parse_tag illustrates the basic use of the **TParser** class. First, **The_parser** is constructed with the call **Parse(The_tag)**, as shown in the code snippet below. Error-raising is turned off, because the first thing we're going to look for is a space after the first keyword. We probably won't find one; many tags don't take arguments. Failure to find the space means we have a simple one-word tag, like </U>. The first or single **Word** is taken as the **Remainder** if **Find** returns an **Error**. Otherwise **The_parser** advances past the space, placing the string before the space into **Last_found**; from there, we put it into **Word**. Finally, we turn error-raising on again. As a rule, we should only turn off errors when we know that we've handled all of the errors that could possibly occur.

```
The_parser := TParser.Parse(The_tag);
with The_parser do begin
   { Get main keyword. }
   No_errors;
   Find(' ');
   if Error then
      Word := strNew(Remainder)
    else
      Word := strNew(Last_found);
   Raise_errors;
```

Then we call **Process_tag** to do all of the work, catching the exception **EParseError**, so a simple tag problem won't break our hypermedia engine. Finally, we dispose the **Word** we created to hold the main tag and **Free The_parser**, as shown in the code snippet below:

```
{ Process, based on the Word. }
try
    Process_tag(strUpper(Word));
  except
    on EParseError do {nothing};
  end;
strDispose(Word);
Free;
end;
```

Processing a Tag: Identification

There isn't much to the routine **Process_tag**. However, it is very long. The basic structure is that of a giant **if...then...else** statement, as shown in the code snippet below:

```
procedure Process_tag(
  const Word : pchar
  );
    begin with Format do begin
      if Word[0] = '!' then
          { Comment -- Do nothing. NOT STANDARD HTML! }
        else if StrComp(Word,'HTML') = 0 then
          { Nothing special to do. }
        else if StrComp(Word,'/HTML') = 0 then
          { Nothing special to do. }
        :
        { Lots of other cases }
        :
        else
          { It's a currently unsupported tag. }
          :
      end; end;
```

Here we can see three really simple tags, the Comment tag (which, by the way, doesn't follow the standard HTML syntax), and the **<HTML>... </HTML>** bracketing pair that some browsers take as their cue to process hypertext. Our engine *always* processes hypertext, so we ignore these tags. This might give you an idea, though, about how you could implement your own data format and have it work hand-in-hand with HTML in the same document.

Simple effects are handled in-line, for instance, the Bold tag, **<B>**.

```
        else if StrComp(Word,'B') = 0 then
           include(Font.specStyle,fsBold)
        else if StrComp(Word,'/B') = 0 then
           exclude(Font.specStyle,fsBold)
```

Other tags, like the Horizontal Rule tag, **<HR>**, and the Heading tag, **<H*n*>**, call local routines.

```
        else if StrComp(Word,'HR') = 0 then
           Parse_HR_tag
        else if StrLComp(Word,'H',1) = 0 then
           Parse_Heading_tag(Word)
        else if StrLComp(Word,'/H',2) = 0 then
           Parse_end_Heading_tag(Word)
```

Note that we must isolate the **<HR>** tag before looking for the Heading tags; since we try to identify all of them, **<H1>** through **<H6>**, in one fell swoop, as any tag starting with an "H" (except "HR"). We tackle the validity of the remainder of the **Word** (as being "1" through "6") in the local routines **Parse_Heading_tag** and **Parse_end_Heading_tag**.

We are going to study two of these local routines in detail, **Parse_A_tag** and **Parse_end_A_tag**, as shown in the code snippet below. For the rest, you're on your own.

```
        else if StrComp(Word,'A') = 0 then
           Parse_A_tag
        else if StrComp(Word,'/A') = 0 then
           Parse_end_A_tag
```

Parsing the HREF Tag

To get started, let's look at the basic form of the **<A>** tag. Here's an example of a sentence with a hotlink:

```
This sentence uses the word <A HREF="L1">hotlink</A> as the link.
```

In this case, the word "hotlink" serves as the *hyperlink* or *hotspot*. The word "L1" serves as the target link or *label*. Whenever the hotspot is selected, a jump is made to the location of the document where the label "L1" is placed. We'll forgo this connection in *Hyper II*; it will be implemented in *Hyper III*. The **<A>** tag is one of the most important tags used in writing HTML documents. This versatile and much used tag is used to denote the beginning of a link. The link can be to another document, to a point within the same document, to an image, or any file the author desires.

The initial letter **A** introduces a link; **HREF** indicates that the quoted text that follows contains the link information. Following the initial mark is text treated as a hotspot and usually displayed with some form of highlighting. The final **/A** (proceeded by the forward slash) marks the end of the link text and returns the text display to its previous format.

Tackling this syntax in code isn't difficult. Remember, **The_parser** is global to us and has already been moved past the "A," as shown in the code snippet below:

```
procedure Parse_A_tag;
    begin with The_parser do begin
        Expect('HREF');
        Expect('=');
        Expect('"');
        Find('"');
        Expect(' ');
```

This is pretty basic stuff. We look for the argument "HREF," which must be followed by an equal sign (=) and a quoted reference. After we **Find** the last closing quote, we **Expect** to be finished with the tag; and **Last_found** contains the reference. Now we can adjust the **Format**'s **Font** and add the reference to **HREF_anchors**, a **tNamed_rectangle_list**. **Add_name** returns an ID that we can use to uniquely identify this hot element of text, and all of the elements until we find the **</A>** tag. As each element is placed on the display later on, by **Break_into_lines**, they will each add a hot rectangle that shares this common ID to the display. We record the ID as the **Format**'s **Anchor_reference**; this will be unchanged on subsequent formats until we process the **</A>** tag, as shown in the code snippet below:

```
            with Format.Font do begin
                Font_before_A := Format.Font;
                include(specStyle,fsUnderline);
                Anchor_reference := HRef_anchors.Add_name(Last_found);
                end;
        end; end;
```

You'll notice that before we plugged the underlining font style, **fsUnderline**, into the **Font**, we saved the **Font** in the program-scope global variable **Font_before_A**. This way, we'll be able to return the **Font** to its original setting when we close the tag in **Parse_end_A_tag**, as shown in the code snippet below:

```
procedure Parse_end_A_tag;
    begin with Format do begin
```

```
Anchor_reference := -1;
with Font do begin
    specStyle := Font_before_A.specStyle;
    end;
end; end;
```

When we close the tag, we set the **Format**'s **Anchor_reference** to -1, so we know we're dealing with unanchored text again. Since all we adjusted was the **Font**'s **specStyle**, that's all we have to restore when the tag closes.

Modifications to the Units Font and FmtText

To support the introduction of the expanded **tHTML_format** and its **Rule_height** and **Anchor_reference** fields, we need to make some minor changes to the units **Font** and **FmtText**. In **Font**, all we did was remove the declaration of **tHTML_format** that we moved to our new unit, **HTML**. This results in the first change required to **FmtText**, also; we must now use **HTML** in the interface's **uses** clause to get to the fields of a **tHTML_format**.

By using **HTML** in **FmtText**, we also gain use of **Process_special_characters**. Before we add text to a formatted text list, we can do the transformation of the HTML-safe special character strings to the special characters, themselves. We can do this here, because now we're totally finished with HTML parsing. We add the call to the **tFormatted_text.Create** constructor, where we create the object that is placed in the **tFormatted_text_list**. This is shown in Listing 3.12.

Listing 3.12   Modifications to unit FmtText from *Hyper I*

```
unit FmtText;
implementation
uses
    Windows, Classes,
    Font, HTML;
:
interface
:
constructor tFormatted_text.Create...
    begin
        inherited Create;
        Text    := strNew(_Text);
        Format  := _Format;
        Direct  := false;
        Process_special_characters(Text);
        end;
:
end.
```

Modifications to DispBuf

We have several modifications to make to **DispBuf** to handle horizontal rules and hotspots. They are shown in Listing 3.13.

Listing 3.13 Modifications to unit DispBuf

```
unit DispBuf;

interface

uses
    Classes, Graphics, Controls,
    Font, FmtText, HyperLnk;

type
    tGraphicControlWithCanvas = class(TGraphicControl)
        property Canvas;
        end;

    tDisplay_buffer = class
      :
      public
        { Hyperlink support lists, built by "Breaker" }
        Reference_anchors : tNamed_rectangle_list;
        { Display Positioning and Height, calc'd by "Breaker" }
        Display_top,
        Display_bottom : integer;
      :

implementation

uses
    SysUtils, Windows, Dialogs,
    MiscLib, HTML;

const
    Length_of_buffer = 1024-1;

constructor tDisplay_buffer.Create(
  const _Control : tGraphicControlWithCanvas
  );
    begin
        :
        Reference_anchors := tNamed_rectangle_list.Create;
        end;

destructor tDisplay_buffer.Destroy;
    begin
        Reference_anchors.Free;
        :
        end;
```

```
procedure tDisplay_buffer.Load_HTML_file(
    :
    procedure Process_HTML_string(
        :
        procedure Parse_HTML(
            :
            procedure Reset_buffer;
                :
            procedure Add_buffer_to_list;
                :
            procedure Set_format(
                :
            procedure New_line;
                :

            procedure Horizontal_rule(
              const Height : integer
              );
                begin
                    Add_buffer_to_list;
                    inc(Pending_newlines);
                    with Current_format do begin
                        Rule_height := Height;
                        Leading_newlines := Pending_newlines;
                        end;
                    Formatted_text_list.Add(
                      tFormatted_text.Create(Current_format,'')
                      );
                    Current_format.Rule_height := 0;
                    Pending_newlines := 0;
                    end;

            procedure Emit(
                :
            function Is_whitespace(const C : char) : boolean;
                :
            function Is_word(const C : char) : boolean;
                :
            var
                Need_a_newline,
                Preceeding_newline,
                Preceeding_space    : boolean;
                Space_format        : tHTML_format;
                Rule_height         : integer;
                The_end : pchar;
                Saved   : char;
                EOL     : pchar;
                Word    : pchar;

            begin
                :
                if Text^ = '<' then begin
                    { Process a Tag }
                    inc(Text);
```

Building a Hypermedia Engine

```
                    The_end^ := #0;
                    Parse_tag(Text,
                      Format,
                      Reference_anchors,
                      Need_a_newline,
                      Rule_height
                      );
                    Text := The_end + 1;
                    Preceeding_newline :=
                      Preceeding_newline or Need_a_newline;
                    if Preceeding_newline then
                        Preceeding_space := false;
                    if Rule_height > 0 then
                        Horizontal_rule(Rule_height);
                    Set_format(Format);
                    end
                  :
procedure Break_into_lines;
  :
    procedure Start_new_line(
      const Line_count : integer
      );
        begin
          :
                          with tFormatted_text(
                              Formatted_text_list.Items[I]
                              ), { .Base_Left_Corner, .Meas, .Format}
                              Base_left_corner, { .X and .Y }
                              Meas { .Width, .Ascent, .Descent }
                          do begin
                            Base_Left_Corner := Line_pos;
                            if Anchor_reference <> -1 then
                                Reference_anchors.Add_rect(
                                  Anchor_reference,
                                  Rect(
                                    X, Y - Ascent,
                                    X + Width, Y + Descent
                                    )
                                  );
                            inc(Line_pos.X,Width);
                            end;
          :
        end;

    begin
      :
                    P := Text;
                    Broken := false;
                    if Rule_height > 0 then begin
                      with Current_line_meas do begin
                        Height := 2 + Rule_height + 2;
                        Width  := Canvas_width;
                        Ascent := 2 + Rule_height;
```

```
                                        Descent := 2;
                                      end;
                                 Meas := Current_line_meas;
                               end
                            else begin
                              Start_width := Current_line_meas.Width;
                              while (not Broken) and (P <> nil) do begin
                                :
                                end;
                              end;
                        :
                      end;
              begin
                  with Format, Font do begin
                      Leading_newlines := 0;
                      Serial_number   := 0;
                      specStyle       := [];
                      Rule_height     := 0;
                      Anchor_reference := -1;
                      end;
                  Parse_HTML(Text,Format);
                  Break_into_lines;
                  end;


      :
    begin
        :
        end;

procedure Draw_rule(
  const Canvas             : TCanvas;
  const Lower_left_corner  : TPoint;
  const Width, Height      : integer
   );
      var
          Saved_pen : TPen;
      begin with Canvas, Lower_left_corner do begin
          Saved_pen := TPen.Create;
          Saved_pen.Assign(Pen);
          Pen.Width := 1;
          Pen.Style := psSolid;
          if Height = 1 then begin
              Pen.Color := clBlack;
              MoveTo(X, Y);
              LineTo(X + Width - 1, Y);
              end
            else begin
              Pen.Color := clWhite;
              MoveTo(X,             Y );
              LineTo(X + Width - 1, Y );
              LineTo(X + Width - 1, Y - Height + 1);
              Pen.Color := clBlack;
              MoveTo(X + Width - 2, Y - Height + 1);
              LineTo(X,             Y - Height + 1);
```

```
            LineTo(X,          Y + 1);
          end;
        Pen.Assign(Saved_pen);
        Saved_pen.Free;
      end; end;

procedure tDisplay_buffer.Display;

    function Line_after(
      :

    function Line_before(
      :

    begin with Formatted_text_list do begin
      :
      for I := First_elem to Last_elem do
        with tFormatted_text(Items[I]), Format do
          if Rule_height > 0 then
            Draw_rule(Control.Canvas,
              Point(Base_left_corner.X,
                    Base_left_corner.Y - Display_top),
              Meas.Width,Rule_height
              )
          else
            if Text <> nil then begin
              Set_font_from_spec(Control.Canvas.Font,Format.Font);
              Control.Canvas.TextOut(
                Base_left_corner.X, Base_left_corner.Y - Display_top,
                Text
                );
            end;
      :
      end; end;

{initialization}
    end.
```

Displaying Horizontal Rules

We need to make two changes to the routine **Parse_HTML**. First, we can now call **Parse_tag** from unit **HTML** to eliminate some in-line decision-making. We now get back a **Rule_height**, and give **Parse_tag** the opportunity to add to our **tDisplay_buffer**'s **Reference_anchors** list of named rectangles.

If **Parse_tag** returns a **Rule_height** (from an **<HR>** tag), we call the new local procedure **Horizontal_rule** to handle the **Buffer** and **Formatted_text_list** housekeeping, as shown in the code snippet below:

```
procedure Horizontal_rule(
  const Height : integer
  );
```

```
begin
    Add_buffer_to_list;
    inc(Pending_newlines);
    with Current_format do begin
        Rule_height := Height;
        Leading_newlines := Pending_newlines;
        end;
    Formatted_text_list.Add(
      tFormatted_text.Create(Current_format,'')
      );
    Current_format.Rule_height := 0;
    Pending_newlines := 0;
    end;
```

We need to add the buffer of text in the old format to **Formatted_text_list**, then increment **Pending_newlines** to ensure that we have a line break before we attempt to display the rule. We then modify the current format, forcibly adding a new **tFormatted_text element** to **Formatted_text_list**, with no text (a null string) attached. This ensures that the current format, with its **Rule_height** set, gets into the **Formatted_text_list**. Finally, we set the **Rule_height** back to zero, since it's now in the pipeline; and since forcibly adding our element handles the new lines, **Pending_newlines** is reset to zero.

When we break the **Formatted_text_list**, we need to handle elements with a **Rule_height** a little differently. Before we even get to the key code, we have already acted upon the fact that these elements start a new line, as shown in the code snippet below:

```
if Leading_newlines > 0 then
    Start_new_line(Leading_newlines);
P := Text;
Broken := false;
if Rule_height > 0 then begin
    with Current_line_meas do begin
        Height  := 2 + Rule_height + 2;
        Width   := Canvas_width;
        Ascent  := 2 + Rule_height;
        Descent := 2;
        end;
    Meas := Current_line_meas;
    end
  else begin
    :
    { Process other non-rule elements as before. }
    :
    end;
```

All we need to do for a rule when we are breaking lines, then, is to measure it; if the rest of the code thinks that the line was filled up with the rule, it will break the line (with the rule on it) when more text is encountered, correctly positioning it.

We will draw the rule from the baseline, up, so our **Ascent** could be just the **Rule_height**. We don't want to actually touch the text above us on the display, so we'll add a two-pixel margin to either side of the rule, giving us an **Ascent** of **2 + Rule_height**, and a **Descent** of **2**. The **Height** is taken as the **Ascent** and **Descent** together, or **2 + Rule_height + 2**. The **Width** is taken as the **Canvas_width**. We could do a partial rule and have text with no intervening Paragraph-type tags show up on the same line—but that's a little too frilly for this project.

Later on, after our **Formatted_text_list** has been broken into lines and our calling routine invokes the **Display** method, we need to actually draw the horizontal rule. This is done by the rather straight-forward routine **Draw_rule**, that draws a rule of specified dimensions on a **Canvas**. We *do* go to the trouble of preserving the current **Pen** of the **Canvas**, using the **Assign** method, which copies all of the fields of an original object (rather than just a reference to the original object) to a new object.

Building the Reference Anchor URL List

Adding reference anchor support is easy. The anchors will be stored in the **public** field **Reference_anchors**. This is a **tNamed_rectangle_list**, declared in unit **HyperLnk**. Aside from dealing with it in **tDisplay_buffer.Create** and **Destroy**, we only have to do two things. First, when we are parsing the file, we must add an entry to record the reference URL. We've already seen this in the **Parse_tag** procedure in unit **HTML**.

When we are breaking the lines of our **Formatted_text_list** and positioning the text, we have a good opportunity to set the hot rectangle, as shown in the code snippet below:

```
Base_Left_Corner := Line_pos;
if Anchor_reference <> -1 then
    Reference_anchors.Add_rect(
      Anchor_reference,
      Rect(
        X, Y - Ascent,
        X + Width, Y + Descent
        )
      );
inc(Line_pos.X,Width);
```

In this section of code, all we need to do is look at **Format.Anchor_reference** and record the rectangle surrounding the text. If **Anchor_reference** contains a valid ID in the **Reference_anchors** list, we simply add a rectangle for the **Anchor_reference**. The rectangle stretches horizontally from **X** to **X + Width**, and vertically from **Y - Ascent** (which will be the top of the text) to **Y + Descent** (the bottom of the text).

Mods to Main

Finally, we are ready to support hotspot detection. All we need to do is add **HyperLnk** to our implementation's **uses** list and add the **OnMouseDown** event handler, shown in Listing 3.14.

Listing 3.14   The **OnMouseDown** event handler in unit **Main**

```
procedure TForm1.PaintBox1MouseDown(Sender: TObject; Button: TMouseButton;
  Shift: TShiftState; X, Y: Integer);
    var
        Target : string;
    begin
        with Output, Reference_anchors do
            Target := Name_of_point(X,Y + Display_top);
        if Target <> '' then
            MessageDlg(Target,mtInformation,[mbOK],0);
        end;
```

We call the **Name_of_point** method to get the anchor reference URL for the location of the mouse click. **Name_of_point** will return the null string if the click is not within a valid location. This could be used to implement a default action of some sort. In this project, just so that we can see this mechanism work, we'll throw up a message box.

One last point: Even though we aren't really using **Display_top** right now, we need to remember that the hotspot locations stored in the **Reference_anchors** refer to document coordinates—not window coordinates. If the screen starts at document pixel line 423 (i.e. **Display_top = 423**), a click at window point (40,62) would refer to document coordinate (40,485).

A Stopping Place?

We've done a lot with our hypertext engine! We've illustrated all of the techniques—and then some—that you can use in developing your own system or enhancing this one. We're not going to stop here, though. We have only a few cosmetic features left before we can call this a professional-grade hypertext engine.

Finishing the Hypertext Engine

We're on the verge of having created a professional-quality hypermedia engine. In the last project of this chapter, we're going to polish the engine with some enhancements to HTML that will give us full support of Windows' font abilities and preformatted text. We're also going to put the finishing touches on our display-handling, as we add full hyperlinking capability to other documents and to specific locations within the current document and other documents altogether.

With an almost trivial change to the final project of this chapter, we'll introduce full hypermedia capability to our engine in Chapter 4. So, without further ado, let's jump into the code.

Hyper III: A Finished Hypertext Engine

This project will add additional HTML features, including support for the font's typeface, size, and color. The Anchor tag will now allow specification of both referenced URLs *and* named destinations. Some new tags, including the Preformatted Text tag, **<PRE>**, will be added. Finally, the user interface will be modified with a scroll bar to view long segments of text—and, most importantly, full hyperlinking.

This builds on the existing source code of *Hyper II*, so we'll be able to use everything we've done so far.

1. We're going on to version three, so let's make a new project directory, *Hyper3*, and an output subdirectory beneath this, *Bin*. With the *Explorer*, copy the project files from your *Hyper2* directory to your *Hyper3* directory. Rename your "Hyper2" files to "Hyper3." You'll need the *.DPR*, *.PAS*, and *.DFM* files.

2. Open your **Hyper3** Project file in Delphi. The compiler will complain that its name is wrong ("Module header is missing or incorrect."). Change its program name from **Hyper2** to **Hyper3**. In the *Project Options* dialog box (from *Project | Options*), set the Application Title to "Hyper III," and its output directory to "Bin."

3. View **Form1** from unit **Main**. In the *Object Inspector*, change its **Caption** from "Hyper II" to "Hyper III."

4. While you have **Form1** up, add a ScrollBox outside the edge of **PaintBox1**. You might need to change its **Kind** to **sbVertical**. You can see where we positioned it in Figure 3.7.

6. Make the required minor modifications to the existing units **Font** (Listing 3.16) and **HTML** (Listing 3.17) to add full font support and parsing of our additional tags.
7. Make the required modifications to **DispBuf** (Listing 3.18).
8. Finally, modify the **OnMouseDown** handler to **PaintBox1**, **PaintBox1MouseDown**, in unit **Main** (Listing 3.19) to support full hyperlinking with the new procedure **Jump_to**.

At this point, the full source code for *Hyper III* can be found in the listings of **MiscLib** (Listing 3.1 from *Hyper I*); **FmtText** (Listing 3.3 from *Hyper I*, with modifications from Listing 3.12 from *Hyper II*); **Parser**, **HyperLnk** (Listings 3.9 and 3.10 from *Hyper II*); and **Font**, **HTML**, **DispBuf**, and **Main** (Listings 3.16, 3.17, 3.18, and 3.19 in this project.)

This project, Hyper3.DPR, and all of its support files, can be found on the accompanying CD-ROM, in the directory \Programs\Chap03\Hyper3. Sample data can be found in the directory \Media\HyperTxt.

Running Hyper III

To see the improved rendition of our sample hypertext, click the **Open File...** button and choose *Sample.Htm* from the *\Media\HyperTxt* directory, yet again. You can also simply enter the filename directly into the Edit control, and press [enter] to load the file. *Hyper III*, running with the sample loaded, is shown in Figure 3.7.

Hotlinks appear as blue underlined text in *Hyper III*. *Sample.HTM* links to *Sample2.HTM*, and to a named anchor in itself. Click the links, work the scroll bar, and convince yourself that the system works. If the program has trouble finding the files to load, you may need to specify their names more explicitly in the Anchor tags. Now that we're really serious about hypertext, we'll show you the source for our sample files in Listing 3.15. We are also interpreting some new tags. Our subset of HTML support is shown in Table 3.3.

Listing 3.15 Sample files *Sample.HTM* and *Sample2.HTM* for testing *Hyper III*

Sample.HTM

```
<HTML>
<H1>Our Sample for Hyper III</H1>
```

Building a Hypermedia Engine

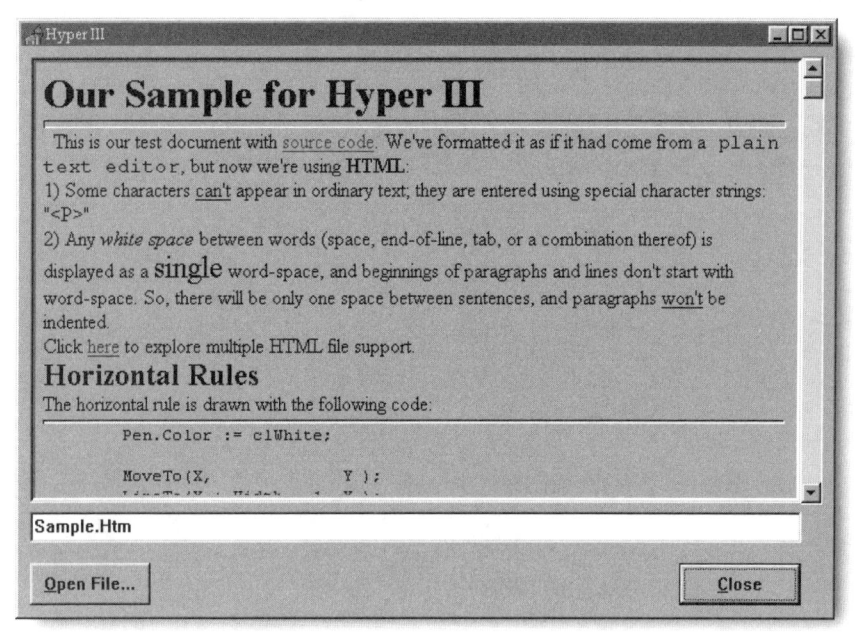

Figure 3.7 *Finished hypertext display with Hyper III. Hyperlinks are now colored, and actually take you to other hyperdocuments.*

```
<HR SIZE=6>
      This is our test document with <A HREF="#codelink">source
code</a>.  We've
    formatted it as if it had come from
    a<TT> plain text editor</TT>, but now we're using
    <B>HTML</B>:
    </P>
<P>
    1) Some characters <U>can't</U> appear in ordinary text; they are
    entered using special character strings: &quot;&lt;P&gt;&quot;
<P>
    2) Any <I>white space</I> between words
    (space, end-of-line, tab, or a combination
    thereof) is displayed as a <font size=+2>single</font>
    word-space, and beginnings of paragraphs and lines
    don't start with word-space.  So, there will be only one space
    between sentences, and paragraphs <U>won't</U>
    be indented.
<P>
    Click <a href="Sample2.Htm">here</a> to explore
    multiple HTML file support.
<P>
<H2><A NAME="codelink">Horizontal Rules</a></H2>
<P>
    The horizontal rule is drawn with the following code:
<HR SIZE = 3>
<PRE>
```

```
        Pen.Color := clWhite;

        MoveTo(X,              Y );
        LineTo(X + Width - 1, Y );
        LineTo(X + Width - 1, Y - Height + 1);<HR size=1>
        Pen.Color := clBlack;

        MoveTo(X + Width - 2, Y - Height + 1);
        LineTo(X,              Y - Height + 1);
        LineTo(X,              Y + 1);<HR size=2>
</PRE>
    It's not hard to see how this works.
</HTML>

Sample2.HTM

<HTML>
<H1>Hyper III Multiple File Support</H1>
<HR SIZE=6>
    This is our <A HREF="Sample.Htm#codelink"> link </A> back
    to the code sample in
    <A HREF="Sample.Htm">Sample.Htm</a>.
<HR SIZE=12>
<H1>Heading 1</H1>
<H2>Heading 2</H2>
<H3>Heading 3</H3>
<H4>Heading 4</H4>
<H5>Heading 5</H5>
<H6>Heading 6</H6>
<FONT SIZE=1>X1X
<FONT SIZE=2>X2X
<FONT SIZE=3>X3X
<FONT SIZE=4>X4X
<FONT SIZE=5>X5X
<FONT SIZE=6>X6X
<FONT SIZE=7>X7X
<P>
<FONT SIZE=1>X1X
<P>
<FONT SIZE=2>X2X
<P>
<P>
<P>
<FONT SIZE=3>X3X
<P>
<FONT SIZE=4>X4X
<P>
<FONT SIZE=5>X5X
<P>
<FONT SIZE=6>X6X
<P>
<FONT SIZE=7>X7X
<P>
</HTML>
```

Table 3.3 The HTML tags implemented in Hyper II

Tag		Description
<!text>		Comment. This syntax is not standard HTML.
<HTML>	</HTML>	Tells browser that following text is HTML. Ignored by our program.
<B>	</B>	Displays text in bold-face.
<I>	</I>	Displays text in italics.
<U>	</U>	Displays underlined text.
<STRONG>	</STRONG>	Displays text in "Strong" format.
<EM>	</EM>	Displays text in "Emphasized" format.
<CITE>	</CITE>	Displays text as a citation.
<HR SIZE=*height*>		Displays a horizontal rule.
<H1>	</H1>	Displays text as a top-level heading.
...		
<H6>	</H6>	Displays text as the lowest-level heading.
<P>	</P>	Starts and ends a paragraph. **</P>** is optional and ignored.
 		Forces a line break.
<A HREF="*url*"> *text* </A>		Defines a reference anchor, highlighting the text between the tags.
<A NAME="*url*"> *text* </A>		Defines a name anchor. No highlighting is performed. New to *Hyper III*.
<TT>	</TT>	Displays text using a teletype font; each character has the same width. New to *Hyper III*.
<PRE>	</PRE>	Displays preformatted text that is not word-wrapped. To aid in lining up columns, the teletype font is used. New to *Hyper III*.
<FONT SIZE=*[+/-]size*>		Sets the font size. The optional +/- indicates that the *size* should be used to increase or decrease the current size, otherwise it is an absolute size. Allowable sizes run from 1, the smallest type, to 7, the largest type. New to *Hyper III*.
</FONT>		Returns the font to its state before the preceeding **<FONT>** tag.

Adding More Font Capability

As our project stood up until now, the only Windows font feature we supported in a **tHTML_font** was *font style*: underlining, bold face, and so on. We are now going to add three other attributes: a *face* (the font name; Windows calls this attribute the *name*), a *size*, and a *color*. To support font size, we need to establish a translation between the HTML device-independent size number, and the size, in points, that Windows uses. The modifications to unit **Font** highlighted in Listing 3.16 add this support.

Listing 3.16 Unit **Font**, modified for full font support in *Hyper III*

```
unit Font;

interface

uses
    Windows, Graphics;

const
    HTML_font_size_in_points : array[1..7] of integer =
      (8, 10, 12, 14, 18, 24, 36);

type
    tHTML_font_spec = record
        specStyle : TFontStyles;
        specName  : string[40]; { Hardcoded limit! }
        specSize  : integer;
        specColor : TColor;
        end;

procedure Set_font_from_spec(
  const Font : TFont;  { var .properties }
        Spec : tHTML_font_spec
  );

type
    tText_measurement = record
        case boolean of
          false : (
            Width,
            Height,
            Ascent,
            Descent : integer;
            );
          true : (
            Extent : TSize
            );
        end;

function Measurement_of(
  const Text    : pchar;
```

```
    const lnText : integer;
    const Canvas : TCanvas;  { var .Font }
    const Font   : tHTML_font_spec
    ) : tText_measurement;

implementation

uses
    SysUtils;

procedure Set_font_from_spec(
  const Font : TFont;  { var .properties }
        Spec : tHTML_font_spec
  );
    begin with Font, Spec do begin
        Style := specStyle;
        Name  := specName;
        if specSize < 1
          then specSize := 1
          else if specSize > 7 then specSize := 7;
        Size  := HTML_font_size_in_points[specSize];
        Color := specColor;
        end; end;

function Measurement_of(
  const Text    : pchar;
  const lnText  : integer;
  const Canvas  : TCanvas;  { var .Font }
  const Font    : tHTML_font_spec
  ) : tText_measurement;
    var
        DC : HDC;
        TM : TTextMetric;
    begin with result do begin
        Set_font_from_spec(Canvas.Font,Font);
        DC := Canvas.Handle;
        GetTextExtentPoint(DC,
          Text,lnText,
          Extent
          );
        GetTextMetrics(DC,TM);
        Ascent  := TM.tmAscent;
        Descent := TM.tmDescent;
        end; end;

{initialization}
    end.
```

Changes to Unit HTML

We take advantage of these new font capabilities in unit **HTML** by adding support for some new tags and letting existing tags modify the font. Along the way, we also add another parameter to **Parse_tag** so that we can store named destination anchors in **tNamed_rectangle_lists**, like we store reference anchors' URLs. Finally, we add a field to the **tHTML_format** record to support preformatted text. The changes are highlighted in Listing 3.17.

Listing 3.17   Unit **HTML**, with support for new tags and font capabilities

```
unit HTML;

interface

uses
    Classes,
    Font,
    HyperLnk;

procedure Process_special_characters(
  S : pchar { var S^ }
  );

type
    tHTML_format = record
        Serial_number      : integer;
        Leading_newlines   : integer;
        Font               : tHTML_font_spec;
        Rule_height        : integer;
        Anchor_reference   : integer;
        Anchor_dest_name   : integer;
        Preformatted       : boolean;
        end;

procedure Parse_tag(
  const         The_tag       : pchar;
  var {in/out}  Format        : tHTML_format;
  const         HRef_anchors  : tNamed_rectangle_list;
  const         Name_anchors  : tNamed_rectangle_list;
  var           Do_a_newline  : boolean;
  var           Rule_height   : integer
  );

implementation

uses
    SysUtils, Graphics,
    MiscLib, Parser;

function Special_character_of(
  S : pchar
  ) : char;
    const
        Err_char = '*';
        SC_table : array[1..4] of
                    record
                        Name      : pchar;
                        Character : char;
                        end = (
            (Name : 'lt';   Character : '<'),
```

```
            (Name : 'gt';   Character : '>'),
            (Name : 'amp';  Character : '&'),
            (Name : 'quot'; Character : '"')
            );
    var
        Found : boolean;
        I     : integer;
    begin
        result := Err_char;
        if S^ = '#' then
            try
                {$R+}
                { Delphi32 did not yet actually raise Range
                  Check errors when this code was written. }
                result := char(StrToInt(S+1));
                {$R-}
            except
                on EConvertError do {nothing};
                on ERangeError   do {nothing};
            end
        else begin
            Found := false;
            I := low(SC_table);
            while not Found and (I <= high(SC_table)) do
                with SC_table[I] do begin
                    Found := strComp(Name,S) = 0;
                    if Found then
                        result := Character
                      else
                        inc(I);
                end;
        end;
    end;

procedure Process_special_characters(
  S : pchar { var S^ }
  );

    function Special_character_from(
      var P : pchar
      ) : char;
        var
            B     : pchar;
            Found : boolean;
        begin
            inc(P);
            B := P;
            Found := false;
            while (P^ <> #0) and (P^ <> ';') do inc(P);
            if P^ = ';' then begin
                P^ := #0;
                inc(P);
                result := Special_character_of(B);
            end
```

```
                else
                   result := #0;
             end;

   var
         P : pchar;
   begin
         P := S;
         while P^ <> #0 do
            case P^ of
               '&' : begin
                   S^ := Special_character_from(P);
                   inc(S)
                   end;
               #10 :
                  inc(P);
               else begin
                   S^ := P^;
                   inc(P);
                   inc(S);
                   end;
               end;
         S^ := #0;
         end;

var
    Font_before_Hn     : tHTML_font_spec;
    Font_before_A      : tHTML_font_spec;
    Last_A_type        : (at_HREF, at_NAME);
    Font_before_TT     : tHTML_font_spec;
    Font_before_FONT   : tHTML_font_spec;
    Font_before_PRE    : tHTML_font_spec;

procedure Parse_tag(
   const          The_tag          : pchar;
   var {in/out}   Format           : tHTML_format;
   const          HRef_anchors     : tNamed_rectangle_list;
   const          Name_anchors     : tNamed_rectangle_list;
   var            Do_a_newline     : boolean;
   var            Rule_height      : integer
   );

    var
         The_parser : TParser;

    procedure Parse_HR_tag;
       var
            Trial_rule_height : integer;
       begin with The_parser do begin
            try
                Expect('SIZE');
                Expect('=');
                Trial_rule_height := StrToInt(Remainder);
                   {Could raise errors}
```

```
          if Trial_rule_height <= 0 then exit;
          Rule_height := Trial_rule_height;
        except
          on EConvertError do {nothing};
          on ERangeError   do {nothing};
        end;
      end; end;

procedure Parse_Heading_tag(
  const Word : pchar
  );
    begin with Format, Font do begin
      if strLen(Word) <> 2 then exit;
      if not (Word[1] in ['1'..'6']) then exit;
      Font_before_Hn := Font;
      specSize := 7 - (ord(Word[1]) - ord('0'));
      include(specStyle,fsBold);
      Do_a_newline := true;
      end; end;

procedure Parse_end_Heading_tag(
  const Word : pchar
  );
    var
      Prev_format : tHTML_format;
    begin with Format, Font do begin
      if strLen(Word) <> 3 then exit;
      if not (Word[2] in ['1'..'6']) then exit;
      specSize  := Font_before_Hn.specSize;
      specStyle := Font_before_Hn.specStyle;
      Do_a_newline := true;
      end; end;

procedure Parse_A_tag;
    const
      HREF_or_NAME : array[1..2] of pchar = (
        'HREF',
        'NAME'
        );
    var
      Token : integer;
    begin with The_parser do begin
      Token := Expect_one_of(HREF_or_NAME);
      Expect('=');
      Expect('"');
      Find('"');
      Expect('');
      case Token of
        1 : with Format,Font do begin
          { HREF anchor }
          Font_before_A := Format.Font;
          specColor := clBlue;
          include(specStyle,fsUnderline);
```

```
                    Anchor_reference := HRef_anchors.Add_name(Last_found);
                    Last_A_type := at_HREF;
                    end;
                2 : with Format do begin
                    { NAME destination }
                    Anchor_dest_name := Name_anchors.Add_name(Last_found);
                    Last_A_type := at_NAME;
                    end;
                end;
            end; end;

procedure Parse_end_A_tag;
    begin with Format do begin
        case Last_A_type of
            at_HREF : begin
                Anchor_reference := -1;
                with Font do begin
                    specColor := Font_before_A.specColor;
                    specStyle := Font_before_A.specStyle;
                    end;
                end;
            at_NAME :
                Anchor_dest_name := -1;
            end;
        end; end;

procedure Parse_FONT_tag;
    var
        Font_size : integer;
    begin with The_parser do begin
        try
            Expect('SIZE');
            Expect('=');
            Font_size := StrToInt(Remainder); {Could raise errors}
            with Format, Font do begin
                Font_before_FONT := Font;
                { Relative/Absolute font size. }
                if Remainder[0] in ['+','-'] then
                    inc(specSize,Font_size)
                  else
                    specSize := Font_size;
                end;
          except
            on EConvertError do {nothing};
            on ERangeError   do {nothing};
          end;
        end; end;

procedure Parse_end_FONT_tag;
    begin
        Format.Font.specSize := Font_before_FONT.specSize;
        end;
```

```
procedure Parse_PRE_tag;
    begin with Format, Font do begin
        Font_before_PRE := Font;
        specName     := 'Courier New';
        specSize     := 2;
        Preformatted := true;
        Do_a_newline := true;
        end; end;

procedure Parse_end_PRE_tag;
    begin with Format, Font do begin
        specName := Font_before_PRE.specName;
        specSize := Font_before_PRE.specSize;
        Preformatted := false;
        Do_a_newline := true;
        end; end;

procedure Process_tag(
  const Word : pchar
  );
    begin with Format do begin
        if Word[0] = '!' then
            { Comment -- Do nothing. NOT STANDARD HTML! }
          else if StrComp(Word,'HTML') = 0 then
            { Nothing special to do. }
          else if StrComp(Word,'/HTML') = 0 then
            { Nothing special to do. }
          else if StrComp(Word,'B') = 0 then
            include(Font.specStyle,fsBold)
          else if StrComp(Word,'/B') = 0 then
            exclude(Font.specStyle,fsBold)
          else if StrComp(Word,'I') = 0 then
            include(Font.specStyle,fsItalic)
          else if StrComp(Word,'/I') = 0 then
            exclude(Font.specStyle,fsItalic)
          else if StrComp(Word,'U') = 0 then
            include(Font.specStyle,fsUnderline)
          else if StrComp(Word,'/U') = 0 then
            exclude(Font.specStyle,fsUnderline)
          else if StrComp(Word,'STRONG') = 0 then
            include(Font.specStyle,fsBold)
          else if StrComp(Word,'/STRONG') = 0 then
            exclude(Font.specStyle,fsBold)
          else if StrComp(Word,'EM') = 0 then begin
            include(Font.specStyle,fsItalic);
            include(Font.specStyle,fsBold);
            end
          else if StrComp(Word,'/EM') = 0 then begin
            exclude(Font.specStyle,fsItalic);
            exclude(Font.specStyle,fsBold);
            end
          else if StrComp(Word,'CITE') = 0 then
            include(Font.specStyle,fsItalic)
          else if StrComp(Word,'/CITE') = 0 then
```

```
            exclude(Font.specStyle,fsItalic)
        else if StrComp(Word,'HR') = 0 then
          Parse_HR_tag
        else if StrLComp(Word,'H',1) = 0 then
          Parse_Heading_tag(Word)
        else if StrLComp(Word,'/H',2) = 0 then
          Parse_end_Heading_tag(Word)
        else if StrComp(Word,'P') = 0 then
          Do_a_newline := true
        else if StrComp(Word,'/P') = 0 then
          { No action to take }
        else if StrComp(Word,'BR') = 0 then
          Do_a_newline := true
        else if StrComp(Word,'A') = 0 then
          Parse_A_tag
        else if StrComp(Word,'/A') = 0 then
          Parse_end_A_tag
        else if StrComp(Word,'TT') = 0 then begin
          Font_before_TT := Font;
          Font.specName := 'Courier New';
          end
        else if StrComp(Word,'/TT') = 0 then
          Font.specName := Font_before_TT.specName
        else if StrComp(Word,'FONT') = 0 then
          Parse_FONT_tag
        else if StrComp(Word,'/FONT') = 0 then
          Parse_end_FONT_tag
        else if StrComp(Word,'PRE') = 0 then
          Parse_PRE_tag
        else if StrComp(Word,'/PRE') = 0 then
          Parse_end_PRE_tag
        else
          { It's a currently unsupported tag. }
          ;
    end; end;

var
    Word : pchar;

begin
    Do_a_newline := false;
    Rule_height  := 0;
    inc(Format.Serial_number);
    if The_tag^ = #0 then exit;  { Null tag. }

    The_parser := TParser.Parse(The_tag);
    with The_parser do begin

        { Get main keyword. }
        No_errors;
        Find(' ');
        if Error then
            Word := strNew(Remainder)
        else
```

```
                Word := strNew(Last_found);
            Raise_errors;

            { Process, based on the Word. }
            try
                Process_tag(strUpper(Word));
            except
                on EParseError do {nothing};
            end;

            strDispose(Word);
            Free;
            end;
        end;
    end;
{initialization}
    end.
```

Anchor Tag Parsing, Revisited

The Anchor tag now supports the arguments **HREF** and **NAME**. The parsing isn't quite as straightforward as it was in *Hyper II*, where we only needed to look for the word "HREF." At last, we get to call on the **Expect_one_of** method of our **TParser** class! To use this, we need to set up an array of **pchar**s that point to tokens in null-terminated strings, as shown in the code snippet below. This isn't as difficult as it sounds, but we need to remember that our **TParser** handles expected text in uppercase.

```
const
    HREF_or_NAME : array[1..2] of pchar = (
      'HREF',
      'NAME'
      );
```

Then, we can get a **Token** number back from **Expect_one_of**. This could raise an error, so its a good thing we're trapping parser errors above us in **Process_tag**. We'll just drop out of the code if we can't find one of our tokens. We can take advantage of the fact that the layout of the **A HREF** and **A NAME** tags are the same: **A** *xxxx***="***string***"**, as shown in the code snippet below.

```
Token := Expect_one_of(HREF_or_NAME);
Expect('=');
Expect('"');
Find('"');
Expect(' ');
```

Once we're finished parsing the tag, we can act on the information we've gleaned from it. We have a couple of more chores than last time for an **HREF** tag. First, we set the **specColor** to **clBlue**, to further highlight the link. Secondly, so that we can properly handle the Anchor closing tag, we need to remember the type of the last Anchor tag encountered. We stash this in a program-scope global variable, **Last_A_type**, as shown in the code snippet below:

```
case Token of
  1 : with Format,Font do begin
    { HREF anchor }
    Font_before_A := Format.Font;
    specColor := clBlue;
    include(specStyle,fsUnderline);
    Anchor_reference := HRef_anchors.Add_name(Last_found);
    Last_A_type := at_HREF;
    end;
```

The **NAME** Anchor tag is a little easier. We don't want to highlight the text at the destination of a link (although we could), so all we need to do is record the destination name in the **Name_anchors** list. Later on, when we position text with an **Anchor_dest_name** ID, we'll record the location of the name; then we can just set up the display to show the hypertext from that location, as shown in the code snippet below:

```
  2 : with Format do begin
    { NAME destination }
    Anchor_dest_name := Name_anchors.Add_name(Last_found);
    Last_A_type := at_NAME;
    end;
  end;
```

When it becomes time to close the anchor, **Parse_end_A_tag** handles the details, as shown in the code snippet below:

```
procedure Parse_end_A_tag;
  begin with Format do begin
    case Last_A_type of
      at_HREF : begin
        Anchor_reference := -1;
        with Font do begin
          specColor := Font_before_A.specColor;
          specStyle := Font_before_A.specStyle;
          end;
        end;
      at_NAME :
        Anchor_dest_name := -1;
        end;
      end; end;
```

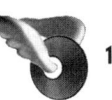

Based on the **Last_A_type**, we either revert the **Format**'s **Anchor_reference** or **Anchor_dest_name** ID to -1. If we are closing a reference tag, we also need to change the font back to what it was before the anchor highlighting.

Supporting Preformatted Text

In unit **DispBuf**, we need to make some minor additions to support preformatted text. We've gone to a whole lot of work to handle text in a device-independent fashion, to the point of ignoring new lines and treating spaces as "word-breaks." Now, we're going to have to circumvent some of that processing. The modification for this—and to support the tracking and storage of named destinations as well as referenced URLs—are highlighted in Listing 3.18. This is a long listing, because the changes are sparse, so hang on.

Listing 3.18 Unit **DispBuf**, with support for preformatted text and named destinations

```
unit DispBuf;

interface

uses
    Classes, Graphics, Controls,
    Font, FmtText, HyperLnk;

type
    tGraphicControlWithCanvas = class(TGraphicControl)
        property Canvas;
        end;

    tDisplay_buffer = class
      private
        { Formatted Text Storage }
        Formatted_text_list : tFormatted_text_list;
        { "Breaker" Data -- Line Breaking list }
        Line_list : TList; {of integer}
        { "Displayer" Data }
        Control : tGraphicControlWithCanvas;
      public
        { Hyperlink support lists, built by "Breaker" }
        Reference_anchors : tNamed_rectangle_list;
        Dest_name_anchors : tNamed_rectangle_list;
        { Display Positioning and Height, calc'd by "Breaker" }
        Display_top,
        Display_bottom : integer;
      public
        constructor Create(
          const _Control : tGraphicControlWithCanvas
          );
```

```
            destructor Destroy; override;
            procedure Load_HTML_file(
              const Filename : string
              );
            procedure Display;
            end;

implementation

uses
    SysUtils, Windows, Dialogs,
    MiscLib, HTML;

const
    Length_of_buffer = 1024-1;

constructor tDisplay_buffer.Create(
  const _Control : tGraphicControlWithCanvas
  );
    begin
        inherited Create;
        Formatted_text_list := tFormatted_text_list.Create;
        Line_list          := TList.Create;
        Control := _Control;
        Display_top := 0;
        Display_bottom := 0;
        Reference_anchors := tNamed_rectangle_list.Create;
        Dest_name_anchors := tNamed_rectangle_list.Create;
        end;

destructor tDisplay_buffer.Destroy;
    begin
        Dest_name_anchors.Free;
        Reference_anchors.Free;
        Line_list.Free;
        Formatted_text_list.Free;
        inherited Destroy;
        end;

procedure tDisplay_buffer.Load_HTML_file(
  const Filename : string
  );

    procedure Process_HTML_string(
      const Text : pchar
      );

        procedure Parse_HTML(
          Text   : pchar;
          Format : tHTML_format
          );

            { Format state variables}
            var
```

```
        Current_format          : tHTML_format;
        Pending_newlines        : integer;

{ Buffer Data Structure }
var
    Buffer,
    End_of_buffer           : pchar;
    Remaining_buffer_length : integer;

procedure Reset_buffer;
    begin
        Buffer^ := #0;
        End_of_Buffer := Buffer;
        Remaining_buffer_length := Length_of_buffer;
        end;

procedure Add_buffer_to_list;
    var
        S : pchar;
    begin
        S := Buffer;
        if  (Pending_newlines > 0)
          and
            not Current_format.Preformatted
          then
            while (S^ <> #0) and (S^ <= ' ') do inc(S);
        if S^ <> #0 then begin
            Current_format.Leading_newlines :=
               Pending_newlines;
            Formatted_text_list.Add(
              tFormatted_text.Create(Current_format,S)
              );
            Pending_newlines := 0;
            end;
        Reset_buffer;
        end;

{ Buffer building }

procedure Set_format(
  var F : tHTML_format
  );
    var
        S : pchar;
    begin
        Add_buffer_to_list;
        Current_format := F;
        end;

procedure New_line;
    begin
        Add_buffer_to_list;
        if Current_format.Preformatted then
            inc(Pending_newlines)
```

```
                    else
                        Pending_newlines := 1;
                end;

        procedure Horizontal_rule(
          const Height : integer
          );
            begin
                Add_buffer_to_list;
                inc(Pending_newlines);
                with Current_format do begin
                    Rule_height := Height;
                    Leading_newlines := Pending_newlines;
                    end;
                Formatted_text_list.Add(
                  tFormatted_text.Create(Current_format,'')
                  );
                Current_format.Rule_height := 0;
                Pending_newlines := 0;
                end;

        procedure Emit(
          S   : pchar;
          lnS : integer
          );
            var
                Chars_to_take       : integer;
            begin
                while lnS > 0 do begin
                    Chars_to_take :=
                      Int_min(Remaining_buffer_length,lnS);
                    strLCopy(End_of_Buffer,S,Chars_to_take);
                    inc(End_of_buffer,Chars_to_take);
                    End_of_buffer^ := #0;
                    dec(Remaining_buffer_length,Chars_to_take);
                    dec(lnS,Chars_to_take);
                    inc(S,Chars_to_take);
                    if Remaining_buffer_length = 0 then
                        Add_buffer_to_list;
                    end;
                end;

        function Is_whitespace(const C : char) : boolean;
            begin
                result := (C <> #0) and (C <= ' ');
                end;

        function Is_word(const C : char) : boolean;
            begin
                result := (C <> #0) and (C > ' ') and (C <> '<');
                end;

        var
            Need_a_newline,
```

```
        Preceeding_newline,
        Preceeding_space   : boolean;
        Space_format       : tHTML_format;
        Rule_height        : integer;
        The_end : pchar;
        Saved   : char;
        EOL     : pchar;
        Word    : pchar;

begin
        Buffer := strAlloc(Length_of_buffer+1);

        Current_format.Serial_number := -1;
        Pending_newlines             := 0;
        Reset_buffer;

        Preceeding_newline := false;
        Preceeding_space := false;
        while Text^ <> #0 do

            if Text^ = '<' then begin

                { Process a Tag }

                The_end := strPos(Text,'>');
                if The_end = nil then begin
                    { Oops, there was no closing ">" on the tag. }
                    { We'll handle this here, trivially.         }
                    Text := strEnd(Text);
                    exit;
                    end;

                inc(Text);
                The_end^ := #0;
                Parse_tag(Text,
                  Format,
                  Reference_anchors,
                  Dest_name_anchors,
                  Need_a_newline,
                  Rule_height
                  );
                Text := The_end + 1;
                Preceeding_newline :=
                  Preceeding_newline or Need_a_newline;
                if Preceeding_newline then
                    Preceeding_space := false;
                if Rule_height > 0 then
                    Horizontal_rule(Rule_height);
                Set_format(Format);
                end

            else if Format.Preformatted then begin

                { Process Preformatted Text }
```

```
            The_end := strPos(Text,'<');
            if The_end = nil then The_end := strEnd(Text);
            Saved := The_end^;
            The_end^ := #0;
            repeat
                EOL := strPos(Text,#13);
                if EOL <> nil then begin
                    EOL^ := #0;
                    Emit(Text,EOL-Text);
                    New_line;
                    Text := EOL+1
                    end
                  else
                    Emit(Text,The_end-Text);
               until EOL = nil;
            The_end^ := Saved;
            Text := The_end
            end

        else if Text^ <= ' ' then begin

          { Process Whitespace }

          if not Preceeding_newline then begin
              Preceeding_space := true;
              Space_format := Format;
              end;
          while Is_whitespace(Text^) do inc(Text);
          end

        else begin

          { Process Words }

          Word := Text;
          while Is_word(Text^) do inc(Text);
          The_end := Text;
          Saved := The_end^;
          The_end^ := #0;
          if Preceeding_newline then
              New_line
            else if Preceeding_space then
              if   Space_format.Serial_number
                 =
                   Format.Serial_number
                 then
                   Emit(' ',1)
                 else begin
                   {Re-} Set_format(Space_format);
                   Emit(' ',1);
                   {Re-} Set_format(Format);
                   end;
          Emit(Word,The_end-Word);
          The_end^ := Saved;
```

```
                    Preceeding_newline := false;
                    Preceeding_space   := false;
                    end;

            Add_buffer_to_list; { Last little bit. }

            strDispose(Buffer);
            end;

procedure Break_into_lines;

    var
        Current_item_index      : integer;
        EOW                     : pchar;
        Last_EOW                : pchar;
        Last_EOW_item_index     : integer;
        Line_pos                : TPoint;
        Last_line_meas,
        Current_line_meas       : tText_measurement;

    procedure Start_new_line(
        const Line_count : integer
        );
        var
            L, I : integer;
        begin
            for L := 1 to Line_count do begin
                Line_pos.Y :=
                    Display_bottom + Current_line_meas.Ascent;

                if L = 1 then begin
                    Line_pos.X := 0;
                    for I :=
                        integer(Line_list.Items[Line_list.Count-1])
                          to
                            Current_item_index-1
                          do
                            with tFormatted_text(
                                Formatted_text_list.Items[I]
                                ), { .Base_Left_Corner, .Meas, .Format}
                                Format,
                                  {.Anchor_reference, .Anchor_dest_name}
                                Base_left_corner,
                                  { .X and .Y }
                                Meas
                                  { .Width, .Ascent, .Descent }
                              do begin
                                Base_Left_Corner := Line_pos;
                                if Anchor_reference <> -1 then
                                    Reference_anchors.Add_rect(
                                        Anchor_reference,
                                        Rect(
                                            X, Y - Ascent,
                                            X + Width, Y + Descent
```

```
                                        )
                                      );
                                    if Anchor_dest_name <> -1 then
                                        Dest_name_anchors.Add_rect(
                                          Anchor_dest_name,
                                          Rect(
                                            X, Y - Ascent,
                                            X + Width, Y + Descent
                                            )
                                          );
                                    inc(Line_pos.X,Width);
                                    end;
                    end;

                Display_bottom :=
                   Line_pos.Y + Current_line_meas.Descent;
                end;

            with Current_line_Meas do begin
                Width   := 0;
                Height  := 0;
                Ascent  := 0;
                Descent := 0;
                end;
            Line_list.Add(pointer(Current_item_index));
            Last_EOW := nil;
            end;

    var
        P, BOW       : pchar;
        Real_EOW     : boolean;
        Saved        : char;
        Broken       : boolean;
        Start_width  : integer;
        Canvas_width : integer;
    begin
        with Control.ClientRect do
            Canvas_width := Right - Left;
        with Last_line_meas do begin
            Width   := 0;
            Height  := 0;
            Ascent  := 0;
            Descent := 0;
            end;
        Current_line_meas := Last_line_meas;
        Line_pos.Y := 0;
        Display_bottom := Line_pos.Y;
        Current_item_index := 0;
        Line_list.Add(pointer(Current_item_index));
        with Formatted_text_list do begin
            while Current_item_index < Count do
                with tFormatted_text(
                        Items[Current_item_index]
                        ),
```

```
   Format
do begin
  if Current_item_index = 0 then
      Leading_newlines := 0;
  if Leading_newlines > 0 then
      Start_new_line(Leading_newlines);
  P := Text;
  Broken := false;
  if Rule_height > 0 then begin
      with Current_line_meas do begin
          Height  := 2 + Rule_height + 2;
          Width   := Canvas_width;
          Ascent  := 2 + Rule_height;
          Descent := 2;
          end;
      Meas := Current_line_meas;
      end
    else if Preformatted then begin
      Meas := Measurement_of(P,strLen(P),
                 Control.Canvas,
                 Font
                 );
      with Current_line_meas do begin
          Height :=Int_max(Height, Meas.Height);
          Width  :=Width + Meas.Width;
          Ascent :=Int_max(Ascent, Meas.Ascent);
          Descent:=Int_max(Descent,Meas.Descent);
          end;
      end
    else begin
      Start_width := Current_line_meas.Width;
      while (not Broken) and (P <> nil) do begin

          { Get to Space or Null at end of next
            word, advance P. }
          BOW := P;
          EOW := strScan(P,' ');
          Real_EOW := EOW <> nil;
          if Real_EOW then
              P := EOW + 1
            else begin
              EOW := strEnd(P);
              P := nil;
              end;
          Saved := EOW^;
          EOW^ := #0;
          StrXlate(BOW,#160,' ');
          EOW^ := Saved;

          { Measure word; if adding it passes
            right edge, then break line. }
          Meas := Measurement_of(Text,EOW-Text,
                     Control.Canvas,
                     Font
                     );
```

```
                                if (Start_width + Meas.Width)
                                  >
                                   Canvas_width
                                 then
                                   if Last_EOW <> nil then begin
                                       Break_at(
                                         Last_EOW_item_index,
                                         Last_EOW
                                         );
                                       Current_item_index :=
                                         Last_EOW_item_index;
                                       tFormatted_text(
                                         Items[Current_item_index + 1]
                                         ).Format.Leading_newlines := 1;
                                       Broken := true;
                                       end;
                                if not Broken then begin
                                    if Real_EOW then begin
                                      { Track previous space to
                                        break on. }
                                      Last_EOW := EOW;
                                      Last_EOW_item_index :=
                                        Current_item_index;
                                      end;
                                    with Current_line_meas do begin
                                        Height  := Int_max(Height,
                                                        Meas.Height);
                                        Width   := Start_width +
                                                        Meas.Width;
                                        Ascent  := Int_max(Ascent,
                                                        Meas.Ascent);
                                        Descent := Int_max(Descent,
                                                        Meas.Descent);
                                        end;
                                      end;
                                  end;
                                end;
                           inc(Current_item_index);
                           end;
                  Start_new_line(1);
                  Line_list.Delete(Line_list.Count-1);
                  end;
            end;

      var
          Format      : tHTML_format;
          The_Text    : pchar;
          InThe_Text  : integer;
      begin
          with Format, Font do begin
              Leading_newlines := 0;
              Serial_number    := 0;
              specStyle        := [];
              specName         := 'Times New Roman';
```

Building a Hypermedia Engine

```
                    specColor          := clBlack;
                    specSize           := 3;
                    Rule_height        := 0;
                    Anchor_reference   := -1;
                    Anchor_dest_name   := -1;
                    Preformatted       := false;
                    end;
                Parse_HTML(Text,Format);
                Break_into_lines;
                end;

        var
            C : char;
        begin
            if Filename = '' then exit;
            with TMemoryStream.Create do
                try
                    try
                        { Load Document. }
                        LoadFromFile(Filename);
                        Seek(-1,soFromEnd); { Last character }
                        Read(C,sizeof(C));
                        { Add a CR if necessary. }
                        if C <> #13 then begin
                            C := #13;
                            Write(C,sizeof(C));
                            end;
                        { Null termination }
                        C := #0;
                        Write(C,sizeof(C));
                        { Do it. }
                        Process_HTML_string(Memory);
                    except on E : EInOutError do
                        MessageDlg(E.Message,mtWarning,[mbOk],0);
                    end;
                finally
                    Free;
                end;
        end;

    procedure Draw_rule(
      const Canvas             : TCanvas;
      const Lower_left_corner  : TPoint;
      const Width, Height      : integer
      );
        var
            Saved_pen : TPen;
        begin with Canvas, Lower_left_corner do begin
            Saved_pen := TPen.Create;
            Saved_pen.Assign(Pen);
            Pen.Width := 1;
            Pen.Style := psSolid;
            if Height = 1 then begin
                Pen.Color := clBlack;
```

```pascal
          MoveTo(X, Y);
          LineTo(X + Width - 1, Y);
          end
        else begin
          Pen.Color := clWhite;
          MoveTo(X,               Y );
          LineTo(X + Width - 1, Y );
          LineTo(X + Width - 1, Y - Height + 1);
          Pen.Color := clBlack;
          MoveTo(X + Width - 2, Y - Height + 1);
          LineTo(X,               Y - Height + 1);
          LineTo(X,               Y + 1);
          end;
      Pen.Assign(Saved_pen);
      Saved_pen.Free;
      end; end;

procedure tDisplay_buffer.Display;

    function Line_after(
      const Pixel_row : integer
      ) : integer;
        begin with Formatted_text_list do begin
          result := 0;
          while
              (result < Line_list.Count)
            and {then}
              (
                tFormatted_text(Items[integer(Line_list.Items[result])])
                  .Base_left_corner.Y
                <
                Pixel_row
              )
            do
              inc(result);
          end; end;

    function Line_before(
      const Pixel_row : integer
      ) : integer;
        begin with Formatted_text_list do begin
          result := 0;
          while
              (result < Line_list.Count)
            and {then}
              (
                tFormatted_text(Items[integer(Line_list.Items[result])])
                  .Base_left_corner.Y
                <=
                Pixel_row
              )
            do
              inc(result);
          if result > 0 then dec(result);
          end; end;
```

```
        var
            First_line,
            Last_line,
            First_elem,
            Last_elem   : integer;
            I           : integer;

        begin with Formatted_text_list do begin
            if Count = 0 then exit;
            First_line := Line_before(Display_top);
            First_elem := integer(Line_list.Items[First_line]);
            Last_line  := Line_after(Display_top +
                                        Control.ClientRect.Bottom);
            if Last_line >= (Line_list.Count-1) then
                Last_elem := Count - 1
              else
                Last_elem := integer(Line_list.Items[Last_line+1]) - 1;

            with Control.Canvas do begin
                Brush.Color := Color;
                FillRect(ClientRect);
                SetTextAlign(Handle,TA_BASELINE);
            end;
            for I := First_elem to Last_elem do
                with tFormatted_text(Items[I]), Format do
                    if Rule_height > 0 then
                        Draw_rule(Control.Canvas,
                            Point(Base_left_corner.X,
                                Base_left_corner.Y - Display_top),
                            Meas.Width,Rule_height
                            )
                      else if Text <> nil then begin
                        Set_font_from_spec(Control.Canvas.Font,Format.Font);
                        Control.Canvas.TextOut(
                            Base_left_corner.X, Base_left_corner.Y - Display_top,
                            Text
                            );
                        end;

        end; end;

{initialization}
    end.
```

Changes to Support Preformatted Text

In the next few sections, we'll review the changes we've made to support preformatted text. Some are common-sense, some are mechanical. Our goal, though, is to retain all of the spaces and all of the line-breaks from the original document.

Changes in Building the Formatted_text_list

You may remember the very heart of the parsing system. In this code, we fill a buffer, word by word, with text of the same format. When a tag is processed, changing the current format, we add the **Buffer** we've been filling to the **Formatted_text_list**. In this code, we would strip off the leading spaces from the **Buffer** if its format indicated that it would start a new line. We don't want to remove leading spaces on new lines in preformatted text, so we add a condition to avoid this, as shown in the code snippet below:

```
procedure Add_buffer_to_list;
    var
        S : pchar;
    begin
        S := Buffer;
        if (Pending_newlines > 0)
          and
            not Current_format.Preformatted
          then
            while (S^ <> #0) and (S^ <= ' ') do inc(S);
        if S^ <> #0 then begin
            Current_format.Leading_newlines :=
              Pending_newlines;
            Formatted_text_list.Add(
              tFormatted_text.Create(Current_format,S)
              );
            Pending_newlines := 0;
            end;
        Reset_buffer;
        end;
```

In the same area of the code, we implemented another function to handle the **Buffer** when we encountered a tag that called for a new line, such as a Paragraph tag. This procedure, **New_line**, can now take advantage of the fact that **Pending_newlines** is a counter, and not just a flag. By calling **New_line** when we find consecutive line breaks in the text, we can accumulate multiple new lines, as shown in the code snippet below:

```
procedure New_line;
    begin
        Add_buffer_to_list;
        if Current_format.Preformatted then
            inc(Pending_newlines)
          else
            Pending_newlines := 1;
        end;
```

Changes in Scanning the Document Text

Parse_HTML is home to the loop than scans through the document text, pulling off tags, skipping whitespace, and processing words, one by one. Those last two aspects of the processing are anathema to preformatted text. The routines above ensure that the spacing and line-break information we pass to them is preserved in the **Formatted_text_list**. Here, we must make sure we don't destroy this information before it has a chance to arrive.

We do this by introducing what is, essentially, another mode of processing. When we are handling preformatted text, we just want to send the text straight to the **Formatted_text_list**. We do need to be able to handle tags in the list, though, so we add another condition to the loop that decides what kind of text we're handling. It recognizes tags, whitespace, and words; now it can scan for preformatted text, also. The loop is shown in the code snippet below:

```
while Text^ <> #0 do
    if Text^ = '<' then begin
        { Process a Tag }
    else if Format.Preformatted then begin

        { Process Preformatted Text }

        The_end := strPos(Text,'<');
        if The_end = nil then The_end := strEnd(Text);
        Saved := The_end^;
        The_end^ := #0;
        repeat
            EOL := strPos(Text,#13);
            if EOL <> nil then begin
                EOL^ := #0;
                Emit(Text,EOL-Text);
                New_line;
                Text := EOL+1
                end
              else
                Emit(Text,The_end-Text);
          until EOL = nil;
        The_end^ := Saved;
        Text := The_end
        end

    else if Text^ <= ' ' then begin
        { Process Whitespace }
    else begin
        { Process Words }
        end;
```

Our strategy for handling preformatted text is to try to grab all of the text, up to the next tag. We have to stop at the tag; otherwise, we could never turn off preformatted text. This means we can't just dump anything into preformatted text. If we have greater-than signs in something like source code, we still need to replace them with HTML's special character strings.

Once we have identified the text we wish to send off to the **Formatted_text_list**, we need to find out where its line-breaks are, so that we can properly chunk the text out into lines by calling **New_line** after **Emit**-ing the text.

Measuring Lines of Preformatted Text

In the procedure **Break_into_lines**, we basically go through the entire **Formatted_text_list**, measuring our lines and breaking the elements that fall over the right edge of the display on the space before the edge (if there *is* a space before the edge), as shown in the code snippet below:

```
while Current_item_index < Count do
    with tFormatted_text(
            Items[Current_item_index]
            ),
         Format
    do begin
      if Current_item_index = 0 then
          Leading_newlines := 0;
      if Leading_newlines > 0 then
          Start_new_line(Leading_newlines);
      P := Text;
      Broken := false;
      if Rule_height > 0 then begin
         { Measure the rule. }
         end
       else if Preformatted then begin
         Meas := Measurement_of(P,strLen(P),
                   Control.Canvas,
                   Font
                   );
         with Current_line_meas do begin
            Height :=Int_max(Height, Meas.Height);
            Width  :=Width + Meas.Width;
            Ascent :=Int_max(Ascent, Meas.Ascent);
            Descent:=Int_max(Descent,Meas.Descent);
            end;
         end
       else begin
         Start_width := Current_line_meas.Width;
         while (not Broken) and (P <> nil) do begin
             { Go word-by-word, measuring until it breaks. }
             end;
         end;
      inc(Current_item_index);
      end;
```

```
Start_new_line(1);
Line_list.Delete(Line_list.Count-1);
```

Since we don't want to break our preformatted text, we need to avoid this section of code in the same manner we avoided it for horizontal rules. For rules, we just wanted to advance the measurement to the point that the next text would fall on the line after the rule. To handle preformatted text we do the same thing, except that we actually have some text to measure. If the text happens to be wider than the display, Windows will clip the output text to the **Control**'s **ClientRect**, and the next line of text (which was discovered by looking for carriage returns and calling **New_line** in **Parse_HTML**) will appear, as it should, on the next display line.

Named Destinations in Preformatted Text

There are some other changes to **DispBuf** to support named destination anchors. These changes parallel the changes we made in *Hyper II*, so we won't go into them here. They are highlighted, though, so you might want to review them anyway.

We mentioned earlier how they could be used, but we'll cover that in a little more detail as a segue to the user-interface code in unit **Main** that uses this information.

tDisplay_buffer has a **Display_top** field that we didn't use until we embarked on this project. This is how we use it to accomplish a jump to a named destination. The field **Dest_name_anchors**, a named rectangle list, is built and maintained exactly as **Reference_anchors** with one exception: The names of the rectangles are destination names, rather than referenced URLs, and they were built from **<A NAME>** tags, rather than **<A HREF>** tags. Thus, we can check to see if a mouse click occurred in text that is marked as a name, just as easily as we could for text marked as a reference. This isn't a very useful feature, though.

What we will do, instead, involves the inverse: When we discover that the user wants to go to a named destination, and we have that name in hand, we will use the method **tNamed_rectangle_list.First_rect_of_name** to find out where the text marked as a name is displayed. With that information, all we need to do to accomplish the "jump" is to set the **Display_top** to start at the top of the named text.

Hyperlinking in the User Interface

The section above covered the groundwork for jumping to a named destination. What was missing was a discussion of how we accomplish a jump to another file. Listing 3.19 shows the final version of unit **Main**, with the modifications needed to support hyperlinking and scrolling. These two topics go hand-in-hand, as we'll see, because the technique we use for scrolling translates into exactly the same code we use for named destination hyperjumps.

Listing 3.19 The final unit **Main**, supporting hyperlinking and scrolling

```
unit Main;

interface

uses
  SysUtils, WinTypes, WinProcs, Messages, Classes, Graphics, Controls,
  Forms, Dialogs, StdCtrls, ExtCtrls;

type
  TForm1 = class(TForm)
    Filename: TEdit;
    Panel1: TPanel;
    ScrollBar1: TScrollBar;
    Open_button: TButton;
    Close_button: TButton;
    OpenDialog1: TOpenDialog;
    PaintBox1: TPaintBox;

    procedure FormCreate(Sender: TObject);
    procedure FormResize(Sender: TObject);
    procedure PaintBox1MouseDown(Sender: TObject; Button: TMouseButton;
      Shift: TShiftState; X, Y: Integer);
    procedure ScrollBar1Change(Sender: TObject);
    procedure FilenameKeyPress(Sender: TObject; var Key: Char);
    procedure Open_buttonClick(Sender: TObject);
    procedure Close_buttonClick(Sender: TObject);
    procedure PaintBox1Paint(Sender: TObject);
  private
    { Private declarations }
  public
    { Public declarations }
  end;

var
  Form1: TForm1;

implementation

    uses
        MiscLib, DispBuf, HyperLnk, Parser;

{$R *.DFM}

var
    Output : tDisplay_buffer;
```

```
procedure Set_scrollbar(
  const Top_pixel : integer
  );
    begin with Form1.ScrollBar1 do begin
        if (Output.Display_bottom < Form1.PaintBox1.Height)
          and
            (Top_pixel = 0)
          then
            Hide
          else begin
            Min := 0;
            Max := Output.Display_bottom;
            Position := Top_pixel;
            SmallChange := 10;
            LargeChange := Form1.PaintBox1.Height - 20;
            Show;
            end;
        Output.Display_top := Top_pixel;
        end; end;

procedure Load_HTML;
    begin
        Output.Free;
        Output := tDisplay_buffer.Create(
                    tGraphicControlWithCanvas(Form1.PaintBox1)
                    );
        Output.Load_HTML_file(Form1.Filename.Text);
        Set_scrollbar(0);
        end;

procedure Load_new_HTML_file;
    begin
        Load_HTML;
        Form1.PaintBox1.Refresh;
        end;

procedure Jump_to(
  const Target : string
  );
    begin with TParser.Parse(pchar(Target)) do begin
        No_errors;
        Find('#');
        if Error then begin
            { Just "filename". }
            Form1.Filename.Text := Remainder;
            Load_HTML;
            end
          else begin
            if Last_found^ <> #0 then begin
                { There was a filename in "filename#label".
                  <label> is in Remainder. }
                Form1.Filename.Text := Last_found;
                Load_HTML;
                end
```

```
              else
                { Just "#label". };
              Set_scrollbar(
                Int_max(
                  Output.Dest_name_anchors.First_rect_of_name(Remainder).Top,
                  0
                  )
                );
              end;
            Form1.PaintBox1.Refresh;
          Free;
          end; end;

procedure TForm1.PaintBox1MouseDown(Sender: TObject; Button: TMouseButton;
  Shift: TShiftState; X, Y: Integer);
    var
       Target : string;
    begin
       with Output, Reference_anchors do
           Target := Name_of_point(X,Y + Display_top);
       if Target <> '' then Jump_to(Target);
       end;

procedure TForm1.ScrollBar1Change(Sender: TObject);
     begin
        Set_scrollbar(ScrollBar1.Position);
        PaintBox1.Refresh;
        end;

procedure TForm1.FilenameKeyPress(Sender: TObject; var Key: Char);
     begin
        if Key = #13 then begin
            Load_new_HTML_file;
            Key := #0;
            end;
        end;

procedure TForm1.Open_buttonClick(Sender: TObject);
     begin
        if OpenDialog1.Execute then begin
            Filename.Text := OpenDialog1.Filename;
            Load_new_HTML_file;
            end;
        end;

procedure TForm1.Close_buttonClick(Sender: TObject);
     begin
        Close;
        end;

procedure TForm1.PaintBox1Paint(Sender: TObject);
     begin
        Output.Display;
        end;
```

```
var
    Resizing_ourselves : boolean;
    Form1s_old_width,
    Form1s_old_height  : integer;

procedure TForm1.FormCreate(Sender: TObject);
    begin
        Resizing_ourselves := false;
        Form1s_old_width   := Form1.Width;
        Form1s_old_height  := Form1.Height;
        Output := nil;
        end;

procedure TForm1.FormResize(Sender: TObject);
    var
        Minimum_width,
        Panel1s_new_width,
        Panel1s_new_height,
        Catchup_width,
        Catchup_height     : integer;
    begin
        if Resizing_ourselves then exit;

        Panel1s_new_width  := Panel1.Width  + (Width  - Form1s_old_width);
        Panel1s_new_height := Panel1.Height + (Height - Form1s_old_height);

        Minimum_width := Open_button.Width + Close_button.Width + 30;
          { 30 pixels between &O and &C}

        Catchup_width := 0;
        Catchup_height := 0;
        if Panel1s_new_width < Minimum_width then
            Catchup_width := Minimum_width - Panel1s_new_width;
        if Panel1s_new_height < 30 then
            Catchup_height := 30 - Panel1s_new_height;
        inc(Panel1s_new_width, Catchup_width);
        inc(Panel1s_new_height,Catchup_height);

        Resizing_ourselves := true;
        with Form1 do begin
            if Catchup_width <> 0 then
                Width  := Width  + Catchup_width;
            if Catchup_height <> 0 then
                Height := Height + Catchup_height;
            end;
        with PaintBox1 do begin
            Width  := Panel1s_new_width  - (Panel1.Width  - Width);
            Height := Panel1s_new_height - (Panel1.Height - Height);
            end;
        with Panel1 do begin
            Width  := Panel1s_new_width;
            Height := Panel1s_new_height;
            end;
```

```
with ScrollBar1 do begin
    Top    := Panel1.Top;
    Height := Panel1.Height;
    Left   := Panel1.Left + Panel1.Width;
    end;
with Filename do begin
    Width := Panel1.Width;
    Top   := Top + Form1.Height - Form1s_old_height;
    end;
with Open_button do
    Top := Top + Form1.Height - Form1s_old_height;
with Close_button do begin
    Top  := Open_button.Top;
    Left := Panel1.Left + Panel1.Width - Close_button.Width;
    end;
Resizing_ourselves := false;

Form1s_old_width  := Form1.Width;
Form1s_old_height := Form1.Height;

Load_new_HTML_file;

Form1.Refresh;
end;
```

end.

We just discussed the use of **Display_top** to accomplish a jump to a named destination in the text. **Display_top** can also be used to easily implement text scrolling. By adjusting the value of **Display_top** to some value controlled by a scroll bar, and redisplaying the **Output** when the scroll bar changes, we completely implement this feature.

Hyperjumps and URLs

Hyperjumps are accomplished with the addition of one routine: **Jump_to**. It is relatively complex, because it needs to parse a reference anchor's *URL*—which we haven't defined until now. Out on the Internet, a URL is a location of *something*. It may be a World Wide Web site address, a news article, a person's email address, or a file's location. All of these, and more, are *resources* provided by the Internet. Hence the name, *Uniform Resource Locator*.

In Hyper III, we've co-opted the term and dummied-down its meaning a little bit. We aren't out on the Web yet with our Browser, so we will assume that all of the URLs are just filenames on our own machines.

The hypertext Reference Anchor tag, **<A HREF>**, actually has two parts to its quoted reference. The first part is a document's URL (a fancy word for "filename" at this point). The second part is a local destination name within the document. The URL and the name are both optional. The name starts with a pound sign (#) and follows the URL, if present. Here are some variations on a theme, shown in the code snippet below:

```
<A HREF="Sample.Htm#codelink">
<A HREF="Sample2.Htm">
<A HREF="#codelink">
```

To instigate a hyperjump, we must first detect a click on a reference anchor. We've done this already, in Hyper II; all we need to do is call the routine to do the hyperjump, instead of only putting up a message box, as shown in the code snippet below:

```
procedure TForm1.PaintBox1MouseDown(Sender: TObject; Button: TMouseButton;
  Shift: TShiftState; X, Y: Integer);
    var
        Target : string;
    begin
        with Output, Reference_anchors do
            Target := Name_of_point(X,Y + Display_top);
        if Target <> '' then Jump_to(Target);
        end;
```

Jump_to parses the reference that is passed to it, loads the file, and scrolls to the local destination, as shown in the code snippet below:

```
procedure Jump_to(
  const Target : string
  );
    begin with TParser.Parse(pchar(Target)) do begin
        No_errors;
        Find('#');
        if Error then begin
            { Just "filename". }
            Form1.Filename.Text := Remainder;
            Load_HTML;
            end
          else begin
            if Last_found^ <> #0 then begin
                { There was a filename in "filename#label".
                  <label> is in Remainder. }
                Form1.Filename.Text := Last_found;
                Load_HTML;
                end
              else
                { Just "#label". };
            Set_scrollbar(
              Int_max(
                Output.Dest_name_anchors.First_rect_of_name(Remainder).Top,
```

```
          0
         )
      );
    end;
    Form1.PaintBox1.Refresh;
    Free;
end; end;
```

If there is no pound-sign, the reference is just a URL. To load the file, we put the reference into the **Filename** Edit control and call **Load_HTML** (which loads the file specified in the **Filename** control and scrolls to its top).

If there was a pound sign with an URL before it, the document would be loaded. Whether a new document was loaded, or if we are still working with the original one, we then look through the **Dest_name_anchors** list to find the top coordinate of the named rectangle. This might come back as −1, so we use **Int_max** to start at the top of the document if the local name isn't found. We use this to set our **Display_top**, indirectly through **Set_scrollbar**. This way, the scroll bar can track our positioning at a label.

When we have completed the jump, we call **Output.Display** to actually display the hypertext to which we've jumped.

Scrolling the Hypertext

Set_scrollbar does a lot more with the **ScrollBar1** control than the **Output** Display Buffer. Before we start adjusting the scroll bar, we make sure it's needed. If the document fits on the screen and starts at the top of the screen, we can hide the scroll bar.

If we can't simply hide it, we set its range to run from the top of the document (document pixel row 0) to the bottom of the document at **Display_bottom**. We then set the thumb position to the top pixel row we've requested. We set the small change to 10, and the large change to the height of the display, less 20 pixels for visual continuity. A rather complicated enhancement would be to make the small change move the display up or down by one line (which may vary in height from line to line), instead of moving by a fixed amount. Finally, we call **Show**, to make sure the scroll bar is visible.

When we're finished, we set **Output.Display_top** to the requested **Top_pixel** row, as shown in the code snippet below:

```
procedure Set_scrollbar(
    const Top_pixel : integer
    );
        begin with Form1.ScrollBar1 do begin
            if (Output.Display_bottom < Form1.PaintBox1.Height)
                and
```

```
          (Top_pixel = 0)
        then
          Hide
        else begin
          Min := 0;
          Max := Output.Display_bottom;
          Position := Top_pixel;
          SmallChange := 10;
          LargeChange := Form1.PaintBox1.Height - 20;
          Show;
          end;
    Output.Display_top := Top_pixel;
    end; end;
```

The only thing still needed to implement full scroll bar support is hooking something up to the scroll bar's **OnChange** event; this way the user, and not just the hyperjump code, can scroll through the text in the window, as shown in the code snippet below. It couldn't be easier.

```
procedure TForm1.ScrollBar1Change(Sender: TObject);
   begin
      Set_scrollbar(ScrollBar1.Position);
      PaintBox1.Refresh;
      end;
```

A Firm Foundation for Nimble Navigation

We've now constructed the most essential mechanisms for a hypertext—or a hypermedia—platform that is based on the flexible HTML. We discovered that the PaintBox control offered us the most flexibility with the fewest obstacles for creating our hypertext system. We then developed the data structures and algorithms that we used to parse HTML, place hyperlinks on the screen, detect clicks on those links, and retrieve and display the text to which those links point.

The projects in this chapter have taken us on a tour of Delphi's powerful features. From this point on, we'll be making liberal use of Delphi and its new (and old) abilities, as we further develop our concept of presentation HTML and finally develop a Web-capable multimedia presentation engine. Along the way, we'll be accumulating a *repertoire* of multimedia presentation techniques. By combining these with Delphi's power and your own ingenuity, you'll be able to create the most fun, powerful, enchanting, and adventuresome multimedia presentations you could ever imagine!

Chapter 4

To develop great multimedia apps with Delphi, you'll want to learn everything you can about the Windows 95 Multimedia API.

Introducing the Windows 95 Multimedia System

Dan Haygood

Thanks to Windows 95 and Visual Basic, the step from hypertext to full hypermedia is shorter than you might suspect. The Windows Multimedia API offers several interfaces to help you get there. In Chapter 1, you learned about ways to call the simple **mciExecute** function to plug in multimedia features. Now, we are going to explain the Windows 95 multimedia system in much more detail.

This system provides both low-level and high-level sets of functions. The low-level set, which includes numerous functions for WAV, MIDI (musical instrument digital interface), and movie player operations, is the largest of the two. The high-level set, which consists primarily of six functions, provides an easy-to-use, high-level interface. As you might guess, the low-level functions call device drivers and require more programming. The high-level functions, on the other hand, hide the details as they pass messages to the *Media Control Interface* (*MCI*), which interprets the messages and calls the low-level functions to access the appropriate device drivers.

To perform important low-level tasks, such as writing utilities for mixing and editing WAV files or synchronizing sounds with other multimedia activities such as animation, we'll need the flexibility and precision timing of the low-level interface. For now, since we only want to play existing multimedia files, the high-level interface will work just fine.

Let's continue where we left off in Chapter 3 and expand on our HTML-driven hypermedia engine. After we explore the high-level multimedia interface, we'll add a multimedia connection to our engine. Then, we'll work our way through the levels of the multimedia interface by exploring a couple of ways to play WAV files. In Chapter 5, we'll move down a few levels and show you how to get closer to the MCI and work with low-level audio functions.

A Look at the High-Level

Although the high-level MCI imposes a few limitations, it's still packed with useful features. It exists mainly to isolate us from the actual device drivers by providing a common interface for all multimedia devices. Using this interface, many of the same instructions will work whether we want to play CD audio, WAV files, MIDI sequences, or video discs.

The MCI comes in two flavors: the Command-Message Interface and the Command-String Interface. The difference between the two interfaces is simple. When you call the Command-Message function **mciSendCommand**, you pass it a numeric constant and a data structure filled with constants, strings, or pointers to other structures that indicate what operation you want the MCI to perform. When you call the Command-String function **mciSendString**, you pass it a text string. The two functions execute the same commands—they just expect the commands in different formats.

In their *Multimedia Programmer's Workbook*, Microsoft states that the Command-Message Interface is "more versatile if your application controls an MCI device directly." They also say that the Command-String Interface is slower. (After all, it's really just a translator that converts string commands into data structures for the Command-Message interface.) Both statements may well be true, but the Command-String Interface offers a couple of advantages. First, you don't need a long list of data structures and constant declarations to establish names for all the command messages. Second—and this Microsoft *does* mention—the Command-String Interface can execute scripts provided by the end user without intermediate interpretation. (You can pass operator text directly to the **mciSendString** function, that is, if the operator knows the MCI command syntax.)

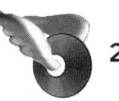

Adding Multimedia to the HTML Hypertext Engine

Our goal now is to extend the HTML-based hypertext engine we constructed in the previous chapter by adding sound. You'll be pleasantly surprised at how simple this is, relative to the intricate algorithms we developed for text display. We can easily do this by using **mciExecute**—the function that strips the Command-String Interface down to its bare bones. This function accepts a plain English text string as its single parameter. Unlike other MCI command functions, **mciExecute** doesn't return an error code. Instead, when we call **mciExecute**, the MCI performs its own error trapping and displays message boxes whenever errors occur. Because these errors are non-fatal, your programs can go about their business, even when one or more multimedia devices aren't working. Although this function won't support a complex application that requires a dialogue between the user and various multimedia devices, it does offer the easiest way to play back WAV (digitized sound), MIDI (synthesized music and sound effects), MMM (movie/animation), AVI (audio/video interleave), and other standard multimedia files.

Hyper IV: Plugging into the High-Level MCI

This project allows you to play a multimedia file when a hyperlink is selected. To incorporate the MCI interface, follow these steps:

1. Using the *Explorer*, create a new project directory, *Hyper4*. Beneath this, create an output directory, *Bin*. Copy the project files from your *Hyper3* directory to your *Hyper4* directory. Rename your "Hyper3" files to "Hyper4". You'll need the *DPR*, *PAS*, and *DFM* files.
2. Open your **Hyper4** Project file in Delphi. The compiler will complain that its name is wrong ("Module header is missing or incorrect."). Change its program name from **Hyper3** to **Hyper4**. In the *Project Options* dialog box (from *Project | Options*), set the Application Title to "Hyper IV", and its output directory to "Bin".
3. View **Form1** from unit **Main**. In the *Object Inspector*, change its **Caption** from "Hyper III" to "Hyper IV".
4. Modify the the Form's **Jump_to** procedure, in unit **Main**, as described below (Listing 4.1).
5. Create new hypertext files to test out the multimedia interface (Listing 4.2).

> This project, Hyper4.DPR, and all of its support files, can be found on the accompanying CD-ROM in the directory \Programs\Chap04\Hyper4. The multimedia hyperdocument can be found in the files \Media\HyperTxt\MM-1.HTM, MM-2.HTM, and MM-3.HTM.

Setting Up for Multimedia

We only need to modify one unit: **Main**. We need to use the Delphi unit **MMSystem**, and then modify our existing **Jump_to** procedure (Recall that this is called from the **TForm1.PaintBox1MouseDown** event procedure once the mouse click position has been resolved to a URL.) If no local label is specified, we will now perform a little extra parsing on the destination URL. We can play any multimedia file by passing the command string **"Play filename.ext"** to **mciExecute**. Since we already have the ability to determine if a destination URL is a local link label, a filename, or both all we need to do is determine whether or not the destination URL specifies a "playable" multimedia file. The easiest way to do this it to use Delphi's **ExtractFileExt** function from its **SysUtils** unit to pull the file extension from the filename. Then, with a simple **if...then...else**, we decide which file type we are dealing with. We'll write this so that if the extension is equal to "**HTM**", we'll fall through to our previous project's code to open a new HTML file. If the extension is equal to "**WAV**", "**MID**", or "**AVI**", we know we are dealing with a multimedia filename. If we find such an extention, we'll feed it to **mciExecute** as the object of a **"Play"** command sentence. Listing 4.1 provides the new version of **Jump_to**.

Listing 4.1 TForm1.Jump_to Event Procedure from *Main.Pas*

```
:
:
   uses
       MMSystem,
       MiscLib, Parser, HyperTxt, HyperLnk, DispBuf;
:
:
procedure Jump_to(
  const Target : string
  );
    var
        Re_show : boolean;
        Ext     : string;
        Command : ansiString;
```

Introducing the Windows 95 Multimedia System

```
begin with TParser.Parse(pchar(Target)) do begin
    Re_show := true;
    No_errors;
    Find('#');
    if Error then begin
        { Just "filename".  Could be a media file. }
        Re_show := false;
        Ext := uppercase(extractFileExt(Remainder));
        if  (Ext = '.WAV')
          or
            (Ext = '.MID')
          or
            (Ext = '.AVI')
        then begin
            Command := 'Play ' + strPas(Remainder);
            mciExecute(pchar('Play ' + strPas(Remainder)));
            end
        else begin
            { 'HTM', et al. }
            Form1.Filename.Text := Remainder;
            Load_HTML;
            Re_show := true;
            end
        end
    else begin
        if Last_found^ <> #0 then begin
            { There was a filename in "filename#label".
              <label> is in Remainder. }
            Form1.Filename.Text := Last_found;
            Load_HTML;
            end
        else
            ; { Just "#label". }
        Set_scrollbar(
            Int_max(
                Output.Dest_name_anchors.First_rect_of_name(Remainder).Top,
                0
                )
            );
        end;
    if Re_show then Form1.PaintBox1.Refresh;
    Free;
    end; end;
```

The function **mciExecute** returns an integer (that we ignore) indicating if it succeeds or fails. Later on, we'll learn what to do with return values like this, but for now it's okay to just ignore it.

That's it! You can add a hotlink to the HTML source file that specifies a multimedia filename, including the path if necessary, and try it out. Listing 4.2 provides a couple of sample HTML files. If you still aren't up to speed with writing HTML tags, you should review Chapter 3 and Appendix A. To help you navigate, we'll give you a quick guided tour of the structures of the two HTML files presented in Listing 4.2.

Listing 4.2 HTML Source Files: *MM-1.Htm*, *MM-2.Htm*, and *MM-3.Htm*

MM-1.Htm:
```
<H1>Hypertext</H1>
<HR Size = 4>
<P>
    Want to try some <A HREF="MM-3.Htm"><I>multimedia</I>?</A>
<HR SIZE=3>
<P>
    <A HREF="MM-2.Htm">Hypertext systems</A> enable readers to
    jump from topic to topic by selecting key words or phrases
    embedded in the text.  These special words are sometimes known
    as <A HREF="MM-2.Htm#Hot Links">hot links</A>.
<P>  <BR>
    Here are some formatting tags in action:<BR>
        <I>Italics</I><BR>
        <B>Bolding</B><BR>
        <U>Underlined</U><BR>
        
        <I><B><U>Italic-Bold-Underlined</U></B></I><BR>
<HR SIZE=3>
<H2>Heading Size 2</H2>
<H4>Heading <FONT SIZE=-2>SIZE</FONT> 4</H4>
<H6>Heading Size 6</H6>
<HR SIZE=4>
```

MM-2.Htm:
```
<H1>Hypertext Systems</H1>
<HR SIZE = 4>
<P>
    Hypertext systems are generally fairly simple, because few
    authors have the willingness to develop meaningful multipath
    content. As you can discover for yourself, though, even a
    simple linear document can be explored in ways that you never
    thought possible with the addition of a few well-placed hot
    links.
<P>
     
<H2><A NAME="Hot Links">Hot Links</A></H2>
<HR SIZE = 3>
<P>
    Hot links are a powerful addition to even a simple linear
    document.  When used to bring
    <A HREF="MM-3.Htm">multimedia</A>
    into a document's content, demonstration and illustration of
    concepts can be done more powerfully than in any pure-text
    application.
<P>
```

```
        The most artful hypertext, though,
    is developed by authors with a concious awareness of the medium
    in which they are working.  As concepts diverge, so can the
    hyperdocument.  As ideas coalesce, so can the hyperdocument.
<HR SIZE=1>
<P>
    (Since we haven't yet implemented navigational buttons, we'll
    need this to get back to our <A HREF="MM-1.Htm">first
    page</A>.)
<HR SIZE = 3>
```

MM-3.Htm:

```
<H1>How About Multimedia...</H1>
<HR SIZE = 3>
<P>
Here are some simple multimedia demonstrations:<BR>
1.  <A HREF="c:\Windows\Media\Chord.Wav">
    Windows <CITE>Chord</CITE></A><BR>
2.  <A HREF="c:\Windows\Help\Explorer.AVI">
    Windows <CITE>Explorer</CITE> Demo</A><BR>
3.  <A HREF="c:\Windows\Media\Canyon.Mid">
    Microsoft <CITE>Canyon</CITE></A><BR>
<P>
 
<P>Back to <A HREF="MM-1.Htm">Hypertext</A>
<HR SIZE = 3>
```

The file *MM-1.Htm* starts with a main heading enclosed in a pair of **<H1>** tags. This is the top-level heading that can be created with HTML. Any text included between these tags will be displayed in the heading font we specify in the unit **HyperTxt**. The HTML spec recommends bold face. If the terminating tag **</H1>** is omitted, everything in the document will be formatted as a top-level heading. For looks, we put a horizontal rule, with a height of 4 pixels, after the heading. Although we haven't yet implemented this feature yet, wouldn't it be convenient if there were some default height, so we could simply use the tag "**<HR>**" ?

The next tag used is **<P>,** which forces a line break. Everything contained within an HTML file is displayed as one continuous stream unless manual breaks are specified by using the **<P>** or **
** tags. Since we haven't implemented any different "look" for these tags, for now, we can use them interchangably. However, we should try to use them logically: Use **<P>** to block out a paragraph (along with the vestigal **</P>**, which even the HTML spec says can be ignored); use **
** only to force a line break. Keep this distinction in mind. In the future, you may want to make your hypertext display system automatically indent paragraphs, but not line breaks; or you may want to put some extra vertical space before a new paragraph, but keep normal line spacing for line breaks.

The first link defined in the file is found in this sentence:

```
Want to try some <A HREF="MM-3.Htm"><I>multimedia</I>?</A>
```

Here, when the user clicks on the word "multimedia" (appearing in italics in addition to the format we've implemented for a hot link), the HTML file *MM-3.Htm* will be automatically loaded and displayed. Recall that the **HREF** parameter is assigned the name of a file to load when used with the **<A>** (anchor) tag. The first part of the tag, **<A HREF="MM-3.Htm">**, specifies the action that should occur when a link is selected, the second part, "multimedia," specifies the highlighted link, and the final part, **</A>**, terminates the anchor definition. Again, if you left out the terminating tag, all the text in the document until the next **</A>** would be displayed as the link.

After the first anchor is defined, you'll find more text and a few more anchors. One worth noting is the one found as part of this line of text:

```
as <A HREF="MM-2.Htm#Hot Links">hot links</A>.
```

This is actually similar in format to the other anchor definition we looked at. But look closely and you'll see the "**#**" character used with the **HREF** variable assignment. In this case, we are defining a link to an actual *location* in another file. The file that will be opened is named *MM-2.Htm* and the location in the file that we'll jump to is referenced by the label **"Hot Link"**. Looking at *MM-2.Htm*, you'll find the anchor's destination label in the middle of the file (and, incidently, nested in a heading):

```
<H2><A NAME="Hot Links">Hot Links</A></H2>
```

This is the actual spot to which the user is taken when the link "hot links" is selected. It is important to realize that we didn't implement any sort of case-insensitive comparison in the routines that locate hyperlink labels (You can find this code in the unit **HyperLnk**). Because of this, labels *are* case-sensitive.

The remainder of the HTML tags in HYPRTXT4.HTM perform some formatting magic. Here's a trick for putting "blank lines" in our text (since we tried so hard to avoid them in ordinary parsing):

```
<P>  <BR>
```

We take advantage of our "hard-space" character to put something on a line, even though the user won't be able to see it. Next, we demonstrate that text can be displayed in italics, bold, underline, and different heading sizes.

Notice that we can also group formatting tags together to put text in more than one format. For example, these lines display text in three formats at the same time, indenting it, also:

```
    
    <I><B><U>Italic-Bold-Underlined</U></B></I><BR>
```

And this line changes font sizes, even for text nested in the middle of a heading tag:

```
<H4>Heading <FONT SIZE=-2>SIZE</FONT> 4</H4>
```

The *MM-3.Htm* file contains the required tags to play sound files. Here we are showing how WAV, AVI, and MID files can be played. When one of the corresponding links are selected, the appropriate media file will be loaded and played. If you have sound, AVI, or MIDI files of your own that you'd like to play, simply edit one of the **<A>** tag definitions. That's all there is to it.

The best part about our system is that you can add other multimedia features. For example, you might want to display a bitmap or activate a CD player. For true hypermedia, you may even want to create hotspot regions on bitmapped images. We'll do all of these things in later chapters using a combination of Delphi and a few Windows 95 API functions. But first, let's look at the Windows Multimedia System in more detail.

Exploring the Windows Multimedia System

The Windows multimedia system functions are located in several dynamic link libraries, or DLLs. In fact, all Windows operating system functions reside in DLLs. The Windows 95 operating system, *sans* multimedia, comes in three libraries: Kernel32, GDI32 (graphic device interface), and User32. These files contain all of the more than 1,000 or so functions that define Windows 95 services.

Almost all graphics functions reside in the GDI32. When you create a multimedia project, you will inevitably call numerous GDI32 functions, which include functions for drawing shapes, writing text, defining and changing colors, and many other graphics operations. Because the three main Windows libraries are more fundamental to Windows programming than to the multimedia system, we'll skip them for now and return to them in later chapters.

A Tour of the Multimedia API

The multimedia system provides an interface to several services:

- WAV audio playback and recording
- Synthesizer audio and MIDI
- Animation playback
- Video playback
- Joystick services
- High-resolution timing
- Operation of external media devices

Except for the lower-level animation functions, which you'll find in MMP.DLL, the functions that control these services reside in WINMM.DLL. These functions can be further divided into two classes: the low-level and high-level multimedia interfaces. The function **mciExecute**, which we used earlier to add multimedia playback capabilities to our hypertext system, belongs to the high-level interface. In fact, you might say that **mciExecute** represents the *highest* level of the high-level interface because it parses MCI commands and performs its own error trapping.

Let's descend into the multimedia interface one level at a time. We'll do this by calling upon several of the functions that we can use to play WAV files.

Using High-Level Multimedia Functions: MessageBeep and sndPlaySound

As we mentioned earlier, the high-level interface includes the MCI—a kind of universal control language for media devices—and two sound functions: **MessageBeep** and **sndPlaySound**. You could say that **MessageBeep** and **sndPlaySound** sit atop the summit of the multimedia interface. Why? Because they perform a single high-level function—playing WAV files. In addition, you don't need to know anything about the underlying data structures—such as the WAV audio data itself—to use them.

Of theses two functions, **MessageBeep** is the most specialized. It takes a single parameter, a flag that indicates a system alert level. You may be familiar to the Windows API call MessageBox, or Delphi's encapsulation, MessageDlg, already. The system alert levels are idenified in Table 4.1.

Now if you use the registry editing program *RegEdit*, you can look through the default system sounds, or peek at some of the sound schemes. Look in HKEY_USERS/.DEFAULT/APPEVENTS/SCHEMES/APPS/.DEFAULT to find all current sound possibilities and their associated WAV files. You'll find a list that looks something like Figure 4.1.

These entries assign sounds, in the form of WAV files, to system events. Notice that four of the events in this list correspond to the four Windows

Introducing the Windows 95 Multimedia System

Table 4.1 MessageBeep System Alert Levels.

MessageBox	MessageDlg	Visual Cue	Audio Cue Name
MB_ICONASTERISK MB_ICONINFORMATION	mtInformation	A blue "I"	SystemAsterisk
MB_ICONEXCLAMATION	mtWarning	An exclamation-point	SystemExclamation
MB_ICONHAND MB_ICONSTOP	mtError	A stop-sign	SystemHand
MB_ICONQUESTION	mtConfirmation	A question-mark	SystemQuestion

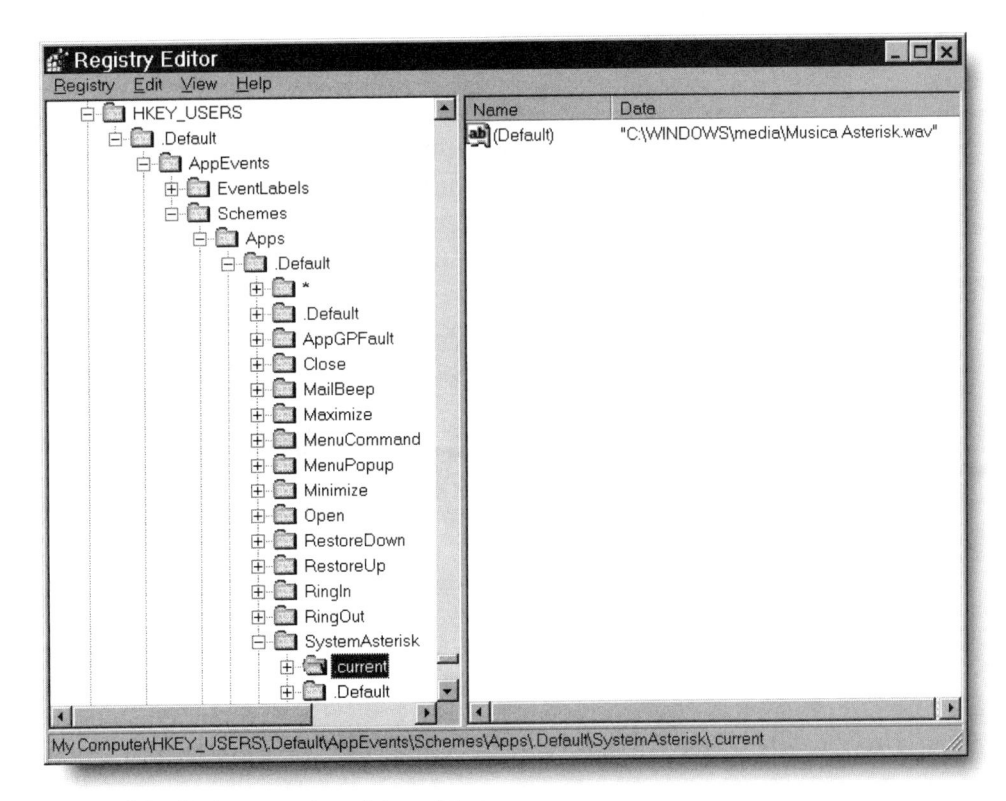

Figure 4.1 System sounds registry entries.

message flags. By calling **MessageBeep** with one of these four flags, you will cause Windows to look up the appropriate sound in the Registry, and play it.

Actually, **MessageBeep** is not a function at all; it's a procedure because it doesn't return anything—no error code, no handles, no success flag—nothing. If you hand it a flag value that it doesn't recognize, it simply plays the **SystemDefault** sound. If that's what you *want*, you can pass it the constant **MB_OK**.

You can also use **sndPlaySound** to play message beeps. This function is actually more useful than **MessageBeep** because it can play other WAV files in your system—not just the sounds that have been assigned to system events in the Registry. The **sndPlaySound** function takes two arguments and returns a **Bool** value (an **integer** that represents a boolean result).

MCI Play I: Playing WAV Files with MessageBeep

Let's begin a new project that demonstrates **MessageBeep**. We'll call it **MCIPlay1**. As we descend into the multimedia interface, we'll add to this project, adding in new functions that demonstrate the various ways to play WAV and other types of multimedia files.

To test out **MessageBeep**, follow these steps:

1. Create a new application in a new project directory named *MCIPlay1*, that has, of course, a *Bin* subdirectory. Save **Unit1** as *Main.Pas*, and **Project1** as *MCIPlay1.DPR*.
2. From the *Project Options* dialog box, set the Application Title to "MCI Play I", and the Output Directory to "Bin".
3. Set **Form1**'s **Caption** to "MCI Play I".
4. Add a Button named **Message_beep_button** to the form..
5. Add code for the **Message_beep_buttonClick** event procedure (Listing 4.3), so the Button can play a WAV file.

> *This project, MCIPlay1.DPR, and all of its support files, can be found on the accompanying CD ROM in the directory \PROGRAMS\CHAP04\MCIPLAY0. Yes, "0". This isn't really MCI Play I until we add another button! We thought it would be nice, though, to include this very first step on the CD ROM.*

Creating the MCIPlay I Project

To start, add a Button to the new main form. Set its caption to "Message&Beep", as shown in Figure 4.2. It also wouldn't hurt to change its **Name** property to something more descriptive than Button1. I recommend "Message_beep_button". Other properties of interest are shown in Table 4.2.

The code is nearly trivial. Double-click the Button, and add one statement in the **TForm1.Message_beep_buttonClick** event procedure as shown in

Introducing the Windows 95 Multimedia System

Table 4.2 *Properties for the MCI Play I project.*

Class	Property	Value
TForm	Name	Form1 (default)
	Caption	'MCI Play I'
TButton	Name	Message_beep_button
	Caption	'Message&Beep'
	OnClick	Message_beep_buttonClick

Figure 4.2 *The first step of our Windows sound system.*

Listing 4.3. If you haven't already, save **Form1**'s unit as *Main.Pas*, and the project as *MCIPlay1.DPR*.

Listing 4.3 Message_beep_buttonClick Event Procedure from unit *Main.Pas*

```
unit Main;

interface

uses
  SysUtils, Windows, Messages, Classes, Graphics, Controls, Forms, Dialogs,
  StdCtrls;

type
  TForm1 = class(TForm)
    Message_beep_button: TButton;
    procedure Message_beep_buttonClick(Sender: TObject);
  private
    { Private declarations }
  public
    { Public declarations }
```

```
    end;

var
  Form1: TForm1;

implementation

{$R *.DFM}

procedure TForm1.Message_beep_buttonClick(Sender: TObject);
begin
    MessageBeep(MB_ICONEXCLAMATION);
    end;

end.
```

Note: *If you wish, you can use the Sound applet in the Windows Control Panel to change the system sounds. Windows 95 even allows you to create entire schemes of sounds, so you can fully customize your interface.*

MessageBeep allows us to abandon old-fashioned beeps in favor of digitized sounds for system signals. Because of its limited capabilities, you wouldn't want to use it as a multimedia presentation function. However, when you build your multimedia apps, you could use message beeps for system signals, just as you would with other types of applications. The system sounds variables are there to ensure that all Windows apps produce the same message beeps, whether those are the default sounds, or sounds installed by the user.

MCI Play I: Playing WAV Files with sndPlaySound

This second sound project allows you to play any WAV file using the **sndPlaySound** function. You can refer to Table 4.3 when assembling this project.

1. Add an Edit control, **Name**d "Command_string_text", and its Label, **Caption**ed "Command String", to **Form1**. Be sure to blank out the default **Text**.

2. Add another Edit control, **Name**d "Error_text", and its Label, **Caption**ed "Error", to **Form1**. Blank out its **Text**.

3. Add a second Button, named **Play_sound_button**, to **Form1**, and set its **Caption** to "snd&PlaySound". Add code for the **Play_sound_buttonClick** event (Listing 4.7). This will call **sndPlaySound**, declared in Delphi's unit **MMSystem**, so we'll need add a **uses** clause, too.

Introducing the Windows 95 Multimedia System 225

> *This project, MCIPlay1.DPR, and all of its support files, can be found on the accompanying CD ROM in the directory \Programs\Chap04\MCIPlay1.*

Running the Updated MCIPlay I Project

To test **sndPlaySound**, run the program (after updating it, as described below) and type the name of a WAV file, including its path, into the "Command String" Edit control that appears at the top of the form. Then, click on the **snd<u>P</u>laySound** Button. Figure 4.3 shows an example of the program as it is running.

You can also enter the name of a system sound, such as "SystemAsterisk" or "SystemExit." **sndPlaySound** first searches the sounds section of the Registry and WIN.INI for a matching string. If it doesn't find one, it looks in the disk directory. If it still doesn't find a match, it plays the "SystemDefault" sound.

The only way we have found to produce a return value of **false** is to disable the device driver for the sound card. **sndPlaySound** is remarkably robust, which makes it handy for simple sound playback applications.

Table 4.3 Properties for the MCI Play I project.

Class	Property	Value
TForm	Name	Form1 (default)
	Caption	'MCI Play I'
TButton	Name	Message_beep_button
	Caption	'Message&Beep'
	OnClick	Message_beep_buttonClick
TEdit	Name	Command_string_text
	Text	<blank>
TLabel	Name	Label1 (default)
	Caption	'Command String'
TEdit	Name	Error_text
	Text	<blank>
TLabel	Name	Label2 (default)
	Caption	'Error'
TButton	Name	Play_sound_button
	Caption	'snd&PlaySound'
	OnClick	Play_sound_buttonClick

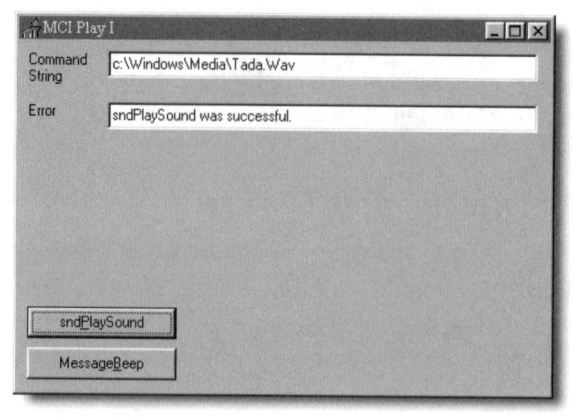

Figure 4.3 *The sndPlaySound function in action.*

By the way, all of the high-level MCI functions will play system sounds. We won't bother to explore that option further, but it's there if you need it.

Expanding the MCIPlay I Project

Instead of creating a whole new project, we'll just add some controls to **Form1**, and a little code to unit **Main** from the previous project. The short section of code revolves around the **sndPlaySound** function, which resides in Delphi's **MMSystem** unit.

For the first parameter to **sndPlaySound**, we pass a pchar-based string that contains either a filename or the name of a system sound. The second parameter is a combination of various *flags*.

Many of the Windows API functions take **flag** parameters. These parameters are also an integral component of *windows messages*. In decimal terms, the value of each flag is a factor of two. The first flag has a decimal value of 1 (2 raised to the power of 0), the second flag has a decimal value of 2, the third has a value of 4, and so on. So each flag value represents one bit in the two byte integer. An **integer** flag block can therefore hold up to 32 flags simultaneously (occasionally, **flag** parameters are declared as **smallint**s, familiar to "old-timers" as 8 and 16-bit platform **integer**s, which are 16 bits long, and thus, hold 16 flags). To set multiple flags, just add their values together, or better yet, combine them with a logical **or** operation.

The declaration of **sndPlaySound** and the six flags that it supports come along from the unit **MMSystem**: We won't go into the details of the declaration, but this is what the constants look like:

```
{ flag values for wFlags parameter }
const
    SND_SYNC       = $0000;   { play synchronously (default) }
    SND_ASYNC      = $0001;   { play asynchronously }
    SND_NODEFAULT  = $0002;   { don't use default sound }
    SND_MEMORY     = $0004;   { lpszSoundName points to a memory file }
    SND_LOOP       = $0008;   { loop the sound until next sndPlaySound }
    SND_NOSTOP     = $0010;   { don't stop any currently playing sound }
```

For now, we'll only use the first two **SND** flags. **SND_SYNC** causes the system to play a WAV file *synchronously*. This means that a program will stand at attention until **sndPlaySound** has finished playing the sound. Since **SND_SYNC** has a 0 value, it actually represents the absence of a flag. It also represents the default behavior of the function. **SND_ASYNC** causes **sndPlaySound** to return control to a program immediately after starting playback, even as the WAV file continues to play *asynchronously* in the background. If **sndPlaySound** succeeds, it returns **true**; otherwise, it returns **false**.

To demonstrate this function, we'll add three more controls to MCIPlay: a Button named **Play_sound_button**, and two Edit controls, **Command_string_text** and **Error_text**, which are shown in Figure 4.4. Let's also label the Edit controls and clear their initial **Text** properties.

In the **Play_sound_buttonClick** event procedure, we'll use the **Command_string_text.Text** as the user's input sound name. We'll then interpret the result of the play operation and display a message in **Error_text** to indicate success or failure. The new version of this event is shown in Listing 4.4.

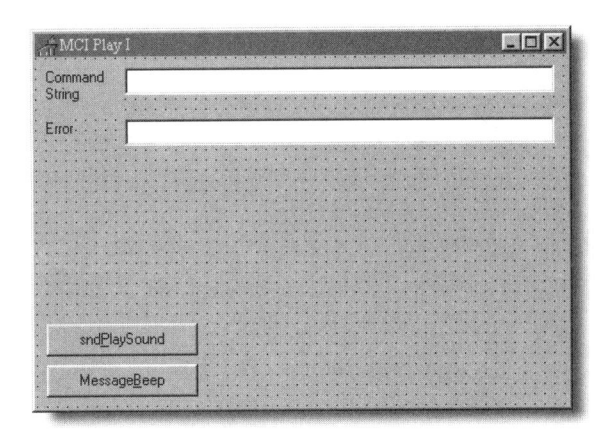

Figure 4.4 Form layout for the simple sounds project.

Listing 4.4   Play_sound_buttonClick Event Procedure from unit *Main.Pas*

```
unit Main;

interface

uses
  SysUtils, Windows, Messages, Classes, Graphics, Controls, Forms, Dialogs,
  StdCtrls;

type
  TForm1 = class(TForm)
    Message_beep_button: TButton;
    Play_sound_button: TButton;
    Label1: TLabel;
    Label2: TLabel;
    Command_string_text: TEdit;
    Error_text: TEdit;
    procedure Message_beep_buttonClick(Sender: TObject);
    procedure Play_sound_buttonClick(Sender: TObject);
  private
    { Private declarations }
  public
    { Public declarations }
  end;

var
  Form1: TForm1;

implementation

    uses
        MMSystem;

{$R *.DFM}

procedure TForm1.Message_beep_buttonClick(Sender: TObject);
begin
    MessageBeep(MB_ICONEXCLAMATION);
    end;

procedure TForm1.Play_sound_buttonClick(Sender: TObject);
begin
    if sndPlaySound(pchar(Command_string_text.Text),SND_ASYNC) then
        Error_text.Text := 'sndPlaySound was successful.'
      else
        Error_text.Text := 'sndPlaySound failed.';
    end;

end.
```

In the next chapter, we'll add four more buttons to this program to demonstrate some of the other ways to play sound.

Scratching the Surface

We've looked at two Windows Multimedia System API calls: **mciExecute** and **sndPlaySound**. Before we go too much further, let's take a look at where these come from. Twice, we've included the declaration **uses MMSystem;** so that's a good place to start. Let's look at Borland's source code, shown in Listing 4.5, wherein these routines are declared so that we may use them.

Listing 4.5 Declarations of **mciExecute** and **sndPlaySound** from Borland's *MMSystem.Pas*

```
unit MMSystem

    interface
        :
        function sndPlaySound(lpszSoundName: PChar; uFlags: UINT): BOOL;
stdcall;
        :
        function mciExecute(pszCommand: LPCSTR): BOOL; stdcall;
        :
    const
        :
        mmsyst = 'winmm.dll';

    implementation
        :
        function mciExecute; external mmsyst name 'mciExecute';
        :
        function sndPlaySound; external mmsyst name 'sndPlaySoundA';
        :
    end.
```

Ahh. The secrets, exposed. You don't really have to rely on Borland's declarations, at all, since you could easily write your own. But, for the thousands of documented calls, wouldn't it be simpler just to use the declarations that ship with Delphi? The structure of the true declaration, in the implementation, is simple: declare the routine (on which they have abbreviated the parameter list, since they declared the parameters in the interface section), and then tell the compiler that it's an external routine, living in a DLL (specified by **mmsyst**, which points to *WinMM.DLL*), and what the routine is called inside the DLL.

Try this: Open a new project, and view the project source. Remove **Unit1**. Gut **Project1**, and make it read:

```
program PlayIt;

    uses
        Forms;

    function Play(P : pchar; F : integer) : integer;
      stdcall; external 'WinMM.DLL' name 'sndPlaySoundA';

begin
    Play('c:\Windows\Media\Tada.Wav',0);
    end.
```

> *This project, PlayIt.DPR, can be found on the accompanying CD-ROM in the directory \Programs\Chap04\PlayIt.*

Save it as *PlayIt.DPR*. This is a quite-minimal Delphi program, and thus exhibits some strange behavior when run in the Integrated Development Environment. So, choose *Project | Build All* from the Delphi menu bar, to produce the executable. Run the program by double clicking it after finding it with the Windows 95 *Explorer*.

All we've done is recreate the declaration that Delphi itself uses. That's all there is to it. In the next chapter, we'll investigate the Windows Multimedia System in much greater depth, and show you how to work with Delphi to gain powerful control over the smallest facets of the System.

Chapter 5

It's time for us to get under the hood and take an in-depth look at the Windows 95 Media Control Interface.

Inside the Windows Multimedia System

Dan Haygood

The Windows Media Control Interface, or MCI, provides a common interface to a variety of multimedia devices, including *Audio Video Interleave* (AVI) playback, animation players, VCRs, video disk players, CD players, and the wave audio and synthesizer systems on our sound cards. Continuing on from where we ended in Chapter 4, we'll show you how to play WAV and MIDI files using MCI functions. Then we'll move down to the basement to show you how to use low-level audio functions.

Using the MCI

With the MCI functions, we can send commands—such as start, stop, and pause—to any of these devices, as if we were pushing a button on the front panel of a VCR or CD player. The particular commands available for each device depend on the capabilities of the device itself. For example, a wave audio device can record, but a CD player can only play. To send MCI commands to multimedia devices, we pass them as arguments to any of three MCI command functions. Along with the command functions, the MCI includes two support functions.

All MCI function names begin with the prefix *mci* and are arranged in three short groups:

- Command-Message Interface
  mciSendCommand
  mciGetDeviceID
- Command-String Interface
  mciSendString
  mciExecute
- Command-String *and* Command-Message Interfaces
  mciGetErrorString
  mciSetYieldProc

The extra function, **mciSetYieldProc**, enables the MCI to carry on a dialog with your application when you issue an MCI command with the **WAIT** flag. The **WAIT** flag instructs the MCI not to return control to the program until the current operation is complete. For example, if you instruct the MCI to play a several-minute-long MIDI music sequencer file and issue the command with the **WAIT** flag, the MCI will freeze your program until the entire sequence has played. However, if you do not include the **WAIT** flag in your command, the MCI will immediately return control to your program and play the MIDI file in the background. Both methods have their uses. **mciSetYieldProc** enables a program to track the progress of a command executed with the **WAIT** flag. Although it's not too difficult to take advantage of this feature; by coding your own "yielded-to procedure", and passing the address to the multimedia system with **mciSetYieldProc**, we can do everything we want to without resorting to this relatively complex low level of control.

The two high-level command interfaces, *Command-Message* and *Command-String*, both perform the same functions. They send commands to the multimedia system, instructing it to play WAV files, MIDI files, and so on, thereby executing operations similar to those you would perform with the remote control on your home entertainment system. Recall that the difference between these two interfaces is mainly the difference between words and numbers. You've already seen one of the easiest ways to play a wave audio file—**mciExecute**. For the sake of completeness, we've added a demonstration function for **mciExecute**. We won't bother to make this a separate project,

Inside the Windows Multimedia System

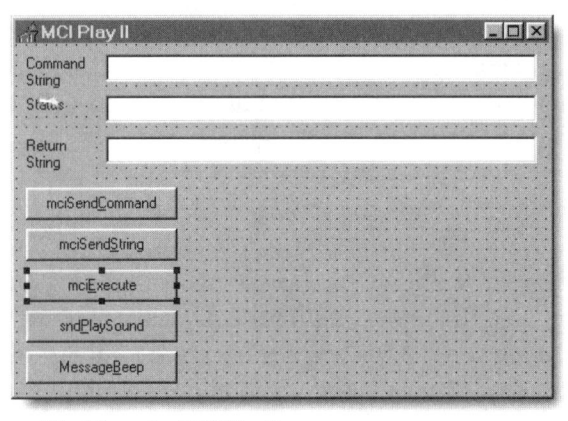

Figure 5.1 *The modified form for **MCIPlay2**.*

but you can easily test it out with the button **Execute_button** we added to **Form1**, with code in *Main.Pas*. Figure 5.1 shows the modified form for **MCIPlay2**; Listing 5.1 shows the code.

Listing 5.1   Execute_buttonClick Event Procedure from *Main.Pas*

```
procedure TForm1.Execute_buttonClick(Sender: TObject);
begin
    if mciExecute(pchar(Command_string_text.Text)) then
       Status_text.Text := 'mciExecute was successful.'
     else
       Status_text.Text := 'mciExecute failed.';
    end;
```

Making WAVes with mciSendString and mciSendCommand

Let's scoot down the ladder another rung and explore **mciSendString** and **mciSendCommand**. These functions are useful for playing WAV files. Since **mciSendString** is the simplest, we'll start with it first.

Delphi's declaration (known in Windows SDK C circles as its *prototype*) of **mciSendString**, found in Delphi's **MMSystem** unit, looks like this:

```
function mciSendString(
  lpstrCommand,
  lpstrReturnString : PChar;
  uReturnLength     : UINT;
  hWndCallback      : HWND
  ): MCIERROR;
    stdcall;
```

The identifiers look a little cryptic; we'll examine them later. There's only one real mystery: **stdcall**. This keyword simply instructs the Delphi compiler to use the ordinary Pascal calling convention when calling this routine; that is, to use the **standard calling** mechanism. This is necessary because Delphi 2.0 introduces some very fast and new calling conventions that are so specialized they are incompatible with Windows API calls. (For those of you coming in late, or without all of the prerequisites, a "calling convention" is a specification of the location in which particular pieces of data will be stored and what machine language should be used when calling a subroutine.)

To confound matters, we have to show you a couple of other versions of this same function. The first is a Delphi redeclaration that explicitly supports its new *ANSI character* type, **ANSIChar**. These are familiar to us as the characters we use every day—simple 8-bit characters. We might as well use **char**, except **ANSIChar** distinguishes 8-bit characters from *Unicode* characters, for which Delphi uses the built-in type **WideChar**. Unicode characters are 16-bit characters which can be used to represent characters in languages with more than 256 unique characters. For example, Japanese is represented by two competing printable character sets, Kanji, with 5700 characters (actually, pictographs, but to us, Unicode characters), and Katakana, with 19,000 characters.

```
function mciSendStringA(
  lpstrCommand,
  lpstrReturnString : PAnsiChar;
  uReturnLength     : UINT;
  hWndCallback      : HWND
  ): MCIERROR;
    stdcall;

function mciSendStringW(
  lpstrCommand,
  lpstrReturnString : PWideChar;
  uReturnLength     : UINT;
  hWndCallback      : HWND
  ): MCIERROR;
    stdcall;
```

Each of these functions takes a pointer to a null-terminated string (however it's represented), and gives it to the multimedia system for processing. We'll look at the parameters more closely in just a moment

We can also play WAV files with **mciSendCommand**. Like **mciSendString**, it comes in an **ANSI** and **Wide** version—but the declarations are identical. Let's take a look at the simple declaration:

```
function mciSendCommand(
  mciId   : MCIDEVICEID;
  uMessage : UINT;
```

```
  dwParam1,
  dwParam2 : DWORD
): MCIERROR;
   stdcall;
```

We could redeclare this function more clearly by naming the third and fourth parameters more descriptively than they are put forth in the Multimedia Development Kit (MDK) documentation:

```
function mciSendCommand(
  mciId               : MCIDEVICEID;
  uMessage            : UINT;
  dwFlags,
  dwCommandParameters : DWORD
): MCIERROR;
   stdcall;
```

(Although we'll never actually use this re-declaration, it will aid in learning how this function works.)

Here, an MCI message, specified by **uMessage**, requires a group of parameters, which we've temporarily named **dwCommandParameters.** We deliver these parameters by wrapping them in a **record** structure and passing that structure by reference. We can accomplish this by passing a pointer to our structure. The pointer is, more generically, four bytes, or a *double-word*, which explains the "dw" prefix. That's how the folks at Microsoft managed to consolidate all the myriad MCI operations into a single interface function. Otherwise, a separate function would be necessary for each operation, each with its own parameter list. Instead of all those functions with separate parameter lists, we call a single function and tell it where to find its parameters.

MCI Play II : Playing MIDI Files with mciSendString

In this second version of the *MCI Play* project, we'll add Buttons that call both **mciSendString** and **mciSendCommand**. Playing a WAV file with the MCI command strings requires these steps:

1. We're going on to version two, so let's make a new project directory, *MCIPlay2*, and an output subdirectory beneath this, *Bin*. With the *Explorer*, copy the project files from your *MCIPlay1* directory to your *MCIPlay2* directory. Rename your "MCIPlay1" files to "MCIPlay2". You'll need the *DPR, PAS*, and *DFM* files.

2. Open your **MCIPlay2** Project file in Delphi. The compiler will complain that its name is wrong ("Module header is missing or incorrect."). Change its program name from **MCIPlay1** to **MCIPlay2**. In the *Project Options* dialog box (from *Project | Options*), set the Application Title to "MCI Play II", and its output directory to "Bin".
3. View **Form1** from unit **Main**. In the *Object Inspector*, change its **Caption** from "MCI Play I" to "MCI Play II".
4. Now that that's out of the way, add the **mciExecute** demonstration Button to **Form1**, as we discussed above. **Name** it "Execute_button", **Caption** it "mci&Execute", and add the **OnClick** handler **Execute_buttonClick** (Listing 5.1, above).
5. Add another Button to **Form1**, **Name**d "SendString_button", an Edit box to catch the result when its **OnClick** handler calls **mciSendString** (Listing 5.2), and a Label for the Edit box. The properties are listed in Table 5.1.

Starting with this version, we're going to adopt a better naming convention for our Buttons. Whereas we had declared the button that calls **mciPlaySound** "Play_sound_button", from now on we'll try to echo the exact name of the function to be called in the **Name** of our button. Thus, the button that calls **mciSendString** is named "SendString_button", *without* the underscore that might separate "Send" and "String" if we were to continue as we had. One of the natural processes of software development is discovering techniques that work a little better than what you had used before; even little things, like the placement of underscores in variable names, can be improved upon. We aren't going to go back and fix what we've already done in this small project, but we'll try and keep the reasoning behind it stored in our minds for later use.

This project, MCIPlay2.DPR, and all of its support files, can be found on the accompanying CD-ROM in the directory \PROGRAMS\CHAP05\MCIPLAY2. The Project there includes yet another button that we'll be adding later.

Table 5.1 Properties for the MCI Play II project.

Class	Property	Value
TForm	Name	Form1 (default)
	Caption	'MCI Play II'
TButton	Name	Message_beep_button
	Caption	'Message&Beep'
	OnClick	Message_beep_buttonClick
TEdit	Name	Command_string_text
	Text	<blank>
TLabel	Name	Label1 (default)
	Caption	'Command String'
TEdit	Name	Error_text
	Text	<blank>
TLabel	Name	Label2 (default)
	Caption	'Error'
TButton	Name	Play_sound_button
	Caption	'snd&PlaySound'
	OnClick	Play_sound_buttonClick
TButton	Name	Execute_button
	Caption	'mci&Execute'
	OnClick	Execute_buttonClick
TLabel	Name	Label3 (default)
	Caption	'Return String'
TEdit	Name	Return_string_text
	Text	<blank>
TButton	Name	SendString_button
	Caption	'mci&SendString'
	OnClick	SendString_buttonClick

Creating the MCIPlay2 Project

In the sample project **MCIPlay2**, we begin where we left off with **MCIPlay1** in Chapter 4. If you are creating this project yourself, you'll find it helpful to copy the files from the previous project before you begin. You can go ahead and add the **Execute_button** we talked about above. If you prefer not to take that step, it's not critical.

Add a new Edit control, and set its **Name** property to **Return_string_text**, and blank out its **Text**. Add a Label for the Edit box, and set its **Caption** to "Return String". Next, drop in another Button, set its **Name** property to **SendString_button**, and set its **Caption** property to "mciSend&String". Finally, we'll add some code for the **OnClick** event of the **SendString_button**. The new version of MCIPlay is shown in Figure 5.2.

You *could* play sounds by simply inserting the following trial version of the **SendString_buttonClick** event:

```
procedure TForm1.SendString_buttonClick(Sender: TObject);
begin
   mciSendString('play c:\Windows\Media\Canyon.MID', nil, 0, 0);
   end;
```

This minimalistic procedure illustrates how little code needs to be written to exercise the Command-String Interface, but it also ignores some useful (and essential) features. Unlike **mciExecute**, **mciSendString** doesn't benefit from the built-in error trapping dialog boxes. When a command fails, you will receive no feedback unless you collect the error code returned by the function and act upon it.

In addition to error codes, the Command-String Interface can also return information about an MCI device, which it does by setting the null-terminated string pointed to by **lpstrRtnString**. This opens the door to a variety of new capabilities not available with **mciExecute**. To add error checking support, we'll use the version of **SendString_buttonClick** shown in Listing 5.2.

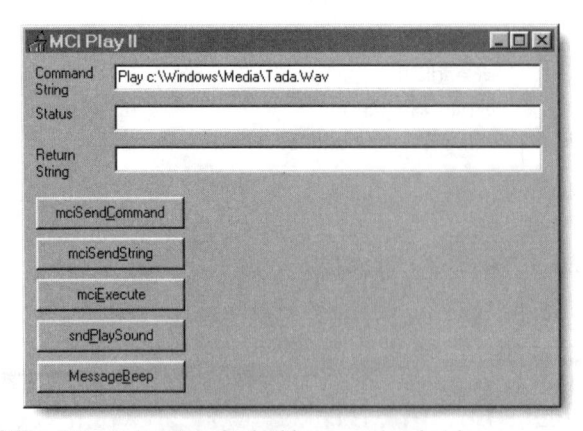

Figure 5.2   MCIPlay2 loaded and cocked with a command string.

Listing 5.2 SendString_buttonClick Event Procedure from *Main.Pas*

```
procedure TForm1.SendString_buttonClick(Sender: TObject);
const
   lnReturn_string = 511;
   lnError_string  = 255;
var
   Return_string : array[0..lnReturn_string] of char;
   Error_string  : array[0..lnError_string]  of char;
   MCI_error     : integer;
   Dummy         : boolean;
begin
   (* mciSendString('play c:\Windows\Media\Canyon.MID', nil, 0, 0); *)
   Status_text.Text := ''; { Blank previous message immediately. }
   MCI_error := mciSendString(pchar(Command_string_text.Text),
      Return_string, lnReturn_string,
      0 { No callback window. }
      );
   Dummy := mciGetErrorString(MCI_error,
            Error_string, lnError_string
            );
   Status_text.Text := Error_string;
   Return_string_text.Text := Return_string;
   end;
```

Notice that neither the **Play** command nor the target filename appear in this procedure because we have not hard coded them. That way the filename and action can be easily entered and changed while running the program.

To play a WAV file, type the entire command into the Edit box labeled "Command String", then click on the **mciSendString** button, as shown in Figure 5.3. To actually see the benefits of capturing the return string and the error text, you might want to start with the command "**Play c:\Windows\Media\Canyon.MID**",

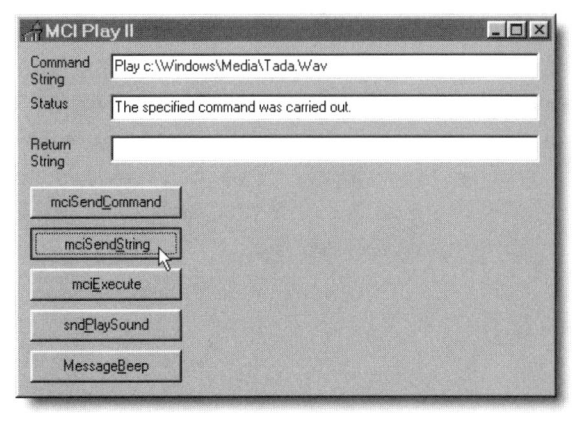

Figure 5.3 The **mciSendString** function in action.

and then mis-type the filename or the word "Play". This will set the **Error_string**. You'll need to read on, though, to find commands that will set the **Return_string**—"Play" won't do it.

A Closer Look at mciSendString and mciGetErrorString

A closer inspection of Listing 5.2 shows that **mciSendString** takes four parameters. This first parameter is a string that tells the MCI what to do. The second parameter supplies the memory address of a buffer through which the MCI can return a message. The third parameter specifies the length of the return buffer. The MCI uses this information to determine the length of the message that it can return. Finally, the fourth parameter sets up a *callback* function (we'll explain this a little later).

If you look at the names of the first and second parameters, **lpstrCommand** and **lpstrRtnString**, you'll notice that their prefixes identify them as long pointers (lp) to strings (str). When we pass strings from Delphi to API functions, we normally pass them as **pchar**s. If the string we are passing is declared as a **pchar**, and we have allocated space for it (with **strNew** or **strAlloc**, for example), we can simply pass the **pchar**. Delphi performs a convenient *automatic type conversion* for us. If we declare the string as an **array[0..*length*] of char**, it will automatically treat our variable as a **pchar** when needed. With this syntax, we have the added benefit that the length is the true length of the longest string we can store, and the zero element serves to make room for one extra byte for our null terminator. If you are taking advantage of string fields from the VCL, or declare your own **ANSIString**s, Delphi will perform a puff of magic for you if you cast the **ANSIString** to a **pchar** as we have done throughout **MCIPlay**: Delphi will send a pointer to the **ANSIString**'s null-terminated character data instead of the beginning of the real **ANSIString** itself. Although the mechanics of this are outside the scope of this chapter, it's a nifty feature that comes in very handy. Finally, having your string declared as a **shortString** could spell trouble: **ShortString**s are not null-terminated, so you must either carefully insert a null after the last valid character in the string, if there is room, and pass a pointer to the first character (not the length byte!) of the string. The other fix is to use **strPCopy** to copy your **shortString** to a **pchar** or assign it to an **ANSIString**.

> ### Different String Types
> A string, from the very genesis of Borland's Turbo Pascal, has always been a structure consisting of a length byte, followed by up to 255 character bytes. With Delphi 2.0 comes the advent of more string and character

> types than the average programmer can shake a stick at, and this kind of string has therefore been specifically named "**shortString**".
>
> The most significant (and somewhat frightening) change is that the programmer can now set a compiler option to indicate whether the identifier "string" refers to the age-old **shortString** or the new-fangled **ANSIString**. Which means that you "experienced coders" may be declaring **ANSIString**s without even realizing it. The most remarkable thing about this situation is that all of these string types work together almost identically and flawlessly with automatic type conversions.

Many MCI commands produce return strings containing such information as track lengths, numbers of tracks, and device mode. The **Play** command, however, does not produce a return string. So, rather than provide a useless buffer, we can tell the API function that no buffer exists. We do this by sending it **nil** in place of a valid pointer. We haven't taken this step here; we really need to explain the mechanism that **mciSendString** uses to set the return string (and that **mciGetErrorString** uses to set the error string).

In Chapter 16, you'll see how we can use the **lpstrRtnString** parameter to retrieve status and position information from MCI devices. When we do need **lpstrRtnString**, we pass it a valid pointer to a null-terminated string, as described above. Remember, the string space must be pre-allocated—the Windows API won't automatically make room for its own return values, because it can't be sure that you'll responsibly dispose of the space it might allocate. When **mciSendString** fills in a return string, it starts with the first byte pointed to by the string reference, then continues filling as many subsequent bytes as it needs to hold the entire string, stopping only when it has copied the number of characters specified by **uReturnLength**. Finally, it puts out the final null. If you were counting, that's a total of **uReturnLength + 1** bytes written. If we were to pass a pointer to a buffer shorter than **uReturnLength**, **mciSendString** would write into memory not allocated to the string, quite possibly overwriting some other crucial data. By declaring and passing a fixed-length array of characters, we simplify the task of telling **mciSendString** how long a return string it can write.

We're now ready to get back to the last parameter of **mciSendString**. It performs a function, known as a *callback*. Although this is available to us with Delphi (but not in less powerful programming environments, such as Microsoft's *Visual Basic 3*), it does introduce a level of complexity we'll want to avoid. However, many API functions perform callbacks. A callback is a means by which an API function can notify a program that it has completed an operation. Callbacks work in one of two ways: They either call an independent function written by the programmer to service the callback; or, like **mciSendString**, they send a message to a window, which must contain event handler code to service the callback message. In the latter case, the callback works just like any other Windows event, except that instead of responding to an action performed by the user—like a mouse click or a resize event—the program responds to an action requested by an API function. These are issues you'll want to tackle only when you've decided you must have that functionality. For now, we'll just tell **mciSendString** not to send a notification message by passing a zero value as the callback handle. Actually, it wouldn't even send the **MM_MCINOTIFY** message unless we changed the command string to:

```
"play c:\windows\media\canyon.mid notify"
```

Along with **mciSendString**, we've slipped in another new function, **mciGetErrorString**. Take a look at its declaration (Again, notice the *A*NSI and *W*ide string versions.):

```
function mciGetErrorString(
  mcierr  : MCIERROR;
  pszText : PChar;
  uLength : UINT
  ): BOOL;
    stdcall;
```

In the first parameter, we pass the error code returned by **mciSendString** (or by **mciSendCommand**, as you'll soon see). The second and third parameters once again define a buffer for a return string and its length, respectively. The return value of **mciGetErrorString** is—believe it or not—an error code. After all, we could feed it an invalid error code to begin with, which would be an error (error trapping can become very convoluted).

MCI Play II: Playing WAV Files with mciSendCommand

One more Button, and we are finished with the high-level MCI.

- Add yet another Button, **Named** "**SendCommand_button**". Set its **Caption** to "mciSend&Command". Add the code for the **SendCommand_buttonClick** event procedure (Listing 5.4).

Table 5.2 One more Button for the MCI Play II project.

Class	Property	Value
TButton	Name	SendCommand_button
	Caption	'mci&SendString'
	OnClick	SendCommand_buttonClick

> This project, MCIPlay2.DPR, and all of its support files, can be found on the accompanying CD-ROM in the directory \PROGRAMS\CHAP05\MCIPLAY2.

Expanding the MCIPlay2 Project

To play a WAV file using the **mciSendCommand**, we need to add another Button. First, we'll examine the record types that will hold the parameters for the commands we'll be sending, as presented in Listing 5.3.

Listing 5.3 Data Structures Needed to Play a WAV File with the MCI Command-Message Interface, Declared in *MMSystem.Pas*

```
{ parameter block for MCI_OPEN command message }

type
    PMCI_Wave_Open_ParmsA = ^TMCI_Wave_Open_ParmsA;
    PMCI_Wave_Open_ParmsW = ^TMCI_Wave_Open_ParmsW;
    PMCI_Wave_Open_Parms  = PMCI_Wave_Open_ParmsA;

    TMCI_Wave_Open_ParmsA = record
        dwCallback       : DWORD;
        wDeviceID        : MCIDEVICEID;
        lpstrDeviceType  : PAnsiChar;
        lpstrElementName : PAnsiChar;
        lpstrAlias       : PAnsiChar;
        dwBufferSeconds  : DWORD;
    end;

    TMCI_Wave_Open_ParmsW = record
        dwCallback       : DWORD;
        wDeviceID        : MCIDEVICEID;
        lpstrDeviceType  : PWideChar;
        lpstrElementName : PWideChar;
        lpstrAlias       : PWideChar;
        dwBufferSeconds  : DWORD;
    end;

    TMCI_Wave_Open_Parms = TMCI_Wave_Open_ParmsA;
```

```
{ parameter block for MCI_PLAY command message }

type
    PMCI_Play_Parms = ^TMCI_Play_Parms;
    TMCI_Play_Parms = record
        dwCallback : DWORD;
        dwFrom     : DWORD;
        dwTo       : DWORD;
        end;
```

The **Play** message in the Command-Message Interface does not perform implied open and close operations. To play a WAV file, we will need to issue three command messages: open, play, and close. Two of these, open and play, take the parameter blocks shown above. Although you can see the detritus of the Wide characters, we won't really need them. Interestingly enough, the simple forms we'll be using are actually just redeclarations of the ANSI character types.

TMCI_Wave_Open_Parms is just a slightly extended version of the more generic structure **TMCI_Open_Parms**, which lacks the field **dwBufferSeconds**. If you do not wish to specify a buffer length, you can use **TMCI_Open_Parms**. **TMCI_Play_Parms** holds the parameters for the play command, although we won't use any of them in this example.

The next step involves adding the **SendCommand_buttonClick** event procedure code in Listing 5.4.

Listing 5.4   The **SendCommand_buttonClick** Event Procedure from *Main.Pas*

```
procedure TForm1.SendCommand_buttonClick(Sender: TObject);
const
    lnError_string = 255;
var
    Error_string : array[0..lnError_string] of char;
    Open_params  : TMCI_Wave_Open_Parms;
    Play_params  : TMCI_Play_Parms;
    MCI_error    : integer;
begin
    Status_text.Text := ''; { Blank previous message immediately. }
    with Open_params do begin
        dwCallback       := 0;
        wDeviceID        := 0;
        lpstrDeviceType  := 'waveaudio';
        lpstrElementName := 'c:\Windows\RingIn.Wav';
        lpstrAlias       := nil;
        dwBufferSeconds  := 0;
        end;
    with Play_params do begin
        dwCallback := 0;   { No callback. }
        dwFrom     := 0;   { From beginning... }
```

```
            dwTo        := 0;   { ...to end. }
            end;

    MCI_error := mciSendCommand(
                    0, { No device yet. }
                    MCI_OPEN,
                    MCI_OPEN_TYPE or MCI_OPEN_ELEMENT,
                    DWORD(@Open_params)
                    );
    if MCI_error = 0 then
        MCI_error := mciSendCommand(
                        Open_params.wDeviceID, { Our device from Open. }
                        MCI_PLAY,
                        MCI_WAIT,
                        DWORD(@Play_params)
                        );
    mciSendCommand(Open_params.wDeviceID,MCI_CLOSE,0,DWORD(nil));

    mciGetErrorString(MCI_error,Error_string,lnError_string);
    Status_text.Text := Error_string;
    end;
```

This procedure, which is actually a complete little program except for declarations, uses several constants. Remember when we said that the difference between the Command-String Interface and the Command-Message Interface was largely the difference between words and numbers? This is what we meant. You'll find definitions of all of the capitalized constants in the Microsoft *Multimedia Programmer's Reference*, but not their values. For their numeric values, you'll have to look in the file *MMSystem.Pas* if you have the Delphi Run-time source, or track down their values with Delphi's Browser.

The first several lines of the **SendCommand_buttonClick** event procedure set the parameter values required by the **Open** command message. The first two are easy.

```
dwCallback      := 0;
wDeviceID       := 0;
```

We aren't going to handle callbacks, so we set the first field to 0. We don't know the **wDeviceID** yet; the MCI will assign one and return its value in the **wDeviceID** field when we execute the **Open** command.

Next, we tell the MCI that we're going to deal with a waveaudio file, as well as the name of that file.

```
lpstrDeviceType    := 'waveaudio';
lpstrElementName   := 'c:\Windows\RingIn.Wav';
```

We don't want to assign an alias to the device, and we don't need to specify a buffer length, so we set both of these parameters to 0.

```
lpstrAlias       := nil;
dwBufferSeconds  := 0;
```

Let's look at the flags that tell the Command-Message Interface how to interpret the information we'll be passing in the **TMCI_Wave_Open_Parms** structure when we call **mciSendCommand**:

```
MCI_OPEN_TYPE or MCI_OPEN_ELEMENT
```

Boolean operations like **or** can be misleading. Unlike a Boolean decision, such as those found in **if** statements and **while** loops, the **or** operator in this assignment statement performs a *bitwise* operation that actually combines the two flags. Let's look first at a trivial case.

Bits can carry one of two values, 0 or 1. Let's say we have two bits, A and B. If both A and B start out with 0 values, then the expression "A **or** B" returns 0. If either A or B, or both A and B are set to 1, then the expression "A **or** B" returns 1. Now let's expand that one step to two whole bytes full of bits.

```
A = 00000001
B = 00000010
```

When we **or** A and B, Delphi performs the **or** operation on each bit, comparing the first bit (or more correctly, the lowest-order bit, counting from right to left) of A with the first bit of B, then the second bit of A with the second bit of B, and so on. The result of "A **or** B" in this case will produce a byte with two bits set to 1:

```
A or B = 00000011
```

The flag parameter is a four-byte value. Each bit in the four bytes represents one flag, for a total of 32 possible flags. The flags we use are shown in Table 5.3.

By the way, these flags notify the MCI that we're supplying both the device type and the name of the file or *element* that we want it to play. We could actually omit the device type in the **MCI_PLAY** call to **mciSendCommandString** by passing a zero (instead of **Open_params.wDeviceID** as shown below) as the device. The MCI can determine the device type by looking up the file extension in the system registry.

Table 5.3 Flags Defined for the MCI_Open Command.

Flag	Hexadecimal	Binary Value
MCI_OPEN_TYPE	$00002000	00000000 00000000 00100000 00000000
MCI_OPEN_ELEMENT	$00000200	00000000 00000000 00000010 00000000
MCI_OPEN_TYPE or MCI_OPEN_ELEMENT	$00002200	00000000 00000000 00100010 00000000

Once we've set all our flags, pointers to strings, and other parameters, we can send the messages:

```
MCI_error := mciSendCommand(
               0, { No device yet. }
               MCI_OPEN,
               MCI_OPEN_TYPE or MCI_OPEN_ELEMENT,
               DWORD(@Open_params)
               );
if MCI_error = 0 then
    MCI_error := mciSendCommand(
               Open_params.wDeviceID, { Our device from Open. }
               MCI_PLAY,
               MCI_WAIT,
               DWORD(@Play_params)
               );
mciSendCommand(Open_params.wDeviceID,MCI_CLOSE,0,DWORD(nil));
```

The **MCI_WAIT** flag that accompanies the **MCI_PLAY** message instructs the MCI not to return control to our program until the play operation is complete. Without this flag, we can go on about our business while the WAV file plays in the background. However, when we send the **MCI_CLOSE** message, the MCI aborts the play operation. To play the WAV file *asynchronously,* we would need to find some other way to close the device upon completion. For this reason you might want to implement a callback routine—if you're doing a lot of asynchronous sound work.

In one way, we've taken a step backward by hard-coding the commands to play a WAV file. Unfortunately, because of the data structures required for its parameters, the Command-Message Interface doesn't easily adapt to a little exerciser function like the one we created for the Command-String Interface. However, if you've been learning about all of Delphi's string-handling, you might take a stab at setting up the **Open_params** to use the **Command_string_text.Text**.

For most multimedia applications that we're likely to write, the Command-Message Interface dwells in limbo between the simple, friendly Command-String Interface and the complex but truly powerful low-level functions that speak directly to the multimedia device drivers. Now you know how to use it. Relax. We won't need **mciSendCommand** for any of the other projects or exercises in *this* book.

Combing the Depths of the Low-Level Audio Functions

Clearly, the MCI functions that we've investigated do lots of work behind the scenes. Wave audio data resides in files, which contain not only the *digital sample* values, but also descriptive information that identifies the particular format of that audio data. To replay a WAV file, the multimedia system has to open the file, read and interpret its header information, load the audio data into memory, open the wave audio device, prepare the header, play the sound, unprepare the header, and close both the device and the file. Whew! That's a lot of work!

To accomplish all this, the MCI functions call upon the services of several low-level functions. To perform low-level replay of WAV files, we need to call about a dozen functions. These fall into two groups: functions that read *Resource Interchange File Format (RIFF)* files, and functions that manage wave audio playback.

Before you can even open the wave audio device, you have to know some things about the data you intend to send. WAV data comes in several formats, various combinations of sampling rate, multiple channels (mono or stereo), and different resolutions (number of bits per sample). We'll talk about WAV formats in greater detail in Chapter 14. For now, you only need to know that this information appears in a format block—known in RIFF terminology as a *chunk*—near the beginning of each WAV file.

The Mysteries of RIFF Files

As Figure 5.4 indicates, RIFF files are hierarchical structures—chunks contain chunks, which may again contain chunks.

The highest-level chunk is the RIFF chunk itself. Chunks carry labels, known officially as *chunk IDs*. If you peek at a WAV file with a file viewer, you'll see that the first four bytes literally contain the characters *R, I, F,* and *F*.

To read and write RIFF files, you use a standard data structure called **TMMCKInfo**, for "multimedia chunk information". Delphi uses declarations from its unit *MMSystem.Pas*:

```
{ RIFF chunk information data structure }
type
    TMMCKInfo = record
        ckid          : FOURCC;   { chunk ID }
```

```
cksize         : DWORD;   { chunk size }
fccType        : FOURCC;  { form type or list type }
dwDataOffset   : DWORD;   { offset of data portion of chunk }
dwFlags        : DWORD;   { flags used by MMIO functions }
end;
```

The first and third fields actually contain simple four-character, fixed-length strings.

```
type
    FOURCC = DWORD;   { a four character code }
```

This **FOURCC** substructure is just a convention created for C programmers who don't have such straightforward string operations. Delphi bends over

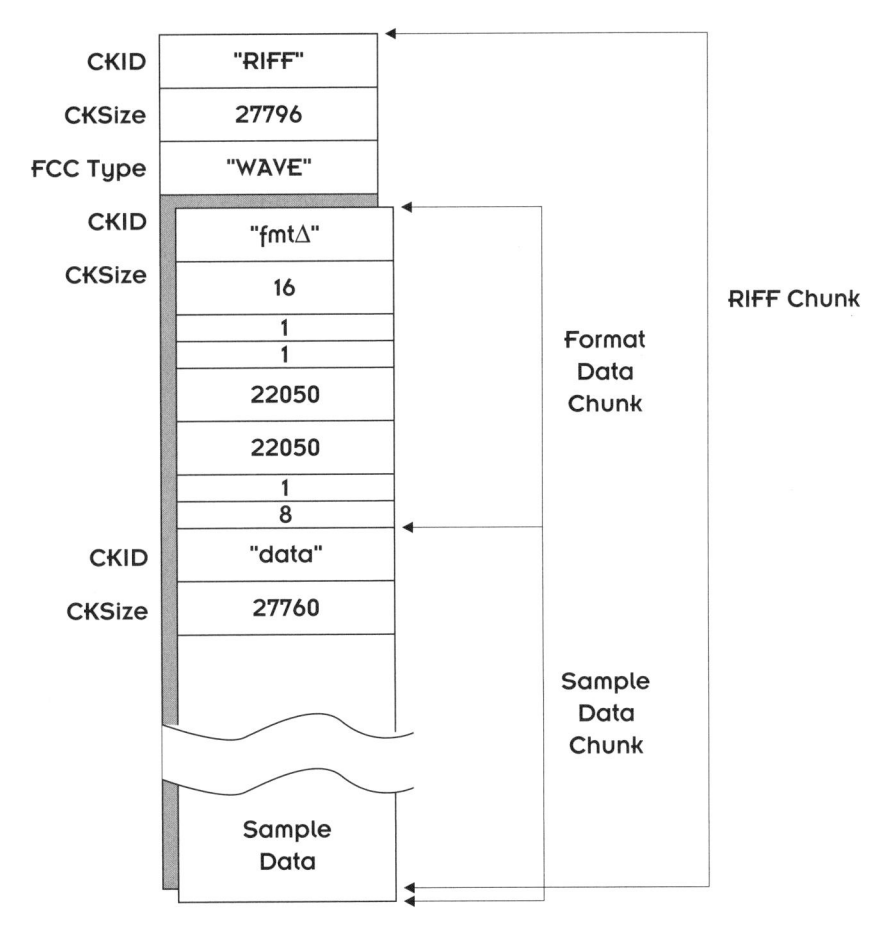

Figure 5.4 *The RIFF file structure.*

backwards respecting these C conventions and declares **FOURCC** as a **DWORD** (or double-word), which is in turn declared as an **integer**—which, on a 32-bit platform, is a 32-bit, or four-**byte**, and thus, four-**char** structure.

To keep you from becoming as confused as we were, let us state now that **TMMCKInfo** *does not define a data file record!* We use **TMMCKInfo** only to exchange information with the *multimedia file I/O functions*. Although chunks do adhere to a couple of well-defined structures, they vary in size; which means we can't just read them into, or write them from simple fixed-length record buffers.

All chunks start with at least two common fields: the *chunk ID* and the *chunk size*, which, coincidentally, correspond to the first two fields of **TMMCKInfo**. When we use the low-level multimedia function **mmioDescend** to read a chunk, we will pass it the address of a structure of type **TMMCKInfo**, which it will then fill with the appropriate values. This is an important distinction. When we read records from a fixed-length data file with Delphi, we often use the **read** statement. In this case, **Read** usually takes two arguments: the file, and the variable into which we want the data copied. To read a record that contains multiple fields, we can define a **record** in our program's **type** section, declare a variable of that type, then **read** a record of the same structure from the disk file. If **TMMCKInfo** were a file record type—which it is not—we could do something like this:

```
var
    The_chunk : TMMCKInfo;
    The_file  : file of TMMCKInfo;
:
read(The_file, The_chunk);   { Don't even think about doing this! }
```

Don't do it! It won't work.

A RIFF file doesn't contain a series of records of uniform structure—chunks vary in size. The only efficient way to read a RIFF file is to walk through it in the prescribed manner, using the **mmio** (multimedia I/O) functions.

To navigate a RIFF file, you use the functions **mmioDescend** and **mmioAscend**. These functions are used to position the file pointer in a chunk. Depending on what type of chunk you want to find, you set either the chunk ID (**ckid**) or the form type (**fccType**), set a search flag and call **mmioDescend**. This function will locate the next chunk in the file with the **ckid** or **fccType** you have specified. If you want the next chunk in line, you can descend without specifying the **ckid** or the **fccType**, and the descent function will fill in those fields with the four-character codes it finds in the next chunk.

The WAV File Structure

To better understand how WAV files are accessed, let's look at a sample file. Table 5.4 shows a breakdown of the WAV file *Tada.Wav* from 16-bit Windows.

At the very minimum, a WAV file contains three chunks. The **RIFF** chunk is the largest container. The whole WAV file is actually a **RIFF** chunk. The **ckSize,** which appears immediately after the **RIFF ckid**, contains a value equal to the file size minus eight bytes—the eight bytes is required to store the **RIFF** chunk's own **ckid** and **ckSize**. The second and third chunks, known as *subchunks*, are contained within the **RIFF** chunk. The first of these, the **fmt** chunk, contains the information necessary to fill in a **PCMWAVEFORMAT** structure. The second subchunk, the **data** chunk—by far the largest portion of the file—immediately follows the **fmt** subchunk, and contains all the digital waveform data. The end of the **data** subchunk corresponds to the end of the RIFF chunk. The **ckSize** of the RIFF chunk equals the total number of bytes occupied by the **fmt** and **data** subchunks.

Table 5.4 The Structure of a Sample WAV File.

Position Hex	Dec	Size in Bytes	Contents	Comments
0000	0	4	"RIFF"	Each byte contains one character, ckId
0004	4	4	27796	Equals the file size minus eight bytes, ckSize
0008	8	4	"WAVE"	fccType
000C	12	4	"fmt "	Next ckID; notice the blank, must be four characters
0010	16	4	16	The WAV format chunk is 16 bytes, ckSize
0014	20	2	1	1 indicates a PCM WAV format, wFormatTag
0016	22	2	1	Number of channels, nChannels
0018	24	4	22050	Sampling rate, nSamplesPerSec
001C	28	4	22050	nAvgBytesPerSec
0020	32	2	1	Effectively bytes per sample, nBlockAlign
0022	34	2	8	wBitsPerSample
0024	36	4	"data"	Next ckID; this chunk contains the wave data itself
0028	40	4	27760	Next ckID; size of wave data
002C	44	Depends on Data		The digitized audio data

To make matters worse, RIFF files may contain another type of chunk called a **LIST** chunk. **LIST** chunks hold additional information, such as copyright notices and other data that describes the content of the main **data** chunk or chunks. At this point, it won't help us to discuss **LIST** chunks; very few WAV files have any information embedded in them. However, the WAV files that come with Windows 95 *do* contain information about copyrights and subject matter. Most of these files are the ones used for the different sound schemes available in Windows 95. We only mention them because their presence—or at least their potential presence—highlights the value of the multimedia file I/O functions, which Microsoft custom-designed for RIFF data files. You'll see what we mean shortly.

A Peek at the Multimedia I/O Functions

You *could* read RIFF files with conventional file I/O functions by calculating offsets and reading blocks of the appropriate sizes with Delphi's powerful BlockRead and BlockWrite built-in procedures. But Windows' multimedia file I/O functions provide intrinsic support for the RIFF format. The best way to understand these functions is to use them.

All multimedia file I/O functions begin with the prefix *mmio*. Here is the complete set:

```
mmioOpen     (A, W)
mmioClose
mmioRename  (A, W)
mmioSeek
mmioRead
mmioWrite
mmioSetBuffer
mmioFlush
mmioDescend
mmioAscend
mmioCreateChunk
mmioStringToFOURCC (A, W)
mmioAdvance
mmioGetInfo
mmioSetInfo
mmioInstallIOProc (A, W)
mmioSendMessage
    (A, W) signifies that both an ANSI chracter and Wide character verion of
this function are also available.
```

Of these seventeen functions, we'll need just five to read and play a WAV file: **mmioOpen**, **mmioClose**, **mmioRead**, **mmioDescend**, and **mmioAscend**.

All of these functions can return errors, so to use them properly we must check the result of each function call to make sure that the operation is performed correctly. Since we need to make several calls to read the WAV file, this error-checking process can become a little lengthy. To minimize confusion and make the code more manageable, we'll wrap these functions in a class. We'll do the same with the wave-audio output routines, which we'll be introducing shortly. Finally, we'll develop the small class **tWave_audio** with two straight-forward methods, one to open and read a WAV file and one to play it. That's three more units according to the way we've divided up the project, so let's get started!

MCI Play III: Playing WAV Files Using Low-Level Functions

This project shows you how to read and play WAV files using the low-level multimedia I/O functions. Just as MCIPLAY2 began where MCIPLAY1 left off, this new project, MCIPLAY3, will begin with the files from MCIPLAY2. By the time we're finished, the final project will have six Buttons, each offering a different way to play WAV and other audio files. Here are the steps:

1. For version three, make a new project directory, *MCIPlay3*, and an output subdirectory beneath this, *Bin*. With the *Explorer*, copy the project files from your *MCIPlay2* directory to your *MCIPlay3* directory. Rename your "MCIPlay2" files to "MCIPlay3", You'll need the *DPR*, *PAS*, and *DFM* files.

2. Open your **MCIPlay3** Project file in Delphi. The compiler will complain that its name is wrong ("Module header is missing or incorrect"). Change its program name from **MCIPlay2** to **MCIPlay3**. In the *Project Options* dialog box (from *Project | Options*), set the Application Title to "MCI Play III", and its output directory to "Bin".

3. View **Form1** from unit **Main**. In the *Object Inspector*, change its **Caption** from "MCI Play II" to "MCI Play III".

4. Add the last Button. **Name** it **WaveOut_button** and set its **Caption** to "waveOut&Write". We'll use its **OnClick** handler, **WaveOut_buttonClick**, to open and play a WAV file. It isn't time to add the handler, yet. The full list of properties is given in Table 5.5.

5. We will need three additional support units. From the menu, choose *File | New*. From the *New* tab of the *New Items* dialog box, choose

"Unit". Delphi will open a new *Editor* page for **Unit2** (or whatever it thinks the sequence number should be). Save it immediately with the new name *MMIOWrap.Pas*, using *File | Save As*.

6. Following the same process, add the support unit *WaveWrap.Pas*.
7. Add the final unit, *WavePlay.Pas*.
8. Flesh out the units with the code discussed below. Even though **WavePlay** is dependent on both **MMIOWrap** and **WaveWrap**, we'll discuss them in this order:
   - **MMIOWrap** (Listing 5.5)
   - **WavePlay** (Listing 5.6)
   - **WaveWrap** (Listing 5.7)
9. Finally, add the new Button's **OnClick** handler, **WaveOut_buttonClick** (Listing 5.8).

This project, MCIPlay3.DPR, and all of its support files, can be found on the accompanying CD-ROM in the directory \PROGRAMS\CHAP05\MCIPLAY3.

Table 5.5 Properties for the MCI Play III project.

Class	Property	Value
TForm	Name	Form1 (default)
	Caption	'MCI Play II'
TButton	Name	Message_beep_button
	Caption	'Message&Beep'
	OnClick	Message_beep_buttonClick
TEdit	Name	Command_string_text
	Text	<blank>
TLabel	Name	Label1 (default)
	Caption	'Command String'
TEdit	Name	Error_text
	Text	<blank>
TLabel	Name	Label2 (default)
	Caption	'Error'
TButton	Name	Play_sound_button
	Caption	'snd&PlaySound'
	OnClick	Play_sound_buttonClick

Continued

Table 5.5 *Properties for the MCI Play III project (Continued).*

Class	Property	Value
TButton	Name	Execute_button
	Caption	'mci&Execute'
	OnClick	Execute_buttonClick
TLabel	Name	Label3 (default)
	Caption	'Return String'
TEdit	Name	Return_string_text
	Text	<blank>
TButton	Name	SendString_button
	Caption	'mci&SendString'
	OnClick	SendString_buttonClick
TButton	Name	SendCommand_button
	Caption	'mci&SendString'
	OnClick	SendCommand_buttonClick
TButton	Name	WaveOut_button
	Caption	' waveOut&Write'
	OnClick	WaveOut_buttonClick

Wrapping up the API

To read and play a WAV file, we'll create three more units—one to wrap up the **mmio** API calls we'll be making, one to wrap up the **wave** calls, and one for the wave-audio class we're going to build. Before we go off on an object-oriented binge (*OOB*, for short), let's make sure we understand why we want to wrap up a perfectly good API into a class. Here are three good reasons.

- **Consistent Exception Handling** First, we need to implement exception handling that is completely under our control. When we wrap up the API, we'll be forced to *cap* the native API functions. Capping, in its simplest form, is just redeclaring the functions—perhaps with a more palatable interface. Since we already have to cap each function, why don't we look for the error conditions we could encounter for each one and raise a Delphi exception? If we do this, we won't need to test the outcome of each function call before going on to the next; we can take advantage of Delphi's exception handling, instead.
- **A Cleaner Interface** We just alluded to the fact that we can put a slightly easier-to-use interface on top of the API functions. *This* project

exposes the all of the functions for demonstration purposes. But operations such as **mmioOpen** and **mmioClose** can easily be hidden within your own wrapper's **Create** and **Destroy** methods to clean up the interface.

- **Hidden Data** In the portion of the mmio API we're using, we will find ourselves constantly passing the same handle to function, after function, after function. By encapsulating the API in a class, we can keep *state* data (data that must be remembered from step to step, but data that has no interest to the calling programmer), like this handle which is hidden from the calling code. And this, in turn, simplifies the interface. Additionally, we're about to make some very specialized assumptions about our use of the **mmio** API. Because we know exactly what we intend to do, places exist where a general declaration would have to handle, say, a set of flags, as a parameter. If we know we'll always be using the same flags, we can eliminate the parameter and hard-code the flags within our class. This may make the code harder to generalize later (So, beware!), but it can also render the code much easier to understand.

Reading and Processing a WAV File

We're building toward a wave-audio class with a Read method and a Play method. Before we can read, the first step we need to take is opening a wave file, so let's declare a cap for the low-level multimedia function, **mmioOpen**. Here's the code for this method; we'll shortly incorporate it into our new class, called **tMMIO_file**, declared in the new unit, *MMIOWrap.Pas*.

```
function tMMIO_file.Open(
  const Filename : string
  ) : HMMIO;
    begin
        result := mmioOpen(pchar(Filename),nil,MMIO_READ);
        Handle := result;
        if result = 0 then
            raise eMMIO_error.Create(result,
              'Error opening tMMIO_file with file "' + Filename + '"'
              );
        end;
```

Our **Open** method function returns an **HMMIO**, a handle to an MMIO file. The API function, **mmioOpen**, takes a **pchar** to a null-terminated string, but we can take advantage of Delphi's new **ANSIString** (the default base type of **string**) to simplify the parameter list. **mmioOpen** performs several operations and each is selectable by passing flags in the third parameter. For this example, since we'll only be reading the file, we need only one flag,

MMIO_READ. We can hard-code this. We'll ignore the second parameter. (We could pass a pointer to a **TMMIOInfo** record with more specialized information about how to open the file.) Our **Open**'s return value, represented by Delphi's **result** identifier, is set to the handle that the multimedia system returns to us. By returning the handle, we can make it easily available to the calling program; although, like our program, most will probably just throw the result away when they call **Open**.

The handle, you'll notice, is saved in the variable **Handle**. As you'll see very shortly, this is a field of our object. We can store the **Handle** within the object, and the caller won't even need to know it's there (even though they *could* get it from **Open**'s returned value).

mmioOpen returns a handle of 0 when something fails. In this case, we raise an exception—Hey, it looks like we should be seeing the declaration of our custom exception, **eMMIO_error**, any time now! We **Create** our exception with the result (which must be zero, in this case) as a numeric representation of the error, an error message that indicates which **mmio** call errored-out and (in this case) the name of the unopenable file.

Here, in Listing 5.5, is the whole **tMMIO_file** wrapper in the unit **MMIOWrap**:

Listing 5.5   Class tMMIO_file in *MMIOWrap.Pas*

```
unit MMIOWrap;

interface

   uses
       SysUtils, Windows, MMSystem;

   type
       FourChars = array[0..3] of char;

       eMMIO_error = class(Exception)
           MMIO_result : integer;
           constructor Create(
             const Err : integer;
             const Msg : string
             );
           end;

       tMMIO_file = class
           Handle : HMMIO;

           constructor Create;

           function Open(
             const Filename : string
             ) : HMMIO;
```

```
        function Close : MMRESULT;

        function Read(
          const Pointer_to_buffer : pchar;
          const Size_of_buffer    : UINT
          ) : longint;

        function Ascend(
          var Chunk_info : TMMCKInfo
          ) : MMRESULT;

        function Descend(
          var   Chunk_info,
                Parent_chunk_info : TMMCKInfo;
          const Flags             : UINT
          ) : MMRESULT;

        function First_descend(
          var   Chunk_info : TMMCKInfo;
          const Flags      : UINT
          ) : MMRESULT;

        end;

implementation

    constructor eMMIO_error.Create(
      const Err : integer;
      const Msg : string
      );
        begin
            inherited Create(Msg);
            MMIO_result := Err;
            end;

    constructor tMMIO_file.Create;
        begin
            inherited Create;
            Handle := 0;
            end;

    function tMMIO_file.Open(
      const Filename : string
      ) : HMMIO;
        begin
            result := mmioOpen(pchar(Filename),nil,MMIO_READ);
            Handle := result;
            if result = 0 then
                raise eMMIO_error.Create(result,
                    'Error opening tMMIO_file with file "' + Filename + '"'
                    );
            end;
```

```
function tMMIO_file.Close : MMRESULT;
    begin
        result := mmioClose(Handle,0);
        if result <> 0 then
            raise eMMIO_error.Create(result,
              'Error closing tMMIO_file'
              );
        end;

function tMMIO_file.Read(
  const Pointer_to_buffer : pchar;
  const Size_of_buffer    : UINT
  ) : longint;
    begin
        result := mmioRead(Handle,Pointer_to_buffer,Size_of_buffer);
        if result = 0 then
            raise eMMIO_error.Create(result,
              'Error reading tMMIO_file'
              );
        end;

function tMMIO_file.Ascend(
  var Chunk_info : TMMCKInfo
  ) : MMRESULT;
    begin
        result := mmioAscend(Handle,@Chunk_info,0);
        if result <> 0 then
            raise eMMIO_error.Create(result,
              'Error ascending in tMMIO_file'
              );
        end;

function tMMIO_file.Descend(
  var   Chunk_info,
        Parent_chunk_info : TMMCKInfo;
  const Flags             : UINT
  ) : MMRESULT;
    begin
        result := mmioDescend(Handle,@Chunk_info,@Parent_chunk_info,Flags);
        if result <> 0 then
            raise eMMIO_error.Create(result,
              'Error descending in tMMIO_file'
              );
        end;

function tMMIO_file.First_descend(
  var   Chunk_info : TMMCKInfo;
  const Flags      : UINT
  ) : MMRESULT;
    begin
        result := mmioDescend(Handle,@Chunk_info,nil,Flags);
        if result <> 0 then
            raise eMMIO_error.Create(result,
              'Error doing first descend in tMMIO_file'
```

```
      );
   end;

{initialization}
   end.
```

Since we made such a big deal about it, let's look at our exception.

```
eMMIO_error = class(Exception)
   MMIO_result : integer;
   constructor Create(
     const Err : integer;
     const Msg : string
     );
   end;
```

We declare one field, **MMIO_result**, to hold the actual error result that the various functions will return. After an exception occurs, we'll be able to check it. Because we want to pass that number in, we declare our own constructor that can take the actual error value, as well as the message.

```
constructor eMMIO_error.Create(
  const Err : integer;
  const Msg : string
  );
    begin
        inherited Create(Msg);
        MMIO_result := Err;
        end;
```

Before we start to use this code somewhere else, let's look at **Close**, to see how the **Handle** field is really used:

```
function tMMIO_file.Close : MMRESULT;
    begin
        result := mmioClose(Handle,0);
        if result <> 0 then
            raise eMMIO_error.Create(result,
              'Error closing tMMIO_file'
              );
        end;
```

This is pretty simple. Since we saved the **Handle** in **Open**, we can just call **mmioClose** with the same **Handle**. We also send in 0 for the flags, we don't want anything special.

At this point, we can start writing some pseudocode for the routine that will read the WAV file. It's pretty short right now, though. Note that, although we capped all the functions to return their original values, we can ignore these return values and let Delphi handle any exceptions. We'll go so far as to call the functions like procedures and ignore the returned result.

```
try
   Open(Filename);
   :
   Close;
except
   on E : eMMIO_error do
       MessageDlg('MMIO error ' + IntToStr(E.MMIO_result) + ': ' + E.Message);
end;
```

After we've opened the file, we have to locate the *parent chunk* of the **RIFF** chunk. RIFF files can't contain more than a single parent chunk in the current version of the multimedia I/O system. This process may seem nonsensical, but future releases will probably support *compound* files (RIFF files that could, for example, contain more than one WAV sound). Besides, the search operation automatically positions the file pointer at the beginning of the data section of the chunk (in this case, the 13th byte in the file); so it isn't a completely wasted effort.

To search for chunks, we'll call upon **mmioDescend**, capped by our Descend method function.

```
function tMMIO_file.Descend(
   var   Chunk_info,
         Parent_chunk_info : TMMCKInfo;
   const Flags             : UINT
   ) : MMRESULT;
   begin
       result := mmioDescend(Handle,@Chunk_info,@Parent_chunk_info,Flags);
       if result <> 0 then
           raise eMMIO_error.Create(result,
             'Error descending in tMMIO_file'
             );
       end;
```

To search for a particular type of RIFF chunk—in this case, a RIFF chunk that contains WAV data—we have to specify the *form type*. The form type, which is the third field at the head of a RIFF chunk, identifies the type of data stored in the RIFF chunk. It's also the third field in **TMMCKInfo**. We'll assume we have a variable of type **TMMCKInfo** called **Parent_chunk_info** in our pseudocode. To search for a RIFF chunk with a form type of WAV, we set the **fccType** field in this record to "WAVE" and call **Descend**, like this:

```
try
   Open(Filename);
   Parent_chunk_info.fccType := 'WAVE';
   Descend(Parent_chunk_info, <The parent has no parent>, MMIO_FINDRIFF);
   :
   Close;
except
   on E : eMMIO_error do
      MessageDlg('MMIO error ' + IntToStr(E.MMIO_result) + ': ' + E.Message);
end;
```

What's that notation? "The parent has no parent?" When the multimedia system descends a logical level into a RIFF chunk, it needs to know about the chunk it's already at (called the *Parent* chunk) and the chunk into which it's descending (called the *Child* chunk). Since we're going from the very top, we're actually going from *no parent* into the chunk that *will be* our parent from now on. Without the wrapper, we could make this call like this:

```
result := mmioDescend(Handle,@Parent_chunk_info,nil,Flags);
  { Get into the RIFF. }

result := mmioDescend(Handle,@Child_chunk_info,@Parent_chunk_info,Flags);
  { Get down into a "fmt" or "data" chunk. }
```

To indicate that we have no parent, we pass **nil** as the parent. We have *so conveniently* capped off our functions to the point that we can't pass **nil** in from the outside, so we have to write another cap method specifically for this case. Some might argue that this is *better*, because it forces the called to acknowledge the difference between going in from the top, and going further down from inside. We call it **First_descend**.

```
function tMMIO_file.First_descend(
   var   Chunk_info : TMMCKInfo;
   const Flags      : UINT
   ) : MMRESULT;
   begin
      result := mmioDescend(Handle,@Chunk_info,nil,Flags);
      if result <> 0 then
         raise eMMIO_error.Create(result,
            'Error doing first descend in tMMIO_file'
            );
      end;
```

Descending is kind of like reading. The difference is that **mmioDescend** reads only the fields that describe the chunk. That is, it reads the rind—not the fruit, the data inside the chunk. As we mentioned earlier, all chunks begin with two data fields, the chunk ID (**ckid**) and the chunk size (**ckSize**). Instead of defining two different structures for chunks, Microsoft muddies the definition of a chunk with a kludge: a chunk may also contain a third data field, the form type or list type (**fccType**), which is contained in the first four bytes of the data section of the chunk. Only **RIFF** and **LIST** chunks include this "extra" field (form type for **RIFF** chunks, and list type for **LIST** chunks, both known as **fccType**).

When you descend into a chunk, **mmioDescend** fills in the field **dwDataOffset** in the **TMMCKInfo** record, which in this case is **Parent_chunk_info**. If you're descending into a **RIFF** or **LIST** chunk, **mmioDescend** will also automatically fill in the **ckid** with either "RIFF" or "LIST".

In the call to **Descend**, we set the form type to "WAVE" and pass the flag **MMIO_FINDRIFF**. **mmioDescend** will quickly search the file for its first (and currently, its only) **RIFF** chunk. When it has finished, we will have a complete description of the **RIFF** chunk contained in a record called **Parent_chunk_info**.

```
try
   Open(Filename);
   Parent_chunk_info.fccType := 'WAVE';
   First_descend(Parent_chunk_info,MMIO_FINDRIFF);
   :
   Close;
 except
   on E : eMMIO_error do
       MessageDlg('MMIO error ' + IntToStr(E.MMIO_result) + ': ' + E.Message);
 end;
```

The RIFF chunk with the form type "WAVE" is the mother of all chunks—at least mother of all other chunks in a WAV file.

Reading the fmt Chunk

To search for any other type of chunk, we need to specify the **ckid** and pass (by reference) a record of type **TMMCHKInfo** for the parent chunk as the third parameter:

```
try
   Open(Filename);
   Parent_chunk_info.fccType := 'WAVE';
   First_descend(Parent_chunk_info,MMIO_FINDRIFF);
   Chunk_info.ckid := 'fmt ';
   Descend(Chunk_info,Parent_chunk_info,MMIO_FINDCHUNK);
   :
   Close;
```

```
except
  on E : eMMIO_error do
      MessageDlg('MMIO error ' + IntToStr(E.MMIO_result) + ': ' + E.Message);
end;
```

Notice that **Chunk_info.ckid** is blank-padded to four characters. In this statement, **mmioDescend** searches the parent chunk for a *format chunk*. This takes little effort because the format chunk begins right after the form type field, at the 13th byte in the file. You can't assume, however, that this will always be the case. Someday you may encounter a WAV file that includes **LIST** chunks which appear ahead of the format chunk. If you were to read the file in a conventional fashion, either with standard file I/O, or with the function **mmioRead**, you would have to identify and skip the **LIST** chunks. But when we call **mmioDescend** with the flag **MMIO_FINDCHUNK** and a **ckid** of **fmt**, it will automatically hop directly to the format chunk.

Now we get to read some data:

```
try
    Open(Filename);
    Parent_chunk_info.fccType := 'WAVE';
    First_descend(Parent_chunk_info,MMIO_FINDRIFF);
    Chunk_info.ckid := 'fmt ';
    Descend(Chunk_info,Parent_chunk_info,MMIO_FINDCHUNK);
    Read(@Format,Chunk_info.ckSize);
    :
    Close;
except
  on E : eMMIO_error do
      MessageDlg('MMIO error ' + IntToStr(E.MMIO_result) + ': ' + E.Message);
end;
```

mmioRead, capped by our **Read** method function, does what you would expect. It reads from the file specified by our object's **Handle** field, the number of bytes specified by **Read**'s second parameter. It then places the data in memory, beginning at the address specified by **Read**'s first parameter. Since we're passing the record **Format**, of type **TWaveFormatEx** by reference in the second parameter, when we return from **mmioRead**, we should find that it has filled in the wave format record. You may have noticed the "@" (at-sign) in front of Format. Our **Read** cap doesn't make any assumptions about what it will be reading to where, so we used the **@**-operator to generate a pointer to the data. We then pass this pointer to **Read**, and **Read** passes it to **mmioRead**.

```
function tMMIO_file.Read(
  const Pointer_to_buffer : pchar;
```

```
    const Size_of_buffer   : UINT
    ) : longint;
  begin
      result := mmioRead(Handle,Pointer_to_buffer,Size_of_buffer);
      if result = 0 then
          raise eMMIO_error.Create(result,
            'Error reading tMMIO_file'
            );
      end;
```

The API gets a little tricky, so we're going to get a little tricky, too. We've just read a format chunk into a **TWaveFormatEx** structure. If you've already had some experience with digital sound, you might already know that WAV files are based on a technology called *Pulse Code Modulation*, or *PCM* for short. If you look at Delphi's **MMSystem** unit, you'll see a very specific set of declarations for dealing just with this type of wave audio file; they follow the declaration of the general waveform structure.

```
{ general waveform format structure (information common to all formats) }
type
    PWaveFormat = ^TWaveFormat;
    TWaveFormat = record
        wFormatTag       : Word;    { format type }
        nChannels        : Word;    { number of channels (i.e. mono, stereo,
etc.) }
        nSamplesPerSec   : DWORD;   { sample rate }
        nAvgBytesPerSec  : DWORD;   { for buffer estimation }
        nBlockAlign      : Word;    { block size of data }
        end;

{ flags for wFormatTag field of WAVEFORMAT }
const
    WAVE_FORMAT_PCM = 1;

{ specific waveform format structure for PCM data }
type
    PPCMWaveFormat = ^TPCMWaveFormat;
    TPCMWaveFormat = record
        wf            : TWaveFormat;
        wBitsPerSample : Word;
        end;
```

So why have we been planning to use a **TWaveFormatEx** structure?

```
{ extended waveform format structure used for all non-PCM formats. this
  structure is common to all non-PCM formats. }

    PWaveFormatEx = ^TWaveFormatEx;
    TWaveFormatEx = record
```

```
    wFormatTag       : Word;  { format type }
    nChannels        : Word;  { number of channels (i.e. mono, stereo, etc.) }
    nSamplesPerSec   : DWORD; { sample rate }
    nAvgBytesPerSec  : DWORD; { for buffer estimation }
    nBlockAlign      : Word;  { block size of data }
    wBitsPerSample   : Word;  { number of bits per sample of mono data }
    cbSize           : Word;  { the count in bytes of the size of }
end;
```

The answer is simple. When we read a waveform file, we won't necessarily be sure that it's a PCM file. If the sound designer used the extended waveform format structure in building the file, we could be in a heap of trouble. The size of the specialized **TPCMWaveFormat** is smaller than the size of **TWaveFormatEx** (By our count, **TWaveFormatEx** has one more field, **cbSize**). Since we need to be able to hold the largest possible format structure, we'll use **TWaveFormatEx**.

This could become a problem for us if we wanted to query the format structure. For example, the number of channels is accessed with **TPCMWaveFormat.wf.nChannels** in the PCM format, but accessed by **TWaveFormatEx.nChannels** in the extended format (Note the **wf** subrecord). For just reading in and passing around, though, we're safe if we use the largest structure available and read in only the number of bytes specified by out format chunk's **Chunk_info.ckSize**.

And another thing—we Pascal programmers like to keep everything as safe as possible, so we might be tempted to write (and we actually *did*, the first time we tried this)

```
Read(@Format,sizeof(Format));
```

This way, we'd never be in danger of overwriting memory outside of **Format**. On the other hand, unless we actually had a file with an extended wave format chunk; we'd *overread* the file, which is almost as bad. Therefore, we are forced to rely on the multimedia system to accurately tell us how many bytes to read.

Reading the data *Chunk*

Somewhere after the format chunk, we should find the data chunk. To find the data chunk without making any assumptions about its location, we'll again want to use **Descend** to search the parent chunk for it. But before we can do that, we first have to *ascend* out of the format chunk:

```
try
   Open(Filename);
   Parent_chunk_info.fccType := 'WAVE';
```

```
    First_descend(Parent_chunk_info,MMIO_FINDRIFF);
    Chunk_info.ckid := 'fmt ';
    Descend(Chunk_info,Parent_chunk_info,MMIO_FINDCHUNK);
    Read(@Format,Chunk_info.ckSize);
    Ascend(Chunk_info);
    :
    Close;
  except
    on E : eMMIO_error do
        MessageDlg('MMIO error ' + IntToStr(E.MMIO_result) + ': ' + E.Message);
  end;
```

The first parameter of **mmioAscend** once again identifies the file, and the second parameter identifies the chunk from which to ascend. The third parameter may someday accept flags, but none have been defined yet by Microsoft, so we'll always set it to 0.

```
function tMMIO_file.Ascend(
  var Chunk_info : TMMCKInfo
  ) : MMRESULT;
    begin
        result := mmioAscend(Handle,@Chunk_info,0);
        if result <> 0 then
            raise eMMIO_error.Create(result,
              'Error ascending in tMMIO_file'
              );
        end;
```

At the end of our ascent, the file pointer will stand at the threshold of the next chunk—which, coincidentally, is the next chunk into which we'll descend.

```
try
    Open(Filename);
    Parent_chunk_info.fccType := 'WAVE';
    First_descend(Parent_chunk_info,MMIO_FINDRIFF);
    Chunk_info.ckid := 'fmt ';
    Descend(Chunk_info,Parent_chunk_info,MMIO_FINDCHUNK);
    Read(@Format,Chunk_info.ckSize);
    Ascend(Chunk_info);
    Chunk_info.ckid := 'data';
    Descend(Chunk_info,Parent_chunk_info,MMIO_FINDCHUNK);
    :
    Close;
  except
    on E : eMMIO_error do
        MessageDlg('MMIO error ' + IntToStr(E.MMIO_result) + ': ' + E.Message);
  end;
```

Throughout this odyssey, our parent chunk has steadfastly remained the RIFF chunk. To locate the data chunk, we set the **ckid** in **Chunk_info** (our child) to **data** and call **Descend** again with the flag **MMIO_FINDCHUNK**. If we strike paydirt, it's time to dig out the prize—waveform audio data.

To read in the waveform data we need to supply a buffer. We'll demonstrate this here using **strAlloc**, for two reasons. First, the API treats the wave data as characters with declarations using **pchar**, so it makes sense to use a character-based data structure. Secondly, by playing some offset allocation games, **strAlloc** receives memory in such a way that the amount of memory allocated is automatically remembered. This way, we won't need to keep some global variable handy telling us how much space to deallocate when the time comes. It just so happens, by the way, that the required size is already available to us in the **ckSize** field of **Chunk_info**.

WAV files tend to be large—very large. The lowest-fidelity WAV format requires 11,025 bytes per second of audio. The WAV files that contain the Windows 95 message beep sounds were recorded at the next highest sampling rate of 22.05 KHz, which means that they occupy 22,050 bytes for each second of playback time. After thinking this through, you may want to consider switching to a data structure and program architecture that will allow you to play long WAV files in bits and pieces. For the moment, we'll probably be able to safely **strAlloc** all the space we need from Windows' global heap.

Now that we know how much information to pull in, how to get the space for it, and where we are going to place it, we can add the code that actually reads in the WAV information:

```
try
    Open(Filename);
    Parent_chunk_info.fccType := 'WAVE';
    First_descend(Parent_chunk_info,MMIO_FINDRIFF);
    Chunk_info.ckid := 'fmt ';
    Descend(Chunk_info,Parent_chunk_info,MMIO_FINDCHUNK);
    Read(@Format,Chunk_info.ckSize);
    Ascend(Chunk_info);
    Chunk_info.ckid := 'data';
    Descend(Chunk_info,Parent_chunk_info,MMIO_FINDCHUNK);
    Data := strAlloc(Chunk_info.ckSize);
    Read(Data,Chunk_info.ckSize);
    with Header do begin
        lpData          := Data;
        dwBufferLength  := Chunk_info.ckSize;
        dwFlags         := 0;
        dwLoops         := 0;
        end;
    Close;
except
    on E : eMMIO_error do
        MessageDlg('MMIO error ' + IntToStr(E.MMIO_result) + ': ' + E.Message);
end;
```

We call **Read**, passing **Data**, a **pchar**-type pointer to the first "character" of the WAV data. Note that we don't use the **@**-operator here, because **Data** is *already* a pointer. **Chunk_info.ckSize** is passed as the number of bytes to read; fortunately, this is identical to the amount of memory space we allocated with **strAlloc**, above.

Finally, if **Read** returns successfully, we have all the information we need to construct a **TWaveHdr** record. Wave headers are the structures that describe individual WAV buffers. For a variety of reasons, we might wish to play wave audio data by passing it to the driver in segments. We treat each segment as a separate buffer with its own header. The format record, a structure of type **TWaveFormatEx**, describes the format of a single wave audio recording. Each segment of that recording will have its own header, a structure of type **TWaveHdr**. Here is the full **TWaveHdr** declaration from Delphi's unit **MMSystem**.

```
{ wave data block header }
type
    PWaveHdr = ^TWaveHdr;
    TWaveHdr = record
        lpData          : PChar;    { pointer to locked data buffer }
        dwBufferLength  : DWORD;    { length of data buffer }
        dwBytesRecorded : DWORD;    { used for input only }
        dwUser          : DWORD;    { for client's use }
        dwFlags         : DWORD;    { assorted flags (see defines) }
        dwLoops         : DWORD;    { loop control counter }
        lpNext          : PWaveHdr; { reserved for driver }
        reserved        : DWORD;    { reserved for driver }
    end;
```

While the **Format** record describes the sampling rate, number of channels, and bit resolution of a wave audio file, the main purpose of a wave **Header** is to hold the length and location of the wave audio data. In **tWave_audio**'s **Play** method, we'll use the **Format** record to *open* the wave-playing device, and the **Header** to *play* the data.

We've developed a little piece of pseudocode to illustrate each **mmio** function's part in reading a WAV file. Now, we'll flesh it out. What we've covered so far, shown in Listing 5.6, implements the **Read** method of the **tWave_audio** class. Next, we're headed to the **Play** method.

Listing 5.6 The **tWave_audio** Class from *WavePlay.Pas*

```
unit WavePlay;

interface
```

```
uses
    MMSystem, MMIOWrap, WaveWrap;

type
    tAudio_waveform = class
        Header : TWaveHdr;
        Data   : pchar;
        Format : TWaveFormatEx;

        destructor Destroy; override;

        function Read(
          const Filename : string
          ) : boolean;
        procedure Play;
        end;

implementation

uses
    SysUtils, Forms, Dialogs;

destructor tAudio_waveform.Destroy;
    begin
        strDispose(Data);
           { ...which was set to nil automatically by
             Delphi, since it is a pointer field of
             a class structure. }
        end;

function tAudio_waveform.Read(
  const Filename : string
  ) : boolean;
    var
        Parent_chunk_info,
        Chunk_info         : TMMCKInfo;
    begin
        result := false;
        strDispose(Data);
        Data := nil;
        with tMMIO_file.Create do
            try
                Open(Filename);

                { Find the "WAVE" audio Parent Chunk. }
                FourChars(Parent_chunk_info.fccType) := 'WAVE';
                First_descend(Parent_chunk_info,MMIO_FINDRIFF);

                { Find the "fmt " format chunk. }
                FourChars(Chunk_info.ckid) := 'fmt ';
                Descend(Chunk_info,Parent_chunk_info,MMIO_FINDCHUNK);

                { Read PCM wave format record. }
                Read(@Format,Chunk_info.ckSize);
```

```
            { Here, we could instantiate a tWave_device
              and do a WAVE_FORMAT_QUERY to see if we are
              able to handle the wave format, and whether
              we should go any fuurther. }

            { Go back up to the WAVE level, and then find
              the "data" chunk. }
            Ascend(Chunk_info);
            FourChars(Chunk_info.ckid) := 'data';
            Descend(Chunk_info,Parent_chunk_info,MMIO_FINDCHUNK);

            { Allocate the wave data buffer, and read it in. }
            Data := strAlloc(Chunk_info.ckSize);
            Read(Data,Chunk_info.ckSize);

            { Fill in the Wave_header }
            with Header do begin
                lpData         := Data;
                dwBufferLength := Chunk_info.ckSize;
                dwFlags        := 0;
                dwLoops        := 0;
                end;
            result:= true;
          finally
            Free;
          end;
      end;

    procedure tAudio_waveform.Play;
      begin
        with tWave_device.Create do
          try
            Open(Format,WAVE_FORMAT_QUERY);
              { Die here if we can't handle the format. }
            Open(Format,0);
            Prepare_header(Header);
            Write(Header);
            while (Header.dwFlags and WHDR_DONE) = 0 do
                Application.ProcessMessages;
            Unprepare_header(Header);
            Close;
          finally
            Free;
          end;
      end;

{initialization}
    end.
```

We don't have to ascend back out to the RIFF chunk before we close the file. Even if we did, we would still be in the same position—at the end of the file. If multimedia file I/O ever supports compound files someday—RIFF files that contain multiple RIFF chunks—we may wish to ascend out of one RIFF chunk before descending into, or searching for the next one.

One final note, now that we have all of the code in front of us. The field **tWave_audio.Data** is our classes' way of keeping track of where the waveform data is stored. We don't really need this field, because we could operate on **tWave_audio.Header.lpData** directly. We just think it's better to extract the maintenance of this dynamic data structure out of a sub-record to a place where we can see it clearly. We get a fringe benefit from Delphi, too: Since **Data** is a pointer field, it will automatically be initialized to **nil** when objects of class **tWave_audio** are instantiated, saving us an explicit step. Delphi isn't able to do this with the sub-record field **lpData**.

Playing the WAV File

Once we've extracted the data from the RIFF file and created the three essential data structures (the Format record, the wave audio **Data**, and the wave data **Header**), we can use the wave audio device to play the sound. Five steps are required to play the wave audio from the structures stored in memory:

1. Open the wave audio device.
2. Prepare the wave header.
3. Write the data to the device.
4. Unprepare the wave header.
5. Close the device.

As you might assume from the discussion so far, we cannot just call the five functions that perform these steps in rapid-fire succession. Like **Read,** our next method, **Play**, will rely on the same type of class-wrapping we did for the **mmio** functions. This time, we'll wrap the **wave** functions. Here, in Listing 5.7, is the complete **WaveWrap** unit.

Listing 5.7   Class **tWave_device** Wrapper in *WaveWrap.Pas*

```
unit WaveWrap;

interface

    uses
        SysUtils, Windows, MMSystem;

    type
        eWave_error = class(Exception)
            Wave_result : integer;
```

```
        constructor Create(
          const Err : integer;
          const Msg : string
          );
        end;

    tWave_device = class
        Handle : HWaveOut;

        constructor Create;

        function Open(
          var   Format : TWaveFormatEx;
          const Flags  : DWORD
          ) : MMRESULT;

        function Close : MMRESULT;

        function Prepare_header(
          var   Header : TWaveHdr
          ) : MMRESULT;

        function Unprepare_header(
          var   Header : TWaveHdr
          ) : MMRESULT;

        function Write(
          var   Header : TWaveHdr
          ): MMRESULT;

        end;

implementation

    constructor eWave_error.Create(
      const Err : integer;
      const Msg : string
      );
        begin
            inherited Create(Msg);
            Wave_result := Err;
            end;

    constructor tWave_device.Create;
        begin
            inherited Create;
            Handle := 0;
            end;

    function tWave_device.Open(
      var   Format : TWaveFormatEx;
      const Flags  : DWORD
      ) : MMRESULT;
```

```
    begin
        result := waveOutOpen(
                    @Handle,
                    WAVE_MAPPER,    { Let Windows choose device. }
                    @Format,
                    DWORD(nil),     { No callback. }
                    0,              { No instance. }
                    Flags
                    );
        if result <> 0 then
            raise eWave_error.Create(result,
                'Error opening output wave device'
                );
        end;

function tWave_device.Close : MMRESULT;
    begin
        result := waveOutClose(Handle);
        if result <> 0 then
            raise eWave_error.Create(result,
                'Error closing output wave device'
                );
        end;

function tWave_device.Prepare_header(
  var   Header : TWaveHdr
  ) : MMRESULT;
    begin
        result := waveOutPrepareHeader(Handle,
                    @Header,
                    sizeof(Header)
                    );
        if result <> 0 then
            raise eWave_error.Create(result,
                'Error preparing header for output wave device'
                );
        end;

function tWave_device.Unprepare_header(
  var   Header : TWaveHdr
  ) : MMRESULT;
    begin
        result := waveOutUnprepareHeader(Handle,
                    @Header,
                    sizeof(Header)
                    );
        if result <> 0 then
            raise eWave_error.Create(result,
                'Error unpreparing header for output wave device'
                );
        end;

function tWave_device.Write(
  var   Header : TWaveHdr
```

```
            ): MMRESULT;
          begin
              result := waveOutWrite(Handle,
                          @Header,
                          sizeof(Header)
                          );
              if result <> 0 then
                  raise eWave_error.Create(result,
                    'Error writing to output wave device'
                    );
          end;

{initialization}
    end.
```

We begin by opening the device. Here, it is a two-step process. First, we do a trial opening to demonstrate the code you could use when reading the WAV file to determine (before you actually read the wave data) whether or not you can **Play** the file. To do this, we call **waveOutOpen** from our wrapper **tWave_device.Open**. We pass it the flag **WAVE_FORMAT_QUERY**, which will compare the contents of the wave format record with the device capabilities as defined in the wave audio device driver. If the file is compatible with the device, **waveOutOpen** returns zero and Open generates no exception.

We still haven't actually opened the wave audio device. We need to call **Open** one more time with no flags at all, which really *will* open the device.

```
procedure tAudio_waveform.Play;
    begin
        with tWave_device.Create do
            try
                Open(Format,WAVE_FORMAT_QUERY);
                  { Die here if we can't handle the format. }
                Open(Format,0);
                Prepare_header(Header);
                Write(Header);
                while (Header.dwFlags and WHDR_DONE) = 0 do
                    Application.ProcessMessages;
                Unprepare_header(Header);
                Close;
            finally
              Free;
            end;
    end;
```

waveOutOpen expects six parameters. The first parameter is the address of an empty device handle, which the function will fill in if it successfully opens a wave audio device. This handle is used to perform all subsequent operations with the device, so it is saved in the **Handle** field of the class. For the second parameter, we specify which wave audio device to open. A Windows system may contain several wave audio devices (the MPC specification requires only one). These will be numbered sequentially, beginning with device 0, if your system contains more than one compatible device. If you want the multimedia system to select the first available driver, you can specify the constant **WAVE_MAPPER**—which, incidentally, has an integer value of –1.

```
function tWave_device.Open(
   var   Format : TWaveFormatEx;
   const Flags  : DWORD
   ) : MMRESULT;
   begin
      result := waveOutOpen(
                @Handle,
                WAVE_MAPPER,   { Let Windows choose device. }
                @Format,
                DWORD(nil),    { No callback. }
                0,             { No instance. }
                Flags
                );
      if result <> 0 then
         raise eWave_error.Create(result,
            'Error opening output wave device'
            );
   end;
```

For the third parameter, we pass the address of the wave format structure (that we probably read from a wave file, but we could create one in memory and pass it in, too). The fourth and fifth parameters specify a callback function and information to be used by the callback function. We could use the callback function to carry on a dialog with the wave playback function. Again, we'll skip callbacks here by passing zeros.

For the last parameter of **waveOutOpen**, we could pass **WAVE_FORMAT_QUERY**. The only other flags available specify the callback method; because we won't be using callbacks, we can pass a zero to **Open** when we simply wish to open the file for real.

The activities of **waveOutPrepareHeader** and **waveOutUnprepareHeader** remain mysterious to us. We know that you must prepare the header before sending wave audio data to the device driver, and that you must unprepare the header before you release the memory occupied by the header and wave audio data. But we have to confess, we can't find any explanation—not even a poor one—of what this preparation actually does.

```
function tWave_device.Prepare_header(
   var   Header : TWaveHdr
   ) : MMRESULT;
```

```
            begin
                result := waveOutPrepareHeader(Handle,
                             @Header,
                             sizeof(Header)
                             );
                if result <> 0 then
                    raise eWave_error.Create(result,
                       'Error preparing header for output wave device'
                       );
            end;
    function tWave_device.Unprepare_header(
      var    Header : TWaveHdr
      ) : MMRESULT;
        begin
            result := waveOutUnprepareHeader(Handle,
                         @Header,
                         sizeof(Header)
                         );
            if result <> 0 then
                raise eWave_error.Create(result,
                   'Error unpreparing header for output wave device'
                   );
        end;
```

We would guess that whatever these functions do, they have been separated from the function **waveOutWrite** to facilitate performance. Digital audio output devours processor cycles. When you consider that the Windows multimedia system can play 16-bit stereo wave data at 44.1 KHz, you realize that the output functions can't be bothered with any tasks other than those that must occur in real time. Because they are external to the output function, **waveOutPrepareHeader** and **waveOutUnprepareHeader** enable **waveOutWrite** to offload some overhead. With these functions we can prepare the buffers and headers in advance and feed them to the output function in quick succession. As the device driver finishes with each buffer, it can spit it out and leave the cleanup for us to perform later. Of course, when we call the prepare and unprepare functions, we're still using the processor, but not during the critical handoff between buffer segments.

```
procedure tAudio_waveform.Play;
    begin
        with tWave_device.Create do
            try
                Open(Format,WAVE_FORMAT_QUERY);
                  { Die here if we can't handle the format. }
                Open(Format,0);
                Prepare_header(Header);
                Write(Header);
                while (Header.dwFlags and WHDR_DONE) = 0 do
```

```
            Application.ProcessMessages;
          Unprepare_header(Header);
          Close;
        finally
          Free;
        end;
  end;
```

After we prepare our **Header** field, we send it to the wave audio device with **Write**.

```
function tWave_device.Write(
      var   Header : TWaveHdr
      ): MMRESULT;
    begin
      result := waveOutWrite(Handle,
                  @Header,
                  sizeof(Header)
                  );
      if result <> 0 then
        raise eWave_error.Create(result,
          'Error writing to output wave device'
          );
    end;
```

Our cap just takes the **Header**; however, **waveOutWrite** takes three arguments: the **Handle** we received when we opened the device (now stored in our wrapper), the memory location of the **Header**, and the size of the **Header**, (Since we built the Header ourselves, we can simply use Delphi's sizeOf function to determine this value). **waveOutWrite** looks at the **lpData** field of the **Header** for the data it will actually "write" to the device.

After we **Write** out the audio data, we need to unprepare the header and close the device. But we can't do that until the device completes playback, so we loop until **waveOutWrite** sets the flag **WHDR_DONE** in **Header**. This is the poor man's alternative to a callback function. If we *did* supply a callback, either in the form of a function or a window handle, we could then instruct **waveOutWrite** to notify us when it's complete. For us, it's easier to just watch for the signal. The signaling mechanism is actually kind of interesting. When you passed **waveOutWrite,** the pointer to the **Header**, the multimedia system remembered that place. The multimedia system can go on playing the sound, perhaps offloading the chore to specialized hardware, without your application needing to worry about it. We've actually developed a kind of parallel execution here: the sound plays while our program loops. When the sound is finished, Windows will look at where we told it our header would be, and sets the **WHDR_DONE** flag in the **dwFlags** field.

```
procedure tAudio_waveform.Play;
   begin
      with tWave_device.Create do
         try
            Open(Format,WAVE_FORMAT_QUERY);
              { Die here if we can't handle the format. }
            Open(Format,0);
            Prepare_header(Header);
            Write(Header);
            while (Header.dwFlags and WHDR_DONE) = 0 do
               Application.ProcessMessages;
            Unprepare_header(Header);
            Close;
         finally
           Free;
         end;
   end;
```

Notice that this "wait" loop repeatedly executes **Application.ProcessMessages**. Under 16-bit Windows, the **ProcessMessages** method is very useful because it allows us to process other messages while an application is waiting for something to happen. Without the **ProcessMessages** call, it is easy to hang 16-bit Windows if the requirements of a loop are never met. (This condition is known as *non-preemptive multihanging* in 16-bit Windows.) Fortunately, the preemptive multitasking operation of the 32-bit Windows environment provides much more flexibility for dealing with problems like this.

If we don't include the **ProcessMessages** call in our loop, and the requirements to exit the loop are never met; only our application will hang. Windows 95 and other applications will continue to run. With 32-bit Windows, the scope of the **ProcessMessages** function has been reduced from a global function to one that only effects the program that calls the function. Even so, we still don't want our program hanging so badly that we can not exit out of it, so we retain the **ProcessMessages** call in.

When we spot the **WHDR_DONE** flag, we unprepare the header. Then, as always, we must close the wave audio device before we terminate our program, or we'll be unable to reopen the device until we restart Windows

Adding Low-Level Playback to MCIPlay

Now we can add the low-level playback functions to our test program, with another button on Form1 and event-handling code in Main.Pas. We're going to revisit the methods Read and Play in Chapter 14, so we'll be able to re-use the three new units we've discussed: WavePlay, and MMIOWrap and WaveWrap.

Add a new Button to Form1. Set its **Name** property to WaveOut_button, and its **Caption** property to "waveOut&Write", as shown in Figure 5.5. While

Chapter 5

Figure 5.5 The **MCIPlay3** form as it appears with all six play buttons.

we're at it, we're going to fix a little "user-interface issue" with our **MessageBeep** routine by inserting the code that appears in Listing 5.8.

Listing 5.8 WaveOut_buttonClick Event Procedure from *Main.Pas*

```
procedure TForm1.WaveOut_buttonClick(Sender: TObject);
begin
    WaveOut_button.Enabled := false;
    with tAudio_waveform.Create do
        try
            try
                Read(pchar(Command_string_text.Text));
                Play;
                Status_text.Text := 'Low-level .WAV Play OK';
            except
              on E : eMMIO_error do
                  Status_text.Text :=
                     'MMIO Error ' + IntToStr(E.MMIO_result) + ': ' +
                     E.Message;
              on E : eWave_error do
                  Status_text.Text :=
                     'Wave Error ' + IntToStr(E.Wave_result) + ': ' +
                     E.Message;
            end;
        finally
          Free;
          WaveOut_button.Enabled := true;
        end;
    end;

procedure TForm1.Message_beep_buttonClick(Sender: TObject);
begin
    MessageBeep(MB_ICONEXCLAMATION);
    Status_text.Text := 'MessageBeep called.'
    end;
```

This may seem like too much trouble just to play WAV files, especially when there are at least five other much simpler methods. It is. But in the most intimate form of interactivity, we will often want to manipulate not only the playback process, but the form and content of the data itself. Wave audio data consists of lengthy streams of binary amplitude values. Those values, when used to drive an analog amplifier and speaker, translate back into sound. Once we have our hands on the binary data, we can chop it, filter it, loop it, splice it, mix it, and otherwise modify it—perhaps in real time—to suit our own purposes—and more importantly, to reflect the actions of our users.

You may also notice that the low-level functions we just implemented do not work with all WAV files—in particular, the new compressed WAV files. These files can be read into our buffer without any problems, but when we attempt to actually open the WAV device, it does not know how to handle the compressed data. We need to find a way to decompress the data that is in our buffer *before* we try and open the device. For the moment, don't worry about this—we will discuss compressed wave audio in more detail in Chapter 15.

The View from the Cellar

We've taken such a direct route down into the multimedia API that we've neglected to pause at each level and survey the territory. The MCI, for example, offers a whole bunch of commands that enable you to manipulate multimedia files as if they were physical media, like audio cassettes or video tapes. You can change your position, ask for the number of tracks, select tracks, set the volume, alter the playback speed, record, pause, and resume. Each device supports a few standard commands, along with a selection of commands unique to its medium.

Although we've focused on wave audio playback, the multimedia system supports several kinds of media, including MIDI for synthesizer control, the Audio Video Interleave format (AVI), graphic animation through the multimedia movie player (MMM), as well as external devices such as video tape recorders, video disk players, CD audio players, and Digital Audio Tape (DAT) decks.

At the low level, the Windows multimedia system includes functions to perform all kinds of operations, including buffered file I/O and MIDI sequencing and mapping. In fact, we haven't yet really reached the bottom level; we're standing on the catwalk in the deepest sub-basement, still a few feet above the floor. To perform such time-critical operations as wave audio or MIDI output, the device control functions depend on even lower-level functions—in particular, the multimedia timer, which offers much higher resolution timing than the standard Windows timer. The multimedia system even provides a standard interface for joystick input.

Essentially, we have discovered that the Windows multimedia system offers a variety of approaches to multimedia operation, each technique offering unique advantages and disadvantages. For any given multimedia project (or for that matter, for any element of any project), choose the approach that provides the most appropriate mixture of accessibility, performance, and control over the data, from simple asynchronous message beeps to byte-by-byte manipulation of digitized sound.

In upcoming chapters, we'll apply many of these techniques, not only to wave audio, but to the other multimedia services as well. So stay tuned.

Chapter 6

Master Windows palettes and you'll be in command of the most important element of multimedia—Color!

Exploring Imaging—From Pixels to Palettes

Chris D. Coppola

As a multimedia developer, you are always striving to get the most out of the hardware and software you have available. Understanding colors and palettes is a key to making that effort successful.

In this chapter, we'll explore how Delphi and Windows work together to display images. You'll learn about bitmaps, color display systems, and palettes. Before we delve into palette management functions, we'll take a peek at the anatomy of a bitmap and the attributes of display systems. Then we'll jump right in and start discovering how palettes work.

The Graphics Device interface

The *Graphics Device Interface (GDI)* is the part of Windows that controls everything that you see on your screen. The window borders, menus, captions, even the contents of a DOS window are all graphics displayed by the GDI. Fortunately, all of the work that Microsoft's team did to develop the functions that display windows, borders, and the like are available to programmers through the Windows API. Delphi encapsulates the API and does most of the tedious work of displaying windows and borders and buttons for us. Delphi also gives us the power to customize any of those functions, if the situation requires it. Most of the time we'll let Delphi take care of the boring stuff, and we'll stick to the creative endeavors.

Display Contexts

All of the GDI functions that can be accessed through the Windows API are performed on a *device context (DC)*. Actually GDI functions are performed on a specific type of device context called a *display context*. What is a device context? It is a reference to a bunch of settings that describe the attributes of a device to the system. For a complete reference of all the settings contained in a device context search for "GetDeviceCaps" in the Delphi Help. A display context, also commonly referred to as a *DC*, is the device that we'll be dealing with in this chapter. For our discussion, we'll being using display context to describe such attributes as the number of colors that the display supports, and the dimensions of the display in pixels.

Understanding Bitmaps

The PC's video system displays a matrix of dots with varying color intensities. These dots, called pixels (*picture elements*), are arranged on an *x-y* coordinate system where, in most cases, *x* ranges from left to right and *y* ranges from top to bottom. Everything in Windows is a bitmap. Bitmaps are made up of pixels. The text that I'm typing right now, the window borders, everything that you see in the Windows environment is a bitmap. You probably already know that a good understanding of bitmaps is essential to developing multimedia titles under Windows. Fortunately, bitmaps are very easy to understand. Windows bitmaps come in a variety of color resolutions, which are described in Table 6.1.

Table 6.1 Bitmap Color Resolutions

Bit Depth	Number of Colors
24 bit	16.7 million
16 bit	65,535
8 bit	256
4 bit	16
1 bit	2 (black & white)

There are two different bitmap structures under Windows: a device-dependent bitmap (DDB), and a device-independent bitmap (DIB). The distinction is simple. A DIB is a bitmap that is not associated with a DC. All of its bit and color information are intact. A DDB is a bitmap that is associated with a DC. Its color table is mapped to the system palette of its device context. We'll actually get into the structure of bitmaps in Chapter 8.

Windows Color

Windows describes colors based on their individual red, green, and blue (RGB) components. Each component, represented by one byte, can have a value in the range of 0 through 255. This range represents the intensity of that color where 0 is no intensity and 255 is full intensity. Using this system, white is described as (255,255,255), and black is described as (0,0,0).

The Windows display system can, depending on hardware, be either *true color* or *palettized*. A true-color device uses 24 bits to describe each pixel of the display, whereas a palettized device commonly uses either 8 or 4 bits.

First let's look what *true color* means. A true-color device can display any one of 16.7 million different colors (2^{24}) for each pixel at any given time. Devices that use 24 bits to describe a pixel's color are often called true color because 16.7 million colors is considerably more than our eyes can detect. All that color, however, comes at a price. A single 640x480 pixel, true-color image uses 921,600 bytes of memory. Even a compressed image that may only consume 10 K of disk space will consume nearly 1 MB of precious memory when displayed. It is for this reason that most games and performance-demanding multimedia titles stick with 8 bit or 256 colors.

Of *palettized* displays, 8 bit is by far the most common. The Windows 256 color mode uses a palette so that it can display each pixel with any of 256 different colors. The palette, rather than representing the red, green, and blue components of the color for each pixel, specifies an index to the system palette. The system palette contains *indexes* and *RGB values*. Figure 6.1 shows how this process works. We'll work with palettes next.

The Magic of Color Palettes

Multimedia demands color. Between that jazzy interface and the awesome collection of images and video you want to include in your title, you're going to need a miracle to make it come out right. You need a miracle, but what you have to work with is the Windows Palette Manager. A miracle would require far less effort on your part, but you can still achieve some pretty amazing effects with palettes.

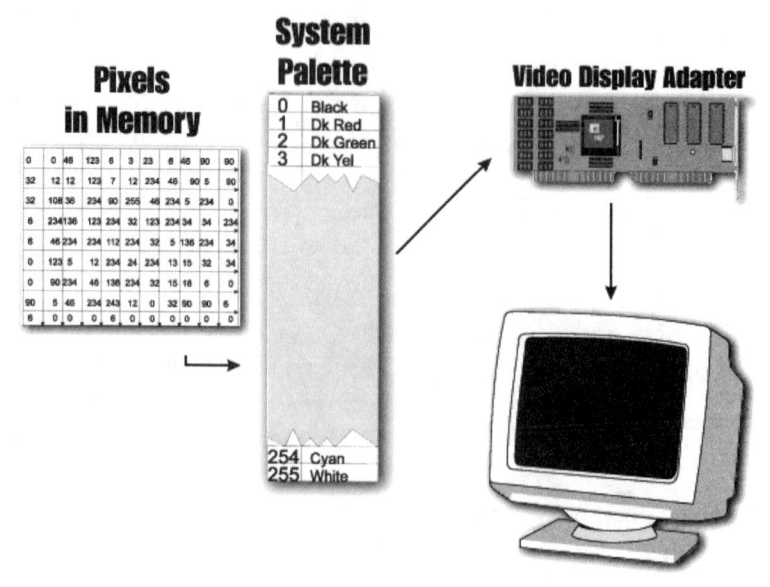

Figure 6.1 *How palette indexes get to colors on the display.*

Imagine working on a project showing highlights of the 50 states. A picture of waterfalls on the Hawaiian Islands would require an entirely different set of colors than would a shot of the Grand Canyon. With only 256 colors to choose from, neither picture would be very spectacular if one of them had to use the other's palette. Another option would be to try to merge the palettes of the two images. With the help of the API we could do this, but it still might not leave either image with enough color information to dazzle the viewer. In cases where the picture colors are from two different extremes, we have to display the pictures one at a time to show them in their full splendor. Between the time we remove one picture from the screen and display the next, we'll swap the color palettes and both images will look their best. When you finish this chapter, you'll have enough knowledge of Windows palettes to handle the situation whichever way the situation requires.

Every *DC* in an 8-bit display has an associated *logical palette* with 256 entries. (Logical palettes are explained more fully in the next section, "Inside the Palette Manager.") Each entry has an associated red, green, and blue color component. The pixels in a DC are represented by a number ranging from 0 to 255 that corresponds to an index in the associated logical palette. To change the color of a pixel, you have two options: You can change the index value of a the pixel so that it references another entry in the palette, or you can change the RGB value of the palette entry. Keep in mind that there can only be one active palette at any given time for the entire display. Changing the RGB value of the palette entry will also change the color of every other pixel on the screen that references that index, including the colors of all other applications that are visible and the colors of Windows itself. For this reason, the system palette maintains 20 static colors that are protected. Figure 6.2 shows the layout of the Windows system palette.

The static entries represent an attempt to maintain consistency of colors throughout the display. The API will let you modify 18 of these static colors (black and white cannot be changed) if you want to, but they are protected so that a change must be deliberate. Just because the API will let you, doesn't mean you should use that ability: Unless you have a full screen application, you should respect the rights of other programs that may be running and work with the 236 remaining colors.

Palettized color has its limitations, but it also offers several advantages. First, an 8-bit image in memory takes about one third the memory of its 24-bit counterpart. Next, you can use the built-in palette-management functions to get a little more bang-for-the-buck by using palette-animation techniques. Finally, by constraining your application to run in an 8-bit environment you can ensure that your application will run on much more of the existing PC hardware already in homes and businesses.

Inside the Palette Manager

As I mentioned previously, each displayed image carries its own color palette. In addition, each active window can manipulate the system palette for its own purposes. Remember that the 256 color constraint applies to the entire screen, not just to each window or application. With such limited seating, someone has to play the role of the bouncer. That's where the Windows *Palette Manager* comes in.

Windows uses the Palette Manager to determine which window has control of the system palette at any given time. The system palette is a logical

Figure 6.2 The System Palette.

palette that the Palette Manager keeps in sync with the display's hardware palette. The active window, the one with the focus, always has priority. If that window doesn't use all the entries in the palette, the priority goes to the next window in the *z-order* (the order in which windows are stacked on the desktop). Once the window with the highest priority "realizes" its palette as the foreground palette, the other windows are signaled in order by the Palette Manager to "realize" their palettes as background palettes.

What does it mean to *realize* a palette? Each image you display has its own logical color palette (several palettes can be kept in memory simultaneously). A palette stored in memory is called a logical palette. The palette in your display system that determines which colors actually appear on the screen is called the system palette. There is only one system palette and the Palette Manager maintains a copy of it. When an application wants to activate its own colors, it must select its logical palette into a display context and realize it, which means that it must ask the Palette Manager to load its logical palette into the system palette. The process of realizing a logical palette is shown in Figure 6.3.

When you realize a palette, the Palette Manager does not just dump the entries in the system palette and replace them with yours. Actually you can instruct it to do just that, but we'll get into that later. The Palette Manager copies each of the entries in the logical palette—in order—to the system palette, respecting the entries that are marked as *static*. The most important colors in your image should appear at the top of the image's logical palette. If you had an image of an Arizona sunset and most of the shades of red were in the entries 236 through 255 of the image's logical palette, the image would not do justice to the sunset. The Palette Manager would do its best to map those shades of red to the closest available colors that made it into the palette, but it would not have much to work with. Images that only use a few colors leave room in the system palette for other images. The system palette can accommodate the colors from multiple logical palettes as long as the total number of colors does not exceed 256.

If the active window does not use all of the entries in the system palette, the remaining slots will be filled with colors in the inactive windows until either all the slots are occupied or until no other windows ask to realize their own palettes. If all of the slots are filled in the system palette before all windows get their colors in, then the Palette Manager will thoughtfully go about matching their palette entries to the closest colors available. You'll see later in this chapter the results of those efforts.

We've got 236 color slots that we can work with and still be friendly to Windows and other running applications. Table 6.2 lists the colors in the

Exploring Imaging—From Pixels to Palettes 289

Logical Palette			
0	85	16	144
1	128	209	0
2	67	11	53
3	0	0	0
4	0	0	128
5	0	0	255
6			
7			

System Palette				
0	0	0	0	
1	128	0	0	
2	0	128	0	
3	128	128	0	
4	0	0	128	First 10 Static Colors (Not Changed by Realizing a Palette)
5	128	0	128	
6	0	128	128	
7	192	192	192	
8	192	220	192	
9	166	202	240	
10	85	16	144	
11	128	209	0	
12	67	11	53	
13				
14				
15				236 Nonstatic Colors (Changed by Realizing a Palette)
16				
17				
18				
19				
245				
246	255	251	240	
247	160	160	164	
248	128	128	128	
249	255	0	0	Last 10 Static Colors (Not Changed by Realizing a Palette)
250	0	255	0	
251	255	255	0	
252	0	0	255	
253	255	0	255	
254	0	255	255	
255	255	255	255	

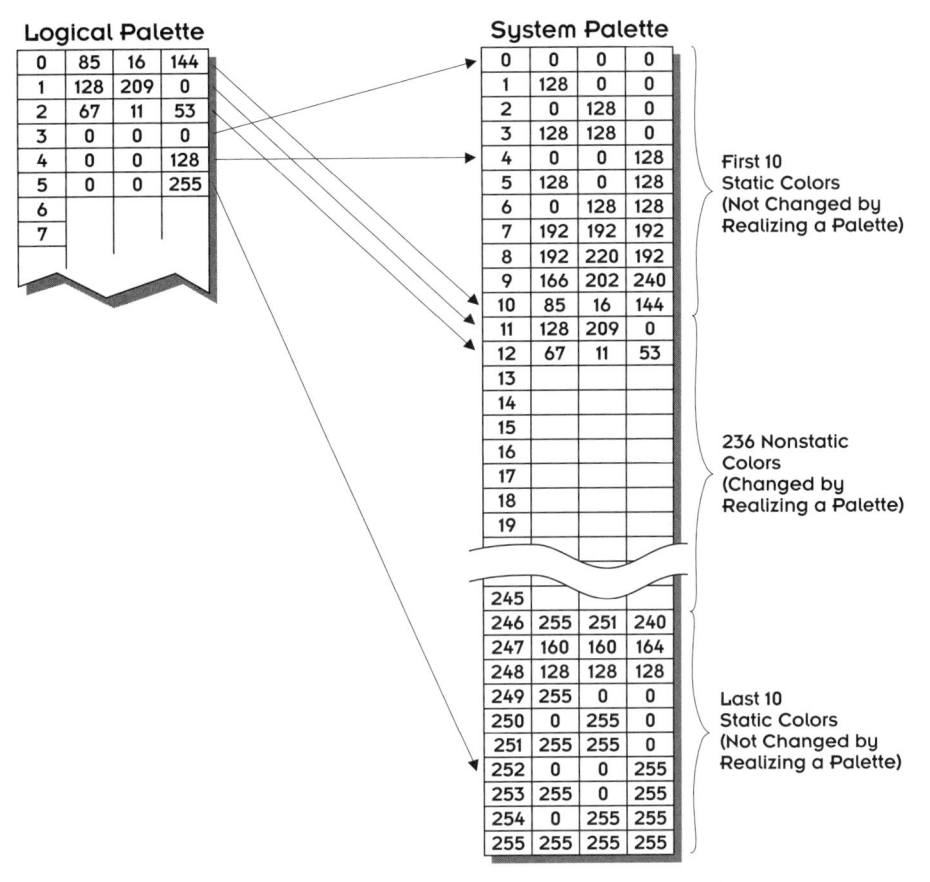

Figure 6.3 *The process of realizing a palette.*

system palette. Notice that the static colors are not contiguous in the system palette. This is so that GDI raster operations like XOR will have meaningful results. We'll talk about raster operations in the next chapter.

It is wise to convert the palette of any 8-bit image into a Windows *identity palette*, which is a palette that includes the 20 static colors (displayed in Table 6.2) and the 236 most important colors of the bitmap that the palette belongs to. The *non-static* palette entries are marked with the **PC_NOCOLAPSE** flag so that the DIB palette gets an exact 1:1 match with the system palette. If your images demand the use of more than 236 colors there is still something you can do. I mentioned earlier that you could tell the Palette Manager, as rude as it is, that you did not want to respect Windows or other applications and you will be using all of the entries in the system palette. The Palette Manager will comply, but it draws the line at 254 colors. It will not give up entries 0 or 255 (black and white).

Table 6.2 *Colors of the System Palette*

Index	Red	Green	Blue	Color
0	0	0	0	Black
1	128	0	0	Maroon
2	0	128	0	Dark Green
3	128	128	0	Dark Yellow
4	0	0	128	Navy
5	128	0	128	Dark Magenta
6	0	128	128	Dark Cyan
7	192	192	192	Light Gray
8	192	220	192	Money Green
9	166	202	240	Sky Blue
246	255	251	240	Cream
247	160	160	164	Medium Gray
248	128	128	128	Dark Gray
249	255	0	0	Red
250	0	255	0	Green
251	255	255	0	Yellow
252	0	0	255	Blue
253	255	0	255	Magenta
254	0	255	255	Cyan
255	255	255	255	White

Exploring Colors with Delphi

Delphi does a great job of hiding the details of color palette operations. If you just want to display bitmaps in Timage controls, you can let Delphi and the Windows Palette Manager take care of it. When Delphi loads a bitmap, it loads and realizes that bitmap's palette automatically. If you load a different image the palette changes again, all behind the scenes. Delphi, as powerful as it is, is not intuitive enough to notice that you have two images displayed with conflicting palettes. It just methodically loads an image and realizes its palette. When you load the next image, it loads and realizes its palette. The first image is then doctored by the Palette Manager to display with colors that are as close as possible. Do not expect Delphi to accurately display two images with dissimilar palettes.

To program applications that have interesting visual effects or dazzling interfaces, you go around Delphi's back and deal directly with the Palette Manager. In this section we'll take a look at color in Delphi firsthand. Let's get started....

Selecting Colors the Easy Way

Before abandoning Delphi's built-in color capabilities, let's see how far they can take us. Delphi gives us access to the **RGB()** function to make it simple to create an RGB color value.

> ## Using the RGB() Function
>
> This project shows you how to use **RGB()** to display different colors. Here are the steps to follow:
>
> 1. Create a new project and name the default form "RGBMain".
> 2. Place 3 trackbars, 3 labels, and a Tpanel control on the form, as shown in Figure 6.4.
> 3. Complete the code module as shown in listing 6.1.
>
> *This project is located in the directory \DELPHIMM\CH06\TESTRGB.*

Creating the RGB() Program

To start, create a new project and name the default form "RGBMain". Place a TPanel component, 3 trackbars, and 3 labels on the form, as shown in Figure 6.4. The TPanel component is going to be the guy that displays the color. The trackbars will change each of the three components of the color (red, green, and blue) independently. The labels will display the value of the trackbar, and subsequently the value of either the red, blue, or green component. Save the project. Name the project's default unit "utestrgb.pas", and name the project "testrgb.dpr".

Before getting into the code, set the important properties of the form and controls using the settings shown in Table 6.3.

Listing 6.1 shows the completed utestrgb.pas unit.

Chapter 6

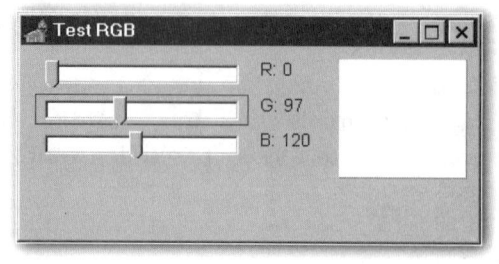

Figure 6.4 *The Test RGB form.*

Table 6.3 *Form and Component Properties*

Component	Property	Setting
Main Form	Name	RGBMain
	Caption	Test RGB
	Position	poScreenCenter
TPanel	Name	pnlColor
	Caption	(clear)
TTrackbars	Name(s)	trbRed, trbGreen, trbBlue
	Min	0
	Max	255
Tlabels	Name(s)	lblRed, lblGreen, lblBlue

Listing 6.1 The Test RGB Form Unit

```
unit utestrgb;

interface

uses
  Windows, Messages, SysUtils, Classes, Graphics, Controls, Forms, Dialogs,
  ExtCtrls, ComCtrls, StdCtrls;

type
  TRGBMain = class(TForm)
    trbRed: TTrackBar;
    trbGreen: TTrackBar;
    trbBlue: TTrackBar;
    pnlColor: TPanel;
    lblRed: TLabel;
    lblGreen: TLabel;
    lblBlue: TLabel;
    procedure FormCreate(Sender: TObject);
    procedure TrackbarChange(Sender: TObject);
```

```
  private
    { Private declarations }
  public
    { Public declarations }
  end;

var
  RGBMain: TRGBMain;

implementation

{$R *.DFM}

procedure TRGBMain.FormCreate(Sender: TObject);
begin
  TrackbarChange(trbRed);
end; {FormCreate}

procedure TRGBMain.TrackbarChange(Sender: TObject);
begin

  { set the label captions }
  lblRed.Caption   := 'R: ' + IntToStr(trbRed.Position);
  lblGreen.Caption := 'G: ' + IntToStr(trbGreen.Position);
  lblBlue.Caption  := 'B: ' + IntToStr(trbBlue.Position);

  {use the RGB function to set the color of the TPanel component}
  pnlColor.Color   := RGB(trbRed.position, trbGreen.position,
                          trbBlue.position);
end; {TrackbarChange}

end.
```

Delphi is going to create most of that code for us. That's the advantage of a visual development environment. Let's examine the code. Delphi created all of the code up to the implementation section except the interface declaration for **TrackbarChange**. I created that declaration so that I could use a single event procedure to handle the **change** event for all of the trackbars. I also created the implementation procedure shell for that event and, of course, I wrote the code inside it.

The procedure call in the **FormCreate** event

```
TrackbarChange(trbRed);
```

calls the **TrackbarChange** event to initialize the labels and the color of the TPanel component. The parameter **trbRed** was an arbitrary choice. The procedure requires **TObject** as a parameter. I could have passed trbGreen or trbBlue with no change in the result. Let's take a closer look at the **TrackbarChange** event procedure:

```
procedure TRGBMain.TrackbarChange(Sender: TObject);
begin
   { set the label captions }
   lblRed.Caption   := 'R: ' + IntToStr(trbRed.Position);
   lblGreen.Caption := 'G: ' + IntToStr(trbGreen.Position);
   lblBlue.Caption  := 'B: ' + IntToStr(trbBlue.Position);

   {use the RGB function to set the color of the TPanel component}
   pnlColor.Color   := RGB(trbRed.position, trbGreen.position,
                           trbBlue.position);
end; {TrackbarChange}
```

In this procedure we display the color values as integers, and we actually set the color value to be displayed. First we set the label captions so they display the correct value for each color component. The Position property of the TTrackBar has a value in the range of 0 to 255. We set the limits when we added the components to the form. Since the range of the TrackBar position directly relates to the color component value, all we have to do is display the value. Next we use the Windows API function RGB() to transform each of the color component values into one color reference. The color reference, or RGB value, that is returned is assigned to the color property of the TPanel component.

Ok, now that the work is done, run the program and experiment with it. I recommend running the program with Windows in 8-bit and also 24-bit (true color).

Let's discuss the results. Quite a difference between running in 256 colors or running in 16 million! With a 256 color driver loaded you should have seen multi-colored hatch patterns as you moved the track bars. This is the Palette Manager using the 20 static system colors to approximate the RGB values that you saw displayed in the labels. Not very pretty is it? You should have noticed also that occasionally there was a color that displayed solid—the 20 static colors. When you ran the program with Windows in true color the Palette Manager took a coffee break. There was nothing do be done—each color was displayed exactly as its red, green, and blue components dictate. What? You don't want to work with 256 colors anymore? Remember the advantages: less memory, greater system compatibility, and palette-animation techniques.

Using More Colors—Loading a Palette

We can do better than dithered colors. The way to go is to use a more extensive palette of "pure colors," which are mixed at the hardware level. This can be done by loading a palette into a specific object that contains a canvas, such as a TImage or TPaintBox control. Actually, if you remember, a palette gets loaded into a DC. In Delphi, a TCanvas encapsulates a Windows display context.

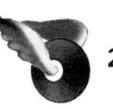

Delphi controls, except the TImage control, do not contain a **Palette** property. The TBitmap object of the TImage control contains a **Palette** property. If you load an image into a TImage component either at design-time or while your program is running, Delphi will load the palette that goes with that image for you. You can even get access to the palette of the image once it is loaded. Unfortunately, by this time you've already lost some control. The palette that you get from the TImage component has already been realized and therefore the image is a DDB and the palette entries are mapped to the currently realized palette. To get the pure palette from the image we have to work around Delphi a bit with the API.

A Closer Look at Colors

Delphi uses the TColor type to describe a color. The Graphics unit that comes with Delphi declares lots of useful constants to specify common Windows colors. You see these constants when you use the object inspector to set the **Color** property of an object. You can also use these constants in your code. When you construct a TColor without the help of these constants, you need to adhere to certain rules: The low-order three bytes represent a byte for each of red, green, and blue components of the color. Table 6.4 shows the results of setting the high-order byte of a color.

The RGB function returns a 32-bit value with the high-order byte $00. In order to change the way that the color is applied, that value should be combined with the logical operator **or**. The following code example tells Windows that I want the color that exists in palette entry #154 of the currently realized logical palette:

```
Panel1.Color := $01000000 or 154;
```

Table 6.4 *High-Order Byte Values of TColor*

Value	Result
$00	Windows dithers the 20 system colors to obtain a color match
$01	The low-order byte represents an index to the currently realized logical palette
$02	Windows locates the palette entry that most closely matches the color determined by the red, green, and blue components specified in the three low-order bytes

Selecting Colors by Numbers

This project uses a handful of API functions to display a palette in a 16×16 grid, as shown in Figure 6.5. Here are the steps to follow:

1. Create a new project and name the default form "PalMain".
2. Add a TImage component about 320x200 pixels in size and then load an image. (There are some in the \IMAGES directory under Delphi 2.0.)
3. Insert the code for the form's **OnActivate** event, as shown in Listing 6.2.

This project is located in the directory \DELPHIMM\CH06\PALEXP1.

Creating the Palette Program

First, create a new project and add a TImage component. Next, set the properties as described in Table 6.5 and load a bitmap into the TImage component by setting the **Picture** property in the object inspector. Save the project. Name the project's default unit "upalexp1.pas", and name the project "palexp1.dpr". Figure 6.5 shows the main form.

Now enter the code for the form's **OnActivate** event, as shown in Listing 6.2.

Table 6.5 Form and Component Properties

Component	Property	Setting
Main Form	Name	PalMain
	Caption	Palette Experiment #1
	Position	poScreenCenter
	Scaled	False
TImage	Name	Image1
	Picture	(TBitmap)
	Width	320
	Height	200
	AutoSize	True
	Stretch	True

Exploring Imaging—From Pixels to Palettes 297

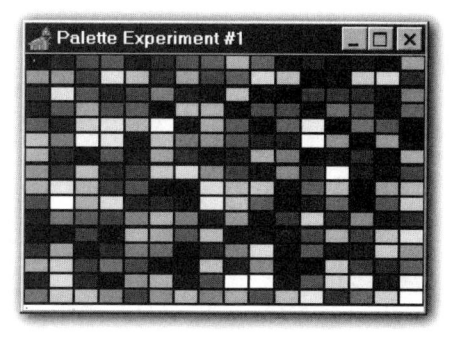

Figure 6.5 *Main form of Palette Experiment #1.*

Listing 6.2 The palexp1 Form Unit

```
unit upalexp1;

interface

uses
  Windows, Messages, SysUtils, Classes, Graphics, Controls, Forms, Dialogs,
  ExtCtrls;

type
  TPalMain = class(TForm)
    Image1: TImage;
    procedure FormActivate(Sender: TObject);
  private
    { Private declarations }
  public
    { Public declarations }
  end;

var
  PalMain: TPalMain;

implementation

{$R *.DFM}


procedure TPalMain.FormActivate(Sender: TObject);
var
  r,c:          integer;       {row and column}
  BoxDim:       TPoint;        {the dimensions (x,y) of a color box}
  colorindex:   longint;       {the index of the palette}
begin
  BoxDim.x := Image1.Width div 16;
  BoxDim.y := Image1.Height div 16;
  Image1.Canvas.Pen.Color := clBlack;
  Image1.Canvas.Brush.Style := bsSolid;
```

```
    for colorindex := 0 to 255 do begin
      r := colorindex div 16 + 1;
      c := colorindex mod 16 + 1;
      Image1.Canvas.Brush.Color := $01000000 or colorindex;
      Image1.Canvas.Rectangle( (c-1) * BoxDim.x, (r-1) * BoxDim.y,
                               c * BoxDim.x, r * BoxDim.y);

    end;
  Image1.Width := 320;
  Image1.Height := 200;
  ClientWidth := Image1.Width;
  ClientHeight := Image1.Height;
end; {FormActivate}

end.
```

Run the program and see what happens. Not very exciting is it? You've actually done quite a bit with this simple little program. Let's take a look at it:

```
  BoxDim.x := Image1.Width div 16;
  BoxDim.y := Image1.Height div 16;
```

Here, we're just dividing the width of the form into 16 equal squares and storing that square size in the variable **BoxDim**. We don't want to do that divide in a loop. It probably wouldn't affect us here, but it's not a good habit. The next two lines set the pen color and the brush style of the Image's canvas:

```
  Image1.Canvas.Pen.Color := clBlack;
  Image1.Canvas.Brush.Style := bsSolid;
```

Remember that a *canvas* is Delphi's encapsulation of a DC. Delphi has actually done quite a bit for us with those two property assignments. Normally the **Pen** and **Brush** would have to be created, modified, and then destroyed when we were finished with them. Delphi takes care of this for us. If you're curious about what you're missing out on, check out what the API says about **SelectObject**. Now for the loop:

```
    for colorindex := 0 to 255 do begin
      r := colorindex div 16 + 1;
      c := colorindex mod 16 + 1;
      Image1.Canvas.Brush.Color := $01000000 or colorindex;
      Image1.Canvas.Rectangle( (c-1) * BoxDim.x, (r-1) * BoxDim.y,
                               c * BoxDim.x, r * BoxDim.y);

    end; {for}
```

Our counter in the loop is **colorindex**. It increments from 0 to 255 (the range of palette index values). For each iteration of the loop, the row and column variables are calculated to increment from left to right across the columns, then down a row. This process is repeated until the row and column point to the lower-right corner grid, which is color index 255. Take a look at that next line:

```
Image1.Canvas.Brush.Color := $01000000 or colorindex;
```

Here we're setting the brush color by index in the logical palette. The **Color** property of the canvas' brush is of the TColor type. Because we're setting the high-order byte to $01 with the logical **or**, the low-order byte represents an index to the currently realized logical palette. We loaded an image into the TImage component, so Delphi graciously loaded and realized its palette for us. The **colorindex** counter increments the color of the brush through the values in the logical palette. The **Rectangle** method, an encapsulation of the GDI function **Rectangle()**, draws a rectangle filled with the brush color.

The last four property settings just make the form a bit bigger so the palette is easier to see. Let's dig a little deeper into the depth of the API. The palette functions that we've used so far have only scratched the surface of the possibilities.

Using the API to Access Colors

Windows provides several functions that control and retrieve information from color palettes. Among these you will find the **RGB()** function that we used in the last project. There are also several important data structures that are used with these functions.

When dealing directly with the API functions used to manage palettes, we use handles to palettes (*hPalette*), logical palettes (*TLogPalette*) that contain palette entries (*TPaletteEntry*), and DCs. A handle to a palette is just an integer number that Windows uses to keep track of a palette. You get a handle back, for example, from the **CreatePalette()** function, which takes a **TLogPalette** structure as a parameter. Take a look at the **TLogPalette** structure:

```
TLogPalette = record
   palVersion: Word;
   palNumEntries: Word;
   palPalEntry: array[0..0] of TPaletteEntry;
 end;
```

This is pretty simple—the **palVersion** field is always $300, the **palNumEntries** field is just the number of entries that are in the palette. The last field, **palPalEntry**, is an array of **TPaletteEntry** structures. **TPaletteEntry** structures are just the red, green, and blue components of each entry in the palette and a flag that specifies how the colors are interpreted. The structure looks like this:

```
TPaletteEntry = record
   peRed: Byte;
   peGreen: Byte;
   peBlue: Byte;
   peFlags: Byte;
 end;
```

The **peRed**, **peGreen**, and **pBlue** fields should be the RGB intensity (0 through 255) unless the **PC_EXPLICIT** flag is used. Then the value of **peRed** designates a specific index in the system palette, and the **peGreen** and **peBlue** fields are ignored. The values for the **peFlags** field are illustrated in Table 6.6.

Changing Colors in the Logical Color Palette

In this project we'll use trackbars again to modify colors. This time we'll get the palette from the desktop. This will give a chance to see what an identity palette looks like with the static colors in place. We'll use the slider bars to make changes to the colors in the logical palette entries.

1. Create a new project and name the default form "PalEdit".
2. Add controls to create a form that looks like the one in Figure 6.6.

Table 6.6 Palette Entry Flags

Flag	Meaning
PC_EXPLICIT	Specifies that the low-order byte (red) designates a system palette index.
PC_NOCOLLAPSE	Specifies that the color will be placed in an unused entry in the system palette instead of being matched to an existing color in the system palette. Once this color is in the system palette, colors in other logical palettes can be matched to this color. If there are no unused entries in the system palette, the color is matched normally.
PC_RESERVED	Specifies that the logical palette entry will be used for palette animation. Because the color will frequently change, using this flag prevents other windows from matching colors to this palette entry. If an unused system-palette entry is available, this color is placed in that entry. Otherwise, the color will not be available for animation.

Exploring Imaging—From Pixels to Palettes 301

3. Modify the properties of the form and controls using Table 6.7.
4. Add the code shown in Listing 6.3.

> This project is located in the directory \DELPHIMM\CH06\PALEXP2.

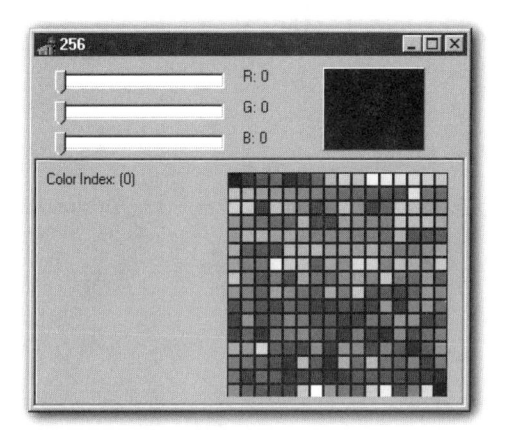

Figure 6.6 Main form of Palette Experiment #2.

Table 6.7 Form and Component Properties

Component	Property/Event	Setting
Main Form	Name	PalEdit
	Caption	Palette Editor
	Position	poScreenCenter
	OnCreate	FormCreate
TPanel	Name	pnlColor
	Caption	(clear)
	OnClick	pnlColorClick
TTrackbars	Name(s)	trbRed, trbGreen, trbBlue
	Min	0
	Max	255
	OnChange	TrackBarChange
Tlabels	Name(s)	lblRed, lblGreen, lblBlue, lblPalText
TPaintBox	Name	pbPalette
	OnMouseDown	pbPaletteMouseDown
	OnPaint	pbPalettePaint

Creating the Palette Edit Program

First, create a new project and add the controls shown in Figure 6.6 to the form. You may wish to copy the form from the RGB program at the beginning of this chapter and modify it for this project. Next set the properties for the form and controls as described in Table 6.7. Save the project. Name the project's default unit "upalexp2.pas", and name the project "palexp2.dpr".

Listing 6.3   The palexp2 Form Unit

```
unit upalexp2;

interface

uses
  Windows, Messages, SysUtils, Classes, Graphics, Controls, Forms, Dialogs,
  ExtCtrls, ComCtrls, StdCtrls;

type
  TPalEdit = class(TForm)
    lblRed: TLabel;
    lblGreen: TLabel;
    lblBlue: TLabel;
    trbRed: TTrackBar;
    trbGreen: TTrackBar;
    trbBlue: TTrackBar;
    pnlColor: TPanel;
    Panel1: TPanel;
    lblPalText: TLabel;
    pbPalette: TPaintBox;
    function DisplayDC: hDC;
    function PaletteFromDesktop: hPalette;
    procedure pbPalettePaint(Sender: TObject);
    procedure pbPaletteMouseDown(Sender: TObject; Button: TMouseButton;
      Shift: TShiftState; X, Y: Integer);
    procedure FormCreate(Sender: TObject);
    procedure TrackBarChange(Sender: TObject);
    procedure FormDestroy(Sender: TObject);
    procedure pnlColorClick(Sender: TObject);
  private
    { Private declarations }
  public
    { Public declarations }
  end;

var
  PalEdit: TPalEdit;

implementation

{$R *.DFM}
```

```
var
  BoxDim:     TPoint;        {dimensions a color tab in the pal display}
  SelColor:   byte;
  hPal:       THandle;
  hOldPal:    hPalette;
  selecting:  boolean;

function TPalEdit.DisplayDC: hDC;
begin
  result := pbPalette.Canvas.Handle;
end; {DisplayDC}

function TPalEdit.PaletteFromDesktop: hPalette;
var
  pNewPal:    PLogPalette;
  size:       longint;
  ScreenDC:   hDC;

begin

  size := sizeof(TLogPalette) + (sizeof(TPaletteEntry) * 256);
  pNewPal := nil;
  ScreenDC := 0;

  try
    ScreenDC := GetDC(0);
    pNewPal := allocmem(size);
    pNewPal^.palVersion := $300;
    pNewPal^.palNumEntries := 256;
    if GetSystemPaletteEntries(ScreenDC, 0, 255, pNewPal^.palPalEntry) > 0 then
      result := CreatePalette(pNewPal^)
    else result := 0;
  finally
    ReleaseDC(0, ScreenDC);
    freemem(pNewPal, size);
  end;

end; {PaletteFromDesktop}

procedure TPalEdit.FormCreate(Sender: TObject);
begin

  {
  set the box dimensions so that each of the 16x16 color tabs
  in the palette fit in 16 rows and 16 columns on the paint box
  }
  BoxDim.x := pbPalette.Width div 16;
  BoxDim.y := pbPalette.Height div 16;
  SelColor := 0;
  TrackBarChange(trbRed);

  hPal := PaletteFromDesktop;
  hOldPal := SelectPalette(DisplayDC, hPal, False);

end; {Create}
```

```
procedure TPalEdit.pbPalettePaint(Sender: TObject);
var
  r,c             integer;        {row and column}
  colorindex:     longint;
  Brush,
  OldBrush:       hBrush;

begin

  Brush := 0;
  OldBrush := 0;
  SelectPalette(DisplayDC, hPal, False);
  Self.Caption := IntToStr(RealizePalette(DisplayDC));
  for colorindex := 0 to 255 do begin
    r := colorindex div 16 + 1;
    c := colorindex mod 16 + 1;
    try
      Brush := CreateSolidBrush($01000000 or colorindex);
      OldBrush := SelectObject(DisplayDC, Brush);
      Rectangle( DisplayDC, ((c-1) * BoxDim.x) + 2, ((r-1) * BoxDim.y) + 2,
                 c * BoxDim.x + 2, r * BoxDim.y + 2);
    finally
      SelectObject(DisplayDC, OldBrush);
      DeleteObject(Brush);
    end; {try}
  end; {for}

end; {pbPalette.OnPaint}

procedure TPalEdit.pbPaletteMouseDown(Sender: TObject;
  Button: TMouseButton; Shift: TShiftState; X, Y: Integer);
var
  r,c:        byte;
  PalEntry:   TPaletteEntry;

begin

  r := Y div BoxDim.y;
  c := X div BoxDim.x;
  SelColor := byte(r * 16 + c);
  if GetSystemPaletteEntries(DisplayDC, SelColor, 1, PalEntry) > 0 then begin
    selecting := True;
    trbRed.Position := PalEntry.peRed;
    trbGreen.Position := PalEntry.peGreen;
    trbBlue.Position := PalEntry.peBlue;
    selecting := False;
    TrackBarChange(trbRed);
    end;

end; {pbPalette.MouseDown}

procedure TPalEdit.TrackBarChange(Sender: TObject);
begin
```

Exploring Imaging—From Pixels to Palettes

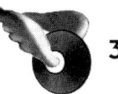

```
    if (not Selecting) and (SelColor >=0) then begin
      {show the RGB values for the slider bar positions}
      lblRed.Caption := 'R: ' + IntToStr(trbRed.Position);
      lblGreen.Caption := 'G: ' + IntToStr(trbGreen.Position);
      lblBlue.Caption := 'B: ' + IntToStr(trbBlue.Position);

      {display the index number of the selected palette entry }
      lblPalText.Caption := 'Color Index: (' + IntToStr(SelColor) + ')';

      {set the color of the panel for a larger display (dithered)}
      pnlColor.Color := RGB(trbRed.Position, trbGreen.Position, trbBlue.Position);

    end; {if}

end; {TrackbarChange}

procedure TPalEdit.FormDestroy(Sender: TObject);
begin
  SelectPalette(DisplayDC, hOldPal, False);
  DeleteObject(hPal);
end; {FormDestroy}

procedure TPalEdit.pnlColorClick(Sender: TObject);
var
  pPalEntry:  PPaletteEntry;

begin
    pPalEntry:=nil;
    try
      pPalEntry := new(PPaletteEntry);
      pPalEntry^.peRed := trbRed.Position;
      pPalEntry^.peGreen := trbGreen.Position;
      pPalEntry^.peBlue := trbBlue.Position;
      pPalEntry^.peFlags := 0;

      SetPaletteEntries(hPal, SelColor, 1, pPalEntry^);
      pbPalette.Repaint;
    finally
      Dispose(pPalEntry);
    end;

end; {pnlColorOnClick}

end.
```

Run the program. You should notice that the palette contains the 20 static colors in the locations that I described earlier. You may also notice that the non-static colors in the palette grid are shades of the colors on your desktop. If you don't have wallpaper on your desktop, or another application that uses more than the system colors, I recommend that you load some 256 color wallpaper temporarily to see the effects of our palette manipulation.

Select a color in the palette other than one of the static colors. The color panel displays that color and the trackbars move to indicate the intensities of the three color components. The label to the left of the grid displays the index in the palette that is currently selected. Now that an index is selected, change the trackbar values so that the color is radically different than it is in the palette. Click on the color panel and the color in the palette is changed to the color you defined with the trackbars! You may have also noticed that the colors in other windows and the desktop have changed to reflect the change in this palette. Your application has the focus and its *identity* palette is realized. Since we are using all 236 of the definable colors, the Palette Manager will be busy trying to map the colors for the desktop and other applications to the closest colors in our palette.

Let's see what happens when we change color index 2. Select the third color from the left on the top row. The color index should be 2. Use the trackbars to change the color, then click on the color panel to replace the color in the palette. It changed! You should now see the new color in its place in the palette display. Click on index 2 again. It should display the original color in the color panel. We'll discover why when we get into the code. But first, let's look at what happens when the form is created:

```
procedure TPalEdit.FormCreate(Sender: TObject);
begin

  {
  set the box dimensions so that each of the 16x16 color tabs
  in the palette fit in 16 rows and 16 columns on the paint box
  }
  BoxDim.x := pbPalette.Width div 16;
  BoxDim.y := pbPalette.Height div 16;
  SelColor := 0;
  TrackBarChange(trbRed);

  hPal := PaletteFromDesktop;
  hOldPal := SelectPalette(DisplayDC, hPal, False);

end; {Create}
```

The first new thing in this procedure is the **PaletteFromDesktop** function. This function uses a few API calls to return an identity palette which it creates from colors on the Windows desktop. It takes four steps to manipulate palettes at the API level:

1. Create the logical palette structure and fill the palette entries with color information.

2. Use **CreatePalette()** to get a handle to the palette.
3. Select the palette into a DC using the handle returned by **CreatePalette()**.
4. Realize the palette in the DC.

The first two steps in this program take place in the **PaletteFromDesktop** function. Take a look at Listing 6.4.

Listing 6.4   The PaletteFromDesktop Function

```
function TPalEdit.PaletteFromDesktop: hPalette;
var
  pNewPal:    PLogPalette;
  size:       longint;
  ScreenDC:   hDC;

begin

  size := sizeof(TLogPalette) + (sizeof(TPaletteEntry) * 256);
  pNewPal := nil;
  ScreenDC := 0;

  try
    ScreenDC := GetDC(0);
    pNewPal := allocmem(size);
    pNewPal^.palVersion := $300;
    pNewPal^.palNumEntries := 256;
    if GetSystemPaletteEntries(ScreenDC, 0, 255, pNewPal^.palPalEntry) > 0 then
      result := CreatePalette(pNewPal^)
    else result := 0;
  finally
    ReleaseDC(0, ScreenDC);
    freemem(pNewPal, size);
  end;

end; {PaletteFromDesktop}
```

This function declares **pNewPal** as *PLogPalette*. This is a pointer to a **TLogPalette** structure. It also uses **ScreenDC**, which is a handle to the display context of the desktop. The first thing that the function does is to get the amount of memory that it will need to hold the palette data. The long integer variable **size** stores this value. After some initialization, the function attempts to get a handle to the screen's display context. **GetDC** is an API call that expects the handle to a window and returns a handle to that window's display context. We allocate memory for the pointer and set the version and number of entries in the palette, then we use **GetSystemPaletteEntries** to fill the logical palette structure. If **GetSystemPaletteEntries** is able to retrieve at least one entry then we use **CreatePalette** to actually create a logical palette. The result of **CreatePalette**, a *handle* to a palette, is returned by the **PaletteFromDesktop** function.

It is worth mentioning here that a resource protection block, **try...finally...end**, makes sure that the memory and resources that get allocated also get released. It is important to release a DC when you are finished with it. Windows only allows five common device contexts to be allocated at any given time.

Back in the **FormCreate** procedure we take the result of CreatePaletteFromDesktop, which is a handle to a palette, and select it into the display context that we will be drawing on. Take a look a the line:

```
hOldPal := SelectPalette(DisplayDC, hPal, False);
```

SelectPalette is an API call that selects a palette into a display context so that its colors can be realized. The first parameter is **DisplayDC**. This is a function that returns a handle to the *canvas* (display context) of the PaintBox that we use to display the palette. A handle to a palette—which we got from the **PaletteFromDesktop** function—is the next parameter. The last parameter, if true, tells the Palette Manager to force this to be a background palette. The return value of **SelectPalette** is a handle to the previously loaded palette. We need to store this value so it can be selected back into the DC before the DC is destroyed and before the palette is deleted. We accomplish this in the **OnDestroy** handler for the form:

```
procedure TPalEdit.FormDestroy(Sender: TObject);
begin
  SelectPalette(DisplayDC, hOldPal, False);
  DeleteObject(hPal);
end; {FormDestroy}
```

The **pbPalettePaint** handler, shown in Listing 6.5, is executed whenever it gets a message from Windows telling it that it should repaint itself. We also cause this event to be fired when we execute the **pbPalette.Refresh** method.

Listing 6.5   The OnPaint Handler

```
procedure TPalEdit.pbPalettePaint(Sender: TObject);
var
  r,c             integer;      {row and column}
  colorindex:     longint;
  Brush,
  OldBrush:       hBrush;
```

```
begin
  Brush := 0;
  OldBrush := 0;
  SelectPalette(DisplayDC, hPal, False);
  Self.Caption := IntToStr(RealizePalette(DisplayDC));
  for colorindex := 0 to 255 do begin
    r := colorindex div 16 + 1;
    c := colorindex mod 16 + 1;
    try
      Brush := CreateSolidBrush($01000000 or colorindex);
      OldBrush := SelectObject(DisplayDC, Brush);
      Rectangle( DisplayDC, ((c-1) * BoxDim.x) + 2, ((r-1) * BoxDim.y) + 2,
                 c * BoxDim.x + 2, r * BoxDim.y + 2);
    finally
      SelectObject(DisplayDC, OldBrush);
      DeleteObject(Brush);
    end; {try}
  end; {for}

end; {pbPalette.OnPaint}
```

The **OnPaint** handler selects and realizes the logical palette we made when the form was created. Then for each of the indexes (0 through 255) of the palette it uses the API to create a drawing brush with the color of the current index, and draw a filled rectangle with that color at the current row and column. The result is a 16x16 grid of colors—one color for each index of the currently realized palette in **DisplayDC**. Take a close look at the first line in the resource protection block:

```
Brush := CreateSolidBrush($01000000 or colorindex);
```

CreateSolidBrush is an API call that takes a color reference (**TColorRef**) as a parameter. The combination of **$01000000** and **colorindex** with the logical operator **or** changes the high-order byte to $01. This tells the function that instead of the three low-order bytes specifying the intesity of red, green, and blue in the color—the low-order byte is used as an index to the currently realized palette. Look back at Table 6.6 if you need to review the construction of a color reference.

Take a look at Listing 6.6. This is the code that is executed when the PaintBox gets a click event.

Listing 6.6 The MouseDown handler for the Paint Box

```
procedure TPalEdit.pbPaletteMouseDown(Sender: TObject;
  Button: TMouseButton; Shift: TShiftState; X, Y: Integer);
```

```
var
  r,c:       byte;
  PalEntry:  TPaletteEntry;

begin

  r := Y div BoxDim.y;
  c := X div BoxDim.x;
  SelColor := byte(r * 16 + c);
  if GetSystemPaletteEntries(DisplayDC, SelColor, 1, PalEntry) > 0 then begin
    selecting := True;
    trbRed.Position := PalEntry.peRed;
    trbGreen.Position := PalEntry.peGreen;
    trbBlue.Position := PalEntry.peBlue;
    selecting := False;
    TrackBarChange(trbRed);
    end;

end; {pbPalette.MouseDown}
```

This event sets the position of the trackbar controls to indicate the RGB value of the color in the selected index of the system palette. The API does most of the work in this handler. We use **GetSystemPaletteEntries** again—this time to get the value of a single entry. The second and third parameters of **GetSystemPaletteEntries** specify the starting index and number of entries to retrieve. If we're able to get the color information from that entry, then we set the position of each of the trackbars and call the **TrackBarChange** procedure to update the labels and color panel.

So far, everything that we've looked at gets information about palettes. We've created them, selected them into DCs, and realized them. Let's take a look at how to modify a palette. Listing 6.7 is the **OnClick** handler for the TPanel control.

Listing 6.7 OnClick Handler for pnlColor

```
procedure TPalEdit.pnlColorClick(Sender: TObject);
var
  pPalEntry:  PPaletteEntry;

begin

    pPalEntry:=nil;
    try
      pPalEntry := new(PPaletteEntry);
      pPalEntry^.peRed := trbRed.Position;
      pPalEntry^.peGreen := trbGreen.Position;
      pPalEntry^.peBlue := trbBlue.Position;
      pPalEntry^.peFlags := 0;
```

```
    SetPaletteEntries(hPal, SelColor, 1, pPalEntry^);
    pbPalette.Repaint;
  finally
    Dispose(pPalEntry);
  end;

end; {pnlColorOnClick}
```

To change color entries in a logical palette, all we have to do is tell the API which palette, which entries, and what we want them to be. If that seems pretty easy, it's because it *is* easy. The **SetPaletteEntries()** API call will change entries based on the same set of parameters that we used on **GetSystemPaletteEntries**. In this case, we're only changing one entry so a single pointer to the **TPaletteEntry** structure will do the job. After we set the changed palette entries, the changed palette must be realized, and the component must be repainted for the changes to take effect. The **OnPaint** handler does this, so all we have have to do is execute the **Repaint** method of **pbPalette**.

The method we used in this project to change entries in a logical palette doesn't do much more than just work. Repainting every time an entry is changed would not be acceptable if we were trying to create a cool effect by cycling the colors of an image. The repaint would be too distracting and ruin the effect. Fortunately, the Windows API gives us another function designed to change color entries on-the-fly. Let's take a look at what the previous project would look like using the **AnimatePalette()** function instead of **SetPaletteEntries()**.

Using AnimatePalette() to Edit the Palette

This project will show you how to avoid that repaint problem by instantly changing any one of the colors in the system palette.

This project is located in the directory \DELPHIMM\CH06\PALEXP3.

Modifying the Code

Copy the files from the palexp2 project that we just finished to a new directory and open the copy of the project so we can make the necessary adjustments. For reference, the finished code for the palexp3 project is in Listing 6.8.

Listing 6.8 The Palette Editor with AnimatePalette()

```
unit upalexp3;

interface
```

```
uses
  Windows, Messages, SysUtils, Classes, Graphics, Controls, Forms, Dialogs,
  ExtCtrls, ComCtrls, StdCtrls;

type
  TPalEdit = class(TForm)
    lblRed: TLabel;
    lblGreen: TLabel;
    lblBlue: TLabel;
    trbRed: TTrackBar;
    trbGreen: TTrackBar;
    trbBlue: TTrackBar;
    pnlColor: TPanel;
    Panel1: TPanel;
    lblPalText: TLabel;
    pbPalette: TPaintBox;
    function DisplayDC: hDC;
    function MakePalette: hPalette;
    procedure pbPalettePaint(Sender: TObject);
    procedure pbPaletteMouseDown(Sender: TObject; Button: TMouseButton;
      Shift: TShiftState; X, Y: Integer);
    procedure FormCreate(Sender: TObject);
    procedure TrackBarChange(Sender: TObject);
    procedure FormDestroy(Sender: TObject);
  private
    { Private declarations }
  public
    { Public declarations }
  end;

var
  PalEdit: TPalEdit;

implementation

{$R *.DFM}
var
  BoxDim:    TPoint;      {dimensions a color tab in the pal display}
  SelColor:  byte;
  hPal:      THandle;
  hOldPal:   hPalette;
  selecting: boolean;

function TPalEdit.DisplayDC: hDC;
begin
  result := pbPalette.Canvas.Handle;
end;

function TPalEdit.MakePalette: hPalette;
var
  pNewPal,
  pHead:   PLogPalette;
  size:    longint;
  index,
  r,g,b:   integer;
```

Exploring Imaging—From Pixels to Palettes

```
begin

  size := sizeof(TLogPalette) + (sizeof(TPaletteEntry) * 256);
  pNewPal := nil;
  pHead := nil;

  try
    pNewPal := allocmem(size);
    pNewPal^.palVersion := $300;
    pNewPal^.palNumEntries := 256;

    pHead := pNewPal;
    GetSystemPaletteEntries(DisplayDC, 0, 10, pNewPal^.palPalEntry);

    {$R-}
    for r := 1 to 6 do
      for g := 1 to 6 do
        for b := 1 to 6 do begin
          index := ((r -1) * 36) + ((g - 1) * 6) + (b - 1) + 10;
          pNewPal^.palPalEntry[index].pered := r * (255 div 6);
          pNewPal^.palPalEntry[index].pegreen := g * (255 div 6);
          pNewPal^.palPalEntry[index].peBlue := b * (255 div 6);
          pNewPal^.palPalEntry[index].peFlags := PC_RESERVED;
        end; {$R+}

    inc(pNewPal,113);
    GetSystemPaletteEntries(DisplayDC, 226, 30, pNewPal^.palPalEntry);

    pNewPal := pHead;
    result := CreatePalette(pNewPal^)

  finally
    freemem(pNewPal, size);
  end;

end; {MakePalette}

procedure TPalEdit.FormCreate(Sender: TObject);
begin

  {
  set the box dimensions so that each of the 16x16 color tabs
  in the palette fit in 16 rows and 16 columns on the paint box
  }
  BoxDim.x := pbPalette.Width div 16;
  BoxDim.y := pbPalette.Height div 16;
  SelColor := 0;
  TrackBarChange(trbRed);

  hPal := MakePalette;
  hOldPal := SelectPalette(DisplayDC, hPal, False);

end; {Create}
```

```
procedure TPalEdit.pbPalettePaint(Sender: TObject);
var
  r,c:          integer;      {row and column}
  colorindex: longint;
  Brush,
  OldBrush:     hBrush;

begin

  Brush := 0;
  OldBrush := 0;
  SelectPalette(DisplayDC, hPal, False);
  Self.Caption := IntToStr(RealizePalette(DisplayDC));
  for colorindex := 0 to 255 do begin
    r := colorindex div 16 + 1;
    c := colorindex mod 16 + 1;
    try
      Brush := CreateSolidBrush($01000000 or colorindex);
      OldBrush := SelectObject(DisplayDC, Brush);
      Rectangle( DisplayDC, ((c-1) * BoxDim.x) + 2, ((r-1) * BoxDim.y) + 2,
                            c * BoxDim.x + 2, r * BoxDim.y + 2);
    finally
      SelectObject(DisplayDC, OldBrush);
      DeleteObject(Brush);
    end; {try}
  end; {for}

end; {pbPalette.OnPaint}

procedure TPalEdit.pbPaletteMouseDown(Sender: TObject;
  Button: TMouseButton; Shift: TShiftState; X, Y: Integer);
var
  r,c:       byte;
  PalEntry:  TPaletteEntry;

begin

  r := Y div BoxDim.y;
  c := X div BoxDim.x;
  SelColor := byte(r * 16 + c);
  if GetSystemPaletteEntries(DisplayDC, SelColor, 1, PalEntry) > 0 then begin
    selecting := True;
    trbRed.Position := PalEntry.peRed;
    trbGreen.Position := PalEntry.peGreen;
    trbBlue.Position := PalEntry.peBlue;
    selecting := False;
    TrackBarChange(trbRed);
    end;

end; {pbPalette.MouseDown}

procedure TPalEdit.TrackBarChange(Sender: TObject);
var
  pPalEntry: PPaletteEntry;
```

Exploring Imaging—From Pixels to Palettes

```
begin

  if (not Selecting) and (SelColor >=0) then begin
    {show the RGB values for the slider bar positions}
    lblRed.Caption := 'R: ' + IntToStr(trbRed.Position);
    lblGreen.Caption := 'G: ' + IntToStr(trbGreen.Position);
    lblBlue.Caption := 'B: ' + IntToStr(trbBlue.Position);

    lblPalText.Caption := 'Color Index: (' + IntToStr(SelColor) + ')';

    pnlColor.Color := RGB(trbRed.Position, trbGreen.Position, trbBlue.Position);

    pPalEntry := new(PPaletteEntry);
    pPalEntry^.peRed := trbRed.Position;
    pPalEntry^.peGreen := trbGreen.Position;
    pPalEntry^.peBlue := trbBlue.Position;
    pPalEntry^.peFlags := PC_RESERVED;

    AnimatePalette(hPal, SelColor, 1, pPalEntry);
    Dispose(pPalEntry);

  end; {if}

  end; {TrackbarChange}
procedure TPalEdit.FormDestroy(Sender: TObject);
begin
  SelectPalette(DisplayDC, hOldPal, False);
  DeleteObject(hPal);
end;

end.
```

There is no **OnClick** event handler in this project for the TPanel control. You can remove the reference in the project. You can also remove the **GetPaletteFromDesktop** function. We won't be needing that anymore either. This time we're going to construct the palette ourselves.

Building the Palette

In this example, instead of just using the palette that the desktop is currently using, we're going to construct our own. Listing 6.9 displays the function **MakePalette**, which creates our palette.

Listing 6.9   The MakePalette Function

```
function TPalEdit.MakePalette: hPalette;
var
  pNewPal,
  pHead:   PLogPalette;
  size:    longint;
```

```
      index,
      r,g,b:    integer;

begin

      size := sizeof(TLogPalette) + (sizeof(TPaletteEntry) * 256);
      pNewPal := nil;
      pHead := nil;

      try
        pNewPal := allocmem(size);
        pNewPal^.palVersion := $300;
        pNewPal^.palNumEntries := 256;

        pHead := pNewPal;
        GetSystemPaletteEntries(DisplayDC, 0, 10, pNewPal^.palPalEntry);

        {$R-}
        for r := 1 to 6 do
          for g := 1 to 6 do
            for b := 1 to 6 do begin
              index := ((r -1) * 36) + ((g - 1) * 6) + (b - 1) + 10;
              pNewPal^.palPalEntry[index].pered := r * (255 div 6);
              pNewPal^.palPalEntry[index].pegreen := g * (255 div 6);
              pNewPal^.palPalEntry[index].peBlue := b * (255 div 6);
              pNewPal^.palPalEntry[index].peFlags := PC_RESERVED;
            end; {$R+}

        inc(pNewPal,113);
        GetSystemPaletteEntries(DisplayDC, 226, 30, pNewPal^.palPalEntry);

        pNewPal := pHead;
        result := CreatePalette(pNewPal^)

      finally
        freemem(pNewPal, size);
      end;

end; {MakePalette}
```

This function is similar to **GetPaletteFromDesktop** in the last project. Let's take a look at the differences. There is a pointer, **pHead**, used in this function that was not used before. We use **pHead** to store the original location of the pointer. We make the first call to **GetSystemPaletteEntries** to get entries 0 through 9. Notice parameters 2 and 3. After filling the top 10 entries of our logical palette with values from the system palette, we get into a nested loop that creates a spectrum of 216 more colors with the flags set to **PC_RESERVED**. Remember from Table 6.6 that we set the **PC_RESERVED** flag so the Palette Manager knows that we intend to use those entries for palette animation and they should not be used for other applications.

Notice that in the **for** loop, we are setting the values of **peRed**, **peGreen**, **peBlue**, and **peFlags** as if they were an array of **TPaletteEntry** structures. Actually, that structure is declared as a single element array, yet we are able to access many more than one element in the array. The reason is this: We allocated memory for the entire size of the palette as if the array were dimensioned to 256 elements. Next, we tell the compiler to close its eyes for a few minutes while we do something we're not supposed to. The {$R} compiler directive, which you will find at either end of the loop, tells the compiler to turn *Range Checking* On or Off.

After the loop is finished, we increment the pointer address to the point in memory where the 226th element of the array should be. We make one more call to **GetSystemPaletteEntries()** for the remaining 30 entries, and the palette is complete. We set the pointer back to its original address and then call **CreatePalette**; with the return value being passed back to the **OnCreate** handler, just like we did in the last project.

Plugging in AnimatePalette

In the previous project, we used the **SetPaletteEntries()** function and then repainted the PaintBox to change entries in the palette. Let's look at how we can modify the **TrackbarChange** event to alter those entries without repainting the control. The new **TrackbarChange**, shown in Listing 6.10, takes on the duties of the **pnlColor OnClick** event in the previous project.

Listing 6.10 TrackbarChange

```
procedure TPalEdit.TrackBarChange(Sender: TObject);
var
  pPalEntry: PPaletteEntry;

begin

  if (not Selecting) and (SelColor >=0) then begin
    {show the RGB values for the slider bar positions}
    lblRed.Caption := 'R: ' + IntToStr(trbRed.Position);
    lblGreen.Caption := 'G: ' + IntToStr(trbGreen.Position);
    lblBlue.Caption := 'B: ' + IntToStr(trbBlue.Position);

    lblPalText.Caption := 'Color Index: (' + IntToStr(SelColor) + ')';

    pnlColor.Color := RGB(trbRed.Position, trbGreen.Position, trbBlue.Position);

    pPalEntry := new(PPaletteEntry);
    pPalEntry^.peRed := trbRed.Position;
    pPalEntry^.peGreen := trbGreen.Position;
    pPalEntry^.peBlue := trbBlue.Position;
    pPalEntry^.peFlags := PC_RESERVED;
```

```
AnimatePalette(hPal, SelColor, 1, pPalEntry);
Dispose(pPalEntry);

end; {if}

end; {TrackbarChange}
```

After **TrackbarChange** is finished updating the labels and the larger color swatch, it sets the palette entry to be changed. In doing so, the **PC_RESERVED** flag must be set as shown in the Listing. **AnimatePalette** only works on palette entries identified by this flag. **AnimatePalette** is called with the same parameters as **SetPaletteEntries()**. The difference is.... Well, just run the program, the difference will be obvious!

A Practical Example

Recently, I was working on a sprite-based screen saver. It was a Delphi 1.0 application that loads DIBs from a resource and uses them as animated sprite characters. Here's what that effort entailed:

When I read the DIB from the resource file, I used the **TBitmapInfo** structure, shown in Listing 6.11, and the **TRGBQuad** structure, shown in Listing 6.12.

Listing 6.11   The TBitmapInfo Structure

```
TBitmapInfo = record
   bmiHeader: TBitmapInfoHeader;
   bmiColors: array[0..0] of TRGBQuad;
end;
```

Listing 6.12   The TRGBQuad Structure

```
TRGBQuad = record
   rgbBlue: Byte;
   rgbGreen: Byte;
   rgbRed: Byte;
   rgbReserved: Byte;
end;
```

We're going to learn about the structure of a bitmap in Chapter 8, but for now look at the byte order of the **TRGBQuad** structure. The colors stored in the **TRGBQuad** are blue, green, and red in that byte order. Recall from working with the **TPaletteEntry** structure that the byte order is red, green, then blue. Normally this is all right because we reference the structure's fields by name (for example, rgbBlue = 244, peRed = 112). In my program however, I was using a pointer to the array of RGB Quads and PaletteEntries and I needed to move the data from one structure to the other. I didn't notice that the byte order was reversed (RGB->BGR), and when my bright red sprite character appeared on the screen it was blue!

It only took me a few seconds to realize what had happened, and I ended up using that as a feature. I wrote a routine to swap the red and blue components in a **TPaletteEntry** structure. With that routine I can change the color of the sprite character in the blink of an eye without the need for additional bitmaps! This is only a small sample of the power that comes with controlling color at the palette level. Use the knowledge that you've gained from this chapter to discover new techniques of your own.

Chapter 7

Discover the secret to creating extraordinary special effects with color palettes and raster operations.

Palette Animation and ROPs

Chris D. Coppola

Would you like to be able to get down to the hardware level and create some animated visual effects? With the help of a few powerful Windows API calls and some unique pixel and raster operations, you can bring your Delphi apps to life.

We're now ready to embark on the second phase of our amazing journey into imaging techniques. This time, we'll go a little deeper into the graphics black hole and see what new mysteries we can uncover. Along the way, we'll add to our imaging construction set. In particular, you'll learn how to use color palettes to perform a useful type of animation. Next, we'll look at some clever techniques for performing animation by manipulating pixels using raster operations. The last part of the chapter explores Delphi's encapsulation of the powerful Windows API **BitBlt()** function for performing magic with bitmap images. We'll show you how this function can be used to quickly copy bitmaps.

The Magic of Color Palette Animations

With direct access to the system palette, we can perform certain kinds of animation—animation that requires no actual changes to the displayed bitmap. With this technique, sometimes known as color cycling, we can simulate running water, atmospheric effects, lighting changes, and even moving objects without resorting to more resource-intensive, multi-frame animation methods. But don't let the terminology mislead you. Remember, **AnimatePalette()** doesn't activate a process; it just sets the palette entries indicated by its second and third parameters to the new colors you specify in its fourth parameter. These changes appear immediately on the screen, without the usual intermediate step of realization. AnimatePalette() instantly changes the RGB values of the hardware palette to the new values specified. The effect can be used to create the illusion of motion.

Marquee Lights with Palette Animation

We'll now draw a series of colored ellipses to represent light bulbs around the perimeter of an otherwise blank form, then use palette animation to set them in motion, much like the traveling lights on a theater marquee. Here's what we'll do:

1. Create a new project and name the default form **Main**.
2. Add a timer component to control the animation.
3. Insert the code.

This project is located in the directory \DELPHIMM\CH07\MARQUEE.

Creating the Marquee Project

Start a new project and set the properties and event procedures according to Table 7.1.

Adding the Event Handler Code

We'll need code for six events: OnActivate, OnCreate, OnDestroy, OnPaint, OnResize, and OnTimer. The OnActivate handler turns on the timer. The OnCreate handler will create the palette and the OnDestroy will free the memory associated with it. The OnPaint handler will draw the ellipses around the border of the form. The OnResize event makes sure that if the user changes

Table 7.1 Form and control properties.

Component	Property/Event	Setting
Default Form	Name	Main
	Caption	Marquee Program
	Position	poScreenCenter
	Color	clBlack
	OnActivate	FormActivate
	OnCreate	FormCreate
	OnDestroy	FormDestroy
	OnPaint	FormPaint
	OnResize	FormResize
TTimer	Name	Timer1
	Enabled	False
	Interval	100
	OnTimer	Timer1Timer

the size of the window, the form clears and puts the *lights* in the correct positions. The OnTimer event triggers the palette change every 100 milliseconds.

Take a look at the code for the form's unit in Listing 7.1.

Listing 7.1 Umarquee.pas

```
implementation

{$R *.DFM}

var
  hSysPal,
  hCurPal:            longint;
  pLogicalPalette:    PLogPalette;
  SizePal:            longint;

procedure TMain.FormCreate(Sender: TObject);
var
  ColorIndex: byte;

begin
  SizePal := SizeOf(TLogPalette) + SizeOf(TPaletteEntry) * 4;
  GetMem(pLogicalPalette, SizePal);
  with pLogicalPalette^ do begin
    palVersion := $300;
    palNumEntries := 4;
    for ColorIndex := 0 to 3 do begin
      palPalEntry[ColorIndex].peRed := 0;
```

```
            palPalEntry[ColorIndex].peGreen := 127 + ColorIndex * 128 div 3;
            palPalEntry[ColorIndex].peBlue  := 127 + ColorIndex * 128 div 3;
            palPalEntry[ColorIndex].peFlags := PC_RESERVED;
          end; {for}
        end; {with}
      hCurPal := CreatePalette(pLogicalPalette^);

end;

procedure TMain.FormDestroy(Sender: TObject);
begin
  FreeMem(pLogicalPalette, SizePal);
  SelectPalette(Main.Canvas.Handle, hSysPal, False);
  DeleteObject(hCurPal);
end;

procedure TMain.FormPaint(Sender: TObject);

  procedure DrawMarquee;
  var
    pos:         TPoint;
    BoxDim:      TPoint;
    DotDiameter: integer;
    CI:          longint;
  begin

    DotDiameter := ClientWidth div 24;
    with Main.Canvas do begin
      Brush.Style := bsSolid;

      {Draw top row of lights}
      pos.y := DotDiameter div 2;
      pos.x := trunc(DotDiameter * 1.5);
      while pos.x < (ClientWidth - trunc(DotDiameter * 2.5)) do begin
        Brush.Color := $01000000 or CI;
        Ellipse(pos.x, pos.y, pos.x + DotDiameter, pos.y + DotDiameter);
        inc(pos.x, trunc(DotDiameter * 1.5));
        inc(CI);
        CI := CI mod 4;
      end; {while}

      {Draw right edge lights}
      while pos.y < (ClientHeight - DotDiameter * 2.5) do begin
        Brush.Color := $01000000 or CI;
        Ellipse(pos.x, pos.y, pos.x + DotDiameter, pos.y + DotDiameter);
        inc(pos.y, trunc(DotDiameter * 1.5));
        inc(CI);
        CI := CI mod 4;
      end; {while}

      {Draw bottom row of lights}
      while pos.x > DotDiameter * 1.5 do begin
        Brush.Color := $01000000 or CI;
        Ellipse(pos.x, pos.y, pos.x + DotDiameter, pos.y + DotDiameter);
```

Palette Animation and ROPs 325

```
        dec(pos.x, trunc(DotDiameter * 1.5));
        inc(CI);
        CI := CI mod 4;
        end; {while}

      {Draw left edge lights}
      while pos.y > DotDiameter  do begin
        Brush.Color := $01000000 or CI;
        Ellipse(pos.x, pos.y, pos.x + DotDiameter, pos.y + DotDiameter);
        dec(pos.y, trunc(DotDiameter * 1.5));
        inc(CI);
        CI := CI mod 4;
        end; {while}

    end; {with Main.Canvas}
  end; {DrawMarquee}

begin

  hSysPal := SelectPalette(Main.Canvas.Handle, hCurPal, False);
  RealizePalette(Main.Canvas.Handle);
  DrawMarquee;

end;

procedure TMain.FormResize(Sender: TObject);
var
  ClientRect:   TRect;

begin
  ClientRect := Rect(0,0,Self.Width, Self.Height);
  with Self.Canvas do begin
    Brush.Color := clBlack;
    FillRect(ClientRect);
    end;
  Self.Repaint;

end;

procedure TMain.Timer1Timer(Sender: TObject);
var
  ci: byte;
  pLogPalHead: PLogPalette;

begin

  pLogPalHead := pLogicalPalette;

  for ci := 4 downto 1 do
    with pLogicalPalette^ do
      palPalEntry[ci] := palPalEntry[ci-1];

  ci := 4;
  pLogicalPalette^.palPalEntry[0] := pLogicalPalette^.palPalEntry[ci];
  AnimatePalette(hCurPal, 0, 4, @pLogicalPalette^.palPalEntry);
```

```
end;

procedure TMain.FormActivate(Sender: TObject);
begin
  Timer1.Enabled := True;
end;

end.
```

Notice that the program listing begins with the implementation section. In this project we did not need to add anything beyond that in the unit. Everything prior to the implementation section Delphi already created.

Four variables are declared globally to the unit: hCurPal, hSysPal, pLogicalPalette, and SizePal. The two palette handles, hCurPal and hSysPal, are used to create, manage, and delete the palette that we create for this example. The variable pLogicalPalette is a pointer to a TLogPalette structure that maintains the color values in our logical palette. Finally, SizePal is needed to allocate and free memory for the pLogicalPalette pointer.

The first event that is triggered when this program is executed is the form's OnCreate. Take a look at the OnCreate handler in Listing 7.2.

Listing 7.2   The OnCreate handler

```
procedure TMain.FormCreate(Sender: TObject);
var
  ColorIndex: byte;

begin
  SizePal := SizeOf(TLogPalette) + SizeOf(TPaletteEntry) * 4;
  GetMem(pLogicalPalette, SizePal);
  with pLogicalPalette^ do begin
    palVersion := $300;
    palNumEntries := 4;
    for ColorIndex := 0 to 3 do begin
      palPalEntry[ColorIndex].peRed := 0;
      palPalEntry[ColorIndex].peGreen := 127 + ColorIndex * 128 div 3;
      palPalEntry[ColorIndex].peBlue := 127 + ColorIndex * 128 div 3;
      palPalEntry[ColorIndex].peFlags := PC_RESERVED;
      end; {for}
    end; {with}
  hCurPal := CreatePalette(pLogicalPalette^);
end;
```

You learned to use the **TLogPalette** and **TPaletteEntry** structures in Chapter 6. Notice that in this procedure we are allocating memory for only four **TPaletteEntry** structures. Notice also that the four entries being created in the logical palette are levels of aqua with the **PC_RESERVED** flag set. Recall from Chapter 6 that the **PC_RESERVED** flag tells the palette manager that these entries are dedicated to palette animation and should not be used by other applications to map background colors. Finally, at the end of this procedure, we get a handle to the logical palette with the **CreatePalette** function.

Next, let's look at the OnPaint handler in Listing 7.3.

Listing 7.3 The form's OnPaint event handler

```
procedure TMain.FormPaint(Sender: TObject);

  procedure DrawMarquee;
  var
    pos:         TPoint;
    BoxDim:      TPoint;
    DotDiameter: integer;
    CI:          longint;
  begin

    DotDiameter := ClientWidth div 24;
    with Main.Canvas do begin
      Brush.Style := bsSolid;

      {Draw top row of lights}
      pos.y := DotDiameter div 2;
      pos.x := trunc(DotDiameter * 1.5);
      while pos.x < (ClientWidth - trunc(DotDiameter * 2.5)) do begin
        Brush.Color := $01000000 or CI;
        Ellipse(pos.x, pos.y, pos.x + DotDiameter, pos.y + DotDiameter);
        inc(pos.x, trunc(DotDiameter * 1.5));
        inc(CI);
        CI := CI mod 4;
        end; {while}

      {Draw right edge lights}
      while pos.y < (ClientHeight - DotDiameter * 2.5) do begin
        Brush.Color := $01000000 or CI;
        Ellipse(pos.x, pos.y, pos.x + DotDiameter, pos.y + DotDiameter);
        inc(pos.y, trunc(DotDiameter * 1.5));
        inc(CI);
        CI := CI mod 4;
        end; {while}

      {Draw bottom row of lights}
      while pos.x > DotDiameter * 1.5 do begin
        Brush.Color := $01000000 or CI;
        Ellipse(pos.x, pos.y, pos.x + DotDiameter, pos.y + DotDiameter);
        dec(pos.x, trunc(DotDiameter * 1.5));
        inc(CI);
        CI := CI mod 4;
        end; {while}
```

```
    {Draw left edge lights}
    while pos.y > DotDiameter  do begin
      Brush.Color := $01000000 or CI;
      Ellipse(pos.x, pos.y, pos.x + DotDiameter, pos.y + DotDiameter);
      dec(pos.y, trunc(DotDiameter * 1.5));
      inc(CI);
      CI := CI mod 4;
      end; {while}

  end; {with Main.Canvas}
end; {DrawMarquee}

begin

  hSysPal := SelectPalette(Main.Canvas.Handle, hCurPal, False);
  RealizePalette(Main.Canvas.Handle);
  DrawMarquee;

end;
```

This handler does only 3 things: Selects the palette that we created into the *dc* of the main form's client area, realizes the selected palette, and Draws the marquee. For clarity, the three statements that the handler executes are:

```
hSysPal := SelectPalette(Main.Canvas.Handle, hCurPal, False);
RealizePalette(Main.Canvas.Handle);
DrawMarquee;
```

The **DrawMarquee** procedure is declared within the **OnPaint** handler. It simply draws ellipses around the edge of the form using the Canvas' ellipse method. The **ellipse** method is an encapsulation of the windows API. The difference between the two functions is that the **ellipse** method does not require a handle to a display context. It always draws on the *dc* of the canvas from which it was initiated.

The other thing to note about the **DrawMarquee** procedure is the color with which the ellipses are drawn. The brush color is set using a binary **or** operation:

```
        Brush.Color := $01000000 or CI;
```

Remember from Chapter 6 that $01000000 and a color index combined with a binary **or** tells the palette manager that we want to use the specific color index in the low order byte to indicate a palette entry in the currently realized palette.

The rest of the procedure is just a few simple loops that move the drawing position around the border of the form.

Palette Animation and ROPs

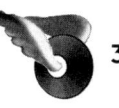

So far we have created, selected, and realized a logical palette. We have also drawn the 'lights' around form's borders. So far so good, but no animation. Lets work on that now using Listing 7.4 as a reference.

Listing 7.4   The timer's OnTimer event handler

```
procedure TMain.Timer1Timer(Sender: TObject);
var
  ci: byte;
  pLogPalHead: PLogPalette;

begin

  pLogPalHead := pLogicalPalette;

  for ci := 4 downto 1 do
    with pLogicalPalette^ do
      palPalEntry[ci] := palPalEntry[ci-1];

  ci := 4;
  pLogicalPalette^.palPalEntry[0] := pLogicalPalette^.palPalEntry[ci];
  AnimatePalette(hCurPal, 0, 4, @pLogicalPalette^.palPalEntry);

end;
```

The timer handler, although one of the simplest procedures in this project, is powerful in its simplicity. The *for* loop cycles through the logical palette entries, changing each to the value of the prior index until the loop gets to entry zero. The two statements following the loop set entry zero to the value of entry four, which was used as temporary storage for entry three. Keep in mind we're only using four entries (0-3).

The last line of this handler is the one that actually makes the visible changes. **AnimatePalette()** is called to change four color values, starting with zero to the values we just changed in the logical palette. Since we are changing the colors in the hardware palette, the changes are visible instantly.

A special mention is in order to explain why these two lines were used:

```
ci := 4;
pLogicalPalette^.palPalEntry[0] := pLogicalPalette^.palPalEntry[ci];
```

instead of:

```
pLogicalPalette^.palPalEntry[0] := pLogicalPalette^.palPalEntry[4];
```

to change index zero to the value of index four. The reason is that Delphi will see the latter as a reference to an array element that is out of bounds. Remember that the declaration for **TPaletteEntry** contains only one element. We could have made a new declaration in which the palette entries' structure contained enough elements to satisfy our requirements. Since we are allocating memory for the structure and all of the elements that we will be using, we can safely address those elements. This gives us flexibility with the array similar to the flexibility that the **ReDim() Preserve** function affords in Visual Basic.

Providing that you've already entered the **OnDestroy** and **OnActivate** handlers, you are ready to take the program for a test drive. If you have not entered the code for **OnDestroy** or **OnActivate,** please refer to Listing 7.1 and do so now before testing the program.

Testing the program should yeild a display similar to Figure 7.1. The most significant difference is that yours should be animated—which is something we couldn't pull off in Figure 7.1!

Pixels and Raster Operations

When you get right down to it, drawing on a graphics display amounts to little more than setting color values for individual pixels. Which is true as long as we begin with a neutral background.

But what is a "neutral" background? White, the most common background color, is represented by 24 bits set to 1 (or true), which literally means the maximum presence of color. The opposite of white is, of course, black, represented by 24 bits set to 0—the total absence of color. To display a bitmapped image, we could disregard the existing colors of the drawing context and replace every bit of every pixel with the bits from our new image. That's exactly what happens when we invoke the **LoadFromFile**() method to display a bitmap.

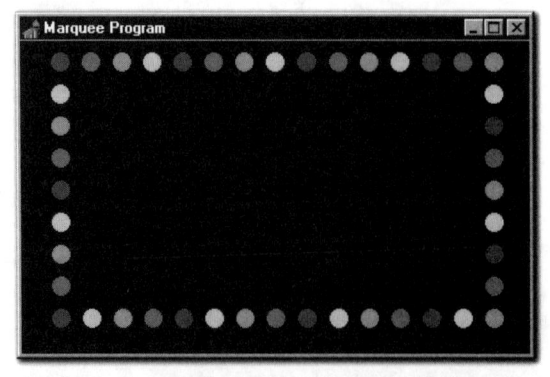

Figure 7.1 *Marquee lights simulated with the AnimatePalette() function.*

Palette Animation and ROPs 331

But sometimes, instead of replacing an existing image altogether, we only need to draw on top of it or combine images. How is this accomplished? It's relatively easy with the addition of *raster operations*, or *ROPs*. Raster operations determine what happens when we try to place one pixel on top of another. (Impossible? Yes and no, but more on this in a moment.) Even more fundamentally, just what is a raster operation? Let's begin another project to see.

When is a Pen a "Not Pen"?

In this simple project we'll take our first look at ROPs. Follow these steps to see how a raster operation affects a line drawing:

1. Create a new project and name the default form **Main**.
2. Set the properties and events for the form.
3. Insert the code.

This project is located in the directory \DELPHIMM\CH07\NOTPEN.

Creating the NotPen Project

Start a new project and set the properties and event procedures according to Table 7.2.

Adding the event handler code

In the **OnCreate** handler, we will set some properties of the pen object associated with the form's canvas. The **OnMouseDown** handler will simply use the pen to draw a line from wherever the user clicks to the center of the form.

Take a look at the code for the form's unit in Listing 7.5.

Table 7.2 Form and control properties.

Component	Property/Event	Setting
Default Form	Name	Main
	Caption	NotPen Experiment
	Color	clAqua
	OnCreate	FormCreate
	OnMouseDown	FormMouseDown

Listing 7.5 Unotpen.pas

```
implementation

{$R *.DFM}

procedure TMain.FormCreate(Sender: TObject);
begin
  with Self.Canvas.Pen do begin
    Style := psSolid;
    Width := 5;
    Color := clBlue;
    Mode := pmNot;
    end;

end;

procedure TMain.FormMouseDown(Sender: TObject; Button: TMouseButton;
  Shift: TShiftState; X, Y: Integer);
begin
  Self.Canvas.MoveTo(X,Y);
  Self.Canvas.LineTo(ClientWidth div 2,ClientHeight div 2);
end;
```

Nothing to it! Run the program and click around on the form. If you clicked in exactly the same places I did, you will see the results shown in Figure 7.2. You probably didn't follow my pattern exactly, but that's not important. You should still see a result *similar* to that in Figure 7.2.

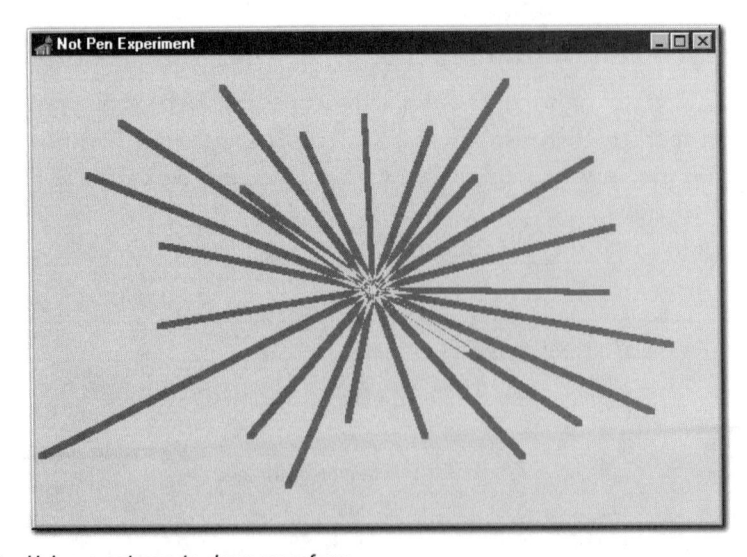

Figure 7.2   *Using a not pen to draw on a form.*

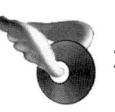

When you click the mouse anywhere on the form's client area, Delphi will draw a line from that point to the center of the form. You may be surprised to learn that the color of the line will depend entirely on the color of the background. To see this, stop the program and change the **Color** property of the form (use the object inspector to do this). Now, when you run the program again and click the mouse, the lines will be drawn in a different color. Ordinarily, you would expect the **Color** property of the pen to determine the current drawing color, but when the pen's **Mode** is set to pmNot, the pen's color is irrelevant. Try it. Change the pen's color (in the **OnCreate** handler) and run the program again. You'll get the same result. The color of the line will always depend exclusively on the background color.

Mixing Pixels

As was pointed out earlier, it is raster operations that determine what happens when we attempt to place one pixel on top of another. This is, of course, impossible. Our display systems can display only one pixel at a time in each pixel position. But by combining the values of pixels in various ways, we can produce digital effects that imitate physical effects such as color blending and transparency. And as an added bonus, we can do things that would be impossible with that goop we call paint.

Let's dissect the raster operation used in the previous project. A raster operation is a Boolean operation performed on two or more pixel values. That's all. Take the simplest case, a black pen on a white background. In the Windows system palette, black is stored in palette location 0, and white is stored in position 255. The logical **Not** operator performs the simplest of all Boolean operations—it flips the bits, so zeros become ones and ones become zeros. If the background is white, then drawing with the **Not** pen changes pixels to black; drawing over the pixels that have changed to black will change them back to white.

This works for other colors, too. If you set the background to the color stored in logical palette position 5, for example, the **Not** pen will change the color to the one stored in position 250.

```
Not  0000 0101   5
  =  1111 1010  250
```

In all, Windows offers 16 binary raster operations. For the complete list, see Table 7.3.

Table 7.3 *The Binary Raster Operations.*

Windows Name	Pen Constant	Pixel Output
R2_BLACK	pmBlack	Always black.
R2_WHITE	pmWhite	Always white.
R2_NOP	pmNop	Unchanged.
R2_NOT	pmNot	Inverse of screen color.
R2_COPYPEN	pmCopy	Pen color specified in Color property.
R2_NOTCOPYPEN	pmNotCopy	Inverse of pen color.
R2_MERGEPENNOT	pmMergePenNot	Combination of pen color and inverse of screen color.
R2_MASKPENNOT	pmMaskPenNot	Combination of colors common to both pen and inverse of screen.
R2_MERGENOTPEN	pmMergeNotPen	Combination of screen color and inverse of pen color.
R2_MASKNOTPEN	pmMaskNotPen	Combination of colors common to both screen and inverse of pen.
R2_MERGEPEN	pmMerge	Combination of pen color and screen color.
R2_NOTMERGEPEN	pmNotMerge	Inverse of pmMerge combination of pen color and screen color.
R2_MASKPEN	pmMask	Combination of colors common to both pen and screen.
R2_NOTMASKPEN	pmNotMask	Inverse of pmMask combination of colors common to both pen and screen.
R2_XORPEN	pmXor	Combination of colors in either pen or screen, but not both.
R2_NOTXORPEN	pmNotXor	Inverse of pmXor combination of colors in either pen or screen, but not both.

ROPs and the Split System Palette

In a true color display system, raster operations are performed on the whole RGB values of the pixels. This approach makes the results predictable. If you invert red, which is RGB value $0000FF, the results will be cyan, RGB value $FFFF00. If you invert blue ($FF0000), you'll have yellow ($00FFFF). But on a palette-based display, the ROPs operate on the pixels' palette references, not on their actual RGB values.

The division of the Windows system colors into two groups of ten, positioned at opposite ends of the palette, is meant to provide some semblance of meaningful behavior when colors are inverted. White inverts to black, navy inverts to yellow, blue inverts to olive, and so on. When raster operations are applied to system palette references 10 through 245, however, the results can become meaningless. If, for example, palette entries 15 and 240 (which are binary complements) contained similar colors, the inversion could become so subtle that it may not even be visible.

Unfortunately, we have to learn to live with this problem. It isn't practical to reorganize the palettes of most 256 color images to pair up the complementary colors. For one thing, the logical palettes of most photographic images tend to contain many similar colors in subtle shades—some images may contain no complementary colors at all. For most purposes, it hardly matters that inverted colors don't produce their complements. The **Not** pen and its close cousin, the **XOr** pen, are used primarily to draw contrasting lines across background bitmaps. In most cases, lines and filled shapes drawn with these pens will contrast enough with the background to stand out.

We've only scratched the surface of the binary raster operations, and they only hint at the power of the ternary raster operations. In later chapters we'll use some of the ROP2 codes. But right now, let's move on to the even more powerful ternary ROP codes, and the API functions that bring them to life.

Processing Bitmaps—Using BitBlt Functions

Delphi provides an excellent encapsulation of most of the Windows API, and the BitBlt function is no exception. Delphi's canvas object uses the Draw, StretchDraw, and CopyRect to draw on a drawing surface or copy pixels from one canvas to another. Let's look at the Windows API function BitBlt:

```
function BitBlt(DestDC: HDC; X, Y, Width, Height: Integer; SrcDC: HDC;
        XSrc, YSrc: Integer; Rop: LongInt): Bool;
```

With nine arguments, the declaration for this function can look pretty intimidating.

DestDC   This is the handle to the *destination* device context. For example, if you were using **BitBlt()** to copy an image from Image1 to Image2, you would pass Image2.canvas.handle as the first argument.

X	A four-byte integer representing the X coordinate, usually in pixels, of the upper-left corner of the destination rectangle. This need not be zero; you may blt the source image to any location within the destination device context.
Y	A four-byte integer representing the Y coordinate of the upper-left corner of the destination rectangle.
nWidth	A four-byte integer representing the width of the destination rectangle. These measurements are given in *logical units*. For most of our purposes that means pixels, but Windows does support other measurement systems, most notably inches and millimeters.
nHeight	A four-byte integer representing the height of the destination rectangle.
hSrcDC	The handle to the *source* device context. In our example, from the description of the first argument, you would pass Image1.canvas.handle as this parameter.
XSrc	A long integer representing the X coordinate of the upper-left corner of the source rectangle. Keep in mind that the *origin* (coordinates 0,0) is in the upper-left corner of any client area. X values increase from left to right; Y values increase from top to bottom. (Although you can change this, we'll stick to the default.)
YSrc	A long integer representing the Y coordinate of the upper-left corner of the source rectangle.
dwROP	A long integer representing one of the 256 raster operation codes. For a simple copy, this would be set to **SRCCOPY**, which is a Windows constant with a value of &HCC0020.

An alternative to **BitBlt()** if you wanted to copy an image from one component to another would be the **CopyRect** method of the destination component. Let's say, for instance, that you wanted to copy the image in Image1 to Image2. Using the **CopyRect** method, the solution would be:

```
Image2.Canvas.CopyRect(rcSrc, Image1.Canvas, rcDest);
```

Let's look at this through the next example.

Palette Animation and ROPs 337

BitBlting—Delphi's simple solution

The easiest way to understand a blt is to see it in action. Lets do a simple experiment in which we'll copy the bitmap in one TImage component to another TImage component:

1. Create a new project and add two TImage components and a SpeedButton to the default form.
2. Arrange the components as shown in Figure 7.3.
3. Set the properties and events for the form and the components.
4. Insert the code.

This project is located in the directory \DELPHIMM\CH07\BITBLTEX.

Creating the BitBltex Project

Start a new project and set the properties and event procedures according to Table 7.4.

Table 7.4 Form and control properties.

Component	Property/Event	Setting
TImage1	AutoSize	True
	Picture	(Tbitmap) load an image of your choice
TImage2	AutoSize	True
TSpeedButton	Caption	&Copy (Blt)
	OnClick	SpeedButton1Click

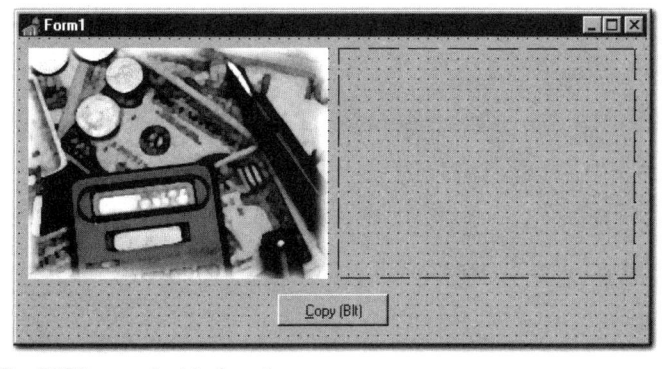

Figure 7.3 The BitBltex project before the copy.

Adding the Event Handler Code

Let's look at the code that supports the SpeedButton's click event in Listing 7.6

Listing 7.6 The SpeedButton's OnClick handler

```
procedure TForm1.SpeedButton1Click(Sender: TObject);
var
  rcSrc,
  rcDest:   TRect;

begin
  rcSrc := Rect(0,0,Image1.Width, Image1.Height);
  rcDest := rcSrc;
  Image2.Canvas.CopyRect(rcSrc, Image1.Canvas, rcDest);
end;
```

We'll show you how to use the blt functions to do a number of exciting things in later chapters. But before you can do much more than blast pieces of pictures from window to window, you have to understand the effects of raster operations. In the our next project, we're going to combine ROPs and Blits to demonstrate what happens when you run bitmaps through the Boolean wringer.

The Standard Windows Raster Operations

In this project we'll try out the fifteen standard raster operations. Because they're so useful, the creators of Windows have given these ROP codes their own names, in the form of Windows constants. Here's what we'll do:

1. Create a new project and add three TImage components and a TListBox to the **Main** form.
2. Arrange the components as shown in Figure 7.4.
3. Set the properties and events for the form and the components.
4. Insert the code.

This project is located in the directory \DELPHIMM\CH07\ROPS.

Creating the ROPs Project

Start a new project and set the properties and event procedures according to Table 7.5.

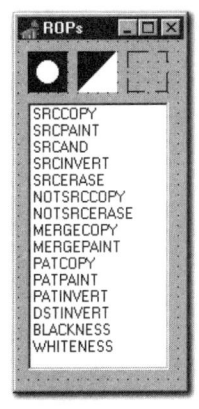

Figure 7.4 *Arrangement of components for the ROPs project.*

For imgSrc and imgDst, we need to load bitmaps at design time. Select imgSrc on the form and then in the object inspector locate the Picture property. Use the property editor to load the **whitedot.bmp** file into the component. Repeat the process to load **halfhalf.bmp** into the picture property of imgDst.

Next, we'll enter the ROP codes into the *Items* property of the listbox. The items property is a TStrings type, so when we change the value at design-time, we get a string list editor dialog. Bring up the string list editor dialog for the *Items* property. Use the right mouse button to access the *load* option and load the file **ropcodes.txt**. You should see a list of raster operations similar to those in Figure 7.5.

Take a quick look at Table 7.6. It describes the 15 ternary ROP codes.

Table 7.5 *Form and control properties.*

Component	Property/Event	Setting
Default Form	Name	Main
	Caption	ROPs Experiment
TImage1	Name	imgSrc
	Autosize	True
TImage2	Name	imgDst
	Autosize	True
TImage3	Name	imgResult
	AutoSize	True
TListBox	Name	lstROPS
	OnClick	lstROPSClick

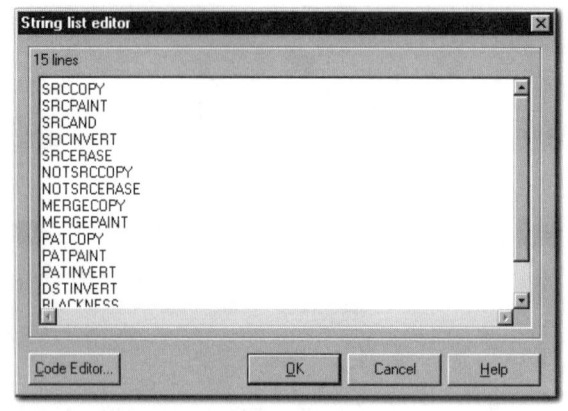

Figure 7.5 *The contents of the lstROPs component.*

Table 7.6 *The 15 Named Ternary ROP Codes.*

Windows Name	Delphi Constant	Action
BLACKNESS	cmBlackness	Turns all output black.
DSTINVERT	cmDstInvert	Inverts the destination bitmap.
MERGECOPY	cmMergeCopy	Combines the pattern and the source bitmap by using the Boolean AND operator.
MERGEPAINT	cmMergePaint	Combines the inverted source bitmap with the destination bitmap by using the Boolean OR operator.
NOTSRCCOPY	cmNotSrcCopy	Copies the inverted source bitmap to the destination.
NOTSRCERASE	cmNotSrcErase	Inverts the result of combining the destination and source bitmaps by using the Boolean OR operator.
PATCOPY	cmPatCopy	Copies the pattern to the destination bitmap with the pattern by using the Boolean XOR operator.
PATINVERT	cmPatInvert	Combines the destination bitmap with the pattern by using the Boolean XOR operator
PATPAINT	cmPatPaint	Combines the inverted source bitmap with the pattern by using the Boolean OR operator. Combines the result of this operation with the destination bitmap by using the Boolean OR operator.
SRCAND	cmSrcAnd	Combines pixels from the destination and source bitmaps by using the Boolean AND operator.
SRCCOPY	cmSrcCopy	Copies the source bitmap to the destination bitmap.

continued

Palette Animation and ROPs 341

Table 7.6 *The 15 Named Ternary ROP Codes (Continued).*

Windows Name	Delphi Constant	Action
SRCERASE	cmSrcErase	Inverts the destination bitmap and combines the result with the source bitmap by using the Boolean AND operator.
SRCINVERT	cmSrcInvert	Combines pixels from the destination and source bitmaps by using the Boolean XOR operator.
SRCPAINT	cmSrcPaint	Combines pixels from the destination and source bitmaps by using the Boolean OR operator.
WHITENESS	cmWhiteness	Turns all output white.

Adding the Event Handler Code

The only event that we need to respond to is the click event of the listbox. It will take care of blting to imgResult based on which ROP code we click on in the list box. Take a look at the code for lstROPSClick in Listing 7.7.

Listing 7.7   The lstROPSClick event handler

```
procedure TMain.lstROPSClick(Sender: TObject);
var
  r: TRect;

begin

  with imgResult.Canvas do begin
    Brush.Style := bsDiagCross;
    CopyMode :=cmSrcCopy;
    Draw(0,0, imgDst.Picture.Bitmap);
    end;

  with imgResult.Canvas do begin
    Case lstROPS.ItemIndex of
        0: CopyMode := cmSrcCopy;
        1: CopyMode := cmSrcPaint;
        2: CopyMode := cmSrcAnd;
        3: CopyMode := cmSrcInvert;
        4: CopyMode := cmSrcErase;
        5: CopyMode := cmNotSrcCopy;
        6: CopyMode := cmNotSrcErase;
        7: CopyMode := cmMergeCopy;
        8: CopyMode := cmMergePaint;
        9: CopyMode := cmPatCopy;
       10: CopyMode := cmPatPaint;
       11: CopyMode := cmPatInvert;
       12: CopyMode := cmDstInvert;
```

```
  13: CopyMode := cmBlackness;
  14: CopyMode := cmWhiteness;

   end; {case}

  Draw(0,0, imgSrc.Picture.Bitmap);
  end;

end;
```

Let's take a look at the first block of code:

```
with imgResult.Canvas do begin
   Brush.Style := bsDiagCross;
   CopyMode :=cmSrcCopy;
   Draw(0,0, imgDst.Picture.Bitmap);
   end;
```

The ternary ROP codes perform their magic by mixing up to three pixels for every pixel of a bitmap. The first couple of statements above set up the Image components to make that possible. We set *the brush style* to **bsDiagCross** so that the ROPs which use a pattern will display a meaningful result. Next we set the *CopyMode* of imgResult to **cmSrcCopy**. We do this because we want the result image to contain a duplicate of the destination bitmap. This is why the *copy mode* must be **cmSrcCopy**.

The result image actually wears two hats in this procedure. It switches hats so quickly, though, that we might miss it if we don't carefully examine its role. We know that the imgResult component will display the final effect, but it also contains the destination bitmap for a fraction of a second. Take a look at the description for PATPAINT in Table 7.6. The PATPAINT operation uses *three* pixels to decide what each pixel of the final image will look like. Let's review this operation step by step using our project as an example. First PATPAINT inverts the source bitmap (imgSrc) and then combines the source with the *pattern* using the boolean **or** operator. The *pattern* that will be used for this operation is the *pattern* contained in imgResult (imgResult.Canvas.Brush.Style), which we have set to **bsDiagCross**. With the result of that first step, PATPAINT adds in the pixels of the destination bitmap (imgResult) using the boolean **or** operator. This last step is the reason that we need to copy the destination bitmap (imgDst) to the result bitmap (imgResult) before we wave the wand and the the ROP does its thing.

The case statement in Listing 7.7 sets the copy mode of imgResult to the one you have selected from the list. The final statement in the procedure draws the source bitmap over the destination bitmap (which is already in imgResult), applying the operation you have selected in the listbox.

Run the program and compare the results you see with the descriptions in Table 7.6.

Pixels in the computer's virtual world, like atoms in our physical world, are the building blocks of bigger and better things. Master the techniques of putting them together, and there's no limit to what you can create!

Chapter 8

Raster operations, pixels, and palettes culminate in this chapter. We'll put them all together and throw in some new stuff to create some brilliant visual effects.

Advanced Imaging—Special Visual Effects

Chris D. Coppola

In the previous two chapters, we explored how Windows displays pictures. You learned how the Palette Manager works in 8-bit color mode, and how to modify and transfer images, or portions of images, with some simple blts and raster operations. Now it's time to pull this information together and expand on it for performing some useful effects, like dissolving one picture into another. The techniques presented in this chapter can easily be incorporated into your own custom multimedia applications. We'll start by exploring a simple dissolve you can use to add an animated effect to images as they are displayed. In order to create the dissolve effect, we'll need to revisit ROPs and the flexible pattern brush. As we work our way into more bitmap trickery, we'll also show you how to combine bitmaps to create eye-catching transition techniques.

Introducing the Dissolve

For decades, filmmakers have used dissolves to produce the visual effect of fading from one scene to the next. To produce this effect on movie film, you only have to expose each frame of the film to both pictures (the original and the end result), gradually decreasing the intensity of one while increasing the intensity of the other, frame by frame, until the original image has vanished.

Creating a dissolve with your computer, however, is another story. You could simulate the photographic process on a true color display by shifting the value of each pixel from its color in the first image to its color in the second image. Unfortunately, this process would take a long time for bitmaps of any significant size—even on a lightning-fast PC. Of course, you could perform the dissolve steps, capture them, then play the whole thing back as an animation. That would be fine if you knew the order of all the transitions you wanted in your presentation, but it could prohibit spontaneous dissolves, especially if you have a large number of images.

Another approach is to replace one image with the other, pixel by pixel. Unfortunately, this process *looks* digital. Also, when you try to use this technique on an 8-bit display, you once again bump into the palette problem. If each image is composed from a palette of 256 colors, then the combined images that appear during the dissolve could require as many as 512 colors, which the display system can't provide. It's easy to dissolve from one image to another if the images share a common palette, or if each of the images uses only a few colors so that their combined palettes don't require more than 256 palette entries. But the general-purpose solution to this problem should anticipate the worst case.

There is a compromise. By combining the pixel-by-pixel replacement technique with a color translation, you can generate a pretty attractive dissolve. Raster operations will work on either a true color or palettized display, but for 8-bit images, the color translation becomes practical only with the assistance of the Palette Manager.

Let's begin by digging deeper into raster operations and bitmaps.

ROPs Revisited

Remember from Chapter 7 that raster operations can work on up to three bitmaps. In Chapter 7 we used a built-in Windows brush to demonstrate its effect on the third bitmap.

The third bitmap is the *Pattern Brush*. Brushes are special square bitmaps, eight pixels on a side, that fill an area with a repeating pattern. You most

Advanced Imaging—Special Visual Effects   347

often see them used with GDI functions that draw shapes. But you can also use them with bitmap drawing routines to add repeating patterns to entire bitmaps or combinations of bitmaps.

In our next project, ROPS2, we'll add a homemade brush to our ROP experiment from the last chapter. To do that, rather than using a built-in brush, we will create the brush; which we can do either by drawing it or by generating it from within our program. Because brushes are such small bitmaps, this is a good time to show you how a bitmap is constructed—from the ground up. Although this will represent a slight digression, building bitmaps is a skill you need to master before we tackle the dissolve project later in this chapter.

Building a Bitmap

In this project we build a brush and use Delphi's built-in drawing routines to see how it affects the outcome of a raster operation. Here's what to do:

1. Copy the files from the ROP experiment in Chapter 7 to a new directory. Then open the project and save it under a new name. I used "ROPS2" for the project name and "UROPS2" as the unit name.
2. Add a **TImage** component between the existing imgDst and imgResult components. You'll probably have to widen the form somewhat as well. Use Figure 8.1 as a guide.
3. Set the new properties and events.
4. Insert and modify code.

This project is located in the directory \DELPHIMM\CH08\ROPS2.

Creating the Rops2 Project

Copy the files from Rops in Chapter 7 to a new directory and save the project under a new name. Add a **TImage** component between imgDst and imgResult on the form using Figure 8.1 as a guide. Now set the properties and event procedures according to Table 8.1.

If you did not copy the previous project, then you'll need to do some additional preparation before we get into the code. For imgSrc and imgDst, you need to load bitmaps at design time. Select imgSrc on the form, and then

Chapter 8

Table 8.1 *Form and component properties.*

Component	Property/Event	Setting
Default Form	Name	Main
	Caption	ROPs Experiment
TImage1	Name	imgSrc
	Autosize	True
TImage2	Name	imgDst
	Autosize	True
TImage3	Name	imgBrush
TImage4	Name	imgResult
TListBox	Name	lstROPS
	OnClick	lstROPSClick

locate the Picture property in the object inspector. Use the property editor to load the **whitedot.bmp** file into the component. Repeat the process to load **halfhalf.bmp** into the picture property of imgDst.

Next, enter the ROP codes into the *Items* property of the listbox. The items property is a TStrings type; when you change the value at design-time, you'll get a string list editor dialog. Bring up the string list editor dialog for the *Items* property. Use the right mouse button to access the *load* option and load the file **ropcode2.txt**.

You should now have a form that looks like this:

Figure 8.1 *The ROPS2 form.*

Advanced Imaging—Special Visual Effects

Adding the Code

This project has three basic steps that need to be handled with the code we're going to write. First, we create the bitmap that we will use as a brush and select the brush into the imgBrush and imgResult canvas. Next, we respond to click events in the ROP list. Finally, we will de-select the brush and destroy it to free resources when the program terminates. Pretty simple, right? Take a look at Listing 8.1 and we'll get started.

Listing 8.1   urops2.pas

```
implementation

{$R *.DFM}

var
  hPatBrush,
  hOldBrush: hBrush;

function TMain.CreateCheckBrush: hBrush;
var
  pDIB:    PBitmapInfo;    {pointer to the packed DIB structure we're creating}
  pBits:   PChar;          {pointer to the bits of the bitmap}
  pQuad:   PRGBQuad;       {pointer to a RGBQuad structure}
  p:       PChar;          {temp pointer for setting bits}
  size:    longint;        {size of the entire dib in memory}
  i:       byte;           {counter variable}
  hBMP:    hBitmap;        {handle to a bitmap}
begin
  size := sizeof(TBitmapInfoHeader) + (2 * sizeof(TRGBQuad)) + 32;
  pDIB := nil;
  hBMP := 0;

  try
    {allocate memory for the DIB}
    pDIB := allocmem(size);
    pQuad := pointer(longint(pDIB) + sizeof(TBitmapInfoHeader));
    pBits := pointer(longint(pQuad) + (2 * sizeof(TRGBQuad)));

    {initialize all of the header information}
    with pDIB^.bmiHeader do begin
      biSize := sizeof(TBitmapInfoHeader);
      biWidth := 8;
      biHeight := 8;
      biPlanes := 1;
      biBitCount := 1;
      biCompression := BI_RGB;
      biSizeImage := 0;
      biXPelsPermeter := 0;
```

```
      biYPelsPermeter := 0;
      biClrused := 0;
      biClrImportant := 0;
      end;

    {set the color table values}
    with pQuad^ do begin
      rgbBlue := 0;
      rgbGreen := 0;
      rgbRed := 0;
      rgbReserved := 0;
      end;

    inc(pQuad);
    with pQuad^ do begin
      rgbBlue := 255;
      rgbGreen := 255;
      rgbRed := 255;
      rgbReserved := 0;
      end;

    {initialize pixel data to all white}
    for i := 0 to 7 do begin
      p := pointer(longint(pBits) + (i * 4));
      if i mod 2 = 0 then
        p^ := Chr($AA)
      else p^ := Chr($55);
      end;
    p := nil;

    hBMP := CreateDIBitmap(imgBrush.Canvas.handle, pDIB^.bmiHeader, CBM_INIT,
                       pBits, pDIB^, DIB_RGB_COLORS);
    result := CreatePatternBrush(hBMP);

  finally
    freemem(pDIB, size);
    if hBMP <> 0 then DeleteObject(hBMP);
  end; {try}

end; {CreateCheckBrush}

procedure TMain.FormCreate(Sender: TObject);
var r: TRect;
begin

  r := Rect(0,0,32,32);
  hPatBrush := CreateCheckBrush;
  hOldBrush := imgBrush.Canvas.Brush.Handle;

  with imgBrush.Canvas do begin
    Brush.handle := hPatBrush;
    FillRect(r);
    end;
```

Advanced Imaging—Special Visual Effects   351

```
    imgResult.Canvas.Brush.handle := hPatBrush;

end; {FormCreate}

procedure TMain.lstROPSClick(Sender: TObject);

begin

  with imgResult.Canvas do begin
    CopyMode :=cmSrcCopy;
    Draw(0,0, imgDst.Picture.Bitmap);
    end;

  with imgResult.Canvas do begin
    Case lstROPS.ItemIndex of
        0: CopyMode := cmSrcCopy;
        1: CopyMode := cmSrcPaint;
        2: CopyMode := cmSrcAnd;
        3: CopyMode := cmSrcInvert;
        4: CopyMode := cmSrcErase;
        5: CopyMode := cmNotSrcCopy;
        6: CopyMode := cmNotSrcErase;
        7: CopyMode := cmMergeCopy;
        8: CopyMode := cmMergePaint;
        9: CopyMode := cmPatCopy;
       10: CopyMode := cmPatPaint;
       11: CopyMode := cmPatInvert;
       12: CopyMode := cmDstInvert;
       13: CopyMode := cmBlackness;
       14: CopyMode := cmWhiteness;

      end; {case}

    Draw(0,0, imgSrc.Picture.Bitmap);
    end;

end; {lstROPSClick}

procedure TMain.FormDestroy(Sender: TObject);
begin
  imgBrush.Canvas.Brush.Handle := hOldBrush;
  imgResult.Canvas.Brush.Handle := hOldBrush;
  DeleteObject(hPatBrush);
end;

end.
```

Let's look at the simple elements first. First, we declare two global variables, hPatBrush and hOldBrush, as handles to a brush object. We'll use these to handle the creation, maintenance, and destruction of the brush we create. The OnCreate handler for the form takes care of the initialization code. Take a look at Listing 8.2.

Listing 8.2 The OnCreate handler

```
procedure TMain.FormCreate(Sender: TObject);
var r: TRect;
begin

  r := Rect(0,0,32,32);
  hPatBrush := CreateCheckBrush;
  hOldBrush := imgBrush.Canvas.Brush.Handle;

  with imgBrush.Canvas do begin
    Brush.handle := hPatBrush;
    FillRect(r);
    end;

  imgResult.Canvas.Brush.handle := hPatBrush;

end; {FormCreate}
```

The first thing we do is to create a **TRect** structure in the variable **r** that is 32 pixels by 32 pixels (the size of a brush). Next, we call the function that actually creates the brush bitmap. The function **CreateCheckBrush** creates a checkerboard pattern brush and returns a handle to that brush. Here we assign that return value to the global variable **hPatBrush**. We'll look at the details of **CreateCheckBrush** in just a moment.

Remember, when you create a GDI object and select it into a device context, you must keep track of the object that is being replaced. That is what we're using **hOldBrush** for. The *handle* for the brush that is currently selected in the **imgBrush** canvas is **imgBrush.Canvas.Brush.Handle**. We store this handle in **hOldBrush** so that we can put it back when we're finished.

Now we can safely select **hPatBrush** into the canvas of **imgBrush** and **imgResult**. The two **TImage** components shared the same brush prior to our selection, so we only need to store the value one time in **hOldBrush**. Once our new brush is selected into the canvas, we can use the **FillRect** method procedure of the canvas to draw the pattern brush. We do this to display the pattern itself. It does not have any effect on the outcome of the raster operations.

The last line of code in the OnCreate handler is:

```
imgResult.Canvas.Brush.handle := hPatBrush;
```

Here we are selecting the pattern brush into the canvas of imgResult. Once the brush is selected, it will be used in all raster operations performed on that canvas that use a brush as a component of the operation.

Let's take a quick look at the cleanup code in the OnDestroy handler for the form. Use Listing 8.3 as a reference.

Listing 8.3 The OnDestroy handler

```
procedure TMain.FormDestroy(Sender: TObject);
begin
  imgBrush.Canvas.Brush.Handle := hOldBrush;
  imgResult.Canvas.Brush.Handle := hOldBrush;
  DeleteObject(hPatBrush);
end;
```

The first step before deleting an object is to make sure that it is not selected in any *dc's*. We select the original brush, **hOldBrush**, into the canvas of **imgBrush** and **imgResult**. Then we use the API function **DeleteObject()** to free the memory used for our pattern brush.

Before we actually create a bitmap in the **CreateCheckBrush** function, let's look at some of the structures that are used to work with bitmaps. In Chapter 6 we briefly looked at the structure of DIB's. To understand the code in this chapter, we're going to have to dig a little more deeply. Look at the illustration in Figure 8.2.

As you can see, the packed DIB contains a BITMAPFILEHEADER, a BITMAPINFOHEADER, a Color Table, and the bits of the bitmap. It is important to note that the BITMAPFILEHEADER is the first part of the bitmap that you will encounter when reading a DIB from a file. It defines some type information and the location of the bits. We will not be using the BITMAPFILEHEADER, but it is important to know its location and size so we can move on to the more important BITMAPINFOHEADER structure. The BITMAPINFOHEADER

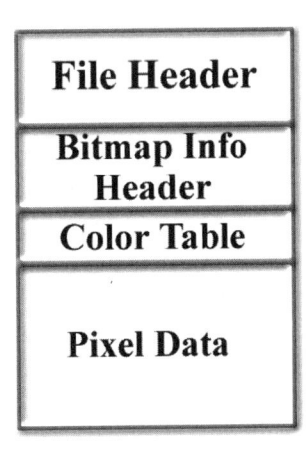

Figure 8.2 *DIB Structure.*

contains all sorts of useful information about the bitmap. The structure looks like this:

```
TBitmapInfoHeader = packed record
    biSize: DWORD;
    biWidth: Longint;
    biHeight: Longint;
    biPlanes: Word;
    biBitCount: Word;
    biCompression: DWORD;
    biSizeImage: DWORD;
    biXPelsPerMeter: Longint;
    biYPelsPerMeter: Longint;
    biClrUsed: DWORD;
    biClrImportant: DWORD;
end;
```

Directly following the BITMAPINFOHEADER is the bitmap's color table. This is an array of TRGBQuad structures large enough to accommodate the number of colors in the DIB. For a 256 color DIB, there is an array of 256 RGBQuad's. The TRGBQuad structure looks like this:

```
TRGBQuad = record
    rgbBlue: Byte;
    rgbGreen: Byte;
    rgbRed: Byte;
    rgbReserved: Byte;
end;
```

The BITMAPINFOHEADER and the color table are both contained in yet another structure called BITMAPINFO. This structure is defined as:

```
TBitmapInfo = record
    bmiHeader: TBitmapInfoHeader;
    bmiColors: array[0..0] of TRGBQuad;
end;
```

Finally, we find the actual bits of the bitmap at the end of the color table. The bits are a contiguous data stream large enough to hold the entire bitmap. The bits of a DIB are arranged beginning with the pixel at the lower left corner of the DIB, moving from left to right until the right boundary is reached, and then the process is repeated for each consecutive scan line from bottom to top. The number of bytes in a DIB scan line must be divisible by four. So each row of a DIB must be padded with enough bytes to keep to this rule. In our case, we're creating a bitmap that is 8 pixels by 8 pixels, 1 bit per pixel.

Advanced Imaging—Special Visual Effects 355

We should be able to store this in 8 bytes. Because of the DIB scan line rule, we must pad each of the eight rows with 3 pad bytes. So in memory, the bits of our bitmap will require 32 bytes instead of 8 bytes.

Now we're ready to build a bitmap! In the OnCreate handler, we used the **CreateCheckBrush** function that gave us a handle to the newly created brush bitmap. Let's step through that process. Listing 8.4 shows the complete function.

Listing 8.4 CreateCheckBrush

```
function TMain.CreateCheckBrush: hBrush;
var
  pDIB: PBitmapInfo; {pointer to the packed DIB structure we're creating}
  pBits:  PChar;     {pointer to the bits of the bitmap}
  pQuad:  PRGBQuad;  {pointer to a RGBQuad structure}
  p: PChar;          {temp pointer for setting bits}
  size: longint;     {size of the entire dib in memory}
  i: byte;           {counter variable}
  hBMP: hBitmap;     {handle to a bitmap}

begin

  size := sizeof(TBitmapInfoHeader) + (2 * sizeof(TRGBQuad)) + 32;
  pDIB := nil;
  hBMP := 0;

  {allocate memory for the DIB}
  pDIB := allocmem(size);

  try
    pQuad := pointer(longint(pDIB) + sizeof(TBitmapInfoHeader));
    pBits := pointer(longint(pQuad) + (2 * sizeof(TRGBQuad)));

    {initialize all of the header information}
    with pDIB^.bmiHeader do begin
      biSize := sizeof(TBitmapInfoHeader);
      biWidth := 8;
      biHeight := 8;
      biPlanes := 1;
      biBitCount := 1;
      biCompression := BI_RGB;
      biSizeImage := 0;
      biXPelsPermeter := 0;
      biYPelsPermeter := 0;
      biClrused := 0;
      biClrImportant := 0;
    end;

    {set the color table values}
    with pQuad^ do begin
      rgbBlue := 0;
```

```
        rgbGreen := 0;
        rgbRed := 0;
        rgbReserved := 0;
        end;

      inc(pQuad);
      with pQuad^ do begin
        rgbBlue := 255;
        rgbGreen := 255;
        rgbRed := 255;
        rgbReserved := 0;
        end;

    for i := 0 to 7 do begin
        p := pointer(longint(pBits) + (i * 4));
        if i mod 2 = 0 then
          p^ := Chr($AA)
        else p^ := Chr($55);
        end;
      p := nil;

      hBMP := CreateDIBitmap(imgBrush.Canvas.handle, pDIB^.bmiHeader, CBM_INIT,
                       pBits, pDIB^, DIB_RGB_COLORS);
      result := CreatePatternBrush(hBMP);

    finally
      freemem(pDIB, size);
      if hBMP <> 0 then DeleteObject(hBMP);
    end; {try}

end; {CreateCheckBrush}
```

In general terms this function does the following:

- Allocates memory for an 8x8 pixel DIB with a 2 color palette.
- Describes the DIB by setting values in the BITMAPINFOHEADER structure.
- Sets the color values.
- Creates the bitmap bits.
- Uses the **CreateDIBitmap()** Windows API function to get a handle to the bitmap.
- Creates the brush.
- Releases memory used to create the bitmap

Let's take a look at each step individually. First we allocate memory for the DIB:

```
size := sizeof(TBitmapInfoHeader) + (2 * sizeof(TRGBQuad)) + 32;
pDIB := nil;
hBMP := 0;
```

```
{allocate memory for the DIB}
pDIB := allocmem(size);

try
  pQuad := pointer(longint(pDIB) + sizeof(TBitmapInfoHeader));
  pBits := pointer(longint(pQuad) + (2 * sizeof(TRGBQuad)));
```

We calculate the number of bytes that the DIB is going to take up in memory and store that in **size**. The size of the bitmap in memory is the number of bytes in TBitmapInfoHeader and the number of bytes in TRGBQuad multiplied by the number of colors in the bitmap (two), plus the number of bytes in the pixel data. We use **allocmem** to allocate enough memory for the DIB, and **pDIB** points to that chunk. Everything after the memory allocation is placed inside a resource protection block so that if anything goes wrong, the memory just allocated will still be freed. The pointer variables pQuad and pBits are for convenient access to the first RGBQuad and the first byte of the pixel stream.

Once the memory is allocated, we need to set some values that describe the bitmap we are creating. Most of these values are in TBitmapInfoHeader:

```
{initialize all of the header information}
   with pDIB^.bmiHeader do begin
     biSize := sizeof(TBitmapInfoHeader);
     biWidth := 8;
     biHeight := 8;
     biPlanes := 1;
     biBitCount := 1;
     biCompression := BI_RGB;
     biSizeImage := 0;
     biXPelsPermeter := 0;
     biYPelsPermeter := 0;
     biClrused := 0;
     biClrImportant := 0;
   end;
```

We access the values in the **BitmapInfoHeader** through the pointer to the DIB (**pDIB**). The fields of TBitmapInfoHeader are fairly self-explanatory. Rather than digressing to discuss each of them here, please look up TBitmapInfo Header in API help reference that ships with Delphi. Included is a detailed description of each field. For our purposes, we're setting the width and height to 8 pixels, no compression (BI_RGB), and we're making it a black and white image (1 bit per pixel, and 1 plane). The color table is represented by two TRGBQuad's. The following code sets the colors to black and white:

```
{set the color table values}
   with pQuad^ do begin
     rgbBlue := 0;
```

```
      rgbGreen := 0;
      rgbRed := 0;
      rgbReserved := 0;
    end;

  inc(pQuad);
  with pQuad^ do begin
    rgbBlue := 255;
    rgbGreen := 255;
    rgbRed := 255;
    rgbReserved := 0;
  end;
```

Remember that we set pQuad to point to the first RGBQuad structure of the DIB. After we set the first one to black, we need to get to the next element of the array. Before we do that, take another look at how TBitmapInfo is declared:

```
TBitmapInfo = record
    bmiHeader: TBitmapInfoHeader;
    bmiColors: array[0..0] of TRGBQuad;
  end;
```

Exactly one element is declared for the bmiColors array. This declaration is from windows.pas. There will be very few times that you will only require one color definition for a bitmap. This brush that we are creating is one of the simpler bitmaps that you will create—and it requires two! The declaration is meant to be used as a template. We have several options for accessing more than one TRGBQuad structure. We could redefine the TBitmapInfo structure to accommodate the number of colors we require. We could also turn off range checking for the section of code and access as many elements of the array as we need, even though only one was declared. We can get away with this because we carefully allocated enough memory to account for the number of colors we need, and we know that the array elements are present. The last method, and the one I used for this piece of code, is to increment the pointer by the size of the TRGBQuad structure. This gives us unidirectional access to each successive TRGBQuad. For this particular situation, that method works just fine. I will introduce several of these methods in other projects. You'll have to decide which one you prefer. You may even devise another method that you like better. I have found that each of the methods I've described works well under different circumstances.

The next part of this function actually creates the bits that make up the bitmap's pattern:

```
for i := 0 to 7 do begin
    p := pointer(longint(pBits) + (i * 4));
    if i mod 2 = 0 then
      p^ := Chr($AA)
    else p^ := Chr($55);
    end;
  p := nil;
```

The loop counter represents a row of pixels: zero is the bottom row, and seven is the top row. The pointer calculation that sets the address of *p* ensures that we are looking at the leftmost byte of the row for each iteration of the loop. Remember that each row is padded with 3 extra bytes. The next statement actually sets the byte to either $AA or $55, using even and odd rows as the deciding factor. The even rows end up set to 01010101, and the odd rows become 10101010. Figure 8.3 demonstrates what the brush will look like.

Next, we turn the DIB into a DDB, and from the DDB create a brush object:

```
    hBMP := CreateDIBitmap(imgBrush.Canvas.handle, pDIB^.bmiHeader, CBM_INIT,
                    pBits, pDIB^, DIB_RGB_COLORS);
    result := CreatePatternBrush(hBMP);

  finally
    freemem(pDIB, size);
    if hBMP <> 0 then DeleteObject(hBMP);
  end; {try}
```

The Windows API function **CreateDIBitmap** is a little misleading by name alone. This function actually takes a DIB and returns a handle to a newly created DDB. The parameters are (in order) the handle to the *dc* with which the bitmap will be associated, the **TBitmapInfoHeader** structure, the Windows constant **CBM_INIT** to initialize a new bitmap, a pointer to the pixel data, the **TBitmapInfo** structure, and a usage flag that indicates whether the bmiColors structure contains RGB values or references to the currently realized palette.

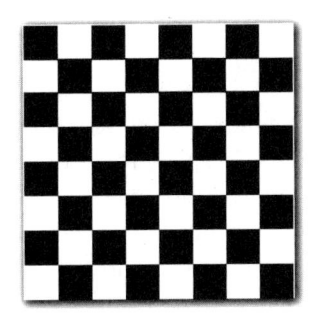

Figure 8.3 *The checkerboard pattern brush.*

The return value is a handle to a bitmap which is then passed to **CreatePatternBrush**. The return value of **CreatePatternBrush** is the fruit of our labor. It is a handle to a newly created checkerboard pattern brush!

The only thing left to do is release some memory that we no longer need. The code that follows *finally* takes care of releasing the memory we used to describe the DIB, and also the bitmap object that we created as a parameter to **CreatePatternBrush**.

We did not go over the event handler code for the listbox click. This code is identical to the code in the first ROP experiment from last chapter. At last, you are ready to test the program. Compare the way this version functions compared to the one from Chapter 7. The difference should be apparent in the ROPs that use a pattern brush.

Combining Bitmaps

We now have a number of tools under our belts for working with palettes, blts, and raster operations. We're well on our way to the image dissolve effect. Next, let's figure out which ROP code will enable us to combine two images.

Imagine that you're holding two photographs in your hand, one on top of the other. You can't see the bottom photo because photographic prints are opaque. You can simulate the digital dissolve process by poking hundreds of tiny holes in the top image, evenly spaced across the entire picture. Through the holes you could then discern little bits of the bottom photo. You could go over the entire image again with your needle, this time adding more holes between the first set. As the holes increase in number, first by hundreds, then by thousands, the bottom image becomes clearer and clearer. After several rounds of hole poking, the top picture disintegrates, leaving the bottom image unobscured.

To speed up the whole process, you could make a little hole puncher by sticking several pins through a piece of cork or rubber. Then you could punch dozens of holes with each pop. And that's exactly what we're going to do with a pattern brush.

The brush created in the ROPS2 project consists of alternating white and black pixels—a checkerboard pattern. If we think of that pattern as a fine mesh rather than a checkerboard, we can easily imagine that we could see a bitmap through the holes represented by the black pixels. Stepping through the dissolve, we'll create brushes with ever increasing numbers of black pixels.

Now we need to deduce which ROP code will combine the brush and the two images to generate the proper effect.

Hunting through Raster Operations

Windows raster operations have an undeserved reputation as a black art. Choosing a raster operation is one of the hardest things to do in Windows graphics programming. But like any programming problem, you only need to break the process into manageable steps. To mix the pixels of two images, we need to do two things:

1. Use the pattern brush to make black holes in the destination bitmap.
2. Fill the holes with the corresponding pixels from the source bitmap.

For the first step, only one logical operator will be necessary. If you **And** a pixel with a binary value of 00000000—representing the black palette entry—with any other pixel value, you will get only one result: 00000000. 10101010 **And** 00000000 equals 00000000; 11110000 **And** 00000000 equals 00000000, and so on. In Boolean logic, only 1 **And** 1 equals 1. But what happens to the pixels in the destination when we **And** them with the white pixels in the pattern brush? Nothing. Because once again, only the pixel bits that equal 1 in the destination will yield 1 when we **And** them with pattern pixel bits that equal 1. 10101010 **And** 11111111 equals 10101010; 11110000 **And** 11111111 equals 11110000. Pixels that are black in the pattern brush become black in the destination bitmap, while pixels that are white in the pattern brush remain unchanged in the destination bitmap. So, step one looks like this:

(Pattern **And** Destination)

Next, we have to combine the source bitmap with the result of step 1 so that only the pixels that lie under the black holes are showing through. This step is trickier. Because any of the three logical operators will blend the bits of the colored pixels from both images, we have to perform another masking operation to eliminate the undesirable pixels from the source image. Step two splits into two tasks. First, we change all the unwanted pixels to black, then we press the two pictures together.

To mask all but the pixels we want to add to our awaiting destination bitmap, we invert the mask with a **Not** operator. In Boolean logic, **Not** changes all 1s to 0s, and all 0s to 1s. Then, in the third step, we use the **And** operator again—this time between the inverted pattern and the source image:

((**Not** Pattern) **And** Source)

Whoops—still one step to go. In this last step, we want to combine the results of steps one through three. We know that **And** won't work; since each pair of pixels includes one colored pixel from either of the images, facing one black pixel from the opposite image. Thus, an **And** would blacken the whole picture. An **Or**, however, will retain the bits from each colored pixel exactly as they appear in their native bitmaps. In fact, since one member of each pixel pair is black, an **Xor** would work just as well. The complete raster operation expression looks like this:

(Pattern **And** Destination) **Or** ((**Not** Pattern) **And** Source)

In Reverse Polish Notation, it looks like this:

PDaSPnao

Don't bother looking in the table of the fifteen named ROP codes for that one—you won't find it. With a little Boolean algebra, we could derive an equivalent expression, one that does appear in the table. But there's an easier way. The Windows API defines a set of pre-defined binary constants, one representing each of the three types of bitmaps, which we can grind through our equation to directly calculate the hexadecimal identification number of the correct ROP code.

Let's work through the steps:

1. Combine the pattern brush and the destination to make black holes in the destination.
   The pattern brush and the destination bitmap are represented by the binary constants 11110000 and 10101010, respectively. 11110000 **And** 10101010 equals 10100000.
2. Invert the pattern brush.
   Not 11110000 equals 00001111.
3. Combine the result of step two with the source bitmap, which is represented by the binary constant 11001100.
   00001111 **And** 11001100 equals 00001100.
4. **Or** the results of steps one and three.
   10100000 **Or** 00001100 equals 10101100.

The ROP code we want is 10101100, which is hexadecimal value &HAC. ROP codes are actually long integers. The highest-order byte always equals

&H00. The second highest-order byte represents the ROP identification number. The two lower-order bytes contain codes that help the ROP engine construct the correct sequence of machine instructions to perform the raster operation. ROPs are like tiny programs, or macros. For the sake of speed, the GDI assembles a temporary program in memory, enabling the blt function to perform the raster operation without calling subfunctions. The lower-order bytes don't help us identify the ROP code, but we must include them when we reference the ROP code in a blt operation.

If we look up raster operation &HAC in the ROP table, we find that its logical expression looks a little different from ours:

SPDSxax

Regardless of appearance, the two expressions are logically equivalent; which we could prove by again grinding the bitmap binary constants. Be my guest.

> **Note:** *The expression given in the ROP table may seem less intuitive than the one we derived by our step-by-step method, but you can still make sense of it by remembering that an **Xor** operation is reversible (just do it over again). In the expression SPDSxax, you see two **Xor** operations. The first combines the source and destination bitmaps. The second de-combines all the pixels untouched by the pattern brush. The middle step combines the effects of the **Not** and both **And** operations from our version of the expression. Instead of performing one **And**, then inverting the pattern to perform the second **And**, you can perform the **And** on the combined bitmaps. When you perform the final **Xor**, the blackened pixels are filled with the pixels from the source bitmap, while simultaneously the source pixels are reversed out of the unblackened destination pixels.*

According to the standard table of Windows ternary ROP codes, the complete hex value of the $AC ROP code is $00AC0744. To test this raster operation, add MergeMask to the ListBox component of ROPS2 and add the statement:

```
15: CopyMode := $00AC0744;
```

to the OnClick handler of the ListBox. When you test the program and select MergeMask, you will see a result similar to that in Figure 8.4.

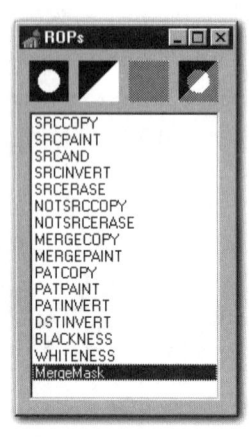

Figure 8.4 *Result of the MergeMask ROP. That takes care of the ROP code. Now we can start the dissolve project.*

Creating the Basic Digital Dissolve

In the program BITBLT which we created in Chapter 7, we simply copied an image from one canvas to another. Let's make that program more interesting by creating a series of black and white pattern brushes, tossing in our newly discovered ROP code, and dissolving the image from one Image component to the other.

The First Dissolve

This project shows you how to dissolve two bitmap images.
1. Create a new project.
2. Add three **TImage** components. Use Figure 8.5 as a guide.
3. Add a **TSpeedButton**.
4. Set the properties and events.
5. Insert and modify code.

This project is located in the directory \DELPHIMM\CH08\DSLVEXP.

Creating the First Dissolve

Create a new project and save the form unit and project file. Add three **TImage** components and a **TSpeedButton** and arrange them on the form as

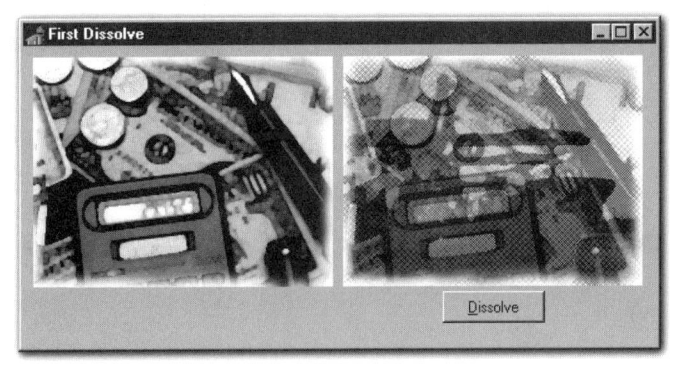

Figure 8.5 *The first dissolve form midway through the dissolve.*

shown in Figure 8.5. Follow Table 8.2 to set the properties and events for the form and components.

Use the object inspector to load bitmaps for the two source **TImage** components. The bitmaps should be the same size for this project. I used finance.bmp and shipping.bmp that come with Delphi in the Images\Splash\256color directory. Use any images you wish.

Adding the Code

This project has two utility routines; **CreateDissolveBrush** and **WaitMil**. **CreateDissolveBrush** is very similar to the **CreateCheckBrush** from the last project with one important exception. It takes a parameter that tells it how much of the brush should be black. This allows us to create a mesh that

Table 8.2 *Form and component properties.*

Component	Property/Event	Setting
Default Form	Name	Main
	Caption	First Dissolve
TImage1	Name	imgSrc1
	Autosize	True
	Picture	(TBitmap)
TImage2	Name	imgSrc2
	Autosize	True
	Picture	(TBitmap)
TImage3	Name	imgDst
TSpeedButton	Name	sbDissolve
	OnClick	sbDissolveClick

Chapter 8

allows increasing amounts of the new image to show through. The **WaitMil** function is used in place of a timer to delay execution for a number of milliseconds. To respond to user actions, we have two event handlers. One responds to the **TSpeedButton** click and the other responds to a click on the destination **TImage** component. Listing 8.5 shows the form **unit udslvexp.pas**.

Listing 8.5   udslvexp.pas

```
unit udslvexp;

interface

uses
  Windows, Messages, SysUtils, Classes, Graphics, Controls, Forms, Dialogs,
  ExtCtrls, Buttons;

type
  TMain = class(TForm)
    imgSrc1: TImage;
    imgSrc2: TImage;
    imgDst: TImage;
    sbDissolve: TSpeedButton;
    procedure sbDissolveClick(Sender: TObject);
    procedure imgDstClick(Sender: TObject);

  private
    { Private declarations }
  public
    { Public declarations }
  end;

var
  Main: TMain;

implementation

{$R *.DFM}

var
  Dissolving: boolean;

function CreateDissolveBrush(step: byte): hBrush;
const
  brushdata: array [0..7,0..7] of Char = (
                        (#$55,#$AA,#$FD,#$FE,#$FD,#$FE,#$FD,#$FE),
                        (#$55,#$AA,#$55,#$AA,#$F5,#$FA,#$F5,#$FA),
                        (#$55,#$AA,#$55,#$AA,#$55,#$AA,#$D5,#$EA),
                        (#$55,#$AA,#$55,#$AA,#$55,#$AA,#$55,#$AA),
                        (#$00,#$00,#$54,#$A8,#$54,#$A8,#$54,#$A8),
                        (#$00,#$00,#$00,#$00,#$00,#$00,#$50,#$A0),
                        (#$00,#$00,#$00,#$00,#$00,#$00,#$40,#$80),
                        (#$00,#$00,#$00,#$00,#$00,#$00,#$00,#$00));
```

Advanced Imaging—Special Visual Effects

```
var
  pDIB:    PBitmapInfo; {pointer to the packed DIB structure we're creating}
  pBits:   PChar;       {pointer to the bits of the bitmap}
  pQuad:   PRGBQuad;    {pointer to a RGBQuad structure}
  p:       PChar;       {temp pointer for setting bits}
  size:    longint;     {size of the entire dib in memory}
  i:       byte;        {counter variable}
  hBMP:    hBitmap;     {handle to a bitmap}

begin

  if (step < 0) or (step > 7) then exit;

  size := sizeof(TBitmapInfoHeader) + (2 * sizeof(TRGBQuad)) + 32;
  pDIB := nil;
  hBMP := 0;

  {allocate memory for the DIB}
  pDIB := allocmem(size);

  try

    pQuad := pointer(longint(pDIB) + sizeof(TBitmapInfoHeader));
    pBits := pointer(longint(pQuad) + (2 * sizeof(TRGBQuad)));

    {initialize all of the header information}
    with pDIB^.bmiHeader do begin
      biSize := sizeof(TBitmapInfoHeader);
      biWidth := 8;
      biHeight := 8;
      biPlanes := 1;
      biBitCount := 1;
      biCompression := BI_RGB;
      biSizeImage := 0;
      biXPelsPermeter := 0;
      biYPelsPermeter := 0;
      biClrused := 0;
      biClrImportant := 0;
      end;

    {set the color table values}
    with pQuad^ do begin
      rgbBlue := 0;
      rgbGreen := 0;
      rgbRed := 0;
      rgbReserved := 0;
      end;

    inc(pQuad);
    with pQuad^ do begin
      rgbBlue := 255;
      rgbGreen := 255;
      rgbRed := 255;
```

```
        rgbReserved := 0;
        end;

      for i := 0 to 7 do begin
        p := pointer(longint(pBits) + (i * 4));
        p^ := brushdata[step, i];
        end;
      p := nil;

      hBMP := CreateDIBitmap(Main.Canvas.handle, pDIB^.bmiHeader, CBM_INIT,
                             pBits, pDIB^, DIB_RGB_COLORS);
      result := CreatePatternBrush(hBMP);

  finally
    freemem(pDIB, size);
    if hBMP <> 0 then DeleteObject(hBMP);
  end; {try}

end; {CreateDissolveBrush}

procedure waitmil(ms : integer);
var
   StartTick : LongInt;

begin

   StartTick := GetTickCount;
   while GetTickCount <= StartTick + ms do
     Application.ProcessMessages;

end;

procedure TMain.sbDissolveClick(Sender: TObject);
var
   i:          byte;
   hOldBrush,
   hCurBrush: hBrush;

begin

   Dissolving := True;
   hCurBrush := 0;
   with imgDst.Canvas do begin
     CopyMode := cmSrcCopy;
     Draw(0,0,imgSrc1.Picture.Bitmap);
     waitmil(2000);
     for i := 0 to 7 do begin
       hOldBrush := hCurBrush;
       hCurBrush := CreateDissolveBrush(i);
       Brush.Handle := hCurBrush;
       if hOldBrush <> 0 then DeleteObject(hOldBrush);
       CopyMode := $AC0744;
       Draw(0,0,imgSrc2.Picture.Bitmap);
       waitmil(25);
```

```
      end;
    end;
  Dissolving := False;

end; {SpeedButtonClick}

procedure TMain.imgDstClick(Sender: TObject);
const
  stage:     byte = 0;
  hOldBrush: hBrush = 0;
  hCurBrush: hBrush = 0;

begin

  if Dissolving then exit;

  if stage > 7 then stage := 0;

  if stage = 0 then begin
    with imgDst.Canvas do begin
      CopyMode := cmSrcCopy;
      Draw(0,0,imgSrc1.Picture.Bitmap);
      end;
    end
  else begin
        with imgDst.Canvas do begin
          hOldBrush := hCurBrush;
          hCurBrush := CreateDissolveBrush(stage);
          Brush.Handle := hCurBrush;
          if hOldBrush <> 0 then DeleteObject(hOldBrush);
          CopyMode := $AC0744;
          Draw(0,0,imgSrc2.Picture.Bitmap);
          end;
        end;

  inc(stage);

end;

end.
```

The procedure **sbDissolveClick**, found in Listing 8.6, activates the dissolve process. First the image in **imgSrc1** is copied to the destination canvas. It remains there for 2 seconds (2000ms). To create the dissolve effect, we iterate through a loop that creates a brush with a decreasing number of black pixels or "holes". Using that brush and the *MergeMask* ROP we derived earlier, we copy **imgSrc2** onto the destination canvas. The only pixels of **imgSrc2** that are actually displayed are the ones that occupy the same location as a white pixel in the pattern brush. The resulting effect is an increasing number of pixels from **imgSrc2** and a decreasing number of pixels that show through from **imgSrc1**—A dissolve!

Listing 8.6 The DissolveClick event handler

```
procedure TMain.sbDissolveClick(Sender: TObject);
var
  i:       byte;
  hOldBrush,
  hCurBrush: hBrush;

begin

  Dissolving := True;
  hCurBrush := 0;
  with imgDst.Canvas do begin
    CopyMode := cmSrcCopy;
    Draw(0,0,imgSrc1.Picture.Bitmap);
    waitmil(2000);
    for i := 0 to 7 do begin
      hOldBrush := hCurBrush;
      hCurBrush := CreateDissolveBrush(i);
      Brush.Handle := hCurBrush;
      if hOldBrush <> 0 then DeleteObject(hOldBrush);
      CopyMode := $AC0744;
      Draw(0,0,imgSrc2.Picture.Bitmap);
      waitmil(25);
      end;
    end;
  Dissolving := False;

end; {SpeedButtonClick}
```

You should be familiar with most of the routines presented in the **sbDissolveClick** handler. A couple exceptions are the **waitmil** procedure and the **CreateDissolveBrush** function. The **waitmil** procedure just receives the number of *ticks* since Windows was started when it is called, and then processes messages until the number of *ticks* elapsed has increased by the value in its parameter:

```
procedure waitmil(ms : integer);
var
  StartTick : LongInt;

begin

  StartTick := GetTickCount;
  while GetTickCount <= StartTick + ms do
    Application.ProcessMessages;

end;
```

GetTickCount is a Windows API function that returns the number of milliseconds that have elapsed since Windows was started.

Advanced Imaging—Special Visual Effects 371

The **CreateDissolveBrush** function in Listing 8.7 should look very familiar. This is a modified version of our **CreateCheckBrush** function from the last project.

Listing 8.7 The CreateDissolveBrush function

```
function CreateDissolveBrush(step: byte): hBrush;
const
  brushdata: array [0..7,0..7] of Char = (
                              (#$55,#$AA,#$FD,#$FE,#$FD,#$FE,#$FD,#$FE),
                              (#$55,#$AA,#$55,#$AA,#$F5,#$FA,#$F5,#$FA),
                              (#$55,#$AA,#$55,#$AA,#$55,#$AA,#$D5,#$EA),
                              (#$55,#$AA,#$55,#$AA,#$55,#$AA,#$55,#$AA),
                              (#$00,#$00,#$54,#$A8,#$54,#$A8,#$54,#$A8),
                              (#$00,#$00,#$00,#$00,#$00,#$00,#$50,#$A0),
                              (#$00,#$00,#$00,#$00,#$00,#$00,#$40,#$80),
                              (#$00,#$00,#$00,#$00,#$00,#$00,#$00,#$00));

var
  pDIB:   PBitmapInfo;  {pointer to the packed DIB structure we're creating}
  pBits:  PChar;        {pointer to the bits of the bitmap}
  pQuad:  PRGBQuad;     {pointer to a RGBQuad structure}
  p:      PChar;        {temp pointer for setting bits}
  size:   longint;      {size of the entire dib in memory}
  i:      byte;         {counter variable}
  hBMP:   hBitmap;      {handle to a bitmap}

begin

  if (step < 0) or (step > 7) then exit;

  size := sizeof(TBitmapInfoHeader) + (2 * sizeof(TRGBQuad)) + 32;
  pDIB := nil;
  hBMP := 0;

  {allocate memory for the DIB}
  pDIB := allocmem(size);

  try

    pQuad := pointer(longint(pDIB) + sizeof(TBitmapInfoHeader));
    pBits := pointer(longint(pQuad) + (2 * sizeof(TRGBQuad)));

    {initialize all of the header information}
    with pDIB^.bmiHeader do begin
      biSize := sizeof(TBitmapInfoHeader);
      biWidth := 8;
      biHeight := 8;
      biPlanes := 1;
      biBitCount := 1;
      biCompression := BI_RGB;
      biSizeImage := 0;
      biXPelsPermeter := 0;
```

```
      biYPelsPermeter := 0;
      biClrused := 0;
      biClrImportant := 0;
    end;

    {set the color table values}
    with pQuad^ do begin
      rgbBlue := 0;
      rgbGreen := 0;
      rgbRed := 0;
      rgbReserved := 0;
    end;

    inc(pQuad);
    with pQuad^ do begin
      rgbBlue := 255;
      rgbGreen := 255;
      rgbRed := 255;
      rgbReserved := 0;
    end;

    for i := 0 to 7 do begin
      p := pointer(longint(pBits) + (i * 4));
      p^ := brushdata[step, i];
    end;
    p := nil;

    hBMP := CreateDIBitmap(Main.Canvas.handle, pDIB^.bmiHeader, CBM_INIT,
                  pBits, pDIB^, DIB_RGB_COLORS);
    result := CreatePatternBrush(hBMP);

  finally
    freemem(pDIB, size);
    if hBMP <> 0 then DeleteObject(hBMP);
  end; {try}

end; {CreateDissolveBrush}
```

Notice that the function now accepts a parameter. The parameter allows the calling routine to specify which stage of the dissolve brush we want to create. My version of the dissolve brush uses eight stages to create the effect. Coincidentally, a two dimensional array of characters represents the bits of the brushes at each stage. To understand how the data in the array represents pixels in the brush, refer to Figure 8.6.

The only other part of this function that has changed is the section of code that actually sets the pixel data of the new bitmap. In the original code, we used an if..then conditional statement to alternate between $AA and $55 for each row of the bitmap. In this version, we use the data from the second dimension of the array in order. Look at the following example:

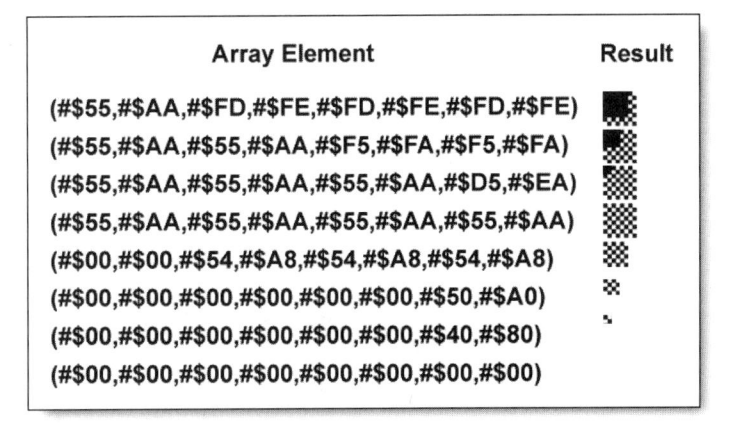

Array Element	Result
(#$55,#$AA,#$FD,#$FE,#$FD,#$FE,#$FD,#$FE)	
(#$55,#$AA,#$55,#$AA,#$F5,#$FA,#$F5,#$FA)	
(#$55,#$AA,#$55,#$AA,#$55,#$AA,#$D5,#$EA)	
(#$55,#$AA,#$55,#$AA,#$55,#$AA,#$55,#$AA)	
(#$00,#$00,#$54,#$A8,#$54,#$A8,#$54,#$A8)	
(#$00,#$00,#$00,#$00,#$00,#$00,#$50,#$A0)	
(#$00,#$00,#$00,#$00,#$00,#$00,#$40,#$80)	
(#$00,#$00,#$00,#$00,#$00,#$00,#$00,#$00)	

Figure 8.6 Visualizing the bitmap array data.

```
for i := 0 to 7 do begin
    p := pointer(longint(pBits) + (i * 4));
    p^ := brushdata[step, i];
    end;
```

Figure 8.7 depicts the data and resulting bitmap generated by this loop, given that **step** is equal to four.

Use Listing 8.5 as a reference to make sure that you have entered the code for the **imgDstClick** event handler and the declaration of the global boolean **Dissolving**. Now that you're finished, run the program.

A Closer Look at the First Dissolve

The dissolve in this project works well in color modes higher than 256. It will also work well if the images are dithered to the same palette or share common colors. In palettized color modes such as 256 colors, the palette manager will map the colors in **imgSrc2** to the palette of **imgSrc1**. To see this demonstrated, load two images that have radically different colors into **imgSrc1** and **imgSrc2** at design time and run the program again.

Brush	Binary	Hex
	10101010	$AA
	01010101	$55
	10101010	$AA
	01010101	$55
	10101010	$AA
	01010101	$55
	10101010	$AA
	01010101	$55

Figure 8.7 Stage four brush.

We usually have to develop down to the level of 256 color systems, and there are still many of them out there. The dissolve we will develop in the next project is very powerful under those conditions. A smooth transition between two 256 color images when the display can only handle 256 colors has always been one of the most frustrating problems to developers of multimedia. In most cases, the developer will transition to a completely black image between each of the 256 color images. This is one way to prevent a palette shift. Another way is to dither all of the images that will be shown to a common palette. This process can be time consuming and leave the images with poor quality if they do not have similar colors. We're going to look at a technique that dissolves smoothly between 256 color images without that dreadful palette shift.

A Palette Aware Dissolve

This project shows you how to dissolve two bitmap images and their associated palettes.

1. Create a new project.
2. Add three **TSpeedButton** components and a TPanel. Figure 8.8 shows the completed form.
3. Create the tDIB class and add it to the *uses* clause of the form unit.
4. Set the properties and events.
5. Insert and modify code.

This project is located in the directory \DELPHIMM\CH08\DISSOLVE.

Creating the Palette Aware Dissolve

Create a new project and add the controls. We'll need a TPanel and three **TSpeedButton**s. Now set the properties and event procedures according to Table 8.3.

The dissolve project draws together just about all of the knowledge that we've developed in Chapters 6, 7, and the beginning of Chapter 8. To develop a smooth dissolve between two images and their palettes, we do the following:

- Load the bitmaps into a DIB memory structure that we can work with.
- Create Windows identity palettes for each of the images.

Advanced Imaging—Special Visual Effects 375

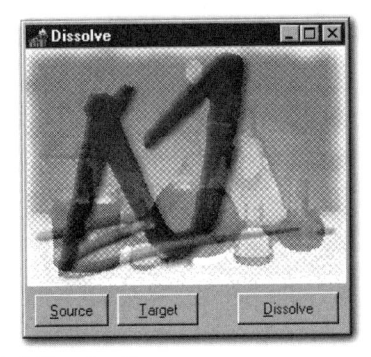

Figure 8.8   *The Completed Dissolve Form.*

Table 8.3   *Form and component properties.*

Component	Property/Event	Setting
Default Form	Name	Main
	Caption	Dissolve
TPanel	Name	pnlDisplay
	Caption	(Leave Blank)
TSpeedButton1	Name	sbSrc
	OnClick	sbSrcClick
TSpeedButton2	Name	sbTgt
	OnClick	sbTgtClick
TSpeedButton3	Name	sbDissolve
	OnClick	sbDissoveClick

- Create an array of RGB values that represents the amount of change between each stage of the dissolve.
- Create an identity palette with the **PC_RESERVED** flag set for the palette animation.
- Apply the dissolve brushes and the palette animation together at each stage of the dissolve

We'll review the event handler code first, so you will have an overview of how the program works. Then we'll get into the nitty-gritty of the supporting functions.

This project has two units. The form unit is the one that we will cover first, given in Listing 8.8. The other module we use is **DIB32c**. This is a class module that makes DIB processing more clear and concise in the calling routines. Be sure to include **DIB32c** in the *uses* clause of the form unit.

Listing 8.8 The uDissolv.pas Form Unit

```pascal
unit udissolv;

interface

uses
  Windows, Messages, SysUtils, Classes, Graphics, Controls, Forms, Dialogs,
  ExtCtrls, Buttons, dib32c;

type
  TMain = class(TForm)
    sbDissolve: TSpeedButton;
    sbSrc: TSpeedButton;
    sbTgt: TSpeedButton;
    pnlDisplay: TPanel;
    procedure FormCreate(Sender: TObject);
    procedure FormDestroy(Sender: TObject);
    procedure sbDissolveClick(Sender: TObject);
    procedure sbTgtClick(Sender: TObject);
    procedure sbSrcClick(Sender: TObject);

  private
    { Private declarations }
  public
    { Public declarations }
  end;

var
  Main: TMain;

implementation

{$R *.DFM}

type
  TRGBDelta = record
    r,g,b: integer;
    end;

  TDeltaPal = array[0..235] of TRGBDelta;

const
  STAGE_COUNT = 8;

var
  Delta_peVals : TDeltaPal;
  hSrcPal,
  hTgtPal,
  hAnimPal,
  hOldPal: hPalette;
  SrcFN, TgtFN:  string;
  SrcDIB,
```

Advanced Imaging—Special Visual Effects

```pascal
    TgtDIB:       tDIB;
    DisplayROP:   longint;
procedure CreateDeltaPaletteVals( pSrc, pTgt: PBitmapInfo;
                                  var peVals: TDeltaPal;
                                  stagecount: byte);
var
  i: byte;
begin

  {$R-}
  for i := 0 to 235 do begin
    Delta_peVals[i].r := (pTgt^.bmiColors[i].rgbRed -
                          pSrc^.bmiColors[i].rgbRed) div stagecount;
    Delta_peVals[i].g := (pTgt^.bmiColors[i].rgbGreen -
                          pSrc^.bmiColors[i].rgbGreen) div stagecount;
    Delta_peVals[i].b := (pTgt^.bmiColors[i].rgbBlue -
                          pSrc^.bmiColors[i].rgbBlue) div stagecount;
    end;
  {$R+}

end; {CreateDeltaPaletteVals}

procedure AnimateInterPal( pSrc, pTgt: PBitmapInfo;
                           DeltaVals: TDeltaPal;
                           stage: byte);
var
  i:       byte;
  pNewPal: PLogPalette;
  size:    longint;

begin

  if stage > STAGE_COUNT then exit;
  size := SizeOf(TLogPalette) + (256 * SizeOf(TPaletteEntry));
  pNewPal := MemAlloc(size);
  try
    pNewPal.palVersion := $300;
    pNewPal.palNumEntries := 256;
    {$R-}
    for i := 0 to 235 do with pNewPal^.palPalEntry[i] do begin
      peRed   := integer(pSrc^.bmiColors[i].rgbRed + (DeltaVals[i].r * stage));
      peGreen := integer(pSrc^.bmiColors[i].rgbGreen + (DeltaVals[i].g * stage));
      peBlue  := integer(pSrc^.bmiColors[i].rgbBlue + (DeltaVals[i].b * stage));
      peFlags := 0;
      end; {for..with}
    {$R+}

    AnimatePalette(hAnimPal,10,235,@pNewPal^.palPalEntry[0]);

  finally
    freemem(pNewPal, size);
  end; {try..finally}
```

```
end; {AnimateInterPal}

function CreateDissolveBrush(step: byte): hBrush;
const
  brushdata: array [0..7,0..7] of Char = (
                                    (#$55,#$AA,#$FD,#$FE,#$FD,#$FE,#$FD,#$FE),
                                    (#$55,#$AA,#$55,#$AA,#$F5,#$FA,#$F5,#$FA),
                                    (#$55,#$AA,#$55,#$AA,#$55,#$AA,#$D5,#$EA),
                                    (#$55,#$AA,#$55,#$AA,#$55,#$AA,#$55,#$AA),
                                    (#$00,#$00,#$54,#$A8,#$54,#$A8,#$54,#$A8),
                                    (#$00,#$00,#$00,#$00,#$00,#$00,#$50,#$A0),
                                    (#$00,#$00,#$00,#$00,#$00,#$00,#$40,#$80),
                                    (#$00,#$00,#$00,#$00,#$00,#$00,#$00,#$00)
                                    );

var
  pDIB:     PBitmapInfo;     {pointer to the packed DIB structure we're creating}
  pBits:    PChar;           {pointer to the bits of the bitmap}
  pQuad:    PRGBQuad;        {pointer to a RGBQuad structure}
  p:        PChar;           {temp pointer for setting bits}
  size:     longint;         {size of the entire dib in memory}
  i:        byte;            {counter variable}
  hBMP:     hBitmap;         {handle to a bitmap}

begin

  if (step < 0) or (step > STAGE_COUNT-1) then exit;

  size := sizeof(TBitmapInfoHeader) + (2 * sizeof(TRGBQuad)) + 32;
  pDIB := nil;
  hBMP := 0;

  {allocate memory for the DIB}
  pDIB := allocmem(size);

  try

    pQuad := pointer(longint(pDIB) + sizeof(TBitmapInfoHeader));
    pBits := pointer(longint(pQuad) + (2 * sizeof(TRGBQuad)));

    {initialize all of the header information}
    with pDIB^.bmiHeader do begin
      biSize := sizeof(TBitmapInfoHeader);
      biWidth := 8;
      biHeight := 8;
      biPlanes := 1;
      biBitCount := 1;
      biCompression := BI_RGB;
      biSizeImage := 0;
      biXPelsPermeter := 0;
      biYPelsPermeter := 0;
      biClrused := 0;
      biClrImportant := 0;
      end;
```

```
    {set the color table values}
    with pQuad^ do begin
      rgbBlue := 0;
      rgbGreen := 0;
      rgbRed := 0;
      rgbReserved := 0;
      end;

    inc(pQuad);
    with pQuad^ do begin
      rgbBlue := 255;
      rgbGreen := 255;
      rgbRed := 255;
      rgbReserved := 0;
      end;

    for i := 0 to 7 do begin
      p := pointer(longint(pBits) + (i * 4));
      p^ := brushdata[step, i];
      end;
    p := nil;

    hBMP := CreateDIBitmap(Main.Canvas.handle, pDIB^.bmiHeader, CBM_INIT,
                           pBits, pDIB^, DIB_RGB_COLORS);
    result := CreatePatternBrush(hBMP);

  finally
    freemem(pDIB, size);
    if hBMP <> 0 then DeleteObject(hBMP);
  end; {try}

end; {CreateDissolveBrush}

procedure waitmil(ms : integer);
var
  StartTick : LongInt;

begin

  StartTick := GetTickCount;
  while GetTickCount <= StartTick + ms do
    Application.ProcessMessages;

end; {waitmil}

procedure TMain.FormCreate(Sender: TObject);
begin

  {load the dibs}
  SrcDIB := tDIB.Create;
  TgtDIB := tDIB.Create;
  SrcDIB.Source := ExtractFilePath(Application.EXEName) + 'chemical.bmp';
  TgtDIB.Source := ExtractFilePath(Application.EXEName) + 'nlcglogo.bmp';
```

Chapter 8

```
    hSrcPal := SrcDIB.Create_IdentPal256(0);
    hTgtPal := TgtDIB.Create_IdentPal256(0);

    {create the array of delta values between the two palettes}
    CreateDeltaPaletteVals( SrcDIB.ptrBitmapInfo,
                            TgtDIB.ptrBitmapInfo,
                            Delta_peVals, STAGE_COUNT);

end; {FormCreate}

procedure TMain.FormDestroy(Sender: TObject);
var
  dc: hDC;

begin
  SrcDIB.Free;
  TgtDIB.Free;
  dc := GetDC(pnlDisplay.Handle);
  try
    SelectPalette(dc, hOldPal, False);
    DeleteObject(hSrcPal);
    DeleteObject(hTgtPal);
  finally
    ReleaseDC(pnlDisplay.Handle, dc);
  end;

end; {FormDestroy}

procedure TMain.sbDissolveClick(Sender: TObject);
var
  i:          byte;
  hOldBrush,
  hDslvBrush: hBrush;
  dc:         hDC;
  w,h:        integer;

begin

  w := pnlDisplay.Width;
  h := pnlDisplay.Height;

  dc := GetDC(pnlDisplay.Handle);

  try

    hAnimPal := SrcDIB.Create_IdentPal256(PC_RESERVED);
    SelectPalette ( dc, hAnimPal, False );
    RealizePalette( dc );

    {paint the source image on the display dc}
    StretchDIBits ( dc, 0, 0, w, h,
                    0,0,SrcDIB.Width, SrcDIB.Height,
                    SrcDIB.ptrBits, SrcDIB.ptrBitmapInfo^,
                    DIB_RGB_COLORS, SRCCOPY);
```

Advanced Imaging—Special Visual Effects

```
    waitmil(1000);

    for i := 0 to STAGE_COUNT-1 do begin

      AnimateInterPal(SrcDIB.ptrBitmapInfo, TgtDIB.ptrBitmapInfo,
                  Delta_peVals, i+1);

      hDslvBrush := CreateDissolveBrush(i);
      hOldBrush := SelectObject(dc, hDslvBrush);

      try

        {paint the new image on the memory dc with the dissolve ROP}
        StretchDIBits ( dc, 0, 0, w, h,
                    0,0,TgtDIB.Width, TgtDIB.Height,
                    TgtDIB.ptrBits, TgtDIB.ptrBitmapInfo^,
                    DIB_RGB_COLORS, $AC0744);

      finally

        {Deselect and delete the brush we created }
        SelectObject(dc, hOldBrush);
        DeleteObject(hDslvBrush);
      end;
      waitmil(2000);
    end;

  finally
    SelectPalette(dc, hOldPal, False);
    DeleteObject(hAnimPal);
    ReleaseDC(pnlDisplay.Handle, dc);
  end;
end; {SpeedButtonClick}

procedure TMain.sbTgtClick(Sender: TObject);
var
  dc: hDC;

begin

  dc := GetDC(pnlDisplay.Handle);
  try
    SelectPalette ( dc, hTgtPal, False );
    RealizePalette( dc );
    StretchDIBits ( dc, 0, 0, pnlDisplay.Width, pnlDisplay.Height,
                  0,0,TgtDIB.Width, TgtDIB.Height,
                  TgtDIB.ptrBits, TgtDIB.ptrBitmapInfo^,
                  DIB_RGB_COLORS, SRCCOPY);
  finally
    ReleaseDC(Main.Handle, dc);
  end;

end;
```

```
procedure TMain.sbSrcClick(Sender: TObject);
var
  dc: hDC;

begin

  dc := GetDC(pnlDisplay.Handle);
  try
    SelectPalette ( dc, hSrcPal, False );
    RealizePalette( dc );
    StretchDIBits ( dc, 0, 0, pnlDisplay.Width, pnlDisplay.Height,
                    0,0,SrcDIB.Width, SrcDIB.Height,
                    SrcDIB.ptrBits, SrcDIB.ptrBitmapInfo^,
                    DIB_RGB_COLORS, SRCCOPY);
  finally
    ReleaseDC(Main.Handle, dc);
  end;

end;

end.
```

The first step in the dissolve process is to load the bitmaps into memory as a DIB so that we can work with them. This happens in the **OnCreate** handler for the form. Listing 8.9 leads the way.

Listing 8.9   The OnCreate handler

```
procedure TMain.FormCreate(Sender: TObject);
begin

  {load the dibs}
  SrcDIB := tDIB.Create;
  TgtDIB := tDIB.Create;
  SrcDIB.Source := ExtractFilePath(Application.EXEName) + 'chemical.bmp';
  TgtDIB.Source := ExtractFilePath(Application.EXEName) + 'nlcglogo.bmp';

  hSrcPal := SrcDIB.Create_IdentPal256(0);
  hTgtPal := TgtDIB.Create_IdentPal256(0);

  {create the array of delta values between the two palettes}
  CreateDeltaPaletteVals( SrcDIB.ptrBitmapInfo,
                          TgtDIB.ptrBitmapInfo,
                          Delta_peVals, STAGE_COUNT);

end; {FormCreate}
```

The tDIB class created for this project encapsulates several of the DIB processing routines that we discussed in the previous projects. The class implementation makes the code for the dissolve in this project more clear and easy to follow. Rather than taking a detour at this point to discuss the class implementation, let's move forward in describing the techniques used to create the dissolve. For now, understand that we're allocating memory for two tDIB objects; **SrcDIB** and **TgtDIB**. We instantiate the objects with the create constructor, and then use the *source* property to open the two bitmaps. Once the bitmaps are loaded, we will need *identity palettes* for each. Remember that an *identity palette* is the first 236 colors in the image's palette sandwiched between the 20 Windows reserved colors. The **Create_IdentPal256** method of the tDIB class does this for us. Next, we need to know how much to increment the color values of the source palette for each step of the dissolve. **CreateDeltaPaletteVals** uses a pointer to the source and destination bitmaps to perform the calculation. The amount of change for each palette entry is stored in **Delta_peVals**. The global constant **STAGE_COUNT** informs several functions and procedures how many stages are in this dissolve.

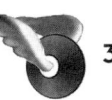

You may be beginning to notice a pattern with the **OnCreate** and **OnDestroy** handlers for the project's main form. They are commonly used to allocate resources as well as free them when the program is terminated. Refer to Listing 8.8 to see the **OnDestroy** handler. Here you'll find some common routines to free resources that we've used in previous projects.

Let's move right into the **sbDissolveOnClick** handler. It is here that the dissolve is actually produced. We've already loaded the bitmaps and created the delta palette values. Now we need to create an identity palette that we will use as the animated palette during the dissolve. This one will have the **PC_RESERVED** flag set. The **PC_RESERVED** flag tells other Windows applications that the palette entries have been designated for palette animation and should not be mapped even as a background palette. The API function **AnimatePalette** will not work on palette entries that do not have this flag set. Once that palette is selected into the *dc* that we're going to use for the dissolve, we're ready to create the effect. The remainder of the process can be found in Listing 8.10.

Listing 8.10 The sbDissolveClick handler

```
procedure TMain.sbDissolveClick(Sender: TObject);
var
  i:         byte;
  hOldBrush,
  hDslvBrush: hBrush;
  dc:        hDC;
  w,h:       integer;

begin
```

```
   w := pnlDisplay.Width;
   h := pnlDisplay.Height;

   dc := GetDC(pnlDisplay.Handle);

   try

      hAnimPal := SrcDIB.Create_IdentPal256(PC_RESERVED);
      SelectPalette ( dc, hAnimPal, False );
      RealizePalette( dc );

      {paint the source image on the display dc}
      StretchDIBits ( dc, 0, 0, w, h,
                      0,0,SrcDIB.Width, SrcDIB.Height,
                      SrcDIB.ptrBits, SrcDIB.ptrBitmapInfo^,
                      DIB_RGB_COLORS, SRCCOPY);

      waitmil(1000);

      for i := 0 to STAGE_COUNT-1 do begin

         AnimateInterPal(SrcDIB.ptrBitmapInfo, TgtDIB.ptrBitmapInfo,
                      Delta_peVals, i+1);

         hDslvBrush := CreateDissolveBrush(i);
         hOldBrush := SelectObject(dc, hDslvBrush);

         try

            {paint the new image on the memory dc with the dissolve ROP}
            StretchDIBits ( dc, 0, 0, w, h,
                         0,0,TgtDIB.Width, TgtDIB.Height,
                         TgtDIB.ptrBits, TgtDIB.ptrBitmapInfo^,
                         DIB_RGB_COLORS, $AC0744);

         finally

            {Deselect and delete the brush we created }
            SelectObject(dc, hOldBrush);
            DeleteObject(hDslvBrush);
         end;
       waitmil(2000);
       end;

   finally
      SelectPalette(dc, hOldPal, False);
      DeleteObject(hAnimPal);
      ReleaseDC(pnlDisplay.Handle, dc);
   end;
end; {SpeedButtonClick}
```

There's a lot of code here, but most of it should be very familiar to you by now. It's actually a very simple procedure. Let's break it into logical steps.

Advanced Imaging—Special Visual Effects

First, we use **GetDC**, an API function, to acquire the *dc* of the TPanel that we use as a display. We then create an identity palette from the source bitmap and set the **PC_RESERVED** flag. That palette, **hAnimPal**, is *selected* and *realized* into the *dc* of **pnlDisplay**. Using **StretchDIBits** we display the source image and hold processing for one second with **waitmil**. At last we get to the *for* loop that iterates through the stages of the dissolve. Within the loop we do 5 things:

- Animate the palette to the next stage of the dissolve.
- Create and select the dissolve brush for this stage.
- Paint the target image with the dissolve ROP.
- Deselect and delete the dissolve brush.
- Wait several milliseconds to see the effect

We repeat this loop **STAGE_COUNT** times until the target image is fully displayed with its original palette. You should be familiar with most of the functions used in the loop. The **CreateDissolveBrush** is identical to the one we developed in the previous project. The one thing that is new in this loop is the **AnimateInterPal** procedure. We'll look at it in just a moment. First you need to see the **CreateDeltaPaletteVals** procedure that was used in the **OnCreate** handler. Let's look at that one now, which you will find in Listing 8.11.

Listing 8.11 The CreateDeltaPaletteVals Procedure

```
procedure CreateDeltaPaletteVals( pSrc, pTgt: PBitmapInfo;
                                  var peVals: TDeltaPal;
                                  stagecount: byte);var
  i: byte;
begin

  {$R-}
  for i := 0 to 235 do begin
    Delta_peVals[i].r := (pTgt^.bmiColors[i].rgbRed -
                          pSrc^.bmiColors[i].rgbRed) div stagecount;
    Delta_peVals[i].g := (pTgt^.bmiColors[i].rgbGreen -
                          pSrc^.bmiColors[i].rgbGreen) div stagecount;
    Delta_peVals[i].b := (pTgt^.bmiColors[i].rgbBlue -
                          pSrc^.bmiColors[i].rgbBlue) div stagecount;
  end;
  {$R+}

end; {CreateDeltaPaletteVals}
```

As you can see, there's not much to this one. For each of the 236 records in the delta values array, we subtract the destination color component from the source color component and divide the result by the number of stages in the dissolve. We'll see how these values are used in the **AnimateInterPal** procedure in Listing 8.12.

Listing 8.12 The AnimateInterPal Procedure

```
procedure AnimateInterPal( pSrc, pTgt: PBitmapInfo;
                           DeltaVals: TDeltaPal;
                           stage: byte);
var
  i:       byte;
  pNewPal: PLogPalette;
  size:    longint;

begin
  if stage > STAGE_COUNT then exit;
  size := SizeOf(TLogPalette) + (256 * SizeOf(TPaletteEntry));
  pNewPal := MemAlloc(size);
  try
    pNewPal.palVersion := $300;
    pNewPal.palNumEntries := 256;
    {$R-}
    for i := 0 to 235 do with pNewPal^.palPalEntry[i] do begin
      peRed   := integer(pSrc^.bmiColors[i].rgbRed + (DeltaVals[i].r * stage));
      peGreen := integer(pSrc^.bmiColors[i].rgbGreen + (DeltaVals[i].g * stage));
      peBlue  := integer(pSrc^.bmiColors[i].rgbBlue + (DeltaVals[i].b * stage));
      peFlags := 0;
    end; {for..with}
    {$R+}

    AnimatePalette(hAnimPal,10,235,@pNewPal^.palPalEntry[0]);

  finally
    freemem(pNewPal, size);
  end; {try..finally}

end; {AnimateInterPal}
```

It is this procedure and its implementation that set this dissolve aside from the dissolve in the previous project. We allocate memory for a logical palette, set the palette entries, implement the new palette entries, and dispose of the memory. It is our method for setting the color values that make this procedure unique. For each stage, 0-7, the individual values for red, green, and blue are set to their starting value + (the delta value * the stage number). This results in colors that gradually change from their original to the color in the destination image. This process, together with the pixel transition, creates a rather attractive dissolve.

Two event handling procedures still need to be discussed. The sbSrcClick and the sbTgtClick handlers are basically the same. One displays the source image with its native palette and the other displays the target image with its native palette. There's nothing new in either of the procedures. Use Listing 8.8 as a reference when entering the code.

I mentioned earlier that this project uses the **DIB32c** unit for clarity of code. The unit is provided in Listing 8.12 as a reference to the necessary methods and properties.

Listing 8.12   The DIB32c Class Unit

```
unit dib32c;

interface
uses
  Windows, SysUtils, Classes, Graphics;

  type
      tDIB = class
        protected
          pDIB    : PBitmapInfo;
          MemSize : longint;

          function Get_biSize : integer;
          function Get_DIBSize : longint;

          procedure ReadFromFile(const fn : string);
          function Get_width : longint;
          function Get_height : longint;
          function Get_ncolors : longint;
          function Get_ptr_to_RGBQuad : PRGBQuad;
          function Get_ptr_to_bits : pointer;

        public
          constructor Create;
          destructor Destroy; override;

          property Source        : string   write ReadFromFile;
          property Width         : longint  read Get_width;
          property Height        : longint  read Get_height;
          property NumColors     : longint  read Get_ncolors;
          property ptrRGBQuad    : PRGBQuad read Get_ptr_to_RGBQuad;
          property ptrBits       : pointer  read Get_ptr_to_bits;
          property ptrBitmapInfo : PBitmapInfo read pDIB;

          function Create_Palette(const palSysFlags,palFlags : byte): hPalette;
          function Create_IdentPal256(const palFlags: byte): hPalette;
      end;

implementation
```

```
constructor tDIB.Create;
begin
  inherited Create;
  MemSize := 0;
end;

destructor tDIB.Destroy;
begin
  if MemSize <> 0 then
    freemem(pDIB,MemSize);

  inherited Destroy;
end;

{
  tDIB.ReadFromFile: loads a bmp file and returns a pointer to the DIB in
                     memory. Also returns the size of the memory image so
                     that the memory can be freed.
}
procedure tDIB.ReadFromFile(const fn : string);
var
  stream: TMemoryStream;

begin
    with TMemoryStream.Create do begin
        LoadFromFile(fn);
        MemSize := size - sizeof(TBitmapFileHeader);
        pDIB := allocmem(MemSize);
        seek(sizeof(TBitmapFileHeader), 0);
        read(pDIB^, MemSize);
        free;
        end;

end; {ReadFromFile}

{
  tDIB.Get_width: returns the width of a dib
}
function tDIB.Get_width : longint;
  begin
    result := pDIB^.bmiHeader.biwidth;
  end; {Get_width}

{
  tDIB.Get_height: returns the height of a dib
}
function tDIB.Get_height : longint;
  begin
    result := pDIB^.bmiHeader.biheight
  end; {dib_height}

{
  tDIB.Get_ncolors: returns the number of colors in a DIB
}
```

```pascal
function tDIB.Get_ncolors : longint;
  begin
    if pDIB^.bmiHeader.biClrUsed > 0 then
      result := pDIB^.bmiHeader.biClrUsed
    else
      result := 1 shl pDIB^.bmiHeader.biBitCount;

  end; {Get_ncolors}

{
  tDIB.Get_biSize: returns the number of bytes in a DIB header including the
                   color table.
}
function tDIB.Get_biSize : integer;
  begin
    result := sizeof(TBitmapInfoHeader) + (Get_ncolors * sizeof(TRGBQuad));
  end; {dib_biSize}

{
  tDIB.Get_DIBSize: returns the number of bytes in a DIB.
}
function tDIB.Get_DIBSize : longint;
  begin
    result := Get_biSize + pDIB^.bmiHeader.biSizeImage;
  end; {Get_DIBSize}

{
  tDIB.Get_ptr_to_RGBQuad: returns a pointer to the first RGBQuad structure
}
function tDIB.Get_ptr_to_RGBQuad : PRGBQuad;
  begin

    {set a pointer to the DIB palette table as an offset from the DIB ptr}
    result := pointer(longint(pDIB) + sizeof(TBitmapInfoHeader));

  end; {Get_ptr_to_RGBQuad}

{
 tDIB.Get_ptr_to_bits: returns a pointer to the pixel data of the DIB
}
function tDIB.Get_ptr_to_bits : pointer;
  begin
    result := pointer(longint(pDIB) + Get_biSize);
  end; {Get_ptr_to_bits}

{
 tDIB.Create_Palette: creates a palette from the DIB's color table and
                      returns a handle.
}
function tDIB.Create_Palette( const palSysFlags,palFlags: byte): hPalette;
var
  DstPal: PLogPalette;
  Colors, n: Integer;
  Size: Longint;
```

```
  DC: HDC;
  Focus: HWND;
  Pal: array[0..15] of TPaletteEntry;
  SysPalSize: Integer;
  I: Integer;

begin
  Result := 0;

  Colors := Get_ncolors;
  if Colors <= 2 then Exit;

  Size := SizeOf(TLogPalette) + ((Colors - 1) * SizeOf(TPaletteEntry));
  DstPal := MemAlloc(Size);
  try
    FillChar(DstPal^, Size, 0);
    with DstPal^ do
    begin
      palNumEntries := Colors;
      palVersion := $300;
      Focus := GetFocus;
      DC := GetDC(Focus);
      try
        SysPalSize := GetDeviceCaps(DC, SIZEPALETTE);
        if (Colors = 16) and (SysPalSize >= 16) then
        begin
          { Ignore the disk image of the palette for 16 color bitmaps use
            instead the first 8 and last 8 of the current system palette }
          GetSystemPaletteEntries(DC, 0, 8, palPalEntry);
          I := 8;
          GetSystemPaletteEntries(DC, SysPalSize - I, I, palPalEntry[I]);
        end
        else
          { Copy the palette for all others (i.e. 256 colors) }
          {$R-}
          for N := 0 to Colors - 1 do
          begin
            palPalEntry[N].peRed   := pDIB^.bmiColors[N].rgbRed;
            palPalEntry[N].peGreen := pDIB^.bmiColors[N].rgbGreen;
            palPalEntry[N].peBlue  := pDIB^.bmiColors[N].rgbBlue;
            if (N < 10) or (N > 245) then
              palPalEntry[N].peFlags := palSysFlags
            else
              palPalEntry[N].peFlags := palFlags;
          end;
          {$R+}
      finally
        ReleaseDC(Focus, DC);
      end;
    end;
    Result := CreatePalette(DstPal^);
  finally
    FreeMem(DstPal, Size);
  end;
end; {Create_Palette}
```

```
{
 tDIB.Create_IdentPal256: returns a handle to the identity palette of a DIB
}
function tDIB.Create_IdentPal256(const palFlags : byte): hPalette;
var
  DstPal: PLogPalette;
  n: Integer;
  Size: Longint;
  DC: HDC;
  Focus: HWND;

begin
  Result := 0;

  Size := SizeOf(TLogPalette) + (256 * SizeOf(TPaletteEntry));
  DstPal := MemAlloc(Size);
  try
    FillChar(DstPal^, Size, 0);
    with DstPal^ do
    begin
      palNumEntries := 256;
      palVersion := $300;
      Focus := GetFocus;
      DC := GetDC(Focus);
      {$R-}
      try
          {use the system palette entries for 0-9, and 246-255}
          GetSystemPaletteEntries(DC, 0, 10, palPalEntry);
          N := 246;
          GetSystemPaletteEntries(DC, 246, 10, palPalEntry[N]);

          {use the entries from 0-236 of the color table and map them to
           entries 10-245 in the new logical palette}
          for N := 10 to 245 do
          begin
            palPalEntry[N].peRed   := pDIB^.bmiColors[N-10].rgbRed;
            palPalEntry[N].peGreen := pDIB^.bmiColors[N-10].rgbGreen;
            palPalEntry[N].peBlue  := pDIB^.bmiColors[N-10].rgbBlue;
            palPalEntry[N].peFlags := palFlags;
          end;
      finally
        ReleaseDC(Focus, DC);
      end;
    {$R-}
    end;
    Result := CreatePalette(DstPal^);
  finally
    FreeMem(DstPal, Size);
  end;
end; {Create_IdentPal256}

end.
```

More About the Palettized Dissolve

As you run the dissolve program, notice that other running applications and the desktop wallpaper will *shift* their palettes to background palettes. Switching back and forth between the source and target images will cause a shift of colors all over the place. This is because each of these images is being displayed with its native palette. When the dissolve is executed, all other applications will map their colors to the 20 *reserved* system colors. Our dissolve takes place without any palette shifting. After we exit the program, the original palette is returned and things return to normal.

One of the drawbacks to the palettized dissolve that we just created is that it won't work in color modes higher than 256. Probably the single most frustrating thing to developers about the evolution of graphics software and hardware is the constant struggle to accommodate the low end of the technology without penalizing the users who have more capable systems. The technique we just used is great for the first part of the equation, but it would not be an acceptable solution because it could not display correctly on a hi-color or true color system. Our first dissolve in this chapter works great in higher color modes, but not in 256 colors. Our suggestion: Combine the two techniques for an all-purpose solution.

Chapter 9

Learn how to bring your Delphi multimedia applications to life by adding interactive hotspots to your images.

The Art of Hyperimaging

Dan Haygood

If something in a picture grabs your attention, you should be able to click on it and find out what it is or what it does. In this chapter we'll look at a few ways to create hotspots on pictures that can activate any of the multimedia features we've presented. We'll explore a few hypermedia projects to see how Windows operates as a hypermedia system. We'll also show you some basic techniques to use to define rectangular hotspots by creating a useful hotspot editor. With this editor, you'll be able to define hotspots and save them in a format so that they can be used in other multimedia apps. In Chapter 10, we'll create a more powerful hotspot editor for defining irregularly-shaped regions. By Chapter 11, we'll be building a powerful hypermedia engine that handles hotspots of any shape or size—an engine you'll be able to use for your own multimedia projects.

We have a lot of ground to cover, so let's get started.

Windows Is Hypermedia!

Every time you click on a button, drag a scroll bar, or select a list box item in a Windows app, you're engaging in a kind of hypermedia. When you click your mouse pointer on a button, Windows detects that the click has occurred within a particular region of the display. It then performs the appropriate actions, which usually include redrawing the button to create the illusion that it has been depressed and released. Some controls even open entire dialog boxes. If you click in the right place on one picture, Windows may display another picture with its own hotspot regions in the form of controls.

Using Controls as Pictures

You probably won't want to use controls for every type of visual hyperlinking, but they do provide a good starting point. Besides, it's a good idea to step back every once in a while and try to imagine new uses for old tools. Figure 9.1 shows a simple experiment where we built a bar chart from a control array of six Buttons.

You might expect Buttons to be short and fat rather than tall and thin. You might also expect them to keep their shapes when you click on them. But in this program, we have turned buttons into bars that shrink and grow.

Rather than stretch them randomly, we set up a simple relationship between them. Any bar (Button), when clicked on, will change its size in proportion to the difference in size between itself and its neighbor to the left. The procedure that performs this operation, **BarButton_Click**, is shown in Listing 9.1.

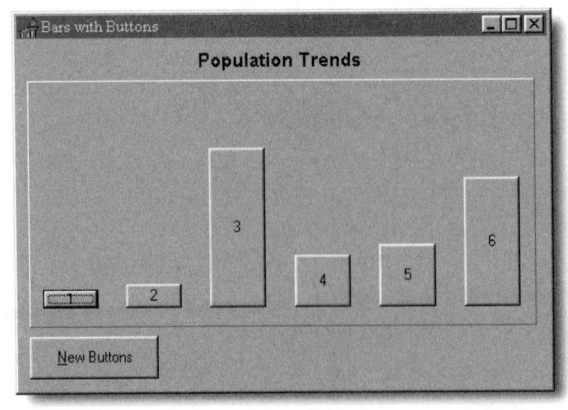

Figure 9.1   *Bars creates this bar chart at runtime.*

> *Although we won't go into the messy details of this project, this code can be found in the unit main.pas, of the project bars.dpr, in the directory \PROGRAMS\CHAP09\BARS on the accompanying CD-ROM.*

Listing 9.1   The **Button_OnClick** Procedure

```
procedure TForm1.Button_OnClick(Sender: TObject);
   var
       This,
       To_left : integer;
begin
       { Get index to left; this can be accomplished
         with the "mod" operator, too. }
       This := TButton(Sender).Tag;
       To_left := This + 1;
       if To_left = 7 then To_left := 1;

       with Button[This] do begin
           Height := Height +
              trunc(0.05 * (Height - Button[To_left].Height));
           Top    := Panel1.Height - 15 - Height;
           end;
end;
```

This code actually exaggerates the curve formed by the tops of the bars in a somewhat less than predictable fashion. You could also use the **OnClick** event to pop up a message box that explains the reasons for the rise or fall in population for that particular year.

To jazz up this demonstration, you could easily substitute Labels or some other control for the Buttons. But Buttons have their own qualities and expect to be touched. You don't need a label that says "Press the Bars for Further Information."

Using Controls as Hotspot Buttons

Now let's move on to the core of this chapter—how to add hotspots to images. By images, we mean bitmap graphics. You could scan photographs or drawings to create your images, or paint them with a drawing program such as *Fractal Painter*. You could even use Delphi to draw them directly into your Image controls. It doesn't matter how you create your images, because pixels are pixels—and as we discovered in Chapter 3, a hotspot is nothing more than a region on the screen. Once you define that region, you can use the **OnMouseDown** event procedure to fire off any multimedia event you wish.

As you discovered in the bar chart program, Buttons don't make the greatest hotspots. For one thing, they're opaque, and we don't want to cover up our attractive images with boring Buttons. Fortunately, Delphi provides us with controls that can sit invisibly on top of pictures while remaining active. These are the Label, the Image control itself, and the PaintBox control. We can also use Delphi's BitBtn (Bitmapped Button) control in an interesting way. Let's see what these controls can do for us.

Control: Creating Hotspots with Assorted Controls

This project uses Label, Image, and PaintBox controls to set up invisible hotspots on an image. We're also going to camouflage a BitBtn for an interesting effect. To create the project, you'll need to make a new form, add a base Image, and include the controls. We'll have some fancy footwork to do underneath the BitBtn, but we'll cover that shortly. To create this project, follow these steps.

1. Create a new directory for the project, *Control*, and an output subdirectory, *Bin*.
2. Open a new application, and in the *Project Options* dialog box, set its Application Title to "Control" and its Output Directory to "Bin".
3. You might want to take this opportunity to save the project in the *Control* project directory.
4. Add controls (Table 9.1) and code (Listing 9.2) as described in the text below.

This project, control.dpr, can be found on the accompanying CD-ROM, in the directory \Programs\Chap09\Control.

Start a new Delphi application and add an Image control that nearly covers the form. This will be our background picture. Set the **Picture** property of **Image1** (its likely name) to any bitmap file that's handy—you'll find some samples on the CD ROM in the directory *\Media\Images*.

Next, place a Label control on the picture. It will appear as blank rectangle, probably named **Label1**. Size **Label1** so it covers some object in the image as closely as possible. In the *Object Inspector*, double-click on its **AutoSize** property, setting it to **False**. Remove the caption from the Label by

Table 9.1 Properties for the Control project.

Class	Property	Value
TForm	Name	Form1 (default)
	Caption	'Control-based Hotspots'
	OnCreate	FormCreate
TImage	Name	Image1 (default)
	Picture	x:\Media\Images\Kaibab.BMP
TLabel	Name	Label1 (default)
	AutoSize	False
	Caption	<blank>
	Transparent	True
	Hint	'Over Label1!'
	ShowHint	True
	OnClick	Label1Click
TImage	Name	Image2 (default)
	Picture	(None)
	Hint	'Over Image2!'
	ShowHint	True
	OnClick	Image2Click
TPaintBox	Name	PaintBox1 (default)
	Hint	'Over PaintBox1!'
	ShowHint	True
	OnClick	PaintBox1Click
TBitBtn	Name	BitBtn1 (default)
	Caption	'Close'
	Hint	'Over BitBtn1!'
	ShowHint	True
	OnClick	BitBtn1Click

clicking on its **Caption** property and then pressing the [delete] key. Set its **Hint** property to "Over Label!" and make sure its **ShowHint** property is set to **True**. When running, the hint text will "magically" appear if the user keeps the cursor over the Label for a little while (actually, 800 milliseconds, but you can override that).

Finally, double-click its **Transparent** property, changing it to **True**. The only remaining evidence of the Label will be its frame handles. Once you click elsewhere on the form, all visible traces of it will vanish from the image. But when you click on the area it covers, it reappears. Double-clicking on the area instructs Delphi to display its **OnClick** event procedure. All you need to do is add the code to kick off the appropriate multimedia event.

You can do the same thing with an Image control. As a bonus, the Image control will work with its default property settings. The other advantage the Image control has over a Label is the ability to display a border during development time so you won't lose track of it. Go ahead and place an Image control on top of **Image1**. It will probably be named **Image2**.

A PaintBox control can be used in exactly the same way as the Image control. Add a PaintBox, **PaintBox1**, on top of the base picture, **Image1**. Since you have both the **Image2** and **PaintBox1** handy, take a moment to compare their properties. An Image has some "overhead" to handle pictures—properties like **AutoSize**, **Stretch**, that control how the Image behaves when a picture is loaded into its **Picture** property. A PaintBox doesn't support any of this picture-loading support, but does have a **Font** property and other properties that support its use as a raw graphics-output area.

To use the control-based method of hyperimaging for a large number of images, you would need a way to create and place controls over the images at runtime. You could keep track of their locations and sizes in a simple database, either using ordinary file I/O, or with Delphi's *BDE* (Borland Database Engine). You could then use an array of controls, generated at runtime, to create as many controls as needed to cover all the hotspots of any particular image. When you finished with an image, you would then free all of those controls. This may seem like a lot of work for a dynamic environment. However, if you have a small set of opening screens or a fixed presentation, these techniques can work well for you.

Uncovering the BitBtn

If you find that control-based hotspots will work for your projects, here's one more trick to spruce up your forms. It reaches back to that basic button interface, but it deals with a picture behind it, too. Choose the BitBtn component from the *Additional* page of the *Component Palette*. Set the button's **Caption** to "Close". The default values of the other properties will do for now, although we're going to manipulate them in code when we create the form at runtime. Add the code shown in Listing 9.2 to **Form1**'s **OnCreate** procedure.

Listing 9.2   Control-based Hotspot Handling in *Main.Pas*

```
unit Main;

interface
```

```
uses
  Windows, Messages, SysUtils, Classes, Graphics, Controls, Forms, Dialogs,
  StdCtrls, Buttons, ExtCtrls;

type
  TForm1 = class(TForm)
    Image1: TImage;
    Image2: TImage;
    PaintBox1: TPaintBox;
    Label1: TLabel;
    BitBtn1: TBitBtn;
    procedure Label1Click(Sender: TObject);
    procedure Image2Click(Sender: TObject);
    procedure PaintBox1Click(Sender: TObject);
    procedure FormCreate(Sender: TObject);
    procedure BitBtn1Click(Sender: TObject);
  private
    { Private declarations }
  public
    { Public declarations }
  end;

var
  Form1: TForm1;

implementation

{$R *.DFM}

procedure TForm1.Label1Click(Sender: TObject);
   begin
      MessageDlg('This is the sky!',mtInformation,[mbOK],0);
      end;

procedure TForm1.Image2Click(Sender: TObject);
   begin
      MessageDlg('This is a hill in the forground!',mtInformation,[mbOK],0);
      end;

procedure TForm1.PaintBox1Click(Sender: TObject);
   begin
      MessageDlg('This is a hill in the background!',mtInformation,[mbOK],0);
      end;

var
    Button_face : TBitmap;
procedure TForm1.FormCreate(Sender: TObject);
    var
        Cap      : string;
        Cap_size : TSize;
    begin
        Image1.Picture.LoadFromFile('c:\DMMAS.IMG\Kaibab.BMP');
          { Rather than LoadFromFile, you could set this at
            design-time, by loading Image1's Picture property. }
```

```
            Cap := BitBtn1.Caption;
            BitBtn1.Caption := '';
            Button_face := TBitmap.Create;
            Button_face.Width  := BitBtn1.Width-6;
            Button_face.Height := BitBtn1.Height-6;
            Button_face.Canvas.CopyRect(
              Button_face.Canvas.ClipRect,
              Image1.Canvas,
              Rect(
                BitBtn1.Left - Image1.Left + 3,
                BitBtn1.Top  - Image1.Top  + 3,
                BitBtn1.Left - Image1.Left + 3 + BitBtn1.Width  - 6,
                BitBtn1.Top  - Image1.Top  + 3 + BitBtn1.Height - 6
                {----------top--------------}   {----height------}   { = bottom }
                )
              );
            GetTextExtentPoint(
              Button_face.Canvas.Handle,
              pchar(Cap), length(Cap),
              Cap_size
              );
            SetBkMode(Button_face.Canvas.Handle,TRANSPARENT);
            Button_face.Canvas.TextOut(
              (Button_face.Width  - Cap_size.cX) div 2,
              (Button_face.Height - Cap_size.cY) div 2,
              Cap
              );
            BitBtn1.Glyph := Button_face;
            end;

procedure TForm1.BitBtn1Click(Sender: TObject);
    begin
        Close;
        end;

end.
```

The BitBtn control accepts a ***Glyph***, a bitmap that can be displayed alongside its **Caption**. When we create the form, we're simply going to put the portion of **Image1** covered up by **BitBtn1** into **BitBtn1**'s **Glyph**. We're also going to display the **Caption**. We have to juggle some things here, since we're going for an effect that isn't native to the **BitBtn**: We want the **Caption** to display on top of, not beside, the **Glyph**.

The first thing we need to do is take the **Caption** off of the button. We save this in the local variable **Cap**; very shortly we'll need to write this back out onto the **Glyph**. At design time, we left the **Glyph** set to "(None)". Therefore, we create a bitmap that we'll call **Button_face**. We set its **Width** and **Height** to be six pixels smaller in each dimension than the button itself. This allows room for the button's 3D effect. Once **Button_face** is created and sized, we copy a rectangle from **Image1** into the **Button_face**. After rewriting the caption, saved in **Cap** over the **Button_face**, we assign our **Button_face** to be **BitBtn1**'s **Glyph**.

Copying the appropriate part of the image looks fearsome, but only because of the specifications of the rectangle to be copied. **CopyRect** copies a rectangle from another specified canvas and rectangle, placing it onto a rectangle on the canvas from which the method is called. Since we call the **CopyRect** method of **Button_face**'s **Canvas**, this will be our destination canvas. The destination rectangle, of type **TRect**, is the first parameter of **CopyRect**. Since we want to fill the **Button_face**, we specify its entire *clipping rectangle* (a **Canvas**' outside border—Graphics drawn outside this area are "clipped," that is, not displayed.), accessible through the property **ClipRect**.

We want to copy the image from the base picture control, **Image1**. The second parameter is the source **Canvas**; therefore, we pass in **Image1.Canvas**. Finally, we need to specify the source rectangle. To convert corner coordinates to a **TRect** for the third parameter, we use Delphi's **Rect** function. The coordinates need to be relative to the **Image1**'s picture. To determine where the left edge of **BitBtn1** falls over the picture in **Image1**, we can take advantage of the fact that **Image1.Left** and **BitBtn1.Left** are both specified relative to the base form. The distance between the controls' left edges, then, is the position of **BitBtn1**'s left edge relative to **Image1**. Remember that we made the **Button_face** bitmap 6 pixels smaller than the button itself? Because of this, we'll offset our rectangle into the image another 3 pixels (half of 6) in both directions, and subtract 6 pixels from the width and height. We add these to the right and bottom, respectively.

```
Button_face.Canvas.CopyRect(
  Button_face.Canvas.ClipRect,
  Image1.Canvas,
  Rect(
    BitBtn1.Left - Image1.Left + 3,
    BitBtn1.Top  - Image1.Top  + 3,
    BitBtn1.Left - Image1.Left + 3 + BitBtn1.Width  - 6,
    BitBtn1.Top  - Image1.Top  + 3 + BitBtn1.Height - 6
    {----------top-------------}   {----height------}   { = bottom }
  )
);
```

Once the rectangle covered by the button has been copied to **Button_face**, we must redraw the original caption. This takes some text manipulation. We want to center the text over the image. To do this, we must know how large the text is, so we know where to output the text. We could make two separate calls to the **Button_face**'s **Canvas**' **GetTextHeight** and **GetTextWidth** methods; however, to make just one call, we can go directly to the Windows API with **GetTextExtentPoint**. You may remember this from Chapters 2 and 3.

```
GetTextExtentPoint(
  Button_face.Canvas.Handle,
  pchar(Cap), length(Cap),
  Cap_size
  );
SetBkMode(Button_face.Canvas.Handle,TRANSPARENT);
Button_face.Canvas.TextOut(
  (Button_face.Width  - Cap_size.cX) div 2,
  (Button_face.Height - Cap_size.cY) div 2,
  Cap
  );
```

SetBkMode, another API call, determines how the drawing of text will affect the background. We will force it to **TRANSPARENT**; otherwise, by default, the text would be black-on-white, not black-on-what's-under-it. Then we simply output the text, using the **TextOut** method. Horizontally, **Button_face.Width - Cap_size.cX** would be the total space remaining on the right of **Button_face** if the text were to be drawn at the left side. To center the text, we divide the remaining space in half and start drawing the text at that position.

When the form is created, the glyph-less BitBtn we placed will now display the image beneath it; yet it retains its button-like qualities. There are some shortcomings to this technique: The ampersand flag "&" won't indicate a keypress shortcut anymore. Unless you happened to load an image consisting entirely of the twenty Windows colors as your base picture, you probably also noticed that your base-picture's colors were mapped to the nearest system palette entries. Still, there's a lot of room here for visual and technical creativity. For instance, you could specify the **CopyRect** brush to accomplish different effects on the button face. While you're playing directly with the **Button_face** bitmap, you could match the picture's colors to their nearest system-palette gray levels for an interesting high-contrast effect. And we're sure you'll want to wrap this up as a class and turn it into a custom control for all of your friends. But that's as far as we'll take this technique. The BitBtn, as we leave it, is shown in Figure 9.2.

To continue exploring image hotspots as we journey toward a full-featured multimedia engine, we'll need to develop some techniques that are not as control-intensive. Follow me to the next project in our multimedia adventure.

*Figure 9.2 This BitBtn control takes its **Glyph** from the Image underneath it.*

Using Rectangular Window Regions

Since you have to keep track of the locations and dimensions of control-based hotspots anyway, it would be nice if you could create them directly on the client area of the Form or PictureBox without scattering controls all over the place. Once again, the Windows API comes to our aid with a pair of almost unbelievably simple functions that do exactly what we need. (Why are we not suprised by this?)

The GDI includes a family of functions that create and manipulate *regions*. A region is simply a bounded area of the screen. Just like the other GDI objects we explored in Chapters 6 and 7, regions have handles. One function, **CreateRectRgn**, constructs a Windows region from two pairs of coordinates that specify the upper-left corner and lower-right corner of a rectangle, returning a handle of type **HRGN**. Delphi declares this in *Windows.Pas*:

```
type
    HRGN = Integer;
function CreateRectRgn(p1, p2, p3, p4: Integer): HRGN; stdcall;
```

Thanks to another GDI function, **PtInRegion**, regions make handy mousetraps.

```
function PtInRegion(RGN: HRGN; p2, p3: Integer): BOOL; stdcall;
```

In Chapter 3, we kept track of hotlink words or phrases in hypertext topic windows by recording their rectangular boundaries. Then, in the

OnMouseDown event procedure, we compared the mouse position coordinates to the rectangular boundaries to determine whether a mouse click occurred within any of those rectangles. With the two API functions just introduced, we can do the same thing with fewer steps.

To intercept mouse clicks in a particular section of the screen, we can mark that area with a region, passing the handle to that region and the coordinates of the **OnMouseDown** event procedure to **PtInRegion**, which will return either **true** or **false**.

Before calling the **CreateRectRgn** and **PtInRegion** functions, we need some way to determine the positions and dimensions of the rectangular regions we want to use as hotspots. Here's our solution: We can write a hotspot editor in Delphi that allows us to draw rectangles over bitmaps, test them, and save them in a file for later use in our hypermedia system. The editor will be a great addition to our multimedia construction set.

Hotspot I: Creating a Basic Hotspot Editor in Delphi

This is one of the bigger projects we've created so far—so hold on to your hat. A number of steps are required, but the editor is actually easy to put together.

1. Create a new project directory, *HotSpot1*, and an output subdirectory, *Bin*.
2. Open a new application, and in the *Project Options* dialog box, set its Application Title to "Hotspot I" and its Output Directory to "Bin".
3. You might want to take this opportunity to save the project in the *HotSpot1* project directory.
4. Add the support unit *hotspots.pas*. Add the declaration of a **tHotspot_record**, and the routines to load and save hotspots from a file (Listing 9.3).
5. Add the handlers for the main form's **OnCreate** and **OnClose** events, and the routine **Clear_for_new_image**. Also, declare all of the variables we'll be using. (Listing 9.4.)
6. Add the form's **Mouse** events for drawing hotspot regions, and the support code for these routines (Listing 9.5). This will manipulate some menu options' **Enabled** properties. Since we'll add the menu in the next step, you'll have to comment out these lines if you want to make the project compile.

7. Add a menu to the project (Menu Table 9.1). From the *Standard* page of the *Component Palette*, select a MainMenu component and click on the Form. Double click the icon that Delphi left on your form (visible only at design time) and build the menu.
6. Add the **OptFile_LoadPictureClick** and **OptFile_Quit** menu event procedures. This will allow us to start using our program by loading an image onto which we'll draw our hotspots, and stop using the program by quitting (Listing 9.6). You'll also need to get an OpenDialog control from the *Dialogs* page of the *Component Palette*.
8. Add the **OptFile_NewHotspotClick** menu event to start a new hotspot, and the **OptMode_TestClick** and **OptMode_DefineClick** menu event procedures to test and define hotspots. Also, add the support routine **Delete_region** (Listing 9.7).
7. To save hotspot records, add the **OptFile_SaveHotspotClick** event procedure (Listing 9.8).
8. Take a detour to "Software Design Land" to build a utility. Add a second Form to the project, that we'll use as a "Select-from-List" dialog box. The Form, named **List_select_dialog**, will come in its own unit, *dlgload.pas*. We'll add some code, here, too (Property Table 9.2, and Listing 9.9).
9. Almost there! Add the **OptFile_EditHotspotClick** (which uses the **List_select_dialog** we just built) and **OptFile_DeleteHotspotClick** event procedures (Listing 9.10).
10. The entire code for unit **Main** is shown in Listing 9.11; unit **Hotspots** in Listing 9.3; and unit **DlgLoad** in Listing 9.9. Since the main Form itself doesn't have anything but the MainMenu control with properties we care about, we haven't included a Property Table for the main Form. The Form's **Caption** is set to "Hotspot I - Rectangular Hotspot Region Editor." Again, the MainMenu properties are listed in Menu Table 9.1.

This project, hotspot1.dpr, as well as all of its support files, can be found on the accompanying CD-ROM, in the directory \Programs\Chap09\HotSpot1.

How the Hotspot Editor Works

Before you explore this project, take a few minutes to run the editor just to become more familiar with how it works. Figure 9.3 shows the editor with a

Figure 9.3   The Rectangular Hotspot Editor.

bitmap image loaded. The editor allows you to load in a bitmap image, draw your hotspots with the mouse and save them.

To display an image, choose *File | Load Picture*, then use the *Open* dialog box to locate and select a bitmap image. When the picture appears on the form, you can use the mouse to draw and test hotspot regions.

Each time you press the mouse button, the editor will begin drawing a new rectangle. You won't see the new figure until you stretch it into one or two dimensions by moving the mouse. When you release the mouse button, the rectangle will remain locked at its last position and size until you restart the process by pressing the mouse button again.

After you draw a rectangle, choose *Mode | Test*. When you click inside the rectangle, you should hear *tada.wav*. When you click outside the rectangle, you should hear *ding.wav*.

Designing the Hotspot Editor

Our editor requires two forms: **Form1** (we kept the default name) in unit **Main** (as we saved Delphi's **Unit1**), and **List_select_dialog** in the unit **DlgLoad**. The first form contains the **OnMouse...** event procedures for drawing hotspot regions and the menu system for the project. We'll create **List_select_dialog** to retrieve and edit hotspots that we have already saved in a file. We'll be taking a closer look at this form later. For now, let's create the main Form, **Form1**.

Set the **Caption** property of the default Form that Delphi starts with to "Hotspot I - Rectangular Hotspot Region Editor." Save the unit as *main.pas*.

Hotspots

Next, we'll need a unit to deal with hotspots. From the *New Items* dialog box (*File | New*), choose "Unit". Save the nearly blank new unit as "hotspots.pas". Flesh out the unit with the code in Listing 9.3.

Listing 9.3   The entire unit *Hotspots.Pas*

```
unit Hotspots;

interface

    type
        tHotspot_record = record
            Image       : string[128];
            Target      : string[128];
            UL_X, UL_Y,
            LR_X, LR_Y  : integer;
            end;

        tHotspot_file = file of tHotspot_record;

    procedure Clear_hotspot(
      var  Hotspot : tHotspot_record
      );

    procedure Save_hotspot_record(
      var    F : tHotspot_file;
      var    I : integer;
      const  H : tHotspot_record
      );

    procedure Load_hotspot_record(
      var    F : tHotspot_file;
      const  I : integer;
      var    H : tHotspot_record
      );

implementation

    procedure Clear_hotspot(
      var  Hotspot : tHotspot_record
      );
        begin
            fillchar(Hotspot,sizeof(Hotspot),0);
            end;

    procedure Save_hotspot_record(
      var    F : tHotspot_file;
      var    I : integer;
      const  H : tHotspot_record
      );
```

```
       var
           Blank_found  : boolean;
           Temp_hotspot : tHotspot_record;
       begin
           if I = -1 then begin
               { Add hotspot }
               Blank_found := false;
               I := 0;
               seek(F,I);
               while not (eof(F) or Blank_found) do begin
                   read(F,Temp_hotspot);
                   Blank_found := Temp_hotspot.Image = '';
                   if not Blank_found then inc(I);
                   end;
               end;
           seek(F,I);
           write(F,H);
           end;

    procedure Load_hotspot_record(
       var   F : tHotspot_file;
       const I : integer;
       var   H : tHotspot_record
       );
         begin
             seek(F,I);
             read(F,H);
             end;

end.
```

This unit does nothing but pure definition and manipulation of hotspot information. Hotspots themselves are declared with the type **tHotspot_record**.

```
tHotspot_record = record
    Image       : string[128];
    Target      : string[128];
    UL_X, UL_Y,
    LR_X, LR_Y  : integer;
    end;
```

The **Image** and **Target** fields are simple **string**s, 128 characters long. Which is enough for some pretty descriptive names! **Image** holds the filename of the image over which the hotspot resides, and **Target** stores the hyperlink destination. The location of the hotspot over the image is recorded as its upper-left and lower-right corners, **UL_X, UL_Y**; and **LR_X, LR_Y**. To facilitate clearing this structure quickly, we declare **Clear_hotspot**—which simply blanks the record to zeros. This sets the length of **Image** and **Target** to zero, effectively nulling them, and sets the rectangle from (0,0) to (0,0). A rectangle consisting of a single point, like this one, is occasionally referred to as a *null rectangle*. This is because most rectangles you'll send to the Windows GDI are *bounding* rectangles: the first coordinate is actually part of the rectangle but the second coordinate is *one pixel to the outside* of the rectangle. Figure 9.4 demonstrates this. In our case, since the second coordinate is the same as the first, but must also be outside of the rectangle, the rectangle must be empty.

The routine **Load_hotspot_record** simply reads a **tHotspot_record** from a given position, **I**, from a file of **tHotspot_records**. **Save_hotspot_record** is a little more tricky: If a position, **I**, other than −1 is specified, a hotspot is saved at that location in the file. Remember, since the position is given in terms of a **seek** index, the first record is in position 0. If a −1 is given as the position, a new record is added to the file. Rather than simply appending the new record to the end of the file, however, the routine looks for a "blank" location first. Thus, we can delete a record by writing out a record with a null **Image** field, later reusing that space without having to enlarge the file. You might want to explicitly code a "**Delete_hotspot_record**" routine, but for now, it's simple enough just to set the **Image** field to null and rewrite it, as we'll do later on.

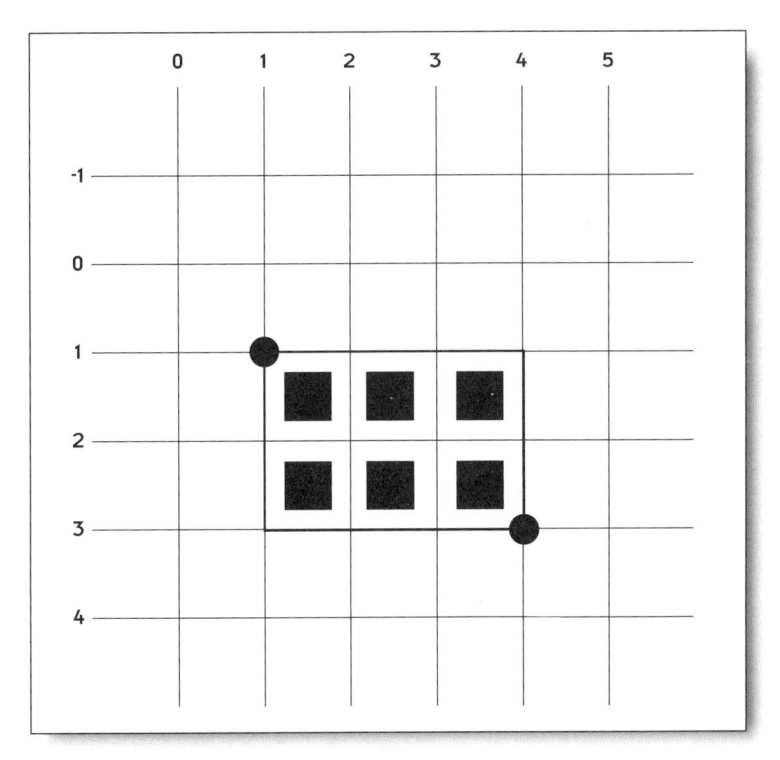

Figure 9.4 The Bounding Rectangle (1,1) - (4,3).

Creating and Closing the Main Form

Now that we've established what hotspots are, how they are represented, and how they will be stored in files, we can begin to address the design of the main program. Back in unit **Main**, our program's Form, **Form1**, will require some associated code as it is created and closed. We will introduce all of our *state variables* that globally (at least to the Form) indicate the current state of our program in this code. Click on the main form and double click on the **OnCreate** and **OnClose** events on the *Events* page of the *Object Inspector*, adding the code shown in Listing 9.4. Some other code needs to be added to unit **Main**, also.

The **uses** clause should be added just after the **implementation**. Since we have not developed the **DlgLoad** unit, the compiler will choke on it in the uses list. If you really want to see the code compile, you could comment it out here. The variables and **Clear_for_new_image** should be added just above the **FormCreate** method.

Listing 9.4 Creation and Closing of **Form1**, from unit **Main**

```
uses
        MMSystem, DlgLoad, Hotspots;

:

var
    Image_link_file        : tHotspot_file;
    Current_hotspot        : integer;
    Current_image_filename : string;
    Drawing_rectangle      : boolean;
    Anchor_X, Anchor_Y,
    End_X,    End_Y        : integer;
    The_region             : HRGN;
    The_hotspot            : tHotspot_record;
    The_image              : TImage;

:

var
    Rectangle_is_visible : boolean;

:

procedure Clear_for_new_image;
    begin
        Clear_hotspot(The_hotspot);
        Current_hotspot := -1; { Not loaded. }
        Anchor_X := 0; Anchor_Y := 0;
        End_X    := 0; End_Y    := 0;
```

```
            Drawing_rectangle := false;
            The_region := 0;
            Rectangle_is_visible := false;
            end;

procedure TForm1.FormCreate(Sender: TObject);
    begin
        assignFile(Image_link_file,
           ExtractFilePath(Application.ExeName)+'ImagLink.Dat'
           );
        {$I-}
        reset(Image_link_file);
        {$I+}
        if ioResult <> 0 then rewrite(Image_link_file);

        The_image := nil;
        Clear_for_new_image;
        end;

procedure TForm1.FormClose(Sender: TObject; var Action: TCloseAction);
    begin
        closeFile(Image_link_file);
        end;
```

The variables indicate something about our current state. The **Image_link_file** is the file containing the hotspots we'll be editing, and is **assign**ed with the filename *imaglink.dat* in the directory in which our application's EXE file resides. This happens in the **FormCreate** method. If the file can't be **reset**, the file is created with **rewrite**. In the future, you may want to change the program so the hotspot database file can be moved, or changed during the editing session. The **Current_hotspot** is the record number (zero-based) of the record of the **Image_link_file** we are currently working on. If we are working on a *new* hotspot, the **Current_hotspot** will be –1.

The **Current_image_filename** is the name of the image on which we'll be drawing the hotspots. **The_image** is a **TImage** we will create at runtime to hold the picture we are currently working with, so we don't need to keep reading from the file specified by **Current_image_filename**.

The_hotspot holds our currently-active hotspot. As we are actually drawing the hotspot, **Anchor_X** and **Anchor_Y** store the location of the **OnMouseDown** event (the first corner of the hotspot rectangle), and **End_X** and **End_Y** store the current location of mouse pointer (cursor) as the rectangle is "rubber-banded" about the screen. The flag **Drawing_rectangle** tells us if we are actually in the process of drawing the rubber-banded rectangle. The flag **Rectangle_is_visible** is used to remind ourselves that the rectangle is visible on the screen, and needs to be erased before we continue.

Finally, **The_region** is a handle to a Windows GDI *region*. As we discussed above, a region is an area of the screen recorded by the GDI so that special manipulations and tests can be performed with it. We'll be most interested in the GDI routine **PtInRegion**, which we'll discuss shortly.

We're obviously going to need some initialization code for all of these variables. **Clear_for_new_image** sets up these variables to edit hotspots on the first image during the run, or on a new image after we have finished editing hotspots on some previous image. We can't assume the existence of a previous image. We clear **The_hotspot**, and set the **Current_hotspot** file index to –1, so we're working with a new hotspot. (If the user loads a hotspot from the file of course, this index will be set to the index of the hotspot from the file.) The **Anchor** and **End** points are set to (0,0), and the handle **The_region** is set to zero. (So, if we were working with a region we created previously, we must already have destroyed it by the time we get here!) As we begin a new hotspot session, the flags **Drawing_rectangle** and **Rectangle_is_visible** are set to **false**, because we have not yet initiated the drawing of a new hotspot.

As we discussed before, **FormCreate** opens the hotspot database file, **Image_link_file**, or creates it if necessary. A key point that may have slipped your attention so far is this: while rewriting a file creates a blank file for writing on, and resetting a file allows you to read from the file, resetting the file also allows you to *write* to the file. You can see how this works back in the **Save_hotspot_record** procedure in unit **Hotspots**.

FormCreate then does a **Clear_for_new_image**, and also sets **The_image** to **nil**. **The_image** is an object of type **TImage**, but as the program starts, **The_image** has not been instantiated. We set it to **nil** because the first thing we'll do when we load a new image is **Free** the previous image. Since we don't want yet another state variable to tell us if we're just starting, we instead set **The_image** to **nil**. That way, the unconditional **The_image.Free** that we'll see below will be OK since **Free** doesn't do anything to **nil** objects.

FormClose simply closes the **Image_link_file**. It could also do a final **The_image.Free**, but we'll let Delphi's exit code take care of this clean-up for us.

Setting the Bait—Outlining Hot Regions

We need to create the three event procedures to support the mouse. So let's move right on through it. Click on the main form and double click on the **OnMouseDown**, **OnMouseMove**, and **OnMouseUp** events on the *Events* page of the *Object Inspector*. As Delphi brings up the code framework, flesh out the events as shown below. Add the support routines **Hide_rectangle** and **Show_rectangle** above the routines. Listing 9.5 shows the required code.

Listing 9.5 The Mouse Events and Rectangle Drawing in Unit **Main**

```
procedure Hide_rectangle;
   begin
      if Rectangle_is_visible then
         Form1.Canvas.Rectangle(Anchor_X,Anchor_Y,End_X,End_Y);
      Rectangle_is_visible := false;
      end;

procedure Show_rectangle;
   begin
      if not Rectangle_is_visible then
         Form1.Canvas.Rectangle(Anchor_X,Anchor_Y,End_X,End_Y);
      Rectangle_is_visible := true;
      end;


procedure TForm1.FormMouseDown(Sender: TObject; Button: TMouseButton;
   Shift: TShiftState; X, Y: Integer);
   begin
      if  (not OptMode.Enabled)
        or
          (Current_image_filename = '')
         then begin
            mciExecute('play c:\Windows\Media\Ding.Wav');
            exit;
            end;
         if OptMode_Define.Checked then begin
            Canvas.Pen.Mode := pmNot;
            Canvas.Brush.Style := bsClear;
            Hide_rectangle; { The old one. }
            Anchor_X := X; Anchor_Y := Y;
            End_X    := X; End_Y    := Y;
            Show_rectangle; { This new, null, one. }
            Drawing_rectangle := true;
            end
          else
            { Test to see if click is in region. }
            if PtInRegion(The_region,X,Y) then
               mciExecute('play c:\Windows\Media\Tada.Wav')
              else
               mciExecute('play c:\Windows\Media\Ding.Wav');
      end;

procedure TForm1.FormMouseMove(Sender: TObject; Shift: TShiftState; X,
   Y: Integer);
   begin
      if not Drawing_rectangle then exit;
      Hide_rectangle;
      End_X := X; End_Y := Y;
      Show_rectangle;
      end;

procedure TForm1.FormMouseUp(Sender: TObject; Button: TMouseButton;
   Shift: TShiftState; X, Y: Integer);
```

```
begin
    if not Drawing_rectangle then exit;
    End_X := X; End_Y := Y;
    Drawing_rectangle := false;
    OptFile_SaveHotspot.Enabled := true;
    OptMode_Test.Enabled        := true;
end;
```

FormMouseDown

FormMouseDown initiates the drawing process. Before we even start, we make sure that the Mode pull-down menu option has been enabled (we'll get to that later), and that we have loaded an image. If not, we play the *Ding* and exit as if nothing happened. Once we start, we look back at the menus to see if we are Defining or Testing hotspots.

When we start defining a hotspot, we first set **Form1**'s **Canvas**' **Pen.Mode** to **pmNot**, and its **Brush.Style** to **bsClear**. The first time we draw a rectangle on the **Canvas**, the interior will show the background image, and a line (of default width 1 pixel) around the outside will be drawn, consisting of inverted pixel colors. The second time we draw a rectangle in the same place, the interior will still show the background image; but the line around the outside will invert the pixel values once more, returning them to their original colors. The rectangle, then, is effectively erased.

After setting the **Pen.Mode** and **Brush.Style**, we hide the previous rectangle, set the **Anchor** and **End** to the **OnMouseDown** point, and draw the new rectangle. This is a null rectangle, so nothing will really happen, but the **OnMouseMove** handler will want to erase the previous rectangle. So to keep in synch, we should draw our null rectangle anyway—just to have a previous one to erase. Finally, to tell the other mouse event procedures that we're in the middle of drawing a rectangle, we set **Drawing_rectangle** to **true**.

If we are just testing a hotspot, we call the Windows GDI function **PtInRegion** with the click location, and play *Tada* or *Ding* if we are inside or outside the region, respectively. **The_region** will have been set up when we chose Testing or Defining from the pull-down menu.

FormMouseMove

Next, we need to add the **FormMouseMove** event procedure. If we are not **Drawing_rectangle**, we exit immediately because we don't care about ordinary cursor motion over our form. Otherwise, we hide the rectangle that was already on the screen, placed there by **FormMouseDown** or by ourselves. We then set our new **End_X** and **End_Y** to the move location and draw a new rectangle to the new cursor location.

FormMouseUp

FormMouseUp doesn't matter to us if we are not **Drawing_rectangle**. If we are, we record the location of the **OnMouseUp** event as our new **End** point, and announce that we are no longer drawing a rectangle by setting **Drawing_rectangle** to **false**. We can leave the old rectangle showing on the screen, because we'll assume Windows always sends us an **OnMouseMove** event before (and in the same location as) the **OnMouseUp** event. Relying upon this assumption, we don't really even have to set the **End** from the **OnMouseUp** location; we already captured it in **FormMouseMove**. Here's the problem: this is only an assumption, based on the documentation we've found so far. It would be far safer (although we don't do it here) to hide the previous rectangle, re-assign **End_X** and **End_Y**, and show the final rectangle instead of just setting the **End** point. We'll leave the fine points to your discretion.

Hide_rectangle and Show_rectangle

How do we actually draw the rectangle? We use **Hide_rectangle** and **Show_rectangle**, which both do the same thing.

```
Form1.Canvas.Rectangle(Anchor_X,Anchor_Y,End_X,End_Y);
```

Since we are using a **pmNot** pen, this code performs double duty. The code around this line makes sure that we don't do what we're attempting to do if we've already done it. By looking at and setting the flag **Rectangle_is_visible**, and calling the routines that reflect what we really want to do, we can ensure that we don't inadvertently draw or undraw the rectangle when it would be inappropriate. In the normal operation of the program, this doesn't pose a big problem, but handling things like **Form1**'s **OnPaint** event can make things go wacky. Rather than relying on our program's own structure, it's nice to have a somewhat more reliable mechanism for making sure we draw the rectangle only when it's appropriate.

Drawing with Inverted Colors

You'll notice that the lines that form the rectangles are not solid, but look more like negative versions of the pixels they cover. The **Pen.Mode** we used, **pmNot**, flips the bits of each pixel value, either from one to zero, or zero to one. The pixel values then reference colors in the opposite side of the system palette. The result often looks like a photographic negative. If you are in High Color or True Color mode, it is; if you are 256 color mode, it isn't—unless each color in the palette happens to be paired with its RGB

> complement at the position in the palette determined by its 8-bit binary complement. Most of the Windows reserved colors try to look like complementary pairs, but even they are impostors. The only colors in the system palette that always enjoy this symmetry are black and white.

Adding the Menu System

It's time to add the menu we've been checking and enabling in the code above. From the *Standard* page of the *Component Palette*, select a MainMenu component and click on **Form1**. Double-click the icon that Delphi puts on the form, and start adding entries using Delphi's *Menu Designer*.

The *Designer* opens with the top-level left menu entry highlighted. In the *Object Inspector*, notice that you are manipulating the **Caption** property of a **TMenuItem** component. Type "File" and press [enter]. Delphi then allows you to enter the **Caption** of the first subitem of the top-level item just entered. You'll see a space to the right of the "File" item you just entered. To set the **Caption** of this next top-level option, click on the box. We'll enter the menu in Delphi's order, though. Table 9.2 will guide you through the menu item property set-up, but we'll also walk you through it.

Go ahead and enter all of the menu's **Caption**s first: "Load Picture", a dash (minus sign), "New Hotspot", "Edit Saved Hotspot", "Save Hotspot", "Delete

*Table 9.2 The Menu **MainMenu1** for Hotspot I.*

Name	Caption	Enabled	Checked
OptFile	'File'	True	False
OptFile_LoadPicture	'Load Picture'	True	False
N1 (default)	'-'	—	—
OptFile_NewHotspot	'New Hotspot'	False	False
OptFile_EditHotspot	'Edit Saved Hotspot'	False	False
OptFile_SaveHotspot	'Save Hotspot'	False	False
OptFile_DeleteHotspot	'Delete Hotspot'	False	False
N2 (default)	'-'	—	—
OptFile_Quit	'Quit'	True	False
OptMode	'Mode'	False	False
OptMode_Test	'Test'	False	False
OptMode_Define	'Define'	True	True

Hotspot", a dash, and "Quit". The dashes are special: They will cause dividing-line breaks in the menu. Now, click on the box to the right of the top-level "File" option. Enter "Mode", and then beneath it, "Test" and "Define". The menu entry screen is shown in Figure 9.5.

Notice that we've established a naming convention for our menu items. The individual menu items' properties, as shown in the *Object Inspector*, don't specifically allow us to set the relationship of a sub-menu-item to a parent item, or to fix their order. To resolve some of this confusion, we start each name with "Opt", for menu *opt*ion, and then the top-level word. For sub-items, we add an underscore, followed by a description of the sub-item option.

Now go back and set the **Name** and **Enabled** properties of each of the entries by highlighting the menu item in the *Menu Designer*, and setting the values in the *Object Inspector*, as specified in Table 9.2. Remember to set the **Checked** property of the **OptMode_Define** menu item. You can leave the **N1** and **N2** items alone; these are the default names Delphi gave to the menu items.

As we continue this project, we'll talk about adding code to handle the menu events. To get the framework of a menu **OnClick** event, you can double-click the **OnClick** event line in the *Object Inspector*, or double-click the desired menu item on the *Menu Designer* window.

Starting and Stopping, as a User

As programmers, we're interested in starting and stopping programs with the **OnCreate** and **OnClose** events. But we must look at this from the user's point of view, too. What options will be available to them when they start the program? How do they quit? A word processor has it easy—it starts with a "blank sheet of paper." Users who want to replace that with a document they

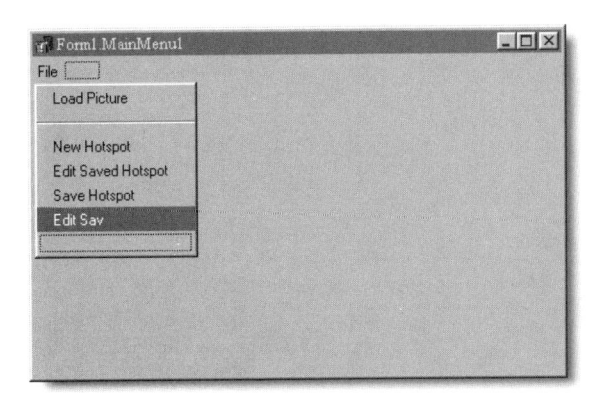

Figure 9.5 *Delphi's Menu Designer in action.*

have already written can just load a file. A general ledger package might not be as simple. You can't post transactions to a set of books until you've chosen the set of books with which you want to work.

In our hotspot editor, our initial settings of the menu items only allow the user to load a picture or quit. This is good—we don't want to be drawing hotspots without a picture already loaded to which we can attach them. The two menu event procedures, **OptFile_LoadPicture** and **OptFile_Quit handle**, are the first and last things a user must do.

Before you can use this code, shown in Listing 9.6, notice that the first line of the **OptFile_LoadPictureClick** method calls the **OpenDialog1.Execute** method. **OpenDialog1** is a Windows Common Control, the *Open* dialog. This is a non-visual component that you can include in your project by retrieving it from the *Dialogs* page of the *Component Palette* and placing it on your form. At this point, your program has the same ability to choose files as any other Windows program. You've seen it a million times, but we'll show it to you once again in Figure 9.6.

Listing 9.6 The Menu Events for Loading a Picture and Quitting in Unit **Main**

```
procedure TForm1.OptFile_LoadPictureClick(Sender: TObject);
   var
      Image : TImage;
   begin
      if not OpenDialog1.Execute then exit;
      Current_image_filename := OpenDialog1.Filename;

      Hide_rectangle;
      Delete_region(The_region);
      The_image.Free;
      The_image := TImage.Create(Self);
```

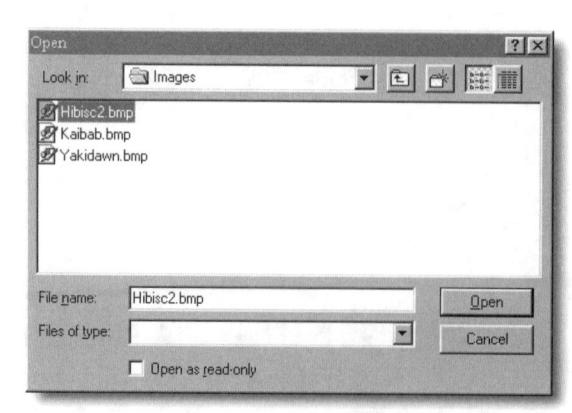

Figure 9.6 *Using the Windows common dialog, encapsulated by Delphi's **TOpenDialog** class.*

```
        with The_image do begin
            AutoSize := true;
            Picture.LoadFromFile(Current_image_filename);
            if Width > 100 then
               Self.ClientWidth := Width
              else
               Self.ClientWidth := 100;
            if Height > 100 then
               Self.ClientHeight := Height
              else
               Self.ClientHeight := 100;
            Self.Canvas.CopyRect(ClientRect,Canvas,ClientRect);
            end;
        Clear_for_new_image;

        OptFile_NewHotspot.Enabled     := true;
        OptFile_EditHotspot.Enabled    := true;
        OptFile_SaveHotspot.Enabled    := false;
        OptFile_DeleteHotspot.Enabled  := false;
        OptMode.Enabled                := true;
        OptMode_Test.Enabled           := false;
        end;

procedure TForm1.OptFile_QuitClick(Sender: TObject);
    begin
        Close;
        end;

procedure TForm1.FormPaint(Sender: TObject);
    begin
        if The_image = nil then exit;
        with The_image do
            Self.Canvas.CopyRect(ClientRect,Canvas,ClientRect);
        Canvas.Pen.Mode := pmNot;
        Canvas.Brush.Style := bsClear;
        Rectangle_is_visible := false;
        Show_rectangle;
        end;
```

With the **OpenDialog** added to **Form1**, the first two lines run the dialog box and retrieve the selected filename into **Current_image_filename**. (To simplify life for your users, you might want to change **OpenDialog1**'s **DefaultExt** property to "BMP", and its **Filter** property to "Pictures|*.BMP;*.DIB".) If no file is selected, we exit right away. Time to clean up what we might have been doing before: We hide any previous rectangle we might have drawn; we delete any test region we might have used, and we free the in-memory copy of the last picture we were using, stored in **The_image**.

To load the new image file, we re-create **The_image**. The parameter, **Self**, is the "owner" of the image. If the owner is destroyed, all of the objects it owns will be destroyed, also. So, Delphi will automatically dispose of our image when it finally disposes of **Form1**. (Since **OptFile_LoadPictureClick** is a method of the **TForm1** type, the **Self** parameter refers to our own instantiation of **TForm1**, which is **Form1** itself.)

We set **The_image.AutoSize** to **true** so that when we load an image, we'll always get the whole picture, and nothing but the whole picture. The picture is loaded with the **LoadFromFile** method of **The_image**'s **Picture** property. After that, we resize the client area of our main form, **Form1** (aka **Self**), to fit the image, or 100 pixels (on each side), whichever is larger. That way, we'll always get a reasonably-sized window, even if we're working with a sixteen-pixel-square image. Once the form has been resized, the form's **Canvas**' **CopyRect** method copies the picture from **The_image** onto the form.

Finally, we call **Clear_for_new_image** to re-initialize our state variables and enable various menu options, now that we have a picture onto which we may draw hotspots. Since we have not yet selected a hotspot for editing, we can't delete it, so that menu option is disabled; and since we can't test a hotspot that we haven't yet drawn, **OptMode_Test** is disabled.

You may be wondering why we go to the trouble of loading the picture into an Image control. The answer is simple: we want the picture on **Form1** itself, but **TForm** doesn't have a "LoadPictureFromFile" method. So, we co-opt the method from **TImage**. Couldn't we then just **Create** and **Free The_image** locally? We could, but if we should need to get to it again, we'd have to reload it. Why would we want to get to it again? To repaint the screen if, say, we were covered up by another program and then uncovered again. **Form1**'s event handler **FormPaint** handles this occurrence. If **The_image** isn't **nil**, **FormPaint** copies it back onto the form. Just in case the **Pen.Mode** or **Brush.Style** changed, we set those back, and then we forcibly redraw the current rectangle.

By the way, when users are finished, they can click *File | Quit* and invoke **OptFile_QuitClick**. This routine simply closes the form.

Drawing or Testing?

Our editor must be set up so that we can switch between drawing mode and testing mode. We've added a menu to the form with an option called *Mode*. This option contains two suboptions labeled *Define* and *Test*. We'll use checkmarks to indicate which option is active. *Define* will turn on the drawing mode, and *Test* will create the rectangular Windows region. Listing 9.7 shows the event handlers for these menu options.

Listing 9.7 Defining and Testing Hotspots in Unit **Main**

```
procedure Delete_region(
  var The_region : HRGN
  );
    begin
        if The_region = 0 then exit;
        if DeleteObject(The_region) then
           The_region := 0
         else
           MessageDlg('Unable to delete region.',mtWarning,[mbOK],0);
        end;

procedure TForm1.OptFile_NewHotspotClick(Sender: TObject);
    begin
        Hide_rectangle;
        Delete_region(The_region);
        Clear_for_new_image;
        OptMode_DefineClick(Self);
        OptFile_SaveHotspot.Enabled   := false;
        OptFile_DeleteHotspot.Enabled := false;
        OptMode_Test.Enabled          := false;
        end;

procedure TForm1.OptMode_TestClick(Sender: TObject);
    begin
        OptMode_Define.Checked := false;
        OptMode_Test.Checked   := true;
        The_region := CreateRectRgn(Anchor_X,Anchor_Y,End_X,End_Y);
        end;

procedure TForm1.OptMode_DefineClick(Sender: TObject);
    begin
        Delete_region(The_region);
        OptMode_Define.Checked := true;
        OptMode_Test.Checked   := false;
        end;
```

Once an image has been loaded, the user will probably want to start working with hotspots. The user ordinarily starts a new hotspot by clicking *File | New Hotspot.* Actually, as long as the user is in Define mode (*Mode | Define*), he/she can draw a new hotspot. Anyway, when the user chooses the *New Hotspot* option, we do a little bit of clean-up, hiding the previously-drawn rectangle and deleting the previous GDI region we might have been using for testing. (We'll see how it's created shortly.) We then re-initialize our state variables with **Clear_for_new_image**, and then adjust the menu.

The first thing we want to do, now that we're working with a new hotspot, is click our own *Define* menu option, placing us in Define mode. To do this, we call **OptMode_DefineClick,** passing our **Self** as the calling object. Since our initialization left us with a null region, we don't want to be able to save it until a rectangle has been drawn. So we disable **OptFile_SaveHotspot**, which is re-enabled when the user completes the drawing of a rectangle, in **FormMouseUp**. We also disable **OptFile_DeleteHotspot**, because we can't delete a hotspot that we didn't recall from the hotspot file. Finally, we disable the **OptMode_Test** menu option, because we can't test a region we haven't yet defined.

When we enable hotspot definition by clicking our own *Define* menu option, or when the user clicks the *Mode | Define* menu option, the handler **OptMode_DefineClick** does very little work. It deletes the previous GDI region used for testing and changes the checkmarks on the menu items.

When the user wants to initiate testing, he/she can click *Mode | Test*, invoking **OptMode_TestClick**. This short handler adjusts the checkmarks on the Mode menu, and then calls the Windows GDI function **CreateRectRgn**. This function registers an "official" region with the GDI, and puts the handle to the region in **The_region**.

When the user clicks the mouse, the **FormMouseDown** event that we saw above is called. Since the user will be in Test mode, the **FormMouseDown** handler can perform a test to see if the **OnMouseDown** location is within **The_region**. To refresh your memory, here is that code:

```
if OptMode_Define.Checked then begin
    :
    end
  else
    { Test to see if click is in region. }
    if PtInRegion(The_region,X,Y) then
        mciExecute('play c:\Windows\Media\Tada.Wav')
      else
        mciExecute('play c:\Windows\Media\Ding.Wav');
```

The call to the **PtInRegion** function takes the handle to the region we created, **The_region**, as well as a location, here the point of the **OnMouseDown** event. **PtInRegion** returns **true** if the point is within the region, and **false**, if not.

Throughout all of this code, whenever we wanted to clean up, we called the routine **Delete_region**. When we are finished with a region that we've created in the GDI, we should let the GDI know that it is complete. This will free some of the GDI's limited resources. To do this, we call the GDI routine **DeleteObject**. This routine deletes all sorts of GDI objects: Pens, Brushes, and so on. As a Delphi programmer, you won't ordinarily code—or even look at code—that handles the deletion of most of the GDI objects you are using; Delphi's VCL takes care of those details behind the scenes.

Since we created **The_region**, we must delete it. We only delete **The_region** if it is a valid, non-zero handle (presumably created in **OptMode_TestClick**); this saves us trouble when we are initializing the program at the start and between hotspots. **DeleteObject** *can* fail. This shouldn't be an issue for us, but if failure occurs, we put up a message box. A failure to delete a region will not prevent the program from continuing, but it will leave an orphan region in memory, which will harmlessly remain there for the rest of the Windows session.

That's all it takes to create and use hotspots with Windows regions. First, you define the boundaries. Then, you create the region. And finally, you test whether a mouse click has occurred within the region.

Saving Hotspots—A Simple Filing System

After you open an image file and draw a hotspot, you'll want to save its coordinates, along with the name of the image file and a hotlink target. That will be the job of the *File | Save Hotspot* menu option and its event procedure **OptFile_SaveHotspotClick**, shown in Listing 9.8. This is just the start of the essential elements of a filing system. Eventually, we will also want to *edit* a hotspot we've saved, and *delete* the ones we don't want.

Listing 9.8 The **OptFile_SaveHotspotClick** Menu Event Procedure from unit **Main**

```
procedure TForm1.OptFile_SaveHotspotClick(Sender: TObject);
    var
        Temp : string;
    begin
        if (Anchor_X = End_X) and (Anchor_Y = End_Y) then begin
            MessageDlg('No Region Defined.',mtWarning,[mbOK],0);
            exit;
            end;
        Hide_rectangle;
        Temp := Trim(
                InputBox(
                   'Enter Target',
                   'Enter a Hyperlink Target string of up to 128 characters:  ',
                   Trim(The_hotspot.Target)
                   )
                );
        Show_rectangle;
        if Temp <> '' then with The_hotspot do begin
            Image := Current_image_filename;
            Target := Temp;
            if Anchor_X <= End_X then begin
                UL_X := Anchor_X; LR_X := End_X;
                end
```

```
      else begin
        UL_X := End_X; LR_X := Anchor_X;
        end;
    if Anchor_Y <= End_Y then begin
        UL_Y := Anchor_Y; LR_Y := End_Y;
        end
      else begin
        UL_Y := End_Y; LR_Y := Anchor_Y;
        end;
    Save_hotspot_record(
      Image_link_file,Current_hotspot,The_hotspot
      );
    end;
end;
```

We already know the filename and path of the image, because we saved it in the string variable **Current_image_filename** when we loaded the picture into the form. We also know the hotspot coordinates, which we created with the drawing operation. The only thing we don't know is the target to which we want the hotspot linked, so we have to ask for it.

Delphi's function **InputBox** will display a simple dialog box with a prompt, a title, and a text box into which the user may type a response. (See Figure 9.7 to see what this function accomplishes.) The third parameter of **InputBox** enables us to display a default response. For a new hotspot, this default will come from a freshly initialized **tHotspot_record**, which means it will be blank. Later, when we implement the *Edit Saved Hotspot* option, we'll be passing the existing target string from the file to **InputBox**.

To avoid confusion when repainting the screen, we hide the rectangle before we put up the input box and show the rectangle again upon completion.

If we're satisfied that the user didn't enter a blank target string, we set the fields of **The_hotspot** to our current values. We go through a little dance to make sure that our **UL_X** and **Y** are really the upper-left corner coordinates; and then we call **Save_hotspot_record** from unit **Hotspots**, passing along the **Current_hotspot** index (which will be -1 if this is a new hotspot, or the previously-retrieved index if we've just edited an existing one). If you look back at Listing 9.3, you'll see that **Current_hotspot** is updated when the hotspot is saved; if we change the hotspot and re-save it, we'll still be updating the same record of the file.

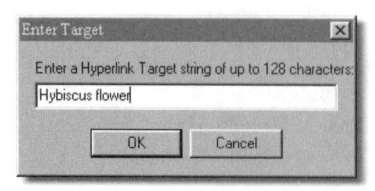

Figure 9.7 The *InputBox* function displays a dialog box.

Retrieving Hotspot Records

Our next requirement is to be able to retrieve and edit hotspots that we have already saved in the file. And that's where the **List_select_dialog** form (shown in Figure 9.8) from the unit **DlgLoad** comes in. Add this unit to the project, and save the blank unit as *dlgload.pas*, after setting the unit's associated Form's **Name** to "List_select_dialog". We're going to see this form again in Chapter 10, so we'll make it as general-purpose as we can.

The form has three controls: a ListBox named **Display**, and two Buttons named **Cancel_button** and **Action_button**. The **DlgLoad** unit, shown in Listing 9.9, contains the event handling code for the controls, and Table 9.3 lists the properties that should be set at design time.

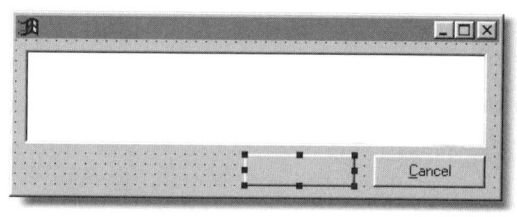

Figure 9.8 The **List_select_dialog** Form.

Table 9.3 Properties for the Form **List_select_dialog** in unit **DlgLoad**.

Class	Property	Value
TForm	Name	List_select_dialog
	BorderIcons	[]
	BorderStyle	bsDialog
	Caption	<blank>
	OnCreate	FormCreate
	Visible	False
TListBox	Name	Display
	Sorted	True
	OnDblClick	DisplayDblClick
TButton	Name	Action_button
	Caption	<blank>
	OnClick	Action_buttonClick
TButton	Name	Cancel_button
	Caption	&Cancel
	Cancel	True
	OnClick	Cancel_buttonClick

Listing 9.9 The Unit **DlgLoad**, for the Form **List_select_dialog**

```
unit DlgLoad;

interface

uses
  Windows, Messages, SysUtils, Classes, Graphics, Controls, Forms, Dialogs,
  StdCtrls;

type
  tLine_and_Data = record
      Line : string;
      Data : pointer;
      end;
  TList_select_dialog = class(TForm)
    Display: TListBox;
    Action_button: TButton;
    Cancel_button: TButton;
    procedure DisplayDblClick(Sender: TObject);
    procedure Action_buttonClick(Sender: TObject);
    procedure Cancel_buttonClick(Sender: TObject);
    procedure FormCreate(Sender: TObject);
  private
    { Private declarations }
    FAction      : string;
    FData_list   : TList;
    FSelected    : tLine_and_Data;
  public
    { Public declarations }
    destructor Destroy; override;

    property Action : string
      read   FAction
      write  FAction;

    procedure Clear;

    procedure Add(
      const Line : string;
      const Data : pointer
      );

    function Execute : boolean;

    property Selected : tLine_and_Data
      read FSelected;

  end;

var
  List_select_dialog: TList_select_dialog;

implementation
```

```
{$R *.DFM}

procedure TList_select_dialog.FormCreate(Sender: TObject);
    begin
        FData_list := TList.Create;
        end;

destructor TList_select_dialog.Destroy;
    begin
        FData_list.Free;
        inherited Destroy;
        end;

procedure TList_select_dialog.Clear;
    begin
        Display.Clear;
        FData_list.Clear;
        end;

procedure TList_select_dialog.Add(
  const Line : string;
  const Data : pointer
  );
    begin
        FData_list.Insert(Display.Items.Add(Line),Data);
        end;

function TList_select_dialog.Execute : boolean;
    var
        I : integer;
    begin
        Action_button.Caption := FAction;
        Action_button.Enabled := Display.Items.Count > 0;
        Display.Enabled := Display.Items.Count > 0;
        ModalResult := mrNone;
        result := ShowModal = mrOK;
        end;

procedure TList_select_dialog.DisplayDblClick(Sender: TObject);
    begin
        with FSelected do begin
            Line := Display.   Items[Display.ItemIndex];
            Data := FData_list.Items[Display.ItemIndex];
            end;
        ModalResult := mrOK;
        end;

procedure TList_select_dialog.Action_buttonClick(Sender: TObject);
    begin with Display do begin
        with FSelected do begin
            Line := Display.   Items[Display.ItemIndex];
            Data := FData_list.Items[Display.ItemIndex];
            end;
```

```
        ModalResult := mrOK;
      end; end;

procedure TList_select_dialog.Cancel_buttonClick(Sender: TObject);
  begin with Display do begin
    with FSelected do begin
      Line := '';
      Data := pointer(-1);
      end;
    ModalResult := mrCancel;
    end; end;

end.
```

This is beginning to look a little bit complicated. OK, a *lot* bit complicated. We haven't often had to add code above the **implementation** section. We'd better take a moment to explain ourselves.

We are essentially trying to implement our own dialog box control. Why? Unfortunately, Delphi doesn't provide us with a "pick-from-list" control. We are still attempting to keep the interface simple, and similar to, say, the **OpenDialog** control. We are also trying to accomplish another goal: we want to attach a piece of extra data to each element of the list box. In our project, the data will be the file index of a record, while the display string will be the target of the indexed record. Just being able to get the display string back isn't very useful to us; we'd have to scan the file again to find the record. (We would have scanned it the first time loading the display list.) By associating the file index with the target, we can get back the file index immediately.

Unlike Microsoft's *Visual Basic*, Delphi's ListBox control does not have a repository for extra data associated with an item. While VB packages some basic functionality for the masses in its list box control, such as the ability to associate a piece of data with each list box entry, Delphi provides you with the tools to maintain any kind of data structure associated with each item in the display list. This is much more versatile, but requires a little more work on your part—even when all you want is one piece of data tied to each item.

These are the properties and methods our **List_select_dialog** will support.

- **Action** This property is the caption of the button that will choose the selected item. Double-clicking an item in the list will also choose it.
- **Clear** This method clears the display list and its list of associated data.
- **Add** This method adds a line of text, and an associated piece of data, passed in as a **pointer**.
- **Execute** This **boolean** function returns **true** if the user clicks the Action button or double-clicks an item in the displayed list, and **false** if the user clicks the Cancel button.

- **Selected** This read-only property is a **tLine_and_Data** record representing the selected item. A **tLline_and_Data** record contains two fields: **Line** (the string displayed) and **Data** (the associated pointer).
- **Caption** This is an inherited property of the **List_select_dialog** form, so we won't have to code it. We mention it because we'll use it to label the window when it is displayed.

There are a couple of holes in this design, but they don't affect us. First, the **Add** method should really be a function like the **Add** methods of the **TStringList** and **TList** sub-components, that returns the position of insertion of the added **Line** and **Data**. Secondly, we must remember that the **Clear** method will not destroy any objects or strings that may be passed to it through **Add**'s **Data** parameter. Since this is the way **TList** works, it isn't actually a "hole"; but we must be careful.

We'll look at each of the methods in detail below, but let's take a quick look at the properties.

```
property Action : string
  read   FAction
  write  FAction;

property Selected : tLine_and_Data
  read FSelected;
```

Action simply sets and gets the value to and from the **private** field **FAction**; **Selected** allows us to control outside access to **FSelected**, making it read-only.

Keeping in Synch

Up in the **interface**, we've added three **private** fields to **TList_select_dialog**, the class of our selection form:

```
FAction      : string;
FData_list   : TList;
FSelected    : tLine_and_Data;
```

As you can see, we've used Delphi's convention of naming our object fields with a leading "F" (for "field"). This helps us avoid confusion with more-easily remembered, and externalized property names like **Selected**. The **FData_list** is where we'll be storing our associated **Data** pointers. Since a **TList** stores pointers, we'll be able to simply **Add** the **Data** to the **FData_list**.

We must create the **FData_list**, which we do when we create the form. Likewise, we must **Free** the list when we're finished. To do this, we declare an overriding **Destroy** routine that frees **FData_list**, and then calls the inherited **Destroy** to finish cleaning up after our ancestors.

```
procedure TList_select_dialog.FormCreate(Sender: TObject);
    begin
        FData_list := TList.Create;
        end;

destructor TList_select_dialog.Destroy;
    begin
        FData_list.Free;
        inherited Destroy;
        end;
```

Here's where the real trick to synchronization between the list box and our **FData_list** is demonstrated. This wouldn't be very difficult if we could keep it simple: We could just add a **Data** item to the end of our **FData_list** every time we added a **Line** to our **Display**. Unfortunately, this only works if all we want to do is append to the end of this list.

```
procedure TList_select_dialog.Add(
  const Line : string;
  const Data : pointer
  );
    begin
        FData_list.Insert(Display.Items.Add(Line),Data);
        end;
```

We thought it might be easier for the user if we kept the **Display** in sorted order. If we do that, though, we can't just append data to the end of our **FData_list**. Fortunately, the methods and properties of the **TListBox** and **TList** can work for us. The **TListBox.Add** method is actually a function; it returns the location where an item was added in the list. If the list isn't sorted, this is just the ever-increasing end of the list. However, if we flip the **TListBox.Sorted** property to true, **Add** returns the location at which the item was actually inserted. That's where we want to **Insert** the data item in our **FData_list**. We've condensed this process into one line, so you'll need to pick apart the calls: **Display.Items.Add(Line)** adds the **Line**, and acts as the insertion location of the call **FData_list.Insert(<*loc*>,Data)**.

A Pop-Up Dialog Box, A La Mode

Now that we can build a sorted **Display** with associated data, we need to be able to display the form. We could just set the form up with its **Visible** property set to **False** at design time, and then show it with the form's **Show** method, or set its **Visible** property to **True** at runtime (though **Show** would be the preferred method). The result would be just another open window in the application. To display the window so that the user cannot proceed without doing something, like choosing a Target from the file or canceling out of the window, we can use a Windows feature, *modal* display.

The word *modal* comes from the three *modes* in which a window can be displayed. Most ordinary program windows work in a normal mode, but the **InputBox** and pop-up dialogs like it, are said to be *Application-Modal*; that is, they become the top and only active window of an application when they are running. The application will not be allowed to continue until the window is closed. There is an even more restrictive mode: *System-Modal* operation. In this case, the user cannot operate *any* application until the window is closed. Generally, this is reserved for catastrophic failures, like Windows itself running out of memory.

Delphi's forms have a **ShowModal** method that will make them visible as an application-modal dialog box. Once a form is showing modally, the form's message loop will look for the form's property **ModalResult** to be given a value other than **mrNone** (one of the allowable values). When this happens, the form will close. Until then, all of the other actions of the form can happen, allowing the user to move the mouse, click buttons, resize the form (if you've allowed the form to be **Sizable**), and so forth.

When the application calls **List_select_dialog.Execute**, we set the form's **ModalResult** to **mrNone**, and then display the form with the **ShowModal** function.

```
function TList_select_dialog.Execute : boolean;
   var
      I : integer;
   begin
      Action_button.Caption := FAction;
      Action_button.Enabled := Display.Items.Count > 0;
      Display.Enabled := Display.Items.Count > 0;
      ModalResult := mrNone;
      result := ShowModal = mrOK;
      end;
```

ShowModal opens the window and keeps it running until some event handler sets a value in **ModalResult**. When that happens, **ShowModal** returns the **ModalResult** value. In this case, **Execute** returns **true** if **ShowModal** returns a **ModalResult** of **mrOK**, and false if otherwise. You'll notice that we do a little housekeeping prior to this, so that the **Action_button** has a **Caption**, and the **Display** only works if there are items in it. You could probably tighten this up even more.

Closing the List_select_dialog

Three actions will close our **List_select_dialog**. The user can double-click an item in the **Display**; select an item, and click the **Action_button**; or click the **Cancel_button**. (Actually the user can press [escape], too, because **Cancel_button** has its **Cancel** property set to **True**.)

```
procedure TList_select_dialog.DisplayDblClick(Sender: TObject);
   begin
      with FSelected do begin
         Line := Display.   Items[Display.ItemIndex];
         Data := FData_list.Items[Display.ItemIndex];
         end;
      ModalResult := mrOK;
      end;

procedure TList_select_dialog.Action_buttonClick(Sender: TObject);
   begin with Display do begin
      with FSelected do begin
         Line := Display.   Items[Display.ItemIndex];
         Data := FData_list.Items[Display.ItemIndex];
         end;
      ModalResult := mrOK;
      end; end;

procedure TList_select_dialog.Cancel_buttonClick(Sender: TObject);
   begin with Display do begin
      with FSelected do begin
         Line := '';
         Data := pointer(-1);
         end;
      ModalResult := mrCancel;
      end; end;
```

Each of the event handlers sets the **FSelected private** field, which can be queried with the **Selected** property. Note that each one sets the **ModalResult**, in effect, closing the form. The form *object* doesn't go away, though; so the **Selected** property can still be used to retrieve the returned **Line** and **Data**.

Defining the Other Menu Options

Back on the main Form in unit **Main**, the *File | Edit Saved Hotspot* option kicks off the process of loading a hotspot record. *File | Delete Hotspot* deletes the currently-loaded hotspot, but is only enabled if the user has loaded a hotspot for editing. Listing 9.10 shows the procedures needed for these tasks.

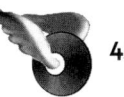

Listing 9.10 Editing and Deleting Hotspots in Unit **Main**

```
procedure TForm1.OptFile_EditHotspotClick(Sender: TObject);
    var
        Link_index : integer;
        Temp_hotspot : tHotspot_record;
    begin
        Hide_rectangle;
        Delete_region(The_region);

        with List_select_dialog do begin
            Caption := 'Load Saved Hotspot';
            Action := '&Load';
            Clear;
            Link_index := 0;
            seek(Image_link_file,Link_index);
            while not eof(Image_link_file) do begin
                read(Image_link_file,Temp_hotspot);
                with Temp_hotspot do
                    if Image = Current_image_filename then
                        Add(
                            Image + ' - ' + Target,
                            pointer(Link_index)
                            );
                inc(Link_index);
            end;
            if Execute then begin
                Current_hotspot := integer(Selected.Data);
                Load_hotspot_record(
                  Image_link_file,Current_hotspot,The_hotspot
                  );
                with The_hotspot do begin
                    Anchor_X := UL_X;
                    Anchor_Y := UL_Y;
                    End_X    := LR_X;
                    End_Y    := LR_Y;
                    end;
                OptFile_SaveHotspot.Enabled   := true;
                OptFile_DeleteHotspot.Enabled := true;
                OptMode_Test.Enabled          := true;
                end;
        end;

        if OptMode_Test.Checked = true then
            The_region := CreateRectRgn(Anchor_X,Anchor_Y,End_X,End_Y);
        Show_rectangle;
        end;


procedure TForm1.OptFile_DeleteHotspotClick(Sender: TObject);
    begin
        if Current_hotspot = -1 then begin
```

```
      MessageDlg(
        'There is no region to delete!',
        mtInformation, [mbOK], 0
        );
      exit;
      end;
  if MessageDlg(
        'Are you sure you want to delete this hotspot?',
        mtWarning, [mbYes,mbNo,mbCancel], 0
        )
    in
      [mrCancel,mrNo]
    then
      exit;

  Hide_rectangle;
  Delete_region(The_region);

  The_hotspot.Image := '';  { Marker for deleted slot. }
  Save_hotspot_record(
    Image_link_file,Current_hotspot,The_hotspot
    );

  Clear_for_new_image;
  OptMode_DefineClick(Self);
  OptFile_SaveHotspot.Enabled   := false;
  OptFile_DeleteHotspot.Enabled := false;
  OptMode_Test.Enabled          := false;
  end;
```

These routines are long, but relatively simple. Let's take them apart, piece by piece. The first thing we'll review is the hotspot handling when we load a new hotspot with the *Edit Saved Hotspot* menu option.

```
Hide_rectangle;
Delete_region(The_region);
:
{ Load a new hotspot for the image from the file. }
:
if OptMode_Test.Checked = true then
    The_region := CreateRectRgn(Anchor_X,Anchor_Y,End_X,End_Y);
Show_rectangle;
```

This bracketing code deletes any previous testing region, and re-creates it if the user is in Test mode. It also hides the old rectangle and shows the new one. That first step wasn't bad, was it?

Next, we set up the **List_select_dialog** we developed above.

```
Caption := 'Load Saved Hotspot';
Action  := '&Load';
```

```
Clear;
Link_index := 0;
seek(Image_link_file,Link_index);
while not eof(Image_link_file) do begin
    read(Image_link_file,Temp_hotspot);
    with Temp_hotspot do
        if Image = Current_image_filename then
            Add(
                Image + ' - ' + Target,
                pointer(Link_index)
                );
    inc(Link_index);
    end;
```

We are within a **with List_select_dialog** here, so the properties we're setting and methods we're calling belong to the **List_select_dialog**. We set its Form **Caption** and **Action_button** text, and then **Clear** the list box. (This clears the data list, too; you can see this in Listing 9.9.) We then read the existing hotspot file, loading the dialog box with a line showing the image filename and hotspot target for each record for the current image, and send along the **Link_index** itself as the data. Remember, **Clear**ing the dialog won't **Free** any objects or **StrDispose** any strings; fortunately, all we're sending is a raw value disguised as a **pointer**.

Next, we invoke the dialog box. If the user chooses a hotspot to edit, we must load it and set up the state variables to reflect the selected hotspot.

```
if Execute then begin
    Current_hotspot := integer(Selected.Data);
    Load_hotspot_record(
      Image_link_file,Current_hotspot,The_hotspot
      );
    with The_hotspot do begin
        Anchor_X := UL_X;
        Anchor_Y := UL_Y;
        End_X    := LR_X;
        End_Y    := LR_Y;
        end;
    OptFile_SaveHotspot.Enabled    := true;
    OptFile_DeleteHotspot.Enabled  := true;
    OptMode_Test.Enabled           := true;
    end;
```

We set the **Current_hotspot** index to the dialog's **Selected.Data**. You'll recall that we had disguised the file index as a **pointer**; now we take off the costume by casting it back to an **integer**. Then we call the **Hotspots** routine **Load_hotspot_record**, sending back the selected **Current_hotspot**. From **The_hotspot** that we have loaded, we set our **Anchor** and **End** points.

When we call **Show_rectangle** at the end of this routine, we'll show the loaded hotspot. Finally, we enable the menu options to save, delete, and test the hotspot.

Deleting hotspots is the only thing we have yet to cover. Again, it's a long hunk o' code, but it's simple. First, we can't delete a hotspot if the user hasn't chosen one, and we shouldn't delete the hotspot if the user doesn't want to take that step.

```
if Current_hotspot = -1 then begin
    MessageDlg(
      'There is no region to delete!',
      mtInformation, [mbOK], 0
      );
      exit;
      end;
if MessageDlg(
      'Are you sure you want to delete this hotspot?',
      mtWarning, [mbYes,mbNo,mbCancel], 0
      )
   in
     [mrCancel,mrNo]
   then
     exit;
```

If we make it past these tests, we can actually delete the hotspot.

```
Hide_rectangle;
Delete_region(The_region);

The_hotspot.Image := ''; { Marker for deleted slot. }
Save_hotspot_record(
   Image_link_file,Current_hotspot,The_hotspot
   );

Clear_for_new_image;
OptMode_DefineClick(Self);
OptFile_SaveHotspot.Enabled   := false;
OptFile_DeleteHotspot.Enabled := false;
OptMode_Test.Enabled          := false;
```

We hide the rectangle and delete any testing region we might have created. Then, to delete the hotspot, we just resave it to the file, with a marker saying that the space is free for someone else to use. This method, of course, never makes the file itself smaller, so you might want to write a "garbage collector" that rewrites the valid records in the file, compressing out unused slots. Finally, we reset our state variables with **Clear_for_new_image**, click our own *Define* menu option, and disable the saving, deleting, and testing of what is now an undefined hotspot. Listing 9.11 shows the entire Main unit.

Listing 9.11   The entire listing of unit Main

```
unit Main;

interface

uses
  Windows, Messages, SysUtils, Classes, Graphics, Controls, Forms, Dialogs,
  Menus, ExtCtrls;

type
  TForm1 = class(TForm)
    MainMenu1: TMainMenu;
    OptFile: TMenuItem;
    OptFile_LoadPicture: TMenuItem;
    OptFile_NewHotspot: TMenuItem;
    OptFile_EditHotspot: TMenuItem;
    OptFile_SaveHotspot: TMenuItem;
    OptFile_DeleteHotspot: TMenuItem;
    OptFile_Quit: TMenuItem;
    N1: TMenuItem;
    N2: TMenuItem;
    OptMode: TMenuItem;
    OptMode_Test: TMenuItem;
    OptMode_Define: TMenuItem;
    OpenDialog1: TOpenDialog;

    procedure FormCreate(Sender: TObject);
    procedure FormClose(Sender: TObject; var Action: TCloseAction);

    procedure FormMouseDown(Sender: TObject; Button: TMouseButton;
      Shift: TShiftState; X, Y: Integer);
    procedure FormMouseMove(Sender: TObject; Shift: TShiftState; X,
      Y: Integer);
    procedure FormMouseUp(Sender: TObject; Button: TMouseButton;
      Shift: TShiftState; X, Y: Integer);

    procedure OptFile_LoadPictureClick(Sender: TObject);
    procedure OptFile_NewHotspotClick(Sender: TObject);
    procedure OptFile_EditHotspotClick(Sender: TObject);
    procedure OptFile_SaveHotspotClick(Sender: TObject);
    procedure OptFile_DeleteHotspotClick(Sender: TObject);
    procedure OptFile_QuitClick(Sender: TObject);
    procedure OptMode_TestClick(Sender: TObject);
    procedure OptMode_DefineClick(Sender: TObject);
    procedure FormPaint(Sender: TObject);
  private
    { Private declarations }
  public
    { Public declarations }
  end;

var
  Form1: TForm1;
```

```
implementation

    uses
        MMSystem, DlgLoad, Hotspots;

{$R *.DFM}

procedure Delete_region(
  var The_region : HRGN
  );
    begin
        if The_region = 0 then exit;
        if DeleteObject(The_region) then
            The_region := 0
          else
            MessageDlg('Unable to delete region.',mtWarning,[mbOK],0);
        end;

var
    Image_link_file         : tHotspot_file;
    Current_hotspot         : integer;
    Current_image_filename  : string;
    Drawing_rectangle       : boolean;
    Anchor_X, Anchor_Y,
    End_X,    End_Y         : integer;
    The_region              : HRGN;
    The_hotspot             : tHotspot_record;
    The_image               : TImage;

var
    Rectangle_is_visible : boolean;

procedure Hide_rectangle;
    begin
        if Rectangle_is_visible then
            Form1.Canvas.Rectangle(Anchor_X,Anchor_Y,End_X,End_Y);
        Rectangle_is_visible := false;
        end;

procedure Show_rectangle;
    begin
        if not Rectangle_is_visible then
            Form1.Canvas.Rectangle(Anchor_X,Anchor_Y,End_X,End_Y);
        Rectangle_is_visible := true;
        end;

procedure Clear_for_new_image;
    begin
        Clear_hotspot(The_hotspot);
        Current_hotspot := -1; { Not loaded. }
        Anchor_X := 0; Anchor_Y := 0;
        End_X    := 0; End_Y    := 0;
        Drawing_rectangle := false;
        The_region := 0;
```

```
            Rectangle_is_visible := false;
        end;

procedure TForm1.FormCreate(Sender: TObject);
    begin
        assignFile(Image_link_file,
          ExtractFilePath(Application.ExeName)+'ImagLink.Dat'
          );
        {$I-}
        reset(Image_link_file);
        {$I+}
        if ioResult <> 0 then rewrite(Image_link_file);

        The_image := nil;
        Clear_for_new_image;
        end;

procedure TForm1.FormClose(Sender: TObject; var Action: TCloseAction);
    begin
        closeFile(Image_link_file);
        end;

procedure TForm1.FormMouseDown(Sender: TObject; Button: TMouseButton;
  Shift: TShiftState; X, Y: Integer);
    begin
        if  (not OptMode.Enabled)
          or
            (Current_image_filename = '')
          then begin
            mciExecute('play c:\Windows\Media\Ding.Wav');
            exit;
            end;
        if OptMode_Define.Checked then begin
            Canvas.Pen.Mode := pmNot;
            Canvas.Brush.Style := bsClear;
            Hide_rectangle; { The old one. }
            Anchor_X := X; Anchor_Y := Y;
            End_X    := X; End_Y    := Y;
            Show_rectangle; { This new, null, one. }
            Drawing_rectangle := true;
            end
          else
            { Test to see if click is in region. }
            if PtInRegion(The_region,X,Y) then
                mciExecute('play c:\Windows\Media\Tada.Wav')
              else
                mciExecute('play c:\Windows\Media\Ding.Wav');
        end;

procedure TForm1.FormMouseMove(Sender: TObject; Shift: TShiftState; X,
  Y: Integer);
    begin
        if not Drawing_rectangle then exit;
        Hide_rectangle;
```

```
            End_X := X; End_Y := Y;
            Show_rectangle;
            end;

procedure TForm1.FormMouseUp(Sender: TObject; Button: TMouseButton;
  Shift: TShiftState; X, Y: Integer);
     begin
         if not Drawing_rectangle then exit;
         End_X := X; End_Y := Y;
         Drawing_rectangle := false;
         OptFile_SaveHotspot.Enabled := true;
         OptMode_Test.Enabled        := true;
         end;

procedure TForm1.OptFile_LoadPictureClick(Sender: TObject);
     var
        Image : TImage;
     begin
         if not OpenDialog1.Execute then exit;
         Current_image_filename := OpenDialog1.Filename;

         Hide_rectangle;
         Delete_region(The_region);
         The_image.Free;
         The_image := TImage.Create(Self);
         with The_image do begin
             AutoSize := true;
             Picture.LoadFromFile(Current_image_filename);
             if Width > 100 then
                Self.ClientWidth := Width
               else
                Self.ClientWidth := 100;
             if Height > 100 then
                Self.ClientHeight := Height
               else
                Self.ClientHeight := 100;
             Self.Canvas.CopyRect(ClientRect,Canvas,ClientRect);
             end;
         Clear_for_new_image;

         OptFile_NewHotspot.Enabled    := true;
         OptFile_EditHotspot.Enabled   := true;
         OptFile_SaveHotspot.Enabled   := false;
         OptFile_DeleteHotspot.Enabled := false;
         OptMode.Enabled               := true;
         OptMode_Test.Enabled          := false;
         end;

procedure TForm1.OptFile_NewHotspotClick(Sender: TObject);
     begin
         Hide_rectangle;
         Delete_region(The_region);
         Clear_for_new_image;
         OptMode_DefineClick(Self);
```

```pascal
            OptFile_SaveHotspot.Enabled   := false;
            OptFile_DeleteHotspot.Enabled := false;
            OptMode_Test.Enabled          := false;
            end;

procedure TForm1.OptFile_EditHotspotClick(Sender: TObject);
    var
        Link_index : integer;
        Temp_hotspot : tHotspot_record;
    begin
        Hide_rectangle;
        Delete_region(The_region);

        with List_select_dialog do begin
            Caption := 'Load Saved Hotspot';
            Action := '&Load';
            Clear;
            Link_index := 0;
            seek(Image_link_file,Link_index);
            while not eof(Image_link_file) do begin
                read(Image_link_file,Temp_hotspot);
                with Temp_hotspot do
                    if Image = Current_image_filename then
                        Add(
                            Image + ' - ' + Target,
                            pointer(Link_index)
                            );
                inc(Link_index);
                end;
            if Execute then begin
                Current_hotspot := integer(Selected.Data);
                Load_hotspot_record(
                   Image_link_file,Current_hotspot,The_hotspot
                   );
                with The_hotspot do begin
                    Anchor_X := UL_X;
                    Anchor_Y := UL_Y;
                    End_X    := LR_X;
                    End_Y    := LR_Y;
                    end;
                OptFile_SaveHotspot.Enabled   := true;
                OptFile_DeleteHotspot.Enabled := true;
                OptMode_Test.Enabled          := true;
                end;
            end;

        if OptMode_Test.Checked = true then
            The_region := CreateRectRgn(Anchor_X,Anchor_Y,End_X,End_Y);
        Show_rectangle;
        end;

procedure TForm1.OptFile_SaveHotspotClick(Sender: TObject);
    var
        Temp : string;
```

```
begin
    if (Anchor_X = End_X) and (Anchor_Y = End_Y) then begin
        MessageDlg('No Region Defined.',mtWarning,[mbOK],0);
        exit;
        end;
    Hide_rectangle;
    Temp := Trim(
             InputBox(
               'Enter Target',
               'Enter a Hyperlink Target string of up to 128 characters: ',
               Trim(The_hotspot.Target)
               )
             );
    Show_rectangle;
    if Temp <> '' then with The_hotspot do begin
        Image := Current_image_filename;
        Target := Temp;
        if Anchor_X <= End_X then begin
            UL_X := Anchor_X; LR_X := End_X;
            end
          else begin
            UL_X := End_X; LR_X := Anchor_X;
            end;
        if Anchor_Y <= End_Y then begin
            UL_Y := Anchor_Y; LR_Y := End_Y;
            end
          else begin
            UL_Y := End_Y; LR_Y := Anchor_Y;
            end;
        Save_hotspot_record(
          Image_link_file,Current_hotspot,The_hotspot
          );
        end;
    end;

procedure TForm1.OptFile_DeleteHotspotClick(Sender: TObject);
    begin
    if Current_hotspot = -1 then begin
        MessageDlg(
          'There is no region to delete!',
          mtInformation, [mbOK], 0
          );
        exit;
        end;
    if  MessageDlg(
          'Are you sure you want to delete this hotspot?',
          mtWarning, [mbYes,mbNo,mbCancel], 0
          )
       in
         [mrCancel,mrNo]
       then
         exit;

    Hide_rectangle;
    Delete_region(The_region);
```

```
            The_hotspot.Image := '';  { Marker for deleted slot. }
            Save_hotspot_record(
              Image_link_file,Current_hotspot,The_hotspot
              );

            Clear_for_new_image;
            OptMode_DefineClick(Self);
            OptFile_SaveHotspot.Enabled   := false;
            OptFile_DeleteHotspot.Enabled := false;
            OptMode_Test.Enabled          := false;
          end;

procedure TForm1.OptFile_QuitClick(Sender: TObject);
    begin
        Close;
        end;

procedure TForm1.OptMode_TestClick(Sender: TObject);
    begin
        OptMode_Define.Checked := false;
        OptMode_Test.Checked   := true;
        The_region := CreateRectRgn(Anchor_X,Anchor_Y,End_X,End_Y);
        end;

procedure TForm1.OptMode_DefineClick(Sender: TObject);
    begin
        Delete_region(The_region);
        OptMode_Define.Checked := true;
        OptMode_Test.Checked   := false;
        end;

procedure TForm1.FormPaint(Sender: TObject);
    begin
        if The_image = nil then exit;
        with The_image do
            Self.Canvas.CopyRect(ClientRect,Canvas,ClientRect);
        Canvas.Pen.Mode := pmNot;
        Canvas.Brush.Style := bsClear;
        Rectangle_is_visible := false;
        Show_rectangle;
        end;

end.
```

What's Next?

Wow. Creating our rectangular hotspot editor was a big job. In our hyperimaging adventures, we've uncovered some powerful Windows programming techniques to help automate the process of defining hotspot regions.

We're now ready to move on and enter the next dimension of hyperimaging. When we arrive, you'll learn how to create a much more versatile hotspot editor for defining irregularly shaped hotspots.

Chapter 10

It's now time to explore real-world objects and create more functional hyperimaging projects.

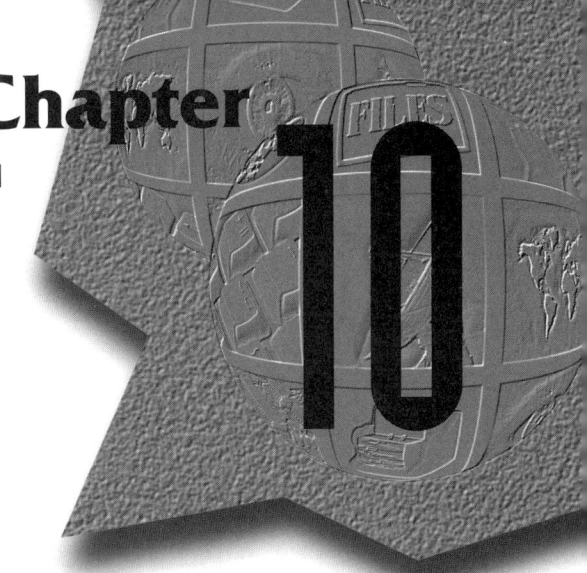

Hyperimaging: The Next Dimension

Dan Haygood

Imagine trying to bring the feel of the Grand Canyon into your home. You could hang up a big photograph in your living room, but that wouldn't be very interactive. You really want to *feel* like you're there—almost as if you could soar over the Canyon like an eagle, locate a hidden gorge, dive down into the Canyon, jump on a raft and splash down the Colorado River.

In Chapter 9, we learned to create rectangular hotspot regions. Unfortunately, the real world isn't made of rectangles. (Think how boring life would be if that were true!) To create multimedia adventures like the real-world Grand Canyon project, you'll need a way to jigsaw pictures of the real world into irregularly-shaped hotspots. Once you accomplish this task, you'll be able to click on any part of a picture and set off a multimedia event, like playing a video or zooming in for greater detail.

Mastering Irregular Hotspots

To bring the non-rectangular world of cars, planes, dinosaurs, and nature into our multimedia apps, we need to create irregularly-shaped hotspots. Let's begin by developing another hotspot editor for our multimedia construction set. For now, we'll start with the drawing and testing features. In the next project, we'll adapt the code we wrote in Chapter 9 for the rectangular hotspot editor, and use it with an editor for irregularly-shaped regions.

Hotspot II: Drawing Irregularly-Shaped Images

This project shows you how to draw irregularly-shaped images using the mouse, and then test the regions you've drawn.

1. Create a new project directory, *HotSpot2*, and an output subdirectory, *Bin*.
2. Open a new application, and in the *Project Options* dialog box, set its Application Title to "Hotspot II" and its Output Directory to "Bin".
3. You might want to take this opportunity to save the project in the *HotSpot2* project directory.
4. Add a menu to the project (Menu Table 10.1).
5. Modify the declaration of the class **TForm1** to include a public method, procedure **Line**. This code, and all of the code you'll add in the next steps, is shown in Listing 10.1.
6. Add the support routines **Dist** and **Delete_region** (familiar to us from Chapter 9), and declare the global variables needed to track polygonal regions.
7. Add the form's **OnMouseDown** and **OnMouseMove** event handlers to draw polygons.
8. Add an **OnPaint** event handler to keep the project looking good! This should give you a better understanding of the polygon's structure.
9. The Form, as well as the mouse event handlers, will need some initialization code, so add an **OnCreate** event handler and the **Init_for_new_poly** procedure. To end the program gracefully, we'll also need an **OnClose** handler.
10. Finally, enable the menu, adding **OptFile_New** and **OptFile_Quit** menu event handlers.

Hyperimaging: The Next Generation   **447**

> This project, HotSpot2.DPR, and all of its support files, can be found on the accompanying CD-ROM, in the directory \PROGRAMS\CHAP10\HOTSPOT2.

Running the Program—Testing the Polygon Hotspots

By running the *Hotspot II* program, you'll see that it starts in testing mode, as shown in Figure 10.1. To begin drawing a polygon, first choose *File | New Region* from the menu. The cursor will change, indicating you are in polygon-definition mode. Click and release the mouse button anywhere on the client area of the form. The first line segment will then follow your cursor until you click and release again, locking in the second point. Then the second line will follow the cursor. Add several sides to the figure. When you feel you've made a complex-enough region, like that drawn by Susan Haygood in Figure 10.1, place the cursor close to the first point and click again. The line that was following you will let go of the cursor and join the first vertex, sealing off the polygon. The program will go back to testing mode. To draw another polygon, you must first select *New* from the *File* menu.

To test the hotspot region once it is closed, click in and around your polygon region to prove that it works. Listen for *Ding* and *Tada*, as in *Hotspot I* from Chapter 9. To stop the program, click the Windows 95 "X", choose *Close* from the control menu of the form or select *Quit* from the *File* menu. If you stop the program from Delphi's IDE, you may end up closing your program after creating a testing region, but before deleting it; you are then relying on Delphi to clean up after your program. In general, this should be avoided.

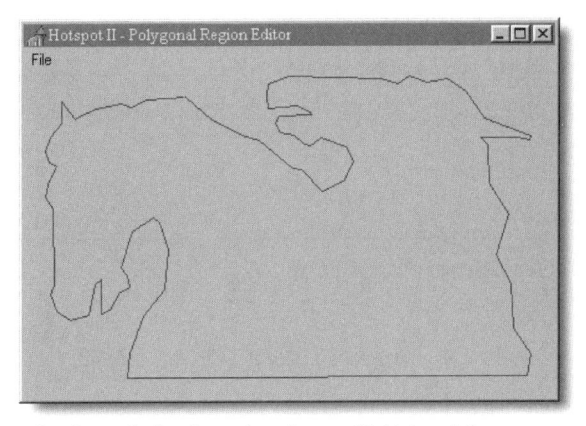

Figure 10.1   *Drawing irregularly-shaped regions with Hotspot II.*

Creating the Form

Begin by creating a new application. With the default Form, **Form1**, we won't need to do anything but **Caption** it: "Hotspot II - Polygonal Region Editor." Drag a MainMenu, **MainMenu1**, onto the form and set it up as shown in Table 10.1. After this, the rest of our work will be in the code, shown in Listing 10.1.

Listing 10.1 The Entire Unit *Main.Pas* for *Hotspot II*

```
unit Main;

interface

uses
  Windows, Messages, SysUtils, Classes, Graphics, Controls, Forms, Dialogs,
  Menus, ExtCtrls;

type
  TForm1 = class(TForm)
    MainMenu1: TMainMenu;
    OptFile: TMenuItem;
    OptFile_New: TMenuItem;
    OptFile_Quit: TMenuItem;

    procedure FormMouseDown(Sender: TObject; Button: TMouseButton;
      Shift: TShiftState; X, Y: Integer);
    procedure FormMouseMove(Sender: TObject; Shift: TShiftState; X,
      Y: Integer);

    procedure FormCreate(Sender: TObject);
    procedure FormClose(Sender: TObject; var Action: TCloseAction);

    procedure OptFile_NewClick(Sender: TObject);
    procedure OptFile_QuitClick(Sender: TObject);

    procedure FormPaint(Sender: TObject);
  private
    { Private declarations }
  public
    { Public declarations }
```

Table 10.1 The Menu **MainMenu1** for Hotspot II.

Name	Caption
OptFile	'File'
OptFile_New	'New Region'
OptFile_Quit	'Quit'

```pascal
    procedure Line(
      const P1, P2 : TPoint
      );
  end;

var
  Form1: TForm1;

implementation

uses
    MMSystem;

{$R *.DFM}

function Dist(
  const P1, P2 : TPoint
  ) : double;
    begin
        Dist := sqrt(sqr(P2.X - P1.X) + sqr(P2.Y - P1.Y));
        end;

procedure Delete_region(
  var The_region : HRGN
  );
    begin
        if The_region = 0 then exit;
        if DeleteObject(The_region) then
            The_region := 0
          else
            MessageDlg('Unable to delete region.',mtWarning,[mbOK],0);
        end;

const
    Max_vertex_count = 100;
var
    Vertices         : array[1..Max_vertex_count] of TPoint;
    Vertex_count     : integer;
    Prev_vertex      : TPoint;
    The_region       : HRGN;
    Drawing_polygon  : boolean;

procedure TForm1.Line(
  const P1, P2 : TPoint
  );
    begin with Canvas do begin
        with P1 do MoveTo(X,Y);
        with P2 do LineTo(X,Y);
        end; end;

procedure TForm1.FormCreate(Sender: TObject);
    begin
        Cursor := crArrow;
```

```
            Canvas.Pen.Mode := pmNot;
            The_region := 0;
            Vertex_count := 0;
            Drawing_polygon := false;
            end;

procedure TForm1.FormClose(Sender: TObject; var Action: TCloseAction);
    begin
        Delete_region(The_region);
        end;

procedure Init_for_new_poly;
    var
        I : integer;
    begin
        if Vertex_count >= 2 then with Form1.Canvas do begin
            with Vertices[1] do MoveTo(X,Y);
            for I := 2 to Vertex_count do
                with Vertices[I] do LineTo(X,Y);
            if not Drawing_polygon then
                with Vertices[1] do LineTo(X,Y); { Do final segment. }
            end;
        Vertex_count := 0;
        Delete_region(The_region);
        Drawing_polygon := true;
        Form1.Cursor := crDrag;
        end;

procedure TForm1.FormMouseDown(Sender: TObject; Button: TMouseButton;
  Shift: TShiftState; X, Y: Integer);

    function Vertex_finishes_polygon(
      const V : TPoint
      ) : boolean;
        begin
            Vertex_finishes_polygon :=
                (Vertex_count = Max_vertex_count)
              or {else}
                (
                    (Vertex_count > 2)
                  and {then}
                    (Dist(V,Vertices[1]) < 10)
                );
            if result then begin
                { Erase previous line, and close the polygon. }
                Line(Vertices[Vertex_count],Prev_vertex);
                Line(Vertices[Vertex_count],Vertices[1]);
                end
              else begin
                { Add the vertex. }
                inc(Vertex_count);
                Vertices[Vertex_count] := V;
                end;
            end;
```

```
    var
        Vertex : TPoint;
    begin
        if Drawing_polygon then begin
            { Start new side from this vertex if still open. }
            Vertex := Point(X,Y);
            if Vertex_finishes_polygon(Vertex) then begin
                Drawing_polygon := false;
                Cursor := crArrow;
                The_region :=
                    CreatePolygonRgn(Vertices,Vertex_count,ALTERNATE);
                end;
            Prev_vertex := Vertex;
            end
          else
            { Test to see if click is in region. }
            if PtInRegion(The_region,X,Y) then
                mciExecute('play c:\Windows\Media\Tada.Wav')
              else
                mciExecute('play c:\Windows\Media\Ding.Wav');
        end;

procedure TForm1.FormMouseMove(Sender: TObject; Shift: TShiftState; X,
  Y: Integer);
    begin
        if (not Drawing_polygon) or (Vertex_count = 0) then exit;
        Line(Vertices[Vertex_count],Prev_vertex);
        Prev_vertex := Point(X,Y);
        Line(Vertices[Vertex_count],Prev_vertex);
        end;

procedure TForm1.OptFile_NewClick(Sender: TObject);
    begin
        { Erase previous line. }
        if Drawing_polygon and (Vertex_count > 0) then
            Line(Vertices[Vertex_count],Prev_vertex);
        Init_for_new_poly;
        end;

procedure TForm1.OptFile_QuitClick(Sender: TObject);
    begin
        Close;
        end;

procedure TForm1.FormPaint(Sender: TObject);
    var
        I : integer;
    begin
        if Vertex_count >= 2 then with Canvas do begin
            with Vertices[1] do MoveTo(X,Y);
            for I := 2 to Vertex_count do
                with Vertices[I] do LineTo(X,Y);
            if not Drawing_polygon then
                with Vertices[1] do LineTo(X,Y); { Do final segment. }
```

```
            end;
       end;

end.
```

You've no doubt noticed some code *above* the implementation. We have declared an additional method to our form which allows us to easily draw lines from end-point to end-point.

```
TForm1 = class(TForm)

:

public
    { Public declarations }
    procedure Line(
      const P1, P2 : TPoint
      );
  end;
```

We could have written a procedure outside of the **TForm1** class, and told it to draw lines specifically on **Form1**'s **Canvas**. However, since this is a pure extension of a Form's functionality, it is stylistically better to add it to the class.

With that declared, let's look at a couple of other general support routines, too.

```
uses
    MMSystem;

{ some code omitted here for brevity }

function Dist(
  const P1, P2 : TPoint
  ) : double;
    begin
        Dist := sqrt(sqr(P2.X - P1.X) + sqr(P2.Y - P1.Y));
        end;

procedure Delete_region(
  var The_region : HRGN
  );
    begin
        if The_region = 0 then exit;
        if DeleteObject(The_region) then
            The_region := 0
          else
            MessageDlg('Unable to delete region.',mtWarning,[mbOK],0);
        end;

const
```

```
    Max_vertex_count = 100;
var
    Vertices         : array[1..Max_vertex_count] of TPoint;
    Vertex_count     : integer;
    Prev_vertex      : TPoint;
    The_region       : HRGN;
    Drawing_polygon  : boolean;
procedure TForm1.Line(
  const P1, P2 : TPoint
  );
    begin with Canvas do begin
        with P1 do MoveTo(X,Y);
        with P2 do LineTo(X,Y);
        end; end;
```

Function **Dist** you probably remember from Euclidean Geometry as the distance between two points on a two-dimensional plane.

We saw **Delete_region** in Chapter 9. To refresh your memory, we will be testing hotspot hits with genuine Windows GDI regions that are accessed through a handle, and that must be destroyed to conserve GDI resources when their job is complete. **Delete_region** accomplishes that destruction while allowing us to be a little careless about knowing whether or not we actually created a region.

Line is the method we declared above. It has lots of pesky **with** statements that some might argue make the source code a little harder to read, especially since any optimizing compiler worth its shrink-wrap won't generate redundant references. Others like to see the fields alone, without the containing record. Just be guided by your own taste.

Tucked in just before the body of **Line** are the unit-global variables we'll be using to track our polygon as it is drawn. (They're stuck in here because they follow the routines **Dist** and **Delete_region**, prime candidates to move out to a general-purpose support unit, but before the methods of **TForm1**.) The polygon itself is represented as a fixed-size array of **Vertices** and a **Vertex_count**. **Prev_vertex** is the location of the last vertex to which a line was drawn, as a "rubber-banded" edge is dragged across the screen in the **OnMouseMove** handler. **Drawing_polygon** indicates that the polygon is actually being drawn, and **The_region** is a region created for testing the polygon for mouse hits once it's closed.

Drawing Polygons

In this project, we'll use the **OnMouseDown** and **OnMouseMove** events to draw the outlines of our polygon hotspot regions. In contrast to the editor in

Chapter 9, this drawing program doesn't use the **OnMouseUp** event to complete a figure.

When we were drawing rectangles, we needed to define only two points, opposite corners. The procedure for drawing a rectangle meshed nicely with the **Down—Move—Up** sequence of events. Unfortunately, it takes more than two points to define a non-rectangular polygon, or even an off-axis rectangle. To mark each corner, or vertex, we need to click and release the mouse button repeatedly—which means we can't use the **OnMouseUp** event to wrap things up.

So, when is a polygon complete? When it's closed. For each mouse click, we'll add a new vertex to the polygon and check the distance to the starting point. We'll close the loop, either when the latest click comes within 10 pixels of the starting point, or when we completely fill up the array in which we're storing the vertices—whichever comes first.

The **FormMouseDown** event procedure has some similarities to the code in *Hotspot I*, with one big difference.

```
procedure TForm1.FormMouseDown(Sender: TObject; Button: TMouseButton;
  Shift: TShiftState; X, Y: Integer);

    { function Vertex_finishes_polygon }

    var
        Vertex : TPoint;
    begin
        if Drawing_polygon then begin
            { Start new side from this vertex if still open. }
            Vertex := Point(X,Y);
            if Vertex_finishes_polygon(Vertex) then begin
                Drawing_polygon := false;
                Cursor := crArrow;
                The_region :=
                    CreatePolygonRgn(Vertices,Vertex_count,ALTERNATE);
                end;
            Prev_vertex := Vertex;
            end
        else
            { Test to see if click is in region. }
            if PtInRegion(The_region,X,Y) then
                mciExecute('play c:\Windows\Media\Tada.Wav')
              else
                mciExecute('play c:\Windows\Media\Ding.Wav');
        end;
```

In *Hotspot I*, the **OnMouseDown** event erased the previously-drawn rectangle by drawing over it with a **Pen.Mode** of **psNot**. It then set the new anchor and end points. The version of **FormMouseDown** in this program doesn't draw or erase anything, leaving that task to the **OnMouseMove** handler. Until the polygon is finished, **FormMouseDown** calls a general function named **Vertex_finishes_polygon** at each click of the mouse button.

```
function Vertex_finishes_polygon(
  const V : TPoint
  ) : boolean;
    begin
        Vertex_finishes_polygon :=
           (Vertex_count = Max_vertex_count)
         or {else}
           (
              (Vertex_count > 2)
            and {then}
              (Dist(V,Vertices[1]) < 10)
           );
        if result then begin
           { Erase previous line, and close the polygon. }
           Line(Vertices[Vertex_count],Prev_vertex);
           Line(Vertices[Vertex_count],Vertices[1]);
           end
         else begin
           { Add the vertex. }
           inc(Vertex_count);
           Vertices[Vertex_count] := V;
           end;
    end;
```

First, this function checks to see if the polygon has more than two vertices and the click is near the starting point, or if the array is full. So, you can see we just lied—if the click closes the polygon, our **FormMouseDown** handler *will* draw the closing segment (using its subroutine **Vertex_finishes_polygon**) after erasing the last segment drawn by the **OnMouseMove** handler. If the click doesn't close the polygon, it's just added to the array.

Finally, back in **FormMouseMove**, if the **Vertex_finishes_polygon**, we indicate to the other routines that we are no longer **Drawing_polygon**. We indicate this fact to the user by changing the cursor to an ordinary **crArrow**. (As we'll see later, the user started drawing with a different cursor.) We then create **The_region** for hit testing.

To create the region, we call another powerful Widows GDI function, **CreatePolygonRgn**. This function returns the handle to a region defined by the **TPoint** list you pass it, and the count of the items in the list. The first parameter is an *untyped **var*** parameter; this Pascal extension allows you to pass any type of data structure you want to the routine. Since the GDI is expecting a sequence of points, it's a good thing we are sending an **array of**

TPoint. The last parameter determines how the GDI will determine the areas both inside and outside of a complex, overlapping polygon. The best way to describe the two allowable values, **ALTERNATE** and **WINDING**, is to show them to you in Figure 10.2.

The **OnMouseMove** event handler, **FormMouseMove**, is a routine we might expect to be complicated, simply because it does the lion's share of the graphics work. But it's almost trivial.

```
procedure TForm1.FormMouseMove(Sender: TObject; Shift: TShiftState; X,
  Y: Integer);
    begin
        if (not Drawing_polygon) or (Vertex_count = 0) then exit;
        Line(Vertices[Vertex_count],Prev_vertex);
        Prev_vertex := Point(X,Y);
        Line(Vertices[Vertex_count],Prev_vertex);
        end;
```

After determining if a polygon is being drawn, or if the first point of a polygon has yet to be clicked, this first draws a **Line** that re-**pmNot**s the line drawn to the **Prev_vertex**, effectively erasing it. After setting the **Prev_vertex** to the current location, it then draws a new line to the current location.

You might be asking yourself how this works on the very first **OnMouseMove** event. The **OnMouseDown** event both added its location as the first element of **Vertices** and set **Prev_vertex** to this location. Thus, the first **Line** draws from one point to the same point; this zero-length line is sometimes referred to as a *null line*. Like the null rectangle described in Chapter 9, Windows simply doesn't draw anything. It won't even light up the pixel at the point, because it knows that the length of the line should be zero—nil—nada—blank, and thus, not there at all.

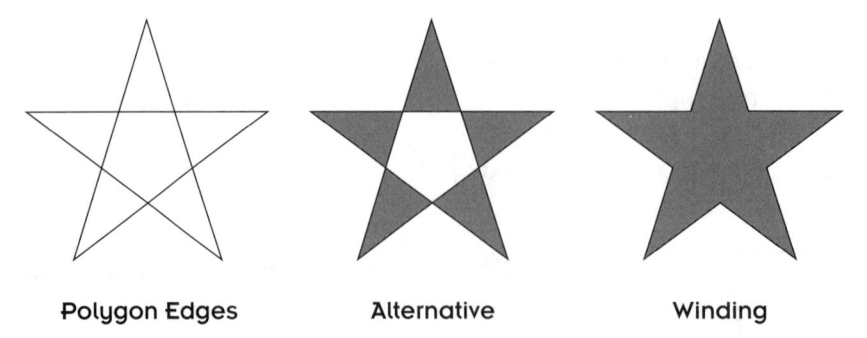

Polygon Edges   **Alternative**   **Winding**

***Figure 10.2** **Alternate** and **winding** interpretations of an overlapping polygon.*

Redrawing Polygons

Event-driven programming really begins to test us when we write drawing programs. For predictable results, we have to consider not only how the various mouse events need to behave, but also the things that can happen to our client area during and after the drawing process. What happens, for example, when you bring the hotspot editor back to the foreground after switching to another application? We expect the program to return the picture to the state it was in before we covered it. And to do that, it's going to need an **OnPaint** event handler.

```
procedure TForm1.FormPaint(Sender: TObject);
    var
        I : integer;
    begin
        if Vertex_count >= 2 then with Canvas do begin
            with Vertices[1] do MoveTo(X,Y);
            for I := 2 to Vertex_count do
                with Vertices[I] do LineTo(X,Y);
            if not Drawing_polygon then
                with Vertices[1] do LineTo(X,Y); { Do final segment. }
            end;
    end;
```

FormPaint will redraw the outline of the polygonal hotspot whenever the client area becomes uncovered or changes size.

Initialization and Clean-up Code

Before we can do any drawing or any painting, we need to set up our variables. We'll do this when our form is created.

```
procedure TForm1.FormCreate(Sender: TObject);
    begin
        Cursor := crArrow;
        Canvas.Pen.Mode := pmNot;
        The_region := 0;
        Vertex_count := 0;
        Drawing_polygon := false;
        end;
```

The first thing we'll do is set the Form's **Cursor** to **crArrow**. This is just the normal mouse pointer cursor. Since this indicates to users that they are in testing mode, we need to set up the rest of our state variables to indicate that there really is *no* available polygon to test yet. Consequently, **The_region** is set to zero (sometimes referred to as a *null* or *nil handle*), the **Vertex_count** is set to zero, and we signify that we are not currently drawing a polygon by setting **Drawing_polygon** to **false**.

If the user should click the mouse button at this point, the **FormMouseDown** handler will try to test the click against the null region of the non-existent polygon. Fortunately, the GDI routine **PtInRegion** behaves predictably when passed a null handle; it realizes the point can't possibly be in the region if the region doesn't exist, and therefore returns **false**.

This is also an excellent place to set the Form's **Canvas.Pen.Mode** to **pmNot**. Since we will not be changing the **Pen** ourselves, we should be able to safely set it only once. This is a departure from the technique shown in Chapter 9—there, we were almost paranoid about the state of our **Pen**. *Hotspot II* shows us that we don't need to be so protective.

When we close the Form, we have only one task: Deleting any testing region we may have created.

```
procedure TForm1.FormClose(Sender: TObject; var Action: TCloseAction);
    begin
        Delete_region(The_region);
        end;
```

Once we create the Form, the user will eventually pick the *New* option from the *File* menu. When this happens, we'll need to be able to set up our drawing variables and our form to draw a new polygon. The procedure **Init_for_new_poly** accomplishes this.

```
procedure Init_for_new_poly;
    var
        I : integer;
    begin
        if Vertex_count >= 2 then with Form1.Canvas do begin
            with Vertices[1] do MoveTo(X,Y);
            for I := 2 to Vertex_count do
                with Vertices[I] do LineTo(X,Y);
            if not Drawing_polygon then
                with Vertices[1] do LineTo(X,Y); { Do final segment. }
            end;
        Vertex_count := 0;
        Delete_region(The_region);
        Drawing_polygon := true;
        Form1.Cursor := crDrag;
        end;
```

We've seen the first part before, in **FormPaint**. Hey, wasn't that used to re*draw* the polygon? Here, we use exactly the same code to *erase* the polygon—remember, we're using the **pmNot** pen. We then clear the polygon by setting its **Vertex_count** to zero; we delete **The_region** with which we've been testing; we tell the mouse event handlers that we're **Drawing_polygon**; and to show this to the user, we set **Form1**'s **Cursor** to **crDrag**. If you were integrating this into a production environment, you might want to use a resource editor to create your own crosshair cursor. Unfortunately, the built-in cursor that sounds like it might work, **crCross**, sometimes takes on different forms on different systems.

Starting a New Polygon

At last, we are ready to handle the user's request to start a new polygonal region, with **OptFile_New**.

```
procedure TForm1.OptFile_NewClick(Sender: TObject);
    begin
        { Erase previous line. }
        if Drawing_polygon and (Vertex_count > 0) then
            Line(Vertices[Vertex_count],Prev_vertex);
        Init_for_new_poly;
    end;

procedure TForm1.OptFile_QuitClick(Sender: TObject);
    begin
        Close;
    end;
```

With all of the groundwork we've laid, all we need to do is erase the last rubber-banded side of the polygon the user could have been drawing, and call **Init_for_new_poly**. Here is one of the contingencies you need to watch out for when you design event-driven programs. It may not be obvious to you, at first glance, that the user *could* start a new polygon, even though the one that was being worked on wasn't finished. There are other ways to handle this—you could simply disable the *File | New Region* option while **Drawing_polygon** is **true**—but before you can come up with any solution to an interaction problem, you have to look for it and know it's there.

Of course, quitting with **OptFile_Quit** is as simple as closing the Form; since the rest of our clean-up code (all one line of it) is in **FormClose**.

Adding Polygon Hotspots to Images

Now we'll combine what we learned in our last two projects, *Hotspot I* and *Hotspot II*, to write a polygon editor that lets us draw irregularly-shaped polygons over bitmapped images and save them in a data file. In the next chapter, we'll pull them back out and put them to work in our hypermedia system.

Although this program resembles *Hotspot I* in its operation, and *Hotspot II* in its drawing technique, it varies considerably from these programs in its actual implementation. We'll highlight the most significant differences here, but don't make any assumptions about the housekeeping procedures. One flaky flag can break the whole thing. Study the code.

Watch for two important differences between this and the two previous projects. Most importantly, we'll implement our hotspot storage using Delphi's *BDE* (the Borland Database Engine) instead of a simple datafile. This buys us a couple of advantages in storage space and flexibility, at the cost of the added complexity (albeit minimal) of managing a database. Secondly, the concept of a drawing or testing "mode" has been extended to support revision of existing hotspots; to help the user, we've added a lot of feedback code.

Hotspot III: The Powerful (Irregular) Hotspot Editor

This editor draws, saves, retrieves, and revises irregular polygonal hotspot regions on BMP images. This would be the third time we've walked you through the process of creating this project, so we won't hold your hand this time.

1. You'll need the same kind of form-and-menu window we've been working with, along with an **OpenDialog** control, as in *Hotspot I*. Of course, we put the project in directory *Hotspot3*, and set the project's options to output to a subdirectory, *Hotspot3\Bin*. We'll title the project "Hotspot III".

2. Like *Hotspot I*, this project uses the unit **Hotspots** and the unit/form combination, **DlgLoad** (our list-selection dialog box). **Hotspots** changes considerably; **DlgLoad** is unchanged from *Hotspot I*. The main project unit is, of course, named **Main**.

3. Set up the hotspot handling routines in Hotspots. This will define how we will use hotspots, as well as how we will interact with the BDE to save and retrieve hotspots.

4. With declarations of hotspots complete, we can then implement the **OnMouse...** event handlers to draw polygons. The code also includes some support routines, including a public method of our form, **Line** (introduced in *Hotspot II*), as well as polygon-drawing initialization and completion code.

Hyperimaging: The Next Generation 461

5. Finally, connect up the menu to save and retrieve hotspots to and from the database.

The **DlgLoad** unit is shown in Chapter 9, Listing 9.9. **Hotspots** is given in Listing 10.2, and **Main** is shown in its entirety in Listing 10.3. **Main**'s **Form1** properties are trivial, following along the lines of *Hotspot I* in Chapter 9; the MainMenu control's options and properties are given in Menu Table 10.2.

> *This project, HotSpot3.DPR, and all of its support files, can be found on the accompanying CD-ROM in the directory \PROGRAMS\CHAP10\HOTSPOT3.*

Running the Hotspot Editor

When you start *Hotspot III*, you'll see the form shown in Figure 10.3—only without the image loaded. The first time you run this program, it will create a Paradox database called *Hotspots*, which is stored in several files named **Hotspots** with the extensions **.db**, **.mb**, **.px**, **.val**, **.xgo**, and **.ygo**. The BDE provides an implementation-independent interface to the database system, so we really don't care what those files are. Had we requested a dBASE table, we'd have a different file scheme.

Before you can begin drawing polygons, you must first load a picture using *File | Load Picture*. Use the resulting dialog box to choose a bitmap file (We used *Hibisc2.BMP*, in the directory *\MEDIA\IMAGES* on the CD ROM.)

Figure 10.3   *Running Hotspot III.*

After starting a new hotspot (*File | New Hotspot*), draw a polygon around some portion of the image, and the choose *File | Save Hotspot*. The program prompts you to enter a hyperlink target. For now, enter anything; we'll create working target strings in the next chapter. When you click on OK, the program will add a new record to the *Hotspots* database.

You'll notice that once you have a hotspot defined, the *Hotspot* menu option is enabled. Here, you have a choice between testing the region (*Hotspot | Test Region*) and re-defining the region (*Hotspot | Re-define Region*). If you've just made a new hotspot, re-defining the region will start you out as if you had chosen *File | New Hotspot*. If you've chosen to edit a saved hotspot (*File | Edit Saved Hotspot*) "however," you'll still be working with the same hotspot, so you'll be able to re-save it.

Of course, you must properly terminate the program to dispose of any active GDI region. Simply choose *File | Quit*, or choose *Close* from the window's *Control* menu, or click the Windows 95 "X". (If you stop the program from Delphi's IDE, there's a chance the region won't be destroyed.) That's all there is to it.

Representing and Storing Polygonal Hotspots

In *Hotspot I*, we used Delphi's ordinary file I/O to store records in a binary data file. We used this record:

```
tHotspot_record = record
    Image       : string[128];
    Target      : string[128];
    UL_X, UL_Y,
    LR_X, LR_Y  : integer;
    end;
```

We then used read and write to retrieve and save records in the data file. To use the same method for the polygonal regions we developed in *Hotspot II*, we'll create a hypothetical structure.

```
tPolygon_record = record
    Image         : string[128];
    Target        : string[128];
    Vertex_count  : integer;
    Vertices      : array[1..100] of TPoint;
    end;
```

Although this looks slightly more elegant without those individual corner coordinates, it's much larger. Each **tHotspot_record** was only 274 bytes, the size of the two **string** fields and their length byte, and four four-byte **integer**s. A record of type **tPolygon_record** would fill 1062 bytes, regardless of whether it held 3 vertices or 98 vertices. Remember, a **TPoint** consists of **X** and **Y** four-byte integers. That's 800 bytes in the **Vertices**!

We could split the record into two structures, and therefore, two files: one to hold the image filename and target string, and one to hold individual vertices. Then we could store only as many points as were needed to define each polygon. To keep track of the vertex records, we could use a linked-list structure in the file. If that sounds like a lot of work—believe us, it is!

Even if we were to get all of that working, we would still have to figure out ways to sort and search the primary file and to manage deleted records in both files. Fortunately, Delphi offers us an alternative to building our own database manager, the Borland Database Engine. This Engine enables us to maintain databases in a number of formats—Paradox, dBASE, ASCII (to name a few)—through a relatively simple object-oriented mechanism that doesn't change, regardless of the underlying database representation. We can use simple methods to insert, edit, and delete records—all with built-in sorting. And, to top it all off, the BDE supports a special binary field, the **TBLObField** (**T**ype **B**inary **L**arge **Ob**ject **Field**), in which we may store *blobs* than can vary in length from record to record.

Given **TBLObField**, we can transfer only **Vertex_count** elements of the **Vertices** array to the database record's blob field, and store only the information we need to re-create the region. We'll do a couple of other nice things for the database: First, computers work well with powers of two, but the size of a 128-character string is really 129 bytes. So we'll declare a **tName** type with a maximum character length of 127 bytes, instead, for a total length of 2^7 bytes. Secondly, since many hotspots could refer to the same target, even on the same image, we'll need a unique identifier for each hotspot. In *Hotspot I*, this was the **Current_hotspot** file-seek index. We'll move that variable into our hotspot record, and it will become the *primary key* of our database. Here is our final hotspot record, **tHotspot**:

```
const
    Max_vertex_count = 100;

type
    tName = string[127];
    tHotspot = record
        ID            : integer;
        Image         : tName;
        Target        : tName;
        Vertex_count  : integer;
        Vertices      : array[1..Max_vertex_count] of TPoint;
        end;
```

The unit **Hotspots** is used to manipulate **tHotspot**, and includes the declaration of **tHotspot** and routines to clear a hotspot, as well as to add, retrieve, and delete hotspots in the database. It is also used to create the database from scratch, in code. (Delphi provides ways to define databases using visual tools and provides visual controls for dropping database-bound fields onto your forms. This is a lot of overkill for us, and whole books can be written about the techniques; it's easier for us to do it in pure code.) This unit is shown in Listing 10.2.

Listing 10.2   The unit *Hotspots.Pas*

```
unit Hotspots;

interface

uses
    Windows, DBTables;

const
    Max_vertex_count = 100;

type
    tName = string[127];
    tHotspot = record
        ID            : integer;
        Image         : tName;
        Target        : tName;
        Vertex_count  : integer;
        Vertices      : array[1..Max_vertex_count] of TPoint;
        end;

    tHotspot_table = class(TTable)
        procedure Establish;
        procedure Save(
          var Hotspot : tHotspot { in.all / out.ID }
          );
        procedure Load(
          var Hotspot : tHotspot
          );
        procedure Delete(
          const Hotspot : tHotspot {in.ID / out.ID }
          );
        end;

procedure Clear_hotspot(
  var  Hotspot : tHotspot
  );

implementation
```

```
procedure Clear_hotspot(
  var Hotspot : tHotspot
  );
    begin
        fillchar(Hotspot,sizeof(Hotspot),0);
        end;

procedure tHotspot_table.Establish;
    { Must have properties DatabaseName and TableName
      set already. }
    var
        F : file;
    begin
        assignfile(F,DatabaseName + TableName + '.DB');
        {$I-}
        reset(F,1);
        {$I+}
        if ioResult = 0 then
            closefile(F)
          else begin
            Active    := False;
            TableType := ttParadox;
            with FieldDefs do begin
                Clear;
                Add('ID',      ftAutoInc, 0,             true);
                Add('Image',   ftString,  sizeof(tName), true);
                Add('Target',  ftString,  sizeof(tName), true);
                Add('Vertices', ftBLOb,   0,             true);
                end;
            with IndexDefs do begin
                Clear;
                Add('By_ID',
                    'ID',[ixPrimary,ixUnique]);
                Add('By_Image_Target',
                    'Image;Target',[ixCaseInsensitive]);
                end;
            CreateTable;
            end;
        end;

procedure tHotspot_table.Save(
  var Hotspot : tHotspot { in.all / out.ID }
  );
    var
        V_stream : TMemoryStream;
    begin with Hotspot do begin
        if ID = 0 then begin
            { New record -
              Don't care about key or current record. }
            Open;
            Insert;
            end
          else begin
```

```
                    { Update existing record. }
                    IndexName := '';
                    Open;
                    SetKey;
                    FieldByName('ID').AsInteger := ID;
                    GotoKey;
                    Edit;
                    end;
                FieldByName('Image') .AsString := Image;
                FieldByName('Target').AsString := Target;
                V_stream := TMemoryStream.Create;
                try
                    V_stream.Write(Vertices,Vertex_count * sizeof(TPoint));
                    V_stream.Seek(0,soFromBeginning);
                    TBLObField(FieldByName('Vertices'))
                      .LoadFromStream(V_stream);
                    Post;
                    ID := FieldByName('ID').AsInteger;
                finally
                    V_stream.Free;
                    Close;
                end;
            end; end;

procedure tHotspot_table.Load(
  var Hotspot : tHotspot
  );
    var
        V_stream : TMemoryStream;
    begin with Hotspot do begin
        IndexName := '';
        Open;
        SetKey;
        FieldByName('ID').AsInteger := ID;
        GotoKey;
        Image := FieldByName('Image') .AsString;
        Target := FieldByName('Target').AsString;
        V_stream := TMemoryStream.Create;
        TBLObField(FieldByName('Vertices'))
          .SaveToStream(V_stream);
        Vertex_count := V_stream.Size div sizeof(TPoint);
        V_stream.Seek(0,soFromBeginning);
        V_stream.Read(Vertices,V_stream.Size);
        V_stream.Free;
        Close;
        end; end;

procedure tHotspot_table.Delete(
  const Hotspot : tHotspot
  );
    begin
        IndexName := '';
        Open;
        SetKey;
```

```
            FieldByName('ID').AsInteger := Hotspot.ID;
            GotoKey;
            inherited Delete;
            Close;
        end;

end.
```

Building the Hotspot Database

Unlike ordinary binary data files, BDE databases are not built from records defined with a **type** declaration. Instead, the BDE views a database as collections of *field objects*, called *table objects*. We will only need to work with one table, *Hotspots*. Since many database representations use many files, the BDE views the database itself as an ordinary file directory. This directory's name *is* the database name. In your other reading, you'll come across the concept of an *alias*. This is a formal name that can be used in place of a directory name; however, it needs to be specially set up in the BDE, so we'll just use the application's directory as the database name. The table's files, all named *Hotspots* with different extensions, will end up residing in this directory.

Let's look at the technique for creating a table in code. The BDE doesn't require anything to be defined at the database level as long as a directory exists in which the database can reside, so we are able to concentrate only on the creation of a table. The database level will come along for the ride without any work on our part.

A **TTable** object has three properties we must set before we can do anything: **TableType** tells the BDE which implementation of a database it should create and use, while **DatabaseName** and **TableName** actually name it.

With these out of the way, we need to describe the table. The two key properties here are the **FieldDefs** and the **IndexDefs**. Yes, these are plural—they are array properties, and as objects themselves, they have their own **Add** method (so we won't have to muck with array references). **FieldDefs.Add** takes four parameters: a name, a data type, the byte-size (used for types without a natural size), and a flag indicating if the field is required in each record. **IndexDefs.Add** takes a name, a field-name list of the fields that are concatenated to rank records for the index, and a set of attributes that describe how the index behaves (ascending or descending, only unique entries allowed, and so forth).

After adding the appropriate fields and indices, creating the table is as simple as calling the table's **CreateTable** method. (Who would've guessed?)

As we've mentioned before, we want to create a Paradox table in the application's directory named *Hotspots*. That takes care of our first three properties. We set up the names in the main program's **FormCreate** event handler:

```
DatabaseName := ExtractFilePath(Application.ExeName);
TableName    := 'Hotspots';
```

In the method **Establish**, we specify the table type:

```
TableType := ttParadox;
```

The fields we'll store will be based on the fields of our **tHotspot** record's fields. **ID** is an auto-incrementing field; each time we add a record, it receives the next serial number in line, starting with one (1). This field is a four-byte integer, so it will be a long time before we run out, and since we know it's four bytes, we don't need to specify a size. The **Image** and **Target** string fields are specifically sized to the size of a **tName**. The **Vertices** blob field is sized for each individual record, which eliminates the need to specify a size. All of the fields are required.

What happened to the **Vertex_count**? That's easy. Blob fields already know how big they are; and since we know a vertex is the size of a **TPoint**, we just need to make sure we store the right number of bytes when we save a record. We only have to divide the blob field's size by the size of a **TPoint** when we read a record to calculate **Vertex_count**.

We'll use two indices: **By_ID** is our primary, unique key, and is composed of the field **ID**. **By_Image_Target** is a secondary index we'll use to retrieve records in order when we build a list of targets for editing.

```
procedure tHotspot_table.Establish;
    { Must have properties DatabaseName and TableName
      set already. }
    var
        F : file;
    begin
        assignfile(F,DatabaseName + TableName + '.DB');
        {$I-}
        reset(F,1);
        {$I+}
        if ioResult = 0 then
            closefile(F)
          else begin
            Active    := False;
            TableType := ttParadox;
            with FieldDefs do begin
                Clear;
                Add('ID',       ftAutoInc, 0,              true);
                Add('Image',    ftString,  sizeof(tName),  true);
                Add('Target',   ftString,  sizeof(tName),  true);
                Add('Vertices', ftBLOb,    0,              true);
                end;
```

```
    with IndexDefs do begin
        Clear;
        Add('By_ID',
          'ID',[ixPrimary,ixUnique]);
        Add('By_Image_Target',
          'Image;Target',[ixCaseInsensitive]);
        end;
    CreateTable;
    end;
end;
```

You've probably noticed that we actually coded a subclass, called **tHotspot_table**, even though we've been discussing **TTable**. That's because we don't really want to deal with the database on its own terms in our application. We want only a few functions with each one using several of **TTable**'s methods. By encapsulating them in our own methods, our main application won't need to worry about little details.

The Four Basic Database Functions

Many programmers have an intuitive grasp of the use of a database, both as an implementor and an end-user. But they seldom think about the basic functionality of the databases they use. With any system for storing and retrieving data, four basic functions must be provided:

- **Add** A database with nothing in it, is—well, not a database. You must be able to create new items to store in the database. Often confused with this ability is the ability to Revise the data already stored—even in our code presented here, the difference exhibits itself only between the methods **Insert** and **Edit**.
- **Retrieve** If you can't retrieve the data you put into the database, you have a tool as useful as a locked file cabinet. Trash cans and garbage disposers are other examples of storage systems without retrieval capabilities. Computer scientists often refer to these as *write-only file systems*.
- **Delete** The ability to delete records is essential to the health of your database. Without it, your database would be destined to grow forever. Even more importantly, if you can Add, Retrieve, and Delete records from a database, you have the intrinsic ability to Revise entries in the database, also: You simply retrieve a record, delete it from the database, change the record, and re-add it as if it were new. This is so cumbersome and the alternative so easy to implement, that we can't imagine a professional database project without the ability to re-save a revised record directly.

- **Order** This is what makes a file system a database. Without it, all of your little bits of data are just so much worthless information. It has the same effect as sorting, but it's accomplished internally, by the database itself, rather than externally, by some other program. The data processing community (people who are into computers strictly for record-keeping, like accountants) sometimes confuses this with another derived function, reporting. Reporting is really just looping built around ordered retrieval, so it's not one of the four essentials. However, in the world of record-keeping, it is quite common to enter little bits of data one by one, over time, and then spit it back out all at once. This is a quite different act on the user's part than pulling up just one of those little bits for inspection (retrieval), so DPers always separate these two aspects.

In our unit **Hotspots**, we've encapsulated only three of the basic functionalities: add (and revise), retrieve, and delete. We also do some reporting in **Main**; that's how we load the **List_select_dialog** with our hotspot names for retrieval. To simplify the mainline code, you might want to try your hand at encapsulating this sorting and retrieval, too.

Saving Hotspots

Now that we have our database, we're going to add records. Don't worry—adding records to a BDE database is easy. Just call the **Insert** method, set up the field values, and call the **Post** method. In a simpler world, the only thing needed to replace a record is a call to **Edit**, rather than **Insert**; but, as we've seen, nothing is quite that simple. Easy, but not simple.

Unlike conventional file systems in which you explicitly read or write a whole record at once, the BDE deals with data on a field level. With the BDE, you position yourself "over" a record, assigning values to or from individual fields in a virtual record buffer. This record buffer is like a sliding porthole. To edit an existing record, you ask the BDE to go to the record, using simple navigation methods like **First**, **Next**, and **Prior**—or using slightly more complicated searching, with **SetKey** and **GotoKey**. Once positioned on the record, you indicate to the BDE that you intend to change the record by calling the **Edit** method. You can copy data to one field or several; you don't need to update them all. When you ask to add a new record with the **Insert** method, you are positioned over a blank record. Other than that, there is no difference between adding a new record and editing an existing record. In either case, calling the **Post** method commits your changes to the database.

Before posting, the first thing to watch for is filling in all required fields. The second thing may be somewhat more difficult to code: If you are using unique indices, you must make sure that the record's fields comprising the key are unique in the database. (This can be very simple in the case of a one-field key, with the field being and autoincrement field.)

We have introduced a little complexity, however. We have two indices, the primary index (**By_ID**) and a secondary index, **By_Image_Target**. Note that we always call the primary index the "primary index". We won't often refer to it by name, because the database knows it only by name of the null string, even though we created it with a perfectly good name. We can only change indices when the file is closed; this is a severe limitation of the BDE. Therefore, we will always need to open the database after choosing the appropriate index and close it when we're finished using it.

In the way we've allowed events to unfold in our application, the following scenario *could* happen: The user chooses a hotspot to edit from the list. The user decides the incorrect hotspot was chosen and tries to choose another hotspot from the list. Choosing the first time puts the record buffer over a perfectly editable hotspot record; but by choosing again, we cause the record buffer to move through another part of the file, over different records, as we rebuild the hotspot display list. If the user decides, "No, that *was* the right hotspot," and cancels the list, our record buffer is now invalid—it contains the record after the last record displayed in the list. Now, every time we want to edit a record; we must reposition ourselves over the correct record.

```
if ID = 0 then begin
    { New record -
      Don't care about key or current record. }
    Open;
    Insert;
    end
  else begin
    { Update existing record. }
    IndexName := '';
    Open;
    SetKey;
    FieldByName('ID').AsInteger := ID;
    GotoKey;
    Edit;
    end;
```

After this code is executed, we can now manipulate the fields and then **Post** the record. This isn't simple, either—we used a blob.

Fields and Streams

Blobs are supported well in Delphi with *stream* objects. Often times, treating a binary large object as a binary file results in elegant code. Delphi's stream objects do just that, providing a file-like interface to blobs. **TBLOBField** supports two stream-related methods, **LoadFromStream** and **SaveToStream**. Unfortunately for us, our blobs are not streams, just an ordinary variable of which we want to save only a portion. This means we need to put the portion of our **Vertices** array that we wish to save into a stream, and then move it from the stream to the field. So, let's grab the rifle and the fly rod.

```
FieldByName('Image') .AsString := Image;
FieldByName('Target').AsString := Target;
V_stream := TMemoryStream.Create;
try
   V_stream.Write(Vertices,Vertex_count * sizeof(TPoint));
   V_stream.Seek(0,soFromBeginning);
   TBLObField(FieldByName('Vertices'))
      .LoadFromStream(V_stream);
   Post;
   ID := FieldByName('ID').AsInteger;
finally
   V_stream.Free;
   Close;
end;
```

TMemoryStream is a basic stream class. It is a class, so instances of it must be created. This, of course, means they must also be freed. And since we're working in database code, where a zillion (well, maybe not that many) things can go wrong, we should make sure that regardless of any problems, our stream is freed.

When a stream is created, our *current position* is at the beginning of the stream. After we **Write** to the stream, our current position is at the end of what we have just written. Since we don't trust **LoadFromStream** to reset the current position to the beginning of our stream, we do it ourselves with a call to **Seek**.

Once the blob field is loaded, we can post the record. By the way, if we are inserting a new record, the autoincrementing **ID** field will receive a new, unique value, one greater than the last **ID** value handed out. As you can see, we pass this back to the application by updating the hotspot's **ID** field.

Loading Hotspots

Loading hotspots is a bit more straight forward, since we don't need to worry about the difference between inserting and replacing data. To read a hotspot record from the database table, we first locate the record with the **SetKey** and **GotoKey** methods we used to re-locate a record for updating.

```
begin with Hotspot do begin
   IndexName := '';
   Open;
   SetKey;
   FieldByName('ID').AsInteger := ID;
   GotoKey;
   Image := FieldByName('Image') .AsString;
   Target := FieldByName('Target').AsString;
   V_stream := TMemoryStream.Create;
   TBLObField(FieldByName('Vertices'))
      .SaveToStream(V_stream);
   Vertex_count := V_stream.Size div sizeof(TPoint);
   V_stream.Seek(0,soFromBeginning);
   V_stream.Read(Vertices,V_stream.Size);
   V_stream.Free;
   Close;
   end; end;
```

We choose the primary key as our index, and call **SetKey** to announce that we're building a search key. We set the **ID** (the only component of the key) to the **ID** we wish to load, and pass in the **Hotspot** from the database record. To position our record buffer over the appropriate record, we call **GotoKey**.

Finally, we reverse the process we used above to put the **Vertices** into the blob field in order to get them back out. Along the way, we calculate the **Vertex_count** for the main program.

Drawing Polygonal Hotspots

Back in unit **Main**, the **FormMouseMove** and **FormMouseDown** event handlers have hardly changed from *Hotspot II*. **FormMouseMove** illustrates how we now refer to many of our state variables as fields of **The_hotspot**, which is a **tHotspot**.

```
procedure TForm1.FormMouseMove(Sender: TObject; Shift: TShiftState; X,
  Y: Integer);
    begin with The_hotspot do begin
        if (not Drawing_polygon) or (Vertex_count = 0) then exit;
        Line(Vertices[Vertex_count],Prev_vertex);
        Prev_vertex := Point(X,Y);
        Line(Vertices[Vertex_count],Prev_vertex);
        end; end;
```

Drawing_polygon is still a global variable, but the **Vertices** and **Vertex_count** are now part of **The_hotspot** instead of standing all alone.

We use the same technique to dereference **The_hotspot** in **FormMouseDown** and its local function, **Vertex_finishes_polygon**. The only other difference is that now we call **Have_new_poly** to adjust our state, change the menu items, and give feedback to the user, instead of trying to do it in-line. This gives us an advantage: Now, whether we load a polygon or draw a new one, we can use one routine to set our state.

```
procedure TForm1.FormMouseDown(Sender: TObject; Button: TMouseButton;
  Shift: TShiftState; X, Y: Integer);

    { function Vertex_finishes_polygon }

var
      Vertex : TPoint;
  begin
      if Drawing_polygon then begin
          { Start new side from this vertex if still open. }
          Vertex := Point(X,Y);
          if Vertex_finishes_polygon(Vertex) then Have_new_poly;
          Prev_vertex := Vertex;
          end
        else
          { Test to see if click is in region. }
          if PtInRegion(The_region,X,Y) then
              mciExecute('play c:\Windows\Media\Tada.Wav')
            else
              mciExecute('play c:\Windows\Media\Ding.Wav');
      end;
```

Have_new_poly is straight-forward.

```
procedure Have_new_poly;
   begin with Form1 do begin
      Drawing_polygon := false;
      OptMode.Enabled := true;
      OptMode_Test.Enabled := true;
      OptMode_TestClick(Form1);
      OptFile_Save.Enabled := true;
      Cursor := crArrow;
      if The_hotspot.ID = 0 then
         Caption := Main_form_caption + ' (Save Your Hotspot)'
        else
         Caption := Main_form_caption + ' (' + The_hotspot.Target + ')';
      end; end;
```

We'll get to the menu-interaction parts later; right now, it's only important to note that we set **Drawing_polygon** to false, to tell our mouse handlers not to rubber-band edges anymore, and give the user some feedback. We set the form's **Cursor** back to an ordinary **crArrow** and place an appropriate message on the screen as part of the window's **Caption**. In **FormCreate**, we capture the form's base **Caption** in **Main_form_caption**. Throughout the rest of the code, we'll put messages like "(Save Your Hotspot)" up in the

Caption by simply assigning the base caption, plus our message, to **Form1.Caption**. In this case, we know that if we loaded a hotspot, **The_hotspot.ID** must be non-zero; after we've loaded it, we just want to tell the user its **Target**. If the **ID** is zero, we know we just completed a new hotspot, so we remind the user to save it.

Of course, we must have a way to initialize our drawing. As in *Hotspot II*, we call **Init_for_new_poly**.

```
procedure Init_for_new_poly(
  const Save_db_info : boolean
  );
    var
      Save_ID     : integer;
      Save_target : string;
  begin with Form1 do begin
    Draw_polygon;
    if Save_db_info then with The_hotspot do begin
      Save_ID     := ID;
      Save_Target := Target;
      Clear_hotspot(The_hotspot);
      ID     := Save_ID;
      Target := Save_Target;
      end
    else
      Clear_hotspot(The_hotspot);
    Delete_region(The_region);
    OptMode.Enabled := false;
    OptFile_Save.Enabled := false;
    Cursor := crDrag;
    Drawing_polygon := true;
    end; end;
```

What we can't see here is that it will be called in two different cases: when drawing a new polygon from scratch, and when redefining an existing polygon from the database. When we start from scratch, with *File | New Hotspot*, we will want to start with a hotspot having a blank **Target** and a zero **ID** (which will cause a new hotspot to be added to the database when *File | Save Hotspot* is chosen). When we are revising an existing hotspot, we'll send in **Save_db_info** as **true**, so we won't clear the **ID** and **Target** fields.

Feedback

Feedback is one of the keys of interaction. We've put feedback into motion in a number of ways in this project, alone. Although we seem to know intuitively what feedback is and how to use it effectively, it seems we can always improve a program by simply analyzing and improving its feedback to the user.

Feedback is a system's external response to its operator's input. A bulldozer's blade tips forward under the eye of an operator pushing a lever: the tipping of the blade is the response; it's the fact that the operator can see the blade move that makes it feedback. Similarly, in *Hotspot III*, when the user clicks *File | New Hotspot* and moves the mouse over the window's client area, the mouse cursor changes from an ordinary pointer to an icon that indicates that a hotspot may then be drawn. Setting **Drawing_polygon** to **true** is the response; changing the cursor is *feedback*.

Multimedia is all *about* feedback—visual and aural feedback for most of us—but tactile feedback, too, for those of us with access to a six-degrees-of-freedom flight simulator platform or a "push-back" steering wheel. That doesn't mean multimedia itself is *necessarily* feedback. You know this if you've ever removed a CD ROM disc from your drive and whittled it into shavings with a kitchen knife while watching yet another boring slide-show. Sometimes, the only feedback you want is for the presentation to stop when you hit the escape key!

Your application's users are going to want feedback at every step of the way. Some users wait about 2.5 seconds after clicking a button, and decide their computer must be hung if they don't see an hourglass. The same users will contentedly wait 2.5 hours before they decide their computer is hung once an hourglass appears. This is one improvement you could make to this editor. When the system is low on resources, Windows 95 can take quite a while to display the *Open* dialog box. Initializing the BDE can take some time, too.

There are other things you could do also: Rubber-banding is nice feedback when drawing polygons, but it's possible that a custom crosshair cursor would do a better job than the cursor we selected. If you were to extend the editor so that vertices could be moved or deleted, handles (those little black boxes) would help the user zero-in on them faster. The list goes on, making your application easier and easier to use.

Which leads us to our last point: If you go too far with all of this, your users might not be able to see the forest with all those darn trees blocking their view. It *is* possible to add so many feedback features to your program that users can no longer tell what they're doing. The judicious use of accurate feedback is the key to a clean, usable product.

User Interaction With The Editor

User interaction is handled much the same way in *Hotspot III* as it was in *Hotspot I*. There are a few changes, especially with the actual drawing (as you've seen). Because we can't redefine a whole polygon with a simple down-drag-up mouse click sequence, we've also been forced to reconsider our drawing and testing "modes". First, we still have modes; but now there's a natural automatic sequence to defining hotspots: Choose to draw a new one, and then click, click, click, until it's closed. At this point, the program can automatically fall through to testing, and from there, the user can click on the image or choose to draw another new hotspot again. Of course, along the way, users can save their hotspots and load them instead of drawing them. But as soon as a hotspot is complete, the program automatically goes into testing mode.

We've renamed our "Mode" menu option to *Hotspot*, because it is now only valid when we have a complete hotspot defined. When the word "Hotspot" appears on the menu, the user knows they have a polygon to test. The "Define" option is now *Re-define Region*, and *Test Region* happens automatically. Of course, we enable and disable the menu options where appropriate; for instance, it's not very useful to be able to test a region that is currently being defined.

The Usual Gang

We continue to service the same menu events as *Hotspot I: Load Picture, New Hotspot, Edit Saved Hotspot, Save Hotspot,* and *Delete Hotspot.* We can still *Quit*, which remains as trivial as before—and we have our "Mode" routines, though we renamed them.

All of our picture handling when loading a picture and repainting stays the same. Although saving and deleting hotspots happen almost identically, now we use the new **tHotspot_table** class. We need to look a little more closely at **OptFile_NewClick** and **OptFile_EditClick**, though, to see how we handle menu option enabling and how we access the database to build a list of hotspots.

```
procedure TForm1.OptFile_NewClick(Sender: TObject);
   begin
      Init_for_new_poly(false);
      Caption := Main_form_caption + ' (Drawing New Hotspot)';
      OptFile_Delete.Enabled := false;
      end;
```

Since we've made **Init_for_new_polygon** erase the old polygon, we have little else to do here. We set the caption to describe the action upon which the user is embarking. Since the user has decided to draw an entirely new hotspot, we no longer have an **ID** to use to delete an existing hotspot, so we disable **OptFile_Delete**. This is similar to the code used to re-define a hotspot.

```
procedure TForm1.OptMode_DefineClick(Sender: TObject);
   begin
      if The_hotspot.ID = 0 then
         OptFile_NewClick(Self)
       else begin
```

```
   { Same as ...NewClick, but we don't disable
     deletion like ...NewClick does.  This allows
     you to delete an edited hotspot while rubber-
     banding a revision. }
   Init_for_new_poly(true);
   Caption :=
     Main_form_caption+' (Redefining: '+The_hotspot.Target+')';
   end;
end;
```

The first test makes sure we treat the re-definition of a new hotspot we haven't yet saved in the same way as simply choosing *New Hotspot*. If we are re-defining a hotspot from the database, we call **Init_for_new_polygon**, but we save the **ID** and **Target** information by passing in **true**. We set the **Caption**, as well, but we don't disable deletion—we're still working with a hotspot from the database. By the way, with all of the user interface work being handled in a standard way, **OptFile_DeleteClick** becomes a matter of dealing with the database and starting a new hotspot, just as if the user had.

```
procedure TForm1.OptFile_DeleteClick(Sender: TObject);
   begin
      :
      Hotspot_table.Delete(The_hotspot);
      OptFile_NewClick(Self);
      end;
```

Revising Existing Hotspots

OptFile_EditClick is much the same, but we now build our selection list using BDE methods, instead of our own binary file manipulation.

```
procedure TForm1.OptFile_EditClick(Sender: TObject);
   begin
      with List_select_dialog do begin
         Caption := 'Load Saved Hotspot';
         Action := '&Load';
         Clear;

         with Hotspot_table do begin
            IndexName := 'By_Image_Target';
            Open;
            SetKey;
            FieldByName('Image' ).AsString := Current_image_filename;
            FieldByName('Target').AsString := '';
            GotoKey;
            while
                (not EOF)
              and {then}
                (
                   Uppercase(FieldByName('Image').AsString)
```

```
                  =
            Uppercase(Current_image_filename)
          )
        do begin
          Add(
             Current_image_filename + ' - '
             +
             FieldByName('Target').AsString,
             pointer(FieldByName('ID').AsInteger)
             );
          Next;
        end;
      Close;
    end;
{ some code omitted here for brevity }
```

We begin by using the **By_Image_Target** index. This naturally views the database with all of the hotspots for one image grouped together. That way, we won't have to scan the entire database to find all of the records for the image we currently have loaded. To get to the first hotspot of our **Image**, we set the **Image** to our image's name and blank the **Target** string. We will then loop, executing **Next** to move us through the records. We loop while there are still records (indicated by "**not EOF**"), and we are still looking at hotspots for our image. Note that, while we declared the key as case-insensitive in unit **Hotspots**, we still need to do our own desensitizing here, because the data is *stored* in upper- and lowercase.

```
{ some code omitted here for brevity }
if Execute then begin
           Init_for_new_poly(false);
           The_hotspot.ID := integer(Selected.Data);
           Hotspot_table.Load(The_hotspot);
           Have_new_poly;
           Draw_polygon;
           OptFile_Delete.Enabled := true;
           Form1.Caption :=
              Main_form_caption + ' (' + The_hotspot.Target + ')';
           end
      end;

   end;
```

Once we **Load The_hotspot**, we call **Have_new_poly**, just as if we had completed a polygon with the **OnMouseDown** event. We didn't actually do all of the drawing work along the way, so we have to draw it ourselves. We are then allowed to delete the loaded hotspot, and we let the user know what hotspot was selected by placing it in the form's **Caption**.

Table 10.2 The Menu **MainMenu1** for Hotspot III.

Name	Caption	Enabled	Checked
OptFile	'File'	True	False
OptFile_LoadPicture	'Load Picture'	True	False
N1 (default)	'-'	—	—
OptFile_New	'New Hotspot'	False	False
OptFile_Edit	'Edit Saved Hotspot'	False	False
OptFile_Save	'Save Hotspot'	False	False
OptFile_Delete	'Delete Hotspot'	False	False
N2 (default)	'-'	—	—
OptFile_Quit	'Quit'	True	False
OptMode	'Hotspot'	False	False
OptMode_Test	'Test Region'	True	False
OptMode_Define	'Re-define Region'	True	True

The Hot Irregular-Spot Editor

We've touched on the just about all of the major parts of this project, but we haven't shown you the whole unit **Main**, yet. See Listing 10.3 and Table 10.2 which, all together, describe the menu layout.

Listing 10.3   Unit **Main**, of Project **Hotspot3**

```
unit Main;

interface

uses
  Windows, Messages, SysUtils, Classes, Graphics, Controls, Forms, Dialogs,
  Menus, ExtCtrls, StdCtrls;

type
  TForm1 = class(TForm)
    MainMenu1: TMainMenu;
    OptFile: TMenuItem;
    OptFile_LoadPicture: TMenuItem;
    OptFile_New: TMenuItem;
    OptFile_Edit: TMenuItem;
    OptFile_Save: TMenuItem;
    OptFile_Delete: TMenuItem;
    OptFile_Quit: TMenuItem;
    N1: TMenuItem;
    N2: TMenuItem;
```

```
    OpenDialog1: TOpenDialog;
    OptMode: TMenuItem;
    OptMode_Test: TMenuItem;
    OptMode_Define: TMenuItem;

    procedure FormCreate(Sender: TObject);
    procedure FormClose(Sender: TObject; var Action: TCloseAction);
    procedure FormMouseDown(Sender: TObject; Button: TMouseButton;
      Shift: TShiftState; X, Y: Integer);
    procedure FormMouseMove(Sender: TObject; Shift: TShiftState; X,
      Y: Integer);
    procedure FormPaint(Sender: TObject);

    procedure OptFile_LoadPictureClick(Sender: TObject);
    procedure OptFile_NewClick(Sender: TObject);
    procedure OptFile_QuitClick(Sender: TObject);
    procedure OptFile_EditClick(Sender: TObject);
    procedure OptFile_SaveClick(Sender: TObject);
    procedure OptFile_DeleteClick(Sender: TObject);
    procedure OptMode_TestClick(Sender: TObject);
    procedure OptMode_DefineClick(Sender: TObject);
  private
    { Private declarations }
  public
    { Public declarations }
    procedure Line(
      const P1, P2 : TPoint
      );
  end;

var
  Form1: TForm1;

implementation

    uses
        MMSystem, Hotspots, DLgLoad;

{$R *.DFM}

function Dist(
  const P1, P2 : TPoint
  ) : double;
    begin
        Dist := sqrt(sqr(P2.X - P1.X) + sqr(P2.Y - P1.Y));
        end;

procedure Delete_region(
  var The_region : HRGN
  );
    begin
        if The_region = 0 then exit;
        if DeleteObject(The_region) then
            The_region := 0
```

```
        else
            MessageDlg('Unable to delete region.',mtWarning,[mbOK],0);
      end;

var
    Main_form_caption : string;

    The_Hotspot    : tHotspot;
    Hotspot_table  : tHotspot_table;

    Prev_vertex    : TPoint;
    The_region     : HRGN;
    Drawing_polygon : boolean;

    The_image              : TImage;
    Current_image_filename : string;

procedure TForm1.Line(
  const P1, P2 : TPoint
  );
    begin with Canvas do begin
        with P1 do MoveTo(X,Y);
        with P2 do LineTo(X,Y);
        end; end;

procedure Draw_polygon;
    var
        I : integer;
    begin with The_hotspot, Form1 do begin
        if Vertex_count >= 2 then with Canvas do begin
            with Vertices[1] do MoveTo(X,Y);
            for I := 2 to Vertex_count do
                with Vertices[I] do LineTo(X,Y);
            if not Drawing_polygon then
                with Vertices[1] do LineTo(X,Y); { Do final segment. }
            end;
        if Drawing_polygon and (Vertex_count > 0) then
            Line(Vertices[Vertex_count],Prev_vertex);
        end; end;

procedure TForm1.FormCreate(Sender: TObject);
    begin
        Cursor := crArrow;
        Canvas.Pen.Mode := pmNot;
        The_region := 0;
        Clear_hotspot(The_hotspot);
        Drawing_polygon := false;

        Hotspot_table := tHotspot_table.Create(Self);
        with Hotspot_table do begin
            DatabaseName := ExtractFilePath(Application.ExeName);
            TableName    := 'Hotspots';
            Establish;
```

```
            end;
        The_image := nil;

        Main_form_caption := Caption;
        Caption := Main_form_caption + ' (No Hotspot Loaded)';
        end;

procedure TForm1.FormClose(Sender: TObject; var Action: TCloseAction);
    begin
        Delete_region(The_region);
        Hotspot_table.Free;
        end;

procedure Init_for_new_poly(
  const Save_db_info : boolean
  );
    var
        Save_ID     : integer;
        Save_target : string;
    begin with Form1 do begin
        Draw_polygon;
        if Save_db_info then with The_hotspot do begin
            Save_ID     := ID;
            Save_Target := Target;
            Clear_hotspot(The_hotspot);
            ID     := Save_ID;
            Target := Save_Target;
            end
          else
            Clear_hotspot(The_hotspot);
        Delete_region(The_region);
        OptMode.Enabled := false;
        OptFile_Save.Enabled := false;
        Cursor := crDrag;
        Drawing_polygon := true;
        end; end;

procedure Have_new_poly;
    begin with Form1 do begin
        Drawing_polygon := false;
        OptMode.Enabled := true;
        OptMode_Test.Enabled := true;
        OptMode_TestClick(Form1);
        OptFile_Save.Enabled := true;
        Cursor := crArrow;
        if The_hotspot.ID = 0 then
            Caption := Main_form_caption + ' (Save Your Hotspot)'
          else
            Caption := Main_form_caption + ' (' + The_hotspot.Target + ')';
        end; end;

procedure TForm1.FormMouseDown(Sender: TObject; Button: TMouseButton;
  Shift: TShiftState; X, Y: Integer);
```

```
    function Vertex_finishes_polygon(
      const V : TPoint
      ) : boolean;
      begin with The_hotspot do begin
          Vertex_finishes_polygon :=
              (Vertex_count = Max_vertex_count)
            or {else}
              (
                  (Vertex_count > 2)
                and {then}
                  (Dist(V,Vertices[1]) < 10)
              );
          if result then begin
            { Erase previous line, and close the polygon. }
            Line(Vertices[Vertex_count],Prev_vertex);
            Line(Vertices[Vertex_count],Vertices[1]);
            end
          else begin
            { Add the vertex. }
            inc(Vertex_count);
            Vertices[Vertex_count] := V;
            end;
          end; end;

    var
       Vertex : TPoint;
    begin
        if Drawing_polygon then begin
           { Start new side from this vertex if still open. }
           Vertex := Point(X,Y);
           if Vertex_finishes_polygon(Vertex) then Have_new_poly;
           Prev_vertex := Vertex;
           end
         else
           { Test to see if click is in region. }
           if PtInRegion(The_region,X,Y) then
              mciExecute('play c:\Windows\Media\Tada.Wav')
            else
              mciExecute('play c:\Windows\Media\Ding.Wav');
        end;

procedure TForm1.FormMouseMove(Sender: TObject; Shift: TShiftState; X,
  Y: Integer);
    begin with The_hotspot do begin
        if (not Drawing_polygon) or (Vertex_count = 0) then exit;
        Line(Vertices[Vertex_count],Prev_vertex);
        Prev_vertex := Point(X,Y);
        Line(Vertices[Vertex_count],Prev_vertex);
        end; end;

procedure TForm1.FormPaint(Sender: TObject);
    begin
        if The_image <> nil then
```

```
            with The_image do
                Self.Canvas.CopyRect(ClientRect,Canvas,ClientRect);
        Draw_polygon;
        end;

procedure TForm1.OptFile_LoadPictureClick(Sender: TObject);
    var
        Image : TImage;
        P     : TPoint;
    begin
        if not OpenDialog1.Execute then exit;
        Current_image_filename := OpenDialog1.Filename;

        { Erase the previous polygon. }
        Draw_polygon;

        The_image.Free;
        The_image := TImage.Create(Self);
        with The_image do begin
            AutoSize := true;
            Picture.LoadFromFile(Current_image_filename);
            if Width > 100 then
                Self.ClientWidth := Width
              else
                Self.ClientWidth := 100;
            if Height > 100 then
                Self.ClientHeight := Height
              else
                Self.ClientHeight := 100;
            Self.Canvas.CopyRect(ClientRect,Canvas,ClientRect);
            end;

        { Renew the previous polygon. }
        Draw_polygon;

        OptFile_New .Enabled := true;
        OptFile_Edit.Enabled := true;
        end;

procedure TForm1.OptFile_NewClick(Sender: TObject);
    begin
        Init_for_new_poly(false);
        Caption := Main_form_caption + ' (Drawing New Hotspot)';
        OptFile_Delete.Enabled := false;
        end;

procedure TForm1.OptFile_EditClick(Sender: TObject);
    begin
        with List_select_dialog do begin
            Caption := 'Load Saved Hotspot';
            Action := '&Load';
            Clear;

            with Hotspot_table do begin
```

```
                IndexName := 'By_Image_Target';
                Open;
                SetKey;
                FieldByName('Image' ).AsString := Current_image_filename;
                FieldByName('Target').AsString := '';
                GotoKey;
                while
                    (not EOF)
                  and {then}
                    (
                        Uppercase(FieldByName('Image').AsString)
                      =
                        Uppercase(Current_image_filename)
                      )
                  do begin
                    Add(
                        Current_image_filename + ' - '
                      +
                        FieldByName('Target').AsString,
                      pointer(FieldByName('ID').AsInteger)
                        );
                    Next;
                    end;
                Close;
                end;

            if Execute then begin
                Init_for_new_poly(false);
                The_hotspot.ID := integer(Selected.Data);
                Hotspot_table.Load(The_hotspot);
                Have_new_poly;
                Draw_polygon;
                OptFile_Delete.Enabled := true;
                Form1.Caption :=
                    Main_form_caption + ' (' + The_hotspot.Target + ')';
                end
            end;

        end;

procedure TForm1.OptFile_SaveClick(Sender: TObject);
    var
        Temp : string;
    begin
        if The_hotspot.Vertex_count < 3 then begin
            MessageDlg('No Region Defined.',mtWarning,[mbOK],0);
            exit;
            end;
        if Drawing_polygon then begin
            MessageDlg('You must close the polygon.',mtWarning,[mbOK],0);
            exit;
            end;
        Temp := Trim(
```

```
                    InputBox(
                      'Enter Target',
                      'Enter a Hyperlink Target string of up to 128 characters:',
                      Trim(The_hotspot.Target)
                      )
                    );
            if Temp <> '' then with The_hotspot do begin
                Image  := Current_image_filename;
                Target := Temp;
                Hotspot_table.Save(The_hotspot);
                Caption := Main_form_caption + ' (' + Target + ')';
                end;
            end;

    procedure TForm1.OptFile_DeleteClick(Sender: TObject);
        begin
            if The_hotspot.ID = 0 then begin
                { This shouldn't happen if we manage our menu
                  options correctly. }
                MessageDlg('No region to delete!',mtInformation,[mbOK],0);
                exit;
                end;
            if MessageDlg(
                   'Are you sure you want to delete this hotspot?',
                   mtWarning, [mbYes,mbNo,mbCancel], 0
                   )
              in
                [mrCancel,mrNo]
              then
                exit;

            Hotspot_table.Delete(The_hotspot);

            OptFile_NewClick(Self);
            end;

    procedure TForm1.OptFile_QuitClick(Sender: TObject);
        begin
            Close;
            end;

    procedure TForm1.OptMode_TestClick(Sender: TObject);
        begin
            OptMode_Test  .Checked := true;
            OptMode_Define.Checked := false;
            Delete_region(The_region);
            with The_hotspot do
                The_region := CreatePolygonRgn(
                                Vertices,
                                Vertex_count,
                                ALTERNATE
                                );
            end;
```

```
procedure TForm1.OptMode_DefineClick(Sender: TObject);
   begin
      if The_hotspot.ID = 0 then
         OptFile_NewClick(Self)
       else begin
         { Same as ...NewClick, but we don't disable
           deletion like ...NewClick does.  This allows
           you to delete an edited hotspot while rubber-
           banding a revision. }
         Init_for_new_poly(true);
         Caption :=
           Main_form_caption+' (Redefining: '+The_hotspot.Target+')';
         end;
      end;
end.
```

Hotspots: The Next Generation

The programs we've written in this chapter work just well enough to get some hotspots onto our images. You'll find many other ways to expand their abilities—just keep looking. For one thing, as we said in an earlier chapter, you should take even greater pains to trap errors. You may also want to add an option that displays or tests all the hotspots for an image simultaneously, just as they'll be used in a working presentation. Or you may want to fix up *Hotspot III* so you can edit a polygon vertex by vertex. The more you search, the more you'll discover.

As a matter of fact, there's one great way to improve on polygon regions we've used in *Hotspot II* and *III*. The API function we used, **CreatePolygonRgn**, helps us make either one polygon, or multiple polygons joined at common vertices (like the star shown back in Figure 10.2). But what do you do when you have several separate hotspots on your image that all have the same hyperlink target? Right now, you must make separate hotspots regions for each of them. But, you *could* call upon the services of yet another API function, **CreatePolyPolygonRgn**. Here you see its declaration in Delphi's *Windows.Pas*:

```
function CreatePolyPolygonRgn(
  const pPtStructs;
  const pIntArray;
        p3,
        p4 : Integer
  ): HRGN;
    stdcall;
```

The difference between this function and **CreatePolygonRgn** is in the second argument, **pIntArray**. In this parameter, you pass a pointer to a second array. This is simply an array of integers in which each (4-byte) integer specifies how many points in the **pPtStructs** belong to each separate polygon. **p3** tells the function exactly how many polygons are represented in **pIntArray**, and **p4** indicates the fill mode.

For example, let's say we have a **pPtStructs** array of 25 vertices, and a **pIntArray** of three integers containing the values 3, 12, and 10. We would, of course, pass 3 to **p3**, indicating that we are defining three distinct polygons: The first three points in **pPtStructs** define a triangle; the next 12 points, a dodecagon, and finally, a decagon. (Get used to the Greek; you're working in a system named after the Oracle of Apollo!)

When we call **PtInRegion** with the handle to the PolyPolygon region just defined, it will return **true** if our point—say, a mouse click—occurs anywhere within any of the three regions. Three regions act as one. Pretty neat, huh?

To implement PolyPolygon regions, both the drawing functions of the program and the storage system would have to be modified. On the other hand, if you've managed to design a system that needs this much flexibility; you should be up to the task of making these modifications.

Now that you know how to create and activate hotspots in both text and images, let's put all this knowledge to work. Our next adventure takes us into a true hypermedia realm—one of sound, music, images, and video.

Chapter 11

With basic support for images, we'll be able to build a presentation-quality multi-media engine.

Expanding the VB Multimedia Engine

Dan Haygood

Get ready for a culminating project. It's time to pull together some of the things we've learned in the first 10 chapters and build a much more powerful multimedia engine that will let us link hotspots with text, sound, music, and video.

In Chapter 1, we showed you how easy it is to use Delphi to trigger multimedia events. We also looked at the basic techniques involved in parsing HTML files. In Chapter 3, we used Delphi to build a hypertext engine that allowed us to jump from topic to topic by clicking on hotlinked words in the text itself. Chapter 4 added some multimedia features to the hypertext engine so that hotlinked words in the hypertext could play back video, MIDI music, or any other event supported by the Windows Multimedia API. Chapter 5 delved more deeply into the API, using waveform audio to try a variety of functions. Chapters 6, 7, and 8 covered the elements of image display and special effects. And in the previous two chapters, we built an editor that enabled us to map out hotspots on our images. We've come a long way.

In this chapter, we're going to draw upon all this knowledge to expand our hypermedia system. First, we'll hook in basic image support, so we can hop back and forth between pictures and text. After we make it look good, we'll add hyperlinks to the pictures themselves, using the Irregular Hotspot Editor from the previous chapter.

Magic I: Basic Image Support

This project presents the steps for creating the new and improved hypertext engine.

1. We're going to build upon our multimedia-enabled engine from Chapter 4, *Hyper4*, so we need to start a new project using the old files. Make a new project directory, *Magic1*, and an output subdirectory beneath this, *Bin*. With the *Explorer*, copy the project files from your *Hyper4* directory to your *Magic1* directory. Rename your "Hyper4" files to "Magic1." You'll need the *DPR*, *PAS*, and *DFM* files.

2. Open your **Magic1** Project file in Delphi. The compiler will complain that its name is wrong ("Module header is missing or incorrect."). Change its program name from **Hyper4** to **Magic1**. In the *Project Options* dialog box (from *Project | Options*), set the Application Title to "Magic I," and its output directory to "Bin."

3. We'll re-arrange the existing controls for a more effective interface and add places for the images, and an Image control within a Panel control.

4. We'll add support to handle images that we "Jump_to," which are images that we'll be able to place in Reference Anchor tags, or enter in the "Goto" box, implemented with the **Filename** Edit control.

5. Finally, we'll go into to the actual HTML engine code to add support for images that can be loaded by a document itself, rather than as the result of the user clicking a reference.

Most of the source units from project **Hyper4** stay the same. At this point, the full source code for *Magic I* can be found in the listings of **MiscLib** (Listing 3.1 from *Hyper I*); **FmtText** (Listing 3.3 from *Hyper I*, with modifications from Listing 3.12 from *Hyper II*); **Parser**, **HyperLnk** (Listings 3.9 and 3.10 from *Hyper II*); and **Font** (Listing 3.16 from *Hyper III*). Modifications are made to units **Main**

(Listing 11.1 modifies Listings 3.19 and 4.1), **HTML** (Listing 11.2 modifies Listing 3.11), and **DispBuf** (Listing 11.3 modifies Listing 3.18).

> *You'll find this project in the subdirectory \PROGRAMS\CHAP11\ MAGIC1 on the accompanying CD-ROM. For our examples here, we'll be using the files Magic1.HTM through magic4.HTM from \MEDIA\HYPERTXT.*

Modifying the Form

In *Hyper IV*, we had the control buttons on the bottom of the form. In practice, though, it's better to group controls in the those places where users expect to find them. In Windows applications, we only rarely see important controls at the bottom of the screen. The title bar and pull-down menus are almost always at the top of the window—as are, typically, speedbars, rulers, and other items with which the user needs to interact. Without having to fall back to one of the formal style guides available for user interface design, we can see that, as we add functionality, it will be better to have controls on the top of the form.

Accomplishing the move is going to be tricky since the form is so tight, and we've used Panel controls. Panel controls can be difficult to work around, because they can take "ownership" of other controls and "suck them inside." To see what we mean, highlight **PaintBox1**, inside **Panel1**. If you click and drag the Paint Box to the side, you'll see that it is clipped by the Panel. We want to avoid putting controls into Panels if they *should* be on the main Form.

You can "leap-frog" the controls: First, we'll make the hypertext display area smaller and move it down, freeing some room at the top of the form; then we'll move the controls from the bottom of the form to the top. Select **PaintBox1** and drag its lower edge up. Then select **Panel1** and drag its lower edge up. Since we're going to move the text display area to the right of the form in order to present images on the left, take this opportunity to drag the right sides of the Paint Box and Panel to the left, also.

You should now have a significantly smaller Panel, and should be able to move it just above the Close Button. Move the Open Button to the top left corner of the form, and the Close button next to it.

We are going to try something special for the **Filename** Edit control. We're going to enhance its appearance by putting it on a raised Bevel with a label, "Go to:" Lay down the Bevel first (from the *Additional* page of the *Component Palette*), and set its **Style** property to **bsRaised**. Then set a Label on its right side, with its **Caption** set to "Go to:" Finally, move the existing **Filename**

Edit control over the left side. You can do fine alignments, even when "Snap To Grid" is turned on in the environment, by using the arrows keys with the [control] key pressed down.

Lastly, we need to add a Panel (it's a nice effect) and an Image to hold the images we'll be loading. Lay down the Panel first. Since one "default-named" control per form is plenty, set this Panel's name to **Image_panel**. For visual interest, we set **BevelOuter** to **bvLowered**, **BevelWidth** to 6, **BorderStyle** to **bsSingle**, and we leave **BorderWidth** at 0. Finally, we place an Image control on the Panel—by doing that we can use the mouse to click down, drag, and release—all on **Image_panel** during the Image control's placement. For the time being, we don't care about the exact size of the image; we're going to force it to fit inside the panel at runtime.

We have a lot of changes to make, so carefully study Figure 11.1, which shows the completed form at design time. The important property settings are shown in Property Table 11.1. Ready and running, *Magic I* is shown in Figure 11.2.

Supporting Referenced Images

Referenced images are the easiest to support. We simply need to alter the procedure **Jump_to** in unit **Main** to load an image when it is passed an image-type filename. **Jump_to** is, in fact, going to become the hub of our file loading; so you'll see the effects of another change. The procedure **Load_new_HTML_file** is now replaced with calls to **Jump_to**, instead. These changes, along with others we'll discuss shortly, appear in the code for *main.pas* in Listing 11.1.

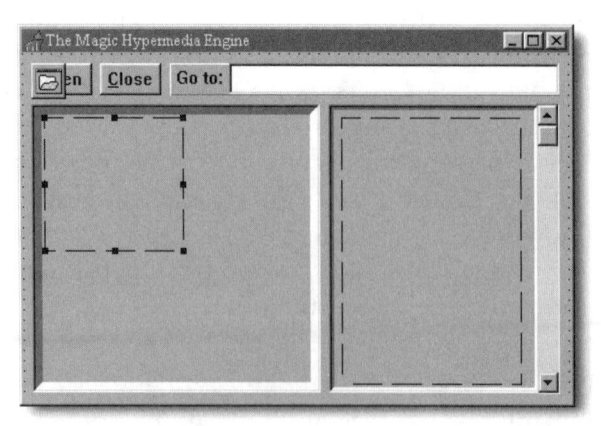

Figure 11.1   The form for Magic I at design time.

Table 11.1 *Properties for the Magic I project.*

Class	Property	Value
TForm	Name	Form1 (default)
	Caption	'The Magic Hypermedia Engine'
TOpenDialog	Name	OpenDialog1 (default)
	Filter	Hypertext*.Htm
		Plain Text*.Txt
		Wave *.Wav
		MIDI *.MID
		Audio/Video *.AVI
		Bitmap *.BMP
		Bitmap (RLE) *.RLE
		Windows Metafile *.WMF
		Icon *.Ico
		All Files *.*
TButton	Name	Open_button
	Caption	'&Open'
	OnClick	Open_buttonClick
TButton	Name	Close_button
	Caption	'&Close'
	OnClick	Close_buttonClick
TBevel	Name	Bevel1 (default)
TLabel	Name	Label1 (default)
	Caption	'Go to:'
TEdit	Name	Filename
	Text	<blank>
	OnKeyPress	FilenameKeyPress
TPanel	Name	Panel1 (default)
	BevelOuter	bvLowered
	BevelWidth	2
	BorderStyle	bsSingle
	BorderWidth	0
TPaintBox	Name	PaintBox1 (default)
	Font	Times New Roman, Regular, 10pt.
TScrollBar	Name	ScrollBar1 (default)
	Kind	sbVertical

Continued

Table 11.1 Properties for the Magic I project (Continued).

Class	Property	Value
TPanel	Name	Image_panel
	BevelOuter	bvLowered
	BevelWidth	6
	BorderStyle	bsSingle
	BorderWidth	0
TImage	Name	Image1
	Stretch	True

Figure 11.2 Magic I, with an image loaded.

Procedure Jump_to still isn't intimidating, but it is getting longer, as shown in the code snippet below.

```
procedure Jump_to(
  const Target : string
  );
    var
      Re_show : boolean;
      Ext     : string;
      Command : ansiString;
```

Expanding the VB Multimedia Engine

```
begin with TParser.Parse(pchar(Target)) do begin
    Re_show := true;
    No_errors;
    Find('#');
    if Error then begin
        { Just "filename".  Could be a media file. }
        Re_show := false;
        Ext := uppercase(extractFileExt(Remainder));
        if  (Ext = '.WAV')
          or
            (Ext = '.MID')
          or
            (Ext = '.AVI')
          then begin
            Command := 'Play ' + strPas(Remainder);
            mciExecute(pchar('Play ' + strPas(Remainder)));
            end
          else if
            (Ext = '.BMP')
          or
            (Ext = '.RLE')
          or
            (Ext = '.WMF')
          or
            (Ext = '.ICO')
          then
            Form1.Image1.Picture.LoadFromFile(Remainder)
          else begin
            { 'HTM', et al. }
            Form1.Filename.Text := Remainder;
            Load_HTML;
            Re_show := true;
            end
      end
    else begin
      if Last_found^ <> #0 then begin
          { There was a filename in "filename#label".
            <label> is in Remainder. }
          Form1.Filename.Text := Last_found;
          Load_HTML;
          end
        else
          ; { Just "#label". }
      Set_scrollbar(
        Int_max(
          Output.Dest_name_anchors.First_rect_of_name(Remainder).Top,
          0
          )
        );
      end;
    if Re_show then Form1.PaintBox1.Refresh;
    Free;
    end; end;
```

All we do is spot the extensions BMP, RLE, WMF, and ICO, and slip their files into **Image1** with its **LoadFromFile** method.

This takes care of two cases of image display for us: First, if the user opens a file with the **Open_button**, or by typing within the **Filename** Edit control, the file is directly loaded with a call straight to **Jump_to**. Secondly, if we find the target attached to a hot rectangle in the **Reference_anchors** rectangle list in the **Output tDisplay_buffer** object; we will **Jump_to** that file, just like any other. It's easy for the hyperdocument designer to get an image into the **Reference_anchors**. All they need to do is specify a suitable image filename, instead of the name of a media file or another hyperdocument.

In these two cases, the user must take some action to load the image. A third case is also possible—the case where the document itself specifies an image to load.

Loading the Documents' Images

Supporting images specified by the document itself, rather than in Reference Anchor tags, is a little more difficult. Instead of dealing with a filename within an arbitrary string in the **<A HREF>** tag, we must come up with a way to specify images directly. We'll use a variation of the HTML Image tag, **<IMG>**. Now it's time to roll up our sleeves and enhance our HTML engine.

Introducing the HTML IMG Tag

In order to support images with our hypermedia engine, we'll need to implement the HTML image (IMG) tag. The IMG tag is perhaps one of the most complicated tags in HTML. It has more variables than most other tags. It is also treated differently in different browsers. Table 11.2 lists the IMG tag variables, their possible values, and their function.

When used in conjunction with each other, you can come up with some really interesting ways to display images. For example, look at the following HTML:

```
<IMG ALIGN=LEFT BORDER=5 HSPACE=10 VSPACE=5 WIDTH=150 HEIGHT=200
SRC="FACE.GIF">
<IMG ALIGN=RIGHT BORDER=5 HSPACE=10 VSPACE=5 WIDTH=150 HEIGHT=200
SRC="FACE.GIF">
<CENTER><H1> The Quick Brown Fox Jumped Over the Lazy Dog!</H1>
</CENTER>
```

If you are using a newer browser, this entry will display the FACE.GIF image on the left side of the display, and on the right side of the display at the same height. Both images will be stretched to fit into a region that is

> 150 pixels wide and 200 pixels tall. The images will have borders that are 5 pixels wide, and the text that wraps around them will be offset by 10 pixels horizontally and five pixels vertically. Finally, the text will be wrapped between them and centered. Check out Figure 11.3 to see how this looks. With a little practice, you can come up with some pretty neat effects by using images in different ways. For more information on the image tag and HTML in general, see Appendix B.

The variation we'll be supporting is almost trivial. We'll take one argument, specified by the **NAME** keyword. Here is an example:

```
<IMG NAME="YAKIDAWN.BMP">
```

When we run across this in a document, we want to put the named image into **Image1**. Since all of our text, and other items of interest like the Horizontal Rule, end up in the **Formatted_text_list**, it seems sensible for Image

Table 11.2   *The IMG Tag Variables.*

Variable	Arguments	Description
SRC	Filename	Image to Display
ALT	Any text string	The text if images are turned off
ALIGN	TOP	Aligns the top edge of the image with the top of the tallest text
	MIDDLE	Aligns the center of the image with the bottom of the text
	BOTTOM	Aligns the bottom of the image with the bottom of the text
	ABSMIDDLE	Aligns the center of image with the center of the text
	LEFT	Aligns the image to the left side of the screen and allows text to wrap around the right side of the image
	RIGHT	Aligns the image to the right side of the screen and allows text to wrap around the left side of the image
LOWSRC	Filename	Low res image to display while large image is loading
HSPACE	Integer	Horizontal space between image and text
VSPACE	Integer	Vertical space between image and text
WIDTH	Integer	Image is stretched to this width
HEIGHT	Integer	Image is stretched to this height
BORDER	Integer	Sets the width of the border around an image. Can be used to create borders on normal images, or can get rid of borders on linked images by setting it to 0.

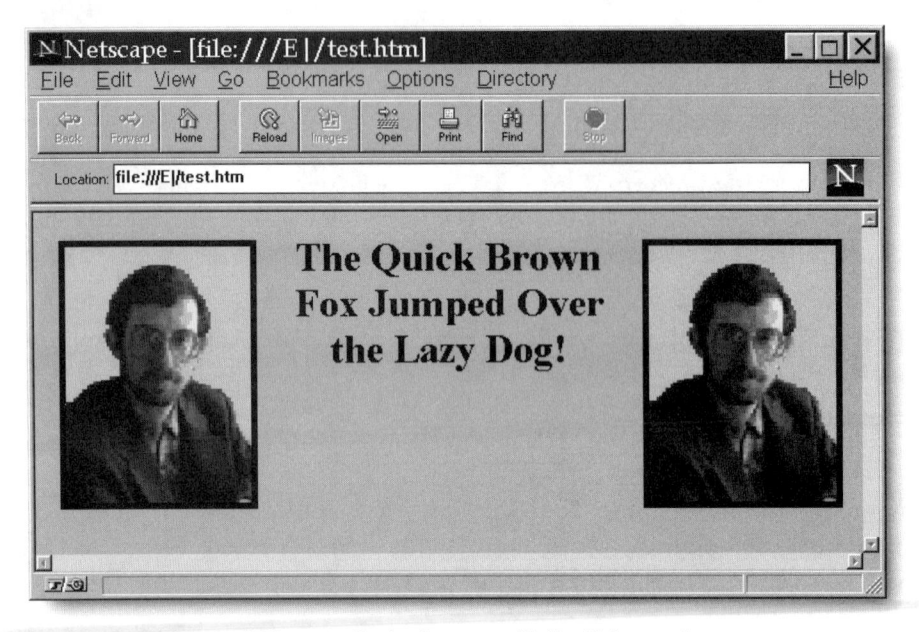

Figure 11.3 *Using the IMG tag to display images with the Netscape browser.*

tags to be recorded there also. In fact, we will treat Image tags in much the same way as we treat Horizontal Rules.

Changes to Unit HTML

We have a field in **tHTML_format**, defined in unit **HTML**, to indicate the height (and thus, the presence) of a horizontal rule at some point in the text. As shown in the code snippet below, we are going to add another field to indicate the presence of an image. The full modifications of the unit are shown later on in the chapter, in Listing 11.2.

```
type
    tHTML_format = record
        Serial_number      : integer;
        Leading_newlines   : integer;
        Font               : tHTML_font_spec;
        Rule_height        : integer;
        Anchor_reference   : integer;
        Anchor_dest_name   : integer;
        Preformatted       : boolean;
        Image_name         : string;
    end;
```

Image_name is a "string"—It's a good thing this is Delphi 2.0: In Delphi 1.0 and Borland Pascal, an unqualified **string** took 256 bytes. That's a lot of wasted RAM for each format record. In Delphi 2.0, though, strings default to the **ANSIString** type, which is dynamically managed for us, so we don't need to worry about so much wasted overhead. Some waste does occur, however; so if speed is critical, you might want to consider re-coding this to use a **pchar**, or even **ShortString** implementation.

The procedure **Parse_tag** must be taught to recognize the **<IMG>** tag. Like the horizontal rule and the new line, images will no doubt require special processing later down the line; rather that set the image name straight into the **Format** that **Parse_tag** modifies, we simply let **Parse_tag** set a returned **var** parameter, as shown in the code snippet below.

```
procedure Parse_tag(
   const          The_tag         : pchar;
   var {in/out}   Format          : tHTML_format;
   const          HRef_anchors    : tNamed_rectangle_list;
   const          Name_anchors    : tNamed_rectangle_list;
   var            Do_a_newline    : boolean;
   var            Rule_height     : integer;
   var            Image_name      : string
   );
```

You may recall the large **if..then..else** statement in Parse_tag; we just add another case to it. (If you don't recall, check out Listing 11.2 of unit **HTML**, below.)

```
else if StrComp(Word,'/PRE') = 0 then
  Parse_end_PRE_tag
else if StrComp(Word,'IMG') = 0 then
  Parse_IMG_tag
else
{ It's a currently unsupported tag. }
;
```

The local procedure **Parse_IMG_tag** doesn't have much work to do. In fact, faster ways to do this are probably available.

```
procedure Parse_IMG_tag;
   begin with The_parser do begin
      Expect('NAME');
      Expect('=');
      Expect('"');
      Find('"');
      Expect(' ');
      Image_name := Last_found
      end; end;
```

All we are doing is grabbing the quote-delimited string from the tag.

Changes to Unit DispBuf

When we are spinning through the document, we will eventually parse out an Image tag. When this happens, we need to give it the same style of special treatment that we would give to a Horizontal Rule. Below, you can see a fragment of **Parse_HTML** in unit **DispBuf** that handles both cases. The full code is given in Listing 11.3.

```
inc(Text);
                        The_end^ := #0;
                        Parse_tag(Text,
                          Format,
                          Reference_anchors,
                          Dest_name_anchors,
                          Need_a_newline,
                          Rule_height,
                          Image_name
                          );
                        Text := The_end + 1;
                        Preceeding_newline :=
                            Preceeding_newline or Need_a_newline;
                        if Preceeding_newline then
                            Preceeding_space := false;
                        if Rule_height > 0 then
                            Horizontal_rule(Rule_height);
                        if Image_name <> '' then
                            Image(Image_name);
                        Set_format(Format);
```

However, the local procedure Image actually does the work, as shown in the code snippet below.

```
procedure Image(
  const _Image_name : string
  );
    begin
      Add_buffer_to_list;
      Current_format.Image_name := _Image_name;
      Current_format.Leading_newlines := 0;
        { If there were Pending_newlines and text
          to go with them, Add_buffer_to_list got
          them.  If they were saved, then
          Pending_newlines isn't adjusted, and will
          be taken the next time ABTL gets called. }
      Formatted_text_list.Add(
        tFormatted_text.Create(Current_format,'')
        );
      Current_format.Image_name := '';
    end;
```

This procedure forces a new item into the **Formatted_text_list**, with no text in it. It first empties the previous **Buffer** into the list, and then sets up the **Current_format** for the image. The **Image_name** is set, of course, along with the **Leading_newlines**. **Leading_newlines** is set to zero on this item, because we don't want to cause line breaks in the text output just because we put an image onto the screen somewhere else. After we force the element onto the list, we set the **Image_name** back to null.

During line breaking, we have nothing special to do. Even though we handle our cousin, the Horizontal Rule, with kid gloves in **Break_into_lines**, we want image elements to have no effect on line breaking. Since they don't have any **Text** and have their **Leading_newlines** set to 0, we can ignore them and let them be treated as zero-length text normally would be.

Finally, it is time to display the image when the document itself is displayed. The **Display** method handles this, and is now passed the additional information needed to present the image. Although we know the image's name, we need to be passed a control in which to display it, as shown in the code snippet below.

```
procedure tDisplay_buffer.Display(
  const Aux_image : TImage
  );
```

Again, we look for a parallel with the horizontal rule and inside the display loop; as we are going through the **Formatted_text_list**, we can see that horizontal rule elements are excepted out, as shown in the code snippet below.

```
if Rule_height > 0 then
    Draw_rule(Control.Canvas,
      Point(Base_left_corner.X,
            Base_left_corner.Y - Display_top),
      Meas.Width,Rule_height
      )
  else if (Aux_image <> nil) and (Image_name <> '') then
    Aux_image.Picture.LoadFromFile(Image_name)
  else if Text <> nil then begin
    Set_font_from_spec(Control.Canvas.Font,Format.Font);
    Control.Canvas.TextOut(
      Base_left_corner.X, Base_left_corner.Y - Display_top,
      Text
      );
```

We also take care of the images here. Note that we've made it possible to send in a **nil Aux_image** to have the ultimate effect of the Image tag ignored.

You may have noticed something odd: There is only one **Aux_image**, but there is no built-in limit on the number of **<IMG>** tags in the document. There are several ways you could handle this: We have decided to let it be known that the last **<IMG>** tag's image will be the last one displayed after all of the previous images may have flashed up before.

Starting Out

Up until now, we've just assumed that the Image control would be the correct size for what we wanted to do. Returning to unit **Main**, though, we still have some work to be done. We have neglected the **Image_panel** and its relationship to **Image1** itself. We also need to discuss an important part of the user interface: resizing.

Very early in the game, we said that we would fit **Image1** to the **Image_panel** at runtime. We do this when we create the form, as shown in the code snippet below. Before we change **Image1**'s dimensions and placement, we must first figure out where it is to go. With some container controls, this would be easy. However, Panels have some special problems; they draw their bevel in the client area they allow other controls to use.

```
procedure TForm1.FormCreate(Sender: TObject);
   :
      with Image_panel do begin
         Total := 0;
         if BorderStyle = bsSingle then
            Control_border := 2
           else
            Control_border := 0;
         Total := Total + Control_border;
         if BevelInner = bvNone then
            if BevelOuter = bvNone then
               Total := Total + BorderWidth {Optionally}
              else
               Total := Total + BevelWidth + BorderWidth {Optionally}
           else
            if BevelOuter = bvNone then
               Total := Total + BevelWidth + BorderWidth
              else
               Total := Total + (2 * BevelWidth) + BorderWidth;
      end;
```

This section of code is practically a general-purpose routine for figuring out the important dimensions of a Panel. Before we can consider the effects of the bevel on the "usable" area inside a panel, we must consider the control border common to many controls. If there is a **bsSingle** border on a control, a single-pixel line is drawn around the control's border, within the control's space, taking away one usable pixel from each edge. Then a one-pixel margin is achieved by setting the control's client area one pixel inside of that boundary. We lose 2 pixels on each edge if we use a **bsSingle** border. If we don't, the area is all our own. We record this in **Control_border**.

Within the control's area, then, we need to account for an outer bevel, a border width, and an inner bevel. If there is no inner bevel, the border width between the bevels will appear to be part of the panel *floor* (the usable area). We could just ignore the **BorderWidth** in these cases if we always wanted to maximize the area available inside. However, in order to have more control at design time, we kept the **BorderWidth** operative. If there is an outer or inner bevel, we need to add **BevelWidth** to the total border thickness, **Total**, for each one. We also need to add in the **BorderWidth**.

We are then left with two values. The **Total** is the total thickness of the control's border and beveling at each edge. This controls the maximum **Width** of anything we want to put inside the Panel: the maximum **Width** (or **Height**, for that matter) is the Panel's **Width**, less **Total**—once for each side. If there is a **Control_border**, though, the client area actually starts two pixels in from the edge; so when we deal with coordinates inside the Panel (for instance, when we want to offset something away from the edge to avoid overdrawing the bevels), we need to subtract off the **Control_border**. These are the equivalent adjustments we make to **Image1** so that it fits inside the **Image_panel**, as shown in the code snippet below.

```
with Image1 do begin
  { Panel window coordinates start with the point
    (0,0) inside the control's 2-pixel border that
    is present if TPanel.BorderStyle is bsSingle.
    Usable area is still calculated from the Form
    coordinates. }
  Left   := Total - Control_border;
  Top    := Total - Control_border;
  Width  := Image_panel.Width  - (2 * Total);
  Height := Image_panel.Height - (2 * Total);
end;
```

Springing Towards the Finish

Resizing the form is the last issue we'll review. Resizing this form is complicated by the presence of two work areas that must share the same space. We'll take the simplest way out here by keeping the relative proportions of the areas the same as their design-time setting. This is referred to as *springing*. It would be a lot of work, without much benefit in most cases, to develop a splitter-bar to divide the areas; but in the Windows 95 *Explorer*, the users' ability to change the use of horizontal space is critical to the application. It's important to realize that this is an option.

We keep the **Left** position of **Panel1**, the left panel, relative to the Form, as a proportional constant. We chose **Panel1.Left** because this is the placement that will change; the **Image_panel** will always have its **Left** just inside the form. Each of the Panels' **Width**s will change also, but with this one midpoint position value, we'll be able to calculate both **Width**s. The spring constant is calculated as a **single** real number in the **FormCreate** handler, as:

```
Panel1_on_Form1 := Panel1.Left / Form1.Width;
```

Now, we can multiply any Form **Width** by this constant and **round** the value to an approximate location giving the same proportionate positions. We do this in **FormResize**. To aid in the overall movement of controls, at this point we've already calculated **Incr_X** and **Incr_Y** as the increase in the size of the Form in both directions, after enforcing the minimum size of the Form, as shown in the code snippet below:

```
with Panel1 do begin
    Old_left  := Left;
    Old_width := Width;
    Left   := round(Form1.Width * Panel1_on_Form1);
    Width  := ScrollBar1.Left - Left;
    Height := Height + Incr_Y;
    Image_panel_incr_X := Left - Old_left;
    end;
```

The amount by which the text Panel moved to the left on the form is given by its new location, **Panel1.Left**, less its old location, **Old_Left**. Since the **Left** side of the control has moved (relative to the Form) that far, the **Width** of the image area on the right can increase by that much and still keep the same distance from the text area. Thus, we name this **Image_panel_incr_X**, the increase in the size of the **Image_panel**, as shown in the code snippet below.

```
with Image_panel do  begin
    Width  := Width + Image_panel_incr_X;
    Height := Height + Incr_Y;
    end;
with PaintBox1 do begin
    Width  := Width + (Panel1.Width - Old_width);
    Height := Height + Incr_Y;
    end;
with Image1 do begin
    Image1.Width := Image1.Width + Image_panel_incr_X;
    Image1.Height:= Image1.Height + Incr_Y;
    end;
```

The Listings

Here are the cut-down listings of the changes to units **Main**, **HTML**, and **DispBuf**. Refer to the CD-ROM for the full source code for these units. Remember, if a line begins with a colon (:), it means that some code has been omitted at that point in the listing.

Listing 11.1   Unit **Main** from *Magic I*, with changes from *Hyper IV* highlighted

```
unit Main;

interface

uses
  SysUtils, WinTypes, WinProcs, Messages, Classes, Graphics, Controls,
  Forms, Dialogs, StdCtrls, ExtCtrls;

type
  TForm1 = class(TForm)
    Panel1: TPanel;
    ScrollBar1: TScrollBar;
    Open_button: TButton;
    OpenDialog1: TOpenDialog;
    PaintBox1: TPaintBox;
    Image_panel: TPanel;
    Image1: TImage;
    Close_button: TButton;
    Filename: TEdit;
    Label1: TLabel;
    Bevel1: TBevel;

    procedure FormCreate(Sender: TObject);
    procedure FormResize(Sender: TObject);
    procedure PaintBox1MouseDown(Sender: TObject; Button: TMouseButton;
      Shift: TShiftState; X, Y: Integer);
    procedure ScrollBar1Change(Sender: TObject);
    procedure FilenameKeyPress(Sender: TObject; var Key: Char);
    procedure Open_buttonClick(Sender: TObject);
    procedure Close_buttonClick(Sender: TObject);
    procedure PaintBox1Paint(Sender: TObject);
  private
    { Private declarations }
  public
    { Public declarations }
  end;

var
  Form1: TForm1;

implementation
```

```
    uses
        MMSystem,
        MiscLib, DispBuf, HyperLnk, Parser;

:

procedure Jump_to(
  const Target : string
  );
    var
        Re_show : boolean;
        Ext     : string;
        Command : ansiString;
    begin with TParser.Parse(pchar(Target)) do begin
        Re_show := true;
        No_errors;
        Find('#');
        if Error then begin
            { Just "filename".  Could be a media file. }
            Re_show := false;
            Ext := uppercase(extractFileExt(Remainder));
            if  (Ext = '.WAV')
              or
                (Ext = '.MID')
              or
                (Ext = '.AVI')
              then begin
                Command := 'Play ' + strPas(Remainder);
                mciExecute(pchar('Play ' + strPas(Remainder)));
                end
              else if
                (Ext = '.BMP')
              or
                (Ext = '.RLE')
              or
                (Ext = '.WMF')
              or
                (Ext = '.ICO')
              then
                Form1.Image1.Picture.LoadFromFile(Remainder)
              else begin
                { 'HTM', et al. }
                Form1.Filename.Text := Remainder;
                Load_HTML;
                Re_show := true;
                end
            end
          else begin
            if Last_found^ <> #0 then begin
                { There was a filename in "filename#label".
                  <label> is in Remainder. }
                Form1.Filename.Text := Last_found;
                Load_HTML;
                end
```

```
                    else
                        ; { Just "#label". }
                    Set_scrollbar(
                       Int_max(
                          Output.Dest_name_anchors.First_rect_of_name(Remainder).Top,
                          0
                          )
                       );
                    end;
            if Re_show then Form1.PaintBox1.Refresh;
            Free;
            end; end;

:

procedure TForm1.FilenameKeyPress(Sender: TObject; var Key: Char);
    begin
        if Key = #13 then begin
            Jump_to(Filename.Text);
            Key := #0;
            end;
        end;

procedure TForm1.Open_buttonClick(Sender: TObject);
    begin
        if OpenDialog1.Execute then begin
            Filename.Text := OpenDialog1.Filename;
            Jump_to(Filename.Text);
            end;
        end;

:

procedure TForm1.PaintBox1Paint(Sender: TObject);
    begin
        Output.Display(Form1.Image1);
        end;

var
    Resizing_ourselves : boolean;
    Form1s_old_width,
    Form1s_old_height  : integer;
    Panel1_on_Form1    : single;

procedure TForm1.FormCreate(Sender: TObject);
    var
        Total,
        Control_border : integer;
    begin
        Resizing_ourselves := false;
        Form1s_old_width   := Form1.Width;
        Form1s_old_height  := Form1.Height;
        Panel1_on_Form1    := Panel1.Left / Form1.Width;
```

```pascal
        with Image_panel do begin
            Total := 0;
            if BorderStyle = bsSingle then
                Control_border := 2
              else
                Control_border := 0;
            Total := Total + Control_border;
            if BevelInner = bvNone then
                if BevelOuter = bvNone then
                    Total := Total + BorderWidth {Optionally}
                  else
                    Total := Total + BevelWidth + BorderWidth {Optionally}
              else
                if BevelOuter = bvNone then
                    Total := Total + BevelWidth + BorderWidth
                  else
                    Total := Total + (2 * BevelWidth) + BorderWidth;
            end;
        with Image1 do begin
            { Panel window coordinates start with the point
              (0,0) inside the control's 2-pixel border that
              is present if TPanel.BorderStyle is bsSingle.
              Usable area is still calculated from the Form
              coordinates. }
            Left   := Total - Control_border;
            Top    := Total - Control_border;
            Width  := Image_panel.Width  - (2 * Total);
            Height := Image_panel.Height - (2 * Total);
            end;
        Output := nil;
        end;

procedure TForm1.FormResize(Sender: TObject);
    var
        Minimum_width,
        Incr_X,
        Incr_Y,
        Old_left,
        Old_width,
        Image_panel_incr_X : integer;
    begin
        if Resizing_ourselves then exit;

        Minimum_width := Filename.Left + 100;
        with Form1 do begin
            if Width < Minimum_width then
                Width := Minimum_width;
            if Height < 100 then
                Height := 100;
            Incr_X := Form1.Width  - Form1s_old_width;
            Incr_Y := Form1.Height - Form1s_old_height;
            end;
        Filename.Width := Filename.Width + Incr_X;
        Bevel1.Width   := Bevel1.Width   + Incr_X;
```

```
       with ScrollBar1 do begin
           Left   := Left   + Incr_X;
           Height := Height + Incr_Y;
           end;
       with Panel1 do begin
           Old_left  := Left;
           Old_width := Width;
           Left   := round(Form1.Width * Panel1_on_Form1);
           Width  := ScrollBar1.Left - Left;
           Height := Height + Incr_Y;
           Image_panel_incr_X := Left - Old_left;
           end;
       with Image_panel do  begin
           Width  := Width + Image_panel_incr_X;
           Height := Height + Incr_Y;
           end;
       with PaintBox1 do begin
           Width  := Width + (Panel1.Width - Old_width);
           Height := Height + Incr_Y;
           end;
       with Image1 do begin
           Image1.Width := Image1.Width + Image_panel_incr_X;
           Image1.Height:= Image1.Height + Incr_Y;
           end;
       Resizing_ourselves := false;

       Form1s_old_width  := Form1.Width;
       Form1s_old_height := Form1.Height;

       Load_HTML; { To re-parse }

       Form1.Refresh;
       end;

end.
```

Listing 11.2 Unit HTML from *Magic I*, with changes from *Hyper IV* highlighted

```
unit HTML;

interface

uses
    Classes,
    Font,
    HyperLnk;

procedure Process_special_characters(
  S : pchar { var S^ }
  );

type
    tHTML_format = record
```

```
            Serial_number     : integer;
            Leading_newlines  : integer;
            Font              : tHTML_font_spec;
            Rule_height       : integer;
            Anchor_reference  : integer;
            Anchor_dest_name  : integer;
            Preformatted      : boolean;
            Image_name        : string;
            end;

procedure Parse_tag(
    const          The_tag        : pchar;
    var {in/out}   Format         : tHTML_format;
    const          HRef_anchors   : tNamed_rectangle_list;
    const          Name_anchors   : tNamed_rectangle_list;
    var            Do_a_newline   : boolean;
    var            Rule_height    : integer;
    var            Image_name     : string
    );

implementation

uses
    SysUtils, Graphics,
    MiscLib, Parser;

  :

procedure Parse_tag(
    const          The_tag        : pchar;
    var {in/out}   Format         : tHTML_format;
    const          HRef_anchors   : tNamed_rectangle_list;
    const          Name_anchors   : tNamed_rectangle_list;
    var            Do_a_newline   : boolean;
    var            Rule_height    : integer;
    var            Image_name     : string
    );

    :

    procedure Parse_IMG_tag;
        begin with The_parser do begin
            Expect('NAME');
            Expect('=');
            Expect('"');
            Find('"');
            Expect(' ');
            Image_name := Last_found
            end; end;

    procedure Process_tag(
      const Word : pchar
        );
```

Expanding the VB Multimedia Engine 513

```
        begin with Format do begin
            if Word[0] = '!' then
                { Comment -- Do nothing. NOT STANDARD HTML! }
            else if StrComp(Word,'HTML') = 0 then

                :

            else if StrComp(Word,'/PRE') = 0 then
                Parse_end_PRE_tag
            else if StrComp(Word,'IMG') = 0 then
                Parse_IMG_tag
            else
                { It's a currently unsupported tag. }
                :
        end; end;

:

    begin
        :
        end;

{initialization}
    end.
```

Listing 11.3   Unit **DispBuf** from *Magic I*, with changes from *Hyper IV* highlighted

```
unit DispBuf;

interface

uses
    Classes, Graphics, Controls, ExtCtrls,
    Font, FmtText, HyperLnk;

:

    tDisplay_buffer = class
      private
        { Formatted Text Storage }
        Formatted_text_list : tFormatted_text_list;
        { "Breaker" Data -- Line Breaking list }
        Line_list : TList; {of integer}
        { "Displayer" Data }
        Control : tGraphicControlWithCanvas;
      public
        { Hyperlink support lists, built by "Breaker" }
        Reference_anchors : tNamed_rectangle_list;
        Dest_name_anchors : tNamed_rectangle_list;
        { Display Positioning and Height, calc'd by "Breaker" }
        Display_top,
        Display_bottom : integer;
```

```
      public
        constructor Create(
          const _Control : tGraphicControlWithCanvas
          );
        destructor Destroy; override;
        procedure Load_HTML_file(
          const Filename : string
          );
        procedure Display(
          const Aux_image : TImage
          );
        end;

implementation

  :

procedure tDisplay_buffer.Load_HTML_file(
  const Filename : string
  );

    procedure Process_HTML_string(
      const Text : pchar
      );

        procedure Parse_HTML(
          Text   : pchar;
          Format : tHTML_format
          );

            :

          procedure Reset_buffer;

          procedure Add_buffer_to_list;

          procedure Set_format(

          procedure New_line;

          procedure Horizontal_rule(

          procedure Image(
            const _Image_name : string
            );
              begin
                Add_buffer_to_list;
                Current_format.Image_name := _Image_name;
                Current_format.Leading_newlines := 0;
                  { If there were Pending_newlines and text
                    to go with them, Add_buffer_to_list got
                    them.  If they were saved, then
                    Pending_newlines isn't adjusted, and will
                    be taken the next time ABTL gets called. }
```

Expanding the VB Multimedia Engine

```
            Formatted_text_list.Add(
              tFormatted_text.Create(Current_format,'')
              );
            Current_format.Image_name := '';
            end;

procedure Emit(

function Is_whitespace(const C : char) : boolean;

function Is_word(const C : char) : boolean;

var
    Need_a_newline,
    Preceeding_newline,
    Preceeding_space    : boolean;
    Space_format        : tHTML_format;
    Rule_height         : integer;
    Image_name          : string;
    The_end : pchar;
    Saved   : char;
    EOL     : pchar;
    Word    : pchar;

begin
    :
    while Text^ <> #0 do
        if Text^ = '<' then begin
            { Process a Tag }
            :
            inc(Text);
            The_end^ := #0;
            Parse_tag(Text,
              Format,
              Reference_anchors,
              Dest_name_anchors,
              Need_a_newline,
              Rule_height,
              Image_name
              );
            Text := The_end + 1;
            Preceeding_newline :=
              Preceeding_newline or Need_a_newline;
            if Preceeding_newline then
                Preceeding_space := false;
            if Rule_height > 0 then
                Horizontal_rule(Rule_height);
            if Image_name <> '' then
                Image(Image_name);
            Set_format(Format);
            end

        else if Format.Preformatted then begin
          { Process Preformatted Text }
```

```
                    :
                  else if Text^ <= ' ' then begin
                    { Process Whitespace }
                    :
                    end
                  else begin
                    { Process Words }
                    :
                    end;
              :
            end;

      procedure Break_into_lines;


      begin
        with Format, Font do begin
            Leading_newlines := 0;
            Serial_number    := 0;
            specStyle        := [];
            specName         := 'Times New Roman';
            specColor        := clBlack;
            specSize         := 3;
            Rule_height      := 0;
            Anchor_reference := -1;
            Anchor_dest_name := -1;
            Preformatted     := false;
            Image_name       := '';
            end;
        Parse_HTML(Text,Format);
        Break_into_lines;
        end;

  :
  begin
      :
      end;

procedure Draw_rule(

procedure tDisplay_buffer.Display(
  const Aux_image : TImage
  );

    function Line_after(

    function Line_before(

:

    begin with Formatted_text_list do begin
        :
        for I := First_elem to Last_elem do
            with tFormatted_text(Items[I]), Format do
```

```
            if Rule_height > 0 then
                Draw_rule(Control.Canvas,
                  Point(Base_left_corner.X,
                        Base_left_corner.Y - Display_top),
                  Meas.Width,Rule_height
                  )
                else if (Aux_image <> nil) and (Image_name <> '') then
                  Aux_image.Picture.LoadFromFile(Image_name)
                else if Text <> nil then
                  with Control.Canvas do begin
                    Set_font_from_spec(Font,Format.Font);
                    SetTextAlign(Handle,TA_BASELINE);
                    TextOut(
                      Base_left_corner.X,
                      Base_left_corner.Y - Display_top,
                      Text
                      );
                  end;

       end; end;

{initialization}
    end.
```

Simple, But Effective

This completes our discussion of basic image support. One thing we did to keep things simple—far too simple to meet the needs of most real presentation packages—was to set our Image control's **Stretch** property to **True**. We've opened up the subject now, and in our next project, we'll address this issue with a vengeance.

You may find yourself with a simple, fixed-size slide presentation project, though; and in this case, you could fix the size of the Image control to that of your slides, and be finished. Since that's not likely to happen, though—Onward!

Refining the Hypermedia Engine

At this stage of development of the hypermedia engine, we are going to fix the image distortion problem and add support for hotspots within the images. It will not be at all difficult to implement these features, especially the hotspots, because we have already completed all required background work. Back in Chapter 10 we created a completely independent unit, **Hotspots**, that has a great deal of the basic hotspot support we need to implement hotspots in images. We will now extend the code module from *Magic I* so that it can handle image hotspots, as well as image scaling and justification.

Magic II: Images with Hotspots—A Finished Presentation Engine

With the addition of three more units, we'll complete a finished multimedia presentation system, *The Magic Hypermedia Engine*. One new unit will handle proportionally-resized images; another new unit will support hotspot regions on the images. We'll also go back to the *Irregular Hotspot Editor* of Chapter 10 and reuse the basic hotspot database definition unit, **Hotspots**, from project **Hotspot3**.

1. We're going on to the second version of our Magic project, *Magic II*; so we need to start yet another new project, using the files we've been using all along. Make a new project directory, *Magic2*, and an output subdirectory beneath this, *Bin*. With the *Explorer*, copy the project files from your *Magic1* directory to your *Magic2* directory. Rename your "Magic1" files to "Magic2". You'll need the *DPR*, *PAS*, and *DFM* files.

2. Open your **Magic2** Project file in Delphi. The compiler will complain that its name is wrong ("Module header is missing or incorrect."). Change its program name from **Magic1** to **Magic2**. In the *Project Options* dialog box (from *Project | Options*), set the Application Title to "Magic II," and its output directory to "Bin."

3. We'll tackle the problems that revolve about displaying images with the correct proportions first, in unit **ImgPanel** (Listing 11.4). This unit contains three general purpose procedures that do not actually implement a whole new class of display elements, but they can help you corral Images within Panels. A fourth routine contains hooks to support hotpsot region lists, which are defined at the next step.

4. Unit **RgnList** (Listing 11.5) implements a list of Windows GDI regions associated with a particular image and holds their target references as well. This unit relies on the **Hotspots** unit from **Hotspot3**, and we'll tackle that next.

5. Copy the unit **Hotspots** from your **Hotspot3** project directory to your **Magic2** directory. From Delphi's menu, choose *File | Add to project...* and add the unit. We don't need to make any changes. We won't be using several of the procedures, but Delphi's dead code elimination will take care of trimming the extra code from the project when it is compiled.

Expanding the VB Multimedia Engine   519

6. To finish up this project, we need to make some minor changes to the units **DispBuf** and **Main**. These are simple, because the difficult work was already moved off into **ImgPanel** and **RgnList**.

Most of the source units from Hyper4 stay the same. At this point, the full source code for *Magic II* can be found in the listings of **MiscLib** (Listing 3.1 from *Hyper I*); **FmtText** (Listing 3.3 from *Hyper I*, with modifications from Listing 3.12 from *Hyper II*); **Parser**, **HyperLnk** (Listings 3.9 and 3.10 from *Hyper II*); **Font** (Listing 3.16 from *Hyper III*); and HTML (Listing 3.11 with mods in Listing 11.2). Further modifications are made to the units **Main** (Listing 11.6), and **DispBuf** (Listing 11.7).

> *You'll find this project in the subdirectory \PROGRAMS\CHAP11\MAGIC2 on the accompanying CD-ROM. For our examples here, we'll be using the files magic1.HTM through magic4.HTM from \MEDIA\HYPERTXT.*

Running the Magic Hypermedia Engine

By running the program, you'll see the window shown in Figure 11.4. Notice that the subject "HyperMedia" is displayed just as it was in all the previous hypertext projects. But this time, *The Kaibab Plateau* scaled correctly, and clicking on the copyright information causes a WAV file to be played. This illustrates how a hotspot can be added to an image.

We have also placed the compiled version of *Hotspot III*, the *Irregular Hotspot Editor*, in the application directory so that you can easily create new hotspots or edit the ones we have created.

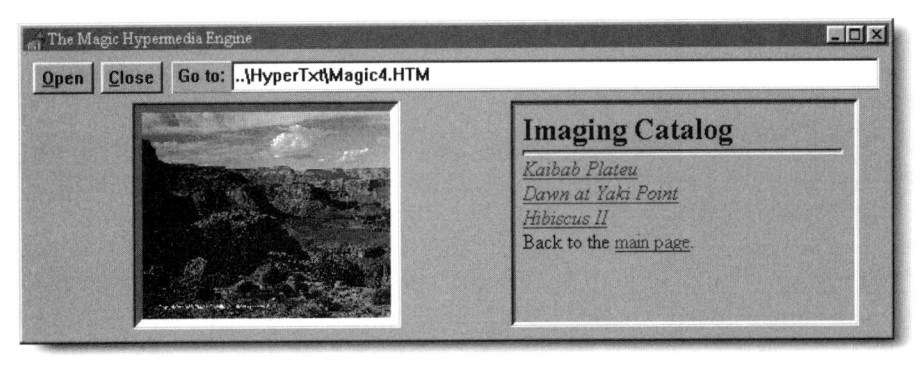

Figure 11.4 *Magic2*, The Magic Hypermedia Engine at work.

Try adding your own images to the system. Use the hotspot editor to define the hotspots, then add hotlinks to the HTML file that point to the pictures. Remember not to create any dead ends—although if you do, you can always stop the program.

Proportionally-sized Images and their Panels

In *Magic I*, we had some in-line code in the main form's **OnCreate** event handler to determine the size of an Image that could fit within a Panel. We've moved this functionality out to a new unit, **ImgPanel**, that supports relationships like this.

The routine **Get_panel_specs** measures a Panel's edges for us. **Set_image_in_panel** uses this information to change the size of an Image to fit it within the working portion of the client area of a Panel. With some re-arrangement of terms, these routines are not significantly different than the in-line code for **TForm1.FormCreate** in *Magic I*. The entire unit is shown in Listing 11.4.

Listing 11.4   Unit **ImgPanel** from *Magic II*

```
unit ImgPanel;

interface

uses
    Windows, ExtCtrls,
    Hotspots, RgnList;

procedure Get_panel_specs(
  const Panel : TPanel;
  var   Border_width : integer;
  var   Bevel_width  : integer
  );

procedure Set_image_in_panel(
  const Image : TImage;
  const Panel : TPanel
  );

procedure Stretch_panel_on_image_in_rect(
  const Panel : TPanel;
  const Image : TImage;
  const Rect  : TRect;
  var   Scale : single
  );

procedure Load_image(
  const Filename : string;
  const Panel    : TPanel;
  const Image    : TImage;
```

```
    const Rect       : TRect;
    var   Scale      : single;
    const Regions    : tRegion_list;
    const HS_table   : tHotspot_table
    );

implementation

uses
    Forms;

procedure Get_panel_specs(
  const Panel : TPanel;
  var   Border_width : integer;
  var   Bevel_width  : integer
  );
    begin
        Border_width := 0;
        Bevel_width  := 0;
        with Panel do begin
            if BorderStyle = bsSingle then Border_width := 2;
            if BevelInner = bvNone then
                if BevelOuter = bvNone then
                    Bevel_width := BorderWidth {Optionally}
                  else
                    Bevel_width := BevelWidth + BorderWidth {Optionally}
              else
                if BevelOuter = bvNone then
                    Bevel_width := BevelWidth + BorderWidth
                  else
                    Bevel_width := (2 * BevelWidth) + BorderWidth;
            end;
        end;

procedure Set_image_in_panel(
  const Image : TImage;
  const Panel : TPanel
  );
    var
        Border, Bevel : integer;
    begin
        Get_panel_specs(Panel,Border,Bevel);
        with Image do begin
            { Panel window coordinates start with the point
              (0,0) inside the control's 2-pixel border that
              is present if TPanel.BorderStyle is bsSingle.
              Usable area is still calculated from the Form
              coordinates. }
            Left   := Bevel;
            Top    := Bevel;
            Width  := Panel.Width  - (2 * (Bevel + Border));
            Height := Panel.Height - (2 * (Bevel + Border));
            end;
        end;
```

```
procedure Stretch_panel_on_image_in_rect(
  const Panel : TPanel;
  const Image : TImage;
  const Rect  : TRect;
  var   Scale : single
  );
    var
        Border, Bevel : integer;
        Max_width,
        Max_height    : integer;
    begin
        Get_panel_specs(Panel,Border,Bevel);
        with Rect do begin
            Max_width  := Right  - Left - (2 * (Bevel + Border));
            Max_height := Bottom - Top  - (2 * (Bevel + Border));
            end;
        with Image do begin
            Stretch :=    (Picture.Width  > Max_width)
                       or
                          (Picture.Height > Max_height);
            if Stretch then begin
                Scale := Max_width / Picture.Width;
                if round(Scale * Picture.Height) > Max_height then
                    { It won't fit vertically. }
                    Scale := Max_height / Picture.Height;
                end
              else
                Scale := 1;
            Width  := round(Picture.Width  * Scale);
            Height := round(Picture.Height * Scale);
            Left   := Bevel;
            Top    := Bevel;
            end;
        with Panel do begin
            Width  := Image.Width  + 2 * (Border + Bevel);
            Height := Image.Height + 2 * (Border + Bevel);
            Left   := Rect.Left +
                      (Rect.Right  - Rect.Left - Width ) div 2;
            Top    := Rect.Top +
                      (Rect.Bottom - Rect.Top  - Height) div 2;
            end;
        end;

procedure Load_image(
  const Filename : string;
  const Panel    : TPanel;
  const Image    : TImage;
  const Rect     : TRect;
  var   Scale    : single;
  const Regions  : tRegion_list;
  const HS_table : tHotspot_table
  );
    begin
        Image.Visible := false;
```

```
      Image.Picture.LoadFromFile(Filename);
      Stretch_panel_on_image_in_rect(
        Panel,Image,Rect,Scale
        );
      Image.Visible := true;
      Regions.Add_regions_for(Filename,HS_Table);
      end;

end.
```

Proportionally Sizing Images

Stretch_panel_on_image_in_rect is a long name for a powerful procedure. Our goal is to display a resized copy of an image in a space that fits on the form, whatever its current size. We accomplished that in *Magic I* by setting **Image1**'s **Stretch** property to **True**; this, however, causes horrible vertical and horizontal exaggeration of the image in most cases. To preserve the quality of the image, we need to restrict the image's display area to the same proportions as the image itself.

When we load a picture into an Image control with its **Picture.LoadFromFile** method, the picture is stored separately from the actual image displayed on the screen. That way, when the Image control needs to be repainted or resized, the control can simply copy the original image from its **Picture** property to its client area, stretching it when the Image's **Stretch** property is set to **True**.

For us, this means we always have access to the image's actual size, and thus, its proportions. All we need to do is figure out which dimension, the horizontal or vertical, limits the size of the image, and then size the other dimension accordingly. Actually, it isn't quite that simplistic: We also need to take into account the total area which we're able to use for image display and the edge dimensions of the surrounding Panel.

```
Get_panel_specs(Panel,Border,Bevel);
with Rect do begin
    Max_width  := Right  - Left - (2 * (Bevel + Border));
    Max_height := Bottom - Top  - (2 * (Bevel + Border));
    end;
```

Rect is passed in as the total area of the form that we are allowed to use. This is equivalent to the footprint of the Panel from *Magic I,* but since we'll have some excess space, we need to treat the actual free form area differently. We keep it as a rectangle here, and later you'll see how we maintain the size of the rectangle during the Form's **OnResize** event. The maximum width of the image that can fit into the area specified by **Rect**, **Max_width**, and the maximum height, **Max_height**, are calculated based on the measurements of the **Panel**'s edges, as shown in the code snippet below.

```
with Image do begin
   Stretch :=   (Picture.Width  > Max_width)
             or
                (Picture.Height > Max_height);
   if Stretch then begin
      Scale := Max_width / Picture.Width;
      if round(Scale * Picture.Height) > Max_height then
         { It won't fit vertically. }
         Scale := Max_height / Picture.Height;
      end
   else
      Scale := 1;
   Width  := round(Picture.Width  * Scale);
   Height := round(Picture.Height * Scale);
   Left   := Bevel;
   Top    := Bevel;
   end;
```

We only need to shrink the image if it won't fit in the allowed area, so we check this to set the **Stretch** property of the **Image**. There is nothing preventing us from enlarging the image beyond its original size, but since image quality degrades rapidly when enlarging pictures in this way, we don't do that here. If we have to **Stretch** the **Image**, we try fitting the picture in horizontally to see if its vertical size fits when its horizontal size fills the available area. If the picture won't fit this way, it will definitely fit the other way, so we calculate the **Scale** based on fitting the picture into the area horizontally. Once we have calculated a **Scale** for our **Image** to make it fit the maximum available area of our footprint **Rect**, we can go ahead and resize the **Image**.

After that, all we need to do is wrap the Panel around the Image. We also take this opportunity to center the **Panel** within the **Rect** area, as shown in the code snippet below.

```
with Panel do begin
   Width  := Image.Width  + 2 * (Border + Bevel);
   Height := Image.Height + 2 * (Border + Bevel);
   Left   := Rect.Left +
             (Rect.Right  - Rect.Left - Width ) div 2;
   Top    := Rect.Top +
             (Rect.Bottom - Rect.Top  - Height) div 2;
   end;
```

You may have noticed that the **Scale** is set here and passed out as a **var** parameter. Why? In order to detect mouse-clicks in a scaled-down image, we'll need to be able to transform the mouse-click coordinates from their location on the scaled-down size, back up to the image's real size.

Loading Scaled Images

This unit provides one last utility routine, **Load_image**, that handles all of the required operations to load a scaled image. As we've coded it here, it also loads the hotspots for the image. Depending on your point of view, this may or may not be a good thing. Hotspot region lists, which we'll discuss below, are not tightly related to this code; and you could argue that the calling code should call a cut-down **Load_image** without the hotspot support, and then call **Add_regions_for** independently. We've chosen to do this here, as shown in the code snippet below, because this ensures that we always load the hotspot regions when we load an **Image**.

```
procedure Load_image(
  const Filename : string;
  const Panel    : TPanel;
  const Image    : TImage;
  const Rect     : TRect;
  var   Scale    : single;
  const Regions  : tRegion_list;
  const HS_table : tHotspot_table
  );
  begin
     Image.Visible := false;
     Image.Picture.LoadFromFile(Filename);
     Stretch_panel_on_image_in_rect(
       Panel,Image,Rect,Scale
       );
     Image.Visible := true;
     Regions.Add_regions_for(Filename,HS_Table);
  end;
```

There are no surprises: we make the **Image** disappear during the resizing, load the new picture from the specified **Filename**, stretch everything out, and make the **Image** visible again. Then we load the regions for the image's hotspots from the **Hotspots** table, with the call to **Add_regions_for**. We'll look into this next. Again, notice that we pass the **Scale** back out to the caller; the regions will be created using the image's real hotspot coordinates, and we'll still need to transform the coordinates.

Hotspots and their Region Lists

Images can have more than one hotspot on them, so we need some sort of dynamic structure to hold the hotspots for an image. We are going to take advantage of GDI regions, so that we don't need to write our own "point-in-polygon" routine. This gives us another advantage: all we have to store in the list is a handle to a region, rather than a whole list of vertices. The class

tRegion_list (implemented in unit **RgnList** and shown in Listing 11.5) handles the conversion from vertice lists in the database to regions in a searchable list.

Listing 11.5 Unit **RgnList** from *Magic II*

```
unit RgnList;

interface

uses
    Windows, Classes, DBTables,
    Hotspots;

type
    tRegion = class
      public
        Target : string;
        Region : HRgn;
        constructor Create(
          const _Target       : string;
          const Vertex_count  : integer;
          const Vertices      : pointer
          );
        destructor Destroy; override;
        end;

    tRegion_list = class(TList)
      public
        destructor Destroy; override;
        procedure Clear;
        function Add(
          const Target        : string;
          const Vertices_BLOb : TBLObField
          ) : integer;
        procedure Add_regions_for(
          const Current_image_filename : string;
          const Hotspot_table          : tHotspot_table
          );
        function Target_reference_of(
          const X, Y : integer
          ) : string;
        end;

implementation

uses
    SysUtils;

constructor tRegion.Create(
  const _Target       : string;
  const Vertex_count  : integer;
  const Vertices      : pointer
  );
```

```
    type
        tPoint_array_ptr = ^tPoint_array;
        tPoint_array     = array[1..1] of TPoint;
    var
        I : integer;
    begin
        inherited Create;
        (*
        {$R-} { For array indexing... }
        for I := 1 to Vertex_count do
            with tPoint_array_ptr(Vertices)^[I] do begin
                X := round(X * Scale);
                Y := round(Y * Scale);
                end;
        {$R+}
        *)
        Target := _Target;
        Region := CreatePolygonRgn(
                    Vertices^,
                    Vertex_count,
                    ALTERNATE
                    );
        end;

destructor tRegion.Destroy;
    begin
        DeleteObject(Region);
        inherited Destroy;
        end;

destructor tRegion_list.Destroy;
    begin
        Clear;
        inherited Destroy;
        end;

procedure tRegion_list.Clear;
    var
        I : integer;
    begin
        for I := 0 to Count - 1 do
            tRegion(Items[I]).Free;
        inherited Clear;
        end;

function tRegion_list.Add(
  const Target        : string;
  const Vertices_BLOb : TBLObField
  ) : integer;
    var
        V_stream     : TMemoryStream;
        Vertex_count : integer;
    begin
        V_stream := TMemoryStream.Create;
```

```
                Vertices_BLOb.SaveToStream(V_stream);
                Vertex_count := V_stream.Size div sizeof(TPoint);
                result := inherited Add(
                                  tRegion.Create(
                                    Target,
                                    Vertex_count,
                                    V_stream.Memory
                                    )
                                  );
          V_stream.Free;
          end;

procedure tRegion_list.Add_regions_for(
  const Current_image_filename : string;
  const Hotspot_table           : tHotspot_table
  );
    begin
        Clear;
        with Hotspot_table do begin
            Open;
            First;
            while not EOF do begin
                if  Uppercase(ExtractFileName(FieldByName('Image').AsString))
                    =
                    Uppercase(ExtractFileName(Current_image_filename))
                then
                    Add(
                      FieldByName('Target').AsString,
                      TBLObField(FieldByName('Vertices'))
                      );
                Next;
                end;
            Close;
            end;
        end;

function tRegion_list.Target_reference_of(
  const X, Y : integer
  ) : string;
    var
        I     : integer;
        Found : boolean;
    begin
        result := '';
        Found := false;
        I := 0;
        while (I < Count) and not Found do
            with tRegion(Items[I]) do begin
                Found := PtInRegion(Region,X,Y);
                if Found then
                    result := Target
                  else
                    inc(I);
```

```
          end;
     end;
end.
```

Because we want to fall back on Delphi's built-in **TList**, we need to declare the class of objects we want to store in the region list. The objects themselves are **tRegion**s, as shown in the code snippet below.

```
tRegion = class
  public
    Target : string;
    Region : HRgn;
    constructor Create(
      const _Target       : string;
      const Vertex_count  : integer;
      const Vertices      : pointer
      );
    destructor Destroy; override;
  end;
```

A **tRegion** holds a **Target**, which is the reference of the hotspot, and a handle to a region, named **Region**, that we'll later be able to test a mouse-click against, using the GDI function **PtInRegion**. To create the **tRegion** with its constructor **Create**, we'll accept a vertex list and vertex count, and use these in a call to **CreatePolygonRgn**. When we **Free** a **tRegion**, our overriding destructor **Destroy** will be called. It simply deletes the **Region** that was created, as shown in the code snippet below.

```
constructor tRegion.Create(
  const _Target       : string;
  const Vertex_count  : integer;
  const Vertices      : pointer
  );
  begin
    inherited Create;
    Target := _Target;
    Region := CreatePolygonRgn(
              Vertices^,
              Vertex_count,
              ALTERNATE
              );
  end;

destructor tRegion.Destroy;
  begin
    DeleteObject(Region);
    inherited Destroy;
  end;
```

The list of regions, class **tRegion_list**, descends as we had planned from **TList**. We need to implement our own **Clear** method, so that when we load a new image and clear the list, we have an opportunity to **Free** the **tRegion**s stored in the list. The **Add** method we'll write takes a **TBLObField** from the database that holds a vertices list for the hotspot. In order to load all of the regions for an image at once, we're adding the method **Add_regions_for**, which takes an image's filename and retrieves all of the hotspots from the database for that image, and places them in the list, using **Add**. Finally, we need a way to tell if a hotspot in the **tRegion_list** has been hit. **Target_reference_of** returns the **Target** of the first region it finds that contains the given point, as shown in the code snippet below.

```
tRegion_list = class(TList)
  public
    destructor Destroy; override;
    procedure Clear;
    function Add(
      const Target         : string;
      const Vertices_BLOb : TBLObField
      ) : integer;
    procedure Add_regions_for(
      const Current_image_filename : string;
      const Hotspot_table          : tHotspot_table
      );
    function Target_reference_of(
      const X, Y : integer
      ) : string;
  end;
```

Destroy and **Clear** are so simple we won't look at them closely. **Add**, however, is required to make sense of the data in a **TBLObField** as a vertices list, as shown in the code snippet below.

```
function tRegion_list.Add(
  const Target         : string;
  const Vertices_BLOb : TBLObField
  ) : integer;
    var
        V_stream      : TMemoryStream;
        Vertex_count : integer;
    begin
        V_stream := TMemoryStream.Create;
        Vertices_BLOb.SaveToStream(V_stream);
        Vertex_count := V_stream.Size div sizeof(TPoint);
        result := inherited Add(
                        tRegion.Create(
                            Target,
                            Vertex_count,
                            V_stream.Memory
                            )
```

```
                        );
    V_stream.Free;
    end;
```

We extract the vertex data from the field into a **TMemoryStream** object, **V_stream**, using the method **SaveToStream**. Once in a memory stream, it's a simple task to **Create** a **tRegion** using the vertices and **Add** it to the list. If we have a lot of hotspots for an image, and if we intend to call this method repeatedly from **Add_regions_for**, we'll end up creating and freeing **TMemoryList**s like they're going out of style! You might want to add your own special handling to make this more efficient.

Add_regions_for relies on the methods of a **tHotspot_table**, declared in the unit **Hotspots** from Chapter 10. We've implemented a rather wishy-washy version of this code—it will accept any directory at all in front of the image's name on a hotspot. We had to go out of our way a little bit to do this, but it saved us the trouble of having to know exactly in which directory all of our files are kept, as shown in the code snippet below.

```
Clear;
with Hotspot_table do begin
    Open;
    First;
    while not EOF do begin
        if Uppercase(ExtractFileName(FieldByName('Image').AsString))
            =
            Uppercase(ExtractFileName(Current_image_filename))
        then
            Add(
                FieldByName('Target').AsString,
                TBLObField(FieldByName('Vertices'))
                );
        Next;
        end;
    Close;
    end;
```

The flow of control is no great mystery. We **Clear** the existing list, and then traverse the database looking for matching image filenames, adding them when we find them.

Finally, the search for a hotspot hit in **Target_reference_of** is equally straight-forward. All we do is loop though the **tRegion_list**, looking for a region that returns **true** from the **PtInRegion** test, as shown in the code snippet below.

```
function tRegion_list.Target_reference_of(
  const X, Y : integer
  ) : string;
```

```
var
    I     : integer;
    Found : boolean;
begin
    result := '';
    Found := false;
    I := 0;
    while (I < Count) and not Found do
        with tRegion(Items[I]) do begin
            Found := PtInRegion(Region,X,Y);
            if Found then
                result := Target
            else
                inc(I);
        end;
end;
```

Putting it All Together

In *Magic I*, all we needed to do to get an image into **Image1** was call its **Picture.LoadFromFile** method. We now have at our disposal the **Load_image** procedure from unit **ImgPanel**, but its call is not quite so simple. The code snippet below shows what the call looks like in procedure **Jump_to**, in unit **Main**.

```
Load_image(
  Remainder,
  Form1.Image_panel,
  Form1.Image1,
  Image_panel_Rect,
  Scale,
  Region_list,
  Hotspot_table
  )
```

The **Remainder**, at this point, is the filename of the image we wish to load. Instead of worrying about **Image1** alone, now we must send **Load_image** the Panel that will be adjusted, **Image_panel**; the rectangular area of the form over which the **Image_panel** is allowed to sprawl, **Image_panel_rect**; and for processing mouse clicks, we must retrieve the **Scale** of the loaded image. Since **Load_image** also handles our hotspot chores, we need to pass it the **Region_list** and the **Hotspot_table**.

We are going to declare the **Image_panel_rect**, **Scale**, **Region_list**, and **Hotspot_table** as global to the unit's implementation. **Image_panel_rect** is so tightly bound to the form that it might make sense to make it a field of the **TForm1** object, but that's unnecessary over-scoping.

Of course, these same parameters must now be passed to the **Output.Display** method, which has been redeclared to use them in unit **DispBuf**, as shown in the code snippet below.

```
procedure tDisplay_buffer.Display(
  const Aux_image       : TImage;
  const Aux_panel       : TPanel;
  const Aux_area        : TRect;
  var   Scale           : single;
  const Aux_region_list : tRegion_list;
  const Aux_table       : tHotspot_table
  );
```

At long last, it's time to detect a mouse click on **Image1**. With so much going before, **Image1**'s **OnMouseDown** handler seems simple, as shown in the code snippet below.

```
procedure TForm1.Image1MouseDown(Sender: TObject; Button: TMouseButton;
  Shift: TShiftState; X, Y: Integer);
    var
        Target : string;
    begin
        Target := Region_list.Target_reference_of(
                        round(X / Scale),round(Y / Scale)
                        );
        if Target <> '' then Jump_to(Target);
        end;
```

Details

Before we leave this code, we should look at some final details. First, we have some housekeeping to do when we create and destroy the form, as shown in the code snippet below.

```
procedure TForm1.FormCreate(Sender: TObject);
    begin
        Resizing_ourselves := false;
        Form1s_old_width   := Form1.Width;
        Form1s_old_height  := Form1.Height;
        Panel1_on_Form1    := Panel1.Left / Form1.Width;
        with Image_panel do
            Image_panel_rect :=
                Rect(Left,Top,Left+Width,Top+Height);
        Set_Image_in_panel(Image1,Image_panel);
        Output := nil;
        Region_list := tRegion_list.Create;
        Hotspot_table := tHotspot_table.Create(Self);
        with Hotspot_table do begin
            DatabaseName := ExtractFilePath(Application.ExeName);
```

```
            TableName       := 'Hotspots';
            Establish;
            end;
      end;
```

FormCreate is much the same as it was; but now, instead of doing in-line calculations to synchronize the size of **Image1** to the available interior of the **Image_panel**, it simply makes a call to **Set_image_in_panel**. Just before that, it looks at the **Image_panel** and extracts its design-time "footprint" rectangle on the form. This rectangle, **Image_panel_rect**, will be resized along with the rest of the form, so that it is always the area in which a proportionally-sized Image and Panel can roam.

We also instantiate the **Region_list** and **Hotspot_table**, and call the **Establish** method of our **tHotspot_table** class to make sure the **Hotspot_table** is ready to go. When we destroy the form, **FormDestroy** cleans up these structures, as shown in the code snippet below.

```
procedure TForm1.FormDestroy(Sender: TObject);
    begin
        Hotspot_table.Free;
        Region_list.Free;
        end;
```

When we resize the form, we now need to resize the **Image_panel_rect**, rather than **Image1** and **Image_panel**, themselves. After the rectangle is resized, a call to **Stretch_panel_on_image_in_rect** handles the proportional resizing of the **Image_panel** and **Image1**, as shown in the code snippet below.

```
with Image_panel_rect do begin
    Image_panel_rect := Rect(
                            Left,Top,
                            Right  + Image_panel_incr_X,
                            Bottom + Incr_Y
                            );
    Stretch_panel_on_image_in_rect(
      Image_panel,Image1,Image_panel_rect,Scale
      );
    end;
```

Listings

These modifications to unit **Main** (Listing 11.6) and **DispBuf** (Listing 11.7) stand on top of the modifications made earlier in Listings 11.1 and 11.3. Remember, when a line begins with a colon, it means that some code has been omitted at that point in the listing.

Listing 11.6 Unit **Main** from *Magic II*, with changes from *Magic I* highlighted

```
unit Main;

interface

uses
  SysUtils, WinTypes, WinProcs, Messages, Classes, Graphics, Controls,
  Forms, Dialogs, StdCtrls, ExtCtrls, ComCtrls;

type
  TForm1 = class(TForm)
    :
    procedure FormDestroy(Sender: TObject);
    procedure Image1MouseDown(Sender: TObject; Button: TMouseButton;
      Shift: TShiftState; X, Y: Integer);
  private
    { Private declarations }
  public
    { Public declarations }
  end;

var
  Form1: TForm1;

implementation

    uses
        MMSystem,
        MiscLib, DispBuf, HyperLnk, Parser, ImgPanel, Hotspots, RgnList;

:

var
    Image_panel_Rect : TRect;
    Scale            : single;
    Region_list      : tRegion_list;
    Hotspot_table    : tHotspot_table;

:

procedure Jump_to(
  const Target : string
  );
    var
        Re_show : boolean;
        Ext     : string;
        Command : ansiString;
    begin with TParser.Parse(pchar(Target)) do begin
        :
            else if
              (Ext = '.BMP')
            or
              (Ext = '.RLE')
            or
              (Ext = '.WMF')
```

```
                    or
                       (Ext = '.ICO')
                    then
                      Load_image(
                        Remainder,
                        Form1.Image_panel,
                        Form1.Image1,
                        Image_panel_Rect,
                        Scale,
                        Region_list,
                        Hotspot_table
                        )
                    else begin
                      { 'HTM', et al. }
                      Form1.Filename.Text := Remainder;
                      Load_HTML;
                      Re_show := true;
                      end
                 end
              else begin

                 :

                 end;
              if Re_show then Form1.PaintBox1.Refresh;
              Free;
              end; end;

    :

procedure TForm1.Image1MouseDown(Sender: TObject; Button: TMouseButton;
   Shift: TShiftState; X, Y: Integer);
     var
        Target : string;
     begin
        Target := Region_list.Target_reference_of(
                                round(X / Scale),round(Y / Scale)
                                );
        if Target <> '' then Jump_to(Target);
        end;

    :

procedure TForm1.PaintBox1Paint(Sender: TObject);
     begin
        Output.Display(
           Form1.Image1,
           Form1.Image_panel,
           Image_panel_rect,
           Scale,
           Region_list,
           Hotspot_table
           );
        end;
```

Expanding the VB Multimedia Engine

```pascal
var
    Resizing_ourselves : boolean;
    Form1s_old_width,
    Form1s_old_height : integer;
    Panel1_on_Form1   : single;

procedure TForm1.FormCreate(Sender: TObject);
    begin
        Resizing_ourselves := false;
        Form1s_old_width   := Form1.Width;
        Form1s_old_height  := Form1.Height;
        Panel1_on_Form1    := Panel1.Left / Form1.Width;
        with Image_panel do
            Image_panel_rect :=
                Rect(Left,Top,Left+Width,Top+Height);
        Set_Image_in_panel(Image1,Image_panel);
        Output := nil;
        Region_list := tRegion_list.Create;
        Hotspot_table := tHotspot_table.Create(Self);
        with Hotspot_table do begin
            DatabaseName := ExtractFilePath(Application.ExeName);
            TableName    := 'Hotspots';
            Establish;
            end;
        end;

procedure TForm1.FormDestroy(Sender: TObject);
    begin
        Hotspot_table.Free;
        Region_list.Free;
        end;

procedure TForm1.FormResize(Sender: TObject);
    var
        Minimum_width,
        Incr_X,
        Incr_Y,
        Old_left,
        Old_width,
        Image_panel_incr_X : integer;
    begin
        if Resizing_ourselves then exit;

        Minimum_width := Filename.Left + 100;
        with Form1 do begin
            if Width < Minimum_width then
                Width := Minimum_width;
            if Height < 100 then
                Height := 100;
            Incr_X := Form1.Width - Form1s_old_width;
            Incr_Y := Form1.Height - Form1s_old_height;
            end;
        :
```

```
            with Panel1 do begin
                Old_left  := Left;
                Old_width := Width;
                Left   := round(Form1.Width * Panel1_on_Form1);
                Width  := ScrollBar1.Left - Left;
                Height := Height + Incr_Y;
                Image_panel_incr_X := Left - Old_left;
                end;
            with PaintBox1 do begin
                Width  := Width + (Panel1.Width - Old_width);
                Height := Height + Incr_Y;
                end;
            with Image_panel_rect do begin
                Image_panel_rect := Rect(
                                        Left,Top,
                                        Right  + Image_panel_incr_X,
                                        Bottom + Incr_Y
                                        );
                Stretch_panel_on_image_in_rect(
                   Image_panel,Image1,Image_panel_rect,Scale
                   );
                end;
            Resizing_ourselves := false;

            Form1s_old_width  := Form1.Width;
            Form1s_old_height := Form1.Height;

            Load_HTML; { To re-parse }

            Form1.Refresh;
            end;

end.
```

Listing 11.7 Unit **DispBuf** from *Magic II*, with changes from *Magic I* highlighted

```
unit DispBuf;

interface

uses
    Windows, Classes, Graphics, Controls, ExtCtrls,
    Font, FmtText, HyperLnk, Hotspots, RgnList;
:

    tDisplay_buffer = class
      private
        { Formatted Text Storage }
        Formatted_text_list : tFormatted_text_list;
        { "Breaker" Data -- Line Breaking list }
        Line_list : TList; {of integer}
```

```
      { "Displayer" Data }
      Control : tGraphicControlWithCanvas;
    public
      { Hyperlink support lists, built by "Breaker" }
      Reference_anchors : tNamed_rectangle_list;
      Dest_name_anchors : tNamed_rectangle_list;
      { Display Positioning and Height, calc'd by "Breaker" }
      Display_top,
      Display_bottom : integer;
    public
      constructor Create(
        const _Control : tGraphicControlWithCanvas
        );
      destructor Destroy; override;
      procedure Load_HTML_file(
        const Filename : string
        );
      procedure Display(
        const Aux_image      : TImage;
        const Aux_panel      : TPanel;
        const Aux_area       : TRect;
        var   Scale          : single;
        const Aux_region_list : tRegion_list;
        const Aux_table      : tHotspot_table
        );
    end;

implementation

uses
    SysUtils, Dialogs,
    MiscLib, HTML, ImgPanel;

    :

procedure tDisplay_buffer.Display(
  const Aux_image      : TImage;
  const Aux_panel      : TPanel;
  const Aux_area       : TRect;
  var   Scale          : single;
  const Aux_region_list : tRegion_list;
  const Aux_table      : tHotspot_table
  );

    :

    begin with Formatted_text_list do begin
        :
        for I := First_elem to Last_elem do
          with tFormatted_text(Items[I]), Format do
            if Rule_height > 0 then
              :
              else if Image_name <> '' then
```

```
                    if Aux_image = nil then
                      { Skip it. }
                    else
                      Load_image(
                        Image_name,
                        Aux_panel,
                        Aux_image,
                        Aux_area,
                        Scale,
                        Aux_region_list,
                        Aux_table
                        )
                else if Text <> nil then
                  with Control.Canvas do begin
                    Set_font_from_spec(Font,Format.Font);
                    SetTextAlign(Handle,TA_BASELINE);
                    TextOut(
                      Base_left_corner.X,
                      Base_left_corner.Y - Display_top,
                      Text
                      );
                  end;

         end; end;

{initialization}
    end.
```

Extending the Multimedia Engine

Well, that's it! You now have a great base for building your ultimate multimedia project. Don't be afraid to experiment with the HTML, database-driven engine. Look for ways to customize it, and make it run faster and smoother. If we had time, we could probably write an entire book about things you could do to customize the engine. We will suggest that customizing the look and feel of the interface would be a good place to start. Try using custom graphics, tool bars, and non-standard images. If you were creating a program for an accounting office, it would be alright to use the standard Windows look and feel. But this is hypermedia, and it is important to find your own "custom" design.

Now that we have created the hypermedia project, let's go back to the hypertext engine at the beginning of this chapter and turn it into a Web browser!

Chapter 12

We're now going to turn our hypermedia application into a powerful World Wide Web Browser, that connects to the Internet with some powerful OCX-based custom controls.

The Hypermedia Engine at Work—Building a Web Browser

Dan Haygood

The hypermedia project we created in the previous chapter pulled together many of the core elements of a multimedia presentation system. From there, we could expand the interface to build all kinds of exciting multimedia projects. But there's another aspect of interactive multimedia: the online connection. The World Wide Web, a suburb (if you will) of the Internet, serves up multimedia on a global scale. The very future of multimedia lies online. So in this chapter, we're going to take the same hypermedia engine, and build it into a highly-functional Web browser. To accomplish this, we need to take a step backward before we leap forward. We will start with the first version of *The Magic Hypermedia Engine*, in project **Magic1**, and build upon it. Only this time, we will concentrate on displaying documents rather than on displaying multimedia elements.

We need to start by developing a plan for building our Web browser. Here are some of the initial design questions we need to consider.

- What should the form look like?
- What type of interface should we use?
- Should we provide a menu for the HTML viewer?
- Should we include a status bar or buttons?
- What additional HTML features should the browser support?

Building a Web browser is a big undertaking. There are a number of features we can include and topics to cover, including page layout, coding style, user interface design, HTML standards, Web page navigation techniques, and on and on. We could have easily written an entire book about the construction of a Web browser. Obviously, we'll have to scale back our discussion somewhat, but fortunately, most of the HTML engine has been developed and explained in previous chapters. So, in this chapter, we can focus on the finer points of developing a user-friendly interface and customizing our HTML engine.

We'll start by using the multimedia application developed in the previous chapter. We'll modify the code for this project so that we can add user interface features to our browser. Then, as in Chapter 11, we'll need to consider the entire issue of image display—this time, co-mingling images with our text! Our browser will implement many of the basic HTML tags, but the best part is that you'll easily be able to extend the browser and provide support for additional HTML features as the World-Wide Web continues to grow.

User Interface Issues

The multimedia application we built in the previous chapter had a fairly standard user-interface. If you were going to update the engine further for inclusion in a distributed product, you would probably update the interface by including fancy buttons, interesting graphics, and a good color scheme. This is the wise approach to take for a consumer-oriented multimedia product, but what about a more utility-oriented product like a Web browser?

When you create your own multimedia product, you can easily use non-standard colors, fancy graphics, and unique icons and buttons to improve the look and feel of your product, because you are in control of the content that will be displayed. However, with an application like a Web browser, the program serves merely as a shell or a tool for displaying information created by other people. Thus, you need to design your interface accordingly.

Our first requirement is to determine who is going to be using our HTML browser. If we were planning to create a browser to be used by all types of people we would want a standard interface that is very intuitive and easy to use. If our browser was going to be used for a specialized application, such as an in-house document viewer, we could customize it further, maybe adding features like a company-logo splash-screen or company colors.

Since we don't know how you'll be using this technology, we are going to develop a fairly standard-looking—some might say Spartan—Windows 95 application, using only the interface elements that come with Delphi. We'll use a couple of powerful OCX-based shareware controls to hit the Internet, but even though we'll see them, the user won't. We will not use any custom fonts, non-standard color schemes, or anything else that is unnecessary for this application. Of course, after learning how the browser works, you can easily add your own customizing features.

Repackaging the Hypermedia Engine

Let's begin by looking at the first project presented in the previous chapter. In that project, we created *Magic I*, incorporating both basic image support and an easier-to-use interface than the basic hypertext engine. It's a great place to begin.

Let's examine what that project did, and determine which features we need to add or subtract. First, we can get rid of the image display area, and all of the code that supports it. In exchange, we'll add code that places the images directly into the text window—mixing freely with the text—just as in other Web browsers. Next, we can widen the text area to fill the entire form. We'll add a simple "Back" button, to get us out of sticky dead-end situations, and we'll add a status bar to give some feedback, such as hotlink destinations, to the user.

Behind the scenes, we'll take care of a nagging problem. As *Magic I* stands, each time the form is resized, the current document must be re-loaded and re-wordwrapped. By maintaining two copies of the parsed document, one unbroken, and the other, a fugitive line-broken version of the original, we'll be able to avoid re-hitting the Web.

We have a lot of work to do, so let's get going!

Browser I: Bringing Images Inside

This project presents the changes to our HTML engine that will turn it into a full-blown HTML document browser. It doesn't hit the Web yet, but our goal here is to make that task seem trivial.

1. Copy the first project from Chapter 11, *Magic I*, to a new directory named *Browser1*. If you need help with this, look back to previous projects, like *Hyper III* or *Magic II* for more detailed instructions.
2. Modify the main form, **Form1**, as discussed below (Figure 12.2).
3. Modify the unit **HTML** to support the new **<IMG>** tag format we'll be using to load pictures into our document (Listing 12.1).
4. To store pictures for later display, as we parse the document, we'll need a list of pictures. Add unit **PicList** to implement this structure (Listing 12.2).
5. We talked about more efficient line-breaking, and we need to add in-line images to our **tDisplay_buffer** class. Modify unit **DispBuf** to make these enhancements (Listing 12.3).
6. Finally, in unit **Main**, we need to hook up the new features of our user interface, and we need to clean up old support code that was left over from the image display area (Listing 12.4).

All of the listings we'll provide in this chapter highlight only the changes to existing code that was presented earlier in the book. Consult the CD-ROM for full listings.

You'll find this project in the subdirectory \Programs\Chap12\Browser1 on the accompanying CD-ROM. For our examples here, we'll be using the files Browser1.HTM through Browser4.HTM from \Media\HyperTxt.

Modifying the Form

We'll make the minor modifications to the form first. To help you through this discussion, Figures 12.1 and 12.2 show the form as it looked in *Magic I*, and what it will look like in *Browser I*.

Delete the **Image_panel** Panel control. It will take **Image1**, where we used to display pictures with it. Stretch **Panel1** back out to fill the width of the Form, and stretch **PaintBox1** back to fill the Panel. Then, slide the bottom of **PaintBox1**, and then the bottom of **Panel1**, upwards to make room for a new Status Bar.

The Status Bar control is a Windows 95-specific control that is very handy for displaying status information such as key states, date and time, or "help"

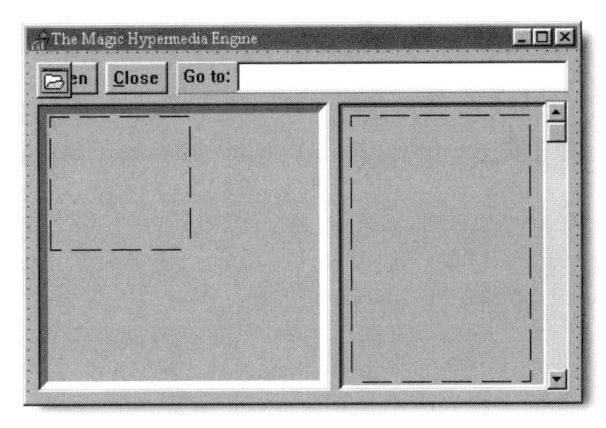

The Hypermedia Engine at Work—Building a Web Browser

Figure 12.1   Form1, as it appears in project Magic I.

information. The Status Bar control offers the advantages of automatic positioning and sizing when the form is resized, and it can also handle multiple panels of information. Hand-coding these features with Panel controls is not particularly difficult, but making them work together and resizing them properly can be a burden. So why not let the Status Bar control do the work for us?

We will use the Status Bar simply to show the destination URL of any hotspots the mouse might pass over. We will show you how to create the code for that at the end of this project. To add the Status Bar, click on the *Win95* page of the *Component Palette*. There you will see Windows 95 custom controls that Delphi recognizes. This set of powerful controls can be very useful in many programming situations. Click the Status Bar, and click-and-drag the area into which it will be placed on the bottom of the form.

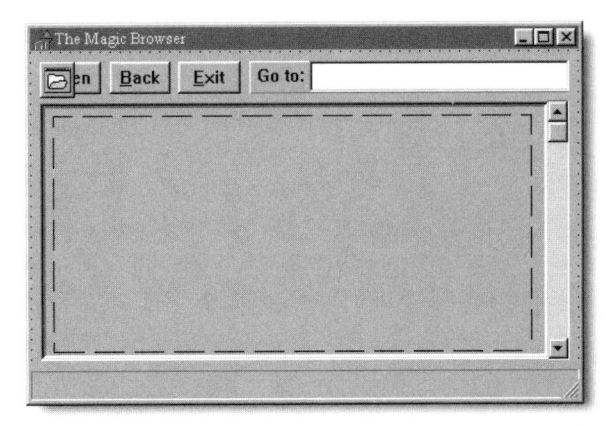

Figure 12.2   Form1, with the necessary modifications made for Browser I.

We need to set only one property of **StatusBar1**, as it is now called. Its **SimplePanel** property must be set to **True**. This allows us to use the Status Bar itself as the presentation device, through its property **SimpleText**. Otherwise, we would have to define interior Status Panels through the *Object Inspector*, as well.

The other thing we want to do here is scrunch the "Go to:" box over a little bit, to make room for a "Back" Button between the Open and Close buttons. We'll hook code up to this button later. For right now, set its **Enabled** property to **False**, since we'll have nothing to go back to when the program starts. Finally, we should change the **Caption** of our Close button—it doesn't really "close" anything like a document or a connection; it actually exits the program. Let's set **Close_button.Caption** to "&Exit" instead.

Other little things, like **Form1**'s **Caption**, you may adjust at you discretion. We've called this project *The Magic Web Browser*.

Handling In-Line Images with Text

Just as we had to carefully consider how images would be incorporated into *The Magic Hypermedia Engine*, we must now consider how they will work with *The Magic Web Browser*. We are going to offer only basic Web functionality for images—no fancy alignments, no text wrapping, not even (gasp) image mapping, whereby hotlinks in images can be defined in the Web. Now that we're not bound to our own computer, we won't be able to pre-define hotspots. Even though we could easily implement a floating image window into which we could load these directly, that's an extra task we won't cover.

That said, all we need to do is identify image references in the HTML document, and work them into our **tDisplay_buffer** control for display. We've already tackled this problem in Chapter 11, but we'll change things slightly to support tags that look more like ordinary HTML.

Supporting the <IMG> Tag

We are going to define a new Image tag that takes a required argument specifying the name of the image (though we won't really enforce that—so be careful), and two optional arguments specifying alignment (or, in our case, simple justification) and scale (though this isn't real HTML). Here is the basic scheme:

```
<IMG SRC=" name"    ALIGN=L[EFT]|M[IDDLE]|R[IGHT]    SCALE=scale%
```

(The percent sign is required, but we'll only look at the first character of the **ALIGN** parameter.)

The Hypermedia Engine at Work—Building a Web Browser

We will handle the parsing chores, and make room in our **tHTML_format** for this image-related information in unit **HTML**. The important changes from this unit's incarnation in *Magic I* are shown in Listing 12.1.

Listing 12.1   Unit **HTML** from *Browser I*

```
unit HTML;

interface

:

type
    Picture_alignments = (pa_Left, pa_Center, pa_Right);
    tHTML_format = record
        Serial_number      : integer;
        Leading_newlines   : integer;
        Font               : tHTML_font_spec;
        Rule_height        : integer;
        Anchor_reference   : integer;
        Anchor_dest_name   : integer;
        Preformatted       : boolean;
        Picture_index      : integer;
        Picture_scale      : integer;
        Picture_align      : Picture_alignments;
        end;

:

implementation

:

procedure Parse_tag(
    const        The_tag        : pchar;
    var {in/out} Format         : tHTML_format;
    const        HRef_anchors   : tNamed_rectangle_list;
    const        Name_anchors   : tNamed_rectangle_list;
    var          Do_a_newline   : boolean;
    var          Rule_height    : integer;
    var          Image_name     : string
    );

    :

    procedure Parse_IMG_tag;
        const
            Tokens : array[1..3] of pchar = (
              'SRC',
              'SCALE',
              'ALIGN'
              );
        var
            Token : integer;
```

```
            Done    : boolean;
            P       : pchar;
       begin with The_parser, Format do begin
            Picture_scale := 100;
            Picture_align := pa_Left;
            No_errors;
            repeat
                Token := Expect_one_of(Tokens);
                Done := Error;
                if not Done then
                    case Token of
                        1: begin
                            Raise_Errors;
                            Expect('=');
                            Expect('"');
                            Find('"');
                            Image_name := strNew(Last_found);
                            end;
                        2: begin
                            No_errors;
                            Expect('=');
                            Find('%');
                            try
                                if Error then
                                    Picture_scale := 100
                                  else
                                    Picture_scale := StrToInt(Last_found);
                              except
                                on EConvertError do Picture_scale := 100;
                                on ERangeError   do Picture_scale := 100;
                              end;
                            end;
                        3: begin
                            No_errors;
                            Expect('=');
                            Find(' ');
                            if Error then P := Remainder else P := Last_found;
                            case upcase(P^) of
                              'L' : Picture_align := pa_Left;
                              'M' : Picture_align := pa_Center;
                              'R' : Picture_align := pa_Right;
                              else  Picture_align := pa_Left;
                              end;
                            end;
                        end;
            until Done;
            Raise_errors;
            end; end;

   procedure Process_tag(
     const Word : pchar
     );
       begin with Format do begin
           if Word[0] = '!' then
```

The Hypermedia Engine at Work—Building a Web Browser

```
              { Comment -- Do nothing. NOT STANDARD HTML! }
              :
            else if StrComp(Word,'IMG') = 0 then
              Parse_IMG_tag
            else
              { It's a currently unsupported tag. }
              ;
          end; end;

    :

    begin
      :
      end;
{initialization}
    end.
```

What We Must Know

In order to display an image with our **tDisplay_buffer** class, we will need to remember particular attributes about the image, as well as the picture itself, between the time we parse the **<IMG>** tag and the time we actually draw the picture on a text-display canvas.

The additional fields **Picture_index**, **Picture_scale**, and **Picture_align** become part of the **tHTML_format** that we save for each formatted segment of text, in much the same way the **Rule_height** field is kept to support horizontal rules. You may wish to alter this structure in the future, so that "special" formatted text elements are maintained is a less wasteful manner. For now, we're going to build on code that's already familiar to us.

Picture_index is a peculiar field—index to what? Our pictures must be loaded and stored in much the same way our formatted text list is built. As we encounter Image tags while parsing an HTML document, we'll load the source image into a list of pictures. We'll discuss the mechanics of this later; for now, it is enough to know that the **Picture_index** uniquely identifies an image to be displayed at a particular point in the document.

How We Discover It

The three fields above are parsed out the **<IMG>** tag by the relatively lengthy procedure **Parse_IMG_tag**. It basically loops through the tag arguments, separately handling each argument it finds. This allows the arguments to appear in any order.

```
const
    Tokens : array[1..3] of pchar = (
```

```
    'SRC',
    'SCALE',
    'ALIGN'
    );

:

Picture_scale := 100;
Picture_align := pa_Left;
No_errors;
repeat
    Token := Expect_one_of(Tokens);
    Done := Error;
    if not Done then
        case Token of
            1: { Do SRC argument }
            2: { Do SCALE argument }
            3: { Do ALIGN argument }
        end;
until Done;
Raise_errors;
```

Each of the arguments is processed when encountered. The **SRC** argument is the simplest; it doesn't rely on any error-handling, so it calls **Raise_errors** to generate an exception if the syntax is wrong.

```
Raise_Errors;
Expect('=');
Expect('"');
Find('"');
Image_name := strNew(Last_found);
```

This code sets the **Image_name** parameter for the calling routine to look at, rather than actually getting the picture and setting the picture index. This more complicated code doesn't really belong here in pure parsing code.

The **SCALE** argument is more complicated; a parsing error could occur, and if that doesn't happen, there's no guarantee that the number will convert without error. Both of these exceptions are trapped, and the **Picture_scale** is forced to 100 percent.

```
No_errors;
Expect('=');
Find('%');
try
    if Error then
        Picture_scale := 100
    else
        Picture_scale := StrToInt(Last_found);
```

```
except
  on EConvertError do Picture_scale := 100;
  on ERangeError  do Picture_scale := 100;
end;
```

The **ALIGN** argument is processed by grabbing whatever token falls after the "="; we only check the first letter; you could use **Expect_one_of** to make this more rigorous.

```
No_errors;
Expect('=');
Find(' ');
if Error then P := Remainder else P := Last_found;
case upcase(P^) of
   'L' : Picture_align := pa_Left;
   'M' : Picture_align := pa_Center;
   'R' : Picture_align := pa_Right;
   else  Picture_align := pa_Left;
end;
```

A Picture-Perfect Memory

In the last section, we said we'd have to remember pictures from the time they were encountered in parsed document text until they were displayed on the screen. That isn't strictly true—we could reload an image each time we needed to scroll it back on to the screen or repaint it when uncovered. If you've ever waited for an image to be downloaded from the Internet on a slow day, though, you'll realize that this approach is plain stupid. We'll load the images once per reference, and save them for repainting, because we're smart. To make things even better, you could detect multiple references to the same picture. Then you would only have to download it once, and save only one copy in memory. This is a hack that could be quite useful in dealing with text having neat graphic bullets.

We'll save the pictures in a list of—obviously—**TPicture**s. To do this, we'll descend a class, **tPicture_list**, from Delphi's versatile **TList** class, and add a member function to add a picture by loading it from a file. The entire unit is shown in Listing 12.2.

Listing 12.2 The Complete Unit **PicList** from *Browser I*

```
unit PicList;

interface

uses
    Classes;
```

```
type
    tPicture_list = class(TList)
        destructor Destroy; override;
        function Add_file(
          const Filename : string
          ) : integer;
        end;

implementation

uses
    Graphics;

destructor tPicture_list.Destroy;
    var
        I : integer;
    begin
        for I := 0 to Count - 1 do
            TPicture(Items[I]).Free;
        inherited Destroy;
        end;

function tPicture_list.Add_file(
  const Filename : string
  ) : integer;
    begin
        result := Add(TPicture.Create);
        TPicture(Items[result]).LoadFromFile(Filename);
        end;

end.
```

The method **Add_file**, instead of taking an already-created object like **TList.Add**, would instead take the **Filename** of a picture. **Add_file** creates the **TPicture** object itself, and then uses **LoadFromFile** to actually get the picture. This saves the calling code some work, and fits in well with the methods available here.

Bringing Pictures In-Line

Now that we've built some good support structures and can identify and track images in our HTML documents, we need alter unit **DispBuf** to actually manipulate the images. We have three basic tasks: We must recognize that we've parsed an Image tag; we must load the image, saving it for later; we must be able to display the image on the screen. In order to save the images, we'll add a field to the class declaration that puts unit **PicList** to work.

The Hypermedia Engine at Work—Building a Web Browser

```
tDisplay_buffer = class
  private
    { Formatted Text Storage }
    Formatted_text_list : tFormatted_text_list;
    Image_list          : tPicture_list;
    { "Breaker" Data -- Line Breaking list }
    Broken_text_list    : tFormatted_text_list;
    Line_list           : TList; {of integer}
    { "Displayer" Data }
    Control             : tGraphicControlWithCanvas;
    procedure Break_into_lines;
  public
    { Hyperlink support lists, built by "Breaker" }
    Reference_anchors : tNamed_rectangle_list;
    Dest_name_anchors : tNamed_rectangle_list;
    { Display Positioning and Height, calc'd by "Breaker" }
    Display_top,
    Display_bottom : integer;
  public
    constructor Create(
      const _Control   : tGraphicControlWithCanvas
      );
    destructor Destroy; override;
    procedure Load_HTML_file(
      const Filename : string
      );
    procedure Reformat;
    procedure Display;
    end;
```

(There are some other modifications here that we'll get to later. They support a means for re-wordwrapping text without reloading the document. The important changes to unit **DispBuf** between *Magic I* and *Browser I* are shown in Listing 12.3, below.)

Recognizing that we've encountered an image is easy; as we did in *Magic I*, we just look for unit **HTML**'s **Parse_tag** function to pass us back a non-null image name. This happens in the body of the local routine **Parse_HTML**:

```
Parse_tag(Text,
  Format,
  Reference_anchors,
  Dest_name_anchors,
  Need_a_newline,
  Rule_height,
  Image_name
  );
Text := The_end + 1;
Preceeding_newline :=
  Preceeding_newline or Need_a_newline;
if Preceeding_newline then
    Preceeding_space := false;
```

```
if Rule_height > 0 then
    Horizontal_rule(Rule_height);
if Image_name <> '' then
    Image(Image_name);
Set_format(Format);
```

Just as we call **Horizontal_rule** to handle rules, we call **Image** to handle images.

```
procedure Image(
  const _Image_name : string
  );
    begin
        Add_buffer_to_list;
        inc(Pending_newlines);
        with Current_format do begin
            Picture_index :=
              Image_list.Add_file(_Image_name);
            Picture_scale := Format.Picture_scale;
            Picture_align := Format.Picture_align;
            Leading_newlines := Pending_newlines;
            end;
        Formatted_text_list.Add(
          tFormatted_text.Create(Current_format,'')
          );
        Current_format.Picture_index := -1;
        Pending_newlines := 0;
        end;
```

We add the existing contents of the **Buffer** to the **Formatted_text_list**, and use **Pending_newlines** to start a new line in the output, so that our image always appears between lines of text. You might want to add the ability, with more advanced alignment tags, to make this optional: Right now, you can't use images as graphical bullets.

Next, the **Current_format**'s **Picture_index**, **Picture_scale**, and **Picture_align** are specified. The **Picture_index** is set to the position in the **tDisplay_buffer**'s **Image_list** at which the image's file is loaded; this happens in one fell swoop.

We force the element into the **Formatted_test_list**, and then return the **Picture_index** of the **Current_format** to -1, an illegal list index value, and marker specifying that an element has no associated image.

This code, by the way, parallels the handling of Horizontal Rules in the local routine **Horizontal_rule**.

Breaking Lines Around Images

It is during the line-breaking process that we reserve space in the document for the images. To make the line-breaking process as smooth as possible, we

The Hypermedia Engine at Work—Building a Web Browser

play a little trick, and make every image take up a full line of text, with the statement **Width := Canvas_width**. This might be a good opportunity to do the horizontal positioning, but it interferes with the measurement mechanism to do it here; we'll save that for **Display** time. We do need to reserve the proper amount of vertical space now, however. This code fragment shows what happens when an element of the **Formatted_text_list** (Actually, we're breaking the **Broken_text_list**, but we'll get to that...) pointing to a picture is encountered.

```
else if Picture_index <> -1 then begin
    Pic := TPicture(Image_list.Items[Picture_index]);
    with Current_line_meas do begin
        Height  :=
          10 +
          round(Pic.Height * Picture_Scale / 100.0) +
          2;
        Width   := Canvas_width;
        Ascent  :=
          10 +
          round(Pic.Height * Picture_Scale / 100.0);
        Descent := 2;
        end;
    Meas := Current_line_meas;
    end
```

Pic is a temporary variable used to reference the picture in the list, without writing out all of the necessary dereferencing each time. We could have used a **with** statement, but this causes confusion for the **Width** and **Height** fields. The "magic" numbers 10 and 2 give us a ten-pixel margin for text above the image, and a two-pixel margin for text below the image. There are **<IMG>** tag arguments you could implement to do this. Note that we have to scale the picture space vertically here.

Displaying Saved Images

After all the work we did to load images and reserve space for them, we finally get to display them in **tDisplay_buffer.Display**. This fragment shows how elements of the text list that reference pictures are displayed.

```
else if Picture_index <> -1 then
    with TPicture(Image_list.Items[Picture_index]) do begin
        H := round(Height * Picture_scale / 100);
        W := round(Width  * Picture_scale / 100);
        case Picture_align of
          pa_Left   : TCX := 0;
          pa_Center : TCX := (Meas.Width - W) div 2;
          pa_Right  : TCX := Meas.Width - W;
          else        TCX := 0;
```

```
      end;
   TCY := Base_left_corner.Y - Display_top - H;
   if Picture_scale = 100 then
      Control.Canvas.Draw(TCX,TCY,Graphic)
   else
      Control.Canvas.StretchDraw(
         Rect(TCX,TCY,TCX+W,TCY+H),
         Graphic
         );
end;
```

We rely upon the methods **Canvas.Draw** and **Canvas.StretchDraw** to copy pictures from the **Image_list** to the **Canvas** of our text display **Control**. The picture itself is stored in the **Graphic** property of a **TPicture** object. **Draw** copies the picture directly to the **Canvas**, given the top-left corner of the destination area. **StretchDraw** will stretch the picture into a specified rectangle on the **Canvas**. In both cases, we need to know the top-left corner.

This is a problem, because when we reserved space for the image, we specified the baseline-left "corner," with the base of the image at the baseline. To get the vertical coordinate of the top-left corner, we need to add the Picture's scaled height to the **Base_left_corner.Y** coordinate. The horizontal coordinate is also tricky. We previously reserved the whole "line" for the image; now we need to act on the alignment of the picture.

We begin by calculating the scaled size of the Picture. We then set its horizontal position. To set its vertical position, we need to adjust for both the height of the scaled picture, and the **Display_top** field (which, you'll recall, tells us how far down the top of our display screen is from the top of the document).

Once we have the top-left corner, we check the **Picture_scale**. If it is 100-percent, we simply call **Draw**, specifying our top-left corner and the **Graphic**. If it needs to be scaled, we construct a rectangle, and stretch the graphic into it.

No Time To Reload!

We promised that by the time we hit the Internet, we wouldn't be reloading the entire document just to re-wordwrap it. The technique is simple: We preserve the original **Formatted_text_list** field of our **tDisplay_buffer** by copying it to a new field, **Broken_text_list**. You can see the new list in the declaration:

```
tDisplay_buffer = class
     private
       { Formatted Text Storage }
       Formatted_text_list : tFormatted_text_list;
```

The Hypermedia Engine at Work—Building a Web Browser

```
    Image_list          : tPicture_list;
    { "Breaker" Data -- Line Breaking list }
    Broken_text_list    : tFormatted_text_list;
    Line_list           : TList; {of integer}
    { "Displayer" Data }
    Control             : tGraphicControlWithCanvas;
    procedure Break_into_lines;
  public
    { Hyperlink support lists, built by "Breaker" }
    Reference_anchors : tNamed_rectangle_list;
    Dest_name_anchors : tNamed_rectangle_list;
    { Display Positioning and Height, calc'd by "Breaker" }
    Display_top,
    Display_bottom : integer;
  public
    constructor Create(
      const _Control   : tGraphicControlWithCanvas
      );
    destructor Destroy; override;
    procedure Load_HTML_file(
      const Filename : string
      );
    procedure Reformat;
    procedure Display;
    end;
```

Now we can provide a new **public** method, **Reformat**, to destroy an existing **Broken_text_list**, and re-create it. We will still automatically do the initial line-breaking in **Load_HTML_file**, but now we can re-line-break anytime we want.

The first step in modifying the code to support this is extricating **Break_into_lines**. Fortunately, it uses no global variables, and operates purely on fields of the class. This means we can yank it right out of its nesting and make it a private method with no code changes!

Second, **Break_into_lines** must free the old **Broken_line_list**, then create a new one. Then we simply loop through the **Formatted_text_list**, adding copies of its elements to the **Broken_text_list**.

```
Broken_text_list.Free;
Broken_text_list := tFormatted_text_list.Create;
with Formatted_text_list do
    for I := 0 to Count - 1 do
        with tFormatted_text(Items[I]) do
            Broken_text_list.Add(
              tFormatted_text.Create(Format,Text)
              );
Line_list.Clear;
```

Now we have to **Clear** the **Line_list**, because we're about to rebuild it.

At this point, the only thing left to do is change references to the **Formatted_text_list** into references to the **Broken_text_list** in the routines **Break_into_lines** and **Display**.

We finally hand this functionality to the user in the **public** routine **Reformat**. All it does is call **Break_into_lines**. We've added this intermediate method in case your future development requires you to do more processing when you re-break your lines. These changes are highlighted in Listing 12.3.

Listing 12.3   Changes to Unit **DispBuf** to Support In-Line Images and Reformatting in *Browser I*

```
unit DispBuf;

interface

uses
    Classes, Graphics, Controls, ExtCtrls,
    Font, FmtText, HyperLnk, PicList;

:
    tDisplay_buffer = class
      private
        { Formatted Text Storage }
        Formatted_text_list : tFormatted_text_list;
        Image_list          : tPicture_list;
        { "Breaker" Data -- Line Breaking list }
        Broken_text_list    : tFormatted_text_list;
        Line_list           : TList; {of integer}
        { "Displayer" Data }
        Control             : tGraphicControlWithCanvas;
        procedure Break_into_lines;
      public
        { Hyperlink support lists, built by "Breaker" }
        Reference_anchors : tNamed_rectangle_list;
        Dest_name_anchors : tNamed_rectangle_list;
        { Display Positioning and Height, calc'd by "Breaker" }
        Display_top,
        Display_bottom : integer;
      public
        constructor Create(
          const _Control   : tGraphicControlWithCanvas
          );
        destructor Destroy; override;
        procedure Load_HTML_file(
          const Filename : string
          );
        procedure Reformat;
        procedure Display;
        end;
```

The Hypermedia Engine at Work—Building a Web Browser

```
implementation

 :

constructor tDisplay_buffer.Create(
  const _Control   : tGraphicControlWithCanvas
  );
    begin
        :
        Broken_text_list := nil;
        Image_list := tPicture_list.Create;
        end;

destructor tDisplay_buffer.Destroy;
    begin
        Image_list.Free;
        Broken_text_list.Free;
        :
        end;

procedure tDisplay_buffer.Break_into_lines;
    :
    procedure Start_new_line(
      const Line_count : integer
      );
        var
            L, I : integer;
        begin
            for L := 1 to Line_count do begin
                Line_pos.Y :=
                    Display_bottom + Current_line_meas.Ascent;

                if L = 1 then begin
                    Line_pos.X := 0;
                    for I :=
                        integer(Line_list.Items[Line_list.Count-1])
                        to
                        Current_item_index-1
                        do
                        with tFormatted_text(
                            Broken_text_list.Items[I]
                            ), { .Base_Left_Corner, .Meas, .Format}
                            Format,
                                {.Anchor_reference, .Anchor_dest_name,
                                 .Picture_index}
                            Base_left_corner,
                                { .X and .Y }
                            Meas
                                { .Width, .Ascent, .Descent }
                        do begin
                            :
                            end;
                    end;
                :
```

```
            end;
    :
        end;

var
    P, BOW        : pchar;
    Real_EOW      : boolean;
    Saved         : char;
    Broken        : boolean;
    Start_width   : integer;
    Canvas_width  : integer;
    I             : integer;
    Pic           : TPicture;
begin
    Broken_text_list.Free;
    Broken_text_list := tFormatted_text_list.Create;
    with Formatted_text_list do
        for I := 0 to Count - 1 do
            with tFormatted_text(Items[I]) do
                Broken_text_list.Add(
                    tFormatted_text.Create(Format,Text)
                    );
    Line_list.Clear;
    :
    with Broken_text_list do begin
        while Current_item_index < Count do
            with tFormatted_text(
                    Items[Current_item_index]
                    ),
                Format
            do begin
                :
                if Rule_height > 0 then begin
                    with Current_line_meas do begin
                        Height  := 2 + Rule_height + 2;
                        Width   := Canvas_width;
                        Ascent  := 2 + Rule_height;
                        Descent := 2;
                        end;
                    Meas := Current_line_meas;
                    end
                else if Picture_index <> -1 then begin
                    Pic := TPicture(Image_list.Items[Picture_index]);
                    with Current_line_meas do begin
                        Height :=
                          10 +
                          round(Pic.Height * Picture_Scale / 100.0) +
                          2;
                        Width   := Canvas_width;
                        Ascent :=
                          10 +
                          round(Pic.Height * Picture_Scale / 100.0);
                        Descent := 2;
                        end;
```

```
                        Meas := Current_line_meas;
                        end
                    else if Preformatted then begin
                        :
                        end
                    else begin
                        :
                        end;
                    inc(Current_item_index);
                    end;
                :
            end;
        end;

procedure tDisplay_buffer.Reformat;
    begin
        Break_into_lines;
        end;

procedure tDisplay_buffer.Load_HTML_file(
  const Filename : string
  );

    procedure Process_HTML_string(
      const Text : pchar
      );

        procedure Parse_HTML(
          Text   : pchar;
          Format : tHTML_format
          );
            :
            procedure Reset_buffer;

            procedure Add_buffer_to_list;

            procedure Set_format(

            procedure New_line;

            procedure Horizontal_rule(
              const Height : integer
              );
                begin
                    Add_buffer_to_list;
                    inc(Pending_newlines);
                    with Current_format do begin
                        Rule_height := Height;
                        Leading_newlines := Pending_newlines;
                        end;
                    Formatted_text_list.Add(
                      tFormatted_text.Create(Current_format,'')
                      );
```

```
                    Current_format.Rule_height := 0;
                    Pending_newlines := 0;
                    end;

            procedure Image(
              const _Image_name : string
              );
                begin
                    Add_buffer_to_list;
                    inc(Pending_newlines);
                    with Current_format do begin
                        Picture_index :=
                            Image_list.Add_file(_Image_name);
                        Picture_scale := Format.Picture_scale;
                        Picture_align := Format.Picture_align;
                        Leading_newlines := Pending_newlines;
                        end;
                    Formatted_text_list.Add(
                      tFormatted_text.Create(Current_format,'')
                        );
                    Current_format.Picture_index := -1;
                    Pending_newlines := 0;
                    end;

            procedure Emit(

            function Is_whitespace(const C : char) : boolean;

            function Is_word(const C : char) : boolean;

                :

            begin
                Buffer := strAlloc(Length_of_buffer+1);

                Current_format := Format;
{replaces:      Current_format.Serial_number := -1;}
                Pending_newlines        := 0;
                Reset_buffer;

                Preceeding_newline := false;
                Preceeding_space := false;
                while Text^ <> #0 do

                    if Text^ = '<' then begin
                        { Process a Tag }
                        :
                        inc(Text);
                        The_end^ := #0;
                        Parse_tag(Text,
                          Format,
                          Reference_anchors,
                          Dest_name_anchors,
                          Need_a_newline,
```

The Hypermedia Engine at Work—Building a Web Browser

```
                        Rule_height,
                        Image_name
                        );
                    Text := The_end + 1;
                    Preceeding_newline :=
                        Preceeding_newline or Need_a_newline;
                    if Preceeding_newline then
                        Preceeding_space := false;
                    if Rule_height > 0 then
                        Horizontal_rule(Rule_height);
                    if Image_name <> '' then
                        Image(Image_name);
                    Set_format(Format);
                    end
                else if Format.Preformatted then begin
                    { Process Preformatted Text }
                    :
                else if Text^ <= ' ' then begin
                    { Process Whitespace }
                    :
                else begin
                    { Process Words }
                    :
                    end;

            Add_buffer_to_list; { Last little bit. }

            strDispose(Buffer);
            end;

    :
    begin
        with Format, Font do begin
            Leading_newlines := 0;
            Serial_number    := -1;
            specStyle        := [];
            specName         := 'Times New Roman';
            specColor        := clBlack;
            specSize         := 3;
            Rule_height      := 0;
            Anchor_reference := -1;
            Anchor_dest_name := -1;
            Preformatted     := false;
            Picture_index    := -1;
            Picture_scale    := 100;
            Picture_align    := pa_Left;
            end;
        Parse_HTML(Text,Format);
        Break_into_lines;
        end;

:
begin
    :
    end;
```

:
```
procedure tDisplay_buffer.Display;

    function Line_after(
      const Pixel_row : integer
      ) : integer;
        begin with Broken_text_list do begin
          :
            end; end;

    function Line_before(
      const Pixel_row : integer
      ) : integer;
        begin with Broken_text_list do begin
          :
            end; end;

    :
    begin with Broken_text_list do begin
      :
        for I := First_elem to Last_elem do
            with tFormatted_text(Items[I]), Format do
                if Rule_height > 0 then
                    Draw_rule(Control.Canvas,
                      Point(Base_left_corner.X,
                            Base_left_corner.Y - Display_top),
                      Meas.Width,Rule_height
                      )
                  else if Picture_index <> -1 then
                    with TPicture(Image_list.Items[Picture_index]) do begin
                        H := round(Height * Picture_scale / 100);
                        W := round(Width  * Picture_scale / 100);
                        case Picture_align of
                          pa_Left   : TCX := 0;
                          pa_Center : TCX := (Meas.Width - W) div 2;
                          pa_Right  : TCX := Meas.Width - W;
                          else        TCX := 0;
                          end;
                        TCY := Base_left_corner.Y - Display_top - H;
                        if Picture_scale = 100 then
                            Control.Canvas.Draw(TCX,TCY,Graphic)
                          else
                            Control.Canvas.StretchDraw(
                              Rect(TCX,TCY,TCX+W,TCY+H),
                              Graphic
                              );
                        end
                  else if Text <> nil then begin
                    Set_font_from_spec(Control.Canvas.Font,Format.Font);
                    Control.Canvas.TextOut(
                      Base_left_corner.X, Base_left_corner.Y - Display_top,
                      Text
                      );
                    end;
```

```
        end; end;

{initialization}
    end.
```

Improving the Interface

We have a few things to do in unit **Main** to use our new ability to reformat code on the fly, and to back our new controls, the **Back_button** and **StatusBar1**. The changes are detailed in Listing 12.4.

The only time we need to **Reformat** our code is when we resize the form. We had some other code in this routine left over form *Magic I*, so we should look at the whole routine again, briefly.

```
procedure TForm1.FormResize(Sender: TObject);
    var
        Minimum_width,
        Incr_X,
        Incr_Y,
        Old_left,
        Old_width,
        Image_panel_incr_X : integer;
    begin
        if Resizing_ourselves then exit;

        Minimum_width :=
            Filename.Left + 100;
        with Form1 do begin
            if Width < Minimum_width then
                Width := Minimum_width;
            if Height < 150 then
                Height := 150;
            Incr_X := Form1.Width - Form1s_old_width;
            Incr_Y := Form1.Height - Form1s_old_height;
            end;
        Filename.Width := Filename.Width + Incr_X;
        Bevel1.Width   := Bevel1.Width   + Incr_X;
        with Panel1 do begin
            Width  := Width  + Incr_X;
            Height := Height + Incr_Y;
            end;
        with PaintBox1 do begin
            Width  := Width  + Incr_X;
            Height := Height + Incr_Y;
            end;
        with ScrollBar1 do begin
            Left   := Left   + Incr_X;
            Height := Height + Incr_Y;
            end;
        Resizing_ourselves := false;
```

```
Form1s_old_width   := Form1.Width;
Form1s_old_height  := Form1.Height;

if Output <> nil then Output.Reformat;
(*Load_HTML; { To re-parse }*)

Form1.Refresh;
end;
```

Something subtle has changed here. When a form is created, its **OnResize** event handler is called as part of the process. In *Magic I*, **FormResize** called **Load_HTML**, which created our **Output tDisplay_buffer**. Now, all we do is **Reformat** the **Output** if the **Output** has been created. So, we actually have to execute **Jump_to** to create **Output** the first time. This means that in other places where we reference **Output** before we've loaded our first document (for instance, a click in the Paint Box), we'll need to check to make sure it's not **nil**.

The new **OnMouseMove** handler for **PaintBox1** is a case in point. All this does is look up the mouse location in the **Output**'s **Reference_anchors** list. The target, which may be null, is placed into **StatusBar1**'s **SimpleText**, telling the user the destination of a hotlink. The user might move the mouse cursor over the Paint Box before a document is loaded, so we need to check for the **nil** condition.

```
procedure TForm1.PaintBox1MouseMove(Sender: TObject; Shift: TShiftState; X,
  Y: Integer);
    begin
        if Output <> nil then
            with Output, Reference_anchors do
                StatusBar1.SimpleText := Name_of_point(X,Y + Display_top);
        end;
```

Back It Up!

The last change to the user interface involves the code behind our Back button. If you carefully near the end of **Jump_to**, you'll see how we remember where we've been.

```
Last_destination    := Refresh_destination;
Refresh_destination := Target;
Form1.Back_button.Enabled := Last_destination <> '';
```

We keep two state variables: one to hold the place we're at, and one to hold the last place we've been. After we've jumped to a new target, we simply trickle the destinations back: the **Refresh_destination** (from before the jump) becomes the **Last_destination**, and the destination we're at now be-

The Hypermedia Engine at Work—Building a Web Browser

comes the **Refresh_destination**. We haven't implemented a "Refresh" control, but we could. Finally, we **Enable** the **Back_button** if the **Last_destination** is not blank. We do this because that's the destination we'll jump to if the user presses the **Back_button**:

```
procedure TForm1.Back_buttonClick(Sender: TObject);
   begin
       Jump_to(Last_destination);
       end;
```

We don't want to do this if the **Last_destination** is blank. Of course, there is some support code behind this mechanism to initialize and declare the variables, but you can see that in Listing 12.4.

There is one more item of particular interest: the variables **Refresh_destination** and **Last_destination** are declared as **ShortStrings**, because for some reason, Delphi's default **string** type, **ANSIString**, becomes confused in the stair-step assignment operation.

Listing 12.4 Changes to Unit Main to Support New Capabilities in *Browser I*

```
unit Main;

interface

:
uses
  SysUtils, WinTypes, WinProcs, Messages, Classes, Graphics, Controls,
  Forms, Dialogs, StdCtrls, ExtCtrls, ComCtrls;

type
  TForm1 = class(TForm)
    Panel1: TPanel;
    ScrollBar1: TScrollBar;
    Open_button: TButton;
    OpenDialog1: TOpenDialog;
    PaintBox1: TPaintBox;
    Close_button: TButton;
    StatusBar1: TStatusBar;
    Back_button: TButton;
    Bevel1: TBevel;
    Label1: TLabel;
    Filename: TEdit;

    procedure FormCreate(Sender: TObject);
    procedure FormResize(Sender: TObject);
    procedure PaintBox1MouseDown(Sender: TObject; Button: TMouseButton;
      Shift: TShiftState; X, Y: Integer);
    procedure ScrollBar1Change(Sender: TObject);
```

```pascal
    procedure FilenameKeyPress(Sender: TObject; var Key: Char);
    procedure Open_buttonClick(Sender: TObject);
    procedure Close_buttonClick(Sender: TObject);
    procedure PaintBox1Paint(Sender: TObject);
    procedure Back_buttonClick(Sender: TObject);
    procedure PaintBox1MouseMove(Sender: TObject; Shift: TShiftState; X,
       Y: Integer);
  private
    { Private declarations }
  public
    { Public declarations }
  end;

:

implementation

{$R *.DFM}

:

var
    Refresh_destination,
    Last_destination    : shortString;

procedure Jump_to(
  const Target : string
  );
    var
       Re_show : boolean;
       Ext     : string;
       Command : ansiString;
    begin with TParser.Parse(pchar(Target)) do begin
       Re_show := true;
       No_errors;
       Find('#');
       if Error then begin
           { Just "filename".  Could be a media file. }
           Re_show := false;
           Ext := uppercase(extractFileExt(Remainder));
           if  (Ext = '.WAV')
             or
               (Ext = '.MID')
             or
               (Ext = '.AVI')
             then begin
               Command := 'Play ' + strPas(Remainder);
               mciExecute(pchar('Play ' + strPas(Remainder)));
               end
             else begin
               { 'HTM', 'html', other web docs. }
               Form1.Filename.Text := Remainder;
               Load_HTML;
```

```
                        Re_show := true;
                    end
                end
            else begin
                if Last_found^ <> #0 then begin
                    { There was a filename in "filename#label".
                      <label> is in Remainder. }
                    Form1.Filename.Text := Last_found;
                    Load_HTML;
                    end
                else
                    ; { Just "#label". }
                Set_scrollbar(
                    Int_max(
                        Output.Dest_name_anchors.First_rect_of_name(Remainder).Top,
                        0
                        )
                    );
                end;
            if Re_show then Form1.PaintBox1.Refresh;
            Free;
            Last_destination    := Refresh_destination;
            Refresh_destination := Target;
            Form1.Back_button.Enabled := Last_destination <> '';
            end; end;

procedure TForm1.PaintBox1MouseDown(Sender: TObject; Button: TMouseButton;
    Shift: TShiftState; X, Y: Integer);
    var
        Target : string;
    begin
        if Output <> nil then begin
            with Output, Reference_anchors do
                Target := Name_of_point(X,Y + Display_top);
            if Target <> '' then Jump_to(Target);
            end;
        end;

procedure TForm1.PaintBox1MouseMove(Sender: TObject; Shift: TShiftState; X,
    Y: Integer);
    begin
        if Output <> nil then
            with Output, Reference_anchors do
                StatusBar1.SimpleText := Name_of_point(X,Y + Display_top);
        end;

⋮

procedure TForm1.Back_buttonClick(Sender: TObject);
    begin
        Jump_to(Last_destination);
        end;
```

```
procedure TForm1.PaintBox1Paint(Sender: TObject);
    begin
        if Output <> nil then Output.Display;
        end;

:
procedure TForm1.FormCreate(Sender: TObject);
    var
        Total,
        Control_border : integer;
    begin
        Resizing_ourselves := false;
        Form1s_old_width   := Form1.Width;
        Form1s_old_height  := Form1.Height;
        Output := nil;
        Refresh_destination := '';
        Last_destination    := '';
        end;

procedure TForm1.FormResize(Sender: TObject);
    :
    begin
        if Resizing_ourselves then exit;

        Minimum_width := Filename.Left + 100;
        with Form1 do begin
            if Width < Minimum_width then
                Width := Minimum_width;
            if Height < 150 then
                Height := 150;
            Incr_X := Form1.Width  - Form1s_old_width;
            Incr_Y := Form1.Height - Form1s_old_height;
            end;
        Filename.Width := Filename.Width + Incr_X;
        Bevel1.Width   := Bevel1.Width   + Incr_X;
        with Panel1 do begin
            Width  := Width  + Incr_X;
            Height := Height + Incr_Y;
            end;
        with PaintBox1 do begin
            Width  := Width  + Incr_X;
            Height := Height + Incr_Y;
            end;
        with ScrollBar1 do begin
            Left   := Left   + Incr_X;
            Height := Height + Incr_Y;
            end;
        Resizing_ourselves := false;

        Form1s_old_width   := Form1.Width;
        Form1s_old_height  := Form1.Height;

        if Output <> nil then Output.Reformat;
        (*Load_HTML; { To re-parse }*)
```

```
    Form1.Refresh;
  end;
end.
```

It's a Great Big World (Wide Web) Out There

At this point, we've built ourselves a full-featured HTML browser. There's only one more big step to take—out the front door, and into the World—Wide Web, that is! To start surfing, all we need is the board. We're going to walk you through adding a couple of custom controls to Delphi. When you place these controls, developed by Edward Toupin, onto our form, you'll be surprised at how easy it is to ride the Web.

We're going to talk about the final trimming on our Browser, too. In *Browser I*, we had a simple "Back" button. To finesse the Web, we're going to add a real history system, that will allow you to go backwards and forwards along your path out into the World.

The Internet Connection

The *TTC Connectivity Custom Controls* package by Edward Toupin contains two OCXs that we can use together to wend our way onto the Web. But before that can happen, we need to bring these controls into Delphi. The OCXs, on the accompanying CD-ROM, are named *GetHost.OCX* and *Socket.OCX*. Use the Windows 95 *Explorer* to copy these to your hard drive. These don't need to be in your *Windows\System* directory, but they do need to be in a place where they'll be easily accessible. As we integrate these controls with Delphi, we'll also be telling Windows where to find them, and Windows won't like it if you move them someday.

Before starting, go ahead and choose *File | Save All* from the main menu. Then, choose *Component | Install...* From the *Install Component* dialog box, press the OCX button. Before we can install the components in Delphi, we must register the OCXs with Windows. Click the Register button on the *Import OLE Control* dialog box, and browse your way to one of the OCXs you've copied to your hard drive. After the OCX is registered, it will appear in the *Registered Controls* list box on the *Import OLE Control* dialog box. You should also register the other OCX at this time.

After registering both OCXs, highlight one in the *Registered Controls* list box, and click OK. Delphi will now write its own "wrapper" for the OCX, and take you back to the *Install Components* dialog box. It will have changed; if you look at the *Installed Units* list, you'll see the name of the wrapper. Don't do anything with that wrapper yet. Press the OCX button again, to go back to the *Import OLE Control* dialog box. This time, choose the other OCX from the *Registered Controls* list, and again, press OK to let Delphi create a wrapper for it.

After the second OCX's wrapper is created, you'll be returned to the *Install Components* dialog box. Find one of your OCX wrapper units in the *Installed Units* list. Highlight it, and click OK. Delphi will recompile a part of itself; this may take several minutes. When it's done, you'll find the control added to the OCX page of the Component Palette. Choose *Component | Install...* again, and this time, choose the other OCX wrapper unit you just made from the *Installed Units* list. Once more, highlight it, and click OK.

When you are done installing the **GetHost** and **Socket** OCXs, you'll find three more controls on the *OCX* page of the *Component Palette*. We are interested in two of these: the **TGetAdrsCtrl** component and the **TSocketCtrl** component. We'll be adding these to our project shortly.

Browser II : Surf's Up!

This project is the culmination of everything we've learned about hypermedia! Instead of giving you the rote steps, we're going to dive right into the code. Here's what to do: Once again, start a new project, named **Browser2**, copied from the previous project, **Browser1**. Modify the main form, **Form1**, by widening it so you can add a "Reload" button and a "Forward" button, as shown in Figure 12.3, below. Put a **TGetAdrsCtrl** and a **TSocketCtrl** on the form, too. Add the unit **Internet**, make the necessary modifications to **DispBuf** and **Main** to support our new ability to retrieve files from the net, and finally, replace the simple **Back_button** mechanics with the new history list mechanics, supporting the Back, Reload, and Forward buttons. The Magic Browser in action is shown in Figure 12.4.

You'll find this project in the subdirectory \Programs\Chap12\Browser2 on the accompanying CD ROM. For our examples here, we'll be using the files Browser1.HTM through Browser4.HTM from \Media\HyperTxt, again, but we'll also be hitting the Web.

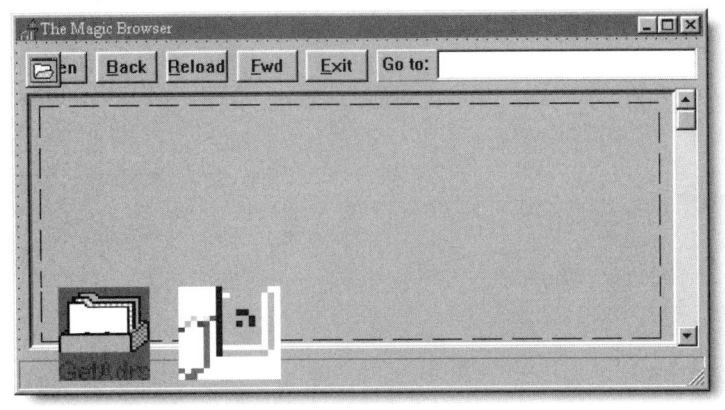

The Hypermedia Engine at Work—Building a Web Browser

Figure 12.3 *The Magic Browser at design time, showing **GetAdrsCtrl1** and **SocketCtrl1**.*

Opening the Door: A Brief Introduction to Sockets

Our strategy for accessing Web files from the Internet is simple: Get the file (somehow) from the net onto the disk, then display it in the usual manner.

The question of course is "How do we get it?" Our approach is to use the TTC Socket custom control, an OCX that provides custom controls for Internet communication via TCP/IP (an Internet protocol) *sockets*. Sockets can be viewed as similar to files; they can be opened, written to, and read from. We will use the custom controls from the TTC package to do exactly that. See the file *Sockets.Hlp* on the CD-ROM for more information about socket communication and the TTC Socket custom control documentation.

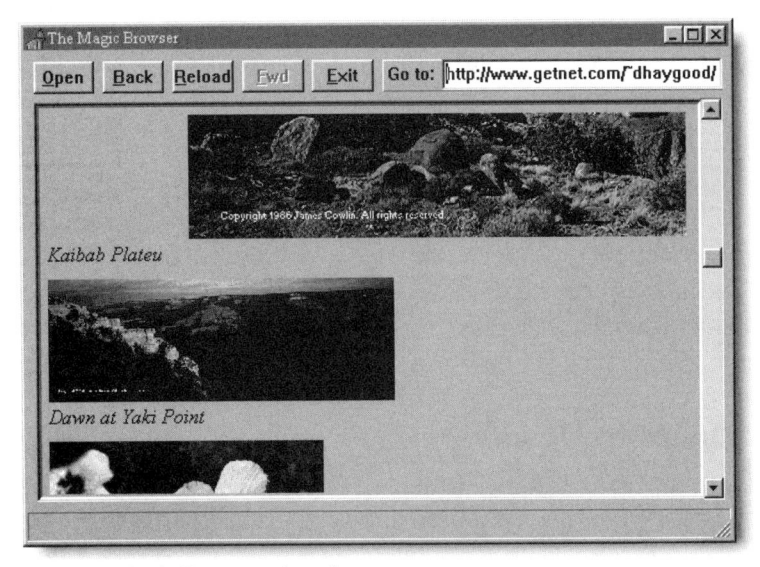

Figure 12.4 *The Magic Browser at work.*

Sockets are opened to specific *ports* on machines: the default port for HTTP (the *H*yper*T*ext *T*ransport *P*rotocol) is port 80. So to talk to a remote webserver (a program that implements HTTP functions), we open port 80 on the machine running the webserver.

While HTTP includes other functions, we will use just one: **GET**. Not surprisingly, **GET** gets the page referred to, and returns it to the socket, from which we can read it.

So here's the basic plan:

1. Parse the URL for the page or object. We are attempting to get into its *hostname* (the web site's name) and its path and filename part. Occasionally, these will be missing; fortunately, HTTP sends a default file, *index.html*, to us if we fail to specify a document name.
2. Get the IP address of the named host, using the **TGetAdrsCtrl** method **GetHostAdrs**. To use the Internet at this low level, we need to know the host machine's numeric address. This method looks up our host's name on a Domain Name Server and returns us the numeric IP address. There are typically four segments in this address, separated with periods, so we'll actually use a string to represent this.
3. Open a socket to the webserver on port 80 of the machine at that IP address.
4. Send the command "GET" plus the path and filename, if we have it, to the webserver (through the socket we've opened to the host).
5. Read what comes back through the socket connection, and write that to a local file.
6. If some error occurs during steps 1-6, we'll write an appropriate error message to the file instead.
7. Read and display the file contents in the usual manner.

For error handling, we have a local procedure, **Load_error_message**, which simply writes an appropriate message to the temporary file (thus "loading" it into the file the browser will display). Each socket function will be written with a conditional which will test for success: if successful, execution will continue on to the next function call; on failure, **Load_error_message** will be called.

Getting Files from the Internet

The last new unit, *Internet.Pas*, implements one routine, **Get_file**, that we'll use to change a URL into a local filename. The entire unit is shown in Listing 12.5. Of course, if the URL points out onto the Web, the major task of this

The Hypermedia Engine at Work—Building a Web Browser

routine will be getting the file from the Web, and putting it into a local file. If the URL is already on the local machine (that is, it doesn't have "http://" in front of it, telling us to look on the Web), we'll just return the URL that was passed into us as the **Filename**. If the URL is on the Web (specified with the prefix "http://"), we'll load it into a temporary file, *HTMLText.HTM*, and return that name as the **Filename**.

Listing 12.5   The New Unit **Internet** from *Browser II*

```
unit Internet;

interface
    uses
        GETHOST, SOCKET;

procedure Get_file(
  const URL      : string;
  var   Filename : string;    {out}
  const GetAdrs  : TGetAdrsCtrl;
  const Soc      : TSocketCtrl
  );

const
    { Socket Parameters }
    {------------------}

    { Socket Types }
    st_STREAM    = 1; { Stream socket }
    st_DGRAM     = 2; { Datagram socket }
    st_RAW       = 3; { Raw-protocol interface }
    st_RDM       = 4; { Reliably-delivered message }
    st_SEQPACKET = 5; { Sequenced packet stream }

    { IP Port Definitions }
    ipp_NETSTAT    =  15; { Network Statistics }
    ipp_FTP        =  21; { File Transfer Protocol }
    ipp_TELNET     =  23; { Telnet }
    ipp_SMTP       =  25; { Simple Mail Transfer Protocol }
    ipp_TIMESERVER =  37; { Network Time }
    ipp_NAMESERVER =  42; { Domain Name Service }
    ipp_WHOIS      =  43; { WHOIS }
    ipp_FINGER     =  79; { Finger }
    ipp_POP3       = 110; { Post Office Protocol v3 }
    ipp_NEWS       = 144; { Newsgroups }
    ipp_SNMP       = 161; { Simple Network Management Protocol }
    ipp_TALK       = 517; { TALK }
    ipp_NTALK      = 518; { NTALK }
    ipp_HTTP       =  80; { HTTP; added by Dan Haygood }

    { Address Format Definitions }
    af_UNSPEC   = 0; { Unspecified }
```

```
af_UNIX        =  1; { Local communications (i.e. pipes, portals, etc.) }
af_INET        =  2; { Internet UDP, TCP, etc. }
af_IMPLINK     =  3; { Arpanet }
af_PUP         =  4; { Pup protocols }
af_CHAOS       =  5; { MIT PUP protocols }
af_IPX         =  6; { IPX and SPX }
af_NS          =  6; { XEROX NS protocols }
af_ISO         =  7; { ISO protocols }
af_ECMA        =  8; { European computer manufacturers }
af_DATAKIT     =  9; { Datakit protocols }
af_CCITT       = 10; { CCITT protocols, X.25 etc }
af_SNA         = 11; { IBM SNA }
af_DECnet      = 12; { DECnet }
af_DLI         = 13; { Direct data link interface }
af_LAT         = 14; { Local Area Transport }
af_HYLINK      = 15; { NSC Hyperchannel }
af_APPLETALK   = 16; { AppleTalk }
af_NETBIOS     = 17; { NetBios-style addresses }

{ Protocol Definitions }
p_IP   =   0; { Dummy for IP }
p_ICMP =   1; { Control message protocol }
p_GGP  =   2; { Gateway^2 }
p_TCP  =   6; { TCP }
p_PUP  =  12; { PUP }
p_UDP  =  17; { User Datagram Protocol }
p_IDP  =  22; { XNS IDP }
p_RAW  = 255; { Raw IP packet }

implementation

uses
    SysUtils, Forms,
    Parser;

procedure Get_file(
  const URL      : string;
  var   Filename : string;    {out}
  const GetAdrs  : TGetAdrsCtrl;
  const Soc      : TSocketCtrl
  );

    procedure Load_document(
      const Filename : string;
      const Doc      : string
      );
      var
          F : text;
      begin
          assignFile(F,Filename);
          rewrite(F);
          write(F,Doc);
          closeFile(F);
          end;
```

```
procedure Load_error_message(
  const Filename : string;
  const Msg      : string
  );
    var
        F : text;
    begin
        assignFile(F,Filename);
        rewrite(F);
        writeln(F,'<HTML>');
        writeln(F,'<H2>Error!</H2>');
        writeln(F,'<P>' + Msg);
        writeln(F,'</HTML>');
        closeFile(F);
        end;

var
    Site,
    File_on_site,
    IP           : string;
    OK           : smallint;
    Document     : string;
begin
    with tParser.Parse(pchar(URL)) do begin
        No_errors;
        Expect('HTTP://');
        if Error then
            Filename := URL
          else begin
            Filename := ExtractFilePath(Application.ExeName)
                       + 'HTMLText.HTM';
            Find('/');
            if Error then begin
                Site := Remainder;
                File_on_site := '/';
                end
              else begin
                Site := Last_found;
                File_on_site := '/' + Remainder;
                end;

            { Get the document. }
            Document := '';
            IP := GetAdrs.GetHostAdrs(Site);
            if IP <> '' then begin
                OK := Soc.OpenSocket(af_INET,st_STREAM,p_TCP);
                if OK = 1 then begin
                    OK := Soc.ConnectRemote(af_INET,ipp_HTTP,IP);
                    if OK = 1 then begin
                        OK := Soc.SendRemote(
                            'GET ' + File_on_site + #13 + #10,5000
                            );
                        if OK = 1 then begin
                            Document := Soc.RecvRemote(5000);
```

```
                            if Document <> '' then
                                Load_document(Filename,Document)
                            else
                                Load_error_message(Filename,
                                    'Could not receive document "' +
                                    File_on_site +
                                    '".'
                                    );
                        end
                    else
                        Load_error_message(Filename,
                            'Could not ask for document "' +
                            File_on_site +
                            '".'
                            );
                    end
                else
                    Load_error_message(Filename,
                        'Could not connect to "' + Site + '".'
                        );
                OK := Soc.CloseSocket;
                end
            else
                Load_error_message(Filename,
                    'Could not open socket.'
                    );
            end
        else
            Load_error_message(Filename,
                'Could not get IP Address for "' +
                Site +
                '" from DNS.'
                );
        end;
    Free;
    end;
end;

end.
```

One of the first things you'll notice is that we use two units we haven't seen before (unless you looked at the **uses** list of unit **Main** after dropping the new OCX controls on it). **GETHOST** and **SOCKET** are the wrappers that Delphi wrote for itself when we imported the custom controls. We use these units here, so we can pass in the controls from the main form when we call **Get_file**. One thing these units don't provide us with is the list of magic numbers that these controls use; we took the list of constants used to specify various configurations to the control from the TTC help files, and gave them meaningful names in our **const** section.

The Hypermedia Engine at Work—Building a Web Browser 579

Once we get into **Get_file**, we first call **tParser.Parse** with the URL, looking for the **HTTP://** prefix; if we don't find it, we assume the URL names a local file, and simply return it as the **Filename** for normal processing. If we do find it, we break the remainder into its host name, **Site**, and the filename of the host, **File_on_site**. If we don't find even a trailing "/", we set the **File_on_site** to "/", which will return the default page, *index.html*, from the server.

Once we know the **Site** and **File_on_site**, we get the IP address of the remote machine by calling **GetAdrs.GetHostAdrs**; if that fails, we write an error message using **Load_error_message** as described above. Then we attempt to open the socket with **Soc.OpenSocket**; again, we continue on success, or write an error message on failure. After opening the socket, we call **Soc.ConnectRemote** to establish a connection to the webserver.

Once we have our opened socket, we can begin interacting with the webserver. We send the **GET** command plus the value of **File_on_site** to the server by calling **Soc.SendRemote**, again writing an error message on failure and continuing on success. Finally, we read what the server returns by calling **Soc.RecvRemote**, and if successful, write the returned document to a temporary file using our local procedure **Load_document**; if we were not successful we (as usual) write an error message.

Note: This code assumes that we will be communicating with a standard webserver on port 80 of the remote machine, as specified by the **ipp_HTTP** constant in the call to **Soc.ConnectRemote**; we do not parse for the optional *:port* argument of the URL. If you anticipate communicating with other webservers that use other ports, you will want to parse for this component and use the port number found there, defaulting to port 80 if it is not specified.

Using Our Internet Support

The only thing left to do to establish connectivity in our program is to call **Get_file** before we actually attempt to load an HTML document. This task has two parts.

First, we must make this call when we load an HTML document from unit **Main**, in the routine **Load_HTML**, so that we can make sure we download Web pages before calling our **tDisplay_buffer**'s **Load_HTML_file** method. The final changes to unit **Main** are shown in Listing 12.7, but here is the simple call to **Get_file**:

```
procedure Load_HTML;
    var
        File_to_use : string;
    begin with Form1 do begin
        Get_file(Filename.Text,File_to_use,
```

```
            GetAdrsCtrl1, SocketCtrl1
              );
        Output.Free;
        Output := tDisplay_buffer.Create(
                    tGraphicControlWithCanvas(PaintBox1),
                    GetAdrsCtrl1,
                    SocketCtrl1
                    );
        Output.Load_HTML_file(File_to_use);
        Set_scrollbar(0);
        end; end;
```

Instead of using the filename directly out of the **Filename** Edit control, we pass this to **Get_file**, along with our TTC controls, to get the file from the Internet if necessary.

Second, we must make sure that when we load our images as we parse the document, that we try to get these from the Web, too. This is a more difficult change; the code fragment above shows one of the necessary modifications in action: We must tell the **tDisplay_buffer** about the custom controls we are using to access the Web, so that it can, in turn, specify these controls to **Get_file**. These changes throughout unit **DispBuf** are highlighted in Listing 12.6.

Listing 12.6 Changes to Unit **DispBuf** to Take Advantage of Unit **Internet** in *Browser II*

```
unit DispBuf;
interface
uses
     Classes, Graphics, Controls, ExtCtrls, GETHOST, SOCKET,
     Font, FmtText, HyperLnk, PicList;
:
tDisplay_buffer = class
       private
         { Internet controls }
         GetAdrs : TGetAdrsCtrl;
         Soc     : TSocketCtrl;
         { Formatted Text Storage }
         Formatted_text_list : tFormatted_text_list;
         Image_list          : tPicture_list;
         { "Breaker" Data -- Line Breaking list }
         Broken_text_list    : tFormatted_text_list;
         Line_list           : TList; {of integer}
         { "Displayer" Data }
         Control             : tGraphicControlWithCanvas;
         procedure Break_into_lines;
       public
         { Hyperlink support lists, built by "Breaker" }
         Reference_anchors : tNamed_rectangle_list;
         Dest_name_anchors : tNamed_rectangle_list;
```

```
        { Display Positioning and Height, calc'd by "Breaker" }
        Display_top,
        Display_bottom : integer;
      public
        constructor Create(
          const _Control : tGraphicControlWithCanvas;
          const _GetAdrs : TGetAdrsCtrl;
          const _Soc     : TSocketCtrl
          );
        destructor Destroy; override;
        procedure Load_HTML_file(
          const Filename : string
          );
        procedure Reformat;
        procedure Display;
        end;
implementation
uses
    SysUtils, Windows, Dialogs,
    MiscLib, HTML, Internet;
:
constructor tDisplay_buffer.Create(
  const _Control : tGraphicControlWithCanvas;
  const _GetAdrs : TGetAdrsCtrl;
  const _Soc     : TSocketCtrl
  );
    begin
      inherited Create;
      Formatted_text_list := tFormatted_text_list.Create;
      Line_list           := TList.Create;
      Control := _Control;
      Display_top    := 0;
      Display_bottom := 0;
      Reference_anchors := tNamed_rectangle_list.Create;
      Dest_name_anchors := tNamed_rectangle_list.Create;
      Broken_text_list := nil;
      Image_list := tPicture_list.Create;
      GetAdrs := _GetAdrs;
      Soc     := _Soc;
      end;
:
procedure tDisplay_buffer.Load_HTML_file(
  const Filename : string
  );
    procedure Process_HTML_string(
      const Text : pchar
      );
        procedure Parse_HTML(
          Text   : pchar;
          Format : tHTML_format
          );
            :
          procedure Reset_buffer;
```

Chapter 12

```
          procedure Add_buffer_to_list;

          procedure Set_format(

          procedure New_line;

          procedure Horizontal_rule(

          procedure Image(
            const _Image_name : string
            );
              var
                File_to_use : string;
              begin
                Get_file(_Image_name,File_to_use,GetAdrs,Soc);
                Add_buffer_to_list;
                inc(Pending_newlines);
                with Current_format do begin
                    Picture_index :=
                      Image_list.Add_file(File_to_use);
                    Picture_scale := Format.Picture_scale;
                    Picture_align := Format.Picture_align;
                    Leading_newlines := Pending_newlines;
                    end;
                Formatted_text_list.Add(
                  tFormatted_text.Create(Current_format,'')
                  );
                Current_format.Picture_index := -1;
                Pending_newlines := 0;
                end;

          procedure Emit(

          function Is_whitespace(const C : char) : boolean;

          function Is_word(const C : char) : boolean;

          begin
              :
             end;
      :
      begin
          :
         end;

    :
    begin
        :
       end;
  :
{initialization}
    end.
```

The Hypermedia Engine at Work—Building a Web Browser

A Sense of History

The last feature we'll add to *The Magic Browser* is a real history list, instead of a simple "Back" button. Hopefully, you've already added the buttons necessary to accomplish this to **Form1** in unit **Main**; we've called our buttons **Back_button**, **Reload_button**, and **Forward_button**. The last two are new.

Our history list, **History_list**, is implemented as a **TStringList**. We simply save URLs to the list as the user goes to them by clicking or entering "Go to" destinations. If the user hits the navigation buttons, we move backward and forward along the **History_list**, using the index variable **History_index**, and then **Jump_to** the referenced URL.

There is one catch to this scheme. If the user backs up, and then follows a different route, the path forward from the old location won't necessarily make sense anymore. In our implementation, we'll just delete everything forward of the user's current location if they click on a link or enter a new destination, rather than pressing the **Forward_button** or other buttons. A typical example is shown in Figure 12.5.

The code snippet below shows the Buttons' response code.

```
procedure TForm1.Back_buttonClick(Sender: TObject);
   begin
      Was_nav_button := true;
      if History_index > 0 then begin
         dec(History_index);
         Jump_to(History_list.Strings[History_index]);
         end;
   end;
```

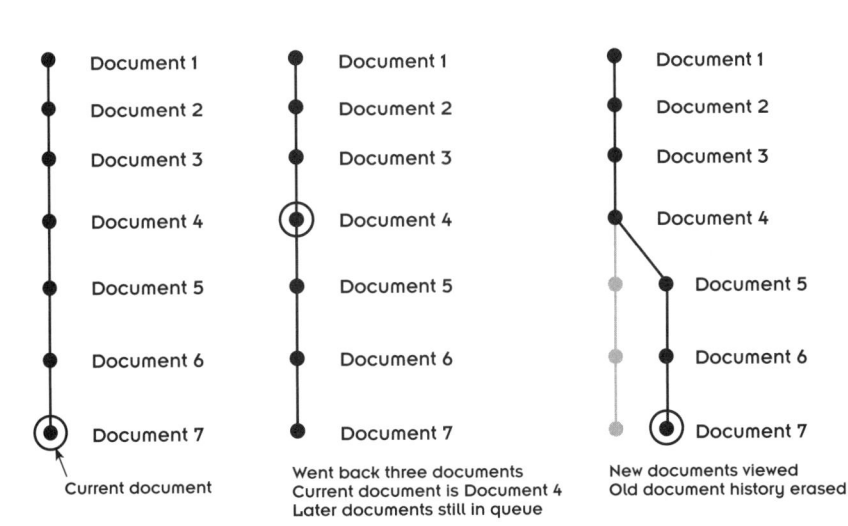

Figure 12.5 *The document history chain.*

```
procedure TForm1.Reload_buttonClick(Sender: TObject);
    begin
        Was_nav_button := true;
        Jump_to(History_list.Strings[History_index]);
    end;

procedure TForm1.Forward_buttonClick(Sender: TObject);
    begin
        Was_nav_button := true;
        if History_index < (History_list.Count - 1) then begin
            inc(History_index);
            Jump_to(History_list.Strings[History_index]);
        end;
    end;
```

The state variable **Was_nav_button** is used to indicate to **Jump_to** that we've just pressed a navigation button, and should *not* delete the portion of the **History_list** after our current **History_index**. After determining if the move backward or forward can be made, we move **History_index** the appropriate direction, and **Jump_to** the URL stored there.

We don't necessarily want to rely on these tests to move backward or forward though, so we can buttress this by disabling the buttons in cases when the user can't move backward or forward. This also gives the user important feedback. After we've made a move, we can **Enable** the buttons appropriately, as shown in the code snippet below.

```
Was_nav_button := false;
with Form1 do begin
    Back_button.Enabled    := History_index>0;
    Forward_button.Enabled := History_index<(History_list.Count-1);
    Reload_button.Enabled  :=
        (History_index >= 0)
      and
        (History_index <= (History_list.Count - 1));
end;
```

We also need to reset our **Was_nav_button** state variable. It is important to set all of these Buttons' Enabled properties to False at design time, so they are disabled when the project starts—we have no history list at this point!

We actually manipulate the **History_list**'s contents in **Jump_to** after we've loaded the document, but before we decide what buttons to **Enable** (the code in this section is actually reversed).

```
if not Was_nav_button then begin
    if History_index <> -1 then
        for I := History_list.Count - 1 downto History_index + 1 do
            History_list.Delete(I);
```

The Hypermedia Engine at Work—Building a Web Browser 585

```
      History_index := History_list.Add(Target);
   end;
```

Before we change the list, we need to establish that we didn't come here from a navigation button. If we did, then all we need to do is move along the existing list, without modifying it. If the user caused this move by explicitly specifying a new destination, or by clicking a hotlink, we need to delete the list that used to be ahead of us, and add our new destination (that we just loaded) to the end of the list. If the **History_index** is at its initial value of –1, indicating that there *is no* **History_list**, we don't need to delete the items ahead of us; if there is a list, we delete everything from the end back to our current location. Finally, we add this location to the list.

The changes, shown in their correct order, are shown in the code for unit **Main**, in Listing 12.7.

Listing 12.7   Changes to Unit **Main** for History and Unit **Internet** Support
Browser II

```
unit Main;
interface
uses
   SysUtils, WinTypes, WinProcs, Messages, Classes, Graphics, Controls,
   Forms, Dialogs, StdCtrls, ExtCtrls, ComCtrls, OleCtrls, GETHOST, SOCKET;
type
   TForm1 = class(TForm)
     Panel1: TPanel;
     ScrollBar1: TScrollBar;
     Open_button: TButton;
     OpenDialog1: TOpenDialog;
     PaintBox1: TPaintBox;
     Close_button: TButton;
     StatusBar1: TStatusBar;
     Back_button: TButton;
     GetadrsCtrl1: TGetadrsCtrl;
     SocketCtrl1: TSocketCtrl;
     Reload_button: TButton;
     Forward_button: TButton;
     Bevel1: TBevel;
     Label1: TLabel;
     Filename: TEdit;

     procedure FormCreate(Sender: TObject);
     procedure FormResize(Sender: TObject);
     procedure PaintBox1MouseDown(Sender: TObject; Button: TMouseButton;
        Shift: TShiftState; X, Y: Integer);
     procedure ScrollBar1Change(Sender: TObject);
     procedure FilenameKeyPress(Sender: TObject; var Key: Char);
     procedure Open_buttonClick(Sender: TObject);
     procedure Close_buttonClick(Sender: TObject);
```

```
    procedure PaintBox1Paint(Sender: TObject);
    procedure Back_buttonClick(Sender: TObject);
    procedure Reload_buttonClick(Sender: TObject);
    procedure Forward_buttonClick(Sender: TObject);
    procedure FormDestroy(Sender: TObject);
    procedure PaintBox1MouseMove(Sender: TObject; Shift: TShiftState; X,
      Y: Integer);
  private
    { Private declarations }
  public
    { Public declarations }
  end;
var
  Form1: TForm1;

implementation
    uses
        MMSystem,
        MiscLib, DispBuf, HyperLnk, Parser, Internet;

procedure Load_HTML;
    var
        File_to_use : string;
    begin with Form1 do begin
        Get_file(Filename.Text,File_to_use,
          GetAdrsCtrl1, SocketCtrl1
            );
        Output.Free;
        Output := tDisplay_buffer.Create(
                    tGraphicControlWithCanvas(PaintBox1),
                    GetAdrsCtrl1,
                    SocketCtrl1
                    );
        Output.Load_HTML_file(File_to_use);
        Set_scrollbar(0);
        end; end;

var
    History_index  : integer;
    History_list   : TStringList;
    Was_nav_button : boolean;

procedure Jump_to(
  const Target : string
  );
    var
        Re_show : boolean;
        Ext     : string;
        Command : ansiString;
        I       : integer;
    begin with TParser.Parse(pchar(Target)) do begin
        Re_show := true;
        No_errors;
        Find('#');
```

```
if Error then begin
    { Just "filename".  Could be a media file. }
    Re_show := false;
    Ext := uppercase(extractFileExt(Remainder));
    if  (Ext = '.WAV')
      or
        (Ext = '.MID')
      or
        (Ext = '.AVI')
      then begin
        Command := 'Play ' + strPas(Remainder);
        mciExecute(pchar('Play ' + strPas(Remainder)));
        end
      else begin
        { 'HTM', 'html', other web docs. }
        Form1.Filename.Text := Remainder;
        Load_HTML;
        Re_show := true;
        end
    end
  else begin
    if Last_found^ <> #0 then begin
        { There was a filename in "filename#label".
          <label> is in Remainder. }
        Form1.Filename.Text := Last_found;
        Load_HTML;
        end
      else
        ; { Just "#label". }
    Set_scrollbar(
      Int_max(
        Output.Dest_name_anchors.First_rect_of_name(Remainder).Top,
        0
        )
      );
    end;
if Re_show then Form1.PaintBox1.Refresh;
Free;
if not Was_nav_button then begin
    if History_index <> -1 then
        for I := History_list.Count - 1 downto History_index + 1 do
            History_list.Delete(I);
    History_index := History_list.Add(Target);
    end;
Was_nav_button := false;
with Form1 do begin
    Back_button.Enabled    := History_index>0;
    Forward_button.Enabled := History_index<(History_list.Count-1);
    Reload_button.Enabled  :=
        (History_index >= 0)
      and
        (History_index <= (History_list.Count - 1));
    end;
end; end;
```

```
:
procedure TForm1.Back_buttonClick(Sender: TObject);
    begin
        Was_nav_button := true;
        if History_index > 0 then begin
            dec(History_index);
            Jump_to(History_list.Strings[History_index]);
            end;
        end;

procedure TForm1.Reload_buttonClick(Sender: TObject);
    begin
        Was_nav_button := true;
        Jump_to(History_list.Strings[History_index]);
        end;

procedure TForm1.Forward_buttonClick(Sender: TObject);
    begin
        Was_nav_button := true;
        if History_index < (History_list.Count - 1) then begin
            inc(History_index);
            Jump_to(History_list.Strings[History_index]);
            end;
        end;
:
end.
```

Upgrading the HTML Browser

When we started this book, a browser like the one we just finished might have been pretty hot—but nowadays, HTML is changing so rapidly that you'll have to play catch-up just to keep up with the latest standards and enhancements. In fact, you might want to jump in and start adding some of the newer HTML 2.0 and HTML 3.0 features that remain unimplemented here: backgrounds, tables, scaleable images, and different text colors; just to name a few. Here are some design and implementation suggestions.

"Relaxed" Parsing

In the first place, we are implementing a fairly rigid subset of the HTML specification: this includes the ability to display text and graphics, and play sounds, but our syntax is more restrictive: for instance, in true HTML, either apostrophes or double quotes can be used when quoting target addresses (URLs); we require double quotes. As a result of our overly-zealous enforcement of the Anchor tag, many real-world documents will turn on an anchor, but won't turn it off.

Backgrounds

While parsing the document, get the image for the background, and paint it repeatedly across the **tDisplay_buffer**'s **Canvas** in the **Display** method.

Image Maps

We already have a structure, **tPicture_list**, that holds the images for display, and their size. Coupled with their placement information in the Display Buffer's **Formatted_text_list**, we have almost enough information to create an image map. By parsing out the **ISMAP** argument of the **<IMG>** tag, you can build map information directly into the Display Buffer's **Reference_anchors** field.

Tables

Tables might be one of the more difficult features to add because there are so many options and variables with which to work. You could develop a structure storing pertinent information while parsing Table tags, such as bounding-box information, border type and thickness, and so forth.

Different Text Colors

This HTML 3.0 feature is almost trivial to implement; we already support color in our output—we just never implemented a tag to allow a document to specify text color. At the beginning of HTML 3.0 documents, sometimes colors for both ordinary text and link text are specified. You could capture these values into a variable, and use those colors instead of the fixed colors we used in our projects.

GIF and JPEG Support

Here's a big one—our browser does not support GIF (*G*raphics *I*nterchange *F*ormat) image files. As the graphics *lingua franca d'Internet*, without this support, our browser is pretty limited. Another popular format, JPEG, is used almost exclusively for graphics images stored for non-Web downloading from the Internet. Adding support for GIFs and JPEGs is trivial with a custom control, and they're out there. We couldn't explain how to decode these popular formats here—that would be a book in itself!

Additional Tags

As previously mentioned, we've implemented a subset of the HTML specification: we have omitted, for instance, the **<title>** tag, among others, all of the new tags in the HTML 2.0 specification, and the 3.0 specification (which is not yet finalized), and many popular extensions (from Netscape, Microsoft, and other vendors) which have been submitted for consideration as part of the HTML 3.0 spec. The beauty of building a system from scratch is that these tags can be added as they appear on the scene.

A few hours with any current browser will reveal lots of other tags and features we haven't gotten around to, including tables, frames, wrapping text around images, background colors and images, image maps, the ability to run external programs in Sun's Java or other languages, and so forth.

Relative URLs

We require full (absolute) URLs even in the pages we visit, with one exception noted below. A full URL consists of six parts: a *facility* name, a *host* or *device name*, a *port number* (optional), a (web) *pathname*, a *file name*, a *file type*, and an optional *named-target name*: a typical example would be:

```
http://www.getnet.com:80/~gwood/index.html#top
```

Schematically, this looks like:

```
facility://hostname:port/pathname/filename#target
```

Some Facilities on the Web are shown in Table 12.1. We are only implementing the HTTP facility and a localized version of the FILE facility.

Internet hostnames typically consists of two or more parts connected by periods, e.g. **www.getnet.com**, **roscoe.phx.cox.com**, **hulaw1.harvard.edu**, **getnet.com**. The **:port** component identifies the port that the remote machine has its webserver attached to. This is port 80 by default, and is often omitted. Pathnames on multi-user webservers often include tilde's (~) in front of usernames (like the **~gwood** above), which means **gwood**'s web home directory.

Table 12.1 Some Facilities on the World Wide Web.

Facility	Function
file:	Local file access
http:	HyperText Transport Protocol (World Wide Web) access
ftp:	(Internet) File Transport Protocol
Telnet:	Opens a Telnet (Internet virtual terminal) session to host

Absolute versus relative URLs.

As a shortcut, when a web page refers to another page using the same facility and on the same host and possibly in the same directory, an author is allowed to leave out those portions of the URL: For instance, in a document whose URL is **http://www.getnet.com/gethelp/unix.html**, the author may include a reference like this:

```
<a href="tips.html">the tips page</a>
```

Here, "tips.html" is a "relative" URL, and is relative to the URL of the page which refers to it: the absolute URL for this page would add the facility, host, and pathnames from the referring page—in this case, **http://www.getnet.com/gethelp/**, producing the absolute (or "fully-qualified") URL **http://www.getnet.com/gethelp/tips.html**. This is like me saying to a friend, "Julie lives at 40132 North Monroe;" I don't have to add "Phoenix, Arizona, 85003, USA, Earth, Left Spiral Arm of the Milky Way Galaxy, ..."

Having said all that, we should repeat: We are not implementing relative addresses, only absolute ones. Adding the ability to process relative addresses requires parsing URLs into their components, noting which components are missing, and filling in those components from the left.

The exception noted above is this: if the URL (entered, or encountered in a document) does not include **HTTP://** it is assumed to be a local file. To be consistent with other web browsers, you will probably wish to require the explicit use of the **FILE** facility name; in *The Magic Browser* we do not use the **FILE** facility. Anything without a leading **HTTP://** is assumed to be a local filename (with device letter and pathname, if required).

Bookmarks mechanism

A bookmark list is a list of URLs similar to a history list except that it is non-volatile (it is saved to a permanent file instead of disappearing between sessions) and the user must choose to add something to it. Advanced browsers allow the user to edit the bookmark list, and to create bookmark folders that expand and collapse like the folders in file manager.

History List and Tree

We implemented the "Back," "Forward," and "Reload" buttons connected to an internal history list, but we do not have a drop-down list the user can pick from (to jump back and forth more than one step at the time). A drop-down menu for the history list would look like the history list in other browsers: if you back up and go off on another branch, the branch you have been down disappears. For example, if your list is:

```
http://www.getnet.com/~gwood
http://www.getnet.com/~gwood/bio.html
http://hulaw1.harvard.edu/pericles/intro.html
http://leland.stanford.edu/~mdb
```

The most recent page appears at the bottom, and you back up to the second entry then go from there to **http://www.cs.cmu.edu**, the history list just drops the Harvard and Stanford links. It would be nice if a history mechanism constructed a tree of where you've been instead of keeping only the current branch.

Cache

When fetching objects from the Internet over a dial-up line, image loading can be very slow; it makes sense, then, to store local copies of such objects so that the next time they are loaded they can be fetched from your local copy. On the other hand, you don't want to keep local copies forever, and you don't want them to fill your available disk space, so you would want to have some method for selecting which ones to keep, how much space to allow for cache storage, etc. Most browsers that have local caching use a variant on the "least-most-recently-used" algorithm for deciding which files to remove from the cache when it fills. The simplest mechanism would be to simply delete the oldest elements; the smartest would be to assign weights based on file size, access frequency, and timeliness, and delete files with the lowest scores.

We're already some of the way to caching: The mechanism we use for displaying files downloaded from the Internet simplifies caching implementation, since the file is already saved to disk before being displayed. All that is needed is an indexing system and the cache-size maintenance mechanism we just discussed.

Chapter 13

Animation is the pinnacle of multimedia. It breathes life into otherwise lifeless images and brings the computer environment a step closer to our own environment. In this chapter we begin our extensive coverage of this exciting technology.

The Magic of Animation

Chris D. Coppola

Animation packs a potent punch when used correctly. Here's an amazing fact: Last year video games generated more income than movies in the U.S. What was their big attraction? Dazzling interactive animation. If you want your multimedia apps to really grab your user's attention, don't underestimate the power of pictures in motion.

The animation used in interactive multimedia comes in two basic forms:

- Movies or video clips
- Sprite or Cell Animation

In this chapter, we'll introduce you to some basic graphics animation techniques, including cell animation and sprite animation. These are the techniques that multimedia and game developers use to create fast action and exciting interfaces. We'll continue our animation adventures in Chapter 14 as we show you how to create fast, smooth, flicker-free animation using some more advanced sprite animation techniques.

Exploring Cell Animation

Cell animation is probably the most basic type of animation available to you as a multimedia developer. Perhaps you recall paper flip books, or maybe you've seen how animated movies are made. The principle is simple. To create a paper flip book you would draw the character to be animated in several different positions on separate pages of paper. Each page represents a *cell* of the animation.

To give the cells the illusion of motion, they must be displayed one over the next in rapid succession. For the paper flip book example, the pages must be aligned so that you can drag your thumb across the edge of the paper, creating a motion where each drawing rapidly replaces the previous one.

In Delphi's digital environment, we can apply the same technique. We'll use image components to replace the paper, and we'll digitally replace each cell with the next one to give the illusion of motion.

The Flip Book

In this simple project, we'll use a specially formatted bitmap to create the illusion of motion from a static image. Follow these steps:

1. Start a new project.
2. Add two TImage components, a Timer, and a Button.
3. Set the properties and events as shown in Table 13.1.
4. Insert the code.

This project is located in the directory \DELPHIMM\CH13\CELLANIM.

Creating the CellAnim Project

Create a new project. Add two TImage components and a TTimer. Don't worry about the placement of these; we'll handle that at run-time. Add a TButton component and position it in the lower right-hand corner of the form. Set the properties and event procedures as indicated in Table 13.1.

We'll use the button to activate and deactivate the animation. The timer acts as our digital 'thumb'—from the flip book example—to make the pages *flip*. One of the image components will store and display the source cells, while the other will display the animation. The code that makes all this happen appears in Listing 13.1.

The Magic of Animation 595

Table 13.1 Form and component properties.

Component	Property/Event	Setting
Default Form	Name	Main
	Caption	Cell Animation
	OnCreate	FormCreate
	OnDestroy	FormDestroy
TImage1	Name	imgSrc
	Stretch	True
TImage2	Name	imgDisplay
TTimer	OnTimer	Timer1Timer
TButton	Caption	Start
	OnClick	Button1Click

Listing 13.1 ucellani.pas

```
implementation

{$R *.DFM}
type
  TCellAnim = record
    Source:     TBitmap;
    CellCount:  integer;
    CellWidth:  integer;
    CellHeight: integer;
    Initialized: boolean;
    end; {TCellAnim}

var
  Anim: TCellAnim;

procedure ShowCell(CellIndex: byte);
var
  SourceRect,
  DestRect:   TRect;

begin
  { Reading the cells bitmap from bottom to top }
  SourceRect := Rect( 0, Anim.CellHeight * CellIndex,
           Anim.CellWidth,
           (Anim.CellHeight * CellIndex) + Anim.CellHeight);
  DestRect := Rect(0,0,Main.imgDisplay.Width, Main.imgDisplay.Height);

  with Main.imgDisplay.Canvas do
    CopyRect(DestRect, Anim.Source.Canvas, SourceRect);

end; {ShowCell}
```

```pascal
procedure TMain.FormCreate(Sender: TObject);
var
  fn: string;
  r:  TRect;
  DisplayWidth,
  DisplayHeight: integer;

begin

  {
    Load and display the bitmap containing all of the cells of
    the bitma we'll be using for the cell animation. We're loading
    it into a record that will make it easy to animate.
  }
  fn := ExtractFilePath(Application.EXEName) + 'cells2.bmp';

  Anim.Source := TBitmap.Create;
  Anim.Initialized := True;
  Anim.Source.LoadFromFile(fn);
  Anim.CellCount := 9;
  Anim.CellWidth := Anim.Source.Width;
  if Anim.Source.Height mod Anim.CellCount = 0 then
     Anim.CellHeight := Anim.Source.Height div Anim.CellCount
  else begin
         ShowMessage('Inconsistent size and cellcount');
         Self.Close;
         end;

  {Display the whole strip of cells}
  r := Rect( 0,0,
             round((ClientHeight / Anim.Source.Height) * Anim.CellWidth),
             ClientHeight);

  with imgSrc do begin
    SetBounds(r.left,r.top,r.right, r.bottom);
    AutoSize := False;
    Stretch := True;
    Picture.Bitmap := Anim.Source;
    end;

  { figure out how much of the screen is left to display the animation }
  DisplayWidth := ClientWidth - imgSrc.Width;
  DisplayHeight := ClientHeight;
  imgDisplay.SetBounds( imgSrc.Width + ((DisplayWidth div 2) -
                        (Anim.CellWidth div 2)),
                        (ClientHeight div 2) - (Anim.CellHeight div 2),
                        Anim.CellWidth,
                        Anim.CellHeight);

  Timer1.Interval := 50;

end; {FormCreate}
```

```
procedure TMain.FormDestroy(Sender: TObject);
begin
  if Anim.Initialized then
    Anim.Source.Free;

end;

procedure TMain.Timer1Timer(Sender: TObject);
const
  CellIndex: integer = 0;

begin

    ShowCell(CellIndex);
    dec(CellIndex);
    if CellIndex < 0 then
      CellIndex := Anim.CellCount - 1;

end;

procedure TMain.Button1Click(Sender: TObject);
begin

  Timer1.Enabled := Not Timer1.Enabled;
  if Timer1.Enabled then
    Button1.Caption := 'Stop'
  else
    Button1.Caption := 'Start';
end;

end.
```

The first thing we should examine is the type declaration for **TCellAnim**:

```
type
  TCellAnim = record
    Source:     TBitmap;
    CellCount:  integer;
    CellWidth:  integer;
    CellHeight: integer;
    Initialized: boolean;
    end; {TCellAnim}
```

Five fields are used to describe the cell animation. **Source** is a **TBitmap** that actually contains all of the cells of the animation arranged in order from bottom to top. We need to know how many cells are in the bitmap, which is stored in **CellCount**. **CellWidth** and **CellHeight** are calculated fields that are based on the actual *height* and *width* of the bitmap and on the **CellCount** property. **Initialized** is a boolean field that tells us whether or not the **TBitmap** was created so that we can free the memory appropriately.

The **OnCreate** handler for the form appears in listing 13.2. In this procedure, we load the bitmap and display it on the form as a visual reference. We also do some initialization and move the components into appropriate positions on the form.

Listing 13.2 The Form's OnCreate handler

```
procedure TMain.FormCreate(Sender: TObject);
var
  fn: string;
  r:  TRect;
  DisplayWidth,
  DisplayHeight: integer;

begin

  {
    Load and display the bitmap containing all of the cells of
    the bitmap we'll be using for the cell animation. We're loading
    it into a record that will make it easy to animate.
  }
  fn := ExtractFilePath(Application.EXEName) + 'cells2.bmp';

  Anim.Source := TBitmap.Create;
  Anim.Initialized := True;
  Anim.Source.LoadFromFile(fn);
  Anim.CellCount := 9;
  Anim.CellWidth := Anim.Source.Width;
  if Anim.Source.Height mod Anim.CellCount = 0 then
    Anim.CellHeight := Anim.Source.Height div Anim.CellCount
  else begin
        ShowMessage('Inconsistent size and cellcount');
        Self.Close;
        end;

  {Display the whole strip of cells}
  r := Rect( 0,0,
            round((ClientHeight / Anim.Source.Height) * Anim.CellWidth),
             ClientHeight);

  with imgSrc do begin
    SetBounds(r.left,r.top,r.right, r.bottom);
    AutoSize := False;
    Stretch := True;
    Picture.Bitmap := Anim.Source;
    end;

  { figure out how much of the screen is left to display the animation }
  DisplayWidth := ClientWidth - imgSrc.Width;
  DisplayHeight := ClientHeight;
  imgDisplay.SetBounds( imgSrc.Width + ((DisplayWidth div 2) -
                        (Anim.CellWidth div 2)),
```

```
                        (ClientHeight div 2) - (Anim.CellHeight div 2),
                        Anim.CellWidth,
                        Anim.CellHeight);

  Timer1.Interval := 50;

end; {FormCreate}
```

The first thing we do in the **OnCreate** handler is setup the **Anim** record. We set the variable **fn** so that we're looking in the same directory as the executable for a file called *cells2.bmp*. Next we initialize the **Source** property of **Anim**. Because **Source** is an *object type* we use the **Create** method of the object class to initialize it. Pay close attention to the assignment below:

```
Anim.Source := TBitmap.Create;
```

A common mistake is to do the following:

```
Anim.Create;
```

Which will generate a rather unattractive error at run-time.

Now that the **Source** property is initialized, we can use the **LoadFromFile** method to retrieve the bitmap from the *cells2.bmp* file.

The **CellCount** property must be set manually so the program can figure out the vertical dimension of each cell. Notice that we also check to make sure that the bitmap is consistent with a strip of cells. The total height of the bitmap must be evenly divisible by the number of cells that we've declared. Otherwise, we couldn't guarantee the results. If this condition is not met, there is no point in proceeding; after a brief message, the program terminates.

The next several blocks of code move components around and resize them to be proportional. Since we're doing this at run-time, the program will respond to different sized strips of cells appropriately without having to manually move the components around.

Lastly, we set the **Interval** of the timer to 50 milliseconds. You may want to adjust this after you've run the program to increase or decrease the speed of the animation.

Since we created a **TBitmap** at run time, we also need to make sure we free the associated memory when we're finished. To do this, we call the **Free** method in the **OnDestroy** handler of the form.

The **Button1Click** event, shown in Listing 13.3, will reverse the state of the timer. If it is *enabled*, then clicking the button will *disable* it and vice versa. To be friendly, we also set the caption appropriately to "Stop" or "Start".

Listing 13.3 The Button1Click handler

```
procedure TMain.Button1Click(Sender: TObject);
begin

  Timer1.Enabled := Not Timer1.Enabled;
  if Timer1.Enabled then
    Button1.Caption := 'Stop'
  else
    Button1.Caption := 'Start';
end;

end.
```

Enabling the timer causes the **OnTimer** event to fire at whatever *interval* we have set. In our example, the **OnTimer** event will fire every 50 milliseconds. This is, of course, ignoring the inaccuracy of the timer component. Take a look at the **OnTimer** event in Listing 13.4.

Listing 13.4 The OnTimer event

```
procedure TMain.Timer1Timer(Sender: TObject);
const
  CellIndex: integer = 0;

begin

    ShowCell(CellIndex);
    dec(CellIndex);
    if CellIndex < 0 then
      CellIndex := Anim.CellCount - 1;

end;
```

In the **Timer1Timer** event, we display the current cell of the animation and then change **CellIndex** to the next cell in the strip. **CellIndex** is declared as a *typed constant*, so that the value is retained when we leave and re-enter the procedure. We are decrementing the cells rather than incrementing them, because in our strip of cells the first cell is at the bottom and the last cell is at the top. A **TBitmap** begins with zero at the upper left-hand corner of the bitmap. Because of this, it will make things simpler in the **ShowCell** procedure to start with a high **CellIndex** and work down. If we're below the lower bound of zero after *de*crementing the **CellIndex**, then we reset back to the first cell.

The procedure **ShowCell**, found in Listing 13.5, is called each time the timer is fired. Let's see how it works!

Listing 13.5 The ShowCell procedure

```
procedure ShowCell(CellIndex: byte);
var
  SourceRect,
  DestRect:    TRect;

begin
  { Reading the cells bitmap from bottom to top }
  SourceRect := Rect( 0, Anim.CellHeight * CellIndex,
            Anim.CellWidth,
            (Anim.CellHeight * CellIndex) + Anim.CellHeight);
  DestRect := Rect(0,0,Main.imgDisplay.Width, Main.imgDisplay.Height);

  with Main.imgDisplay.Canvas do
    CopyRect(DestRect, Anim.Source.Canvas, SourceRect);

end; {ShowCell}
```

This is probably the simplest procedure in the program, but without it, nothing would happen. Each time **ShowCell** is called, **SourceRect** is defined as the rectangle that covers the cell to be displayed in the source bitmap. Notice that the assignment depends upon the value of **CellIndex** which is passed by the timer event. **DestRect** is the same each time the procedure is called. It is the rectangle that defines the display area. To actually display the cell, we use the **CopyRect** method of the display's canvas. This just copies the image defined by **SourceRect** over the entire area of the display canvas.

That's it! Run the program. Figure 13.1 shows the cell animation in action.

Don't let the application here narrow your impression of how you can use cell animation. This technique can be used to make interface buttons come alive when they are pressed or when the mouse passes over them. It can also be used to show step-by-step how to assemble a product. Use your imagination.

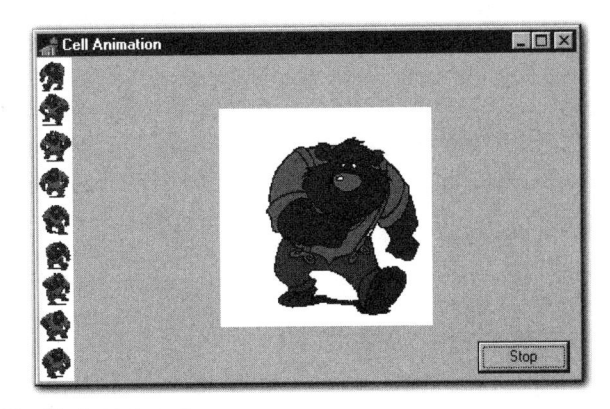

Figure 13.1 *The flip book in action.*

Adventures with Sprite Animation

The most interactive form of animation allows the user to move objects around on the screen. In video games, you often find that you can move objects in different directions at varying speeds, and that other objects (sometimes quite a few of them) whiz around the screen at the same time. If the authors of these games had to create completely rendered frames for every possible combination of background and moving objects, they would find themselves buried in artwork. Every flick of the joystick would need to send the blting engine off on another path, spitting out screen-sized images quickly enough to simulate motion.

Film animators solved a similar problem, decades before the invention of video games—actually, decades before the invention of video. They call their solution cel animation, which comes from the term celluloid animation. A feature-length animated movie requires thousands of drawings. Each second of screen time requires twelve images (in most animation, each frame is photographed twice to produce the standard film speed of 24 frames per second). That's 720 frames per minute. Animated feature films tend to run about 100 minutes, for a total of 72,000 drawings. But most of the stuff in each frame doesn't move, or when it does, it just scrolls (pans in film language) right or left, up or down. So why redraw the background over and over again, hundreds of times for each scene? Instead, the background is drawn once. The characters are then painted on to clear acetate sheets (before the invention of plastics, they were painted on celluloid), which the camera operator lays over the background to compose each frame. This labor-saving method revolutionized animation, and later made it practical to produce television shows like "The Simpsons," because once the cels of a TV cartoon are painted, they can be reused for other scenes and future episodes.

In computer animation, cels become sprites, bitmapped graphical objects that move around on the screen independently of the background—and each other. Just as cels make it practical to produce animated film, sprites make it practical to do real-time computer animation; which means that instead of just playing back pre-recorded animated clips, we can make animated graphics that respond to user activity or move based on algorithms rather than being pre-recorded.

The Magic of Animation

Sprites Over Easy

In this brief project, we'll use the simplest method to move a bitmap around on the screen—with no API function calls:

1. Start a new project.
2. Add two TImage components and a Timer.
3. Set the properties and events as shown in Table 13.2.
4. Insert the code.

This project is located in the directory \DELPHIMM\CH13\SPRITE1.

Creating the Sprite1 Project

First start a new project and add the components. We'll deal with the placement of the controls at run-time. Set the component properties as shown in Table 13.2.

You will find two bitmaps in the project directory. Use the object inspector to load **moth1.bmp** into the **Picture** property of **imgMoth**. Next load **hibisc2.bmp** into the **Picture** property of **imgBackground**. We'll take care of arranging the components on the form in the **OnCreate** event. The form at design time should look similar to Figure 13.2. The **OnTimer** event will take care of moving the moth around the screen with the assistance of a helper procedure called **MoveSprite**. You'll find all of the code in Listing 13.6.

Table 13.2 Form and component properties.

Component	Property/Event	Setting
Default Form	Name	Main
	Caption	Sprite Experiment #1
	OnCreate	FormCreate
TImage1	Name	imgMoth
	AutoSize	True
	Picture	(TBitmap)
	Visible	False
TImage2	Name	imgBackground
	AutoSize	True
	Picture	(TBitmap)
TTimer	OnTimer	Timer1Timer

Figure 13.2 *The Sprite1 form at design time.*

Listing 13.6 usprite1.pas

```
unit usprite1;

interface

uses
  Windows, Messages, SysUtils, Classes, Graphics, Controls, Forms, Dialogs,
  ExtCtrls;

type
  TMain = class(TForm)
    imgBackground: TImage;
    Timer1: TTimer;
    imgMoth: TImage;
    procedure MoveSprite;
    procedure FormCreate(Sender: TObject);
    procedure Timer1Timer(Sender: TObject);
  private
    { Private declarations }
  public
    { Public declarations }
  end;

var
  Main: TMain;

implementation

{$R *.DFM}

procedure TMain.MoveSprite;
const
```

```
    SpritePos: TPoint = (X:0; Y:0);
    Offset:    TPoint = (X:2; Y:2);

begin

  {Deal with horizontal movement}
  if ((SpritePos.x + imgMoth.Width + Offset.x) > ClientWidth) or
     ((SpritePos.x + Offset.x) < 0) then
       Offset.x := -Offset.x
  else inc(SpritePos.x, Offset.x);

  {Deal with vertical movement}
  if ((SpritePos.y + imgMoth.Height + Offset.y) > ClientHeight) or
     ((SpritePos.y + Offset.y) < 0) then
       Offset.y := -Offset.y
  else inc(SpritePos.y, Offset.y);

  imgMoth.SetBounds(SpritePos.x, SpritePos.y, imgMoth.Width, imgMoth.Height);
  if not imgMoth.Visible then imgMoth.Visible := True;

end;

procedure TMain.FormCreate(Sender: TObject);
begin

  Timer1.Interval := 50;
  Timer1.Enabled := True;
  ClientWidth := imgBackground.Width;
  ClientHeight:= imgBackground.Height;
  imgMoth.SetBounds(0,0,imgMoth.Width, imgMoth.Height);

end;

procedure TMain.Timer1Timer(Sender: TObject);
begin
  MoveSprite;
end;

end.
```

Notice that the procedure **MoveSprite** is declared within the form's class. This is done so that, when referring to the form's components, we do not have to explicitly reference **Main**. If we did not set up a forward declaration as part of the **TMain** class, then in **MoveSprite**, we would have to reference **imgSprite** as **Main.imgSprite**. It works either way.

This program simply moves the **TImage** control around the background and bounces it off of the boundaries of the form. As you can see in Listing 13.6, the **OnCreate** handler enables the timer and positions and sizes the components. The timer event is fired every 50ms, and each time it calls the **MoveSprite** procedure. Take a look at the **MoveSprite** procedure in Listing 13.7.

Listing 13.7   The MoveSprite procedure

```
procedure TMain.MoveSprite;
const
  SpritePos: TPoint = (X:0; Y:0);
  Offset:    TPoint = (X:2; Y:2);

begin

  {Deal with horizontal movement}
  if ((SpritePos.x + imgMoth.Width + Offset.x) > ClientWidth) or
     ((SpritePos.x + Offset.x) < 0) then
       Offset.x := -Offset.x
  else inc(SpritePos.x, Offset.x);

  {Deal with vertical movement}
  if ((SpritePos.y + imgMoth.Height + Offset.y) > ClientHeight) or
     ((SpritePos.y + Offset.y) < 0) then
       Offset.y := -Offset.y
  else inc(SpritePos.y, Offset.y);

  imgMoth.SetBounds(SpritePos.x, SpritePos.y, imgMoth.Width, imgMoth.Height);
  if not imgMoth.Visible then imgMoth.Visible := True;

end;
```

Notice that the **SpritePos** and **Offset** variables are declared as *typed constants*. This style of declaration affords two advantages. We can initialize the value, and *typed constants* retain their value when the procedure is finished, like a variable declared *static* in Visual Basic.

Four things happen in this procedure. First we choose the new horizontal position, which is calculated as an offset of the previous position. We also check to make sure that the new position remains within the boundaries of the form's client area. Next the new vertical position is chosen. This is done the same way as the horizontal position. Once both components of the new position are known, we use the **SetBounds** method of the **TImage** component to change the position. Using **SetBounds** lets us move the control in one step instead of setting the **Top** and **Left** properties. The last thing we do in this procedure is to make sure the component is visible. At design time we set the component to be invisible so that it wouldn't appear to jump when the program begins.

That's it! Run the program. As you can see from Figure 13.3, very little difference exists between the running program and the program at designtime. The timer is not visible and the moth box is moving.

This is just scratching the surface of sprite animation. I'm not even sure that it deserves to be called sprite animation. If this were done correctly,

Figure 13.3 *The Sprite1 program in action?*

which we'll do shortly, the moth would appear to be flying around over a background of flowers. When you run this program, it looks like a bitmap being moved around on top of another bitmap. We'll fix some of the shortcomings as we expand our sprite techniques, but first let's define the shortcomings as they appear now:

- The part of the image that moves is rectangular but the moth is not.
- The image moves in a slow jerky motion.
- The image flickers as it moves.
- Moths should move their wings when they are flying.
- The motion is mechanical

We'll address several of these shortcomings in the next project, and the rest in the next chapter.

Animating Sprites with Block Transfer Routines

Moving components around the screen may work for some applications. Most of the time, however, we need to use more powerful techniques in order to reach a higher level of realism.

A faster way to perform sprite animation is to use *bl*ock *t*ransfer (blt) routines to get our sprites to the display. In this project, you'll discover a method to paint the moth on the background without that rectangular border. We'll combine the techniques we learned about cell animation in the first project of this chapter to make the wings appear to flap as the moth moves. By using a blt to get the moth on the display, we'll also reduce the amount of flicker as it moves.

Blt Animation

In this project we'll produce something that is more worthy of the term "sprite animation". The moth will move faster, smoother, and will appear more realistic than the previous version. Here's what to do:

1. Start a new project.
2. Add a TPanel, TTimer, and four TImage components.
3. Set the properties and events as shown in Table 13.3.
4. Insert the code.

This project is located in the directory \DELPHIMM\CH13\SPRITE2.

Creating the Sprite2 Project

First start a new project and add the **TPanel**, **TTimer**, and three **TImage** components. Next add another **TImage** component on top of the **TPanel**. Don't be concerned with the placement or size of the components; we'll deal with that at run-time. Set the component properties as shown in Table 13.3.

The **TImage** component that sits on top of the **TPanel** is **imgDisplay**. Use the file **hibisc2.bmp**, found in the project directory, for the **Picture** property of **imgDisplay**. We will use the **OnCreate** handler to position and size all of the components. Also in **OnCreate,** we will load the sprite and mask bitmaps and initialize the data that we need to define the sprite. As usual, the **OnDestroy** will free memory. The component **imgDisplay** is where all of the action is going to take place. At design-time it contains the background image, and at run-time we'll show the moth flying around on top of it as seen in Figure 13.4. We will use the **imgSprite** and **imgMask** components to display the sprite bitmaps. These components are only for visual reference, they are not used to create or assist in the animation. The last **TImage** component, **imgBuffer**, is used to store a portion of the background before we stomp on it with the moth image. More importantly, it will be used to replace that background so we can move the moth without destroying the background in the process. You might have guessed that the timer will execute the movement of the moth.

Next we'll look at the code in one manageable chunk at a time. In Listing 13.8, you'll find the entire code unit for reference.

Table 13.3 *Form and component properties.*

Component	Property/Event	Setting
Default Form	Name	Main
	Caption	Sprite Animation #2
	OnCreate	FormCreate
	OnDestroy	FormDestroy
TPanel1	Align	alTop
	BevelInner	bvLowered
	BorderStyle	bsNone
TImage1	Name	imgDisplay
	Align	alClient
	AutoSize	True
	Picture	(TBitmap)
TImage2	Name	imgSprite
	Stretch	True
TImage3	Name	imgMask
	Stretch	True
TImage4	Name	imgBuffer
TTimer	OnTimer	Timer1Timer

Figure 13.4 *The Sprite2 program at run time.*

Listing 13.8   usprite2.pas

```pascal
implementation

{$R *.DFM}
const
  SHOW_BUFFERS = true;

type
  TSprite = record
    Source:     TBitmap;
    Mask:       TBitmap;
    CellCount:  integer;
    CellWidth:  integer;
    CellHeight: integer;
    Offset:     TPoint;
    PrvPos,
    CurPos:     TPoint;
    CurCell:    integer;
    Initialized: boolean;
    end; {TSprite}

var
  Moth:     TSprite;

procedure MoveMoth;

begin

  {Deal with horizontal movement}
  with Moth do begin
    PrvPos := CurPos;
    if ((CurPos.x + CellWidth + Offset.x) > Main.imgDisplay.Width) or
       ((CurPos.x + Offset.x) < 0) then
         Offset.x := -Offset.x
    else inc(CurPos.x, Offset.x);

    {Deal with vertical movement}
    if ((CurPos.y + CellHeight + Offset.y) > Main.imgDisplay.Height) or
       ((CurPos.y + Offset.y) < 0) then
         Offset.y := -Offset.y
    else inc(CurPos.y, Offset.y);

    {set the next cell to be displayed}
    dec(CurCell);
    if CurCell < 1 then
      CurCell := CellCount;

    end; {with Moth}

end; {MoveMoth}

procedure DrawMoth;
var
```

```
    SrcRect,
    DstRect: TRect;

begin

  { STEP #1 }
  { First we copy the area of the buffer where the moth was last to the screen }
  with Moth do begin
     SrcRect := Rect( 0,0,CellWidth, CellHeight);
     DstRect := Rect( PrvPos.x, PrvPos.y,
                      PrvPos.x + CellWidth,
                      PrvPos.y + CellHeight);
     end; {with Moth}

  with Main.imgDisplay.Picture.Bitmap.Canvas do begin
    CopyMode := cmSrcCopy;
    CopyRect(DstRect, Main.imgBuffer.Picture.Bitmap.Canvas, SrcRect);
    end;

  { STEP #2 }
  { Next we copy the area from the background where the moth will be so that
    next time around we'll have a clean background for step #1}
  with Moth do begin
     SrcRect := Rect( CurPos.x, CurPos.y,
                      CurPos.x + CellWidth,
                      CurPos.y + CellHeight);
     DstRect := Rect( 0,0,CellWidth, CellHeight);
     end; {with Moth}

  with Main.imgBuffer.Picture.Bitmap.Canvas do
    CopyRect(DstRect, Main.imgDisplay.Picture.Bitmap.Canvas, SrcRect);

  { STEP #3 }
  { In this step we copy the sprite mask to the display dc using SRCAND }
  with Moth do begin
     SrcRect := Rect(
                0,(CellCount * CellHeight) - (CurCell * CellHeight),
                CellWidth-1,
                (CellCount * CellHeight) - (CurCell * CellHeight) +
                CellHeight-1
                );

     DstRect := Rect( CurPos.x, CurPos.y,
                      CurPos.x + CellWidth-1,
                      CurPos.y + CellHeight-1);
     end; {with Moth}

  if Moth.Offset.x < 0 then begin
    inc(DstRect.Left, Moth.CellWidth-1);
    DstRect.Right := DstRect.Left - Moth.CellWidth;
    end;

  with Main.imgDisplay.Picture.Bitmap.Canvas do begin
    CopyMode := cmSrcAnd;
```

```
        CopyRect(DstRect, Moth.Mask.Canvas, SrcRect);
        end;

      { STEP #4 }
      { In this step we copy the sprite to the display dc using SRCPAINT }
      with Main.imgDisplay.Picture.Bitmap.Canvas do begin
        CopyMode := cmSrcPaint;
        CopyRect(DstRect, Moth.Source.Canvas, SrcRect);
        end;

end; {DrawMoth}

procedure TMain.FormCreate(Sender: TObject);
var
  fn:       string;
  SrcRect,
  DstRect: TRect;

begin

  {setup the form}
  Panel1.Align := alClient;
  ClientWidth := imgDisplay.Picture.Bitmap.Width;
  ClientHeight := imgDisplay.Picture.Bitmap.Height;
  Panel1.Align := alNone;

  {initialize the moth sprite}
  with Moth do begin
    Source := TBitmap.Create;
    Mask := TBitmap.Create;
    Initialized := True;
    fn := ExtractFilePath(Application.EXEName) + 'mothspr.bmp';
    Source.LoadFromFile(fn);
    fn := ExtractFilePath(Application.EXEName) + 'mothmsk.bmp';
    Mask.LoadFromFile(fn);
    CellCount := 4;
    CellWidth := Moth.Source.Width;
    CellHeight:= Moth.Source.Height div Moth.CellCount;
    CurPos.x := 285;
    CurPos.y := 85;
    Offset.x := 2;
    Offset.y := 2;
    end;

  {initialize the buffer image}
  with imgBuffer.Picture do begin
    Bitmap := TBitmap.Create;
    Bitmap.width := Moth.CellWidth;
    Bitmap.height := Moth.CellHeight;
    end;

  {finish setting up the form}
  if SHOW_BUFFERS then begin
```

```
   {put the appropriate pictures in the Sprite and Mask components}
   ClientHeight := round(ClientHeight + Moth.CellHeight * 1.5);
   imgSprite.Picture.Assign(Moth.Source);
   imgMask.Picture.Assign(Moth.Mask);

   {relocate the Sprite imgage component}
   imgSprite.Top := round(Panel1.Height + Moth.CellHeight * 0.25);
   imgSprite.Left := Panel1.Left;
   imgSprite.Width := Moth.CellWidth div Moth.CellCount;
   imgSprite.Height := Moth.CellHeight;

   {relocate the Mask image component}
   imgMask.Top := imgSprite.Top;
   imgMask.Left := round(imgSprite.Left + (imgSprite.Width * 1.5));
   imgMask.Width := Moth.CellWidth div Moth.CellCount;
   imgMask.Height := Moth.CellHeight;

   {relocate the Buffer picture component}
   imgBuffer.Width := Moth.CellWidth;
   imgBuffer.Height := Moth.CellHeight;
   imgBuffer.Left := Panel1.Width - imgBuffer.Width * 2;
   imgBuffer.Top := imgSprite.Top;

   {Make sure that the composition components are visible}
   imgSprite.Visible := True;
   imgMask.Visible := True;
   imgBuffer.Visible := True;

   end; {if SHOW_BUFFERS}

 {Enable the timer to start the animation}
 Timer1.Interval := 10;
 Timer1.Enabled := True;

 {setup the buffer with the current section of the background}
 with Moth do begin
    SrcRect := Rect( CurPos.x, CurPos.y,
                     CurPos.x + CellWidth,
                     CurPos.y + CellHeight);
    DstRect := Rect( 0, 0, CellWidth, CellHeight);
    end; {with Moth}

  with Main.imgBuffer.Picture.Bitmap.Canvas do
    CopyRect(DstRect, Main.imgDisplay.Picture.Bitmap.Canvas, SrcRect);

end;

procedure TMain.FormDestroy(Sender: TObject);
begin
  if Moth.Initialized then begin
    Moth.Source.Free;
    Moth.Mask.Free;
    end; {if Moth.Initialized}

end;
```

```
procedure TMain.Timer1Timer(Sender: TObject);
begin

  MoveMoth;
  DrawMoth;

end;

end.
```

Transparent Bitmaps—Sprites and Masks

Before we dive into the code, we should explore for a moment the concept of sprites and masks. In the previous project, the **TImage** component that contained the sprite bitmap cut a rectangular swatch out of the background. It's pretty hard to create the illusion that the sprite belongs to the background when it always appears against its own white matte. But there is a way to trim it neatly around the edges and display just the moth itself. To do that, we need a couple of raster operations and two modified versions of the sprite bitmap.

In effect, we want the sprite bitmap to work like an animation cel. The moth should overlay the background, while the "blank" area that surrounds it should become transparent, allowing the background to show through. This is easier than you might think.

The first thing we need to do is decide which color in the original sprite bitmap will become transparent. The moth bitmaps are drawn on a red background, so let's assume that red pixels are transparent. We can't just blt the sprite to the background in a single operation, because any raster operation we use will either blend the images in some way, ignore the sprite bitmap entirely, or transfer the entire rectangle. The problem is that we need the sprite's own background and foreground to behave differently when we combine them with the background image; the background of the sprite must not appear at all, while the sprite's foreground shape must opaquely cover the background image. Clearly, we need to prepare the sprite and the background image in a way that they can be combined without disrupting each other.

Bear with me while I work backward. Imagine that the red pixels of the sprite bitmap have been changed to black, and that an area in the shape of the moth has been colored black in the background image. If we could get this far, we could use an **or** raster operation (**SRCPAINT**) to align and combine the images; wherever we combined the black pixels in the sprite with the colored pixels in the background, the background pixels would determine the colors of the combined bitmaps; further, wherever we combined the black pixels of the background with the colored pixels in the sprite, the sprite's pixels would determine the colors. (Remember, when you **or** any value with $00, you get the original value.)

That's fine. However, if we can't blt the moth shape onto the background in the first place, how are we supposed to punch a moth-shaped hole? The answer to that question begins with yet another variation of the original sprite. Use your imagination again to visualize what happens when you use an **and** raster operation (**SRCAND**) to blt a monochrome (black and white) bitmap onto a colored background. This time, the pixels in the bitmap that are black will force the colored pixels in the background to turn black, and the pixels that are white will leave the background pixels set to their original colors. So, if we begin with a monochrome version of the sprite in which the moth is colored completely black, and the surrounding pixels are colored white (their original color), then the **SRCAND** raster operation will paint a black silhouette of the moth onto the background. This monochrome version of the sprite bitmap is called a *mask*.

That's all there is to it. We've created the two bitmaps for you because it's tedious work and this is not a graphic design book. In the next project, we'll show you how to create the sprite and mask bitmaps programmatically.

Developing the Sprite2 program

To simplify working with the moth sprite and to clarify the code, we will develop a sprite *type*. That is defined as follows:

```
type
  TSprite = record
    Source:     TBitmap;
    Mask:       TBitmap;
    CellCount:  integer;
    CellWidth:  integer;
    CellHeight: integer;
    Offset:     TPoint;
    PrvPos,
    CurPos:     TPoint;
    CurCell:    integer;
    Initialized: boolean;
  end; {TSprite}
```

The **Source** and **Mask** properties contain the actual sprite and mask bitmaps. Keep in mind that these bitmaps represent all four cells of the sprite and the corresponding cells of the mask. The cells are arranged from bottom to top just like the **CellAnim** project at the beginning of this chapter. You may remember from that project that we used the fields **CellCount**, **CellWidth**, and **CellHeight**. We set the number of cells in the field **CellCount,** and then the program figures out how high and how wide each cell will be. The **Offset** is the number of pixels which the moth will move horizontally and vertically (x and y). **PrvPos** and **CurPos** store the previous and current position of the moth relative to the background. These will be used together with the **Offset** to calculate the movement of the moth. **CurCell** stores the current cell that is being displayed so that we can cycle through each of the four cells and make the moth's wings appear to flap. The last field, **Initialized**, tells us whether the memory allocated to the bitmaps should be freed when the program terminates.

The **OnCreate** handler does things like sizing and arranging components on the form. It also initializes information about the moth sprite like the number of cells and such. The bitmaps for the sprite and the mask are loaded here as well.

We perform two more important tasks in the **OnCreate** handler. We initialize the buffer component (**imgBuffer**) with the contents of the background where the moth is going to be drawn first. We also set the timer interval and enable it.

Each time the timer event is fired, **MoveMoth** and **DrawMoth** are called. These procedures represent the heart of this project. **MoveMoth** should be familiar from the previous project, but a couple of differences are worth noting. Listing 13.9 shows the procedure.

Listing 13.9 MoveMoth

```
procedure MoveMoth;

begin

  {Deal with horizontal movement}
  with Moth do begin
    PrvPos := CurPos;
    if ((CurPos.x + CellWidth + Offset.x) > Main.imgDisplay.Width) or
       ((CurPos.x + Offset.x) < 0) then
         Offset.x := -Offset.x
    else inc(CurPos.x, Offset.x);

    {Deal with vertical movement}
    if ((CurPos.y + CellHeight + Offset.y) > Main.imgDisplay.Height) or
       ((CurPos.y + Offset.y) < 0) then
         Offset.y := -Offset.y
    else inc(CurPos.y, Offset.y);

    {set the next cell to be displayed}
    dec(CurCell);
    if CurCell < 1 then
      CurCell := CellCount;

  end; {with Moth}

end; {MoveMoth}
```

The two main differences between this **MoveMoth** procedure and the **MoveSprite** procedure from the previous project are: **MoveMoth** uses the **PrvPos** and **CurPos** fields of the **Moth** variable to determine position, and **MoveMoth** sets the current cell to be displayed.

The **DrawMoth** procedure is the one that actually makes things happen on the screen. It is here that we apply the concept of transparency using masks and an off-screen buffer. **DrawMoth** is in Listing 13.10.

Listing 13.10 DrawMoth

```
procedure DrawMoth;
var
  SrcRect,
  DstRect: TRect;

begin

  { STEP #1 }
  { First we copy the area of the buffer where the moth was last to the screen }
  with Moth do begin
    SrcRect := Rect( 0,0,CellWidth, CellHeight);
    DstRect := Rect( PrvPos.x, PrvPos.y,
                     PrvPos.x + CellWidth,
                     PrvPos.y + CellHeight);
  end; {with Moth}

  with Main.imgDisplay.Picture.Bitmap.Canvas do begin
    CopyMode := cmSrcCopy;
    CopyRect(DstRect, Main.imgBuffer.Picture.Bitmap.Canvas, SrcRect);
  end;

  { STEP #2 }
  { Next we copy the area from the background where the moth will be so that
    next time around we'll have a clean background for step #1}
  with Moth do begin
    SrcRect := Rect( CurPos.x, CurPos.y,
                     CurPos.x + CellWidth,
                     CurPos.y + CellHeight);
    DstRect := Rect( 0,0,CellWidth, CellHeight);
  end; {with Moth}

  with Main.imgBuffer.Picture.Bitmap.Canvas do
    CopyRect(DstRect, Main.imgDisplay.Picture.Bitmap.Canvas, SrcRect);

  { STEP #3 }
  { In this step we copy the sprite mask to the display dc using SRCAND }
  with Moth do begin
    SrcRect := Rect(
               0,(CellCount * CellHeight) - (CurCell * CellHeight),
               CellWidth-1,
               (CellCount * CellHeight) - (CurCell * CellHeight) +
```

```
                    CellHeight-1
                    );

    DstRect := Rect( CurPos.x, CurPos.y,
                     CurPos.x + CellWidth-1,
                     CurPos.y + CellHeight-1);
  end; {with Moth}

  if Moth.Offset.x < 0 then begin
    inc(DstRect.Left, Moth.CellWidth-1);
    DstRect.Right := DstRect.Left - Moth.CellWidth;
  end;

  with Main.imgDisplay.Picture.Bitmap.Canvas do begin
    CopyMode := cmSrcAnd;
    CopyRect(DstRect, Moth.Mask.Canvas, SrcRect);
  end;

  { STEP #4 }
  { In this step we copy the sprite to the display dc using SRCPAINT }
  with Main.imgDisplay.Picture.Bitmap.Canvas do begin
    CopyMode := cmSrcPaint;
    CopyRect(DstRect, Moth.Source.Canvas, SrcRect);
  end;

end; {DrawMoth}
```

Notice from the code that four steps are being performed:

1. From the off screen buffer we copy the background back to the display to erase the moth.
2. From the background we copy the area of the new moth position to the off screen buffer so step #1 works next time.
3. Then we make a black silhouette of the moth by blting the mask to the display with the SRCAND raster operation.
4. Finally, we combine the silhouette of the moth with the actual sprite colors by blting the sprite to the display with the SRCPAINT ROP.

In the first two steps, we setup our source and destination rectangles so that they define the correct area of the display and either the *sprite*, *mask*, or *buffer*. Steps 1 and 2 use the **TCanvas** method, **CopyRect**, to copy the source rectangle from the source canvas to the destination rectangle of the destination canvas. Although the code is lengthy, it is straightforward. Most of it is just setting up the correct source and destination rectangles.

Step 3 defines the source and destination rectangle for steps 3 and 4. In these steps, we are copying the sprite and the mask to the display. In step 3, we're copying the mask with the **CopyRect** method. To make sure that the moth is displayed appropriately for the direction of travel, we need a condition. Take a look at the code below:

```
if Moth.Offset.x < 0 then begin
   inc(DstRect.Left, Moth.CellWidth-1);
   DstRect.Right := DstRect.Left - Moth.CellWidth;
   end;
```

If **Offset.x** is less than zero, then the moth must be moving left. In this case, we need to display the moth and mask horizontally flipped. This will make it appear to have changed direction. Since the procedure will now draw from right to left, we must offset the Left side of **DstRect** to the right by the width of the cell and then offset the Right side of **DstRect** to the left by the width of the cell.

That's really all there is to it. When you run the program, you will notice a huge improvement over the last project. We've eliminated all but one of the previous complaints. The motion is still mechanical. We'll work on that in the next chapter. We'll also look at methods for decreasing the amount of flicker even further as the moth moves around the screen.

Because of the technique that we are using, this project should actually have more flicker than it does. Let's re-examine the steps we are taking to draw the sprite:

1. Clear the background from the save buffer.
2. Save the background for next time.
3. Blt the mask.
4. Blt the Sprite.

Notice that in step #1, no moth appears on the screen at all. It is this step that introduces flicker. Due to the behavior of the **TImage** component, we do not notice the flicker because of a lag in repainting. We're drawing directly on the underlying bitmap of the **TImage**, so the first step is never really visible. This is not a global solution to the problem of flicker, so in the next chapter we'll introduce a technique that will always produce flickerless sprite animation.

Making Masks and Sprites Automatically

Let's take a short break from sprite animation so we can look into the creation of sprites and masks. We'll create a small utility program that takes a bitmap with a solid background color and creates a sprite and mask bitmap from it. You'll be able to use this utility to create sprites for other projects, and we're going to use some of the code we develop in the next chapter.

The Sprite and Mask Maker

This project takes a solid color bitmap and creates a sprite and a mask from it. Here are the steps to follow:

1. Start a new project.
2. Add a TOpenDialog, TSaveDialog, TMainMenu, and three TImage components.
3. Set the properties and events as shown in Table 13.4.
4. Insert the code.

This project is located in the directory \DELPHIMM\CH13\MAKEMASK.

Creating the MakeMask Project

First start a new project and add the **TOpenDialog**, **TSaveDialog**, **TMainMenu**, and three **TImage** components. Don't be concerned with the placement or size of the components; we'll deal with that at run-time. Set the component properties as shown in Table 13.4.

In the **OnDestroy** event, we'll do some memory cleanup. We'll use the save dialog to save the new bitmap files for the sprite and the mask. The open dialog is used to open the original bitmap which is displayed in **imgOrg**. The other two **TImage** components, **imgSpr** and **imgMsk**, display the completed

Table 13.4   Form and component properties.

Component	Property/Event	Setting
Default Form	Name	Main
	Caption	Sprite and Mask Maker
	OnDestroy	FormDestroy
TSaveDialog	DefaultExt	bmp
	Filter	Bitmap Files|*.bmp
TOpenDialog	DefaultExt	bmp
	Filter	Bitmap Files|*.bmp
TImage1	Name	imgOrg
	AutoSize	True
TImage2	Name	imgSpr
TImage3	Name	imgMsk

The Magic of Animation 621

Figure 13.5 *The MakeMask program.*

sprite and mask images. Figure 13.5 displays the completed form after processing the original moth bitmap. The **TMainMenu** component is the one that controls the program execution. Use the menu designer (double-click on the **TMainMenu** on the form) to add a **File** menu which contains **Open**, **Save**, and **Exit** options. They should be named **mnuFile**, **mnuFOpen**, **mnuFSave**, and **mnuFExit** respectively. Once the menu has been created, exit the menu designer. To add event procedures for the menu options, select the option from the menu at design time. In addition to the event procedures, we'll use a couple of helper procedures called **ConvertImageToSprite** and **ConvertImageToMask**.

Let's take a look at how the program works. Listing 13.11 contains the entire form unit.

Listing 13.11 umakemsk.pas

```
implementation

{$R *.DFM}

var
  MemBmp: TBitmap;

procedure ConvertImageToSprite(bmp: TBitmap);
var
  OrgBackColor: TColor;
  w,h:          longint;

begin
```

```
    OrgBackColor := bmp.Canvas.Pixels[0,0];
    for h := 0 to bmp.Height do
      for w := 0 to bmp.Width do
        if bmp.Canvas.Pixels[w,h] = OrgBackColor then
          bmp.Canvas.Pixels[w,h] := $00000000;

end; {ConvertImageToSprite}

procedure ConvertImageToMask(bmp: TBitmap);
var
  BackColor: TColor;
  w,h:       longint;

begin

  BackColor := bmp.Canvas.Pixels[0,0];
  for h := 0 to bmp.Height do
    for w := 0 to bmp.Width do
      if bmp.Canvas.Pixels[w,h] = BackColor then
        bmp.Canvas.Pixels[w,h] := $00FFFFFF
      else
        bmp.Canvas.Pixels[w,h] := $00000000;

end; {ConvertImageToMask}

procedure TMain.mnuFLoadClick(Sender: TObject);
begin
  if OpenDialog1.Execute then begin

    Cursor := crHourglass;
    {Create a memory bitmap from the selected file and display it}
    MemBmp := TBitmap.Create;
    MemBmp.LoadFromFile(OpenDialog1.FileName);
    imgOrg.Picture.Bitmap.Assign(MemBmp);
    imgOrg.SetBounds(0,0,imgOrg.Width, imgOrg.Height);
    imgOrg.Visible := True;

    {Move the compoenents into position on the form}
    imgSpr.SetBounds(imgOrg.Width, 0, imgOrg.Width , imgOrg.Height);
    imgMsk.SetBounds(imgOrg.Width * 2, 0, imgOrg.Width , imgOrg.Height);

    {convert the original image to a sprite image and display it}
    imgSpr.Picture.Bitmap.Assign(MemBmp);
    ConvertImageToSprite(imgSpr.Picture.Bitmap);
    imgSpr.Visible := True;

    {convert the original image to a sprite image and display it}
    imgMsk.Picture.Bitmap.Assign(MemBmp);
    ConvertImageToMask(imgMsk.Picture.Bitmap);
    imgMsk.Visible := True;
    Cursor := crDefault;

    end;
end;
```

```
procedure TMain.mnuFSaveClick(Sender: TObject);
begin
  SaveDialog1.Title := 'Enter the name for the new sprite file';
  if SaveDialog1.Execute then
    imgSpr.Picture.Bitmap.SaveToFile(SaveDialog1.FileName);

  SaveDialog1.Title := 'Enter the name for the new MASK file';
  if SaveDialog1.Execute then
    imgMsk.Picture.Bitmap.SaveToFile(SaveDialog1.FileName);

end; {mnuFSaveClick}

procedure TMain.mnuFExitClick(Sender: TObject);
begin
  Self.Close;
end;

procedure TMain.FormDestroy(Sender: TObject);
begin

  if MemBmp <> nil then MemBmp.Free;

end;

end.
```

Operationally, the program begins when the **File|Load** option is selected. The Load procedure invokes the **OpenDialog** so the user can select a bitmap file to process. Once a file is selected, that file is loaded into a memory bitmap using the **LoadFromFile** method of the **TBitmap** object. That bitmap is then copied into the bitmap of **imgOrg** for display. Next the form's components are arranged to fit according to the size of the bitmap that has been loaded. Next we create the new sprite bitmap. To do this we copy the memory bitmap, which is the original, into **imgSpr** and call the **ConvertImageToSprite** procedure. We'll go over the details of that procedure shortly. The last part of the Load procedure is to copy the memory bitmap into **imgMsk** and call the **ConvertImageToMask** procedure.

To save the images, we use the **SaveToFile** method of the controls and the **SaveDialog**.

Looking at the **ConvertImageToSprite** function in Listing 13.12, you can see that we are looping through the pixels of the original bitmap searching for whatever color was originally in the upper left-hand corner. This will be considered the transparent color.

Listing 13.12   ConvertImageToSprite

```
procedure ConvertImageToSprite(bmp: TBitmap);
var
```

```
    OrgBackColor: TColor;
    w,h:          longint;

begin

    OrgBackColor := bmp.Canvas.Pixels[0,0];
    for h := 0 to bmp.Height do
      for w := 0 to bmp.Width do
        if bmp.Canvas.Pixels[w,h] = OrgBackColor then
          bmp.Canvas.Pixels[w,h] := $00000000;

end; {ConvertImageToSprite}
```

If we find a pixel that is the color of the original background, we change it to black. In the **ConvertImageToMask** procedure, found in Listing 13.13, we also look at each pixel and compare it to the original background color.

Listing 13.13 ConvertImageToMask

```
procedure ConvertImageToMask(bmp: TBitmap);
var
    BackColor: TColor;
    w,h:       longint;

begin

    BackColor := bmp.Canvas.Pixels[0,0];
    for h := 0 to bmp.Height do
      for w := 0 to bmp.Width do
        if bmp.Canvas.Pixels[w,h] = BackColor then
          bmp.Canvas.Pixels[w,h] := $00FFFFFF
        else
          bmp.Canvas.Pixels[w,h] := $00000000;

end; {ConvertImageToMask}
```

The difference between **ConvertImageToMask** and **ConvertImageToSprite** is that in creating the mask, we want to change the foreground colors and the background color. Our condition becomes: *If* the current pixel *is* the background color, *then* make it white; *otherwise* make it black.

That's the program in a nutshell. Run it and load **moth.bmp** from the project directory. After just a few seconds, you'll have a sprite and mask bitmap that can be saved as new files and used in the sprite2 project—or another program that uses the same techniques.

In the next chapter, we'll develop new and better techniques for sprite animation that take advantage of double-buffering to decrease flicker. We'll also put the conversion techniques that we developed in this project to use.

Chapter 14

In this chapter, we'll develop our sprite animation techniques even further to produce fast, flicker-free, sprite characters.

Better Animation

Chris D. Coppola

The animation techniques we developed in the previous chapter were not as complete as we need them to be. The sequence or step in the draw routine where no sprite is visible represents a fundamental flaw of the technique that we used. The techniques also relied heavily upon the behavior of Delphi's components.

In this chapter, we'll develop a technique to overcome the phantom step when no sprite is visible, and we'll build a sprite library that does not rely on Delphi components. We'll also scrutinize the draw routine to see where improvements can be made to increase speed.

Creating Flicker-Free Animation

In the previous chapter, we discovered that when we reconstructed the background, a brief time occurred where the background existed with no visible moth. This step makes the moth appear to flicker as it moves. If we don't reconstruct the background, we'll get flickerless motion, but the moth will leave trails. So how do we get flickerless animation without trails? We use off-screen buffers..

We'll develop a technique in this chapter that uses two off-screen buffers to eliminate flicker. We'll use one off-screen buffer to store the original background, and another as a temporary construction area. As we apply this technique, the draw routine takes four steps:

1. Copy the *affected area* from the background buffer to the construction buffer.
2. Draw the sprite mask to the construction buffer with the SRCAND operation.
3. Draw the sprite to the construction buffer with the SRCPAINT operation.
4. Copy the *affected area* from the construction buffer to the screen.

Four simple steps! Each time the sprite moves, the area of the screen that is affected can be defined by a rectangle. The *dirty rectangle* is the smallest rectangular area that encompasses the sprite in its previous position as well as the sprite in its new position. This is described visually in Figure 14.1.

We can utilize other techniques to minimize the size of each screen update. One such technique employs a complex region defined by three rectangles. The single rectangle technique that we use is both easy in application, and eliminates most of the pixels that do not require updating.

In the previous chapter we were not concerned with the *dirty rectangle*, because for each move of the sprite, the sprite was erased first. This left us with an area the size of one cell to update for each move. There's nothing to reduce with that technique. It is fast, but it introduces flicker. In the next project, we'll enhance our sprite techniques with *double buffering* and *dirty rectangle* updating.

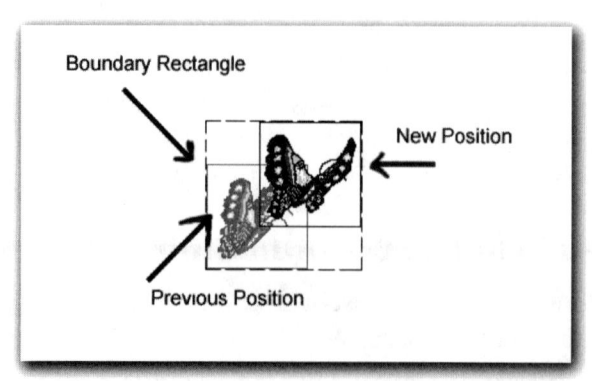

Figure 14.1 *The previous and new positions of the sprite occupy a boundary rectangle.*

Flicker Free Sprite Animation with Delphi Objects

In this project, we make several major revisions to the sprite techniques of Chapter 13. First we'll develop a class from the sprite routines and properties we already developed, making the sprite code more modular and reusable. We'll also modify the draw routine to utilize the new double buffering technique introduced in this chapter.

1. Start a new project.
2. Add a TPanel, TImage, two TCheckBox's and a Button.
3. Set the properties and events as shown in Table 14.1.
4. Insert the code.

This project is located in the directory \DELPHIMM\CH14\SPRITE4.

Creating the Sprite4 Project

Create a new project. Add a **TPanel**, then add a **TImage** on top of the **TPanel**. Add two **TCheckBox**'s and a **TButton**. Arrange the components in a similar configuration to Figure 14.2. The **TPanel** and **TImage** components will be sized at run-time. After the components are added and arranged, set the properties and events as indicated in Table 14.1.

Figure 14.2 *The Sprite4 form at design time.*

Table 14.1 *Form and component properties.*

Component	Property/Event	Setting
Default Form	Name	Main
	Caption	Sprite Animation #4
	OnCreate	FormCreate
	OnDestroy	FormDestroy
TPanel1	Align	alTop
	BevelOuter	bvLowered
TImage1	Name	imgBackground
	Picture	(TBitmap)
	Align	alClient
TCheckBox1	Name	chkFlipH
	Caption	Flip Horizontal
	OnClick	chkFlipHClick
TCheckBox2	Name	chkFlipV
	Caption	Flip Vertical
	OnClick	chkFlipVClick
TButton	Caption	Start
	OnClick	Button1Click

We'll use the button to activate and deactivate the animation. The panel component is there to give a beveled look to the display. The **TImage** will be our drawing surface, and the checkboxes are available so that we can change the sprite properties FlipH and FlipV at run time. Also make sure to load the **hibisc2.bmp** file into the picture property of the **TImage** at design time. There are two units used in this project. Listing 14.1 shows the default form unit that will deal with program control. The other unit, shown in Listing 14.2, contains a sprite class.

Listing 14.1   uSprite4.pas

```
{$DEFINE UseDirtyCalc}
unit uSprite4;

interface

uses
  Windows, Messages, SysUtils, Classes, Graphics, Controls, Forms, Dialogs,
  ExtCtrls, cSprite, MMSystem, StdCtrls;

type
  TMain = class(TForm)
```

```pascal
    Panel1: TPanel;
    imgBackground: TImage;
    chkFlipH: TCheckBox;
    chkFlipV: TCheckBox;
    Button1: TButton;
    procedure FormCreate(Sender: TObject);
    procedure FormDestroy(Sender: TObject);
    procedure chkFlipVClick(Sender: TObject);
    procedure chkFlipHClick(Sender: TObject);
    procedure Button1Click(Sender: TObject);
  private
    { Private declarations }
  public
    { Public declarations }
  end;

var
  Main: TMain;

implementation

{$R *.DFM}

var
  Moth: TSprite;
  BG,
  Composite: TBitmap;

procedure MoveMoth;
var
  NewPos: TPosition;
  NewOffset: TPoint;

  function getrandom(Min, Max : Integer) : Integer;
  begin
    result := Trunc((Max - Min + 1.0) * Random + Min);
  end; {getrandom}

begin

  with Moth do begin

    {generate new offsets to make the motion more realistic}
    NewOffset.x := getrandom(3,5);
    NewOffset.y := getrandom(2,4);

    {set the new offset keeping the old direction}
    if OffsetX < 0 then
      OffsetX := -abs(NewOffset.x)
    else OffsetX := abs(NewOffset.x);

    if OffsetY < 0 then
      OffsetY := -abs(NewOffset.y)
    else OffsetY := abs(NewOffset.y);
```

```
    {decide whether to change direction}
    if getrandom(0,100) > 95 then
      OffsetX := -OffsetX;

    if getrandom(0,100) > 70 then
      OffsetY := -OffsetY;

    {Deal with horizontal movement}
    PrvPos := CurPos;
    NewPos := CurPos;
    if ((CurPos.Left + CellWidth + OffsetX) > Main.imgBackground.Width) or
       ((CurPos.Left + OffsetX) < 0) then
         OffsetX := -OffsetX
    else inc(NewPos.Left, OffsetX);

    {Deal with vertical movement}
    if ((CurPos.Top + CellHeight + OffsetY) > Main.imgBackground.Height) or
       ((CurPos.Top + OffsetY) < 0) then
         OffsetY := -OffsetY
    else inc(NewPos.Top, OffsetY);
    CurPos := NewPos;

    {set the next cell to be displayed}
    CurCellNum := CurCellNum - 1;

    end; {with Moth}

end; {MoveMoth}

procedure DrawMoth;
var
  SrcRect,
  DstRect,
  DirtyRect: TRect;

  StartTime: longint;

const

  Itterations:  longint = 0;
  ItterationsN: longint = 1;
  ItterationsF: longint = 1;
  Step1Time:    longint = 0;
  Step2TimeN:   longint = 0;
  Step2TimeF:   longint = 0;
  Step3TimeN:   longint = 0;
  Step3TimeF:   longint = 0;
  Step4Time:    longint = 0;


begin

  {Timing Stuff}
  inc(Itterations);
```

Better Animation 631

```
{Calculate the dirty rectangle}
{$IFDEF UseDirtyCalc}
  with Moth do begin
    if OffsetX > 0 then begin
      DirtyRect.Left := PrvPos.Left;
      DirtyRect.Right := CurPos.Left + CellWidth;
      end
    else begin
      DirtyRect.Left := CurPos.Left;
      DirtyRect.Right := PrvPos.Left + CellWidth + 1;
      end;

    if OffsetY > 0 then begin
      DirtyRect.Top := PrvPos.Top;
      DirtyRect.Bottom := CurPos.Top + CellHeight;
      end
    else begin
      DirtyRect.Top := CurPos.Top;
      DirtyRect.Bottom := PrvPos.Top + CellHeight + 1;
      end;

    end; {with Moth}

{$ELSE}
  DirtyRect := Rect( 0,0,
                     Main.imgBackground.Width-1,
                     Main.imgBackground.Height-1);
{$ENDIF}

{ STEP #1 }
{ First we copy the saved background to the composite buffer}
StartTime := timeGetTime;
with Composite.Canvas do begin
  CopyMode := cmSrcCopy;
  CopyRect(DirtyRect, BG.Canvas, DirtyRect);
  end;
inc(Step1Time, timeGetTime - StartTime);

{ STEP #2 }
{ In this step we copy the sprite mask to the composite dc using SRCAND }
StartTime := timeGetTime;
SrcRect := Moth.CurCellRect;
DstRect := Moth.CurDestRect;

with Composite.Canvas do begin
  CopyMode := cmSrcAnd;
  CopyRect(DstRect, Moth.Mask.Canvas, SrcRect);
  end;

{timing stuff}
if (DstRect.Right < DstRect.Left) or
   (DstRect.Bottom < DstRect.Top) then
  begin
    inc(Step2TimeF, timeGetTime - StartTime);
```

```
          inc(ItterationsF);
        end
    else begin
      inc(Step2TimeN, timeGetTime - StartTime);
      inc(ItterationsN);
      end;

    { STEP #3 }
    { In this step we copy the sprite to the display dc using SRCPAINT }
    StartTime := timeGetTime;
    with Composite.Canvas do begin
      CopyMode := cmSrcPaint;
      CopyRect(DstRect, Moth.Sprite.Canvas, SrcRect);
      end;

    {timing stuff}
    if (DstRect.Right < DstRect.Left) or
       (DstRect.Bottom < DstRect.Top)
        then inc(Step3TimeF, timeGetTime - StartTime)
    else
      inc(Step3TimeN, timeGetTime - StartTime);

    { STEP #4 }
    { Blt the composite dc to the screen }
    StartTime := timeGetTime;
    with Main.imgBackground.Canvas do begin
      CopyMode := cmSrcCopy;
      CopyRect(DirtyRect, Composite.Canvas, DirtyRect);
      end;
    inc(Step4Time, timeGetTime - StartTime);

    {timing stuff}
    if Itterations mod 100 = 0 then begin
      Main.Caption := '(Step1: ' + IntToStr(Step1Time div Itterations) + 'ms)' +
                      '(Step2: ' + IntToStr(Step2TimeN div ItterationsN) + 'ms' +
                      ', ' + IntToStr(Step2TimeF div ItterationsF) + 'ms)' +
                      '(Step3: ' + IntToStr(Step3TimeN div ItterationsN) + 'ms' +
                      ', ' + IntToStr(Step3TimeF div ItterationsF) + 'ms)' +
                      '(Step4: ' + IntToStr(Step4Time div Itterations) + 'ms)';
      end;

end; {DrawMoth}

procedure TMain.FormCreate(Sender: TObject);
var
  r :TRect;
  FirstPos: TPosition;

begin
  {Arrange the components}
  ClientWidth := imgBackground.Picture.Bitmap.Width;
  Panel1.Height := imgBackground.Picture.Bitmap.Height;
  ClientHeight := round(imgBackground.Picture.Bitmap.Height * 1.25);
```

Better Animation 633

```
  {Setup the Moth}
  Moth := TSprite.Create;
  Moth.CellCount := 4;
  Moth.Source := ExtractFilePath(Application.EXEName) + 'moth.bmp';
  FirstPos.Left := 50;
  FirstPos.Top := 50;
  Moth.CurPos := FirstPos;
  Moth.OffsetX := 2;
  Moth.OffsetY := 2;

  {Setup the buffers}
  BG := TBitmap.Create;
  BG.Assign(imgBackground.Picture.Bitmap);

  Composite := TBitmap.Create;
  Composite.Width := imgBackground.Width;
  Composite.Height := imgBackground.Height;

end;

procedure TMain.FormDestroy(Sender: TObject);
begin
  Moth.Free;
  BG.Free;
  Composite.Free;
end;

procedure TMain.chkFlipVClick(Sender: TObject);
begin
  if chkFlipV.Checked then
    Moth.FlipV := True
  else Moth.FlipV := False;

end;

procedure TMain.chkFlipHClick(Sender: TObject);
begin
  if chkFlipH.Checked then
    Moth.FlipH := True
  else Moth.FlipH := False;
end;

procedure TMain.Button1Click(Sender: TObject);
const
  Interval = 10;
  Quitting: boolean = True;

var
  StartTime: longint;

begin

  Quitting := Not Quitting;
  if Quitting then
```

```pascal
    Button1.Caption := 'Start'
  else Button1.Caption := 'Stop';

  while not Quitting do begin

    StartTime := timeGetTime;
    while (timeGetTime - StartTime) < Interval do
      Application.ProcessMessages;
    MoveMoth;
    DrawMoth;

    end;

end; {Button1Click}

end.
```

Listing 14.2   cSprite.pas

```pascal
unit cSprite;

interface

uses
  Windows, Classes, Graphics;

type
  TPosition = record
    Left,
    Top:  integer;
    end;

  TAnimStyle = (asLoop, asPingPong);
  TOrientationStyleH = (osLeftToRight, osRightToLeft);
  TOrientationStyleV = (osTopToBottom, osBottomToTop);

  TSprite = class(TObject)
    private

      procedure ReadBitmapFile(const fn: string);
      procedure SetCurCellNum(Value: byte);
      function GetCurCellRect: TRect;
      function GetCurDestRect: TRect;

    protected
      FSprite: TBitmap;
      FMask: TBitmap;
      FCellCount: byte;
      FCellWidth: integer;
      FCellHeight: integer;
      FCurCellNum: byte;
      FAnimStyle: TAnimStyle;
```

```pascal
      FCurPos: TPosition;
      FPrvPos: TPosition;
      FOffsetX: integer;
      FOffsetY: integer;

      FOrientationH: TOrientationStyleH;
      FOrientationV: TOrientationStyleV;
      FFlipH:        boolean;
      FFlipV:        boolean;

    public
      constructor Create;
      destructor Destroy; override;

      property Source: string write ReadBitmapFile;
      property Sprite: TBitmap read FSprite;
      property Mask: TBitmap read FMask;

      property CellCount: byte read FCellCount write FCellCount;
      property CellWidth: integer read FCellWidth;
      property CellHeight: integer read FCellHeight;

      property CurPos: TPosition read FCurPos write FCurPos;
      property PrvPos: TPosition read FPrvPos write FPrvPos;
      property OffsetX: integer read FOffsetX write FOffsetX;
      property OffsetY: integer read FOffsetY write FOffsetY;

      property OrientH: TOrientationStyleH read FOrientationH
                                           write FOrientationH
                                           default osLeftToRight;

      property OrientV: TOrientationStyleV read FOrientationV
                                           write FOrientationV
                                           default osTopToBottom;

      property FlipH:    boolean read FFlipH write FFlipH default False;
      property FlipV:    boolean read FFlipV write FFlipV default False;

      property CurCellNum: byte read FCurCellNum write SetCurCellNum;
      property AnimationStyle: TAnimStyle read FAnimStyle write FAnimStyle
                                          default asLoop;
      property CurCellRect: TRect read GetCurCellRect;
      property CurDestRect: TRect read GetCurDestRect;

    end;

implementation

procedure ConvertBitmapToSprite(bmp: TBitmap);
var
  OrgBackColor: TColor;
  w,h:          longint;

begin
```

```
    OrgBackColor := bmp.Canvas.Pixels[0,0];
    for h := 0 to bmp.Height do
      for w := 0 to bmp.Width do
        if bmp.Canvas.Pixels[w,h] = OrgBackColor then
          bmp.Canvas.Pixels[w,h] := $00000000;

end; {ConvertImageToSprite}

procedure ConvertBitmapToMask(bmp: TBitmap);
var
  BackColor: TColor;
  w,h:       longint;

begin

  BackColor := bmp.Canvas.Pixels[0,0];
  for h := 0 to bmp.Height do
    for w := 0 to bmp.Width do
      if bmp.Canvas.Pixels[w,h] = BackColor then
        bmp.Canvas.Pixels[w,h] := $00FFFFFF
      else
        bmp.Canvas.Pixels[w,h] := $00000000;

end; {ConvertImageToMask}

constructor TSprite.Create;
begin
  inherited Create;

end;

destructor TSprite.Destroy;
begin
  if not FSprite.Empty then FSprite.Free;
  if not FMask.Empty then FMask.Free;

  inherited Destroy;
end;

procedure TSprite.ReadBitmapFile(const fn: string);
var
  MemBitmap: TBitmap;

begin

  if FCellCount > 0 then begin
    {Load a file from the disk into a memory bitmap}
    MemBitmap := TBitmap.Create;
    MemBitmap.LoadFromFile(fn);

    {
      The next two blocks create a sprite bitmap and a mask bitmap. This is really
      overkill for the sake of clarity. We don't need to have black and white for
```

```
        the raster operations to do their work. Right now in the sprite bitmap we're
        creating a BLACK background and leaving the actual sprite alone. In the mask
        we're creating a white background with a black silhouette. We could
        eliminate a time consuming step by creating a mask that has a black
        silhouette and a background that is a binary compliment of whatever the
        original background color was.
        }
        FSprite := TBitmap.Create;
        FSprite.Assign(MemBitmap);
        ConvertBitmapToSprite(FSprite);

        FMask := TBitmap.Create;
        FMask.Assign(MemBitmap);
        ConvertBitmapToMask(FMask);

        {setup some of the sprite fields that we know now}
        FCellWidth := FSprite.Width;
        FCellHeight := FSprite.Height div FCellCount;
        FCurCellNum := 1;

        MemBitmap.Free;
        end;

end; {TSprite.ReadBitmapFile}

procedure TSprite.SetCurCellNum(Value: byte);
begin

   Case FAnimStyle of
      asLoop: begin
                  if Value < 1 then
                     Value := FCellCount
                  else if Value > FCellCount then
                       Value := 1;

                  FCurCellNum := Value;
              end;

      asPingPong: begin
                     {this is just a starter routine}

                  end;

      end; {case FAnimStyle of}

end; {TSprite.SetCurCellNum}

function TSprite.GetCurCellRect: TRect;

begin

   result := Rect(
              0,(FCellCount * FCellHeight) - (FCurCellNum * FCellHeight),
```

```
                    FCellWidth-1,
                    (FCellCount * FCellHeight) - (FCurCellNum * FCellHeight) +
                    FCellHeight-1
                    );

end; {TSprite.GetCurCellRect}

function TSprite.GetCurDestRect: TRect;
var
    l,t,r,b: integer;

begin

    if ((OffsetX < 0) and (OrientH = osLeftToRight)) and FlipH then begin
        l := FCurPos.Left + FCellWidth;
        r := FCurPos.Left;
        end
    else begin
        l := FCurPos.Left;
        r := FCurPos.Left + FCellWidth;
        end;

    if ((OffsetY < 0) and (OrientV = osTopToBottom)) and FlipV then begin
        t := FCurPos.Top + FCellHeight;
        b := FCurPos.Top;
        end
    else begin
        t := FCurPos.Top;
        b := FCurPos.Top + FCellHeight;
        end;

    result := Rect(l,t,r,b);

end; {TSprite.GetCurDestRect}

end.
```

The Sprite Class

In the sprite class we create for this project, we encapsulate many of the sprite elements and routines that we've already developed, plus we add some new stuff. Let's break it down into manageable pieces.

The first thing that we do in this unit is to develop some useful *types* that will make some of the property settings seem more straightforward.

```
type
  TPosition = record
    Left,
    Top: integer;
    end;
```

```
TAnimStyle = (asLoop, asPingPong);
TOrientationStyleH = (osLeftToRight, osRightToLeft);
TOrientationStyleV = (osTopToBottom, osBottomToTop);
```

We'll use **TPosition** as an (x,y) reference to the position of a sprite. **TAnimStyle** gives a meaningful value for the cell behavior of a sprite. **TOrientationStyleH** and **TOrientationStyleV** help describe the sprite bitmaps original viewing orientation.

The next part of the unit is the TSprite class definition. The sprite class uses protected fields to store data and gives access to those fields through properties. We have also declared some private functions which I will explain as we examine this unit. Let's take a closer look at the **TSprite** class.

```
public
     constructor Create;
     destructor Destroy; override;
```

Of course we declare the **constructor** and **destructor** methods to create and destroy any sprite object that we instantiate.

```
property Source: string write ReadBitmapFile;
property Sprite: TBitmap read FSprite;
property Mask: TBitmap read FMask;
```

Setting the **Source** property will execute the **ReadBitmapFile** procedure. If the **Source** property is a valid bitmap filename, then the function initializes the **Sprite** and **Mask** properties using the conversion routines we developed in the previous chapter.

```
property CellCount: byte read FCellCount write FCellCount;
property CellWidth: integer read FCellWidth;
property CellHeight: integer read FCellHeight;
```

CellCount is a property that must be set before the **Source** property will do anything. Just as in the previous chapter, we need to know how many cells exist so we can calculate the height of each cell. The width and height of each cell are stored in **CellWidth** and **CellHeight**. These properties are *read-only* and set when the **ReadBitmapFile** procedure is executed.

```
property CurPos: TPosition read FCurPos write FCurPos;
property PrvPos: TPosition read FPrvPos write FPrvPos;
property OffsetX: integer read FOffsetX write FOffsetX;
property OffsetY: integer read FOffsetY write FOffsetY;
```

We store the current and previous positions of the sprite in **CurPos** and **PrvPos** respectively. The offset properties, **OffsetX** and **OffsetY**, store the distance, in pixels, that the sprite should move each time. A negative value indicates that the sprite will be moving opposite to its normal direction.

```
property OrientH: TOrientationStyleH read FOrientationH
                                     write FOrientationH
                                     default osLeftToRight;

    property OrientV: TOrientationStyleV read FOrientationV
                                         write FOrientationV
                                         default osTopToBottom;

    property FlipH:  boolean read FFlipH write FFlipH default False;
    property FlipV:  boolean read FFlipV write FFlipV default False;
```

The orientation properties, **OrientH** and **OrientV**, indicate the original viewing orientation of a sprite cell. These properties are used together with **FlipH** and **FlipV** to decide whether the sprite should be drawn either horizontally or vertically flipped when it is moving backwards.

```
property CurCellNum: byte read FCurCellNum write SetCurCellNum;
    property AnimationStyle: TAnimStyle read FAnimStyle write FAnimStyle
default asLoop;
    property CurCellRect: TRect read GetCurCellRect;
    property CurDestRect: TRect read GetCurDestRect;
```

The property **CurCellNum** returns the sprite's currently active cell. When this property is set, it calls **SetCurCellNum** to validate that the new setting conforms to the **AnimationStyle** property. I've set up this procedure with room to grow. It only handles a sequence of cells such as the moth where the cells loop. Another possibility is to have the cells *Ping-Pong* back and forth. This condition could be handled with a case statement. Whatever the style of animation required, this procedure should calculate the next cell to be displayed. That way the calling program stays simple and easy to follow.

The **CurCellRect** property returns a **TRect** structure indicating the bounding rectangle of the cell in the sprite and mask bitmaps. Similarly, the property **CurDestRect** returns a **TRect** structure that defines the bounding rectangle of the destination canvas where the sprite is to be drawn.

Much of the code in this module is taken directly from projects that we have already developed. The procedures **ConvertBitmapToSprite** and **ConvertBitmapToMask** were developed in the previous chapter to make and save sprites and masks to new bitmap files. We've incorporated the procedures here so that, at the cost of a little time at startup, we only need one bitmap file that does not require any special formatting.

The **ReadBitmapFile** procedure is derived from the **MakeMask** project in the last chapter. Here we just load the bitmap and call the conversion procedures. We also set some of the properties of the sprite based on the dimensions of the file loaded

In the **Sprite2** project from the previous chapter, the drawing routine was responsible for calculating the destination rectangle where the sprite would be drawn, and then testing to see if we were moving from right to left. If the direction was right to left, then the destination rectangle was modified so the sprite would be drawn horizontally flipped. In the sprite class we've developed for this project, the property **CurDestRect** returns a destination rectangle that has already been calculated and tested for reverse motion by the **GetCurDestRect** function. This will simplify and clarify the draw routine.

The Mechanics of the Sprite4 Project

Now that you understand the functionality that the **TSprite** class implements, lets look at the code in **uSprite4.pas**. This is where all of the action is generated, and the entire unit is in Listing 14.1.

Notice that the uses clause references the sprite class unit, and a unit called **MMSystem**. We're referencing **MMSystem** because that unit defines a function, **timeGetTime**, which happens to provide timing information with better resolution and accuracy than **GetTickCount**.

```
uses
    Windows, Messages, SysUtils, Classes, Graphics, Controls, Forms, Dialogs,
    ExtCtrls, cSprite, MMSystem, StdCtrls;
```

We also use a compiler definition {$UNDEF UseDirtyCalc} or {$DEFINE UseDirtyCalc} so that we can test the speed gain we get by updating only the changed region of the screen. Take a look at the **DrawMoth** procedure in Listing 14.3.

Listing 14.3 The DrawMoth procedure

```
procedure DrawMoth;
var
  SrcRect,
  DstRect,
  DirtyRect: TRect;

  StartTime: longint;
```

Chapter 14

```
const

  Itterations:   longint = 0;
  ItterationsN:  longint = 1;
  ItterationsF:  longint = 1;
  Step1Time:     longint = 0;
  Step2TimeN:    longint = 0;
  Step2TimeF:    longint = 0;
  Step3TimeN:    longint = 0;
  Step3TimeF:    longint = 0;
  Step4Time:     longint = 0;


begin

  {Timing Stuff}
  inc(Itterations);

  {Calculate the dirty rectangle}
  {$IFDEF UseDirtyCalc}
    with Moth do begin
      if OffsetX > 0 then begin
        DirtyRect.Left := PrvPos.Left;
        DirtyRect.Right := CurPos.Left + CellWidth;
        end
      else begin
        DirtyRect.Left := CurPos.Left;
        DirtyRect.Right := PrvPos.Left + CellWidth + 1;
        end;

      if OffsetY > 0 then begin
        DirtyRect.Top := PrvPos.Top;
        DirtyRect.Bottom := CurPos.Top + CellHeight;
        end
      else begin
        DirtyRect.Top := CurPos.Top;
        DirtyRect.Bottom := PrvPos.Top + CellHeight + 1;
        end;

      end; {with Moth}

  {$ELSE}
    DirtyRect := Rect( 0,0,
                       Main.imgBackground.Width-1,
                       Main.imgBackground.Height-1);
  {$ENDIF}

  { STEP #1 }
  { First we copy the saved background to the composite buffer}
  StartTime := timeGetTime;
  with Composite.Canvas do begin
    CopyMode := cmSrcCopy;
    CopyRect(DirtyRect, BG.Canvas, DirtyRect);
```

Better Animation 643

```
    end;
inc(Step1Time, timeGetTime - StartTime);

{ STEP #2 }
{ In this step we copy the sprite mask to the composite dc using SRCAND }
StartTime := timeGetTime;
SrcRect := Moth.CurCellRect;
DstRect := Moth.CurDestRect;

with Composite.Canvas do begin
  CopyMode := cmSrcAnd;
  CopyRect(DstRect, Moth.Mask.Canvas, SrcRect);
  end;

{timing stuff}
if (DstRect.Right < DstRect.Left) or
   (DstRect.Bottom < DstRect.Top) then
    begin
      inc(Step2TimeF, timeGetTime - StartTime);
      inc(ItterationsF);
    end
else begin
  inc(Step2TimeN, timeGetTime - StartTime);
  inc(ItterationsN);
  end;

{ STEP #3 }
{ In this step we copy the sprite to the display dc using SRCPAINT }
StartTime := timeGetTime;
with Composite.Canvas do begin
  CopyMode := cmSrcPaint;
  CopyRect(DstRect, Moth.Sprite.Canvas, SrcRect);
  end;

{timing stuff}
if (DstRect.Right < DstRect.Left) or
   (DstRect.Bottom < DstRect.Top)
    then inc(Step3TimeF, timeGetTime - StartTime)
else
  inc(Step3TimeN, timeGetTime - StartTime);

{ STEP #4 }
{ Blt the composite dc to the screen }
StartTime := timeGetTime;
with Main.imgBackground.Canvas do begin
  CopyMode := cmSrcCopy;
  CopyRect(DirtyRect, Composite.Canvas, DirtyRect);
  end;
inc(Step4Time, timeGetTime - StartTime);

{timing stuff}
if Itterations mod 100 = 0 then begin
  Main.Caption := '(Step1: ' + IntToStr(Step1Time div Itterations) + 'ms)' +
                  '(Step2: ' + IntToStr(Step2TimeN div ItterationsN) + 'ms' +
```

```
                  ', ' + IntToStr(Step2TimeF div ItterationsF) + 'ms)' +
                  '(Step3: ' + IntToStr(Step3TimeN div ItterationsN) + 'ms' +
                  ', ' + IntToStr(Step3TimeF div ItterationsF) + 'ms)' +
                  '(Step4: ' + IntToStr(Step4Time div Itterations) + 'ms)';
  end;

end; {DrawMoth}
```

In spite of all the code, it is still fairly simple. The timing code accounts for a fair amount of code in the procedure. We're timing each step of the draw so we can determine where the program is spending its time. For each step of the draw, we do the following to tally the time that step took:

1. Store the result of **timeGetTime**.
2. Perform the draw
3. Increment *StepXTime* by the time elapsed during the draw.

At the end of the draw procedure, we display the average time each step took in the caption bar of the form.

We learned earlier in this chapter that four steps are required to draw a sprite with a double-buffering technique. Let's take a closer look at how each of those steps are implemented. To jog your memory we'll do the following:

1. Copy the *dirty rectangle* from the background buffer to the construction buffer.
2. Draw the sprite mask to the construction buffer with the SRCAND operation.
3. Draw the sprite to the construction buffer with the SRCPAINT operation.
4. Copy the *dirty rectangle* from the construction buffer to the screen.

We're only counting the processes that actually perform some type of draw as steps. We actually have to add a couple of simple calculations too. First, as illustrated below, we need to calculate the area of the screen to be updated (the *dirty rectangle*).

```
{Calculate the dirty rectangle}
  {$IFDEF UseDirtyCalc}
    with Moth do begin
      if OffsetX > 0 then begin
        DirtyRect.Left := PrvPos.Left;
        DirtyRect.Right := CurPos.Left + CellWidth;
      end
      else begin
        DirtyRect.Left := CurPos.Left;
        DirtyRect.Right := PrvPos.Left + CellWidth + 1;
      end;
```

```
    if OffsetY > 0 then begin
      DirtyRect.Top := PrvPos.Top;
      DirtyRect.Bottom := CurPos.Top + CellHeight;
      end
    else begin
      DirtyRect.Top := CurPos.Top;
      DirtyRect.Bottom := PrvPos.Top + CellHeight + 1;
      end;

  end; {with Moth}
{$ELSE}
  DirtyRect := Rect( 0,0,
                     Main.imgBackground.Width-1,
                     Main.imgBackground.Height-1);
{$ENDIF}
```

We're using a compiler definition so that we can time the program, updating the entire window each time and then using the dirty rectangle calculation. This way we'll be able to compare the time required for each technique. Remember that **DirtyRect** is the smallest rectangle that encompasses the sprite's previous and current positions. This was illustrated in Figure 14.1.

In step #1, we copy the *dirty rectangle* from the saved background to the construction buffer:

```
with Composite.Canvas do begin
   CopyMode := cmSrcCopy;
   CopyRect(DirtyRect, BG.Canvas, DirtyRect);
   end;
```

In step #2 we'll copy the mask to the construction buffer. For this we need to know what portion of the mask to copy, and where to copy it. This information can be retrieved from the sprite object in **SrcRect** and **DstRect**:

```
SrcRect := Moth.CurCellRect;
DstRect := Moth.CurDestRect;

with Composite.Canvas do begin
   CopyMode := cmSrcAnd;
   CopyRect(DstRect, Moth.Mask.Canvas, SrcRect);
   end;
```

Step #3 uses the same source and destination rectangles but copies the sprite with SRCPAINT. At this point, the construction buffer contains a portion of the background with the moth drawn transparently over it. We won't actually see anything until after step #4.

```
{ STEP #3 }
{ In this step we copy the sprite to the display dc using SRCPAINT }
StartTime := timeGetTime;
with Composite.Canvas do begin
  CopyMode := cmSrcPaint;
  CopyRect(DstRect, Moth.Sprite.Canvas, SrcRect);
  end;
```

The final step is the only one that actually updates the screen. We copy the dirty rectangle from the construction buffer to the screen:

```
{ STEP #4 }
{ Blt the composite dc to the screen }
StartTime := timeGetTime;
with Main.imgBackground.Canvas do begin
  CopyMode := cmSrcCopy;
  CopyRect(DirtyRect, Composite.Canvas, DirtyRect);
  end;
```

Figure 14.3 illustrates the entire draw process.

Now let's inspect the form's **OnCreate** handler. This is where the offscreen buffers are created and the moth sprite is initialized. The **OnCreate** handler appears in Listing 14.4.

Figure 14.3 The double-buffering draw process for a sprite with transparency.

Listing 14.4 The OnCreate handler

```
procedure TMain.FormCreate(Sender: TObject);
var
  r :TRect;
  FirstPos: TPosition;

begin
  {Arrange the components}
  ClientWidth := imgBackground.Picture.Bitmap.Width;
  Panel1.Height := imgBackground.Picture.Bitmap.Height;
  ClientHeight := round(imgBackground.Picture.Bitmap.Height * 1.25);

  {Setup the Moth}
  Moth := TSprite.Create;
  Moth.CellCount := 4;
  Moth.Source := ExtractFilePath(Application.EXEName) + 'moth.bmp';
  FirstPos.Left := 50;
  FirstPos.Top := 50;
  Moth.CurPos := FirstPos;
  Moth.OffsetX := 2;
  Moth.OffsetY := 2;

  {Setup the buffers}
  BG := TBitmap.Create;
  BG.Assign(imgBackground.Picture.Bitmap);

  Composite := TBitmap.Create;
  Composite.Width := imgBackground.Width;
  Composite.Height := imgBackground.Height;

end;
```

Notice the order in which the moth sprite is initialized. First, the sprite is instantiated with a call to **TSprite.Create**. This allocates memory for the object. Next we set the CellCount property. In order for the sprite to be initialized properly, this must be set before the Source property. The remaining properties of the moth are not order dependent.

Next we set up the off-screen buffers. In this example, the buffers are **TBitmaps**. The background is identical to the Picture property of imgBackground on the form, so we use the **Assign** method to copy the contents. The composite buffer just needs to be created and sized to the same dimensions as the background. It will not contain anything until the draw routine uses it for construction.

The event that sparks the sprite into motion is the click event of the **TButton**. Here, rather than using a timer, we generate a loop that moves and draws the sprite every 10ms. Listing 14.5 contains the **OnClick** event procedure.

Listing 14.5 The Button1Click handler

```
procedure TMain.Button1Click(Sender: TObject);
const
  Interval = 10;
  Quitting: boolean = True;

var
  StartTime: longint;

begin

  Quitting := Not Quitting;
  if Quitting then
    Button1.Caption := 'Start'
  else Button1.Caption := 'Stop';

  while not Quitting do begin

    StartTime := timeGetTime;
    while (timeGetTime - StartTime) < Interval do
      Application.ProcessMessages;
    MoveMoth;
    DrawMoth;

  end;

end; {Button1Click}
```

So you see, all of the action is generated in this procedure. Each iteration of the loop calls the **MoveMoth** procedure and then the **DrawMoth** procedure.

One of the problems with the sprite animation from chapter 13 is very mechanical motion. I've modified the **MoveMoth** procedure slightly to illustrate how easy it is to generate different types of motion. The entire procedure is in Listing 14.6.

Listing 14.6 The MoveMoth procedure

```
procedure MoveMoth;
var
  NewPos: TPosition;
  NewOffset: TPoint;

  function getrandom(Min, Max : Integer) : Integer;
  begin
    result := Trunc((Max - Min + 1.0) * Random + Min);
  end; {getrandom}

begin

  with Moth do begin
```

```
     {generate new offsets to make the motion more realistic}
     NewOffset.x := getrandom(3,5);
     NewOffset.y := getrandom(2,4);

     {set the new offset keeping the old direction}
     if OffsetX < 0 then
       OffsetX := -abs(NewOffset.x)
     else OffsetX := abs(NewOffset.x);

     if OffsetY < 0 then
       OffsetY := -abs(NewOffset.y)
     else OffsetY := abs(NewOffset.y);

     {decide whether to change direction}
     if getrandom(0,100) > 95 then
       OffsetX := -OffsetX;

     if getrandom(0,100) > 70 then
       OffsetY := -OffsetY;

     {Deal with horizontal movement}
     PrvPos := CurPos;
     NewPos := CurPos;
     if ((CurPos.Left + CellWidth + OffsetX) > Main.imgBackground.Width) or
        ((CurPos.Left + OffsetX) < 0) then
           OffsetX := -OffsetX
     else inc(NewPos.Left, OffsetX);

     {Deal with vertical movement}
     if ((CurPos.Top + CellHeight + OffsetY) > Main.imgBackground.Height) or
        ((CurPos.Top + OffsetY) < 0) then
           OffsetY := -OffsetY
     else inc(NewPos.Top, OffsetY);
     CurPos := NewPos;

     {set the next cell to be displayed}
     CurCellNum := CurCellNum - 1;

     end; {with Moth}

end; {MoveMoth}
```

I've added a function called **getrandom()** to the original procedure, which returns a randomly selected number that falls between the two numbers passed as parameters. This is used in the next couple of statements to add some variety to the motion. Notice that the moth has a 5% chance of changing horizontal direction, and a 30% chance of changing vertical direction. A moth's flight tends to be sort of bouncy in vertical movement, but not as much so in horizontal movement. We've haven't accurately reproduced the flight of a moth, but we've given the animation more visual appeal.

Running the Program

The first time you run the program, you should set the compiler definition as follows:

```
{$UNDEF UseDirtyCalc}
```

This will cause the program to run without doing any dirty rectangle calculation. The entire screen will be updated for each movement of the moth. Run the program long enough for the moth to complete several treks across the screen. Make sure that you have the *Flip Horizontal* checkbox checked. This will ensure that we get an accurate timing for a draw that had to flip the bitmap. The numbers in the caption bar should stabilize. Make a mental note of the time required to complete each of the draw steps.

Change the compiler definition to read:

```
{$DEFINE UseDirtyCalc}
```

When the program runs this time, you should notice a drop in the draw times. Table 14.2 indicates the results on a Pentium 60 with 16MB of RAM running Windows 95.

Notice the 9ms drop in time for the steps that use the dirty rectangle calculation. A 9ms drop may seem insignificant, but observation will undoubtedly indicate otherwise.

Improving the Sprite Engine

We've come a long way from the rectangular sprite that jumped and flashed around the screen in Chapter 13. The techniques we've developed here are the very same as the ones employed by many multimedia programs and

Table 14.2 *Draw routine timings.*

Draw Operation	Time without Dirty Rectangle Calc.	Time with Dirty Rectangle Calc.
Step #1	10ms	1ms
Step #2	1ms	1ms
Step #2 flipped	15ms	15ms
Step #3	1ms	1ms
Step #3 flipped	15ms	15ms
Step #4	10ms	1ms

games. In this implementation, the components are dealing with most of the low-level routines like reading bitmap files and allocating memory, while we've concentrated on the sprite techniques. What we've gained in clarity and ease-of use, we've lost in speed. Because Delphi's components are designed to handle many different situations, they are not as fast as they could be. In the next project, we're going to dig a little deeper and reclaim some of the speed. By working at a lower level and bypassing some of the Delphi objects, we'll generate code that performs only what we need it to do. It won't be bloated with code that deals with other contingencies or performs unnecessary tasks. Also, since we'll be working with bitmaps as DIBs, we'll have direct access to some of the faster API drawing routines.

Sprite Animation from the Ground Up

This project is nothing more than a conversion of the SPRITE4 project we completed previously. We'll be converting the routines to work with DIBs, bypassing most of Delphi's drawing surfaces and objects. We'll retain the timing code so we can compare the results to the last project.

1. Copy the SPRITE4 project into a new directory for modification.
2. Add the DIB class module developed in Chapter 8.
3. Modify the sprite class module as indicated.
4. Modify the SPRITE4 code as indicated.

This project is located in the directory \delphimm\ch14\sprite5.

Creating the Sprite5 Project

Begin by copying the SPRITE4 project into a new directory so that we can work from it to create SPRITE5. Rename the file "uSprite4.pas" to "uSprite5.pas". Start a new project and call it SPRITE5. Add "uSprite5.pas", "cDIB.pas", and "cSprite.pas". You will need to copy cDIB.pas from the dissolve project directory in Chapter 8. You could also just load the project from the companion CD-ROM, and follow the code discussion to understand the changes.

For this project, we're not going to make any operational changes. This program will operate identically to the SPRITE4 program. We are going to change the way the sprite is stored and drawn. In SPRITE4, we used Delphi's

TBitmap and **TCanvas** objects. We're going to work at a lower level in this project and work directly with DIBs and *dc*s for drawing. We'll have to add some functionality to the cDIB.pas unit, change some of the procedures in cSprite.pas so that they work with the DIBs instead of **TBitmaps**, and make some minor changes to the draw routine in uSprite5.pas.

The first modification to make is in cDIB.pas. We'll be adding a function called **Get_storagewidth** which returns the number of bytes that are required to store a single scan line of a DIB. Remember that each horizontal line of a DIB is padded to multiples of 4 bytes. To calculate the total number of bytes that the pixels of a DIB require, we multiply the height of the DIB by the storage width. The completed unit appears in Listing 14.7.

Listing 14.7   cDIB.pas

```
unit cDIB;

interface
uses
  Windows, SysUtils, Classes, Graphics;

  type
      TDIB = class(TPersistent)
        protected
          pDIB     : PBitmapInfo;
          MemSize  : longint;

          function Get_biSize : integer;
          function Get_DIBSize : longint;

          procedure ReadFromFile(const fn : string);
          function Get_width : longint;
          function Get_height : longint;
          function Get_storagewidth : longint;
          function Get_ncolors : longint;
          function Get_ptr_to_RGBQuad : PRGBQuad;
          function Get_ptr_to_bits : PByte;

        public
          constructor Create;
          destructor Destroy; override;

          property Source         : string write ReadFromFile;
          property Width          : longint read Get_width;
          property Height         : longint read Get_height;
          property StorageWidth   : longint read Get_storagewidth;
          property NumColors      : longint read Get_ncolors;
          property ptrRGBQuad     : PRGBQuad read Get_ptr_to_RGBQuad;
          property ptrBits        : PByte read Get_ptr_to_bits;
          property ptrBitmapInfo  : PBitmapInfo read pDIB;
```

```pascal
    function Create_Palette(const palSysFlags,palFlags : byte): hPalette;
    function Create_IdentPal256(const palFlags: byte): hPalette;
    procedure Assign(Source : TPersistent); override;

  end;

implementation

constructor TDIB.Create;
begin
  inherited Create;
  MemSize := 0;
end;

destructor TDIB.Destroy;
begin
  if MemSize <> 0 then
    freemem(pDIB, MemSize);

  inherited Destroy;
end;

procedure TDIB.Assign(Source : TPersistent);
begin
  if (TDIB = nil) or not (Source is TDIB) then exit;
  MemSize := TDIB(Source).MemSize;
  pDIB := allocmem(MemSize);
  move(TDIB(Source).pDIB^, pDIB^, MemSize);
end; {Assign}

{
   TDIB.ReadFromFile: loads a bmp file and returns a pointer to the DIB in
                      memory. Also returns the size of the memory image so
                      that the memory can be freed.
}
procedure TDIB.ReadFromFile(const fn : string);

begin
    with TMemoryStream.Create do begin
        LoadFromFile(fn);
        MemSize := size - sizeof(TBitmapFileHeader);
        pDIB := allocmem(MemSize);
        seek(sizeof(TBitmapFileHeader), 0);
        read(pDIB^, MemSize);
        free;
        end;

end; {ReadFromFile}

{
   TDIB.Get_width: returns the width of a dib
}
function TDIB.Get_width : longint;
```

```pascal
  begin
    result := pDIB^.bmiHeader.biwidth;
  end; {Get_width}


{
   TDIB.Get_height: returns the height of a dib
}
function TDIB.Get_height : longint;
  begin
    result := pDIB^.bmiHeader.biheight
  end; {dib_height}


{
   TDIB.Get_storagewidth: returns the width of a dib
}
function TDIB.Get_storagewidth : longint;
  begin
    result := (pDIB^.bmiHeader.biWidth + 3) and not 3;;
  end; {Get_storagewidth}


{
   TDIB.Get_ncolors: returns the number of colors in a DIB
}
function TDIB.Get_ncolors : longint;
  begin
    if pDIB^.bmiHeader.biClrUsed > 0 then
      result := pDIB^.bmiHeader.biClrUsed
    else
      result := 1 shl pDIB^.bmiHeader.biBitCount;

  end; {Get_ncolors}


{
   TDIB.Get_biSize: returns the number of bytes in a DIB header including the
                    color table.
}
function TDIB.Get_biSize : integer;
  begin
    result := sizeof(TBitmapInfoHeader) + (Get_ncolors * sizeof(TRGBQuad));
  end; {dib_biSize}


{
   TDIB.Get_DIBSize: returns the number of bytes in a DIB.
}
function TDIB.Get_DIBSize : longint;
  begin
    result := Get_biSize + pDIB^.bmiHeader.biSizeImage;
  end; {Get_DIBSize}


{
   TDIB.Get_ptr_to_RGBQuad: returns a pointer to the first RGBQuad structure
}
function TDIB.Get_ptr_to_RGBQuad : PRGBQuad;
```

```pascal
  begin
    {set a pointer to the DIB palette table as an offset from the DIB ptr}
    result := pointer(longint(pDIB) + sizeof(TBitmapInfoHeader));

  end; {Get_ptr_to_RGBQuad}

{
 TDIB.Get_ptr_to_bits: returns a pointer to the pixel data of the DIB
}
function TDIB.Get_ptr_to_bits : PByte;
  begin
    result := pointer(longint(pDIB) + Get_biSize);
  end; {Get_ptr_to_bits}

{
 TDIB.Create_Palette: creates a palette from the DIB's color table and
                      returns a handle.
}
function TDIB.Create_Palette( const palSysFlags,palFlags: byte): hPalette;
var
  DstPal: PLogPalette;
  Colors, n: Integer;
  Size: Longint;
  DC: HDC;
  Focus: HWND;
  SysPalSize: Integer;
  I: Integer;

  begin
  Result := 0;

  Colors := Get_ncolors;
  if Colors <= 2 then Exit;

  Size := SizeOf(TLogPalette) + ((Colors - 1) * SizeOf(TPaletteEntry));
  DstPal := MemAlloc(Size);
  try
    FillChar(DstPal^, Size, 0);
    with DstPal^ do
    begin
      palNumEntries := Colors;
      palVersion := $300;
      Focus := GetFocus;
      DC := GetDC(Focus);
      try
        SysPalSize := GetDeviceCaps(DC, SIZEPALETTE);
        if (Colors = 16) and (SysPalSize >= 16) then
        begin
          { Ignore the disk image of the palette for 16 color bitmaps use
            instead the first 8 and last 8 of the current system palette }
          GetSystemPaletteEntries(DC, 0, 8, palPalEntry);
          I := 8;
```

```
            GetSystemPaletteEntries(DC, SysPalSize - I, I, palPalEntry[I]);
         end
         else
           { Copy the palette for all others (i.e. 256 colors) }
           {$R-}
           for N := 0 to Colors - 1 do
           begin
             palPalEntry[N].peRed   := pDIB^.bmiColors[N].rgbRed;
             palPalEntry[N].peGreen := pDIB^.bmiColors[N].rgbGreen;
             palPalEntry[N].peBlue  := pDIB^.bmiColors[N].rgbBlue;
             if (N < 10) or (N > 245) then
               palPalEntry[N].peFlags := palSysFlags
             else
               palPalEntry[N].peFlags := palFlags;
           end;
           {$R+}
      finally
        ReleaseDC(Focus, DC);
      end;
    end;
    Result := CreatePalette(DstPal^);
  finally
    FreeMem(DstPal, Size);
  end;
end; {Create_Palette}


{
 TDIB.Create_IdentPal256: returns a handle to the identity palette of a DIB
}
function TDIB.Create_IdentPal256(const palFlags : byte): hPalette;
var
  DstPal: PLogPalette;
  n: Integer;
  Size: Longint;
  DC: HDC;
  Focus: HWND;

begin

  Size := SizeOf(TLogPalette) + (256 * SizeOf(TPaletteEntry));
  DstPal := MemAlloc(Size);
  try
    FillChar(DstPal^, Size, 0);
    with DstPal^ do
    begin
      palNumEntries := 256;
      palVersion := $300;
      Focus := GetFocus;
      DC := GetDC(Focus);
      {$R-}
      try
          {use the system palette entries for 0-9, and 246-255}
          GetSystemPaletteEntries(DC, 0, 10, palPalEntry);
```

```
          N := 246;
          GetSystemPaletteEntries(DC, 246, 10, palPalEntry[N]);

          {use the entries from 0-236 of the color table and map them to
           entries 10-245 in the new logical palette}
          for N := 10 to 245 do
          begin
            palPalEntry[N].peRed   := pDIB^.bmiColors[N-10].rgbRed;
            palPalEntry[N].peGreen := pDIB^.bmiColors[N-10].rgbGreen;
            palPalEntry[N].peBlue  := pDIB^.bmiColors[N-10].rgbBlue;
            palPalEntry[N].peFlags := palFlags;
          end;
        finally
          ReleaseDC(Focus, DC);
        end;
      {$R-}
      end;
      Result := CreatePalette(DstPal^);
    finally
      FreeMem(DstPal, Size);
    end;
end; {Create_IdentPal256}

end.
```

Next we'll work on the cSprite.pas unit displayed in Listing 14.8. We'll convert several routines so that they work with a TDIB object.

Listing 14.8   cSprite.pas

```
unit cSprite;

interface

uses
  Windows, Classes, Graphics, cDIB;

type
  TPosition = record
    Left,
    Top: integer;
    end;

  TAnimStyle = (asLoop, asPingPong);
  TOrientationStyleH = (osLeftToRight, osRightToLeft);
  TOrientationStyleV = (osTopToBottom, osBottomToTop);

  TSprite = class(TObject)
    private

      procedure ReadBitmapFile(const fn: string);
      procedure SetCurCellNum(Value: byte);
```

```
    function GetCurCellRect: TRect;
    function GetCurDestRect: TRect;

  protected
    FSprite: TDIB;
    FMask: TDIB;
    FCellCount: byte;
    FCellWidth: integer;
    FCellHeight: integer;
    FCurCellNum: byte;
    FAnimStyle: TAnimStyle;

    FCurPos: TPosition;
    FPrvPos: TPosition;
    FOffsetX: integer;
    FOffsetY: integer;

    FOrientationH: TOrientationStyleH;
    FOrientationV: TOrientationStyleV;
    FFlipH:        boolean;
    FFlipV:        boolean;

  public
    constructor Create;
    destructor Destroy; override;

    property Source: string write ReadBitmapFile;
    property Sprite: TDIB read FSprite;
    property Mask: TDIB read FMask;

    property CellCount: byte read FCellCount write FCellCount;
    property CellWidth: integer read FCellWidth;
    property CellHeight: integer read FCellHeight;

    property CurPos: TPosition read FCurPos write FCurPos;
    property PrvPos: TPosition read FPrvPos write FPrvPos;
    property OffsetX: integer read FOffsetX write FOffsetX;
    property OffsetY: integer read FOffsetY write FOffsetY;

    property OrientH: TOrientationStyleH read FOrientationH
                                         write FOrientationH
                                         default osLeftToRight;

    property OrientV: TOrientationStyleV read FOrientationV
                                         write FOrientationV
                                         default osTopToBottom;

    property FlipH:   boolean read FFlipH write FFlipH default False;
    property FlipV:   boolean read FFlipV write FFlipV default False;

    property CurCellNum: byte read FCurCellNum write SetCurCellNum;
    property AnimationStyle: TAnimStyle read FAnimStyle write FAnimStyle
                                        default asLoop;
```

```
    property CurCellRect: TRect read GetCurCellRect;
    property CurDestRect: TRect read GetCurDestRect;

  end;

implementation

procedure ConvertBitmapToSprite(bmp: TDIB);
var
  OrgBackColor: byte;
  TempPtr:      PByte;
  szImageBits:  longint;
  i:            longint;

begin

  TempPtr := bmp.ptrBits;
  OrgBackColor := TempPtr^;

  szImageBits := bmp.StorageWidth * bmp.Height;
  for i := 1 to szImageBits do begin
    if TempPtr^ = OrgBackColor then
      TempPtr^ := 0;
    inc(TempPtr);
    end;

end; {ConvertImageToSprite}

procedure ConvertBitmapToMask(bmp: TDIB);
var
  BackColor:   byte;
  TempPtr:     PByte;
  szImageBits: longint;
  i:           longint;

begin

  TempPtr := bmp.ptrBits;
  BackColor := TempPtr^;

  szImageBits := bmp.StorageWidth * bmp.Height;
  for i := 1 to szImageBits do begin
    if TempPtr^ = BackColor then
      TempPtr^ := 255
    else
      TempPtr^ := 0;

    inc(TempPtr);
    end;

end; {ConvertImageToMask}

constructor TSprite.Create;
begin
  inherited Create;
```

```
end;

destructor TSprite.Destroy;
begin
  FSprite.Free;
  FMask.Free;

  inherited Destroy;
end;

procedure TSprite.ReadBitmapFile(const fn: string);
var
  MemDIB: TDIB;

begin

  if FCellCount > 0 then begin
    MemDIB := TDIB.Create;
    MemDIB.Source := fn;
    {
      The next two blocks create a sprite bitmap and a mask bitmap. This is really
      overkill for the sake of clarity. We don't need to have black and white for
      the raster operations to do their work. Right now in the sprite bitmap we're
      creating a BLACK background and leaving the actual sprite alone. In the mask
      we're creating a white background with a black silhouette. We could
      eliminate a time consuming step by creating a mask that has a black
      silhouette and a background that is a binary compliment of whatever the
      original background color was.
    }
    FSprite := TDIB.Create;
    FSprite.Assign(MemDIB);
    ConvertBitmapToSprite(FSprite);

    FMask := TDIB.Create;
    FMask.Assign(MemDIB);
    ConvertBitmapToMask(FMask);

    {setup some of the sprite fields that we know at this point}
    FCellWidth := FSprite.Width;
    FCellHeight := FSprite.Height div FCellCount;
    FCurCellNum := 1;

    MemDIB.Free;

    end;

end; {TSprite.ReadBitmapFile}

procedure TSprite.SetCurCellNum(Value: byte);
begin

  Case FAnimStyle of
    asLoop: begin
              if Value < 1 then
                Value := FCellCount
```

```
              else if Value > FCellCount then
                  Value := 1;

              FCurCellNum := Value;
            end;

    asPingPong: begin
                 {this is just a starter routine}

              end;

    end; {case FAnimStyle of}

end; {TSprite.SetCurCellNum}

function TSprite.GetCurCellRect: TRect;

begin
  result := Rect(
             0,(FCellCount * FCellHeight) - (FCurCellNum * FCellHeight),
             FCellWidth,
             FCellHeight
             );

end; {TSprite.GetCurCellRect}

function TSprite.GetCurDestRect: TRect;
var
  l,t,r,b: integer;

begin

  if ((OffsetX < 0) and (OrientH = osLeftToRight)) and FlipH then begin
    l := FCurPos.Left + FCellWidth-1;
    r := -FCellWidth;
    end
  else begin
    l := FCurPos.Left;
    r := FCellWidth;
    end;

  if ((OffsetY < 0) and (OrientV = osTopToBottom)) and FlipV then begin
    t := FCurPos.Top + FCellHeight-1;
    b := -FCellHeight;
    end
  else begin
    t := FCurPos.Top;
    b := FCellHeight;
    end;

  result := Rect(l,t,r,b);

end; {TSprite.GetCurDestRect}

end.
```

The first change we notice in this unit is that it now references **cDIB** in the uses clause. The most significant change is that the **Sprite** and **Mask** properties are now stored as **TDIB** instead of **TBitmap**. The remaining changes in this unit revolve around the new bitmap storage type.

In the function **ReadBitmapFile**, instead of creating two **TBitmaps**, we create two **TDIBs**. We use the Source property of the **TDIB** class to load the bitmap from a file into the **Sprite** and **Mask** properties of the sprite. The sprite and the mask are then run through the **ConvertBitmapToSprite** and **ConvertBitmapToMask** functions as in the previous project. The difference is that the parameter is now a **TDIB** instead of a **TBitmap**.

The functions **ConvertBitmapToSprite** and **ConvertBitmapToMask** in the previous project used the array of bits, available through the **TBitmap** object, to change the background and foreground colors of the bitmap pixels. In this project, we don't have access to an array of bits. However, we do have direct access to a pointer that references a stream of pixel data. The two conversion routines only require some minor changes. Looking at Listing 14.9, you can see that the function is relatively the same as it was in the SPRITE4 project, with the exception of the details of the looping mechanism.

Listing 14.9 ConvertBitmapToSprite

```
procedure ConvertBitmapToSprite(bmp: TDIB);
var
  OrgBackColor: byte;
  TempPtr:      PByte;
  szImageBits:  longint;
  i:            longint;

begin

  TempPtr := bmp.ptrBits;
  OrgBackColor := TempPtr^;

  szImageBits := bmp.StorageWidth * bmp.Height;
  for i := 1 to szImageBits do begin
    if TempPtr^ = OrgBackColor then
      TempPtr^ := 0;
    inc(TempPtr);
  end;

end; {ConvertBitmapToSprite}
```

In this function, we determine the total number of bytes to store the image. That value is stored in **szImageBits**. Then we just loop through each byte checking to see if the color is the same as the original background color. If it is, we change it to black (color zero).

The remaining changes to this project will be in the draw routine. Listing 14.10 is the complete uSprite5.pas unit. I'm providing it here for reference. Except for the procedure **DrawMoth**, it is identical to uSprite4.pas. Let's take a closer look at how the draw function has changed. Use Listing 14.11 to follow the discussion.

Listing 14.10   uSprite5.pas

```
unit uSprite5;

interface

uses
  Windows, Messages, SysUtils, Classes, Graphics, Controls, Forms, Dialogs,
  ExtCtrls, cSprite, MMSystem, StdCtrls;

type
  TMain = class(TForm)
    Panel1: TPanel;
    imgBackground: TImage;
    chkFlipH: TCheckBox;
    chkFlipV: TCheckBox;
    Button1: TButton;
    procedure FormCreate(Sender: TObject);
    procedure FormDestroy(Sender: TObject);
    procedure Button1Click(Sender: TObject);
    procedure chkFlipHClick(Sender: TObject);
    procedure chkFlipVClick(Sender: TObject);
  private
    { Private declarations }
  public
    { Public declarations }
  end;

var
  Main: TMain;

implementation

{$R *.DFM}

var
  Moth: TSprite;
  BG,
  Composite: hDC;
  hOldBitmap,
  hCompositeBitmap,
  hBackgroundBitmap: hBitmap;

procedure MoveMoth;
var
```

Chapter 14

```pascal
  NewPos: TPosition;
  NewOffset: TPoint;

  function getrandom(Min, Max : Integer) : Integer;
  begin
    result := Trunc((Max - Min + 1.0) * Random + Min);
  end; {getrandom}

begin

  with Moth do begin

    {generate new offsets to make the motion more realistic}
    NewOffset.x := getrandom(3,5);
    NewOffset.y := getrandom(2,4);

    {set the new offset keeping the old direction}
    if OffsetX < 0 then
      OffsetX := -abs(NewOffset.x)
    else OffsetX := abs(NewOffset.x);

    if OffsetY < 0 then
      OffsetY := -abs(NewOffset.y)
    else OffsetY := abs(NewOffset.y);

    {decide whether to change direction}
    if getrandom(0,100) > 95 then
      OffsetX := -OffsetX;

    if getrandom(0,100) > 70 then
      OffsetY := -OffsetY;

    {Deal with horizontal movement}
    PrvPos := CurPos;
    NewPos := CurPos;
    if ((CurPos.Left + CellWidth + OffsetX) > Main.imgBackground.Width) or
       ((CurPos.Left + OffsetX) < 0) then
         OffsetX := -OffsetX
    else inc(NewPos.Left, OffsetX);

    {Deal with vertical movement}
    if ((CurPos.Top + CellHeight + OffsetY) > Main.imgBackground.Height) or
       ((CurPos.Top + OffsetY) < 0) then
         OffsetY := -OffsetY
    else inc(NewPos.Top, OffsetY);
    CurPos := NewPos;

    {set the next cell to be displayed}
    CurCellNum := CurCellNum - 1;

  end; {with Moth}

end; {MoveMoth}
```

Better Animation

```
procedure DrawMoth;
var
  SrcRect,
  DstRect,
  DirtyRect: TRect;
  dc: hDC;

  StartTime: longint;
const

  Itterations:   longint = 0;
  ItterationsN:  longint = 1;
  ItterationsF:  longint = 1;
  Step1Time:     longint = 0;
  Step2TimeN:    longint = 0;
  Step2TimeF:    longint = 0;
  Step3TimeN:    longint = 0;
  Step3TimeF:    longint = 0;
  Step4Time:     longint = 0;

begin

  {Timing Stuff}
  inc(Itterations);

  {Calculate the dirty rectangle}
  with Moth do begin
    if OffsetX > 0 then begin
      DirtyRect.Left := PrvPos.Left;
      DirtyRect.Right := CellWidth + OffsetX;
      end
    else begin
      DirtyRect.Left := CurPos.Left;
      DirtyRect.Right := CellWidth + Abs(OffsetX);
      end;

    if OffsetY > 0 then begin
      DirtyRect.Top := PrvPos.Top;
      DirtyRect.Bottom := CellHeight + OffsetY;
      end
    else begin
      DirtyRect.Top := CurPos.Top;
      DirtyRect.Bottom := CellHeight + Abs(OffsetY);
      end;

    end; {with Moth}

  { STEP #1 }
  { First we copy the saved background to the composite buffer}
  StartTime := timeGetTime;
  BitBlt(
         Composite,
         DirtyRect.Left, DirtyRect.Top, DirtyRect.Right, DirtyRect.Bottom,
```

```
                BG,
                DirtyRect.Left, DirtyRect.Top,
                SRCCOPY
                );
inc(Step1Time, timeGetTime - StartTime);

{ STEP #2 }
{ In this step we copy the sprite mask to the composite dc using SRCAND }
StartTime := timeGetTime;
SrcRect := Moth.CurCellRect;
DstRect := Moth.CurDestRect;

StretchDIBits(
                Composite,
                DstRect.Left, DstRect.Top, DstRect.Right, DstRect.Bottom,
                SrcRect.Left, SrcRect.Top, SrcRect.Right, SrcRect.Bottom,
                Moth.Mask.ptrBits,
                Moth.Mask.ptrBitmapInfo^,
                DIB_RGB_COLORS,
                SRCAND
                );

{timing stuff}
if (DstRect.Right < 0) or
   (DstRect.Bottom < 0) then
   begin
     inc(Step2TimeF, timeGetTime - StartTime);
     inc(ItterationsF);
   end
else begin
  inc(Step2TimeN, timeGetTime - StartTime);
  inc(ItterationsN);
  end;

{ STEP #3 }
{ In this step we copy the sprite to the display dc using SRCPAINT }
StartTime := timeGetTime;
StretchDIBits(
                Composite,
                DstRect.Left, DstRect.Top, DstRect.Right, DstRect.Bottom,
                SrcRect.Left, SrcRect.Top, SrcRect.Right, SrcRect.Bottom,
                Moth.Sprite.ptrBits,
                Moth.Sprite.ptrBitmapInfo^,
                DIB_RGB_COLORS,
                SRCPAINT
                );

{timing stuff}
if (DstRect.Right < 0) or
   (DstRect.Bottom < 0)
   then inc(Step3TimeF, timeGetTime - StartTime)
else
  inc(Step3TimeN, timeGetTime - StartTime);
```

```
{ STEP #4 }
{ Blt the composite dc to the screen }
StartTime := timeGetTime;
dc := GetDC(Main.Panel1.Handle);
BitBlt(
        dc,
        DirtyRect.Left, DirtyRect.Top+1, DirtyRect.Right, DirtyRect.Bottom,
        Composite,
        DirtyRect.Left, DirtyRect.Top,
        SRCCOPY
        );
ReleaseDC(Main.Panel1.Handle, dc);
inc(Step4Time, timeGetTime - StartTime);

{timing stuff}
if Itterations mod 100 = 0 then begin
   Main.Caption := '(Step1: ' + IntToStr(Step1Time div Itterations) + 'ms)' +
                   '(Step2: ' + IntToStr(Step2TimeN div ItterationsN) + 'ms' +
                   ', ' + IntToStr(Step2TimeF div ItterationsF) + 'ms)' +
                   '(Step3: ' + IntToStr(Step3TimeN div ItterationsN) + 'ms' +
                   ', ' + IntToStr(Step3TimeF div ItterationsF) + 'ms)' +
                   '(Step4: ' + IntToStr(Step4Time div Itterations) + 'ms)';
   end;

end; {DrawMoth}

procedure TMain.FormCreate(Sender: TObject);
var
   FirstPos: TPosition;
   ImageWidth,
   ImageHeight: integer;

begin
   {Arrange the components}
   ClientWidth := imgBackground.Picture.Bitmap.Width;
   Panel1.Height := imgBackground.Picture.Bitmap.Height+2;
   ClientHeight := round(imgBackground.Picture.Bitmap.Height * 1.25);

   {Setup the Moth}
   Moth := TSprite.Create;
   Moth.CellCount := 4;
   Moth.Source := ExtractFilePath(Application.EXEName) + 'moth.bmp';
   FirstPos.Left := 50;
   FirstPos.Top := 50;
   Moth.CurPos := FirstPos;
   Moth.OffsetX := 2;
   Moth.OffsetY := 2;

   {Setup the buffers}
   ImageWidth := imgBackground.Picture.Bitmap.Width;
   ImageHeight := imgBackground.Picture.Bitmap.Height;

   BG := CreateCompatibleDC(imgBackground.Picture.Bitmap.Canvas.Handle);
   hBackgroundBitmap := CreateCompatibleBitmap(
```

```
                              imgBackground.Picture.Bitmap.Canvas.Handle,
                              ImageWidth, ImageHeight
                              );
  hOldBitmap := SelectObject(BG, hBackgroundBitmap);
  BitBlt( BG, 0,0,ImageWidth, ImageHeight,
          imgBackground.Picture.Bitmap.Canvas.Handle,
          0,0,
          SRCCOPY
          );

  Composite := CreateCompatibleDC(imgBackground.Picture.Bitmap.Canvas.Handle);
  hCompositeBitmap := CreateCompatibleBitmap(
                          BG, ImageWidth, ImageHeight
                          );
  SelectObject(Composite, hCompositeBitmap);

end;

procedure TMain.FormDestroy(Sender: TObject);
begin
  Moth.Free;

  SelectObject(BG, hOldBitmap);
  DeleteDC(BG);

  SelectObject(Composite, hOldBitmap);
  DeleteDC(Composite);

  DeleteObject(hBackgroundBitmap);
  DeleteObject(hCompositeBitmap);

end;

procedure TMain.Button1Click(Sender: TObject);
const
  Interval = 10;
  Quitting: boolean = True;

var
  StartTime: longint;

begin

  Quitting := Not Quitting;
  if Quitting then
    Button1.Caption := 'Start'
  else Button1.Caption := 'Stop';

  while not Quitting do begin

    StartTime := timeGetTime;
    while (timeGetTime - StartTime) < Interval do
      Application.ProcessMessages;
    MoveMoth;
    DrawMoth;
```

```
      end;

end; {Button1Click}

procedure TMain.chkFlipHClick(Sender: TObject);
begin
  if chkFlipH.Checked then
    Moth.FlipH := True
  else Moth.FlipH := False;
end;

procedure TMain.chkFlipVClick(Sender: TObject);
begin
  if chkFlipV.Checked then
    Moth.FlipV := True
  else Moth.FlipV := False;
end;

end.
```

Listing 14.11   The DrawMoth procedure

```
procedure DrawMoth;
var
  SrcRect,
  DstRect,
  DirtyRect: TRect;
  dc: hDC;

  StartTime: longint;
const

  Itterations:   longint = 0;
  ItterationsN:  longint = 1;
  ItterationsF:  longint = 1;
  Step1Time:     longint = 0;
  Step2TimeN:    longint = 0;
  Step2TimeF:    longint = 0;
  Step3TimeN:    longint = 0;
  Step3TimeF:    longint = 0;
  Step4Time:     longint = 0;

begin

  {Timing Stuff}
  inc(Itterations);

  {Calculate the dirty rectangle}
  with Moth do begin
    if OffsetX > 0 then begin
      DirtyRect.Left := PrvPos.Left;
      DirtyRect.Right := CellWidth + OffsetX;
      end
```

```
      else begin
        DirtyRect.Left := CurPos.Left;
        DirtyRect.Right := CellWidth + Abs(OffsetX);
        end;

     if OffsetY > 0 then begin
        DirtyRect.Top := PrvPos.Top;
        DirtyRect.Bottom := CellHeight + OffsetY;
        end
      else begin
        DirtyRect.Top := CurPos.Top;
        DirtyRect.Bottom := CellHeight + Abs(OffsetY);
        end;

    end; {with Moth}

{ STEP #1 }
{ First we copy the saved background to the composite buffer}
StartTime := timeGetTime;
BitBlt(
       Composite,
       DirtyRect.Left, DirtyRect.Top, DirtyRect.Right, DirtyRect.Bottom,
       BG,
       DirtyRect.Left, DirtyRect.Top,
       SRCCOPY
       );
inc(Step1Time, timeGetTime - StartTime);

{ STEP #2 }
{ In this step we copy the sprite mask to the composite dc using SRCAND }
StartTime := timeGetTime;
SrcRect := Moth.CurCellRect;
DstRect := Moth.CurDestRect;

StretchDIBits(
              Composite,
              DstRect.Left, DstRect.Top, DstRect.Right, DstRect.Bottom,
              SrcRect.Left, SrcRect.Top, SrcRect.Right, SrcRect.Bottom,
              Moth.Mask.ptrBits,
              Moth.Mask.ptrBitmapInfo^,
              DIB_RGB_COLORS,
              SRCAND
              );

{timing stuff}
if (DstRect.Right < 0) or
   (DstRect.Bottom < 0) then
   begin
     inc(Step2TimeF, timeGetTime - StartTime);
     inc(ItterationsF);
   end
else begin
  inc(Step2TimeN, timeGetTime - StartTime);
  inc(ItterationsN);
  end;
```

Better Animation

```
{ STEP #3 }
{ In this step we copy the sprite to the display dc using SRCPAINT }
StartTime := timeGetTime;
StretchDIBits(
            Composite,
            DstRect.Left, DstRect.Top, DstRect.Right, DstRect.Bottom,
            SrcRect.Left, SrcRect.Top, SrcRect.Right, SrcRect.Bottom,
            Moth.Sprite.ptrBits,
            Moth.Sprite.ptrBitmapInfo^,
            DIB_RGB_COLORS,
            SRCPAINT
            );

{timing stuff}
if (DstRect.Right < 0) or
   (DstRect.Bottom < 0)
    then inc(Step3TimeF, timeGetTime - StartTime)
else
   inc(Step3TimeN, timeGetTime - StartTime);

{ STEP #4 }
{ Blt the composite dc to the screen }
StartTime := timeGetTime;
dc := GetDC(Main.Panel1.Handle);
BitBlt(
       dc,
       DirtyRect.Left, DirtyRect.Top+1, DirtyRect.Right, DirtyRect.Bottom,
       Composite,
       DirtyRect.Left, DirtyRect.Top,
       SRCCOPY
       );
ReleaseDC(Main.Panel1.Handle, dc);
inc(Step4Time, timeGetTime - StartTime);

{timing stuff}
if Itterations mod 100 = 0 then begin
   Main.Caption := '(Step1: ' + IntToStr(Step1Time div Itterations) + 'ms)' +
                   '(Step2: ' + IntToStr(Step2TimeN div ItterationsN) + 'ms' +
                   ', ' + IntToStr(Step2TimeF div ItterationsF) + 'ms)' +
                   '(Step3: ' + IntToStr(Step3TimeN div ItterationsN) + 'ms' +
                   ', ' + IntToStr(Step3TimeF div ItterationsF) + 'ms)' +
                   '(Step4: ' + IntToStr(Step4Time div Itterations) + 'ms)';
    end;

end; {DrawMoth}
```

The **DrawMoth** procedure is structured the same as the previous version. Any difference at all? Where we were previously using a canvas' **CopyRect** method, we now use either **BitBlt** or **StretchDIBits**. That's it.

In Step 1, we blt the contents of the background memory *dc* to the composite *dc*. We're using the dirty rectangle calculation we developed in the

SPRITE4 project. We ditched the compiler directive, since we found that the time it takes to calculate the dirty rectangle is much less than the time wasted by drawing areas of the screen that don't need to be updated.

In Steps 2 and 3, we use an API function called **StretchDIBits** to get the mask and sprite bitmaps to the composite buffer. We'll see when we finally run this version of the program that StretchDIBits is much faster than the **CopyRect** method of **TCanvas**.

Step #4 completes the draw routine by blting the constructed image to the screen.

Running the Program

Either compile the project or run Sprite5.exe from the companion CD-ROM. Check the *Flip Horizontal* checkbox and let the moth fly around for several seconds until timing has stabilized in the program's title bar. Figure 14.4 shows the SPRITE5 program in action, and Table 14.3 shows comparative results between SPRITE4 and SPRITE5. These results were taken from the programs running on a Toshiba Satellite Pro 400CDT with 16MB RAM and a Pentium 75 processor.

We're using **timeGetTime** to gauge the drawing times. The Win32s Developer's Reference claims that **timeGetTime** is precise to 1ms. Since the precision is 1ms and there are four steps involved, each of the four timing calculations introduces a significant amount of error in the overall draw time. The data we're receiving from the timing mechanism is valuable as comparative information, but you should keep in mind that it is not precise.

Figure 14.4 *The Sprite5 program.*

Table 14.3 *Comparative Draw Timings.*

Draw Operation	Sprite4	Sprite5
Step #1	1ms	0ms
Step #2	1ms	1ms
Step #2 flipped	14ms	9ms
Step #3	1ms	1ms
Step #3 flipped	14ms	9ms
Step #4	1ms	1ms

Enhancing the Sprite Animation

You can see from the results in Table 14.3 that each draw when the moth is traveling from right to left spends about 95% of the time performing the stretch. If we were to improve our technique, that would be an excellent place to start. We could create TDIB properties called ReversedSprite and ReversedMask and initialize them once at startup. This alternative would gobble a little more memory, but it would reduce the draw time by about 16ms. That enhancement would not only be valuable for the speed increase, but it would balance the draw speed in each horizontal direction. In its current state, the sprite moves faster in one direction. This erratic behavior would require more code to bring the two speeds into sync.

The motion algorithm could also use some further development. The moth's movement may be slightly too random right now. It jitters about on the screen without any sense of purpose. Depending on the application, the movement may need to take elements of the background into consideration. You may want it to flutter from flower to flower with more purpose than it is displaying.

You could also implement a more sophisticated cell selection method. We're animating the moth by cycling through the cells over and over in the same direction. The simplest improvement to this would be to implement a Ping-Pong motion. That would be better, although it is still rather mechanical. I don't think we would find a moth in nature whose wings opened and closed to the exact same position each time. You could implement a method of changing the order of cell selection periodically.

Now that you know how to display and move sprites, you can expand the construction set we've developed in this chapter to add all kinds of interesting motion to your Delphi programs.

Introducing the Latest Animation Technology

The techniques we've developed in the last couple of chapters are genuinely usable techniques for sprite animation. I've already pointed out several places where they can be enhanced, but they still represent a good base. We discovered that the type of draw routine we use has a dramatic influence on the overall performance independent of the technique. Using BitBlt and StretchDIBits was much faster than the CopyRect method.

There are several other sets of low-level drawing functions that are worth mentioning here. WinG is a technology that Microsoft developed for *fast* display of bitmapped graphics in the Windows 3.x operating environment. WinG provides a fast drawing surface for bitmapped graphics. The same technology that was WinG in Windows 3.x is now built-in to the Windows 95 environment. Programmers access it through the function CreateDIBSection.

The latest technology for game and multimedia development is in Microsoft's Games Software Development Kit (Games SDK). This SDK includes four main components: DirectDraw, DirectSound, DirectPlay, and DirectInput, collectively called the DirectX libraries. DirectDraw, gives programmers direct access to video hardware through a set of low-level APIs. Likewise, DirectSound, DirectPlay, and DirectInput give the programmer direct access to the hardware associated with each technology.

Since the DirectX technologies are intended for very low-level programming, you might like to know that libraries are available for Delphi that encapsulate the technology to provide access at a higher level. One such library is FastGraph for Windows from Ted Gruber Software. At the time of this writing, the FastGraph libraries for Delphi 2.0 are in Beta about to be released. I have used the FastGraph libraries for some time now with Delphi 1.0 and have been very happy with their ease of use and performance. In fact, I had an opportunity to beta test the Delphi 2.0 FastGraph libraries while working on this book. In addition to *lightning speed*, they take advantage of the 32-bit flat memory model. In the 16-bit version several of the routines are limited to 64k blocks, which tends to complicate the code.

Chapter 15

With a mastery of digital audio you'll turn that boring presentation into an exciting, attention grabbing, multimedia showcase.

Exploring Waveform Audio

Chris D. Coppola

We've told you that multimedia is a visual medium. But what about sound? You certainly don't want to underestimate its value when it comes to creating entertaining or educational multimedia applications. After all, imagine what it would be like to see Steven Spielberg's latest action adventure movie with no sound. You'd be missing out on half the fun—after all, it's the roar of the Tyrannosaurus Rex that makes you cling to your seat.

In this chapter, we'll start you on the road to mastering the basics of digital audio. We'll discuss the technologies involved in digital audio, including redbook audio, MIDI, pulse code modulation, and digital sampling. For our first project, we'll create an application that will let us experiment with WAV files. This project illustrates how low-level Windows API calls can be used to play sounds and add echo effects by directly manipulating the audio data. The overall goal is to show you how waveform data can be manipulated at the byte level.

In the second part of the chapter, we'll show you how to manipulate WAV files as they are being played in real time. We'll do this using Microsoft's DirectSound—the state-of-the-art in digital audio technology for Windows.

Audio: A Potent Medium

Movie and television producers spend a small fortune on their soundtracks. The sound production often nearly equals the cost of the visual work. When sitting in a dark theater, watching twenty-feet-high and forty-feet-wide pictures, you probably aren't entirely aware of all the things you hear—the low tones that trigger your anxiety, the reverberating footsteps, and the rhythm of the musical soundtrack.

Few people realize that most of what they hear in a movie theater, on a music CD, or on television, has been carefully fabricated. In the movies, a gunshot may reverberate from cliff to canyon; but when you record the sound of a gunshot, all you usually catch on tape is a popping noise, no more impressive than a kid's cap gun. From there, the sound engineers craft that recording; give it weight, filter out noise, stretch its duration, and mix in low frequency subharmonics. To locate it in space, whether the ringing is confinedto an underground garage or an echoing Rocky Mountain pass, they adjust the volume, balance, and Surround Sound™ effects, running it through a digital effects processor to add reverberation.

If we're going to produce multimedia powerful enough to draw people away from their televisions, we had better learn the methods of sound production and learn how to create the tools necessary for applying them to our projects.

Checking Out the Options

Unfortunately, VB provides no intrinsic support for sound. But as you learned in Chapter 3, that won't hold us back at all. In fact, the Windows multimedia system has so many sound options it can be hard to decide which to use. Let's sort them out.

Redbook Audio

When you pop a music CD into your Discman™ and press the Play button, you're listening to redbook audio. The specifications for the various data formats available on compact disk come in color-coded books; the cover of the standard audio specification is red, hence "redbook audio." With the MCI, you can play audio CDs on your CD-ROM drive. Just plug the analog audio output of your CD-ROM drive into any amplifier; you don't even need a sound card. If both the Microsoft MSCDEX.EXE CD driver and the Windows [MCI] CD Audio drivers are loaded, you can use the Media Player—or the Windows 95 CD player—to operate the drive and listen to your favorite tunes. If you have an internal CD-ROM drive and a sound card, you may have connected the drive to the card with a thin, three-wire audio cable. This cable does nothing more than act as an external audio cable. It simply connects the analog audio outputs of the drive to the line-level analog inputs of the mixer/amplifier on the sound card.

Redbook audio is digital, and many sound cards can play and record digital audio at the same 16-bit, 44.1 kHz sampling rate that redbook uses. However, no standard drivers—and as far as I know, no commercially available CD-ROM drives or sound cards—will let you "read" the digital sound data on the redbook audio tracks. You may use the MCI driver to select tracks, query the drive for timing or other information, play tracks, or manipulate the disk in a variety of other ways. But the conversion of the digital audio into an analog signal is handled entirely by the digital to analog converter (DAC) inside the drive.

Does this mean we can't use redbook audio in our multimedia projects? Not by a long shot. Although the mastering process is different, redbook audio and CD-ROM data can, and often do, cohabit on the same disk. That's how titles like Microsoft/Voyager's Multimedia Beethoven or 7th Level's Tuneland with Howie Mandel work.

MIDI

The musical instrument digital interface (MIDI) actually makes no sound at all. MIDI is just a protocol that enables computers, synthesizers, keyboards, and other musical devices to communicate with each other. Almost every PC sound card available today includes some kind of built-in synthesizer. To play music on it, though, you have to send it messages that tell it which instrument sound (known as a patch) to use and which note to play. You'll also need to provide information for volume control and other sound qualities. MIDI is a specification that defines both the serial interface used by instruments to communicate with each other, and the message codes that travel over those links.

MIDI is the most economical type of multimedia sound. For example, to hold a single synthesizer note for an hour would require just 6 bytes—a 3 byte message to start the note, and a 3 byte message to stop it. In contrast, one hour of the lowest-fidelity waveform data would fill 39,690,000 bytes! MIDI enables you to store lengthy musical passages in just a few kilobytes or tens of kilobytes. As another advantage, it allows you to change music on the fly. For example, you can transpose an entire piece to another key just by adding or subtracting a constant from all the note numbers. You can also change the playback speed of MIDI music without affecting its pitch.

The major disadvantage of MIDI is that the quality of sound it produces depends entirely on the synthesizer on which it is played, whether it be a sound card or an external synthesizer. Even two cards that use the same synthesizer chip can have different sounds programmed into it.

We'll examine MIDI in more detail in the next chapter.

Waveform Audio

Waveform audio is the workhorse of PC multimedia sound. With waveform audio, you can do anything within the practical limitations of memory, disk storage, processor speed, and the capabilities of your sound card. Depending on your needs, you shouldn't necessarily skip MIDI and redbook audio altogether; however, waveform audio offers the most general-purpose sound system. You can record and play music, sound effects, narration—anything you could do with a tape recorder, you can do with waveform audio.

Like CD audio, waveform audio is a digital medium. Unlike CD audio, however, it supports a variety of formats, from 8-bit monophonic at a sampling rate of 11,025 samples per second (11,025 bytes per second) to 16-bit stereo at a rate of 44,100 samples per second (176,400 bytes per second!). Also unlike CD audio, you can read and write it, store and retrieve it—in short, manipulate it to your heart's content.

The waveform data format you choose—in other words, the sampling rate, number of channels (mono versus stereo), and bit resolution (8 versus 16)—should depend not only upon the capabilities of the sound card on which you develop your presentations, but also upon the capabilities of the sound cards on which they must eventually play.

Digital Audio Basics

Waveform audio is stored in a format known as pulse code modulation, or PCM, which is the ten-dollar term for the seven-and-a-half-dollar term "digital sampling." The principle is actually pretty simple.

Sound consists of a pressure wave moving through a medium, such as air. For each wave pulse there is a traveling zone of compressed air, trailed by a zone of rarefied air. To represent sound electronically, the compression is represented by a positive voltage and the rarefaction by a negative voltage. The voltage level determines the amplitude of the wave. A pure sine wave forms a nice rolling voltage, gradually switching from a positive value to a negative value of the same degree, and back again, as illustrated in the top

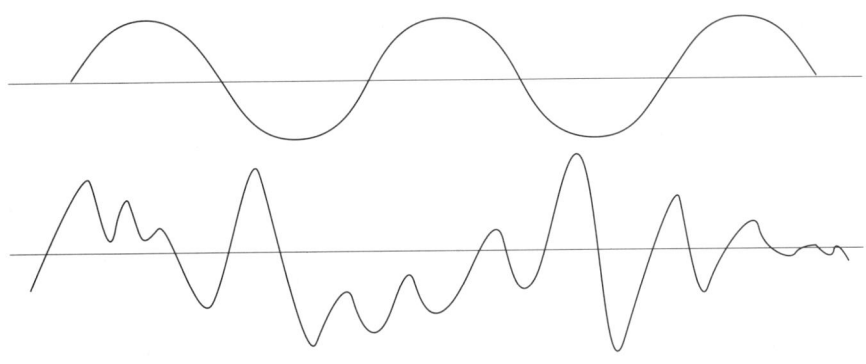

Figure 15.1 *A pure and not-so-pure sound waveform.*

portion of Figure 15.1. But most sounds aren't that pure. They include numerous sine waves and possibly other waveforms, all added together to form an irregular pattern, as shown in the bottom portion of Figure 15.1.

To represent an analog waveform digitally, the voltage levels of the wave are sampled at regular intervals and stored as numbers. Audible frequencies range from about 50 Hz (cycles per second) to over 20,000 Hz. To record a meaningful digital representation, you need to sample the waveform frequently. In fact, it was proven mathematically in 1948, by Claude Shannon of Bell Laboratories, that you can accurately represent any analog signal with a digital sampling rate equal to twice the maximum frequency contained in the source. That's why CD audio is recorded at a frequency of 44.1 kHz—twice the maximum audible frequency (at least to humans).

You needn't preserve the full fidelity of the original analog signal, however. By sampling at lower rates, you don't lose the sound entirely, just the higher frequencies. This can produce the "AM radio" effect—the conversion of rich, full-bodied sound into tinny, cracker-box sound.

Sampling rate isn't the only factor that determines fidelity. The resolution of the sample—that is, the number of bits per sample—can also have a major impact. Regardless of the sampling rate, 8-bit samples cannot accurately represent sound. The human brain, by way of its audio sensors (ears!) can distinguish very subtle differences in amplitude and frequency. With only 256 recordable levels, many of the subtler elements of a complex sound disappear. This loss is called aliasing. This is the audio equivalent of the stairstep aliasing that appears when you blow up bitmap images, or the color banding you often see when you convert a true color image to an 8-bit palette—especially in broad areas of graduated color, such as a clear blue sky. On the other hand, 16-bit sampling can differentiate over 65,000 signal levels, which makes it possible to represent a sound with much greater fidelity by just doubling the storage demand.

Whatever the sampling rate and bit resolution of the digital waveform, the format of the data is simple. In 8-bit samples, each byte represents an amplitude. If the sample contains two channels of audio—in other words, stereo—the left channel is recorded in the even-numbered bytes, beginning with byte zero, and the right channel is recorded in the odd-numbered bytes, beginning with byte one. 8-bit values have no sign, so a value of 128 represents the baseline of the data. Values higher than 128 represent positive amplitudes, and values lower than 128 represent negative amplitudes. Since 8 bits represent an even number of possible values, the choice of 128 as the baseline is arbitrary; although 127 would work just as well, 128 is the standard.

In 16-bit wave files, each sample occupies two bytes, which happen to represent an ordinary signed integer. Amplitudes range in value from −32,768 to 32,767. In stereo 16-bit wave files, every other pair of bytes contains the data for one channel. Consequently, bytes zero and one contain the first sample of the left channel, bytes two and three contain the first sample of the right channel, bytes four and five contain the second sample of the left channel, and so on.

The best way to understand waveform audio and to appreciate its simplicity is to fiddle with it. In the next project, we'll expand on the code we developed in Chapter 5 to read, play, and modify waveform data (WAV) files with the low-level audio API functions.

Playing and Modifying Wave Data

In the last section of Chapter 5, we used the multimedia I/O functions and the low-level audio functions to read and play a wave audio file. We'll use some simple audio processing techniques to adjust the overall loudness, or level, of a sample and to add echo effects. Here are the steps to follow:

1. Start a new project.
2. Setup the main form.
3. Add event handling code in the form's code unit.
4. Copy the units: WaveWrap.pas, WavePlay.pas, and MMIOWrap.pas from the chapter 5 directory to the new project directory.
5. Modify the units as indicated.

This project is located in the directory \delphimm\15\Wave2

Creating the Wave2 Project

Create a new project and save it using uwave2.pas and wave2.dpr for names. Rather than adding components and setting all of the properties manually for the projects main form—we're going to cheat a little. With any text editor (including the editor window in Delphi), open the file uwave2.dfm from the project directory on the CD-ROM. Copy the contents of that file onto the clipboard. Now right-click on the default form in Delphi and select 'view as text' from the menu. The form definition should appear in the editor window under a new tab. Select all of the text and paste to replace it with the text copied from uwave2.dfm. Now right-click on the editor window and select 'view form.' The result should be a main form resembling that in Figure 15.2. If you prefer, the text for the form definition is in Listing 15.1. The text can be directly entered when the form is viewed as text. Next copy the files wavewrap.pas, waveplay.pas, and mmiowrap.pas to the project directory and add them to the project.

Listing 15.1   uWave2.dfm

```
object Main: TMain
  Left = 205
  Top = 116
  Width = 273
  Height = 370
  Caption = 'Digital Audio Effects'
  Font.Color = clWindowText
  Font.Height = -11
```

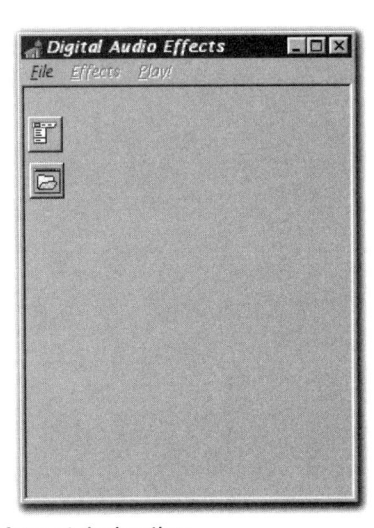

Figure 15.2   *The Wave2 form at design time.*

```
  Font.Name = 'MS Sans Serif'
  Font.Style = []
  Menu = MainMenu1
  Position = poScreenCenter
  WindowMenu = mnuFile
  OnDestroy = FormDestroy
  PixelsPerInch = 96
  TextHeight = 13
  object reCaps: TRichEdit
    Left = 0
    Top = 0
    Width = 265
    Height = 327
    Align = alClient
    Color = clBtnFace
    ReadOnly = True
    ScrollBars = ssVertical
    TabOrder = 0
  end
  object MainMenu1: TMainMenu
    Left = 5
    Top = 25
    object mnuFile: TMenuItem
      Caption = '&File'
      ShortCut = 0
      object mnuFOpen: TMenuItem
        Caption = '&Open'
        ShortCut = 16463
        OnClick = mnuFOpenClick
      end
      object mnuFGetCaps: TMenuItem
        Caption = '&Get Device Caps'
        ShortCut = 16455
        OnClick = mnuFGetCapsClick
      end
      object mnuBreak: TMenuItem
        Caption = '-'
        ShortCut = 0
      end
      object mnuFExit: TMenuItem
        Caption = 'E&xit'
        ShortCut = 0
        OnClick = mnuFExitClick
      end
    end
    object mnuEffects: TMenuItem
      Caption = '&Effects'
      Enabled = False
      ShortCut = 0
      object mnuEVolDown: TMenuItem
        Caption = '&Decrease Volume'
        ShortCut = 0
        OnClick = mnuEVolClick
      end
```

```
      object mnuEVolUp: TMenuItem
        Tag = 1
        Caption = 'I&ncrease Volume'
        ShortCut = 0
        OnClick = mnuEVolClick
      end
      object mnuEEcho: TMenuItem
        Caption = '&Echo'
        ShortCut = 0
        OnClick = mnuEEchoClick
      end
    end
    object mnuPlay: TMenuItem
      Caption = '&Play!'
      Enabled = False
      ShortCut = 0
      OnClick = mnuPlayClick
    end
  end
  object OpenDialog1: TOpenDialog
    DefaultExt = 'wav'
    FileEditStyle = fsEdit
    Filter = 'Digital Audio Files|*.wav'
    Title = 'Select the WAV file to open'
    Left = 6
    Top = 61
  end
end
```

Let's look at the big picture. UWave2.pas, shown in Listing 15.2, is the unit that handles events such as menu clicks. Therefore, it controls the program execution. The program works with one wave file at a time, which is represented by the global variable **WaveForm**. This variable is created in the **File|Open** event procedure with the help of the **TOpenDialog** component and supporting Wave and I/O classes. Also in the same procedure, information about the Wave file is displayed in the **TRichEdit** component. Once the file is loaded successfully, the menu options to play, change volume, and add echo to the Wave are enabled. The File menu also contains an option to retrieve the capabilities of the Wave output device and quit the program.

Listing 15.2   uWave2.pas

```
unit uWave2;

interface

uses
  Windows, Messages, SysUtils, Classes, Graphics, Controls, Forms, Dialogs,
  Menus, ExtCtrls, StdCtrls, ComCtrls, WaveWrap, WavePlay, MMIOWrap;
```

```
type
  TMain = class(TForm)
    MainMenu1: TMainMenu;
    mnuFile: TMenuItem;
    mnuFOpen: TMenuItem;
    mnuEffects: TMenuItem;
    mnuPlay: TMenuItem;
    reCaps: TRichEdit;
    mnuFGetCaps: TMenuItem;
    mnuBreak: TMenuItem;
    mnuFExit: TMenuItem;
    OpenDialog1: TOpenDialog;
    mnuEVolDown: TMenuItem;
    mnuEEcho: TMenuItem;
    mnuEVolUp: TMenuItem;
    procedure mnuFExitClick(Sender: TObject);
    procedure mnuFGetCapsClick(Sender: TObject);
    procedure FormDestroy(Sender: TObject);
    procedure mnuFOpenClick(Sender: TObject);
    procedure mnuPlayClick(Sender: TObject);
    procedure mnuEVolClick(Sender: TObject);
    procedure mnuEEchoClick(Sender: TObject);
  private
    { Private declarations }
  public
    { Public declarations }
  end;

var
  Main: TMain;

implementation

{$R *.DFM}
var
  WaveForm: tAudio_waveform;

function Clip8(Value: integer): byte;
  begin
    if Value > 127 then
      Value := 127;
    if Value < -128 then
      Value := -128;
    result := Value + 128;
  end; {Clip8}

function Clip16(Value: integer): SmallInt;
  begin
    if Value > 32767 then
      Value := 32767;
    if Value < -32768 then
      Value := -32768;
    result := Value;
  end; {Clip16}
```

```
procedure TMain.FormDestroy(Sender: TObject);
begin
  with reCaps.Lines do
    if Count > 0 then Clear;

  WaveForm.Free;

end;

procedure TMain.mnuFExitClick(Sender: TObject);
begin
  Self.Close;
end;

procedure TMain.mnuFGetCapsClick(Sender: TObject);
var
  i: integer;

begin

  with tWave_device.Create do
    try
      try
        GetOutCaps(0);
        with reCaps.Lines do begin
          if Count > 0 then Clear;
          Add('Manufacturer''s Driver ID: ' + IntToStr(Caps.wMid));
          Add('Product ID: ' + IntToStr(Caps.wPid));
          Add('Driver Version: ' +
            IntToStr(hi(Caps.vDriverVersion)) + '.' +
            IntToStr(lo(Caps.vDriverVersion))
            );
          Add('Product Name: ' + StrPas(Caps.szPname) );

          Add('Wave Formats Supported:');
          for i := 0 to NUM_WAVE_FORMATS-1 do
            if Caps.dwFormats and (1 shl i) = (1 shl i) then
              Add('   ' + WaveFormatString(1 shl i));

          Add('Number of Channels: ' + IntToStr(Caps.wChannels));

          Add('Wave Functions Supported:');
          for i := 0 to NUM_WAVE_FUNCTIONS-1 do
            if Caps.dwSupport and (1 shl i) = (1 shl i) then
              Add('   ' + WaveFunctionString(1 shl i));

        end; {with reCaps.Lines}

      except
        on E : eWave_error do
          MessageDlg(
            IntToStr(E.Wave_result) + ': ' + E.Message,
            mtError,
            [mbOK],
```

```
                    0
                    );
            end; {except}
         finally
            Free;
         end; {finally}

end; {GetCapsClick}

procedure TMain.mnuFOpenClick(Sender: TObject);
begin
   if OpenDialog1.Execute then begin
      WaveForm := tAudio_waveform.Create;
      with WaveForm do
         try
            Read(pchar(OpenDialog1.Filename));
            mnuPlay.Enabled := True;
            mnuEffects.Enabled := True;

            {Display Information about the wav file}
            with reCaps.Lines do begin
               if Count > 0 then Clear;
               Add('Wave File Information:');
               Add('File Name: ' + OpenDialog1.FileName);
               if Format.wFormatTag = WAVE_FORMAT_PCM then
                  Add('PCM Digital Audio')
                  else
                     Add('Non-PCM format: ' + IntToStr(Format.wFormatTag));

               if Format.nChannels = 1 then
                  Add('Mono')
                  else
                     Add('Stereo');

               Add('Samples per second: ' + IntToStr(Format.nSamplesPerSec));
               Add('Bits per Sample: ' + IntToStr(Format.wBitsPerSample));
               Add('Avg Data Rate: ' + IntToStr(Format.nAvgBytesPerSec) +
                                 ' bytes/sec' );

            end; {with reCaps.Lines}

         except
            on E : eMMIO_error do
               MessageDlg(
                  'MMIO Error ' + IntToStr(E.MMIO_result) + ': ' + E.Message,
                  mtError,
                  [mbOK], 0
                  );
            on E : eWave_error do
               MessageDlg(
                  'Wave Error ' + IntToStr(E.Wave_result) + ': ' + E.Message,
                  mtError,
                  [mbOK], 0
```

Exploring Waveform Audio

```delphi
                            );
            end; {except}

        end; {if open}

    end; {FOpenClick}

procedure TMain.mnuPlayClick(Sender: TObject);
begin
  try
    WaveForm.Play;
  except
    on E : eMMIO_error do
        MessageDlg(
          'MMIO Error ' + IntToStr(E.MMIO_result) + ': ' + E.Message,
          mtError,
          [mbOK], 0
          );

    on E : eWave_error do
        MessageDlg(
          'Wave Error ' + IntToStr(E.Wave_result) + ': ' + E.Message,
          mtError,
          [mbOK], 0
          );
    end; {except}
end;

procedure TMain.mnuEVolClick(Sender: TObject);
var
  p8bitSample:   ^Byte;
  p16bitSample:  ^SmallInt;
  i:             integer;
  LevelFactor:   real;

begin

  {Check to see which menu option was clicked and then
   set the appropriate level factor to decrease or
   increase the volume of the wave. }
  if TMenuItem(Sender).Tag = 0 then
    LevelFactor := 0.5
  else
    LevelFactor := 1.5;

  {disable functionality while processing}
  Main.reCaps.Cursor := crHourglass;
  mnuEffects.Enabled := False;
  mnuPlay.Enabled := False;

  {process the waveform data to increase/decrease the volume}
  with WaveForm do begin
    if Format.wFormatTag = WAVE_FORMAT_PCM then begin
      if Format.wBitsPerSample = 8 then begin
```

```pascal
            {working with an 8-bit, sample}
            p8bitSample := addr(Data^);
            for i := 0 to Header.dwBufferLength-1 do begin
              p8bitSample^ := Clip8(
                             Round((p8bitSample^ - 128) * LevelFactor)
                             );
              inc(p8bitSample);
              end;
            end
          else if (Format.wBitsPerSample = 16) then begin
            {working with a 16-bit, sample}
            p16bitSample := addr(Data^);
            for i := 0 to ((Header.dwBufferLength-1) div 2) do begin
              p16bitSample^ := Clip16(Round(p16bitSample^ * LevelFactor));
              inc(p16bitSample);
              end; {for}
            end;
          end {if PCM}
        else
          MessageDlg('Non-PCM format audio', mtError, [mbOK], 0);

      end; {with}

    Main.reCaps.Cursor := crDefault;
    mnuEffects.Enabled := True;
    mnuPlay.Enabled := True;

end; {ELevelsClick}

procedure TMain.mnuEEchoClick(Sender: TObject);
const
  Gain = 50;
  Delay = 500;
  TrailingEchos = 3;

var
  pPrev8bitSample,
  p8bitSample:    ^Byte;
  pPrev16bitSample,
  p16bitSample: ^SmallInt;
  i:              integer;
  szNewBuffer:    Cardinal;
  NewData:        PChar;
  GainFactor,
  Period:    integer;


begin

  {disable functionality while processing}
  Main.reCaps.Cursor := crHourglass;
  mnuEffects.Enabled := False;
  mnuPlay.Enabled := False;

  {process the waveform data to add an echo effect}
```

Exploring Waveform Audio

```
with WaveForm do begin
  GainFactor := Gain div 50;
  Period := Delay * Format.nSamplesPerSec div 1000;

  if Format.wFormatTag = WAVE_FORMAT_PCM then begin
    if Format.wBitsPerSample = 8 then begin
      {working with an 8-bit sample}
      if Format.nChannels = 2 then
        Period := Period * 2;

      {Re-allocate memory for the new size of the wave data}
      szNewBuffer := (Header.dwBufferLength + (Period * TrailingEchos)) - 1;
      NewData := strAlloc(szNewBuffer);
      StrMove(NewData, Data, Header.dwBufferLength);
      StrDispose(Data);
      Data := NewData;

      {initialize the new part of the buffer to 128}
      p8bitSample := addr(Data^);
      inc(p8bitSample, Header.dwBufferLength);
      for i := Header.dwBufferLength to szNewBuffer do begin
        p8bitSample^ := 128;
        inc(p8bitSample);
        end; {for}

      {Add the echo effect}
      p8bitSample := addr(Data^);
      pPrev8bitSample := addr(Data^);
      inc(p8bitSample, Period);
      for i := Period to szNewBuffer do begin
        p8bitSample^ := Clip8(((p8bitSample^ - 128) +
                      (pPrev8bitSample^ - 128) * GainFactor) div 2);
        inc(p8bitSample);
        inc(pPrev8bitSample);
        end; {for}

      Header.lpData := Data;
      Header.dwBufferLength := szNewBuffer + 1;

      end
    else if Format.wBitsPerSample = 16 then begin
      {working with a 16-bit sample}
      if Format.nChannels = 2 then
        Period := Period * 4
      else
        Period := Period * 2;

      {Re-allocate memory for the new size of the wave data}
      szNewBuffer := (Header.dwBufferLength +
        (Period * TrailingEchos)) - 1;

      NewData := strAlloc(szNewBuffer);
      StrMove(NewData, Data, Header.dwBufferLength);
      StrDispose(Data);
      Data := NewData;
```

```
      {initialize the new part of the buffer to 0}
      p16bitSample := addr(Data^);
      inc(p16bitSample, Header.dwBufferLength div 2);
      for i := 1 to ((szNewBuffer - Header.dwBufferLength) div 2) do begin
        p16bitSample^ := 0;
        inc(p16bitSample);
        end; {for}

      {Add the echo effect}
      p16bitSample := addr(Data^);
      pPrev16bitSample := addr(Data^);
      inc(p16bitSample, Period div 2);
      for i := 1 to ((szNewBuffer - Period) div 2) do begin
        p16bitSample^ := Clip16((p16bitSample^ + pPrev16bitSample^ *
                        GainFactor) div 2);
        inc(p16bitSample);
        inc(pPrev16bitSample);
        end; {for}

      Header.lpData := Data;
      Header.dwBufferLength := szNewBuffer + 1;

      end;
    end {if PCM}
  else
    MessageDlg('Non-PCM format audio', mtError, [mbOK], 0);

  end; {with}

Main.reCaps.Cursor := crDefault;
mnuEffects.Enabled := True;
mnuPlay.Enabled := True;

end; {EEchoClick}

end.
```

Checking Wave Output Capabilities

Now let's take a closer look at how some of the code works. The event code that displays the capabilities of the Wave output device is in **mnuFGetCapsClick**. This procedure, shown in Listing 15.3, uses the **tWave_device** method, **GetOutCaps**, to fill a **TWaveOutCaps** structure. The member function **GetOutCaps** actually uses the API function **waveOutGetCaps** to fill the structure with information about the device. The device capabilities, stored in the Caps field of the **tWave_device** object, are then displayed in the **TRichEdit** component. The **TWaveOutCaps** structure contains information about the Wave output device as described below:

```
TWaveOutCaps = record
    wMid: Word;                          { manufacturer ID }
```

```
    wPid: Word;                         { product ID }
    vDriverVersion: MMVERSION;          { version of the driver }
    szPname: array[0..MAXPNAMELEN-1] of AnsiChar;   { product name (NULL
terminated string) }
    dwFormats: DWORD;                   { formats supported }
    wChannels: Word;                    { number of sources supported }
    dwSupport: DWORD;                   { functionality supported by driver }
  end;
```

Most of the fields of **TWaveOutCaps** can be interpreted in a line of code or two. The fields **dwFormats** and **dwSupport**, however, use the helper functions **WaveFormatString** and **WaveFunctionString** to interpret the Double-Word flags and return a meaningful string. Table 15.1 shows a list of the standard PCM waveform formats, and Table 15.2 displays the bit masks that represent sound card functionality.

Table 15.1 *The Standard Wave Format Constants.*

Constant Name	Sampling Rate.	Bit Resolution	Channels	Bit Mask
WAVE_FORMAT_1M08	11.025 kHz	8	Mono	$00000001
WAVE_FORMAT_1S08	11.025 kHz	8	Stereo	$00000002
WAVE_FORMAT_1M16	11.025 kHz	16	Mono	$00000004
WAVE_FORMAT_1S16	11.025 kHz	16	Stereo	$00000008
WAVE_FORMAT_2M08	22.05 kHz	8	Mono	$00000010
WAVE_FORMAT_2S08	22.05 kHz	8	Stereo	$00000020
WAVE_FORMAT_2M16	22.05 kHz	16	Mono	$00000040
WAVE_FORMAT_2S16	22.05 kHz	16	Stereo	$00000080
WAVE_FORMAT_4M08	44.1 kHz	8	Mono	$00000100
WAVE_FORMAT_4S08	44.1 kHz	8	Stereo	$00000200
WAVE_FORMAT_4M16	44.1 kHz	16	Mono	$00000400
WAVE_FORMAT_4S16	44.1 kHz	16	Stereo	$00000800

Table 15.2 *The Bit Masks That Indicate Wave Output Functionality of the Device.*

Constant Name	Value	Meaning
WAVECAPS_PITCH	$00000001	Supports changing playback pitch
WAVECAPS_PLAYBACKRATE	$00000002	Supports changing the playback rate
WAVECAPS_VOLUME	$00000004	Supports changing the playback volume
WAVECAPS_LRVOLUME	$00000008	Supports changing the left and right volume separately

Listing 15.3 The File|Get Device Caps menu

```
procedure TMain.mnuFGetCapsClick(Sender: TObject);
var
  i: integer;

begin

  with tWave_device.Create do
    try
      try
        GetOutCaps(0);
        with reCaps.Lines do begin
          if Count > 0 then Clear;
          Add('Manufacturer''s Driver ID: ' + IntToStr(Caps.wMid));
          Add('Product ID: ' + IntToStr(Caps.wPid));
          Add('Driver Version: ' +
            IntToStr(hi(Caps.vDriverVersion)) + '.' +
            IntToStr(lo(Caps.vDriverVersion))
            );
          Add('Product Name: ' + StrPas(Caps.szPname) );

          Add('Wave Formats Supported:');
          for i := 0 to NUM_WAVE_FORMATS-1 do
            if Caps.dwFormats and (1 shl i) = (1 shl i) then
              Add('  ' + WaveFormatString(1 shl i));

          Add('Number of Channels: ' + IntToStr(Caps.wChannels));

          Add('Wave Functions Supported:');
          for i := 0 to NUM_WAVE_FUNCTIONS-1 do
            if Caps.dwSupport and (1 shl i) = (1 shl i) then
              Add('  ' + WaveFunctionString(1 shl i));

        end; {with reCaps.Lines}

      except
        on E : eWave_error do
          MessageDlg(
            IntToStr(E.Wave_result) + ': ' + E.Message,
            mtError,
            [mbOK],
            0
            );
      end; {except}
    finally
      Free;
    end; {finally}

end; {GetCapsClick}
```

The two helper functions **WaveFormatString** and **WaveFunctionString** each use a *case* statement to return meaningful text for each of the supported formats or functions. Look at the excerpt from **WaveFormatString** below:

```
function WaveFormatString(
      const FormatConstant: UINT
      ): string;

      begin
        case FormatConstant of
            WAVE_FORMAT_1M08:
               result := '11.025 kHz. Mono. 8-bit';
            WAVE_FORMAT_1S08:
               result := '11.025 kHz. Stereo 8bit';
            WAVE_FORMAT_1M16:
               result := '11.025 kHz. Mono. 16-bit';
            ...
```

The calling procedure passes a constant, and the function returns the text that is associated with that constant. The calling procedure determines which formats the device supports by checking the bit mask in the **dwFormats** field against each of the format constants shown in Table 15.1. The technique used to check whether a particular value is contained in a *bit mask* is illustrated below:

```
for i := 0 to NUM_WAVE_FORMATS-1 do
     if Caps.dwFormats and (1 shl i) = (1 shl i) then
        Add(' ' + WaveFormatString(1 shl i));
```

This technique is very useful for identifying whether or not a bit mask includes a particular value. Let's look at an example. Assume that:

```
         A =   $00000089   00000000 00000000 00000000 10001001
         B =   $00000001   00000000 00000000 00000000 00000001
A and B =     $00000001   00000000 00000000 00000000 00000001
```

If **A** is the bit mask and we want to know if **B** is a part of that mask, we have Delphi do a *bitwise* comparison to see which bits are in **A** *and* **B**. In the example we're working with, the result is $00000001 which is also the value of **B**. Because the result of **A** *and* **B**, in our example, is B—we know that **B** is contained in the bit mask **A**. If we look at another example where:

```
         A =   $00000089   00000000 00000000 00000000 10001001
         B =   $00000002   00000000 00000000 00000000 00000010
A and B =     $00000000   00000000 00000000 00000000 00000000
```

We'll find that **A** *and* **B** = 0, or in other words, **A** *and* **B** ≠ **B**. This means that **B** is <u>not</u> contained in the bit mask **A**. We check the capabilities of the wave output device by comparing **Caps.dwFormats** *and* each of the wave format constants. If we were to reference each of the constants literally it would look something like this:

```
if Caps.dwFormats and WAVE_FORMAT_1M08 = WAVE_FORMAT_1M08 then
   Add(' ' + WaveFormatString(WAVE_FORMAT_1M08));
if Caps.dwFormats and WAVE_FORMAT_1M16 = WAVE_FORMAT_1M16 then
   Add(' ' + WaveFormatString(WAVE_FORMAT_1M16));
if Caps.dwFormats and WAVE_FORMAT_1S08 = WAVE_FORMAT_1S08 then
   Add(' ' + WaveFormatString(WAVE_FORMAT_1S08));
if Caps.dwFormats and WAVE_FORMAT_1S16 = WAVE_FORMAT_1S16 then
   Add(' ' + WaveFormatString(WAVE_FORMAT_1S16));
...
```

That's actually only one third of the code required to replace the three line *for* loop we're using. The magic being performed in that loop is called a *bitwise shift left* (**shl**). To understand how **shl** works, take a look at a few of the wave format constants in binary form:

```
WAVE_FORMAT_1M08    00000000 00000000 00000000 00000001
WAVE_FORMAT_1S08    00000000 00000000 00000000 00000010
WAVE_FORMAT_1M16    00000000 00000000 00000000 00000100
WAVE_FORMAT_1S16    00000000 00000000 00000000 00001000
```

Based on the constants listed above, the following expressions are also true:

```
WAVE_FORMAT_1S08 = WAVE_FORMAT_1M08 shl 1
WAVE_FORMAT_1S16 = WAVE_FORMAT_1M08 shl 3
WAVE_FORMAT_1M16 = WAVE_FORMAT_1S08 shl 1
```

A *bitwise shift* operation shifts each of the bits in a number either left or right. The expression **A shl** 1 shifts the bits of **A** by 1 position to the left. If **A** = 00000000 00000000 00000000 00000001 then **A shl** 1 = 00000000 00000000 00000000 00000010. In *hexadecimal* notation, the value changes from $00000001 to $00000002. In *wave format constant notation* it changes from **WAVE_FORMAT_1M08** to **WAVE_FORMAT_1S08**.

At this point you should be able to see that, with each iteration of the *for* loop, we're comparing **Caps.dwFormats** *and* each of the wave format constants. The iterations that get a match send the value to **WaveFormatString** to get a meaningful text description of the constant value.

Inside the Waveform Object

Next let's look at how a wave file is loaded. The procedure **mnuFOpenClick** is shown in Listing 15.4. Here we use the **TOpenDialog** component so that the user can choose a waveform file to be opened. Once a file is selected, we use the filename to create a **tAudio_waveform** object, and the file's contents are loaded. If the file is successfully loaded, we display information such as the bit depth and number of channels in the waveform. We also enable the menu options to play and process the Wave.

Listing 15.4 The File|Open menu

```
procedure TMain.mnuFOpenClick(Sender: TObject);
begin
  if OpenDialog1.Execute then begin
    WaveForm := tAudio_waveform.Create;
    with WaveForm do
      try
        Read(pchar(OpenDialog1.Filename));
        mnuPlay.Enabled := True;
        mnuEffects.Enabled := True;

        {Display Information about the wav file}
        with reCaps.Lines do begin
          if Count > 0 then Clear;
          Add('Wave File Information:');
          Add('File Name: ' + OpenDialog1.FileName);
          if Format.wFormatTag = WAVE_FORMAT_PCM then
            Add('PCM Digital Audio')
          else
            Add('Non-PCM format: ' + IntToStr(Format.wFormatTag));

          if Format.nChannels = 1 then
            Add('Mono')
          else
            Add('Stereo');

          Add('Samples per second: ' + IntToStr(Format.nSamplesPerSec));
          Add('Bits per Sample: ' + IntToStr(Format.wBitsPerSample));
          Add('Avg Data Rate: ' + IntToStr(Format.nAvgBytesPerSec) +
                         ' bytes/sec' );

        end; {with reCaps.Lines}

      except
        on E : eMMIO_error do
          MessageDlg(
            'MMIO Error ' + IntToStr(E.MMIO_result) + ': ' + E.Message,
            mtError,
            [mbOK], 0
            );
```

```
          on E : eWave_error do
            MessageDlg(
              'Wave Error ' + IntToStr(E.Wave_result) + ': ' + E.Message,
              mtError,
              [mbOK], 0
              );
        end; {except}

    end; {if open}

end; {FOpenClick}
```

We're not going to open the hood of the **tAudio_waveform** object. The mechanics of the low-level waveform functions were covered in Chapter 5. We'll focus on how to use these classes to work with the waveform data. In the File|Open click procedure, we use the **Read** method to open the file and load its contents. To refresh your memory, calling the **Read** method does the following:

1. Opens the file with **mmioOpen** through the **tMMIO_file** object.
2. Locates the wave format record using successive **mmioDescend** calls.
3. Locates the wave data and loads it into a buffer.
4. Completes the wave header record.

Once we have a waveform loaded, playing it is a piece of cake. We devised the **tAudio_waveform** object with a handy method called **Play**. Behind the scenes, this method takes care of opening the output device and writing the waveform data to the device. These are the steps required to play audio using the low-level waveform services:

1. Load Wave data using the Multimedia File I/O functions.
2. Open a waveform output device capable of handling the waveform data.
3. Write the Wave data to the output device—either all at once or in chunks.

The class structure that we have developed gives us a simple and clean way to load and play waveform audio files without having to deal with the low level I/O and data preparation in the calling program. We've also left the class structure open enough so that we have easy access to the actual waveform data.

Modifying Wave Data to Change the Amplitude of a Waveform

In Listing 15.5, you'll find the event procedure that is executed when the user selects either Decrease Volume or Increase Volume from the menu. In this procedure, we actually increase or decrease the volume of the waveform data by changing the byte data that represents the amplitude of the wave. This is much different than changing the output level of the sound system. Before we actually discuss the process, let's look at how a PCM waveform is stored. Just like bitmaps, digital audio has many formats. We're going to limit our discussion to the standard PCM Wave Audio formats listed in Table 15.1. The most significant difference among uncompressed PCM formats is the difference between the storage of 8-bit and 16-bit formats. Table 15.3 describes the difference.

Because the two formats have different storage requirements, the routines that read audio data must take that difference into account. The number of channels that a waveform uses also makes a difference in how that waveform is stored. For the processing we are doing, the difference is not significant—but a look at Table 15.4 will help you understand how each format is stored.

Table 15.3 Eight- and 16-bit PCM Waveform Data Storage.

Data Format	Max Value	Min Value	Midpoint Value	Storage Requirement
8-bit PCM	255 ($FF)	0	128 ($80)	1 Byte (Byte)
16-bit PCM	32,767 ($7FFF)	−32,768 ($8000)	0	2 Bytes (SmallInt)

Table 15.4 Monaural and Stereo PCM Waveform Data Storage.

Data Format	Storage Description
8-bit Monaural	Each sample is 1 byte, which represents one sample of audio data.
8-bit Stereo	Each sample is 2 bytes. The even numbered bytes (0,2,4,6,…) represent the left channel (channel 0) samples, and the odd bytes (1,3,5,7,…) represent the right channel samples (channel 1).
16-bit Monaural	Each sample is 2 bytes. The first byte is the low order byte of channel 0 and the second byte is the high order byte of channel 0. In other words…the bytes are arranged like this: ($0000 0000)($0000 0000)($0000 0000) where each set in parentheses represents a single sample.
16-bit Stereo	Each sample is 4 bytes. For each sample the first byte is the low order byte of channel 0; the second byte is the high order byte of channel 0; the third byte is the low order byte of channel 1; the fourth byte is the high order byte of channel 1. So the data would look like this: ($0000 0000 $0000 0000)($0000 0000 $0000 0000) where each set in parentheses represents a single sample.

Listing 15.5 The mnuEVolClick Event Procedure

```
procedure TMain.mnuEVolClick(Sender: TObject);
var
  p8bitSample:   ^Byte;
  p16bitSample:  ^SmallInt;
  i:             integer;
  LevelFactor:   real;

begin

  {Check to see which menu option was clicked and then
   set the appropriate level factor to decrease or
   increase the volume of the wave. }
  if TMenuItem(Sender).Tag = 0 then
    LevelFactor := 0.5
  else
    LevelFactor := 1.5;

  {disable functionality while processing}
  Main.reCaps.Cursor := crHourglass;
  mnuEffects.Enabled := False;
  mnuPlay.Enabled := False;

  {process the waveform data to increase/decrease the volume}
  with WaveForm do begin
    if Format.wFormatTag = WAVE_FORMAT_PCM then begin
      if Format.wBitsPerSample = 8 then begin
        {working with an 8-bit, sample}
        p8bitSample := addr(Data^);
        for i := 0 to Header.dwBufferLength-1 do begin
          p8bitSample^ := Clip8(
                            Round((p8bitSample^ - 128) * LevelFactor)
                          );
          inc(p8bitSample);
          end;
        end
      else if (Format.wBitsPerSample = 16) then begin
        {working with a 16-bit, sample}
        p16bitSample := addr(Data^);
        for i := 0 to ((Header.dwBufferLength-1) div 2) do begin
          p16bitSample^ := Clip16(Round(p16bitSample^ * LevelFactor));
          inc(p16bitSample);
          end; {for}
        end;
      end {if PCM}
    else
      MessageDlg('Non-PCM format audio', mtError, [mbOK], 0);

    end; {with}
```

```
Main.reCaps.Cursor := crDefault;
mnuEffects.Enabled := True;
mnuPlay.Enabled := True;

end; {ELevelsClick}
```

This procedure uses the **LevelFactor** to change the amplitude that each byte represents in the waveform data. We set the **Tag** property of each menu item so that we can test the value of Sender.Tag to see which menu option was selected. This procedure is executed when either the *Increase Volume* or *Decrease Volume* menus are selected. Since **Sender** is declared as **Tobject**, we must *typecast* it to **TMenuItem** so that the **Tag** property is accessible. Take a look at the statements below:

```
if TMenuItem(Sender).Tag = 0 then
   LevelFactor := 0.5
  else
   LevelFactor := 1.5;
```

We'll use **LevelFactor** to calculate the new value of each sample. Several conditions determine how the audio data will be processed. The first condition ensures that we're dealing with PCM audio data. If the waveform is a nonstandard format, we don't process it. The next condition distinguishes between 8 and 16-bit waveforms. Let's look at the 8-bit process first:

```
   if Format.wBitsPerSample = 8 then begin
     {working with an 8-bit, sample}
     p8bitSample := addr(Data^);
     for i := 0 to Header.dwBufferLength-1 do begin
       p8bitSample^ := Clip8(
                         Round((p8bitSample^ - 128) * LevelFactor)
                        );
      inc(p8bitSample);
       end;
     end
```

We declared **p8bitSample** as a pointer to a byte. Because of that declaration, when we reference the audio data (**Waveform.Data^**) through **p8bitSample^**, we get a single byte at a time. We used a *for..next* loop because we know the length of the buffer. The loop processes one byte of audio data with the routine **Clip8**, and then increments the pointer to the next byte. This process continues until each byte of audio data has been handled. Now that we know the overall process, let's look at how each byte is changed to effect the amplitude.

A sample of digital audio can have either a value above or below the baseline (The baseline is where no sound occurs). The baseline for 8-bit audio is 128. Basically, what we want to do is to multiply the original value by **LevelFactor**. Before we can do that, we need to convert the original value so it has a baseline of 0. We do this by subtracting 128 from the original value. To illustrate why we have to do this, consider the following example: If the original value is 128 (no sound), and we multiply by a factor of 1.5, we get 192. This means that we've gone from a silent sample to a sample with an amplitude of 62 above the baseline. If we first subtract 128 and then multiply, we get zero. When we are finished with the calculation and range checking, we'll add 128 back in.

The helper function **LevelFactor** performs some range checking on the calculated result and then adds 128 to the verified result. If, by increasing the original value, we exceed the maximum value (255), we need to clip it at 255. By the same token, if we exceed the lower bound of 0, the value should be clipped at 0.

If the waveform is 16-bit, then the following code handles the change:

```
else if (Format.wBitsPerSample = 16) then begin
  {working with a 16-bit, sample}
  p16bitSample := addr(Data^);
  for i := 0 to ((Header.dwBufferLength-1) div 2) do begin
    p16bitSample^ := Clip16(Round(p16bitSample^ * LevelFactor));
    inc(p16bitSample);
    end; {for}
end;
```

This block is similar to the code that deals with 8-bit waveforms. There are several important distinctions to address. First, the pointer variable that references the data is declared as a **SmallInt** (2 byte value ranging from -32,768-32,767). Each iteration of this loop is going to process 2 bytes of data (1 sample). Therefore, we only need the loop to execute once for every two bytes (dwBufferLength div 2). Also, because 16-bit samples have a baseline of zero, no conversion is necessary. We just multiply the original value by **LevelFactor** and use **Clip16** to handle clipping.

It's really fairly simple when broken down into manageable chunks. Let's see what it takes to do something a little different—like add an echo effect to the waveform.

Implementing an Echo Effect

It's a little harder to add echo to waveform audio than it is to adjust the volume, but not *too* much harder. The old-fashioned analog way to create an electronic echo is to take the output of the monitor head on a tape recorder and feed it back to the record head upstream. By adjusting the gain on this feedback loop, an engineer can control the decay rate of the echo—in other words, the change in loudness from one repetition to the next. To change the period of the echo—the delay between repetitions—you have to change the tape speed, because the heads are usually mounted in fixed positions along the tape path. That all sounds pretty complicated, but all we have to do is change a few bits here and there.

We can reproduce the effect of the analog tape loop method and gain some flexibility in the process. Unlike the tape process, we'll be starting with a complete recording of the original sound, to which we will add echo. For each sample in the waveform recording, we'll pick up an earlier sample, adjust its amplitude, and add the two together. The distance between the two samples will depend on the sampling rate, the number of bytes per sample, and the time delay we choose. Take a look at the **mnuEEchoClick** event procedure in Listing 15.6.

Listing 15.6 The mnuEEchoClick Event Procedure

```
procedure TMain.mnuEEchoClick(Sender: TObject);
const
  Gain = 50;
  Delay = 500;
  TrailingEchos = 3;

var
  pPrev8bitSample,
  p8bitSample:    ^Byte;
  pPrev16bitSample,
  p16bitSample: ^SmallInt;
  i:              integer;
  szNewBuffer:  Cardinal;
  NewData:      PChar;
  GainFactor,
  Period:    integer;

begin
    {disable functionality while processing}
    Main.reCaps.Cursor := crHourglass;
    mnuEffects.Enabled := False;
    mnuPlay.Enabled := False;

    {process the waveform data to add an echo effect}
    with WaveForm do begin
```

```
         GainFactor := Gain div 50;
         Period := Delay * Format.nSamplesPerSec div 1000;

         if Format.wFormatTag = WAVE_FORMAT_PCM then begin
           if Format.wBitsPerSample = 8 then begin
             {working with an 8-bit sample}
             if Format.nChannels = 2 then
               Period := Period * 2;

             {Re-allocate memory for the new size of the wave data}
             szNewBuffer := (Header.dwBufferLength + (Period * TrailingEchos)) - 1;
             NewData := strAlloc(szNewBuffer);
             StrMove(NewData, Data, Header.dwBufferLength);
             StrDispose(Data);
             Data := NewData;

             {initialize the new part of the buffer to 128}
             p8bitSample := addr(Data^);
             inc(p8bitSample, Header.dwBufferLength);
             for i := Header.dwBufferLength to szNewBuffer do begin
               p8bitSample^ := 128;
               inc(p8bitSample);
               end; {for}

             {Add the echo effect}
             p8bitSample := addr(Data^);
             pPrev8bitSample := addr(Data^);
             inc(p8bitSample, Period);
             for i := Period to szNewBuffer do begin
               p8bitSample^ := Clip8(((p8bitSample^ - 128) +
                             (pPrev8bitSample^ - 128) * GainFactor) div 2);
               inc(p8bitSample);
               inc(pPrev8bitSample);
               end; {for}

             Header.lpData := Data;
             Header.dwBufferLength := szNewBuffer + 1;

             end
           else if Format.wBitsPerSample = 16 then begin
             {working with a 16-bit sample}
             if Format.nChannels = 2 then
               Period := Period * 4
             else
               Period := Period * 2;

             {Re-allocate memory for the new size of the wave data}
             szNewBuffer := (Header.dwBufferLength +
               (Period * TrailingEchos)) - 1;

             NewData := strAlloc(szNewBuffer);
             StrMove(NewData, Data, Header.dwBufferLength);
             StrDispose(Data);
             Data := NewData;
```

```
      {initialize the new part of the buffer to 0}
      p16bitSample := addr(Data^);
      inc(p16bitSample, Header.dwBufferLength div 2);
      for i := 1 to ((szNewBuffer - Header.dwBufferLength) div 2) do begin
        p16bitSample^ := 0;
        inc(p16bitSample);
        end; {for}

      {Add the echo effect}
      p16bitSample := addr(Data^);
      pPrev16bitSample := addr(Data^);
      inc(p16bitSample, Period div 2);
      for i := 1 to ((szNewBuffer - Period) div 2) do begin
        p16bitSample^ := Clip16((p16bitSample^ + pPrev16bitSample^ *
                        GainFactor) div 2);
        inc(p16bitSample);
        inc(pPrev16bitSample);
        end; {for}

      Header.lpData := Data;
      Header.dwBufferLength := szNewBuffer + 1;

      end;
    end {if PCM}
  else
    MessageDlg('Non-PCM format audio', mtError, [mbOK], 0);

  end; {with}

  Main.reCaps.Cursor := crDefault;
  mnuEffects.Enabled := True;
  mnuPlay.Enabled := True;

end; {EEchoClick}
```

There is some similarity between changing the volume and adding an echo effect. We have to validate that the sample is standard PCM format and the processing is different between 8 and 16-bit samples. That's about where the similarity ends. One of the new conditions that we have to deal with in the echo procedure is that of dynamically changing the buffer size. We also need to keep track of two positions in the waveform data—one for the source of the echo and one for the sample that is modified by the source. To understand how the procedure works let's break it down into chunks that we'll be able to digest.

For both 8 and 16-bit samples, we have to allocate more buffer space to accommodate the trailing echoes. Before we go allocating blocks of memory to be used for waveform audio data, we have to figure out how much memory to allocate. For an 8-bit sample **szNewBuffer**, the size of the new buffer to be allocated is (the original size) *plus* (the number of trailing echoes *times* the size of the echo). The size of the echo, or the echoes **Period**, depends not only on whether the sample is 8 or 16-bit, but also on how many channels the sample has. If the sample is 8-bit mono, then each sample is 1 byte. The Period, measured in samples, is then equal to the number of bytes. On the other hand, 16-bit stereo samples require 4 bytes to store a sample. Therefore the period must also be multiplied by 4 to remain consistent. We do this before calculating the additional buffer requirement.

We have the data buffer declared as a **PChar**. In order to increase the size of the buffer, we allocate a new buffer of the correct size, move the contents from the old buffer to the new, dispose of the old buffer, and set the old buffer (which is a pointer) to the same address of the new buffer. To make sure that the trailing echoes work correctly, we need to set all of the newly allocated bytes to their baseline. For 8-bit samples, the baseline is 128; for 16-bit samples, it is 0. Let's take a close look at the *for* loops that initialize the new buffer memory. When processing 8-bit samples, we're working with a ^**Byte**. When we iterate through the loop using inc(p8bitSample), we are incrementing the pointer by 1 byte each time. When processing 16-bit samples, the pointer is a ^**SmallInt**. Incrementing **p16bitSample** then advances 2 bytes for each step. Since the size of the buffer is still measured in bytes, we only need the loop to do half as many iterations.

Now we're ready to talk about the code that actually creates the effect. First we set both **p8bitSample** and **pPrev8bitSample** to the address of the data buffer. The two pointers represent the current position, and the position 1 period behind the current position. Next we increment **p8bitSample** by the **Period**. Now, from the current position to the length of the new buffer, we change each byte using the following formula:

```
p8bitSample^ := Clip8(((p8bitSample^ - 128) + (pPrev8bitSample^ - 128) *
           GainFactor) div 2);
```

In a nutshell, that statement converts the current and previous samples to a zero baseline, multiplies the previous sample by GainFactor, adds the previous sample to the current sample, and divides the whole thing by 2. That result is then passed to the clipping function so the range of the data type is not exceeded. The last thing that we do is to update the **Waveform** object's **Header** record with the current **dwBufferLength** and a current **Data** address.

Real-Time Audio Effects

In the previous project, we explored ways to manipulate waveform data at the byte level. By using the low-level sound functions in the multimedia API, we were able to load a wave file into memory and trigger instant play. On the other hand, while we also modified the individual digital sample values to change the overall amplitude of the recording and to add echo effects, those operations were anything but instantaneous.

Imagine what we could do if we could manipulate wave data on the fly. We could combine wave files to produce effects for the ears that are as compelling and interactive as sprite animation is to the eyes. But clearly, based on our experience, it wouldn't be possible to do this by working with bytes.

Introducing WaveMix

As Microsoft gurus continue to expand and refine the multimedia features of Windows, they have occasionally tossed us new components with which to tinker. Some time ago, Microsoft released WaveMix as an unsupported library. There were only a few functions, some .ini file settings, and a handful of constants to handle. Truly, this was an incredible product. It was (and is) fairly easy to use and sports 8 buffers that can be mixed together in real-time. WaveMix supports up to 22kHz 16-bit stereo waves.

If you're not interested in converting the C++ header file yourself, several conversions have been posted on the web. We won't get into WaveMix in this book, because we don't have time...at least not if we are going to cover a *real* audio mixer like DirectSound! Actually, WaveMix is probably still the way to go for 16-bit applications. We've included a wrapper for WaveMix and DLL, and documentation on the companion CD-ROM. You'll find it in the \SHAREWAR\WAVEMIX directory.

Cutting Edge Audio Technology

When it comes to digital audio technology for the PC, DirectSound is the state-of-the-art. Like its DirectDraw counterpart, DirectSound was developed to provide direct access to audio hardware. It allows developers to create and maintain audio buffers that can be played and mixed on demand. The number of buffers allowed is limited only by the amount of memory that can be allocated. In addition to real-time mixing, DirectSound has some other goodies like real-time volume attenuation, real-time frequency manipulation, and 3D placement of sounds. 3D positioning is not supported in the currently released version, but they've left room for it, as if to indicate that it isn't too far away.

DirectSound is based on two components—The DirectSound object which is a virtual representation of the sound card, and DirectSound buffers which represent the audio. Because of its close relationship with the hardware,

DirectSound provides very responsive control over the sounds and sound processing.

Let's take a look at DirectSound from an example.

Mixing Audio and Beyond

This project introduces the latest digital audio technology—DirectSound. After completing this project, you'll understand the DirectSound interface and you'll have examples of its most important features in action. Here's what to do:

1. Start a new project.
2. Setup the main form.
3. Create or add the Dsound.pas unit.
4. Create or add the DSWrap.pas unit.
5. Add event handling code in the form's code unit.
6. Copy the units: WaveWrap.pas, WavePlay.pas, and MMIOWrap.pas from the Wave2 directory to the new project directory.
7. Modify the units as indicated.

This project is located in the directory \DELPHIMM\15\DSTEST.

Creating the DirectSound Test Project

Create a new project and save it using udstest.pas and dstest.dpr for names. As with the previous project, we recommend that you create the main form by force-feeding the DFM file with code from the CD-ROM. Open the file udstest.dfm with a text editor. It will be located in the project directory on the CD-ROM. Now copy the contents of that file onto the clipboard. Next, right-click on the default form in Delphi and select *view as text* from the menu. The form definition should appear in the editor window under a new tab. Select all of the text and paste to replace it with the text copied from udstest.dfm on the CD-ROM. Finally, right-click on the editor window and select *view form*. You should now be looking at something similar to Figure 15.3. If you prefer, the text for the form definition is in Listing 15.7. If you like typing, you may wish to view the form as text and then enter the code using Listing 15.7 as a reference. Another option is to add components to the main form and set all of the appropriate properties and events. You could do this using Listing 15.7 as a reference. After the form is complete—however you may decide to do

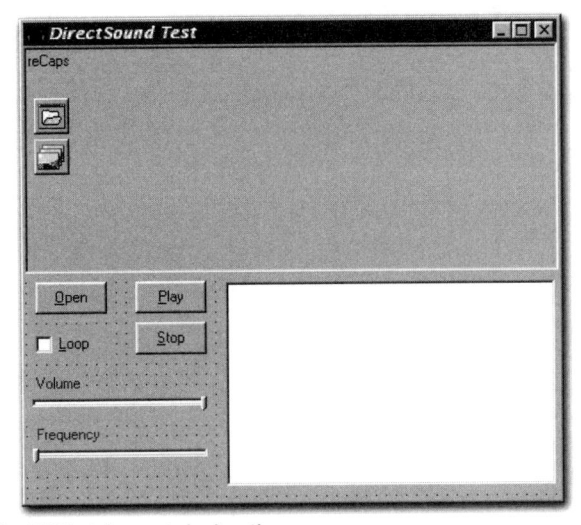

Figure 15.3 *The DSTest form at design time.*

it—you'll need to copy wavewrap.pas, waveplay.pas, and mmiowrap.pas from the previous project to the current project directory and add them to the project. Now you're ready for the new stuff.

Listing 15.7 The udstest.dfm Form Module

```
object Main: TMain
  Left = 100
  Top = 24
  Width = 435
  Height = 382
  Caption = 'DirectSound Test'
  Font.Color = clWindowText
  Font.Height = -11
  Font.Name = 'MS Sans Serif'
  Font.Style = []
  Icon.Data = {
    0000010001002020100000000000E80200001600000028000000200000004000
...
    C98301AFE98001AFE58081AFF18181FFF9818179FE8183593AC19EDD3B799FBC
    BDF99CFE3FF99C9F3FF9CE9FFFF3CE5FFFF3CF1FFFF3E79FFFE7E7FFFFE7F3FF
    FFCFF1FFFF8FF8FFFF1FFC1FFC3FFF00007FFFE003FFFFFFFFFFFFFFFF}
  OnActivate = FormActivate
  OnCreate = FormCreate
  OnDestroy = FormDestroy
  PixelsPerInch = 96
  TextHeight = 13
  object lblVol: TLabel
    Left = 8
    Top = 256
    Width = 35
```

```
      Height = 13
      Caption = 'Volume'
      Color = clBtnFace
      Font.Color = clNavy
      Font.Height = -11
      Font.Name = 'MS Sans Serif'
      Font.Style = []
      ParentColor = False
      ParentFont = False
    end
    object lblFreq: TLabel
      Left = 8
      Top = 296
      Width = 50
      Height = 13
      Caption = 'Frequency'
      Color = clBtnFace
      Font.Color = clNavy
      Font.Height = -11
      Font.Name = 'MS Sans Serif'
      Font.Style = []
      ParentColor = False
      ParentFont = False
    end
    object reCaps: TRichEdit
      Left = 0
      Top = 0
      Width = 427
      Height = 177
      Align = alTop
      Color = clBtnFace
      Lines.Strings = (
        'reCaps')
      ScrollBars = ssVertical
      TabOrder = 0
    end
    object btnOpen: TButton
      Left = 8
      Top = 184
      Width = 57
      Height = 25
      Caption = '&Open'
      TabOrder = 1
      OnClick = btnOpenClick
    end
    object WaveList: TListView
      Left = 160
      Top = 184
      Width = 265
      Height = 161
      OnClick = WaveListClick
      Columns = <>
      ReadOnly = True
      HideSelection = False
```

```
    IconOptions.AutoArrange = True
    SortType = stText
    TabOrder = 2
    ViewStyle = vsList
    LargeImages = ImageList1
    SmallImages = ImageList1
    StateImages = ImageList1
  end
  object btnPlay: TButton
    Left = 88
    Top = 184
    Width = 57
    Height = 25
    Caption = '&Play'
    TabOrder = 3
    OnClick = btnPlayClick
  end
  object btnStop: TButton
    Left = 88
    Top = 216
    Width = 57
    Height = 25
    Caption = '&Stop'
    TabOrder = 4
    OnClick = btnStopClick
  end
  object chkLoop: TCheckBox
    Left = 8
    Top = 224
    Width = 57
    Height = 17
    Caption = '&Loop'
    TabOrder = 5
    OnClick = chkLoopClick
  end
  object trbVolume: TTrackBar
    Left = 0
    Top = 272
    Width = 150
    Height = 20
    LineSize = 100
    Max = 0
    Min = -10000
    Orientation = trHorizontal
    PageSize = 1000
    Frequency = 1
    Position = 0
    SelEnd = 0
    SelStart = 0
    TabOrder = 6
    TickMarks = tmBottomRight
    TickStyle = tsNone
    OnChange = trbVolumeChange
  end
```

```
  object trbFreq: TTrackBar
    Left = 0
    Top = 312
    Width = 150
    Height = 20
    LineSize = 100
    Max = 100000
    Min = 100
    Orientation = trHorizontal
    PageSize = 1000
    Frequency = 1
    Position = 100
    SelEnd = 0
    SelStart = 0
    TabOrder = 7
    TickMarks = tmBottomRight
    TickStyle = tsNone
    OnChange = trbFreqChange
  end
  object ImageList1: TImageList
    Left = 8
    Top = 72
    Bitmap = {
      361800000100000042 4D361800000000000036000000280000004000000002000
...
      00000000677D000000000001AFFD000000000000B7FB000000000000DFFB0101
      01010101CFF7000001010101F00F010101010101FFFF010101010101}
  end
  object OpenDialog: TOpenDialog
    DefaultExt = 'wav'
    FileEditStyle = fsEdit
    Filter = 'Wave Files|*.wav'
    Title = 'Select Wave File to Open'
    Left = 8
    Top = 40
  end
end
```

The form module in Listing 15.7 has two gaps, indicated by ellipses, in the code. The gaps are included so we didn't have to list pages of binary data. The **Icon.Data** of the form and the **TImageList.Bitmap** properties actually contain an icon and a bitmap. You should use the property editor to set those properties, although neither are necessary.

The DirectSound Interface

Let's begin the new material for this project by looking at the Delphi conversion of Microsoft's DirectSound header. Locate dsound.pas in the project directory of the CD-ROM and add it to the project. You should first copy the file to your project directory.

The structures, constants, and functions in dsound.pas are well documented in the GamesSDK help system. Please use that as a reference, and we'll stick to a general explanation of how the DirectSound interface works. As we mentioned earlier, DirectSound consists of two basic structures—**IDirectSound** and **IDirectSoundBuffer**. **IDirectSound** is a class object that represents the system's sound card. The declaration, located in Listing 15.8, displays the 8 methods that represent the object's functionality. We'll end up using 4 of them in this project.

Listing 15.8 The IDirectSound class definition

```
IDirectSound = class ( IUnknown )
    function CreateSoundBuffer(
            const lpDSBufferDesc: DSBUFFERDESC;
            var lplpDirectSoundBuffer: IDirectSoundBuffer;
            pUnkOuter: IUnknown
            ): HRESULT; virtual; stdcall; abstract;
    function GetCaps(
            var lpDSCaps: DSCAPS
            ): HRESULT; virtual; stdcall; abstract;
    function DuplicateSoundBuffer(
            lpDsbOriginal: IDirectSoundBuffer;
            var lplpDsbDuplicate: IDirectSoundBuffer
            ): HRESULT; virtual; stdcall; abstract;
    function SetCooperativeLevel(
            hwnd: HWND;
            dwLevel: DWORD
            ): HRESULT; virtual; stdcall; abstract;
    function Compact: HRESULT; virtual; stdcall; abstract;
    function GetSpeakerConfig(
            var lpdwSpeakerConfig: DWORD
            ): HRESULT; virtual; stdcall; abstract;
    function SetSpeakerConfig(
            dwSpeakerConfig: DWORD
            ): HRESULT; virtual; stdcall; abstract;
    function Initialize(
            lpGuid: PGUID
            ): HRESULT; virtual; stdcall; abstract;
end;
```

IDirectSoundBuffer is also a class object. It represents the audio data that an application plays through DirectSound. The buffer interface provides 18 functions that range in purpose from retrieving the capabilities of a buffer to changing its playback frequency or panning. The complete class definition is located in Listing 15.8.

Listing 15.8 The IDirectSoundBuffer class definition

```
IDirectSoundBuffer = class ( IUnknown )
    function GetCaps (
            var lpDSBufferCaps: DSBCAPS
            ): HRESULT; virtual; stdcall; abstract;
    function GetCurrentPosition (
            var lpdwCurrentPlayCursor: DWORD;
            var lpdwCurrentWriteCursor: DWORD
            ): HRESULT; virtual; stdcall; abstract;
    function GetFormat(
            var lpwfxFormat: TWaveFormatEx;
            dwSizeAllocated: DWORD;
            var lpdwSizeWritten: DWORD
            ): HRESULT; virtual; stdcall; abstract;
    function GetVolume(
            var lplVolume: LongInt
            ): HRESULT; virtual; stdcall; abstract;
    function GetPan(var lplPan: LongInt
            ): HRESULT; virtual; stdcall; abstract;
    function GetFrequency(
            var lpdwFrequency: DWORD
            ): HRESULT; virtual; stdcall; abstract;
    function GetStatus(
            var lpdwStatus: DWORD
            ): HRESULT; virtual; stdcall; abstract;
    function Initialize(
            lpDirectSound: IDirectSound;
            const lpDSBufferDesc: DSBUFFERDESC
            ): HRESULT; virtual; stdcall; abstract;
    function Lock(
            dwWriteCursor: DWORD;
            dwWriteBytes: DWORD;
            var lplpvAudioPtr1: pointer;
            var lpdwAudioBytes1: DWORD;
            var lplpvAudioPtr2: pointer;
            var lpdwAudioBytes2: DWORD;
            dwFlags: DWORD
            ): HRESULT; virtual; stdcall; abstract;
    function Play(
            dwReserved1: DWORD;
            dwReserved2: DWORD;
            dwFlags: DWORD
            ): HRESULT; virtual; stdcall; abstract;
    function SetCurrentPosition(
            dwNewPosition: DWORD
            ): HRESULT; virtual; stdcall; abstract;
    function SetFormat(
            const lpwfxFormat: TWaveFormatEx
            ): HRESULT; virtual; stdcall; abstract;
    function SetVolume(
            lVolume: LongInt
            ): HRESULT; virtual; stdcall; abstract;
```

```
    function SetPan(
            lPan: LongInt
            ): HRESULT; virtual; stdcall; abstract;
    function SetFrequency(
            dwFrequency: DWORD
            ): HRESULT; virtual; stdcall; abstract;
    function Stop: HRESULT; virtual; stdcall; abstract;
    function Unlock(
            lpvAudioPtr1: PChar;
            dwAudioBytes1: DWORD;
            lpvAudioPtr2: pointer;
            dwAudioBytes2: DWORD
            ): HRESULT; virtual; stdcall; abstract;
    function Restore: HRESULT; virtual; stdcall; abstract;
  end;
```

Implementing DirectSound

An application that takes advantage of DirectSound does so by following these basic steps:

1. Create a DirectSound object using the **DirectSoundCreate** function.
2. Specify a cooperative level with **IDirectSound.SetCooperativeLevel**.
3. Create secondary buffers by calling **IDirectSound.CreateSoundBuffer**.
4. Use **IDirectSound.Lock** to set a pointer to the sound data.
5. Use **IDirectSound.Unlock** to set the data to the sound device.
6. Play the audio with **IDirectSoundBuffer.Play**.
7. Terminate playback of each buffer using **IDirectSound.Stop**.
8. Release DirectSound.

There is yet another unit in this project that you'll have to create. Before we begin our implementation of DirectSound—create a new unit called DSWrap.pas. The completed unit is in Listing 15.9.

Listing 15.9 The DSWrap unit

```
unit DSWrap;

interface
uses
  SysUtils, Windows, DSound;

type
  EDSoundErr = class(Exception)
    DSoundResult : HResult;
    constructor Create(const Err : HResult; const Msg : string);
    end;
```

```
  TDSound = class(TObject)
    protected
      FDSObj: IDirectSound;
      FCaps: DSCAPS;

    public
      constructor Create;
      destructor Destroy;

      property Caps: DSCAPS read FCaps;
      property IDS: IDirectSound read FDSObj;

      function Init(hwnd: hWnd; dwLevel: DWORD): HResult;
      function GetCaps: HResult;
      function IsCapable(Flag: DWORD): Boolean;

    end;

  TDSBuffer = class(TObject)
    protected
      FDSBufObj: IDirectSoundBuffer;
      FCaps: DSBCAPS;
      FDesc: DSBUFFERDESC;
      FLoop: Boolean;

    public
      constructor Create;

      property Caps: DSBCAPS read FCaps;
      property Desc: DSBUFFERDESC read FDesc write FDesc;
      property IDSB: IDirectSoundBuffer read FDSBufObj;
      property Loop: Boolean read FLoop write FLoop default True;

      function InitFile(
        DS: IDirectSound;
        flags: DWORD;
        fn: string
        ): HResult;

    end;

implementation
uses
  WavePlay;

constructor EDSoundErr.Create(const Err : HResult; const Msg : string);
begin
  inherited Create(Msg);
  DSoundResult := Err;
end;

constructor TDSound.Create;
begin
  inherited Create;
```

Exploring Waveform Audio

```pascal
end;

destructor TDSound.Destroy;
begin
  FDSObj.Release;
  inherited Destroy;
end;

constructor TDSBuffer.Create;
begin
  inherited Create;
end;

function TDSound.Init(hwnd: hWnd; dwLevel: DWORD): HResult;
{Creates a directsound interface object and sets the cooperative level}
begin

  result := DirectSoundCreate(
    nil,
    FDSObj,
    nil
    );
  if result = DS_OK then
    FDSObj.SetCooperativeLevel(hwnd, dwLevel)
  else
    raise EDSoundErr.Create(
      result,
      'Unable to initialize the DirectSound interface'
      );

end; {TDSound.Init}

function TDSBuffer.InitFile(
  DS: IDirectSound;
  flags: DWORD;
  fn: string
  ): HResult;

var
  WaveForm: tAudio_waveform;
  pAudioBuffer1,
  pAudioBuffer2: pointer;
  nAudioBuffer1Bytes,
  nAudioBuffer2Bytes: DWORD;

begin

  {Read the waveform from a file}
  WaveForm := tAudio_waveform.Create;
  try
    WaveForm.Read(fn);

    {Setup the DSBufferDesc structure}
    FDesc.dwSize := SizeOf(FDesc);
```

```
      FDesc.dwFlags := flags;
      FDesc.dwBufferBytes := WaveForm.Header.dwBufferLength;
      FDesc.lpwfxFormat := @WaveForm.Format;

      result := DS.CreateSoundBuffer(
        FDesc,
        FDSBufObj,
        nil
        );

      if result = DS_OK then begin
        FDSBufObj.Lock(
          0,
          FDesc.dwBufferBytes,
          pAudioBuffer1,
          nAudioBuffer1Bytes,
          pAudioBuffer2,
          nAudioBuffer2Bytes,
          0
          );
        Move(WaveForm.Data^, PByte(pAudioBuffer1)^, nAudioBuffer1Bytes);
        FDSBufObj.UnLock(
          pAudioBuffer1,
          nAudioBuffer1Bytes,
          pAudioBuffer2,
          nAudioBuffer2Bytes
          );

      end
    else
      raise EDSoundErr.Create(
        result,
        'Unable to create sound buffer'
        );
    finally
      WaveForm.Free;
    end;

end; {TDSBuffer.Init}

function TDSound.GetCaps: HResult;
{Retrieves the Capabilities of the DirectSound object}
begin

  FCaps.dwSize := SizeOf(FCaps);
  FCaps.dwFlags := 0;
  result := FDSObj.GetCaps(FCaps);
  if result <> DS_OK then
    raise EDSoundErr.Create(
      result,
      'Unable to initialize the DirectSound interface'
      );

end; {TDSound.GetCaps}
```

```
function TDSound.IsCapable(Flag: DWORD): Boolean;
begin
  result := False;
  if Flag and FCaps.dwFlags = Flag then
    result := True;
end;

end.
```

The DSWrap unit defines two objects that simplify the use of **IDirectSound** and **IDirectSoundBuffer**. The new objects, **TDSound** and **TDSBuffer**, make calls to **IDirectSound** and **IDirectSoundBuffer** and provide a little bit of error checking. These objects are designed to make the explanation of the DirectSound Interface more concise and a foundation for some real DirectSound components.

Since we now have **TDSound**, **IDirectSound**, **TDSBuffer**, and **IDirectSoundBuffer** to work with, I'm going to establish some conventions that I will follow through the remainder of this project. From this point on, I will refer to **IDirectSound**—the actual DirectSound object—as either **IDirectSound** or the 'DirectSound *Interface*'; **TDSound** will be the 'DirectSound *Object*.' Likewise, **IDirectSoundBuffer** will be the 'Buffer *Interface*,' and **TDSBuffer** is the 'Buffer *Object*.'

Now let's take a look at how we implement DirectSound in this project. The first thing that we have to do is create a DirectSound object. We've implemented that step in the form's **OnCreate** handler. Let's take a look at Listing 15.10.

Listing 15.10   FormCreate: Initializing DirectSound

```
procedure TMain.FormCreate(Sender: TObject);

begin

  Loading := True;
  DS := TDSound.Create;
  DS.Init(Self.Handle, DSSCL_NORMAL);

  {retrieve the capabilities of the DSound object and display them}
  DS.GetCaps;
  DisplayCaps;

end;
```

We take care of the first two steps that start a DirectSound session in the **DS.Init** procedure. You'll find the procedure in Listing 15.9. **DS.Init** calls

DirectSoundCreate to create a DirectSound interface. If the interface is created successfully, then **SetCooperativeLevel** is called immediately to establish how this DirectSound interface will behave in a multitasking environment. Next, in the form's **OnCreate** handler, we use **DS.GetCaps** to retrieve useful information about the system's sound card and drivers. **GetCaps** calls the interface function **GetCaps** and does a quick error check. It fills a **DSCAPS** structure as described below:

```
DSCAPS = record
    dwSize: DWORD;
    dwFlags: DWORD;
    dwMinSecondarySampleRate: DWORD;
    dwMaxSecondarySampleRate: DWORD;
    dwPrimaryBuffers: DWORD;
    dwMaxHwMixingAllBuffers: DWORD;
    dwMaxHwMixingStaticBuffers: DWORD;
    dwMaxHwMixingStreamingBuffers: DWORD;
    dwFreeHwMixingAllBuffers: DWORD;
    dwFreeHwMixingStaticBuffers: DWORD;
    dwFreeHwMixingStreamingBuffers: DWORD;
    dwMaxHw3DAllBuffers: DWORD;
    dwMaxHw3DStaticBuffers: DWORD;
    dwMaxHw3DStreamingBuffers: DWORD;
    dwFreeHw3DAllBuffers: DWORD;
    dwFreeHw3DStaticBuffers: DWORD;
    dwFreeHw3DStreamingBuffers: DWORD;
    dwTotalHwMemBytes: DWORD;
    dwFreeHwMemBytes: DWORD;
    dwMaxContigFreeHwMemBytes: DWORD;
    dwUnlockTransferRateHwBuffers: DWORD;
    dwPlayCpuOverheadSwBuffers: DWORD;
    dwReserved1: DWORD;
    dwReserved2: DWORD;
end;
```

The record itself would not be very meaningful if it weren't for the **DisplayCaps** procedure in udstest.pas. You'll find **DisplayCaps** in Listing 15.11. This function interprets the numeric values contained in the record and displays some sort of meaningful description in the **TRichEdit** component.

Listing 15.11 The Display Caps Procedure

```
procedure DisplayCaps;
const FlagString: array[0..11] of string = (
  'Device supports monophonic primary buffers',
  'Device supports stereo primary buffers',
  'Device supports primary buffers with 8-bit samples',
  'Device supports primary buffers with 16-bit samples',
  'Continuous rate (+/- 10Hz)',
  'No DirectSound driver (Emulation Mode Enabled)',
```

```
    'Driver certified by Microsoft',
    '',
    'Device supports hardware-mixed monophonic secondary buffers',
    'Device supports hardware-mixed stereo secondary buffers',
    'Device supports hardware-mixed secondary buffers with 8-bit samples',
    'Device supports hardware-mixed secondary buffers with 16-bit samples'
    );
var
  i: integer;
  NormalFont,
  Heading: TFont;

begin

  {setup the font styles}
  NormalFont := TFont.Create;
  NormalFont.Assign(Main.reCaps.Font);
  Heading := TFont.Create;
  Heading.Assign(NormalFont);
  Heading.Style := [fsBold];
  Heading.Color := clNavy;

  {display capabilities}
  with Main.reCaps.Lines do begin
    if Count > 0 then Clear;
    Main.reCaps.SelAttributes := TTextAttributes(Heading);
    Add('DirectSound Initialized: Priority Normal');

    Main.reCaps.SelAttributes := TTextAttributes(NormalFont);
    for i := 0 to 10 do
      if DS.IsCapable($00000001 shl i) then
        Add('   * '+ FlagString[i]);

    {Sample rate and primary buffer info}
    Add('  Minimum sample rate (Secondary HW Buffers): ' +
        IntToStr(DS.Caps.dwMinSecondarySampleRate)
        );
    Add('  Maximum sample rate (Secondary HW Buffers): ' +
        IntToStr(DS.Caps.dwMaxSecondarySampleRate)
        );
    Add('  Number of primary buffers: ' +
        IntToStr(DS.Caps.dwPrimaryBuffers)
        );

    {Hardware Mixing Caps}
    Main.reCaps.SelAttributes := TTextAttributes(Heading);
    Add('Hardware Mixing Capabilities:');
    Main.reCaps.SelAttributes := TTextAttributes(NormalFont);
    Add('  Total # of buffers: ' +
        IntToStr(DS.Caps.dwMaxHwMixingAllBuffers)
        );
    Add('  Maximum static buffers (onboard RAM): ' +
        IntToStr(DS.Caps.dwMaxHwMixingStaticBuffers)
        );
```

```
Add('  Maximum streaming buffers: ' +
    IntToStr(DS.Caps.dwMaxHwMixingStreamingBuffers)
    );

Main.reCaps.SelAttributes := TTextAttributes(Heading);
Add('Unallocated Hardware Mixing Capabilities:');
Main.reCaps.SelAttributes := TTextAttributes(NormalFont);
Add('  Total # of buffers: ' +
    IntToStr(DS.Caps.dwFreeHwMixingAllBuffers)
    );
Add('  Maximum static buffers (onboard RAM): ' +
    IntToStr(DS.Caps.dwFreeHwMixingStaticBuffers)
    );
Add('  Maximum streaming buffers: ' +
    IntToStr(DS.Caps.dwFreeHwMixingStreamingBuffers)
    );

{3D Positioning Caps (not used in first release of DS)}
Main.reCaps.SelAttributes := TTextAttributes(Heading);
Add('3D Positioning Capabilities:');
Main.reCaps.SelAttributes := TTextAttributes(NormalFont);
Add('  Total # of buffers: ' +
    IntToStr(DS.Caps.dwMaxHw3DAllBuffers)
    );
Add('  Maximum static buffers (onboard RAM): ' +
    IntToStr(DS.Caps.dwMaxHw3DStaticBuffers)
    );
Add('  Maximum streaming buffers: ' +
    IntToStr(DS.Caps.dwMaxHw3DStreamingBuffers)
    );

Main.reCaps.SelAttributes := TTextAttributes(Heading);
Add('Unallocated 3D Positioning Capabilities:');
Main.reCaps.SelAttributes := TTextAttributes(NormalFont);
Add('  Total # of buffers: ' +
    IntToStr(DS.Caps.dwFreeHw3DAllBuffers)
    );
Add('  Maximum static buffers (onboard RAM): ' +
    IntToStr(DS.Caps.dwFreeHw3DStaticBuffers)
    );
Add('  Maximum streaming buffers: ' +
    IntToStr(DS.Caps.dwFreeHw3DStreamingBuffers)
    );

{Onboard memory configuration}
Main.reCaps.SelAttributes := TTextAttributes(Heading);
Add('Sound Card RAM:');
Main.reCaps.SelAttributes := TTextAttributes(NormalFont);
Add('  Total: ' +
    IntToStr(DS.Caps.dwTotalHwMemBytes)
    );
Add('  Free: ' +
    IntToStr(DS.Caps.dwFreeHwMemBytes)
    );
```

```
        Add(' Free (contiguous): ' +
           IntToStr(DS.Caps.dwMaxContigFreeHwMemBytes)
           );

        {Misc. Information}
        Main.reCaps.SelAttributes := TTextAttributes(Heading);
        Add('Misc');
        Main.reCaps.SelAttributes := TTextAttributes(NormalFont);
        Add(' Hardware transfer rate: ' +
           IntToStr(DS.Caps.dwUnlockTransferRateHwBuffers)
           );
        Add(' CPU overhead to mix SW buffers: ' +
           IntToStr(DS.Caps.dwPlayCpuOverheadSwBuffers)
           );

     end; {with}

end; {DisplayCaps}
```

The **DisplayCaps** procedure works a lot like the function from the last project that displayed the capabilities of the wave output device.

That's about as far as we can follow the program's execution. The remainder of the program responds to user-generated events. The next thing we have to do, according to the basic steps we outlined, is create a sound buffer. This is done when the user clicks on the *Open* button. See Listing 15.12.

Listing 15.12 The btnOpenClick event procedure

```
procedure TMain.btnOpenClick(Sender: TObject);
var
  NewItem: TListItem;
  Vol: LongInt;
  Freq: DWORD;
  Result: HRESULT;

begin

  if OpenDialog.Execute then begin
    NewItem := WaveList.Items.Add;
    NewItem.Caption := ExtractFileName(OpenDialog.FileName);
    NewItem.ImageIndex := 0;
    NewItem.Data := TDSBuffer.Create;
    with TDSBuffer(NewItem.Data) do begin
      InitFile(
        DS.IDS,
        DSBCAPS_CTRLDEFAULT or DSBCAPS_STATIC,
        OpenDialog.FileName
        );
      chkLoop.Checked := Loop;

      Result := IDSB.GetVolume(Vol);
      if Result <> DS_OK then
```

```
      trbVolume.Enabled := False
    else begin
      trbVolume.Enabled := True;
      trbVolume.Position := Vol;
      end;

    Result := IDSB.GetFrequency(Freq);
    if Result <> DS_OK then
      trbFreq.Enabled := False
    else begin
      trbFreq.Enabled := True;
      trbFreq.Position := Freq;
      end;
    end; {with}
  end; {if}

end;
```

The click event for the Open button takes care of creating a sound buffer, adding it to the list, loading a wave file, putting the wave data into the DirectSound buffer, and setting the appropriate slider values for volume and frequency. That gets us up to step five of eight in the DirectSound implementation. At the program level, the following code snippet does everything we just mentioned except setting the volume and frequency sliders:

```
NewItem.Data := TDSBuffer.Create;
with TDSBuffer(NewItem.Data) do begin
  InitFile(
    DS.IDS,
    DSBCAPS_CTRLDEFAULT or DSBCAPS_STATIC,
    OpenDialog.FileName
    );
    ...
```

The first line assigns a new **TDSBuffer** (a pointer to a DirectSound buffer object) to the Data property of **NewItem,** which is a **TListItem**. With the buffer interface and buffer object created, the next thing to do is load the wave file and put the associated waveform data into the DirectSound buffer. **NewItem.Data** points to a **TDSBuffer** object, but its type is actually **pointer**. In order to reference its methods and properties, it must be *typecast* to **TDSBuffer**. The InitFile method of TDSBuffer is the workhorse of this event. Let's take a look at what it's doing behind the scenes.

Loading a Waveform File to Play with DirectSound

Listing 15.13 shows the InitFile method of the TDSBuffer object. In this procedure, waveform data is pulled from a disk file and stuffed into a DirectSound buffer so it is ready to play or mix on demand.

Listing 15.13 TDSBuffer.InitFile

```
function TDSBuffer.InitFile(
  DS: IDirectSound;
  flags: DWORD;
  fn: string
  ): HResult;

var
  WaveForm: tAudio_waveform;
  pAudioBuffer1,
  pAudioBuffer2: pointer;
  nAudioBuffer1Bytes,
  nAudioBuffer2Bytes: DWORD;

begin

  {Read the waveform from a file}
  WaveForm := tAudio_waveform.Create;
  try
    WaveForm.Read(fn);

    {Setup the DSBufferDesc structure}
    FDesc.dwSize := SizeOf(FDesc);
    FDesc.dwFlags := flags;
    FDesc.dwBufferBytes := WaveForm.Header.dwBufferLength;
    FDesc.lpwfxFormat := @WaveForm.Format;

    result := DS.CreateSoundBuffer(
      FDesc,
      FDSBufObj,
      nil
      );

    if result = DS_OK then begin
      FDSBufObj.Lock(
        0,
        FDesc.dwBufferBytes,
        pAudioBuffer1,
        nAudioBuffer1Bytes,
        pAudioBuffer2,
        nAudioBuffer2Bytes,
        0
        );
      Move(WaveForm.Data^, PByte(pAudioBuffer1)^, nAudioBuffer1Bytes);
      FDSBufObj.UnLock(
        pAudioBuffer1,
        nAudioBuffer1Bytes,
        pAudioBuffer2,
        nAudioBuffer2Bytes
        );

    end
  else
```

```
      raise EDSoundErr.Create(
        result,
        'Unable to create sound buffer'
        );
    finally
      WaveForm.Free;
    end;

end; {TDSBuffer.Init}
```

The first step in getting waveform data from a disk file to a DirectSound buffer is obviously retrieving the file from the disk. We've done that in several projects now. The **tAudio_waveform**—and its one-step file load procedure **Read**—should be familiar by now. We've used it in two previous projects.

After loading a wave file, we have enough information to fill in the **TDSBUFFERDESC** structure and consequently create a buffer interface with the **CreateSoundBuffer** method of the DirectSound interface. Two methods will aid us in getting the wave data from the **tAudio_waveform** to the DirectSound buffer interface. First we have **Lock**, a method of **IDirectSoundBuffer**. **Lock** returns a write pointer to which we can copy a chunk of memory that represents waveform data. After data is written to that pointer, the application must immediately use **Unlock**, another method of **IDirectSoundBuffer**, to set that data to the device.

At this point, we've established a DirectSound interface, a buffer interface, and we've stuffed the buffer with waveform data. Here is where the real the fun begins. All of DirectSound's functionality is readily available with single statements like Play, Stop, SetFrequency, SetVolume, etc. Before we breeze through that, let's look at the **Lock** and **Unlock** functions again:

```
      function Lock(
        dwWriteCursor:         DWORD;   {start position within the buffer}
        dwWriteBytes:          DWORD;   {how many bytes need to be written}
        var lplpvAudioPtr1:    pointer; {write pointer returned for block #1}
        var lpdwAudioBytes1:   DWORD;   {number of bytes allocated for block #1}
        var lplpvAudioPtr2:    pointer; {write pointer returned for block #2}
        var lpdwAudioBytes2:   DWORD;   {number of bytes allocated for block #2}
        dwFlags:               DWORD    {flags that modify the lock event}
        ): HRESULT; virtual; stdcall; abstract;
```

Notice that the function returns two pointers and two associated sizes. This is due to the cyclic characteristic of an audio buffer. Let's look at an example:

Assume that the audio buffer length is 100 bytes. We'll set **dwWriteCursor** to 75 and **dwWriteBytes** to 50. Since writing 50 bytes, starting at byte 75, would extend past the end of the buffer, DirectSound wraps the write to the beginning of the buffer. The return values would look like this:

```
lplpvAudioPtr1  =  {pointer to address starting at byte 75}
lpdwAudioBytes1 =  25
lplpvAudioPtr2  =  {pointer to address starting at byte 0}
lpdwAudioBytes2 =  25
```

So the total number of bytes written is the same as what we had requested, but because of our starting position within the buffer, DirectSound wrapped around to the beginning of the buffer for us. Now let's move on to the part of the program where all of this hard work pays off.

Testing DirectSound's Features

The functions in Listing 15.14 are all from udstest.pas. They implement the higher-level functionality such as play, stop, change volume, etc. They don't require much by way of explanation; however, you should examine the code before you continue.

Listing 15.14   Multiple Functions from udstest.pas

```pascal
procedure TMain.btnPlayClick(Sender: TObject);
var
  Flags: DWORD;

begin
  Flags := 0;
  if WaveList.Selected <> nil then begin
    If TDSBuffer(WaveList.Selected.Data).Loop then
      Flags := DSBPLAY_LOOPING;
    TDSBuffer(WaveList.Selected.Data).IDSB.Play(0,0,Flags);
  end;

end;

procedure TMain.btnStopClick(Sender: TObject);
begin
  if WaveList.Selected <> nil then
    TDSBuffer(WaveList.Selected.Data).IDSB.Stop;
end;

procedure TMain.chkLoopClick(Sender: TObject);
begin
  if WaveList.Selected <> nil then
    TDSBuffer(WaveList.Selected.Data).Loop := chkLoop.Checked;
end;

procedure TMain.WaveListClick(Sender: TObject);
var
  Vol: LongInt;
  Freq: DWORD;
  Result: HRESULT;
```

```
begin
  if WaveList.Selected <> nil then begin
    chkLoop.Checked := TDSBuffer(WaveList.Selected.Data).Loop;

    Result := TDSBuffer(WaveList.Selected.Data).IDSB.GetVolume(Vol);
    if Result = DS_OK then begin
      trbVolume.Enabled := True;
      trbVolume.Position := Vol;
      lblVol.Caption := 'Volume attenuated by ' +
        IntToStr(trbVolume.Position div 100) + ' db';
      end
    else
      trbVolume.Enabled := False;

    Result := TDSBuffer(WaveList.Selected.Data).IDSB.GetFrequency(Freq);
    if Result = DS_OK then begin
      trbFreq.Enabled := True;
      trbFreq.Position := Freq;
      lblFreq.Caption := 'Frequency: ' + IntToStr(trbFreq.Position) + 'Hz';
      end
    else
      trbFreq.Enabled := False;

    end; {if selection <> nil}

end; {WaveListClick}

procedure TMain.trbVolumeChange(Sender: TObject);
begin
  if WaveList.Selected <> nil then begin
    TDSBuffer(WaveList.Selected.Data).IDSB.SetVolume(trbVolume.Position);
    lblVol.Caption := 'Volume attenuated by ' +
      IntToStr(trbVolume.Position div 100) + ' db';
    end;

end;

procedure TMain.trbFreqChange(Sender: TObject);
begin
  if WaveList.Selected <> nil then begin
    TDSBuffer(WaveList.Selected.Data).IDSB.SetFrequency(trbFreq.Position);
    lblFreq.Caption := 'Frequency: ' + IntToStr(trbFreq.Position) + 'Hz';
    end;

end;
```

Remember that when we reference the **TDSBuffer** object, stored as a *pointer* in **WaveList.Selected.Data**, we have to *typecast* it from **pointer** to **TDSBuffer**. That's really the only trick to the event procedures in Listing 15.14. Now it's time to test the program.

Running the DirectSound Test Program

Make sure that you have added all of the code for this project—or load the project from the CD-ROM. Compile and run the program. If everything goes right, you'll get a screen like the one in Figure 15.4.

Load several wave files using the Open button. Lots of sample waves are available on the companion CD-ROM in the \clips\sounds directory. Once you have a few sounds loaded, try playing one (select it in the list) and press the Play button. You can change the attenuation and frequency in real-time as the audio is playing. But wait—it gets better. Set a file playing with loop checked. Now with that one playing, start another one—better yet, start three or four. DirectSound is only limited by the amount of memory available on the system.

We haven't covered everything that DirectSound is capable of doing. Not by a long shot. For instance, DirectSound has a *primary* buffer that represents a sound actually being heard through the sound card, and *secondary* buffers that DirectSound manages and mixes into the *primary* buffer. As a developer, you can access the primary buffer directly. We also didn't discuss the difference between *static* and *streaming* buffers. We used static buffers exclusively—the sounds were loaded in their entirety and stored for repeated playback. After setting up a callback routine to consistently feed data to DirectSound, we can use streaming buffers that require less memory for longer sounds.

What we have accomplished with this project is to develop a solid understanding of DirectSound basics. With the techniques developed in this project, you should be able to use DirectSound right away to mix audio in real time

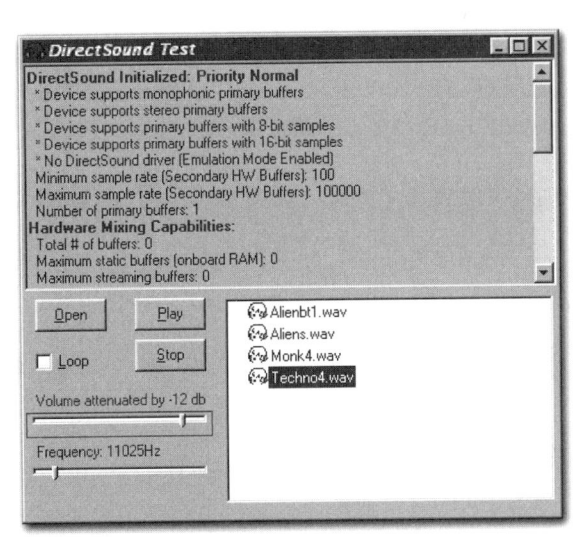

Figure 15.4   *The DirectSound Test Program in Action.*

and change attributes such as volume, panning, and frequency. You may also wish to develop and refine the class structures to create more versatile and re-usable components.

> ### Other DirectX Resources
>
> We mentioned in Chapter 14 that commercially available components for Delphi are available. We found one company that offers a complete suite of DirectX components for Delphi 2.0. Systems Advisory Group Enterprises, Inc., of Amarillo, TX, offers all four DirectX components for a very reasonable price. For a little bit more, they even offer the source code. We only briefly looked at the DirectDraw and DirectSound components and did not have a chance to look at DirectInput or DirectPlay. The components seemed stable and they were very easy to use. If the last project we worked on isn't your idea of a good time, you might want to check these out. Samples of each of the components are on the companion CD-ROM in the \demos\RingZero directory. Also don't forget to check out the FastGraph sample programs in \demos\FastGraph. FastGraph provides access to DirectDraw through their fast, familiar, and time-proven libraries.

Recording Wave Audio

Besides all the playback features we've covered in this chapter and in Chapter 5, the multimedia system also supports wave recording. For many of the waveOut functions, you will find corresponding waveIn functions. To get a more in-depth range of knowledge about wave audio, we're going to use the MCI to record wave audio. This method allows the multimedia system to deal with the low-level I/O that you've become familiar with, and gives you an easy interface to a wealth of multimedia functionality.

> ### Using the MCI to Record Wave Audio
>
> In this brief project, we'll use the API function mciSendString to record wave audio. Follow these steps to see how this works:
>
> 1. Create a simple form with three TButton components.
> 2. Add the form event code to the form's code unit.
>
> *This project is located in the directory \delphimm\15\wavercd.*

Running the Program

When you run the wavercd program, it will display a small form with three TButton components as shown in Figure 15.5.

Make sure you have some kind of input audio source ready, such as a microphone or an audio CD in your CD-ROM drive. You may need to select an input source using the mixer application that came with your sound card. For specific instructions, consult the user guide for your sound card.

When your input source is ready, click on the *Record* button to begin recording. Wait a few seconds, then click on the button labeled *Stop and Save*. You may then click on the *Play* button to replay your recording.

Creating the Form

Place three Tbuttons on a new form and name them btnRec, btnStop, and btnPlay. The complete code unit for the form appears in Listing 15.15.

Listing 15.15   uwavercd.pas

```
unit uwaverec;

interface

uses
   Windows, Messages, SysUtils, Classes, Graphics, Controls, Forms, Dialogs,
   StdCtrls, ComCtrls;

type
   TMain = class(TForm)
     btnRecord: TButton;
     btnStop: TButton;
     btnPlay: TButton;
     procedure btnPlayClick(Sender: TObject);
     procedure btnRecordClick(Sender: TObject);
     procedure btnStopClick(Sender: TObject);
   private
     { Private declarations }
   public
     { Public declarations }
   end;

var
   Main: TMain;
```

Figure 15.5   *The Wave Recorder.*

```pascal
implementation

{$R *.DFM}

uses
  MMSystem;

type
  LastAction = (actPlay, actRec, actStop);

var
  ReturnString: array[0..255] of Char;

procedure TMain.btnPlayClick(Sender: TObject);
begin

  mciSendString(                        //Play the wave file
    'play testfile.wav',
    ReturnString,
    256, 0
    );

end;

procedure TMain.btnRecordClick(Sender: TObject);
begin

  mciSendString(
    'Open New type WaveAudio alias wave',  //Start a new waveaudio file in
                                           //memory
    ReturnString,
    256,
    0
    );

  mciSendString(
    'set wave bitpersample 8',          //Set the bits per sample to 8
    ReturnString,
    256,
    0
    );

  mciSendString(
    'set wave samplespersec 11025',     //Set the sample rate to 11025
    ReturnString,
    256,
    0
    );

  mciSendString(
    'set wave channels 2',              //Set the number of channels to 2
    ReturnString,
    256,
    0
    );
```

```
  mciSendString(
    'record wave',                    //Start recording
    ReturnString,
    256,
    0
    );

end;

procedure TMain.btnStopClick(Sender: TObject);
begin
  mciSendString(
    'stop wave',                      //Stop recording
    ReturnString,
    256,0
    );

  mciSendString(
    'save wave testfile.wav',         //Save the file
    ReturnString,
    256,0
    );

  mciSendString(
    'close wave',                     //Close the file
    ReturnString,
    256,0
    );

end;

end.
```

With a handful of MCI commands, the low-level functions we explored earlier, and DirectSound under your belt—you're on your way to really dynamic multimedia or game titles. Now that you have a thorough understanding of waveform digital audio, let's move on to MIDI.

Chapter 16

Learn how to use MIDI to add music to your programs.

Using the Musical Instrument Digital Interface

Scott Jarol

At the 1982 convention of the National Association of Music Manufacturers, a revolution started in the electronic music industry. Korg and Kawai, two of the largest makers of electronic musical instruments, drove the Golden Spike of the music industry when they linked together their instruments with the new Musical Instrument Digital Interface (MIDI). The music industry has never looked back. MIDI now occupies a prominent place and has appeared in hundreds of thousands of recordings and live performances. Almost any electronic device, from the humblest portable keyboards to 48-channel studio mixers, includes a set of MIDI ports.

These simple five-pin connectors offer some of the most thrilling opportunities for budding multimedia moguls. While it offers phenomenal benefits, MIDI has also opened the door to corridors of confusion. Before you can fully appreciate MIDI's potential, you need to grasp some MIDI fundamentals. Let's take a closer look at what MIDI does and how it works, and then we'll explore how to access MIDI devices from our VB apps.

Everything You Need to Know about MIDI

Most MIDI devices—electronic keyboards, modular synthesizers, audio mixers, drum machines, and so on—are external and talk to each other over a three-wire cable. You might not realize it, but your sound card includes a MIDI compatible synthesizer. This MIDI device lives inside your computer and talks directly to your computer's bus. Most sound cards let you hook up additional MIDI devices through a set of MIDI ports known as *In, Out,* and *Through*.

MIDI is actually a real-time interactive network. In theory, any device that includes at least one MIDI In and one MIDI Out port can talk to any other MIDI device. Many MIDI devices also offer a MIDI Through port to pass along data that comes in the MIDI In port. MIDI devices are not limited to three ports, however. In fact, many products provide several ports in various combinations of the three types.

The Musical Connection

When most people hear the term "MIDI", they think of musical applications. After all, the letter "M" in MIDI stands for Musical. But as we explore MIDI's musical features, keep in mind that it has grown far beyond its original specifications.

At the hardware level, MIDI provides a simple asynchronous serial interface that transmits data in ten bit chunks at a rate of 31.25 kilobaud (31,250 bits per second). The ten bits include a start bit, eight data bits, and a stop bit. Although we won't be dealing with many hardware issues in this chapter, you'll want to remember the transmission rate when you create your MIDI apps.

The data that travels through the MIDI cable controls electronic musical instruments—synthesizers. Before MIDI, in the late 1970s, as these instruments began to acquire the sophistication of digital electronics, their manufacturers developed various proprietary systems for interconnecting their products. Their main goal was to create integrated musical workshops so that musicians could compose and play music on several instruments simultaneously. This required at least one synthesizer, along with a device that could record what was played as a *sequence* of control events, or keypresses, just like a player piano roll. With such a system, you could later substitute a different note, change the duration of a note, or eliminate a note entirely without recording the entire passage again. And because you were only recording keystrokes (rather than analog waveforms), you could even change the tempo of the music without changing its pitch, or transpose the pitch without changing the tempo. These recording devices became known as *sequencers*. Once that problem was solved, it didn't take long for most manufacturers to recognize

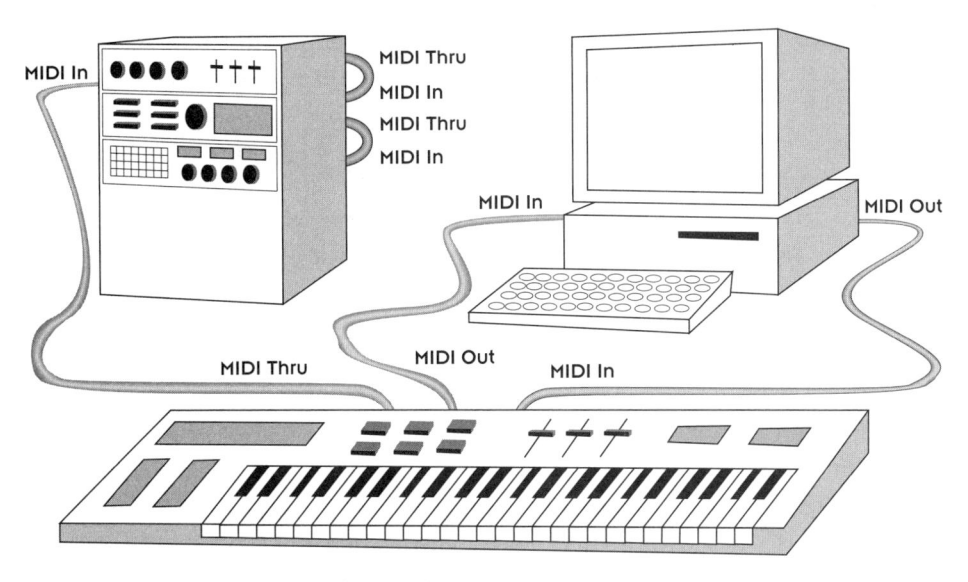

Figure 16.1 *A typical MIDI hardware setup.*

the need for a standard protocol to link sequencers and synthesizers. That's how MIDI was born. Figure 16.1 shows a typical MIDI hardware setup.

Once you can make a sequencer talk to a synthesizer, you can make synthesizers talk to each other. If you plug the MIDI Out port of one instrument into the MIDI In port of a second instrument, you can play the second synthesizer from the keyboard of the first. Most manufacturers now offer major models in two versions, one with a keyboard, and one without. Keyboardless versions are usually called *synthesizer modules* and they often come in "rack mount" cabinets. In the pre-MIDI era, keyboard players like Rick Wakeman and Keith Emerson often appeared on stage in synthesizer pods, surrounded by walls of keyboards. Like space aliens in their cockpits, they flailed around from instrument to instrument, which made for a flashy performance but created a setup nightmare. Today, performing keyboardists may play one or two keyboards on stage while controlling dozens of instruments stacked neatly on racks—out of the way.

A Look at MIDI Messages

MIDI devices communicate by sending each other messages. Messages are divided into two general categories—*channel* and *system*—and into five types—*voice, mode, system common, system real-time,* and *system exclusive*.

The first category, *channel messages*, includes *voice messages* and *mode messages*. These messages are grouped into the channel message category because they are transmitted on individual channels rather than globally to all devices in the MIDI network. To understand how MIDI devices identify channels, let's take some time to review the structure of a MIDI message.

As shown in Figure 16.2, a MIDI message includes a *status byte* and up to two *data bytes*. It's easy to identify a status byte because all status bytes have their most significant bit set to 1. Conversely, the most significant bit of any data byte is set to 0. This convention holds true for all standard MIDI messages and not just channel messages. Therefore, the data in each byte must be encoded in the seven remaining bits.

MIDI devices transmit all messages on the same cable, regardless of their channel assignments. In the early days of MIDI, musicians and recording engineers were accustomed to 48 track audio mixers, tangled patch panels, and fat umbilical cords stuffed with wire. These folks had a hard time understanding that they didn't need a separate cable for each MIDI channel. The four low-order bits of each status byte identify the channel to which it belongs. Four bits produce 16 possible combinations, so MIDI supports 16 channels over a single cable string. (Keep in mind that although MIDI users and vendors number the channels from 1 through 16, internally they are numbered 0 through 15.) The three remaining bits identify the message. Three bits encode eight possible combinations, so channel messages could come in eight flavors—but they don't. A status byte with all four high-order bits set to 1 indicates a system common message: the second general category, which we'll cover after we tackle the channel messages. For that reason, channel messages are limited to seven.

The Channel Voice Messages

Most of the channel messages are voice messages, as shown in Table 16.1. Voice messages:

- Instruct the receiving instrument to assign particular sounds to its *voices*
- Turn notes on and off
- Send *controller* signals that can alter the sound of the currently active note

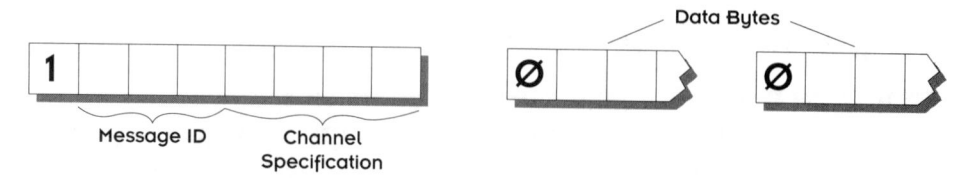

Figure 16.2 *How MIDI messages are structured.*

Table 16.1 MIDI Channel Voice Messages

Voice Message	Status Byte Hex Value	Number of Data Bytes
Note Off	&H8x	2
Note On	&H9x	2
Polyphonic Aftertouch	&HAx	2
Control Change	&HBx	2
Program Change	&HCx	1
Aftertouch	&HDx	1
Pitch Bend	&HEx	1 or 2

A *voice* is the portion of the synthesizer that produces sound. Most modern synthesizers have several voices—that is, they have several circuits that work independently and simultaneously to produce sounds of different *timbre* and *pitch*. Timbre is the sound that the instrument will imitate, such as a flute, cello, or helicopter. Pitch is the musical note that the instrument plays. To play two notes together, the synthesizer uses two voices. Those voices may play two notes with the same timbre or two notes of different timbres. A Control Change message *modulates* the current note by altering its pitch, volume, or timbre to produce various effects such as vibrato or tremolo.

Voice messages are followed by either one or two data bytes. A Note On message, for example, is followed by two bytes: one to identify the note, and one to specify the *velocity*. The velocity specifies how the note should sound. For example, if the synthesizer's voice is set to sound like a piano, the velocity could determine how loudly the note should be played. (In the keyboard world, the faster you strike a piano key, the louder it plays.) To play note number 80 with maximum velocity on channel 13, the MIDI device would send the following three hexadecimal byte values:

&H9C &H50 &H7F

To turn off the note, it would send either the Note Off message:

&H8C &H50 &H00

or the Note On message with a velocity of 0:

&H9C &H50 &H00

Note: The Note Off channel voice message accepts a velocity because some synthesizers can use the release velocity to determine how a note should decay once it has been shut off. Almost any instrument will accept a Note On message with a velocity of 0 in lieu of a Note Off message.

Often, you will hear musicians and synthesizer technicians use the term *patches*. The make and model of each synthesizer offers unique controls for designing and setting timbres. A patch refers to the control settings that define a particular timbre. The actual contents of a patch depends on the particular instrument; so rather than sending the whole patch to the instrument through MIDI (although this is also possible), the Program Change voice message sends a number from 0 to 127, in order to select a patch already stored in the instrument's own *voice bank* memory. For example, to set the instrument on channel 13 to its patch 104, you would send this MIDI message:

```
&HCC &H68
```

Four of the channel voice messages—Control Change, Polyphonic Aftertouch, Aftertouch, and Pitch Bend—signal a *controller* change. For example, when a saxophone player blows harder, his instrument may sound harsher. By cleverly programming the synthetic saxophone, a keyboard musician can use a slider, foot pedal, or some other device to simulate the breath control of a sax player. Let's take a look at these voice message types.

Pitch Bend was so common on synthesizers when the MIDI specification was created, that it was given its own MIDI message (&HEx). This message signals the synthesizer to raise or lower the pitch of currently active notes on the channel. Pitch Bend messages do not contain note values. The value of the Pitch Bend message bytes reflects the degree to which the pitch bend controller (usually a wheel or lever beside the keyboard) has been moved up or down. The degree to which the pitch changes is determined by the instrument itself.

Like Pitch Bend, *Aftertouch* was considered valuable and common enough to be granted its own MIDI message types. The first type of Aftertouch, known as *Polyphonic Aftertouch* (&HAx), transmits a value on a particular channel, for a particular note, that indicates the degree of pressure on the key after it has been struck. Many electronic keyboards now support this feature, which enables keyboard players to have some of the control that other musicians achieve by changing the pressure on their mouthpieces or bows. The other Aftertouch control message (&HDx) is used when an instrument supports aftertouch, but not on individual notes. In other words, a change in pressure on one key will affect all the notes currently playing on the channel.

The creators of the MIDI specification realized that other types of controllers were found on some instruments, and that more would follow. So, they created one general purpose channel voice message (&HBx) to handle them. The first data byte of the Control Change message selects the controller type, and the second byte specifies its current value. You'll find a complete listing of the pre-defined controller types in the *MIDI 1.0 Detailed Specification* (see the bibliography). Actually, the Control Change message supports only 121 controllers, numbered 0 through 120. The remaining 7 values are reserved for the Channel Mode Messages.

The Channel Mode Messages

Mode messages determine how an instrument will process MIDI voice messages. Now that you understand how to send MIDI channel voice messages, you'll have an easier time understanding how to send channel mode messages. Unfortunately, some of the modes themselves have caused more confusion than any other aspect of MIDI.

Channel Mode messages are a special case of the Control Change message. They always begin with a status byte containing the value &HBx, where x is the channel number. The difference between a Control Change message and a Channel Mode message, which share the same status byte value, is in the first data byte. Data byte values 121 through 127 have been reserved in the Control Change message for the channel mode messages. These are listed in Table 16.2.

Table 16.2 The Channel Mode Messages

First Data Byte Value	Description	Meaning of Second Data Byte
&H79	Reset All Controllers	None; set to 0
&H7A	Local Control	0 = Off; 127 = On
&H7B	All Notes Off	None; set to 0
&H7C	Omni Mode Off	None; set to 0
&H7D	Omni Mode On	None; set to 0
&H7E	Mono Mode On (Poly Mode Off)	0 means that the number of channels used is determined by the receiver; all other values set a specific number of channels, beginning with the current basic channel
&H7F	Poly Mode On (Mono Mode Off)	None; set to 0

Of these messages, the least understood—and therefore most creatively interpreted by instrument manufacturers—are Omni Mode On, Omni Mode Off, Mono Mode On, and Poly Mode On. Actually, modes have a life of their own that is independent of the mode messages; most electronic instruments provide a front panel control that allows you to choose the current mode. The Channel Mode messages were added to the MIDI specification to enable remotely controlled mode changes on the fly over the MIDI cable. The intent of these modes is to determine how an instrument responds to incoming channel voice messages.

Omni Mode means that the instrument responds to messages on all 16 channels. If Note On messages are transmitted on all channels, the instrument in Omni Mode will attempt to play them all, up to the maximum number of voices it has available. Some synthesizers, *monophonic* instruments, can only play one note at a time. Others, known as *polyphonic* instruments, can play 8, 16, 32, or other numbers of simultaneous notes. If a device with only 8 voices receives 15 simultaneous Note On messages, it will play only the first or last 8.

For most real-world applications, Omni Mode isn't discerning enough. (In fact, it isn't discerning at all.) Most polyphonic instruments can not only play a multitude of simultaneous notes, they can also play them with a variety of patches. Which enables one synthesizer to sound like a whole band. In Poly Mode, each channel is assigned a patch. All notes on each channel play with the same timbre. For example, you could set channel 1 to play bass, channel 2 to play piano, and channel 3 to play drums. In Mono Mode, only one note can play at a time on each channel. Poly Mode has some powerful capabilities, but we don't have room to discuss them here. For detailed coverage of MIDI modes, order a copy of the *MIDI 1.0 Detailed Specification*.

The System Messages

The second general category of MIDI messages are the *system messages*, which include *system common messages, system real-time messages,* and *system exclusive messages*. These messages carry information that is not channel-specific, such as timing signals for synchronization, positioning information in pre-recorded MIDI sequences, and detailed setup information for the destination device.

The four types of system common messages are shown in Table 16.3.

The six system real-time messages, listed in Table 16.4, primarily affect sequencer playback and recording. These messages have no data bytes.

Table 16.3 *The MIDI System Common Messages*

System Common Message	Status Byte Hex Value	Number of Data Bytes
MIDI Time Code	&HF1	1
Song Position Pointer	&HF2	2
Song Select	&HF3	1
Tune Request	&HF6	None

The third type of system message, the system exclusive message, is used to transfer data between devices. For example, you may wish to store patch setups for an instrument on a computer using a *patch librarian* program. You can then transfer those patches to the synthesizer by means of a system exclusive message. The name *system exclusive* means that these are messages exclusively for a particular device, or type of device, rather than universal messages that all MIDI compatible products should recognize. A system exclusive message is just a stream of bytes, all with their high bits set to 0, bracketed by a pair of system exclusive start and end messages (&HF0 and &HF7).

The MIDI Offspring

Since the introduction of the MIDI protocol, four other MIDI standards have appeared:

- MIDI Show Control 1.0
- MIDI Machine Control 1.0
- Standard MIDI Files 1.0
- General MIDI System, Level 1

Table 16.4 *The MIDI System Real-Time Messages*

System Real Time Message	Status Byte Hex Value
Timing Clock	&HF8
Start Sequence	&HFA
Continue Sequence	&HFB
Stop Sequence	&HFC
Active Sensing	&HFE
System Reset	&HFF

The MIDI Show Control and MIDI Machine Control standards specify a set of system-exclusive messages that can control various types of non-musical equipment. The Show Control focuses specifically on stage lighting and sound control systems, although it is designed to control just about any kind of performance system, including mechanical stages. The Machine Control standard specifies system exclusive messages to operate audio and video recorders.

The biggest problem that surfaced after the widespread adoption of the MIDI protocol was in sequencer file formats. Shortly after the introduction of the first MIDI-equipped synthesizers, several sequencer programs appeared. Sequencer programs allow musicians and composers to record and playback MIDI information. With a sequencer, one person can compose and play an entire symphony, using nothing more than a computer and a few synthesizers. All these programs, no matter which platform they supported, adhered to the MIDI communication protocol. They had to, or they wouldn't work. But the files in which they stored their data were another matter. Each software developer created its own proprietary format, making it impossible to create a music sequence with one program and play it back with another. So in 1988, The International MIDI Association published the second component of the MIDI standard, *Standard MIDI Files 1.0*. Standard MIDI files are built from *chunks*, which contain some header information and a series of data bytes. Sound familiar? Although not identical, MIDI standard files and RIFF files have quite a bit in common. In fact, a Windows MIDI file is actually a standard MIDI file embedded in a RIFF chunk.

Standard MIDI files made it possible for musicians to share their files, regardless of hardware and software platforms. But this new standard brought to light another problem. The *tracks* in a MIDI sequencer file may specify a program number, which determines the instrument sound (or patch) with which that track should be played. But every instrument has its own assortment of patches. So, while program number 30 on one synthesizer might be a brass section patch, the same program number on another instrument could be a tympani drum, or a sci-fi phaser gun. Playback of a standard MIDI file might produce all the right notes; however, they may be on all the wrong instruments. The General MIDI System standard attempts to solve this problem by offering a standard program list, consisting of the 128 most common patch types, from pianos to gunshots (literally—General MIDI program 1 is 'Acoustic Grand Piano,' and program 128 is 'Gunshot'). General MIDI also specifies a layout for percussion instruments, called the General MIDI Percussion Map. Percussion is a special case, because non-melodic percussion sounds, such as drums, cymbals, and cowbells, need to occupy only one note position, so you can theoretically fit up to 128 separate percussion sounds in one patch. General MIDI includes 47 percussion sounds and specifies that percussion should be transmitted on MIDI channel 10.

General MIDI is considered a *system* rather than a *specification,* because not all instruments need to comply. In fact, that would defeat the purpose of programmable synthesizers that enable artists to continually invent new sounds. Some synthesizer modules are designed specifically for use as General MIDI devices, and come pre-programmed with compliant patches. Other synthesizers support a General MIDI mode, but also provide a separate programmable patch bank. And some instruments don't support General MIDI at all, unless you program and arrange the patches yourself.

MIDI and Windows

The Windows Multimedia System fully supports MIDI. Besides the standard MCI commands that enable us to play (but not record) MIDI files, there are 29 low-level MIDI functions in the API, with which we can send and receive MIDI messages over any of the 16 channels. To use these functions, you'll need either a sound card equipped with MIDI ports, or a dedicated MIDI adapter.

MIDI Connections

Most sound cards today provide a combination joystick/MIDI port in the form of a 15-pin connector. To use this port for MIDI, you'll need an adapter cable, usually available from the card's manufacturer, to convert the 15-pin connector to either two or three 5-pin DIN connectors, as shown in Figure 16.3. If your adapter cable provides three MIDI ports, there will be one of

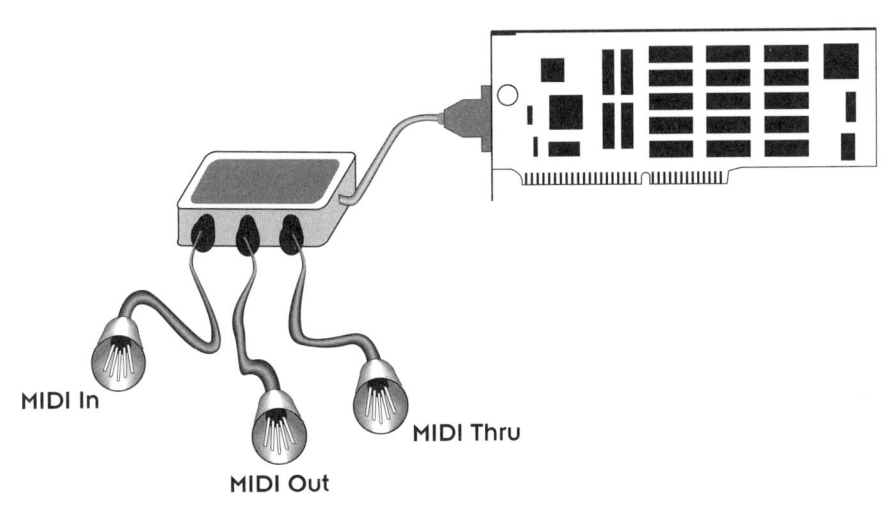

Figure 16.3 *A typical sound card with its MIDI adapter cable attached.*

each type (In, Out, and Through). If only two are present, they are likely to be In and Out ports.

Three of the most common brands of PC sound cards, The Creative Labs Soundblaster series, the Media Vision Pro Audio Spectrum series, and the Advanced Gravis Ultrasound, all use the same type of MIDI cable. The professional level Multisound card from Turtle Beach Systems has no joystick port, but provides a 9-pin connector to which you may attach a special MIDI cable that is available from the manufacturer.

It's important not to confuse the on-board synthesizer on your sound card with the card's MIDI capabilities. You don't need a sound card at all to use the MIDI multimedia functions. You can just install a MIDI port adapter, such as the Roland MPU-401, which would enable you to exchange MIDI data with any external MIDI device, including synthesizers, drum machines, sequencers—even other computers. The synthesizer on your sound card acts like any other MIDI device; you play notes on it by sending it MIDI messages. How your on-board synthesizer responds to MIDI depends partly on the settings in the Windows MIDI Mapper.

The Windows MIDI Mapper

For some reason, the Windows MIDI Mapper has inspired just about as much fear and loathing as any other Windows feature. That could be because Microsoft slipped it in with little fanfare, and even less explanation. However, the purpose and operation of the MIDI Mapper is really pretty simple.

With Windows 3.1, the MIDI Mapper helped achieve some level of device independence between MIDI devices. For example, not all sound cards' internal patches are organized according to General MIDI guidelines. The Patch Maps section of the Windows 3.1 MIDI Mapper provides a way to map General MIDI patch numbers to the actual patches in the sound card, as shown in Figure 16.4.

The Key Maps dialog box from Windows 3.1, shown in Figure 16.5, is used to remap notes. Why would you need to do this, you ask? There are two reasons. The MIDI 1.0 Detailed Specification places middle C at note 60 (&H3C). Some older devices, especially those not specifically designed to support MIDI, may use a different note position mapping. You can use the Key Maps dialog box to remap the device's own note positions to the standard configuration.

You can also use the Key Maps dialog box to map percussion instruments to the General MIDI layout. For example, in General MIDI, note 35 is an Acoustic Bass Drum. Some devices place that instrument at note 47, one octave higher, so the Key Map can be used to remap it.

Using the Musical Instrument Digital Interface 745

MIDI Patch Map: 'MT32'

1 based patches

Src Patch	Src Patch Name	Dest Patch	Volume %	Key Map Name
0	Acoustic Grand Piano	0	100	[None]
1	Bright Acoustic Piano	1	100	[None]
2	Electric Grand Piano	3	100	[None]
3	Honky-tonk Piano	7	100	[None]
4	Rhodes Piano	5	100	[None]
5	Chorused Piano	6	100	[None]
6	Harpsichord	17	100	[None]
7	Clavinet	21	100	[None]
8	Celesta	22	100	[None]
9	Glockenspiel	101	100	[None]
10	Music Box	101	100	[None]
11	Vibraphone	98	100	[None]
12	Marimba	104	100	[None]
13	Xylophone	103	100	[None]
14	Tubular Bells	102	100	[None]
15	Dulcimer	105	100	[None]

OK   Cancel   Help

Figure 16.4 *The Windows 3.1 MIDI Patch Map dialog box allows you to map General MIDI patch numbers to the actual patches in the sound card.*

MIDI Key Map: '+1 octave'

Src Key	Src Key Name	Dest Key
35	Acoustic Bass Drum	47
36	Bass Drum 1	48
37	Side Stick	49
38	Acoustic Snare	50
39	Hand Clap	51
40	Electric Snare	52
41	Low Floor Tom	53
42	Closed Hi Hat	54
43	High Floor Tom	55
44	Pedal Hi Hat	56
45	Low Tom	57
46	Open Hi Hat	58
47	Low-Mid Tom	59
48	High-Mid Tom	60
49	Crash Cymbal 1	61
50	High Tom	62

OK   Cancel   Help

Figure 16.5 *The Windows 3.1 MIDI Key Maps dialog box allows you to remap notes and to map percussion instruments to the General MIDI system.*

Chapter 16

Src Chan	Dest Chan	Port Name	Patch Map Name	Active
1	1	MVI Pro Audio/CDPC MID	[None]	☒
2	2	MVI Pro Audio/CDPC MIDI Output	[None]	☒
3	3	MVI Pro Audio/CDPC MIDI Output	[None]	☒
4	4	MVI Pro Audio/CDPC MIDI Output	[None]	☒
5	5	MVI Pro Audio/CDPC MIDI Output	[None]	☒
6	6	MVI Pro Audio/CDPC MIDI Output	[None]	☒
7	7	MVI Pro Audio/CDPC MIDI Output	[None]	☒
8	8	MVI Pro Audio/CDPC MIDI Output	[None]	☒
9	9	MVI Pro Audio/CDPC MIDI Output	[None]	☒
10	10	MVI Pro Audio/CDPC MIDI Output	[None]	☒
11	11	[None]	[None]	■
12	12	[None]	[None]	■
13	13	Voyetra OPL-3 FM Synth	[None]	☒
14	14	Voyetra OPL-3 FM Synth	[None]	☒
15	15	Voyetra OPL-3 FM Synth	[None]	☒
16	16	Voyetra OPL-3 FM Synth	[None]	☒

Figure 16.6 *The Windows 3.1 MIDI Mapper Setup dialog box allows you to assign a patch map to each MIDI channel.*

The Windows 3.1 MIDI Mapper also includes the MIDI Setup dialog box, shown in Figure 16.6, which enables you to remap channels and select patch maps for each channel individually. The patch map is device-specific. In other words, if you play all music on one instrument—whether the on-board synthesizer on your sound card, or a single external instrument connected to your MIDI Out port—the patch map would be the same on all channels. If you connect multiple instruments into the MIDI chain by linking the Through port of each instrument to the In port of the next, you may need a separate patch map for each one. In this case, you would use the MIDI Mapper to assign the patch map to the channel or channels on which the corresponding instrument is waiting for MIDI messages. This may seem complicated, but it really simplifies things when it comes time to play music. By mapping all instruments to the General MIDI patch numbers, you can send MIDI messages that select the correct patches on each instrument without considering each instrument's unique patch layout. So, device-*specific* MIDI Setups produce device-*independent* operation.

The construction of a complete MIDI setup under Windows 3.1 is a three-step process:

1. Create the necessary key maps.
2. Create the patch maps, using the appropriate key maps if needed.

Using the Musical Instrument Digital Interface

3. Create the MIDI Setup, assigning Source Channels to Destination Channels, Ports, and Patch Maps.

The installation program for your sound card's drivers should have installed the Windows 3.1 MIDI drivers and any required MIDI Mapper setups.

If you look at the setup shown in Figure 16.6, you'll notice that the activated channels are divided into two groups. Channels 1 through 10 are set to MVI Pro Audio/CDPC MIDI Output, while channels 13 through 16 are set to Voyetra OPL-3 FM Synth. The setting on the first ten channels causes them to send their output to an external MIDI device, completely bypassing the on-board synthesizer. The second group of channels do just the opposite; they send all messages to the internal device, the OPL-3 FM synthesizer chip. These groupings reflect Microsoft's own contribution to the standardization of MIDI files and devices, at least as far as Windows 3.1 is concerned!

Windows 95 clearly makes life much easier for us. We no longer have to worry about the MIDI Mapper, because Windows 95 knows which type of audio card is installed, so it figures out how to map the channels and patches to match the card's capabilities. You do have the option of selecting which instrument to play through. On one of our systems, we installed a Creative Labs AWE 32 sound card. Now that Windows 95 has recognized the card and set it up, we can go into the MIDI page of the Multimedia Properties dialog box, where we have three options for MIDI output, as shown in Figure 16.7.

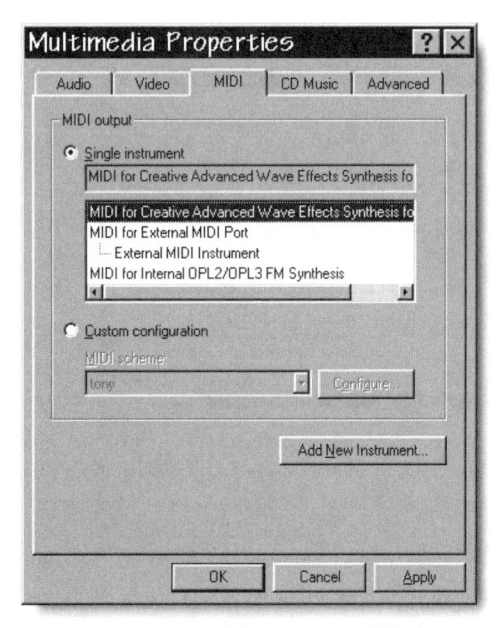

Figure 16.7 The Multimedia Properties dialog box from Windows 95.

If the default setting does not work well for you, then you can try the others. If that fails to give you the desired results, you can custom-build your own output scheme. Windows 95 will probably set things up pretty well on its own, but this is where you want to go if you have problems. To set up your own instrument configuration, click on the Custom Configuration radio button and click on Configure. You will be presented with the MIDI Configuration dialog box, as shown in Figure 16.8. Here, you custom-pick the output device for each channel.

Windows recognizes two general types of synthesizers: *Base-Level* and *Extended-Level.* These two categories reflect the capabilities of the devices. A Base-Level device can play at least three distinct and simultaneous patches, each assigned to its own channel, with at least six simultaneous notes. The notes may be distributed in any way across the three channels. At one point during playback, one channel can be used to play a single note, the second channel can play two notes, and the third channel can play three notes. Then, later in the same sequence, the voices can shift so the first channel can play four notes, while the third channel plays the remaining two notes. This is called *dynamic voice allocation.* In addition to the minimum of six simultaneous melodic notes, a Base-Level device must also support a minimum of three simultaneous percussion notes. The melodic parts are played from MIDI channels 13, 14, and 15; while percussion is played from channel 16.

Extended-Level MIDI devices can play at least nine distinct and simultaneous patches on nine separate channels with a minimum of sixteen simultaneous,

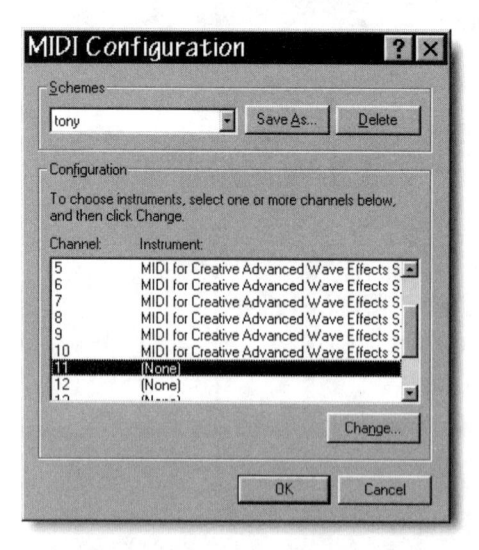

Figure 16.8 The MIDI Configuration properties dialog box from Windows 95.

dynamically allocated notes. The percussion channel should support an additional sixteen simultaneous notes. The melodic voices play on channels 1 through 9, with percussion on channel 10. Channels 11 and 12 are unassigned.

Most of the popular sound cards available today, especially those based on the OPL FM synthesizer chips, meet or exceed the Base-Level requirements. Only a few products meet the Extended-Level specification. Some of the cards that act as if they were Extended-Level devices fail to comply fully with the guidelines, usually by offering fewer than the 32 recommended voices.

To provide device-independent support for MIDI sequencer files, Microsoft recommends that any Windows compatible file should contain two versions of the sequence: one that will play on a Base-Level device and one that will play on an Extended-Level device. The file CANYON.MID, which comes with Windows 95, is an example of such a file. The MIDI playback system will pump out data on all 14 assigned channels, but if the MIDI Setup is correct, as it should be with Windows 95, only one set of tracks will play on any given device. You may run into a situation where both the base-level and extended-level tracks are being played back at the same time. Depending on the MIDI file, you may not notice it at all. With other files, you may distinctly hear two separate tracks. When we were working on the projects for this chapter, we ran into this problem. For many popular sound cards, the channel maps in Windows 95 seem to default to a full sixteen channel configuration. The solution is to set up a custom MIDI configuration using the Windows 95 MIDI configuration editor (see Figure 16.8). For a sound card that supports the Extended-Level, simply highlight channels 1 through 10, either one at a time or as a group, making sure they are pointing to an available device, usually something referred to as the "internal synthesizer". Set channels 11 through 16 to None so that their tracks will not be output, and there you have it. Now only the extended-level tracks will be heard. If you have only Base-Level MIDI support on your sound card, do the opposite: set channels 1 through 12 to None, and set channels 13 through 16 to the appropriate device.

Sending MIDI Messages

You've seen in Chapter 15 how to play a MIDI file with MCI commands. It's as simple as sending the string "Play filename.MID" with either the **mciExecute()** or **mciSendString()** functions. But now that you know something about MIDI messages and where they go, let's use the low-level MIDI API functions to send some messages directly to the device. We'll begin with a simple experiment so you can see how the functions work. Then we'll explore the Delphi MIDI Piano, a nifty little program based on the VB MIDI

Piano, a program originally created in Microsoft Visual Basic by MIDI programming wizard Arthur Edstrom, of Artic Software, Inc.

Sending MIDI Messages

It takes only a handful of API functions to open and use a MIDI device. In this project we'll try them out. Here are the steps to follow:

1. Open a new project named MidiOut, with a singe form named MidiOutForm.
2. Place a label, an edit box, and two button components on the form, as shown in figure 16.9
3. Fill in the code (Listing 16.1).

You'll find this project in the directory \DELPHIMM\CH16\MIDIOUT in the files MidiOut.DPR, MidOutFm.Pas, and MidOutFm.DFM.

Running the Program

When you run the program, it will display a small form with two Command Buttons, as shown in Figure 16.9

Click on the button labeled Open MIDI Device. Its label will then change to Close MIDI Device. Click on the Send Note button once to turn on a note, and again to turn it off. If you hear nothing, make sure the MIDI channel is set properly for your sound card or external MIDI device. Don't forget to check all your volume settings, including those in your multimedia mixer program and on any physical devices such as the amplifier controls and the output level of an external synthesizer.

When testing is complete, click on the Close MIDI Device button and end the program.

The midiOut API Functions

The MIDI API function declarations are located in MMSystem.DLL and are declared as follows:

```
function midiOutOpen(lphMidiOut: PHMidiOut; uDeviceID: Word; dwCallback,
dwInstance, dwFlags: Longint): Word;
function midiOutShortMsg(hMidiOut: HMidiOut; dwMsg: Longint): Word;
function midiOutClose(hMidiOut: HMidiOut): Word;
```

Let's take a look at how these functions work.

Figure 16.9 *The project MidiOut at run-time.*

The **midiOutOpen()** function takes five arguments. In the first argument, **lphMidiOut**, we pass a pointer to variable of type **tHandle**, which the function will fill with a handle to the device. The second argument, **uDeviceId**, specifies which MIDI device to open. Most systems have only one MIDI device, and its **uDeviceId** is 0. To select the MIDI Mapper, you would normally pass the constant **MIDI_MAPPER**, which has an integer value of -1. Unfortunately, the argument **uDeviceId** is declared as a Word, which cannot accept negative integer values, so we'll pass the equivalent hex value, "$FFFF".

The arguments **dwCallback** and **dwInstance** specify either the address of a callback function, or a handle for a window callback. Our simple examples of MIDI output won't need a callback, so we'll set both these arguments to NULL (0). Later in this chapter, when we talk about MIDI input, we'll show you how to use callbacks. The fifth argument, **dwFlags**, also relates to callbacks. Its only defined flags are **CALLBACK_WINDOW** and **CALLBACK_FUNCTION**, both of which will be ignored because **dwCallback** is set to NULL.

The function **midiOutShortMsg()** requires only two arguments. The first, as you might expect, takes the handle set by **midiOutOpen()**. In the second argument, we pass the MIDI message as a four byte long integer. The least significant byte contains the status byte, the actual MIDI command. The next higher-order byte contains the first data byte, if needed. And the third byte contains the second data byte, if needed. The highest-order byte is always set to &H00.

The third and last function declared for this project, **midiOutClose()**, takes nothing but the handle to the device.

All three of these functions return integer values that indicate error conditions. If no error occurs, they return 0.

Adding the Form Code

If you're creating this program from the ground up, start with a small form. Place two buttons on it. Set their **Name** properties to "OpenButton" and "SendMessageButton". Set their initial **Caption** properties to "Open MIDI Device" and "Send Note", respectively. Then place an edit box component on the form. Name it "ChannelText", and give it an initial **Text** property value of 16. You may also want to place a Label beside the Text Box, as we did in

Table 16.5 Control Properties for MidiOut.Pas.

Component	Property	Value
Label1	Caption	'MIDI Channel:'
ChannelEdit	Text	'16'
OpenButton	Caption	'Open MIDI Device'
SendMessageButton	Caption	'Send Note'
	Enabled	false

the sample program on the companion CD. Next, we can fill in the code. Table 16.5 shows the control properties.

This bare-bones program requires only four event procedures and a handful of variables, as shown in Listing 16.1.

Listing 16.1   The MidOutFm Form Unit

```
unit Midoutfm;

interface

uses
  SysUtils, WinTypes, WinProcs, Messages, Classes, Graphics, Controls,
  Forms, Dialogs, StdCtrls, MMSystem;

type
  TMidiOutForm = class(TForm)
    Label1: TLabel;
    ChannelEdit: TEdit;
    OpenButton: TButton;
    SendMessageButton: TButton;
    procedure FormCreate(Sender: TObject);
    procedure FormDestroy(Sender: TObject);
    procedure OpenButtonClick(Sender: TObject);
    procedure SendMessageButtonClick(Sender: TObject);
  private
    { Private declarations }
    NotePlaying    : boolean;
    hMidiOut       : tHandle;
    MidiDeviceOpen : boolean;
    MidiChannel    : integer;
  public
    { Public declarations }
  end;

var
  MidiOutForm: TMidiOutForm;

implementation
```

```
{$R *.DFM}

procedure TMidiOutForm.FormCreate(Sender: TObject);
begin
    MidiDeviceOpen := false;
    NotePlaying := false;
    MidiChannel := 0;
end;

procedure TMidiOutForm.FormDestroy(Sender: TObject);
var
    ReturnValue : integer;
begin
    ReturnValue := midiOutClose(hMidiOut);
end;

procedure TMidiOutForm.OpenButtonClick(Sender: TObject);
var
    ReturnValue : integer;

begin
    if MidiDeviceOpen then begin
        ReturnValue := midiOutClose(hMidiOut);
        OpenButton.Caption := 'Open MIDI Device';
        SendMessageButton.Enabled := false;
        end
      else begin
        ReturnValue := midiOutOpen(@hMidiOut, $FFFF, 0, 0, 0);
        OpenButton.Caption := 'Close MIDI Device';
        SendMessageButton.Enabled := true;
        end;
    MidiDeviceOpen := not MidiDeviceOpen;
end;

procedure TMidiOutForm.SendMessageButtonClick(Sender: TObject);
var
    ErrorCode        : integer;
    ReturnValue      : integer;
    MidiShortMessage : longint;
    MidiChannelValue : integer;
begin
    val(ChannelEdit.Text, MidiChannelValue, ErrorCode);
    if ErrorCode = 0 then
        MidiChannel := (abs(MidiChannelValue) - 1) mod 16;
    NotePlaying := not NotePlaying;
    if not NotePlaying then begin
        { Note On = $9x, where x = channel }
        { Middle C = $3C }
        { Velocity of 64 = $40 }
        MidiShortMessage := $403C90 + MidiChannel;
        sendMessageButton.Caption := 'Stop Note';
        end
      else begin
        { Note On = $9x, where x = channel }
```

```
      { Middle C = $3C }
      { Velocity of 0 = Note Off = $00 }
      MidiShortMessage := $3C90 + MidiChannel;
      SendMessageButton.Caption := 'Send Note';
      end;
    ReturnValue := midiOutShortMsg(hMidiOut, MidiShortMessage);
end;

end.
```

Most of the action takes place in the **TMidiOutForm.SendMessageButtonClick()** event procedure. After we make sure we're transmitting on a valid MIDI channel, we set **NotePlaying**, which determines whether we're about to turn a note on or off. If **NotePlaying** is false, we send a Note On MIDI message, &H9x. By adding the channel number of 0 to 15 to the long integer, we affect only the four low-order bits of the lowest-order byte. The second byte is set to &H3C, which will select Middle C, and the third byte is set to the median velocity, &H40. To turn off the note, we can cheat by retransmitting the Note On message with a velocity of 0.

The Delphi MIDI Piano

This project is based on a Visual Basic program contributed by Arthur Edstrom of Artic Software, Inc., which was originally written as a tutorial for all the folks hanging around in the Visual Basic forum on CompuServe who expressed an interest in VB MIDI programming. Here are the steps to follow to create the Delphi version:

1. Open a new project named MidiPian, with a single form named PianoForm.
2. Begin with a Main Menu component. Then drop in two Group Boxes, ten Panels, nine Labels, and five ScrollBar components to build the general operating controls. And finally, add 53 more Panel components to construct the keyboard, as shown in Figure 16.10.
3. Fill in the code (Listing 16.2).

You'll find this project in the directory \DELPHIMM\CH16\MIDIPIANO in the files MidiPian.DPR, Piano1.Pas, Piano1.DFM, and Patch.Ini.

Playing the Delphi MIDI Piano

When you run the program, it will display its form—a piano keyboard accompanied by five scroll bars, as shown in Figure 16.10.

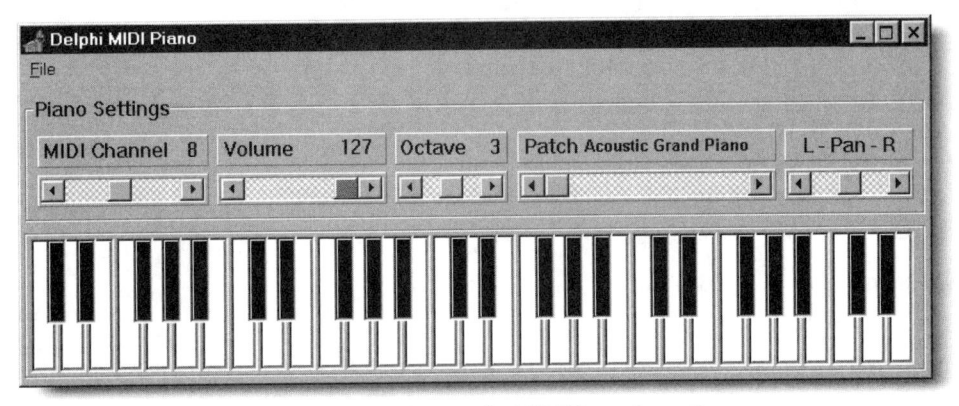

Using the Musical Instrument Digital Interface   755

Figure 16.10 *The Delphi MIDI Piano, from project MidiPian, at run-time.*

Use the scroll bars to select the MIDI channel and set the volume (or in MIDI terms, the *velocity*). You may also shift the octave of the keyboard up or down, change the current patch; and if your sound card supports stereo, set the left-to-right balance, known as the *pan*.

You can press and hold several notes in succession by holding down the mouse button and dragging the pointer across the piano keyboard. To activate selected notes, hold the button and drag off the keyboard, then back on again over the keys of your choice. To release all the currently active notes, release the mouse button while the pointer is over the piano keyboard, or release the mouse button and press it again over another key.

Creating the Form

Although you could burn a lot of time designing a bitmap keyboard with sprites to indicate keypresses, Arthur has found a much simpler and very attractive alternative. The keys are actually a collection of 53 Panel components. To color the keys, the **BackColor** property is set either to pure black (clBlack) or pure white (clWhite). To On all keys, the **BorderWidth** property is set to 2, and the **BevelOuter** is set to bvRaised. The **BevelWidth** property is set on the black keys to 1, and on the white keys to 2. To indicate a keypress, the program changes **BevelOuter** to bvLowered. We're going to do something a little unusual to activate keypresses, which will require us to handle drag and drop operations, so set the **DragMode** property to dmAutomatic. Finally, to help us identify which key has been pressed at runtime, we'll also set the **Tag** property of each control to a unique integer value. So set the **Tag** property of the first key to 0, set the **Tag** of the second key to 1, and so on up to 52. Be sure to follow the normal keyboard order up the musical scale, properly alternating black and white keys from left to right.

The remaining controls consist of Scroll Bars and Labels, set in SSPanel controls to get the 3D effect. For a complete list of the non-keyboard controls and their properties, see Table 16.6.

Table 16.6 The Non-Keyboard Components from Piano1.Pas.

Component	Property	Value
SettingGroupBox	Caption	'Piano Settings'
KeyboardGroupBox		
MainMenu1		
ChannelPanel	BevelOuter	bvRaised
	BevelWidth	1
	BorderStyle	bsNone
	Caption	' '
VolumePanel	BevelOuter	bvRaised
	BevelWidth	1
	BorderStyle	bsNone
	Caption	' '
OctavePanel	BevelOuter	bvRaised
	BevelWidth	1
	BorderStyle	bsNone
	Caption	' '
PatchPanel	BevelOuter	bvRaised
	BevelWidth	1
	BorderStyle	bsNone
	Caption	' '
PanPanel	BevelOuter	bvRaised
	BevelWidth	1
	BorderStyle	bsNone
	Caption	'L - Pan - R'
Label1	Caption	'MIDI Channel'
ChannelLabel	Caption	'16'
Label3	Caption	'Volume'
VolumeLabel	Caption	'128'
Label5	Caption	'Octave'
OctaveLabel	Caption	'3'
Label7	Caption	'Patch'
PatchLabel	Caption	' '

Continued

Table 16.6 The Non-Keyboard Components from Piano1.Pas (Continued).

Component	Property	Value
ChannelScrollPanel	BevelOuter	bvRaised
	BevelWidth	1
	BorderStyle	bsNone
	Caption	''
VolumeScrollPanel	BevelOuter	bvRaised
	BevelWidth	1
	BorderStyle	bsNone
	Caption	''
OctaveScrollPanel	BevelOuter	bvRaised
	BevelWidth	1
	BorderStyle	bsNone
	Caption	''
PatchScrollPanel	BevelOuter	bvRaised
	BevelWidth	1
	BorderStyle	bsNone
	Caption	''
PanScrollPanel	BevelOuter	bvRaised
	BevelWidth	1
	BorderStyle	bsNone
	Caption	''
HScrollMIDIChannel	LargeChange	3
	Max	16
	Min	1
	SmallChange	1
HScrollVolume	LargeChange	16
	Max	127
	Min	0
	SmallChange	1
HScrollOctave	LargeChange	1
	Max	5
	Min	1
	SmallChange	1
HScrollPatch	LargeChange	16
	Max	127
	Min	0
	SmallChange	1

Continued

Table 16.6 *The Non-Keyboard Components from Piano1.Pas (Continued).*

Component	Property	Value
HScrollPan	LargeChange	16
	Max	127
	Min	0
	SmallChange	1

Coding the Delphi MIDI Piano Form Unit

The code for the piano program is shown in Listing 16.2. One difference between this program and the simple experiment we created in MidiOut.DPR is that this code uses decimal values for MIDI messages. In your own programs, use whichever numeric base you wish; the messages will work either way.

Listing 16.2 The Code in Piano1.Pas

```
unit Piano1;

interface

uses
  SysUtils, WinTypes, WinProcs, Messages, Classes, Graphics, Controls,
  Forms, Dialogs, ExtCtrls, StdCtrls, Menus, Mmsystem;

type
  tKeyDownSet = set of 0..52;
  TPianoForm = class(TForm)
    KeyboardGroupBox: TGroupBox;
    Panel2: TPanel;
    Panel3: TPanel;
    Panel4: TPanel;
    Panel5: TPanel;
    Panel6: TPanel;
    Panel7: TPanel;
    Panel8: TPanel;
    Panel9: TPanel;
    Panel10: TPanel;
    Panel11: TPanel;
    Panel12: TPanel;
    Panel13: TPanel;
    Panel1: TPanel;
    Panel14: TPanel;
    Panel15: TPanel;
    Panel16: TPanel;
    Panel17: TPanel;
    Panel18: TPanel;
    Panel19: TPanel;
    Panel20: TPanel;
```

```
Panel21: TPanel;
Panel22: TPanel;
Panel23: TPanel;
Panel24: TPanel;
Panel25: TPanel;
Panel26: TPanel;
Panel27: TPanel;
Panel28: TPanel;
Panel29: TPanel;
Panel30: TPanel;
Panel31: TPanel;
Panel32: TPanel;
Panel33: TPanel;
Panel34: TPanel;
Panel35: TPanel;
Panel36: TPanel;
Panel37: TPanel;
Panel38: TPanel;
Panel39: TPanel;
Panel40: TPanel;
Panel41: TPanel;
Panel42: TPanel;
Panel43: TPanel;
Panel44: TPanel;
Panel45: TPanel;
Panel46: TPanel;
Panel47: TPanel;
Panel48: TPanel;
Panel49: TPanel;
Panel50: TPanel;
Panel51: TPanel;
Panel52: TPanel;
Panel53: TPanel;
MainMenu1: TMainMenu;
File1: TMenuItem;
Exit1: TMenuItem;
SettingsGroupBox: TGroupBox;
ChannelPanel: TPanel;
VolumePanel: TPanel;
OctavePanel: TPanel;
PatchPanel: TPanel;
PanPanel: TPanel;
ChannelScrollPanel: TPanel;
HScrollMIDIChannel: TScrollBar;
Label1: TLabel;
ChannelLabel: TLabel;
Label3: TLabel;
VolumeLabel: TLabel;
Label5: TLabel;
OctaveLabel: TLabel;
Label7: TLabel;
PatchLabel: TLabel;
VolumeScrollPanel: TPanel;
OctaveScrollPanel: TPanel;
```

```
    PatchScrollPanel: TPanel;
    PanScrollPanel: TPanel;
    HScrollVolume: TScrollBar;
    HScrollOctave: TScrollBar;
    HScrollPatch: TScrollBar;
    HScrollPan: TScrollBar;
    procedure Exit1Click(Sender: TObject);
    procedure FormCreate(Sender: TObject);
    procedure FormClose(Sender: TObject; var Action: TCloseAction);
    procedure HScrollMIDIChannelChange(Sender: TObject);
    procedure HScrollOctaveChange(Sender: TObject);
    procedure HScrollPanChange(Sender: TObject);
    procedure HScrollPatchChange(Sender: TObject);
    procedure HScrollVolumeChange(Sender: TObject);
    procedure Panel2DragDrop(Sender, Source: TObject; X, Y: Integer);
    procedure Panel2DragOver(Sender, Source: TObject; X, Y: Integer;
       State: TDragState; var Accept: Boolean);
  private
    { Private declarations }
    NoteCatchCount: integer;
    NoteOnCatcher : array [0..127] of integer;
    KeyDownSet :tKeyDownSet;
    hMidiOutHandle       : HMIDIOUT;
    hMidiOutHandleCopy   : HMIDIOUT;
    MidiOpenError : string;

    MidiPatch    : array [0..15] of integer;
    MidiVolume   : array [0..15] of integer;
    MidiPan      : array [0..15] of integer;
    Octave       : array [0..15] of integer;

    MidiChannelOut : integer;

    procedure MidiOutOpenPort;
    procedure SendMidiOut(MidiNoteOut, MidiEventOut,
       MidiVelOut : longint);
    procedure ReadPatch(PatchNumber : integer);

  public
    { Public declarations }

  end;

var
  PianoForm: TPianoForm;

implementation

{$R *.DFM}

procedure TPianoForm.MidiOutOpenPort;
var
    ReturnValue : integer;
begin
```

Using the Musical Instrument Digital Interface

```pascal
    ReturnValue := midiOutOpen(@hMidiOutHandle, $FFFF, 0, 0, 0);
    str(ReturnValue, MidiOpenError);
    hMidiOutHandleCopy := hMidiOutHandle;

end; { procedure MidiOutOpenPort }

procedure TPianoForm.ReadPatch(PatchNumber : integer);
var
    SName,
    Ret,
    Ext,
    FileName,
    Default1 : string;
    Counter,
    nSize    : integer;
begin
    Ret := '';
    for Counter := 1 to 255 do
        Ret := Ret + #0;
    Default1 := Ret;
    SName := 'General MIDI' + #0;
    Ext := IntToStr(PatchNumber) + #0;
    FileName := ExtractFilePath(Application.ExeName) + '\Patch.Ini' + #0;
    nSize := GetPrivateProfileString(@SName[1], @Ext[1], @Default1[1],
      @Ret[1], length(Ret), @FileName[1]);
    PatchLabel.Caption := copy(Ret, 1, pos(#0,Ret)-1);
    PatchLabel.Alignment := taCenter;
end; { procedure ReadPatch }

procedure TPianoForm.SendMidiOut(MidiNoteOut, MidiEventOut,
    MidiVelOut : longint);
var
    MidiMessage,
    LowInt,
    HighInt     : longint;
    ReturnValue : integer;
begin
    LowInt := (MidiNoteOut * 256) + MidiEventOut;
    HighInt := (MidiVelOut  * 256) * 256;
    MidiMessage := LowInt + HighInt;
    ReturnValue := midiOutShortMsg(hMidiOutHandleCopy, MidiMessage);
end; { procedure SendMidiOut }

procedure TPianoForm.Exit1Click(Sender: TObject);
var
  ReturnValue : integer;
begin
  ReturnValue := midiOutClose(hMidiOutHandleCopy);
  Application.Terminate;
end;

procedure TPianoForm.FormCreate(Sender: TObject);
var
    Counter : integer;
```

```
begin
    { Initialize variables }
    Screen.Cursor := crHourglass;
    MidiOutOpenPort;
    HScrollMIDIChannel.Position := 13;
    ChannelLabel.Caption := '13';
    HScrollPatch.Position := 0;
    HScrollVolume.Position := 100;
    VolumeLabel.Caption := '100';
    HScrollPan.Position := 64;
    HScrollOctave.Position := 3;
    OctaveLabel.Caption := '3';
    Screen.Cursor := crDefault;
    KeyDownSet := [];
    for Counter := 0 to 127 do
        NoteOnCatcher[Counter] := 0;
    NoteCatchCount := 0;
    for Counter := 0 to 15 do begin
        MidiVolume[Counter] := 100;
        MidiPan[Counter] := 64;
        Octave[Counter] := 3 * 12;
        MidiPatch[Counter] := 0;
        SendMidiOut(0, $C0 + Counter,0);
        end;
    ReadPatch(MidiPatch[MidiChannelOut]);
    Left := 0;
    Top := 0;
end;

procedure TPianoForm.FormClose(Sender: TObject; var Action: TCloseAction);
var
    ReturnValue : integer;
begin
    ReturnValue := midiOutClose(hMidiOutHandleCopy);
end;

procedure TPianoForm.HScrollMIDIChannelChange(Sender: TObject);
var
    TempString : string;
begin
    MidiChannelOut := HScrollMIDIChannel.Position - 1;
    { Display the new channel }
    str(HScrollMIDIChannel.Position:2, TempString);
    ChannelLabel.Caption := TempString;
    { Set the patch, volume, pan, and octave for the new channel }
    HScrollPatch.Position := MidiPatch[MidiChannelOut];
    HScrollVolume.Position := MidiVolume[MidiChannelOut];
    HScrollPan.Position := MidiPan[MidiChannelOut];
    HScrollOctave.Position := Octave[MidiChannelOut] div 12;
end;

procedure TPianoForm.HScrollOctaveChange(Sender: TObject);
var
    TempString : string;
```

```
begin
    str(HScrollOctave.Position:2,TempString);
    OctaveLabel.Caption := TempString;
    Octave[MidiChannelOut] := HScrollOctave.Position * 12;
end;

procedure TPianoForm.HScrollPanChange(Sender: TObject);
begin
    MidiPan[MidiChannelOut] := HScrollPan.Position;
    {Send change to Midi device }
    SendMidiOut(0, 176 + MidiChannelOut, MidiPan[MidiChannelOut]);
end;

procedure TPianoForm.HScrollPatchChange(Sender: TObject);
begin
    MidiPatch[MidiChannelOut] := HScrollPatch.Position;
    ReadPatch(MidiPatch[MidiChannelOut]);
    { Send Patch change to MIDI device }
    SendMidiOut(MidiPatch[MidiChannelOut], $C0 + MidiChannelOut, 0);
end;

procedure TPianoForm.HScrollVolumeChange(Sender: TObject);
var
    TempString : string;
begin
    {MidiVelocity := HScrollVolume.Position;}
    MidiVolume[MidiChannelOut] := HScrollVolume.Position;
    str(HScrollVolume.Position:3,TempString);
    VolumeLabel.Caption := TempString;
end;

procedure TPianoForm.Panel2DragDrop(Sender, Source: TObject; X,
  Y: Integer);
var
    Counter : integer;
begin
    for Counter := 0 to NoteCatchCount - 1 do
        SendMidiOut(NoteOnCatcher[Counter], 144 + MidiChannelOut, 0);
    NoteCatchCount := 0;
    for Counter := 0 to KeyboardGroupBox.ControlCount - 1 do begin
            if KeyboardGroupBox.Controls[Counter].Tag in KeyDownSet then begin
                TPanel(KeyboardGroupBox.Controls[Counter]).BevelOuter :=
bvRaised;
                KeyDownSet :=
                  KeyDownSet - [KeyboardGroupBox.Controls[Counter].Tag];
                end ; { if }
        end; { for }
end; { procedure }

procedure TPianoForm.Panel2DragOver(Sender, Source: TObject; X, Y: Integer;
  State: TDragState; var Accept: Boolean);
var
    NoteToPlay : longint;
begin
```

```
    { If cursor still on same note, discard event }
    if not (TControl(Sender).Tag in KeyDownSet) then begin
        TPanel(Sender).BevelOuter := bvLowered;
        NoteToPlay := TControl(Sender).Tag + Octave[MidiChannelOut];
        SendMidiOut(NoteToPlay,
            144 + MidiChannelOut, MidiVolume[MidiChannelOut]);

        { Add this key to the set of currently depressed keys }
        KeyDownSet := KeyDownSet + [TControl(Sender).Tag];

        { Since we're using Drag/Drop, we need to keep track of
          which notes are currently playing }
        NoteOnCatcher[NoteCatchCount] := NoteToPlay;
        if NoteCatchCount < 128 then
            NoteCatchCount := NoteCatchCount + 1;

        end;
    end;

end.
```

The playing action takes place in the **TPianoForm.Panel2DragOver()** event procedure, while the **TPianoForm.Panel2DragDrop()** event procedure handles the Note Off messages. To enable the user to successively press and hold two or more piano keys, the program uses drag and drop operations to activate piano keys, instead of **Click** or **MouseDown** events. A **DragOver** event occurs whenever you press the mouse button on a control that has DragMode enabled—either because its **DragMode** property is set to Automatic, or because one of the control's other event procedures calls the **Drag** method. The **DragOver** event occurs even on the control that started the drag operation. This would cause the procedure to repeatedly activate the same note, also repeatedly and uselessly adding it to **KeyDownSet** until the mouse cursor has moved off the key. The first part of **Panel2DragOver()** checks whether the current panel component is the same as the previous one. If so, it drops to the end of the procedure, as shown in the code snippet below:

```
{ If cursor still on same note, discard event }
if not (TControl(Sender).Tag in KeyDownSet) then begin
```

The next three lines in **Panel2DragOver()** change the appearance of the key, then set up and send the MIDI Note On message, as shown in the code snippet below:

```
TPanel(Sender).BevelOuter := bvLowered;
NoteToPlay := TControl(Sender).Tag + Octave[MidiChannelOut];
```

```
SendMidiOut(NoteToPlay,
    144 + MidiChannelOut, MidiVolume[MidiChannelOut]);
```

The variables **MidiVolume** and **MidiChannelOut** are set by the HScrollVolume and the HScrollMidiChannel Scroll Bars. **SendMidiOut()**, which we'll get to shortly, is a procedure declared as a **private** method of TPianoForm.

To handle the simultaneous notes, the program keeps a set of depressed keys in **KeyDownSet**, and a list of active notes in an array of integers called **NoteOnCatcher**. The variable **NoteCatchCount** is used to keep track of the number of active notes held in the array. The last part of the **Panel2DragOver()** event handler updates these two bookkeeping elements as shown in the code snippet below:

```
{ Add this key to the set of currently depressed keys }
KeyDownSet := KeyDownSet + [TControl(Sender).Tag];

{ Since we're using Drag/Drop, we need to keep track of
  which notes are currently playing }
NoteOnCatcher[NoteCatchCount] := NoteToPlay;
if NoteCatchCount < 128 then
    NoteCatchCount := NoteCatchCount + 1;
```

The **Panel2DragDrop()** event procedure first runs through the **NoteOnCatcher** array, sending Note On messages with 0 velocity to shut off each note, and changing the **BevelOuter** property back to bvRaised. It then steps through the **Controls** array property of the KeyboardGroupBox, checking whether each key belongs to the **KeyDownSet**. For each key it finds in the set, it restores the corresponding panel component's **BevelOuter** property to bvRaised and removes its **Tag** value from the set.

These two event handlers could be named after any of the keyboard panel components—I just happened to choose Panel2 when I first implemented them. Once they've been created, you can attach them to all of the other keyboard panel components. First, select all the keyboard panel components by holding the Shift key as you click each one. Next, click the Events tab in the Object Inspector. Then single-click the OnDragDrop event and use the embedded list to select **Panel2DragDrop**, or whichever DragDrop handler you created first. Finally, single-click the OnDragOver event from the list and select the **Panel2DragOver** event handler. Once you've completed these steps, the two event handlers will be assigned to all 53 keyboard panel components.

The method **TPianoForm.ReadPatch()** calls the Windows API function **GetPrivateProfileString()**, which reads data from INI files. For a complete description of this function, consult any good Windows API reference. The purpose of this function in this program is to read from the list of patch names in the file PATCH.INI. You may also want to investigate Delphi's TINIFile object, which encapsulates access to .INI files.

Receiving MIDI Messages

Receiving MIDI data is a little more difficult than sending it. Unlike WAV audio, which can be recorded with MCI commands, MIDI provides no MCI input support—only low-level functions, which translates into "no shortcuts."

All the low-level recording functions in the Windows Multimedia System use *callbacks* to request buffers or to report activity. In the MIDI functions, the callback is where incoming MIDI messages are passed to an application.

Windows Callbacks

Many Windows API functions support either of two kinds of callbacks: a *callback function*, or a *window message callback*. In general, callback functions are needed to handle precision timing and synchronous processes, while window message callbacks are used for tasks where response time is less critical.

To use a callback function, you pass the actual memory address of the function to the API function. The API function then calls your callback function when it has completed an operation. In some situations, this arrangement enables the API function to perform complex processes, then interrupt all other activity on the system when it's ready to return the result. In *interrupt driven* processes, such as MIDI input, callback functions enable Windows to respond immediately to incoming data.

To use the other type of callback, a window message callback, you pass a handle to the window that needs to receive the callback notification. When messages are used for callbacks, the API function simply posts a message to a window. The message is then delivered when it reaches the front of the message queue.

Some functions, like **midiInOpen()**, support either type of callback. But there is a catch. MIDI data is time-critical. The human ear—or more accurately, the human brain—can detect minute variations in time, down to about two milliseconds. Which means that if you're going to faithfully record MIDI input, you need precision down to one millisecond.

The multimedia high-resolution timer can provide this kind of precision, but only when you use a callback function. For each MIDI message it receives from the Input port, the MIDI device driver calls the specified callback function, passing it the MIDI message and an accurate time stamp. When you request a window message callback for the MIDI input device, however; the multimedia system doesn't even bother to time-stamp the callback message. It is assumed in the design of the MIDI API that window message callbacks can't be used for real-time musical event recording. In spite of the limitations of window message callbacks, you can still do some impressive things.

Receiving MIDI Messages

In this project, we'll use a windows message callback—the easier but less accurate method—to capture incoming MIDI messages. In the next project we'll plug in a callback function to perform MIDI input with accurate time stamping.

1. Open a new project named MidiIn.DPR, with a single form unit named MidiInFm.Pas.
2. Add the control components to the new form.
3. Add the code for the **TMidiInForm.FormCreate()**, **TMidiInForm.MidiDevListClick()**, and **TMidiInForm.StartStopButtonClick()** event handlers.
4. Add event handlers for the MIDI window messages.

You'll find this project in the directory \DELPHIMM\CH16\MIDIIN in the files MidiIn.DPR, MidiInFm.Pas, and MidiInFm.DFM.

Running the Program

To run this program, you'll need an external MIDI controller, such as a professional or portable keyboard with a MIDI Out port. Use a standard MIDI cable to connect the MIDI Out port of the instrument to the MIDI In port on your computer's MIDI adapter. (You can find MIDI cables at most music stores.) This program does not discriminate channels, so you can set your external MIDI device to transmit data on any of the 16 MIDI channels.

Run the program and click on the Start button as shown in Figure 16.11. If the program locates any valid MIDI Input devices, it will display their names in the List Box. These names are determined by the manufacturer of the MIDI adapter or sound card, and its driver. Choose the device whose name contains some reference to the MIDI In port. You can then click on the Start button to open the selected device. If the device is valid, "Device Open" appears in the image component at right, indicating that the form window

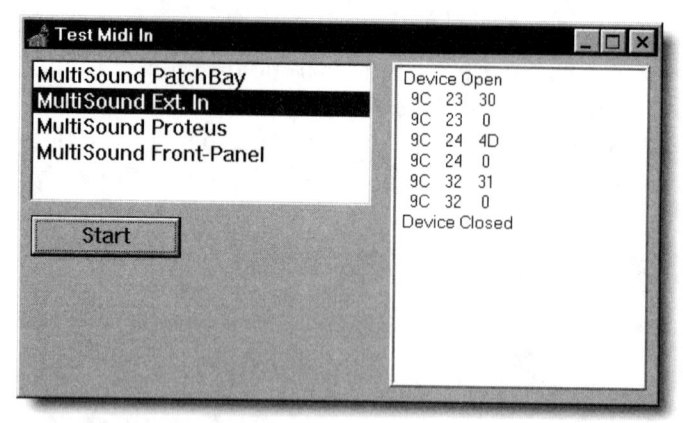

Figure 16.11 *The project MidiIn at runtime.*

has received an **MM_MIM_OPEN** message from the device driver. When you press the keys of your MIDI controller keyboard, you probably won't hear any sound, but you should see the numeric codes for the MIDI Note On and Note Off messages appear in the image component at the right. The messages are displayed as three hexadecimal values. The first number in each line displays the value of the status byte. The second and third numbers display the values of the data bytes.

When you are finished, click on the Command Button, now labeled Stop, then use the form's built-in controls to terminate the program.

> **Note:** *If this, or any other MIDI input program you write closes prematurely, before it has a chance to close the MIDI input device with the **midiInStop()** and **midiInClose()** API functions, the device driver may lock up. If this happens, you will need to restart Windows to reactivate the MIDI device.*

Creating the Form

Set the **Name** property of the form to "MidiInForm", and set its **Caption** to "Test MIDI In", and save it under the filename MidiInFm.Pas. Drop in a TListBox, a TButton, and a TImage component within a TPanel as shown in Figure 16.11. Set the properties of the control components as shown in Table 16.7.

The midiIn API Functions

The midiIn API functions are located in the WinMM.DLL. The Delphi declarations for WinMM are located in the file MMSystem.Pas, which is normally placed by the Delphi setup program in the directory SOURCE\RTL\WIN\.

Table 16.7 *The Components from MidiInFm.Pas.*

Component	Property	Value
MidiInForm	Position	poScreenCenter
MidiDevList	(no changes)	
StartStopButton	Caption	'Start'
Panel1	BevelInner	bvLowered
	BevelOuter	bvRaised
	BevelWidth	2
	Caption	' '
	Color	clWhite
ScrollingTextImage	Align	alClient

For this and the next project, we'll need seven of the thirteen midiIn functions, as shown in the code snippet below.

```
function midiInGetNumDevs: Word;
function midiInGetDevCaps(DeviceID: Word; lpCaps: PMidiInCaps;
  uSize: Word): Word;
function midiInOpen(lphMidiIn: PHMidiIn; uDeviceID: Word;
  dwCallback, dwInstance, dwFlags: Longint): Word;
function midiInClose(hMidiIn: HMidiIn): Word;
function midiInStart(hMidiIn: HMidiIn): Word;
function midiInStop(hMidiIn: HMidiIn): Word;
function midiInReset(hMidiIn: HMidiIn): Word;
```

Adding the Code

The first thing we need to do is query the MIDI device driver for the number of MIDI Input devices and their capabilities. We'll then list that information in the MidiDevList list box, as shown in Listing 16.3.

Listing 16.3 The FormCreate() Event Handler from MidiInFm.Pas

```
procedure TMidiInForm.FormCreate(Sender: TObject);
var
    NumMidiInDevices : integer;
    DevCounter       : integer;
    ReturnValue      : integer;
    DeviceCaps       : tMidiInCaps;
begin
    MidiInActive := false;
    hMidiIn := 0;
    InputDeviceNumber := 0;
    StartStopButton.Enabled := false;
    NumMidiInDevices := midiInGetNumDevs;
```

```
        for DevCounter := 0 to NumMidiInDevices - 1 do begin
            ReturnValue := midiInGetDevCaps(DevCounter,
                @DeviceCaps, sizeOf(DeviceCaps));
            MidiDevList.Items.Add(strPas(DeviceCaps.szPname));
            end;
end;
```

The API function **midiInGetNumDevs**, which takes no arguments, returns the number of MIDI Input devices installed in the system. We use that number, captured in the integer variable **NumMidiInDevices** to step through the devices and interrogate them with **midiInGetDevCaps()**. This function takes three arguments: a zero-based device number, the address of a record of type tMidiInCaps, and the size of that record.

Before we can start MIDI input, we need to open the appropriate device, which we do in the **TMidiInForm.StartStopButtonClick()** event handler, shown in Listing 16.4.

Listing 16.4 The StartStopButtonClick() Event Handler from MidiInFm.Pas

```
procedure TMidiInForm.StartStopButtonClick(Sender: TObject);
var
    ReturnValue : integer;
begin
    if not MidiInActive then begin
        ReturnValue := midiInOpen(@hMidiIn, InputDeviceNumber,
            MidiInForm.handle, 0, CALLBACK_WINDOW);
        if ReturnValue = 0 then begin
            ReturnValue := midiInReset(hMidiIn);
            ReturnValue := midiInStart(hMidiIn);
            MidiInActive := true;
            StartStopButton.Caption := 'Stop';
            MidiDevList.Enabled := false;
            end
        else
            MessageDlg('Unable to open MIDI Device', mtError, [mbOK], 0);
        end
    else begin
        ReturnValue := midiInStop(hMidiIn);
        ReturnValue := midiInClose(hMidiIn);
        MidiInActive := false;
        StartStopButton.Caption := 'Start';
        MidiDevList.Enabled := true;
        end;
    end;
```

The **midiInOpen()** function takes five arguments, as shown in the code snippet below.

```
function midiInOpen(lphMidiIn: PHMidiIn; uDeviceID: Word;
  dwCallback, dwInstance, dwFlags: Longint): Word;
```

The first, **lphMidiIn**, is a pointer to the variable that the function will set to the handle of the device, once it has been opened. In the second argument, **uDeviceID**, we specify which device to open. The device numbers are zero-based, so the first device is number 0, the second is number 1, and so on. In the third argument, **dwCallback**, we pass either the address of a callback function, or the handle to a window that can receive a message callback. The fourth argument, **dwInstance**, is used when **dwCallback** contains a function address; it passes data to the callback function. In this project we'll be using a window callback, not a callback function, so we'll set **dwInstance** to 0. In **dwFlags** we pass a flag that indicates which type of callback to use. In **StartStopButtonClick()** we pass the flag constant **CALLBACK_WINDOW**, which has a value of &H10000.

If we successfully open the device, we call two more functions, **midiInReset()** and **midiInStart()** to reset the device and begin receiving MIDI messages. In your own projects, you may wish to use **midiInStart()** and its sibling, **midiInStop()**, to temporarily suspend MIDI input without closing and reopening the device. When we're ready to shut down the device, we call **midiInStop()** followed by **midiInClose()**. We use the form-level integer variable **MidiInActive** to keep track of whether the device is open or closed. In **StartStopButtonClick()**, we open the device if **MidiInActive** is False; otherwise, we close it.

The Windows Message Event Handlers

If event handlers handle events, what are the events that event handlers handle? Windows messages, of course. Most event handlers provide responses to messages sent by the operating system to a windowed component. The events are defined in the class definitions for tForm, tButton, tImage, and all other components. If you wish, you may *subclass* any of these predefined classes and add your own events to your derived component class. Your new events will then show in the Object Inspector whenever you declare a component of your new class. But you don't need to define a new component just to handle a new message. You can just add a *message handler* to the **protected** section of your application's window class. And that's how we'll handle the messages sent to us by the MIDI Input device, as shown in the code snippet below.

```
protected
    procedure mmMIMClose(var MidiMessage : tMessage); message mm_MIM_Close;
    procedure mmMIMData(var MidiMessage : tMessage); message mm_MIM_Data;
    procedure mmMIMError(var MidiMessage : tMessage); message mm_MIM_Error;
    procedure mmMIMOpen(var MidiMessage : tMessage); message mm_MIM_Open;
```

Message handlers always take the same form, a procedural method that takes just one argument, a var parameter of the message type. The entire procedure declaration is followed by the **message** directive and the integer constant that identifies the message. The Delphi documentation suggests that message handlers should be named after the message constant, without the underscore characters. It's just a convention, but it's a good one.

These four event handlers are triggered, respectively, whenever the MIDI Input device driver sends our window any of four messages: **mm_MIM_Close**, **mm_MIM_Data**, **mm_MIM_Error**, or **mm_MIM_Open**.

As you can see in Listing 16.5, the message handlers themselves are trivially simple. In this program, we're just going to display the messages as they arrive, which we'll do by turning the TImage component into a continuously scrolling text display.

To display the messages, we'll combine the **ScrollDC()** API function with the **ScrollingTextImage** component's own **TextOut()** method in the form's **LineOut()** method (see Listing 16.5). The **TextOut()** method doesn't perform line feeds, so after each line we display, we need to set the pen position to the top of the next line. Once **PenPos.Y** exceeds the **Height** of the **Canvas**'s client area, meaning that it has slipped beyond the bottom edge, we use **ScrollDC()** to slide everything up by an amount equal to the height of one line of text. **ScrollDC()** accepts seven arguments. The first specifies the handle of the DC to scroll, which in this case is the handle of the image component's **Canvas** property. The next two arguments accept the number of units to scroll horizontally and vertically. Arguments four and five specify the area to scroll. If the rectangle passed in the fifth argument, the **Clip** rectangle, is smaller than the first, then only the area within that rectangle will scroll. The final two arguments enable us to pass the handle to an update region, and a pointer to a rectangle that the function will fill with the coordinates of the smallest rectangle that will enclose the area exposed by scrolling. Remember, the function supports simultaneous horizontal and vertical scrolling, so the region actually exposed may not be rectangular. We already know about how much space we're creating at the bottom of the client area, so we'll pass a null handle and a **nil** pointer, which tell the function not to compute the update region at all.

Listing 16.5 The Complete listing of the Unit MidiInFm in MidiInFm.Pas

```
unit Midiinfm;

interface

uses
  SysUtils, WinTypes, WinProcs, Messages, Classes, Graphics, Controls,
  Forms, Dialogs, StdCtrls, Mmsystem, ExtCtrls;
```

Using the Musical Instrument Digital Interface

```pascal
type
  TMidiInForm = class(TForm)
    MidiDevList: TListBox;
    Panel1: TPanel;
    StartStopButton: TButton;
    ScrollingTextImage: TImage;
    procedure FormCreate(Sender: TObject);
    procedure StartStopButtonClick(Sender: TObject);
    procedure MidiDevListClick(Sender: TObject);
    procedure FormClose(Sender: TObject; var Action: TCloseAction);
  protected
    procedure mmMIMClose(var MidiMessage : tMessage); message mm_MIM_Close;
    procedure mmMIMData(var MidiMessage : tMessage); message mm_MIM_Data;
    procedure mmMIMError(var MidiMessage : tMessage); message mm_MIM_Error;
    procedure mmMIMOpen(var MidiMessage : tMessage); message mm_MIM_Open;
  private
    MidiInActive      : boolean;
    hMidiIn           :HMIDIIN;
    InputDeviceNumber : integer;
    procedure LineOut(const LineToPrint : string);
  public
    { Public declarations }
  end;

var
  MidiInForm: TMidiInForm;

implementation

{$R *.DFM}

procedure tMidiInForm.LineOut(const LineToPrint : string);
var
    bReturnValue : boolean;
    AreaToScroll : trect;
    LineHeight   : integer;
    NewYPos      : longint;
    hUpdateRgn   : hRgn;
    UpdateRect   : tRect;
begin
    LineHeight := ScrollingTextImage.Canvas.TextHeight('Ag');
    if (ScrollingTextImage.Canvas.PenPos.Y >
       (ScrollingTextImage.Height - LineHeight)) then begin
       AreaToScroll.Top := 0;
       AreaToScroll.Left := 0;
       AreaToScroll.Right := ScrollingTextImage.Width;
       AreaToScroll.Bottom := ScrollingTextImage.Height;
       hUpdateRgn := $00;
       bReturnValue := ScrollDC(ScrollingTextImage.Canvas.Handle, 0,
            -LineHeight, AreaToScroll, AreaToScroll, hUpdateRgn, nil);
       ScrollingTextImage.Canvas.Brush.Color := clWhite;
       ScrollingTextImage.Canvas.Pen.Color := clWhite;
       ScrollingTextImage.Canvas.Rectangle(0,
           ScrollingTextImage.Height - LineHeight,
           ScrollingTextImage.Width, ScrollingTextImage.Height);
```

```
            ScrollingTextImage.Canvas.MoveTo(5,
                ScrollingTextImage.Height - LineHeight);
            end; { if }
        ScrollingTextImage.Canvas.TextOut(5,
            ScrollingTextImage.Canvas.PenPos.Y, LineToPrint);
        NewYPos := ScrollingTextImage.Canvas.PenPos.Y + LineHeight;
        ScrollingTextImage.Canvas.MoveTo(5,
            ScrollingTextImage.Canvas.PenPos.Y + LineHeight);
        end; { procedure LineOut }

procedure tMidiInForm.mmMIMClose(var MidiMessage : tMessage);
begin
    LineOut('Device Closed');
    end;

procedure tMidiInForm.mmMIMData(var MidiMessage : tMessage);
begin
    if (MidiMessage.LParamLo mod 256) <> 254 then
        LineOut(format('%4x    %4x    %4x',
        [MidiMessage.LParamLo mod 256,MidiMessage.LParamLo div 256,
          MidiMessage.LParamHi]));
    end;

procedure tMidiInForm.mmMIMError(var MidiMessage : tMessage);
begin
    LineOut('MIDI Error Received');
    end;

procedure tMidiInForm.mmMIMOpen(var MidiMessage : tMessage);
begin
    LineOut('Device Open');
    end;

procedure TMidiInForm.FormCreate(Sender: TObject);
var
    NumMidiInDevices : integer;
    DevCounter       : integer;
    ReturnValue      : integer;
    DeviceCaps       : tMidiInCaps;
begin
    MidiInActive := false;
    hMidiIn := 0;
    InputDeviceNumber := 0;
    StartStopButton.Enabled := false;
    NumMidiInDevices := midiInGetNumDevs;
    for DevCounter := 0 to NumMidiInDevices - 1 do begin
        ReturnValue := midiInGetDevCaps(DevCounter,
            @DeviceCaps, sizeOf(DeviceCaps));
        MidiDevList.Items.Add(strPas(DeviceCaps.szPname));
        end;
end;

procedure TMidiInForm.StartStopButtonClick(Sender: TObject);
var
```

```
        ReturnValue : integer;
begin
    if not MidiInActive then begin
        ReturnValue := midiInOpen(@hMidiIn, InputDeviceNumber,
            MidiInForm.handle, 0, CALLBACK_WINDOW);
        if ReturnValue = 0 then begin
            ReturnValue := midiInReset(hMidiIn);
            ReturnValue := midiInStart(hMidiIn);
            MidiInActive := true;
            StartStopButton.Caption := 'Stop';
            MidiDevList.Enabled := false;
            end
          else
            MessageDlg('Unable to open MIDI Device', mtError, [mbOK], 0);
        end
      else begin
        ReturnValue := midiInStop(hMidiIn);
        ReturnValue := midiInClose(hMidiIn);
        MidiInActive := false;
        StartStopButton.Caption := 'Start';
        MidiDevList.Enabled := true;
        end;
    end;

procedure TMidiInForm.MidiDevListClick(Sender: TObject);
begin
    InputDeviceNumber := MidiDevList.ItemIndex;
    StartStopButton.Caption := 'Start';
    StartStopButton.Enabled := true;
    end;

procedure TMidiInForm.FormClose(Sender: TObject; var Action: TCloseAction);
var
    ReturnValue : integer;
begin
    if hMidiIn <> 0 then begin
        ReturnValue := midiInStop(hMidiIn);
        ReturnValue := midiInClose(hMidiIn);
        end;
    end;

end.
```

Receiving Time-Stamped MIDI Messages

If you intend to develop musical MIDI applications that can record and replay MIDI data, you'll need to know more than which notes to play. You'll also need to know when to play them. In this project, we'll drop the window callback in favor of a callback function to capture incoming MIDI messages. The advantage of this method is that the data includes time-stamping, accurate to within one millisecond, which is precise enough for musical applications.

1. Open a new project named MidiCB.DPR, with a singe form unit named MidiCBU.Pas.
2. Code the midiIn callback function and compile it into MidiCB.DLL.
3. Open the project MidiIn.DPR and use the Save Project As menu option to save it under the names MidiIn2.DPR and MidInFm2.Pas.
4. Modify the code in the unit MidInFm2 to receive time-stamped MIDI data by way of the callback function in MidiCB.DPR (Listing 16.6).

> You'll find this project in the directory \DELPHIMM\CH16\MIDIIN2. The files MidiCB.DPR and MidiCBU.Pas contain the source code for the callback DLL. The source code for the MidiIn2 program itself resides in the files MidiIn.DPR, MidiInFm.Pas, and MidiInFm.DFM.

Running the Program

To run this program, follow the instructions given for the previous project. The only difference you will see between this version and the last is the new integer value that appears before each line of MIDI data, as shown in Figure 16.12. This value represents the number of milliseconds that have elapsed since the midiInStart function was last called.

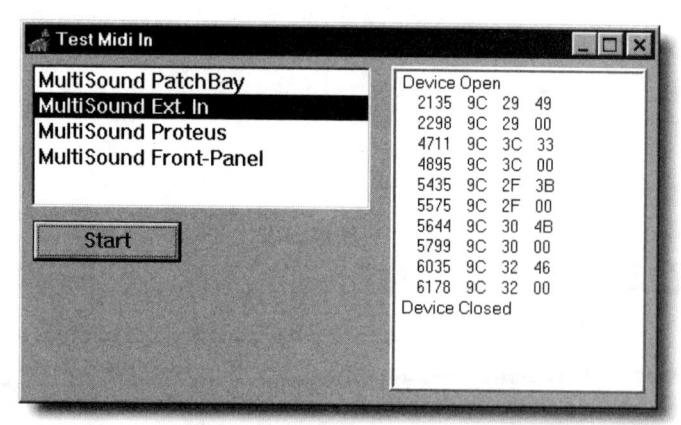

Figure 16.12 The project MidiIn2 at runtime.

Creating the DLL for the Callback Function

A callback function provides a way for Windows to trigger an operation within an application that cannot be accomplished with a simple message notification. One such circumstance is an operation where timing is critical, such as MIDI input. In fact, MIDI input is *interrupt drive*, which means that every time the MIDI In port receives data, it orders the microprocessor to jump to the *device driver* code responsible for handling that data. Where the data goes from there depends on a callback function. By passing the address of a callback function to the device driver, we tell the driver what to do next with the data it has received from the hardware input port.

Most callback functions may reside in the same unit as other code in the project. But a callback function that services an interrupt driven process must reside in its own DLL.

To build the DLL, start a new project. We'll call it MidiCB.DPR. Once we make a few simple changes to the project file, Delphi will compile the project as a DLL rather than as an EXE. To prepare to compile as a DLL, follow these steps:

1. Open the project file by selecting View|Project Source from Delphi's main menu.
2. The first line in the file contains the reserved word **program**. Change it to **library**.
3. Remove the Forms unit from the **uses** list.
4. Below the **uses** list, and before the begin...end block, add the reserved word **exports**. In this section you will list the names of all procedures and functions made available by the DLL to other programs. We'll call our function MidiInCallback.
5. Remove any code that appears in the begin...end block. Do not remove the begin and end reserved words themselves.

For a callback function that services an interrupt, we'll also need to place a couple of restrictions on the DLL. Windows loads, moves and disposes of most DLLs as needed. For an interrupt servicing DLL, however, we need to make sure it stays in one place and never leaves memory until Windows is shut down. This enables the device driver to trigger the callback function at will, without considering whether it might have wandered off into some other part of memory. The compiler directive $C enables us to specify that the DLL's code segment should **PRELOAD**, and should remain at a **FIXED** and **PERMANENT** location.

The completed DPR file appears in Listing 16.6.

Listing 16.6 The Project Source Code from MidiCB.DPR

```
library Midicb;

{$C PRELOAD FIXED PERMANENT}

uses
    Midicbu in 'MIDICBU.PAS';

{$R *.RES}

exports
    MidiInCallback index 1;

begin
end.
```

It's really that easy.

Now we can write the callback function itself. The name of this function is arbitrary. When we open the MIDI In port, we pass the address of the callback function to **midiInOpen()**. The device driver does not expect to find a function of a specific name. The only requirement is that the argument list must match the pre-defined prototype for the callback. We'll call it **MidiInCallback()**. In the **interface**, be sure to add the **export** reserved word to the end of the function's declaration. This is shown in Listing 16.7.

Listing 16.7 The Function MidiInCallback from MidiCBU.Pas

```
unit MidiCBU;

{$C PRELOAD FIXED PERMANENT}

interface

uses
    SysUtils, WinTypes, WinProcs, Messages, Classes, MMSystem;

procedure MidiInCallback(hMidiInHandle : HMIDIIN; wMsg : word;
    dwInstance, dwParam1, dwParam2 : integer); export; stdcall;

implementation

procedure MidiInCallback(hMidiInHandle : HMIDIIN; wMsg : word;
    dwInstance, dwParam1, dwParam2 : integer);

type
MidiShortMessage = record
        MidiTime    : integer;
      case boolean of
        true:
          (RawMidiData : integer);
```

Using the Musical Instrument Digital Interface 779

```
        false:
          (MidiMessage : byte;
           MidiData1    : byte;
           MidiData2    : byte;
           FillByte     : byte);
        end;

var
    lpMidiShort    : pointer;
    hGMem          : thandle;
    hCallingWindow : thandle;
    bReturnValue   : boolean;
begin
    hCallingWindow := dwInstance;
    case wMsg of
      MIM_Open : PostMessage (hCallingWindow, mm_MIM_Open, 0, 0);
      MIM_Error: PostMessage (hCallingWindow, mm_MIM_Error, 0, 0);
      MIM_Data : begin
        hGMem := GlobalAlloc(GMEM_SHARE, sizeOf(MidiShortMessage));
        if hGMem <> 0 then begin
            lpMidiShort := GlobalLock(hGMem);
            with MidiShortMessage(lpMidiShort^) do begin
                MidiTime := dwParam2;
                RawMidiData := dwParam1;
                end; { with }
            bReturnValue := GlobalUnlock(hGMem);
            PostMessage(hCallingWindow, WM_USER, 0, hGMem);
            end; { if }
        end; { MIM_Data }
      MIM_Close: PostMessage (hCallingWindow, mm_MIM_Close, 0, 0);
      else
        { For a complete MIDI application, you should also consider
          MIDI long messages, also known as System Exclusive Messages }
      end; { case wMsg }
    end; { procedure MidiInCallback }


begin
end.
```

As you can see in Listing 16.7, the callback function receives five arguments. When the function is called by the device driver, **hMidiInHandle** will contain the handle to the MIDI Input device. The second argument, **wMsg**, holds a 16-bit value that represents one of six possible MIDI message identifiers:

```
MIM_Open
MIM_Close
MIM_Data
MIM_LongData
MIM_Error
MIM_LongErr
```

The third argument, **dwInstance**, will contain the value passed as the instance argument to the **midiInOpen()** function. This value is user-defined, but usually holds either the handle of the global memory block used to hold a buffer, or, as we'll use it here, the handle of the application window. The two remaining arguments, **dwParam1** and **dwParam2**, contain data passed with the message when needed.

When the callback function receives MIDI data, **dwParam2** will contain the time-stamp; while **dwParam1** will contain the MIDI message itself, consisting of one status byte and up to two data bytes. Having received that information, the callback function needs to pass it along to the application that opened the MIDI In device in the first place. And how does it do that? By using the **PostMessage()** API function to send it a window message! At first this may seem to defeat the entire purpose of the callback function; in fact, it does not. You see, an ordinary window message cannot hold enough information to pass back a three-byte MIDI message and a four-byte time-stamp. The callback function becomes a middleman, collecting input from the device driver in real time with accurate time-stamps, then feeding it back to the application asynchronously, at whatever rate the application can accept it.

Although a window message doesn't have enough cargo space to hold a complete MIDI data message, it can easily accommodate a handle to a global memory block. So instead of passing the data itself, we store it in a global memory block, then pass the handle back to the application in a user-defined window message, WM_USER. The constant WM_USER represents the first integer value available for user-defined message types. When you define your own messages, use WM_USER as your base value. For example:

```
WM_MYMESSAGE := WM_USER;
WM_MYSECONDMESSAGE := WM_USER + 1;
WM_MYTHIRDMESSAGE := WM_USER + 2;
```

To store the data in the global memory block, we *cast* the block as a MidiShortMessage:

```
with MidiShortMessage(lpMidiShort^) do begin
```

Casting is like dropping a template over the raw global memory, effectively partitioning it into the fields defined in the type definition for the MidiShortMessage record.

The definition of MidiShortRecord itself contains another type of multiple casting, known as a *variant*. The **case** boolean **of** statement within the record definition enables that portion of the record to be dereferenced either way:

either as the four-byte **RawMidiData** field, or as the three fields **MidiMessage**, **MidiData1**, and **MidiData2**. Within the callback function, we'll only use one variation, but we'll use the other when we write the code that receives the data. I've expressed it as a variant only to be consistent between the DLL and the application.

When the callback function receives MIM_OPEN, MIM_ERROR, or MIM_CLOSE messages, it will just pass them along without further manipulation.

Updating the MIDI Input Program

There are three differences between the form unit in this project (MidInFm2.Pas) and the form unit in the previous project (MidiInFm.Pas).

First, we need to declare the callback function in the **implementation** section:

```
procedure MidiInCallback(hMidiInHandle : HMIDIIN; wMsg : word;
    dwInstance, dwParam1,
    dwParam2 : integer); far; external 'MidiCB' name 'MidiInCallback';
```

Secondly, we need to modify the call to **midiInOpen()** in the **StartStopButtonClick()** event handler:

```
ReturnValue := midiInOpen(@hMidiIn, InputDeviceNumber,
 integer(@MidiInCallback), MidiInForm.handle, CALLBACK_FUNCTION);
```

This time we pass the address of the callback function, cast as an integer to match the declaration for **midiInOpen()** in MMSystem.Pas. We use the **dwInstance** argument to pass the handle to our window, so the callback function will know where to send back its incoming MIDI data. In the last argument, we pass the CALLBACK_FUNCTION flag so the device driver will know that the **dwCallback** argument specifies an address to a callback function rather than a window handle.

Finally, we replace the **MIMData()** event handler with a new event handler called **WMUser()**, as shown in Listing 16.8.

Listing 16.8 The Code from the Unit MidInFm2.Pas

```
unit Midinfm2;

interface

uses
    SysUtils, WinTypes, WinProcs, Messages, Classes, Graphics, Controls,
    Forms, Dialogs, StdCtrls, Mmsystem, ExtCtrls;
```

```
type
  TMidiInForm = class(TForm)
    MidiDevList: TListBox;
    Panel1: TPanel;
    StartStopButton: TButton;
    ScrollingTextImage: TImage;
    procedure FormCreate(Sender: TObject);
    procedure StartStopButtonClick(Sender: TObject);
    procedure MidiDevListClick(Sender: TObject);
    procedure FormClose(Sender: TObject; var Action: TCloseAction);
  protected
    procedure MIMClose(var MidiMessage : tMessage); message mim_Close;
    procedure WMUser(var MidiMessage : tMessage); message WM_USER;
    procedure MIMError(var MidiMessage : tMessage); message mim_Error;
    procedure MIMOpen(var MidiMessage : tMessage); message mim_Open;
  private
    MidiInActive     : boolean;
    hMidiIn          :HMIDIIN;
    InputDeviceNumber : integer;
    procedure LineOut(const LineToPrint : string);
  public
    { Public declarations }
  end;

var
  MidiInForm: TMidiInForm;

implementation

{$R *.DFM}

procedure MidiInCallback(hMidiInHandle : HMIDIIN; wMsg : word;
    dwInstance, dwParam1,
    dwParam2 : integer); far; external 'MidiCB' name 'MidiInCallback';

procedure tMidiInForm.LineOut(const LineToPrint : string);
var
    bReturnValue : boolean;
    AreaToScroll : trect;
    LineHeight   : integer;
    NewYPos      : longint;
    hUpdateRgn   : hRgn;
    UpdateRect   : tRect;
begin
    LineHeight := ScrollingTextImage.Canvas.TextHeight('Ag');
    if (ScrollingTextImage.Canvas.PenPos.Y >
       (ScrollingTextImage.Height - LineHeight)) then begin
       AreaToScroll.Top := 0;
       AreaToScroll.Left := 0;
       AreaToScroll.Right := ScrollingTextImage.Width;
       AreaToScroll.Bottom := ScrollingTextImage.Height;
       hUpdateRgn := $00;
       bReturnValue := ScrollDC(ScrollingTextImage.Canvas.Handle, 0,
            -LineHeight, AreaToScroll, AreaToScroll, hUpdateRgn, nil);
```

```
            ScrollingTextImage.Canvas.Brush.Color := clWhite;
            ScrollingTextImage.Canvas.Pen.Color := clWhite;
            ScrollingTextImage.Canvas.Rectangle(0,
                ScrollingTextImage.Height - LineHeight,
                ScrollingTextImage.Width, ScrollingTextImage.Height);
            ScrollingTextImage.Canvas.MoveTo(5,
                ScrollingTextImage.Height - LineHeight);
        end; { if }
    ScrollingTextImage.Canvas.TextOut(5,
        ScrollingTextImage.Canvas.PenPos.Y, LineToPrint);
    NewYPos := ScrollingTextImage.Canvas.PenPos.Y + LineHeight;
    ScrollingTextImage.Canvas.MoveTo(5,
        ScrollingTextImage.Canvas.PenPos.Y + LineHeight);
    end; { procedure LineOut }

procedure tMidiInForm.MIMClose(var MidiMessage : tMessage);
begin
    LineOut('Device Closed');
    end;

procedure tMidiInForm.MIMError(var MidiMessage : tMessage);
begin
    LineOut('MIDI Error Received');
    end;

procedure tMidiInForm.MIMOpen(var MidiMessage : tMessage);
begin
    LineOut('Device Open');
    end;

procedure tMidiInForm.WMUser(var MidiMessage : tMessage);
type
    MidiShortMessage = record
            MidiTime    :integer;
         case boolean of
           true:
             (RawMidiData :integer);
           false:
             (MidiMessage : byte;
              MidiData1   : byte;
              MidiData2   : byte;
              FillByte    : byte);
         end;
var
    hGMem         : tHandle;
    lpMidiShort   : pointer;
begin
    hGMem := MidiMessage.lParam;
    lpMidiShort := GlobalLock(hGMem);
    with MidiShortMessage(lpMidiShort^) do
        if (MidiMessage<> $FE) then
            LineOut(format('%8d   %4.2x   %4.2x   %4.2x',
                [MidiTime, MidiMessage, MidiData1, MidiData2]));
```

```
        GlobalUnlock(hGMem);
        GlobalFree(hGMem);
        end;

procedure TMidiInForm.FormCreate(Sender: TObject);
var
    NumMidiInDevices : integer;
    DevCounter       : integer;
    ReturnValue      : integer;
    DeviceCaps       : tMidiInCaps;
    pCallbackfunction: longint;
begin
    MidiInActive := false;
    hMidiIn := 0;
    InputDeviceNumber := 0;
    StartStopButton.Enabled := false;
    NumMidiInDevices := midiInGetNumDevs;
    for DevCounter := 0 to NumMidiInDevices - 1 do begin
        ReturnValue := midiInGetDevCaps(DevCounter,
            @DeviceCaps, sizeOf(DeviceCaps));
        MidiDevList.Items.Add(strPas(DeviceCaps.szPname));
        end;
end;

procedure TMidiInForm.StartStopButtonClick(Sender: TObject);
var
    ReturnValue : integer;
begin
    if not MidiInActive then begin
        ReturnValue := midiInOpen(@hMidiIn, InputDeviceNumber,
            longint(@MidiInCallback), MidiInForm.handle, CALLBACK_FUNCTION);
        if ReturnValue = 0 then begin
            ReturnValue := midiInReset(hMidiIn);
            ReturnValue := midiInStart(hMidiIn);
            MidiInActive := true;
            StartStopButton.Caption := 'Stop';
            MidiDevList.Enabled := false;
            end
          else
            MessageDlg('Unable to open MIDI Device', mtError, [mbOK], 0);
        end
      else begin
        ReturnValue := midiInStop(hMidiIn);
        ReturnValue := midiInClose(hMidiIn);
        MidiInActive := false;
        StartStopButton.Caption := 'Start';
        MidiDevList.Enabled := true;
        end;
    end;

procedure TMidiInForm.MidiDevListClick(Sender: TObject);
begin
    InputDeviceNumber := MidiDevList.ItemIndex;
```

```
    StartStopButton.Caption := 'Start';
    StartStopButton.Enabled := true;
    end;

procedure TMidiInForm.FormClose(Sender: TObject; var Action: TCloseAction);
var
    ReturnValue : integer;
begin
    if hMidiIn <> 0 then begin
        ReturnValue := midiInStop(hMidiIn);
        ReturnValue := midiInClose(hMidiIn);
        end;
    end;

end.
```

One flaw in the Windows MIDI system is the lack of tight coupling between input and output. By using a callback function, we ensure accurate time-stamping of incoming MIDI messages. But those messages are still passed on to our programs by way of window messages, which means that we can't pass them on to the output device with the same chronological precision with which they were received. Many sound cards and stand-alone MIDI interfaces include a MIDI Through port, which passes MIDI data on to the next device in the cable chain without forcing it through the computer. For cards that don't offer a Through port, however, the computer can introduce annoying lags during live performance. To eliminate this problem, make sure that the computer is always the last device in the chain.

Beyond MIDI Basics

The API functions we have used in this chapter represent the core of the MIDI programming interface. The multimedia system contains many other functions. Some handle MIDI System Exclusive messages (known in Windows as MIDI Long Messages). Among the others are functions that control playback volume on the internal mixer, translate error codes into string messages, and manage synthesizer patches. With the help of the MIDI API, you can write your own MIDI utilities and sequencers. Here are some suggestions to help you get started:

- Combine the midiIn and midiOut functions to pass incoming MIDI messages on to your sound card's internal synthesizer.
- Add support for Long Messages, known in the MIDI specification as System Exclusive messages.

- Write a MIDI sequencer that records incoming MIDI data, then plays it back. Here's a hint: you'll need the high resolution timer API functions.
- Build a new component to perform continuously scrolling text display by descending a new class from an existing component class.

Appendix A

32-Bit Application Development

Everyone is talking about Delphi 2 and Windows 95—and has been for quite some time now. And it's no wonder. Microsoft spent more money and resources promoting and launching Windows 95 than most software companies acquire in their lifetime. Of course, critics have been complaining about Windows 95's shortcomings ever since it was introduced to the world—it is not a true 32-bit operating system, it still needs DOS, it won't run all of your old software as well as Windows 3.1 could, and it was released two years late. But most developers, especially those of us who are creating cutting-edge applications like multimedia products, are increasingly won over to Windows 95's enhanced features. Let's face it, Windows 95's true multitasking and multithreading capabilities will certainly make our software run better than ever and its new built-in multimedia capabilities will give it more power and flexibility than any other operating system.

The challenge now is to find a way to take advantage of the 32-bit power of Windows 95. Fortunately, that's where Delphi 2 comes in. Delphi's latest release can bring you into the core of Windows 95 development where you can really take advantage of 32-bit and multimedia programming.

In this chapter, we'll look at Windows 95 to see what new features are in store to help us create powerful multimedia applications. If you haven't done much Windows 95 (32-bit) programming with Delphi, this introduction will help you see what you've been missing.

Windows 95—32 Bits at Last!

When you start up Windows 95, the first thing you'll notice is that its user interface makes Windows 3.1 look like something out of the stone age. The new interface controls, Task Bar and Explorer file manager, provide the types of desktop tools that users have been demanding for years. If you are lucky enough to have a multimedia application developed for Windows 95, you'll soon discover that the built-in multimedia capabilities are the best they've ever been. Windows 3.1 offered a good platform for multimedia development, but Windows 95's speed increase and unique features, including Plug & Play, AutoRun, and better sound and video drivers, make it tough to beat. Many multimedia developers who felt Windows would never be as good as the Mac for creating and running multimedia are starting to take a serious second look.

But the real power of Windows 95 isn't found by just exploring its new interface. When you get under the hood, you'll encounter its biggest change—support for 32-bit applications. What exactly does this do for you? Well, that depends on the actual application you're developing. If you are creating a database-driven multimedia program like the ones we'll be developing in this book, you could possibly double the bandwidth at which information can be moved around in memory. Does this mean that all of your older Delphi programs can be recompiled under Delphi 2 as 32-bit apps, so that they will instantly run twice as fast under Windows 95? Not quite. First, due to compatibility reasons, not all Windows API calls truly take advantage of the full potential of the new 32-bit environment. For example, Delphi's built-in database engine still must handle 16-bit applications as well, so it has to use a little bit of it's processing bandwidth to watch for those exceptions. The more you work with Windows 95, the more you'll find that many API functions that you might have thought were implemented as 32-bit operations are still running as 16-bit tasks. Second, even if you could truly double the data transfer rate of an application, the application won't spend all of its time transferring information to and from memory—it still must perform other operations such as I/O, sending and receiving messages to and from Windows, and performing general housekeeping chores. Unfortunately, because many of these tasks are performed by making Windows API calls that are still written to support both 16- and 32-bit programs, there will be some communication overhead required.

The Power of Multitasking and Multithreading

Where can you get the biggest performance boost with Windows 95? The answer lies in Windows 95's ability to perform preemptive multitasking and multithreading. But isn't Windows 3.1 a multitasking environment? Well yes, but it's a *non-preemptive* multitasking system. This means that an application running under Windows 3.1 must manually tell the operating system when it is ready to hand control over to another program. In other words, a Windows 3.1 application retains control of the system until it decides to give it up—and if it decides not to give up control for one reason or another, the other programs are out of luck. Think of this like trying to catch a shuttle bus at a New York airport. Imagine that a shuttle pulls up and someone in front of you jumps in but stands in the doorway, and the shuttle just sits there idle (with the door open). You can't climb aboard because the person in front of you has taken control over the bus. To get a ride, you'd wait until the person decides to step off the shuttle. Although the shuttle has room for more passengers, you can't use it because it is *non-preemptive*.

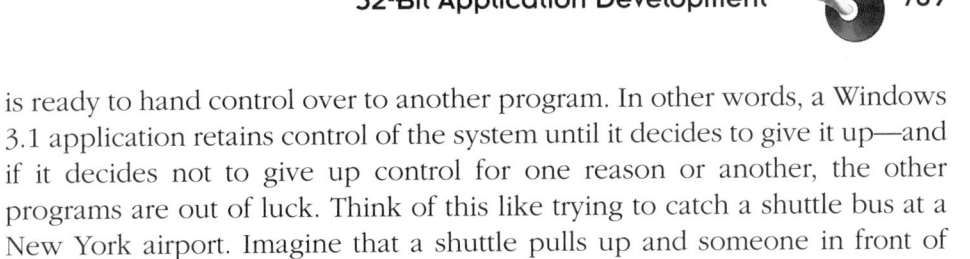

Windows 95, on the other hand, uses preemptive, time-slice-based multitasking that schedules tasks to be completed and hands them off to the CPU when it is ready. When a new application is launched, Windows 95 schedules it to run even though there may be other applications already running. This system is much more efficient, because it allows the operating system to have complete control over how applications are scheduled, rather than the other way around. This approach prevents any single task from dominating the system.

But Windows 95 scheduling system doesn't stop here. It takes the multitasking idea one step further by letting a single application run multiple *threads*. (Windows 3.1 deals only with processes—Windows 95 deals with threads.) A thread can be a single program running somewhere in memory, or it can be just a single operation of the program. So, every application can run on at least one thread at any time, but it can also spawn multiple threads at any time, and therefore may perform multiple tasks simultaneously. Where Windows 3.1 lets you run more than one application at once, Windows 95 lets multiple applications run multiple threads, all at the same time. The key here is figuring out how to take advantage of threads. Once you start thinking about it, you'll realize just how powerful threads can be when used effectively.

In a multimedia context, threads can be used in any number of ways. In this area, you'll see previously undreamed of uses for threads, because developers of mass-market products have not had access to an operating system that could handle threads and true multitasking. One possible use for threads is to make interactive video clips. With Windows 3.1, playback of videos was a very processor-intensive undertaking. Now, with Windows 95, the use of 32-bit addressing increases the throughput and speeds up playback. This gives us a little bit of our processor time back. What do we do with it? How about using the extra processor cycles to run a thread that checks for mouse movement and clicks within a video window? Later in this book we'll show you how to create hotspots in images. You could take this technology one step further and create animated hotspots for videos. Using threads, you could track a region as it moved around in a video and respond to mouse movements and clicks within that region. Under Windows 3.1 this would be a mighty tough task, but with Windows 95 it just takes some initial time and effort to create the hotspot information and develop the code to deal with the mouse.

Multiple Input Queues

Another improvement that Windows 95 has introduced is the addition of multiple input queues. Windows 3.1 provides a single input queue that keeps track of input messages such as key presses and mouse clicks while an open application is busy. Windows 95 gives each open thread its own input queue, which has the advantage that no one process can slow things down if it is responding slowly to its messages.

This is a feature that you may not be aware of because it already does what you would have expected Windows 3.1 to do. When a task has been taken over by the processor, the mouse pointer still functions. When the processor frees up, all the mouse movements and clicks that occurred when the processor was busy are executed. Under Windows 3.1, all the mouse activity that occurs is assigned to a single process. Because Windows 3.1 keeps track only of where a mouse event occurs, such as a mouse click, events can't be assigned to different tasks. For example, assume you are running an application and another window becomes active before you click the mouse. The new windows will get the click, instead of the old window that you thought you had originally clicked on. This problem is fixed under Windows 95. A separate queue is created for each open thread. When a click is registered for a thread, Windows 95 keeps track of not only where the click took place, but what window was clicked, even when the processor is busy.

Text-Based Application Support

Windows 95 gives you more power and flexibility with text-based applications as well. With previous versions of Windows, text-based applications were inconvenient. They either required the full screen, or slowed down the system too much. Now, with Windows 95, a special type of window is available, called a *console*. A console window provides a standard text-based, command-prompt environment. The big advantage that Windows 95 offers is that these programs now run in windows that act just like all the other windows. So, you can resize DOS boxes or use the mouse within any text-based application, just like you can for regular Windows programs.

32-Bit Addressing

Another important feature introduced by Windows 95 is *flat addressing*. Windows 95 applications can use memory from a pool of 4 gigabytes of virtual memory! Not only is this amount significantly higher than the memory pool available with Windows 3.1, but this memory resides in a flat address space. Unlike DOS and Windows 3.1, which use *segmented memory*, Windows 95 treats memory as though it were linear, which means that access speed is improved and memory management is much simpler from a programmer's point of view. Due to the use of virtual memory, each application has as much memory as it could possibly need (as long as you have the RAM and disk space).

The shift to 32-bit addressing has changed the way some messages are passed to a Windows 95 program versus a Windows 3.1 program. Most of the change is in the way the messages are organized, and also in the format of the values being passed. The most common change you will see is the switch from two-byte integers to four-byte *Long* integers. But, be warned, not every message and function has changed, so you can't just expect that all values will come in as Longs if they were regular integers before.

These are not all the changes that have been made to the Windows operating system, just some of the big ones that you will have to pay attention to when programming for the 32-bit environment.

Windows 95 versus Windows NT

Ever since the announcement of Windows 95 more than two years ago, developers have been debating whether Windows NT is a better 32-bit operating system than Windows 95. Originally, it seemed that Microsoft planned Windows 95 to be a user's stepping stone to Windows NT. Microsoft knew they couldn't force everyone to go out and buy a monster machine with 32 MB of RAM to run Windows NT, so why not create an operating system that provided the basic 32-bit features, but wouldn't be as demanding on the hardware budget?

As Windows 95 evolved over the course of its extended beta testing period, many of the features in Windows NT migrated into Windows 95. Of course, Windows NT is a more powerful 32-bit operating system than Windows 95. But you can bet that Windows 95 will remain a popular operating system to run your multimedia applications for quite a few years. Personally, we'd like to see more users running Windows NT in the near future because it is an extremely stable and robust environment. Many of the problems and delays that impacted the release of Windows 95 are associated with compatibility issues. Microsoft needed to ensure that Windows 95 would run all of the major 16-bit Windows applications, otherwise they'd be hearing from a lot of angry customers. So, they sacrificed some speed to gain compatibility. But don't think that having to support the thousands of 16-bit apps has turned Windows 95 into a crippled operating system. It simply means that Microsoft has had to do some incredible work, just to create what they did.

With Windows NT, Microsoft did not need to create a system that was compatible with every Windows program ever created. Their goal was to build a no-compromises, 32-bit environment that would lead them into the next century. Unfortunately, to achieve this goal, Windows NT has become one of the most resource-intensive environments for desktop computers. When NT was released in 1993, those resource demands really hurt its acceptance into the PC marketplace. But as hardware prices have fallen, systems capable of effectively running NT can be purchased for a modest sum. When NT is released with the Windows 95 user interface, many users will migrate toward this system.

But what about today? Well, in terms of personal users, the scales clearly tip towards Windows 95. Its new user interface is much more efficient to use and more aesthetically pleasing. The release of Windows 95 should be one of the biggest boons to the computer hardware market ever seen. Why? Because everyone will want the latest and greatest hardware to keep up with Windows 95. Plug and Play, built-in multimedia features, and higher system demands will push users into acquiring new hardware, especially more memory and larger hard drives. If you plan on doing any serious multimedia work or connecting to a network, you'll want to load your PC with at least 8 megabytes of RAM, and 16 megabytes is even a better idea. At least a gigabyte of hard drive space is probably a safe start. The release of Windows 95, even with the delay, is likely to be the most revolutionary event in the modern era of computing.

Appendix B

HTML 3 Reference Guide

To use one of the HTML-driven multimedia engines or the Web browsers we've created in this book, you'll need to learn HTML. HTML is essentially a basic ASCII *markup language* that can easily be composed and edited with any Windows or DOS editor. In fact, we've included a useful custom HTML editor called Web Spinner on the companion CD ROM to help you create HTML files.

As you probably know, HTML is the formatting language used by the World Wide Web. The acronym *HTML* stands for *Hypertext Markup Language*. The hypertext part means that an HTML document can contain references to other documents. This is why HTML makes a great platform for developing interactive multimedia applications. You can design HTML documents to link to other HTML documents or video, sound, and animation files. The other advantage to using HTML as a multimedia platform is that you can develop multimedia applications that can access and use the power of the Internet and the World Wide Web. This is a whole new field, one we like to call *virtual media*.

Originally, HTML was designed as a typesetting language for documents that were created using a computer. The "markup" part of its name comes from the days when book and magazine editors made special marks on the authors' manuscripts to instruct typesetters how to format the text. This process was called markup, and the term was adopted when people started inserting formatting instructions into their computer files.

Although we discussed some of the basic features of HTML as we presented our programming projects, we covered only a few of the many HTML tags that are available. This appendix provides a useful guide to most of the HTML features supported by leading Web browsers such as Netscape and

Mosaic. You'll want to use this guide as you create HTML documents for the multimedia engine and Web browser presented in this book. But keep in mind that these basic HTML engines developed in this book do not support all the HTML tags introduced by the HTML 3 standard. Of course, you can add the newer tags by studying them in this appendix and adding the necessary support code to the Delphi programs.

HTML—The Language of the Web

The HTML that we use in this book to create our multimedia and Web documents is actually a subset of a language called *SGML*, which stands for *Standard Generalized Markup Language*. HTML commands are enclosed in angle brackets, **<like this>**. Most commands come in pairs that mark the beginning and end of a part of text. The end command is often identical to the start command, except that it includes a forward slash between the opening bracket and the command name. For example, the title of an HTML document called "Multimedia Adventures" would look like this:

```
<TITLE>Multimedia "Adventures</TITLE>"
```

Similarly, a word or phrase that you want to display in bold type would be indicated like this:

```
<B>Display this phrase in bold</B>
```

It's not too hard to mark up your text, but all the bracketed tags can make your source text hard to read and proofread. No one has created a true "Web processor," a WYSIWYG word processor that happens to read and write HTML files, but we're bound to see one soon. For now we have to use word processors, text editors, or simple HTML editors that display the tags, not their effects.

Using an HTML Editor

Many people do prefer using an HTML editor over a word processor like Microsoft Word or a simple text editor like Windows Notepad. In fact, we've included some handy HTML editors on the companion CD-ROM, including Web Spinner and HTMLAssistant. It is easier to start writing HTML with an HTML editor than with a basic text editor, because most HTML editors offer some sort of menu of tags. This can help you get acquainted with the HTML tag set.

The other advantage of an HTML editor is that when it inserts tags for you, it inserts both the start and the end tags. This feature greatly reduces the chance that your whole document will end up in the **<H1>** (first level header) style, or that a bold word will become three bold paragraphs.

HTML Basics

All HTML files consist of a mixture of text to be displayed and HTML tags that describe how the text should be displayed. Normally, extra whitespace (spaces, tabs, and line breaks) is ignored, and text is displayed with a single space between each word. Text is always wrapped to fit within a browser's window in the reader's choice of fonts. Line breaks in the HTML source are treated as any other whitespace, that is, they're ignored—and a paragraph break must be marked with a **<P>** tag.

Tags are always set off from the surrounding text by angle brackets, the less-than and greater-than signs. Most tags come in *begin* and *end* pairs, for example, **<I>** ... **</I>**. The end tag includes a slash between the opening bracket and the tag name. There are a few tags that require only a start tag; we'll point out these tags as they come up.

HTML is case insensitive: **<HTML>** is the same as **<html>** or **<hTmL>**. However, many Web servers run on Unix systems, which *are* case sensitive. This will never affect HTML interpretation, but will affect your hyperlinks: My.gif is not the same file as my.gif or MY.GIF.

Some begin tags can take parameters, which come between the tag name and the closing bracket like this: **<DL COMPACT>**. Others, like description lists, have optional parameters. Still others, such as anchors and images, require certain parameters and can also take optional parameters.

The Structure of an HTML Document

All HTML documents have a certain standard structure, but Netscape and most other Web browsers will treat any file that ends in .HTML (.HTM on PCs) as an HTML file, even if it contains no HTML tags. All HTML text and tags should be contained within this tag pair:

<HTML> ... </HTML>

<HEAD> ... </HEAD> Tag

All HTML documents are divided into a header that contains the title and other information about the document, and a body that contains the actual document text.

While you should not place display text outside the body section, this is currently optional since most Web browsers and HTML readers will format and display any text that's not in a tag. Also, while you can get away with not using the **<HEAD>** tag pair, we recommend you use it.

<BODY> ... </BODY> Tag

The tags that appear within the body of an HTML document do not separate the document into sections. Rather, they're either special parts of the text, like images or forms, or they're tags that say something about the text they enclose, like character attributes or paragraph styles.

Headings and Paragraphs

In some ways, HTML text is a series of paragraphs. Within a paragraph, the text will be wrapped to fit the reader's screen. In most cases, any line breaks that appear in the source file are totally ignored.

Paragraphs are separated either by an explicit paragraph break tag, **<P>**, or by paragraph style commands. The paragraph style determines both the font used for the paragraph and any special indenting. Paragraph styles include several levels of section headers, five types of lists, three different *block formats*, and the normal, or default, paragraph style. Any text outside of an explicit paragraph style command will be displayed in the normal style.

<ADDRESS> ... </ADDRESS> Tag

The last part of the document body should be an **<ADDRESS>** tag pair, which contains information about the author and, often, the document's copyright date and revision history. While the address block is not a required part of the document in the same way that the header or the body is, official style guides urge that all documents have one. In current practice, while most documents use the **<HTML>**, **<HEAD>**, and **<BODY>** tag pairs, almost all documents have address blocks—perhaps because the address block is visible.

The format for using the **<ADDRESS>** tag is as follows:

```
<ADDRESS>Address text goes here</ADDRESS>
```

Comments

Comments can be placed in your HTML documents using a special tag as shown:

```
<!-Comment text goes here->
```

Everything between the <> will be ignored by a browser when the document is displayed.

Header Elements

The elements used in the header of an HTML document include a title section and internal indexing information.

<TITLE> ... </TITLE> Tag

Every document should have a title. The manner in which a title is displayed varies from system to system and browser to browser. The title could be displayed as a window title, or it may appear in a pane within the window. The title should be short—64 characters or less—and should contain just text.

The title should appear in the header section, marked off with a **<TITLE>** tag pair; for example, **<TITLE>**Explore the Grand Canyon**</TITLE>**. Some Web browsers like Netscape are quite easy-going and will let you place the title anywhere in the document, even after the **</HTML>** tag, but future browsers might not be quite so accommodating. Including a title is important because many Web search engines will use the title to locate a document.

The format for using the **<TITLE>** tag is as follows:

```
<TITLE>Title text goes here</TITLE>
```

Other <HEAD> Elements

There are a few optional elements that may only appear in the document's header (**<HEAD>** tag pair). The header elements that browsers use are the **<BASE>** and **<ISINDEX>** tags. Both are empty or solitary tags that do not have a closing **</...>** tag and thus do not enclose any text.

The **<BASE>** tag contains the current document's URL, or Uniform Resource Locator; browsers can use it to find local URLs.

The **<ISINDEX>** tag tells browsers that this document is an index document, which means that the server can support keyword searches based on the document's URL. Searches are passed back to the Web server by concatenating a question mark and one or more keywords to the document URL and then requesting this extended URL. This is very similar to one of the ways that form data is returned. (See the section *Form Action and Method Attributes* for more information.)

HTML includes other header elements, such as **<NEXTID>** and **<LINK>**, which are included in HTML for the benefit of editing and cataloging software. They have no visible effect; browsers simply ignore them.

Normal Text

Most HTML documents are composed of plain, or normal, text. Any text not appearing between format tag pairs is displayed as normal text.

Normal text, like every other type of paragraph style except the preformatted style, is wrapped at display time to fit in the reader's window. A larger or smaller font or window size will result in a totally different number of words on each line, so don't try to change the wording of a sentence to make the line breaks come at appropriate places. It won't work.

*
 Tag*

If line breaks are important, as in postal addresses or poetry, you can use the **
** command to insert a line break. Subsequent text will appear one line down, on the left margin.

The general format for this tag is:

```
<BR CLEAR=[Left|Right]>
```

The section listed between the [] is optional. This is a feature introduced as an HTML enhancement and supported by newer versions of Netscape.

Let's look at an example of how **
** is used. To keep

```
Coriolis Group Books
7339 East Acoma Drive, Suite 7
Scottsdale, Arizona 85260-6912
```

from coming out as

```
Coriolis Group Books 7339 East Acoma Drive, Suite 7 Scottsdale, Arizona 85260-6912
```

you would write:

```
Coriolis Group Books<BR>
7339 East Acoma Drive, Suite 7<BR>
Scottsdale, Arizona 85260-6912<BR>
```

The extended form of the **
** tag allows you to control how text is wrapped. The **CLEAR** argument allows text to be broken so that it can flow to the right or to the left around an image. For example, this tag shows how text can be broken to flow to the left:

```
This text will be broken here.<BR CLEAR=Left>
```

This line will flow around to the right of an image that can be displayed with the **<IMG>** tag.

<NOBR> Tag

This tag stands for *No Break*. This is another HTML extension supported by Netscape. To keep text from breaking, you can include the **<NOBR>** tag at the beginning of the text you want to keep together.

<WBR> Tag

This tag stands for Word Break. If you use the **<NOBR>** tag to define a section of text without breaks, you can force a line break at any location by inserting the **<WBR>** tag followed by the **
** tag.

<P> Tag

The **
** command causes a line break within a paragraph, but more often we want to separate one paragraph from another. We can do this by enclosing each paragraph in a **<P>** tag pair, starting the paragraph with **<P>** and ending it with **</P>**. The actual appearance of the paragraphs will depend on your reader's Web browser: Paragraph breaks may be shown with an extra line or half line of spacing, a leading indent, or both.

The **</P>** tag is optional; most people include a single **<P>** at the beginning of each paragraph, at the end, or alone on a line between two paragraphs.

Physical and Logical Attributes

Character attribute tags let you emphasize words or phrases within a paragraph. HTML supports two different types of character attributes: physical and logical. Physical attributes include the familiar bold, italic, and underline, as well as a tty attribute for monospaced text.

Logical attributes are different. In keeping with the SGML philosophy of using tags to describe content and not the actual formatting, logical attributes let you describe what sort of emphasis you want to put on a word or phrase, but leave the actual formatting up to the browser. That is, where a word marked with a physical attribute like **<B>**bold**</B>** will always appear in bold type, an **<EM>**emphasized**</EM>** word may be italicized, underlined, bolded, or displayed in color.

Web style guides suggest that you use logical attributes whenever you can, but there's a slight problem: Some current browsers only support some physical attributes, and few or no logical attributes. Since Web browsers simply ignore any HTML tag that they don't *understand*, when you use logical tags, you run the risk that your readers will not see any formatting at all!

The standard format for using any of the physical attributes tags is as follows:

```
<tag>text goes here</tag>
```

You can nest attributes, although the results will vary from browser to browser. For example, some browsers can display bold italic text, while others will only display the innermost attribute. (That is, **<B><I>**bold italic**</I></B>** may show up as bold italic.) If you use nested attributes, be sure to place the end tags in reverse order of the start tags; don't write something like **<B><I>**bold italic**</B></I>**! This may work with some Web browsers, but may cause problems with others.

Keep in mind that even if current browsers arbitrarily decide that **<EM>** text will be displayed as italic and **<KBD>** text will be displayed as Courier, future browsers will probably defer these attributes to a setting controlled by the user. So, don't conclude that citations, definitions, and variables all look alike and that you should ignore them and use italic.

<BLINK> ... </BLINK>

This is a new enhanced tag supported by Netscape. Text placed between this pair will blink on the screen. This feature is useful for attention-grabbing, but using it too much could get rather annoying. The format for this tag is:

```
<BLINK>This text will blink</BLINK>
```

<CENTER> ... </CENTER>

This HTML enhancement makes some Web page authors feel like they've died and gone to heaven. Any text (or images) placed between this pair is centered between the left and right margins of a page. The format for this tag is:

```
<CENTER>This text will be centered between the left and right margins</CENTER>
```

<FONT> ... </FONT>

This HTML enhancement allows you to control the sizes of the fonts displayed in your documents. The format for this tag is:

```
<FONT SIZE=font-size>text goes here</FONT>
```

where *font-size* must be a number from 1 to 7. A size of 1 produces the smallest font. The default font size is 3. Once the font size has been changed, it will remain in effect until the font size is changed by using another tag.

<BASEFONT>

To give you even greater control over font sizing, a new HTML tag has been added so that you can set the base font for all text displayed in a document. The format for this tag is:

```
<BASEFONT SIZE=font-size>
```

Again, *font-size* must be a number from 1 to 7. A size of 1 produces the smallest font. The default font size is 3. Once the base font size has been defined, you can display text in larger or smaller fonts using the + or – sign with the **<FONT>** tag. Here's an example of how this works:

```
<BASEFONT SIZE=4>
This text will be displayed as size 4 text.
<FONT SIZE=+2>
This text will be displayed as size 6.
</FONT>
This text will return to the base font size--size 4.
```

Headings

HTML provides six levels of section headers, **<H1>** through **<H6>**. While these are typically short phrases that fit on a line or two, the various headers are actually full-fledged paragraph types. They can even contain line and paragraph break commands.

You are not required to use a **<H1>** before you use a **<H2>**, or to make sure that a **<H4>** follows a **<H3>** or another **<H4>**.

The standard format for using one of the six heading tags is illustrated by this sample:

```
<H1>Text Goes Here</H1>
```

Lists

HTML supports five different list types. All five types can be thought of as a sort of paragraph type. The first four list types share a common syntax, and differ only in how they format their list elements. The fifth type, the *description* list, is unique in that each list element has two parts—a tag and a description of the tag.

All five list types display an element marker—whether it be a number, a bullet, or a few words—on the left margin. The marker is followed by the actual list elements, which appear indented. List elements do not have to fit on a single line or consist of a single paragraph—they may contain **<P>** and **
** tags.

Lists can be nested, but the appearance of a nested list depends on the browser. For example, some browsers use different bullets for inner lists than for outer lists, and some browsers do not indent nested lists. However, Netscape and Lynx, which are probably the most common graphical and text mode browsers, do indent nested lists; the tags of a nested list align with the elements of the outer list, and the elements of the nested list are further indented. For example,

- This is the first element of the main bulleted list.
  - This is the first element of a nested list.
  - This is the second element of the nested list.
- This is the second element of the main bulleted list.

The four list types that provide simple list elements use the list item tag, **<LI>**, to mark the start of each list element. The **<LI>** tag always appears at the start of a list element, not at the end.

Thus, all simple lists look something like this:

```
<ListType>

<LI>
There isn't really any ListType list, however the OL, UL, DIR, and
MENU lists all follow this format.

<LI>
Since whitespace is ignored, you can keep your source legible by
putting blank lines between your list elements. Sometimes, we like to put the
&lt;li&gt; tags on their own lines, too.

<LI>
(If we hadn't used the ampersand quotes in the previous list element,
the "&lt;li&gt;" would have been interpreted as the start of a new
list element.)

</ListType>
```

Numbered List

In HTML, numbered lists are referred to as *ordered lists*. The list type tag is **<OL>**. Numbered lists can be nested, but some browsers get confused by the close of a nested list, and start numbering the subsequent elements of the outer list from 1.

Bulleted List

If a numbered list is an ordered list, what else could an unnumbered, bulleted list be but an unordered list? The tag for an unordered (bulleted) list is **<UL>**. While bulleted lists can be nested, you should keep in mind that the list nesting may not be visible; some browsers indent nested lists; some don't. Some use multiple bullet types; others don't.

Netscape List Extensions

Netscape has added a useful feature called **TYPE** that can be included with unordered and ordered lists. This feature allows you to specify the type of bullet or number that you use for the different levels of indentation in a list.

Unordered List with Extensions

When Netscape displays the different levels of indentation in an unordered list, it uses a solid disk (level 1) followed by a bullet (level 2) followed by a square (level 3). You can use the **TYPE** feature with the **<UL>** tag to override this sequence of bullets. Here's the format:

```
<UL TYPE=Disc|Circle|Square>
```

For example, here's a list defined to use circles as the bullet symbol:

```
<UL TYPE=Circle>
<LI>This is item 1
<LI>This is item 2
<LI>This is item 3
</UL>
```

Ordered List with Extensions

When Netscape displays ordered (numbered) lists, it numbers each list item using a numeric sequence—1, 2, 3, and so on. You can change this setting by using the **TYPE** modifier with the **<OL>** tag. Here's how this feature is used with numbered lists:

```
<OL TYPE=A|a|I|i|1>
```

where **TYPE** can be assigned to any one of these values:

A   Mark list items with capital letters
a   Mark list items with lowercase letters
I   Mark list items with large roman numerals
i   Mark list items with small roman numerals
1   Mark list items with numbers (default)

Wait, there's more. You can also start numbering list items with a number other than 1. To do this, you use the **START** modifier as shown:

```
<OL START=starting-number>
```

where starting-number specifies the first number used. You can use the feature with the **TYPE** tag. For example, the tag

```
<OL TYPE=A START=4>
```

would start the numbered list with the roman numeral IV.

Using Modifiers with List Elements

In addition to supporting the **TYPE** modifier with the **<UL>** and **<OL>** tags, Netscape allows you to use this modifier with the **<LI>** tag to define list elements for ordered and unordered lists. Here's an example of how it can be used with an unordered list:

```
<H2>Useful Publishing Resources</H2>
<UL TYPE=Disc>
<LI>HTML Tips
<LI>Web Page Samples
<LI TYPE=Square>Images
<LI TYPE=Disc>Templates
</UL>
```

In this case, all the list items will have a disc symbol as the bullet, except the third item, *Images*, which will be displayed with a square bullet.

The **TYPE** modifier can be assigned the same values as those used to define lists with the **<UL>** and **<OL>** tags. Once it is used to define a style for a list item, all subsequent items in the list will be changed, unless another **TYPE** modifier is used.

If you are defining **<LI>** list elements for ordered lists **<OL>**, you can also use a new modifier named **VALUE** to change the numeric value of a list item. Here's an example:

```
<H2>Useful Publishing Resources</H2>
<OL>
<LI>HTML Tips
<LI>Web Page Samples
<LI VALUE=4>Images
<LI>Templates
</UL>
```

In this list, the third item would be assigned the number 4 and the fourth item would be assigned the number 5.

Directory and Menu Lists

The directory and menu lists are special types of unordered lists. The menu list, **<MENU>**, is meant to be visually more compact than a standard unordered list; menu list items should all fit on a single line. The directory list, **<DIR>**, is supposed to be even more compact; all list items should be less than 20 characters long, so that the list can be displayed in three (or more) columns.

We're not sure if we've ever actually seen these lists in use, and their implementation is still spotty; current versions of Netscape do not create multiple columns for a **<DIR>** list, and while they let you choose a directory list font and a menu list font, they do not actually use these fonts.

Description List

The description list, or **<DL>**, does not use the **<LI>** tag the way other lists do. Each description list element has two parts, a tag and its description. Each tag begins with a **<DT>** tag, and each description with a **<DD>** tag. These appear at the start of the list element, and are not paired with **</DT>** or **</DD>** tags.

The description list looks a lot like any other list, except that instead of a bullet or a number, the list tag consists of your text. Description lists are intended to be used for creating formats like a glossary entry, where a short tag is followed by an indented definition, but the format is fairly flexible. For example, a long tag will wrap, just like any other paragraph, although it should not contain line or paragraph breaks. (Netscape will indent any **<DT>** text after a line or paragraph, as if it were the **<DD>** text.) Further, you needn't actually supply any tag text; **<DT><DD>** will produce an indented paragraph.

Compact and Standard Lists

Normally, a description list puts the tags on one line, and starts the indented descriptions on the next:

```
Tag 1
Description 1.
Tag 2
Description 2.
```

For a tighter look, you can use a **<DL COMPACT>**. If the tags are very short, some browsers will start the descriptions on the same line as the tags:

```
Tag 1    Description 1
Tag 2    Description 2
```

However, most browsers do not support the compact attribute, and will simply ignore it. For example, with current versions of Windows Netscape, a **<DL COMPACT>** will always look like a **<DL>**, even if the tags are very short.

Inline Images

Using only text attributes, section headers, and lists, you can build attractive-looking documents. The next step is to add pictures.

<IMG ...> Tag

The **<IMG>** tag is a very useful HTML feature. It lets you insert inline images into your text. This tag is rather different from the tags we've seen so far. Not only is it an empty tag that always appears alone, it has a number of parameters between the opening **<IMG** and the closing **>**. Some of the parameters include the image file name and some optional modifiers. The basic format for this tag is:

```
<IMG SRC="URL" ALT="text"
     ALIGN=top|middle|bottom
     ISMAP>
```

Since HTML 3 has emerged and additional Netscape extensions have been added, this tag has expanded more than any other HTML feature. Here is the complete format for the latest and greatest version of the **<IMG>** tag:

```
<IMG SRC="URL" ALT="text"
     ALIGN=left|right|top|texttop|middle|absmiddle|
           baseline|bottom|absbottom
     WIDTH=pixels
     HEIGHT=pixels
     BORDER=pixels
     VSPACE=pixels
     HSPACE=pixels
     ISMAP>
```

The extended version allows you to specify the size of an image, better control image and text alignment, and specify the size of an image's border.

Every **<IMG>** tag must have a **SRC=** parameter. This specifies a URL, or Uniform Resource Locator, which points to a GIF or JPEG bitmap file. When the bitmap file is in the same directory as the HTML document, the file name is an adequate URL. For example, **<IMG SRC=**MySmilingFace.gif**>** would insert a picture of a smiling face.

Some people turn off inline images because they have a slow connection to the Web. This replaces all images, no matter what size, with a standard graphic. This isn't so bad if the picture is ancillary to your text, but if you've used small inline images as bullets in a list or as section dividers, the placeholder graphic will usually make your page look rather strange. For this reason, some people avoid using graphics as structural elements; others simply don't worry about people with slow connections; still others include a note at the top of the page saying that all the images on the page are small, and invite people with inline images off to turn them on and reload the page.

Keep in mind that some people use text-only browsers, like Lynx, to navigate the Web. If you include a short description of your image with the **ALT=** parameter, text-only browsers can show something in place of your graphic. For example, **<IMG SRC=**MySmilingFace.gif could be supplemented by the code: **ALT=**"A picture of the author">, so that no one feels left out.

Since the the value assigned to the **ALT** parameter has spaces in it, we have to put it within quotation marks. In general, you can put any parameter value in quotation marks, but you need to do so only if it includes spaces.

Mixing Images and Text

You can mix text and images within a paragraph; an image does not constitute a paragraph break. However, some Web browsers, like earlier versions of Netscape, did not wrap paragraphs around images; they displayed a single line of text to the left or right of an image. Normally, any text in the same paragraph as an image would be lined up with the bottom of the image, and would wrap normally below the image. This works well if the text is essentially a caption for the image, or if the image is a decoration at the start of a paragraph. However, when the image is a part of a header, you may want the text to be centered vertically in the image, or to be lined up with the top of the image. In these cases, you can use the optional **ALIGN=** parameter to specify **ALIGN=top**, **ALIGN=middle**, or **ALIGN=bottom**.

Using Floating Images

With the extended version of the **<IMG>** tag, you can now create "floating" images that will align to the left or right margin of a Web page. Text that is displayed after the image will either wrap around the right-hand or left-hand side of the image. Here's an example of how an image can be displayed at the left margin with text that wraps to the right of the image:

```
<IMG SRC="limage.gif" ALIGN=left>
```

Text will be displayed to the right of the image.

Specifying Spacing for Floating Images

When you use floating images with wrap-around text, you can specify the spacing between the text and the image by using the **VSPACE** and **HSPACE** modifiers. **VSPACE** defines the amount of spacing in units of pixels between the top and bottom of the image and the text. **HSPACE** defines the spacing between the left or right edge of the image and the text that wraps.

Sizing Images

Another useful feature that has been added to the **<IMG>** tag is image sizing. The **WIDTH** and **HEIGHT** modifiers are used to specify the width and height for an image in pixels. Here's an example:

```
<IMG SRC="logo.gif" WIDTH=250 HEIGHT=310>
```

When a browser like Netscape displays an image, it needs to determine the size of the image before it can display a placeholder or bounding box for the image. If you include the image's size using **WIDTH** and **HEIGHT**, a Web page can be built much faster. If the values you specify for **WIDTH** and **HEIGHT** differ from the image's actual width and height, the image will be scaled to fit.

Using Multiple Images per Line

Since an image is treated like a single (rather large) character, you can have more than one image on a single line. In fact, you can have as many images on a line as will fit in your reader's window! If you put too many images on a line, the browser will wrap the line and your images will appear on multiple lines. If you don't want images to appear on the same line, place a **
** or **<P>** between them.

Defining an Image's Border

Typically, an image is displayed with a border around it. This is the border that is set to the color blue when the image is part of an anchor. Using the **BORDER** modifier, you can specify a border width for any image you display. Here's an example that displays an image with a five pixel border:

```
<IMG SRC="logo.gif" BORDER=5>
```

IsMap Parameter

The optional **ISMAP** parameter allows you to place hyperlinks to other documents in a bitmapped image. This technique is used to turn an image into a clickable map. (See the section *Using Many Anchors in an Image* for more detail.)

Horizontal Rules

The **<HR>** tag draws a horizontal rule, or line, across the screen. It's fairly common to put a rule before and after a form, to help set off the user entry areas from the normal text.

Many people use small inline images for decoration and separation, instead of rules. Although using images in this manner lets you customize your pages, it also takes longer for them to load—and it may make them look horrible when inline images are turned off.

The original **<HR>** tag simply displayed an engraved rule across a Web page. A newer version of the tag has been extended to add additional features including sizing, alignment, and shading. The format for the extended version of **<HR>** is:

```
<HR SIZE=pixels
    WIDTH=pixels|percent
    ALIGN=left|right|center
    NOSHADE>
```

The **SIZE** modifier sets the width (thickness) of the line in pixel units. The **WIDTH** modifier specifies the length of the line in actual pixel units or a percentage of the width of the page. The **ALIGN** modifier specifies the alignment for the line (the default is center) and the **NOSHADE** modifier allows you to display a solid line.

As an example of how some of these new features are used, the following tag displays a solid line, five pixels thick. The line is left justified and spans 80 percent of the width of the page:

```
<HR SIZE=5 WIDTH=80% ALIGN="left" NOSHADE>
```

Hypermedia Links

The ability to add links to other HTML documents or to entirely different sorts of documents is what makes the HTML-driven readers so powerful. The special sort of highlight that your reader clicks on to traverse a hypermedia link is called an anchor, and all links are created with the anchor tag, **<A>**. The basic format for this tag is:

```
<A HREF="URL"
   NAME="text"
   REL=next|previous|parent|made
   REV=next|previous|parent|made
   TITLE="text">

text</A>
```

Links to Other Documents

While you can define a link to another point within the current page, most links are to other documents. Links to points within a document are very similar to links to other documents, but are slightly more complicated, so we will talk about them later. (See the section *Links to Anchors*.)

Each link has two parts: The visible part, or anchor, which the user clicks on, and the invisible part, which tells the browser where to go. The anchor is the text between the **<A>** and **</A>** tags of the **<A>** tag pair, while the actual link data appears in the **<A>** tag.

Just as the **<IMG>** tag has a **SRC=** parameter that specifies an image file, so does the **<A>** tag have an **HREF=** parameter that specifies the hypermedia reference. Thus, **<A HREF=SomeFile.Type>click here</A>** is a link to *somefile.type* with the visible anchor *click here*.

Browsers will generally use the linked document's filename extension to decide how to display the linked document. For example, HTML or HTM files will be interpreted and displayed as HTML, whether they come from an http server, an FTP server, or a gopher site. Conversely, a link can be to any sort of file—a large bitmap, sound file, or movie.

Images as Hotspots

Since inline images are in many ways just big characters, there's no problem with using an image in an anchor. The anchor can include text on either side of the image, or the image can be an anchor by itself. Most browsers show an image anchor by drawing a blue border around the image (or around the placeholder graphic). The image anchor may be a picture of what is being linked to, or for reasons we'll explain shortly, it may even just point to another copy of itself:

```
<A HREF=image.gif><IMG SRC=image.gif></A>.
```

Thumbnail Images

One sort of *picture of the link* is called a thumbnail image. This is a tiny image, perhaps 100 pixels in the smaller dimension, which is either a condensed version of a larger image or a section of the image. Thumbnail images can be transmitted quickly, even via slow communication lines, leaving it up to the reader to decide which larger images to request. A secondary issue is aesthetic: Large images take up a lot of screen space, smaller images don't.

Linking an Image to Itself

Many people turn off inline images to improve performance over a slow network link. If the inline image is an anchor for itself, these people can then click on the placeholder graphic to see what they missed.

Using Many Anchors in an Image

The **<IMG>** tag's optional ISMAP parameter allows you to turn rectangular regions of a bitmap image into clickable anchors. Clicking on these parts of the image will activate an appropriate URL. (A default URL is also usually provided for when the user clicks on an area outside of one of the predefined regions.) While forms let you do this a bit more flexibly, the ISMAP approach doesn't require any custom programming—just a simple text file that defines the rectangles and their URLs—and this technique may work with browsers that do not support forms. An example of how to do this can be found on the Web site at:

```
http://wintermute.ncsc.uiuc.edu:8080/map-tutorial/image-maps.html
```

Links to Anchors

When an HREF parameter specifies a filename, the link is to the whole document. If the document is an HTML file, it will replace the current document and the reader will be placed at the top of the new document. Often this is just what you want. But sometimes you'd rather have a link take the reader to a specific section of a document. Doing this requires two anchor tags: one that defines an anchor name for a location, and one that points to that name. These two tags can be in the same document or in different documents.

Defining an Anchor Name

To define an anchor name, you need to use the **NAME** parameter: **<A NAME=**AnchorName**>**. You can attach this name to a phrase, not just a single point, by following the **<A>** tag with a **</A>** tag.

Linking to an Anchor in the Current Document

To then use this name, simply insert an **<A HREF=**...**>** tag as usual, except that instead of a filename, use a **#** followed by an anchor name. For example, **<A HREF=#**AnchorName**>** refers to the example in the previous paragraph.

Names do not have to be defined before they are used; it's actually fairly common for lengthy documents to have a table of contents with links to names defined later in the document. It's also worth noting that while tag and parameter names are not case sensitive, anchor names are; **<A HREF=#**anchorname**>** will not take you to the AnchorName example.

Linking to an Anchor in a Different Document

You can also link to specific places in any other HTML document, anywhere in the world—provided, of course, that it contains named anchors. To do this, you simply add the # and the anchor name after the URL that tells where the document can be found. For example, to plant a link to the anchor named "Section 1" in a file named complex.html in the same directory as the current file, you could use **<A HREF=**"Complex.html#Section 1"**>**. Similarly, if the named anchor was in http://www.another.org/Complex.html, you'd use **<A HREF=**"http://www.another.org/Complex.html#Section 1"**>**.

Using URLs

Just as a complete DOS filename starts with a drive letter followed by a colon, so a full URL starts with a resource type—HTTP, FTP, GOPHER, and so on—followed by a colon. If the name doesn't have a colon in it, it's assumed to be a local reference, which is a filename on the same file system as the current document. Thus, **<A HREF=**Another.html**>** refers to the file "Another.html" in the same directory as the current file, while **<A HREF=**/html/File.html**>** refers to the file "File.html" in the top-level directory *html*. One thing to note here is that a URL always uses "/" (the Unix-style forward slash) as a directory separator, even when the files are on a Windows machine, which would normally use "\", the DOS-style backslash.

Local URLs can be very convenient when you have several HTML files with links to each other, or when you have a large number of inline images. If you ever have to move them all to another directory, or to another machine, you don't have to change all the URLs.

<BASE> Tag

One drawback of local URLs is that if someone makes a copy of your document, the local URLs will no longer work. Adding the optional **<BASE>** tag to the **<HEAD>** section of your document will help eliminate this problem. While many browsers do not yet support it, the intent of the **<BASE>** tag is precisely to provide a context for local URLs.

The **<BASE>** tag is like the **<IMG>** tag, in that it's a so-called empty tag. It requires an HREF parameter—for example, **<BASE HREF**=http://www.imaginary.org/index.html>—which should contain the URL of the document itself. When a browser that supports the **<BASE>** tag encounters a URL that doesn't contain a protocol and path, it will look for it relative to the base URL, instead of relative to the location from which it actually loaded the document. The format for the **<BASE>** tag is:

```
<BASE HREF="URL">
```

Reading and Constructing URLs

Where a local URL is just a file name, a global URL specifies an instance of one of several resource types, which may be located on any Internet machine in the world. The wide variety of resources is reflected in a complex URL syntax. For example, while most URLs consist of a resource type followed by a colon, two forward slashes, a machine name, another forward slash, and a resource name, others consist only of a resource type, a colon, and the resource name.

The resource-type://machine-name/resource-name URL form is used with centralized resources, where there's a single server that supplies the document to the rest of the net, using a particular protocol. Thus, "http://www.another.org/Complex.html" means "use the Hypertext Transfer Protocol to get file complex.html from the main www directory on the machine www.another.org", while "ftp://foo.bar.net/pub/www/editors/README" means "use the File Transfer Protocol to get the file /pub/www/editors/README from the machine foo.bar.net".

Conversely, many resource types are distributed. We don't all get our news or mail from the same central server, but from the nearest one of many news and mail servers. URLs for distributed resources use the simpler form resource-type:resource-name. For example, "news:comp.infosystems.www.providers"

refers to the Usenet newsgroup comp.infosystems.www.providers, which, by the way, is a good place to look for further information about writing HTML.

Using www and Actual Machine Names

In the HTTP domain, you'll often see "machine names" like "www.coriolis.com". This usually does not mean there's a machine named www.coriolis.com that you can FTP or Telnet to; "www" is an alias that a Webmaster can set up when he or she registers the server. Using the www alias makes sense, because machines come and go, but sites (and, we hope, the Web) last for quite a while. If URLs refer to www at the site and not to a specific machine, the server and all the HTML files can be moved to a new machine simply by changing the www alias, without having to update all the URLs.

Using Special Characters

Since < and > have special meanings in HTML, there must be a way to represent characters like these as part of text. While the default character set for the Web is ISO Latin-1, which includes European language characters like Å and Ñ in the range from 128 to 255, it's not uncommon to pass around snippets of HTML in 7-bit email, or to edit them on dumb terminals, so HTML also needs a way to specify high-bit characters using only 7-bit characters.

Two Forms Numeric and Symbolic

There are two ways to specify an arbitrary character: numeric and symbolic. To include the copyright symbol, ©, which is character number 169, you can use ©. That is, &#, then the number of the character you want to include, and a closing semicolon. The numeric method is very general, but not easy to read.

The symbolic form is much easier to read, but its use is restricted to the four low-bit characters with special meaning in HTML. To use the other symbols in the ISO Latin-1 character set, like ® and the various currency symbols, you have to use the numeric form. The symbolic escape is like the numeric escape, except there's no #. For example, to insert é, you would use "é", or &, the character name, and a closing semicolon. You should be aware that symbol names are case sensitive: É is É, not é, while &EAcute; is no character at all, and will show up in your text as &EAcute;!

Preformatted and Other Special Paragraph Types

HTML supports three special "block" formats. Any normal text within a block format is supposed to appear in a distinctive font.

<BLOCKQUOTE> ... </BLOCKQUOTE> Tag

The block quote sets an extended quotation off from normal text. That is, a **<BLOCKQUOTE>** tag pair does not imply indented, single-spaced, and italicized; rather, it's just meant to change the default, plain text font. The format for this tag is:

```
<BLOCKQUOTE>text</BLOCKQUOTE>
```

<PRE> ... </PRE> Tag

Everything in a preformatted block will appear in a monospaced font. The **<PRE>** tag pair is also the only HTML element that pays any attention to the line breaks in the source file; any line break in a preformatted block will be treated just as a **
** elsewhere. Since HTML tags can be used within a preformatted block, you can have anchors as well as bold or italic monospaced text. The format for this tag is:

```
<PRE WIDTH=value>text</PRE>
```

The initial **<PRE>** tag has an optional **WIDTH=** parameter. Browsers won't trim lines to this length; the intent is to allow the browser to select a monospaced font that will allow the maximum line length to fit in the browser window.

<ADDRESS> ... </ADDRESS> Tag

The third block format is the address format: **<ADDRESS>**. This is generally displayed in italics, and is intended for displaying information about a document, such as creation date, revision history, and how to contact the author. Official style guides say that every document should provide an address block. The format for this tag is:

```
<ADDRESS>text</ADDRESS>
```

Many people put a horizontal rule, **<HR>**, between the body of the document and the address block. If you include a link to your home page or to a page that lets the reader send mail to you, you won't have to include a lot of information on each individual page.

Using Tables

Features like lists are great for organizing data; however, sometimes you need a more compact way of grouping related data. Fortunately, some of the newer browsers like Netscape have implemented the proposed HTML 3 specification for tables. Tables can contain a heading and row and column data. Each unit of a table is called a cell and cell data can be text and images.

<TABLE> ... </TABLE> Tag

This tag is used to define a new table. All of the table-specific tags must be placed within the pair **<TABLE>** ... **</TABLE>**, otherwise they will be ignored. The format for the **<TABLE>** tag is:

```
<TABLE BORDER>table text</TABLE>
```

Leaving out the **BORDER** modifier will display the table without a border.

Creating a Table Title

Creating a title or caption for a table is easy with the **<CAPTION>** tag. This tag must be placed within the **<TABLE>** ... **</TABLE>** tags. Here is its general format:

```
<CAPTION ALIGN=top|bottom>caption text</CAPTION>
```

Notice that you can display the caption at the top or bottom of the table. By default, the caption will be displayed at the top of the table.

Creating Table Rows

Every table you create will have one or more rows. (Otherwise it won't be much of a table!) The simple tag for creating a row is:

```
<TR>text</TR>
```

For each row that you want to add, you must place the **<TR>** tag inside the body of the table, between the **<TABLE>** ... **</TABLE>** tags.

Defining Table Data Cells

Within each **<TR>** ... **</TR>** tag pair come one or more **<TD>** tags to define the table cell data. You can think of the cell data as the column definitions for the table. Here is the format for a **<TD>** tag:

```
<TD ALIGN=left|center|right
    VALIGN=top|middle|bottom|baseline
    NOWRAP
```

```
    COLSPAN=number
    ROWSPAN=number>
text</TD>
```

The size for each cell is determined by the width or height of the data that is displayed. The **ALIGN** parameter can be used to center or left- or right-justify the data displayed in the cell. The **VALIGN** parameter, on the other hand, specifies how the data will align vertically. If you don't want the text to wrap within the cell, you can include the **NOWRAP** modifier.

When defining a cell, you can manually override the width and height of the cell by using the **COLSPAN** and **ROWSPAN** parameters. **COLSPAN** specifies the number of columns the table cell will span and **ROWSPAN** specifies the number of rows to span. The default setting for each of these parameters is 1.

Defining Headings for Cells

In addition to displaying a table caption, you can include headings for a table's data cells. The tag for defining a heading looks very similar to the **<TD>** tag:

```
<TH ALIGN=left|center|right
    VALIGN=top|middle|bottom|baseline
    NOWRAP
    COLSPAN=number
    ROWSPAN=number>
text</TH>
```

Using Forms

The HTML features presented so far correspond with traditional publishing practices: You create a hypermedia document, and others read it. With HTML forms, however, you can do much more. You can create a form that lets your readers search a database using any criteria they like. Or you can create a form that lets them critique your Web pages. Or—and this is what excites business people—you can use forms to sell things over the Internet.

Forms are easy to create. However, to use them, you'll need a program that runs on your Web server to process the information that the user's client sends back to you. For simple things like a "comments page," you can probably use an existing program. For anything more complex, you'll probably need a custom program. While we will briefly describe the way form data looks to the receiving program, any discussion of form programming is beyond this book's scope.

<FORM> ... </FORM> Tag

All input widgets—text boxes, check boxes, and radio buttons—must appear within a **<FORM>** tag pair. When a user clicks on a submit button or an image map, the contents of all the widgets in the form will be sent to the program that you specify in the **<FORM>** tag. HTML widgets include single- and multi-line text boxes, radio buttons and check boxes, pull-down lists, image maps, a couple of standard buttons, and a hidden widget that might be used to identify the form to a program that can process several forms.

Within your form, you can use any other HTML elements, including headers, images, rules, and lists. This gives you a fair amount of control over your form's appearance, but you should always remember that the user's screen size and font choices will affect the actual appearance of your form.

While you can have more than one form on a page, you cannot nest one form within another.

The basic format for the **<FORM>** tag is as follows:

```
<FORM ACTION="URL"
     METHOD=get|post>
text</FORM>
```

Notice that text can be included as part of the form definition.

Form Action and Method Attributes

Nothing gets sent to your Web server until the user presses a Submit button or clicks on an image map. What happens then depends on the **ACTION**, **METHOD**, and **ENCTYPE** parameters of the **<FORM>** tag.

The ACTION parameter specifies which URL the form data should be sent to for further processing. This is most commonly in the cgi-bin directory of a Web server. If you do not specify an action parameter, the contents will be sent to the current document's URL.

The **METHOD** parameter tells how to send the form's contents. There are two possibilities here: Get and Post. If you do not specify a method, Get will be used. Get and Post both format the form's data identically; they differ only in how they pass the form's data to the program that uses that data.

Get and Post both send the forms contents as a single long text vector consisting of a list of WidgetName=WidgetValue pairs, each separated from its successor by an ampersand. For example:

```
"NAME=Tony Potts&Address=aapotts@coriolis.com"
```

(Any & or = sign in a widget name or value will be quoted using the standard ampersand escape; any bare "&" and any "=" sign can therefore be taken as a separator.) You will not necessarily get a name and value for every widget in the form; while empty text is explicitly sent as a WidgetName= with an empty value, unselected radio buttons and check boxes don't send even their name.

Where Get and Post differ is that the Get method creates a "query URL," which consists of the action URL, a question mark, and the formatted form data. The Post method, on the other hand, sends the formatted form data to the action URL in a special data block. The Web server parses the query URL that a Get method creates and passes the form data to the form processing program as a command line parameter. This creates a limitation on form data length that the Post method does not.

Currently, all form data is sent in plain text. This creates a security problem. The optional **ENCTYPE** parameter offers a possible solution, which only allows you to ratify the plain text default. In the future, however, values may be provided that call for an encrypted transmission.

Widgets

From a users' point of view, there are seven types of Web widgets; all of them are generated by one of three HTML tags. Except for the standard buttons, all widgets must be given a name.

<INPUT> Tag

The **<INPUT>** tag is the most versatile, and the most complex. It can create single-line text boxes, radio buttons, check boxes, image maps, the two standard buttons, and the hidden widget. It's somewhat like the **<IMG>** tag in that it appears by itself, not as part of a tag pair, and has some optional parameters. Of these, the **TYPE=** parameter determines both the widget type and the meaning of the other parameters. If no other parameters are provided, the **<INPUT>** tag generates a text box.

The format for the **<INPUT>** tag is:

```
<INPUT TYPE="text"|"password"|"checkbox"|"radio"|"submit"|"reset"|"hidden"|"image"
    NAME="name"
    VALUE="value"
    SIZE="number"
    MAXLENGTH="number"
    CHECKED>
```

The **TYPE** parameter can be set to one of eight values. We'll look at each of these options shortly. Each input must contain a unique name defined with **NAME**. The **VALUE** parameter specifies the initial value of the input. This value is optional. The **SIZE** parameter defines the size of a text line and **MAXLENGTH** is the maximum size allowed for the returned text.

Text Boxes

If the **TYPE=** parameter is set to text (or no parameter is used), the input widget will be a text box. The password input type is just like the text type, except that the value shows only as a series of asterisks. All text areas must have a name. Text areas always report their value, even if it is empty.

Check Boxes and Radio Buttons

Check boxes and radio buttons are created by an **<INPUT>** tag with a checkbox or radio type. Both must have a name and a value parameter, and may be initially checked. The name parameter is the widget's symbolic name, used in returning a value to your Web server, not its onscreen tag. For that, you use normal HTML text next to the **<INPUT>** tag. Since the display tag is not part of the **<INPUT>** tag, Netscape check boxes and radio buttons operate differently from their dialog box kin; you cannot toggle a widget by clicking on its text, you have to click on the widget itself.

Radio buttons are grouped by having identical names. Only one (or none) of the group can be checked at any one time; clicking on a radio button will turn off whichever button in the name group was previously on.

Check boxes and radio buttons return their value only if they are checked.

Image Maps

Image maps are created with the **TYPE=**"image" code. They return their name and a pair of numbers that represents the position that the user clicked on; the form handling program is responsible for interpreting this pair of numbers. Since this program can do anything you want with the click position, you are not restricted to rectangular anchors, as with **<IMG ISMAP>**.

Clicking on an image map, like clicking on a Submit button, will send all form data to the Web server.

Submit/Reset Buttons

The submit and reset types let you create one of the two standard buttons. Clicking on a Submit button, like clicking on an image map, will send all form data to the Web server. Clicking on a Reset button resets all widgets in the form to their default values. These buttons are the only widgets that don't need to have names. By default, they will be labeled Submit and Reset; you can specify the button text by supplying a VALUE parameter.

Hidden Fields

A hidden type creates an invisible widget. This widget won't appear onscreen, but its name and value are included in the form's contents when the user presses the Submit button or clicks on an image map. This feature might be used to identify the form to a program that processes several different forms.

<TextArea> ... </TextArea> Tag

The **<TEXTAREA>** tag pair is similar to a multi-line text input widget. The primary difference is that you always use a <TextArea> tag pair and put any default text between the **<TEXTAREA>** and **</TEXTAREA>** tags. As with **<PRE>** blocks, any line breaks in the source file are honored, which lets you include line breaks in the default text. The ability to have a long, multi-line default text is the only functional difference between a **TEXTAREA** and a multi-line input widget.

The format for the **<TEXTAREA>** tag is:

```
<TEXTAREA NAME="name"
          ROWS="rows"
          COLS="cols"> </TEXTAREA>
```

<SELECT> ... </SELECT> Tag

The **<SELECT>** tag pair allows you to present your users with a set of choices. This is not unlike a set of check boxes, yet it takes less room on the screen.

Just as you can use check boxes for 0 to N selections, or radio buttons for 0 or 1 selection, you can specify the cardinality of selection behavior. Normally, select widgets act like a set of radio buttons; your users can only select zero or one of the options. However, if you specify the multiple option, the select widget will act like a set of check boxes, and your users may select any or all of the options.

The format for the **<SELECT>** tag is:

```
<SELECT NAME="name"
        SIZE="rows"
        MULTIPLE>text/option list</SELECT>
```

Within the **<SELECT>** tag pair is a series of **<OPTION>** statements, followed by the option text. These are similar to **<LI>** list items, except that **<OPTION>** text may not include any HTML markup. The **<OPTION>** tag may include an optional selected attribute; more than one option may be selected if and only if the **<SELECT>** tag includes the **MULTIPLE** option.

For example:

```
Which Web browsers do you use?
<SELECT NAME="Web Browsers" MULTIPLE>
<OPTION>Netscape
<OPTION>Lynx
<OPTION>WinWeb
<OPTION>Cello
</SELECT>
```

For more information on creating HTML documents, go to the following World Wide Web sites:

A Beginner's Guide to HTML
http://www.ncsa.uiuc.edu/General/Internet/WWW/HTMLPrimer.html

The HTML Quick Reference Guide
http://kuhttp.cc.ukans.edu/lynx_help/HTML_quick.html

Information on the Different Versions of HTML
http://www.w3.org/hypertext/WWW/MarkUp/MarkUp.html

Composing Good HTML
http://www/willamette.edu/html-composition/strict-html.html

HTML+ Specifications
http://info.cern.ch/hypertext/WWW/MarkUp/HTMLPlus/htmlplus_1.html

HTML Specification Version 3.0
http://www.hpl.hp.co.uk/people/dsr/html3/CoverPage.html

HTML Editors
http://akebono.stanford.edu/yahoo/Computers/World_Wide_Web/HTML_Editors/

Resources for Converting Documents to HTML
http://info.cern.ch/hypertext/WWW/Tools/Filters.html

An Archive of Useful HTML Translators
ftp://src.doc.ic.ac.uk/computing/information-systems/www/tools/translators/

Appendix C

Using the CD-ROM

All of the Delphi form, code, and data files you'll need to compile and run all the projects in this book are present on the companion CD-ROM. This book is intended for use with Delphi 2.0 under Windows 95 or Windows NT. Most of the techniques will work with Delphi 1.0 under Windows 3.x also.

We've also included some media to use for testing the projects in the book. You'll find some stuff in the \clips directory and also in the \media directory.

Be sure to check out the demo programs in \demos. These are commercially available DirectX components for Delphi 2.0.

In the \shareware directory you'll find some WaveMix code translated to Delphi units and some Internet shareware OCXs.

The DirectX stuff that you need to distribute DirectX applications is located in the \gdk directory. The setup program used for the companion CD-ROM uses the DirectX installer in this directory.

Using the Companion CD-ROM

This CD-ROM is Autoplay enabled so under Windows 95 just put the CD-ROM in the drive and wait a couple of seconds. You'll get the option to install all of the project files to your hard drive, install shortcuts for the project executables and demo programs, or install DirectX to your computer.

Anything that you install with the companion CD-ROM's setup program can be easily undone with the add/remove programs icon in the Windows 95 control panel.

If you are using this book with Windows 3.x, just access the project files from the directory \projects on the CD-ROM.

Index

A

Aliasing, audio, 679
Anchor, hypertext, 36
 data structure, 139
And raster operation, 361, 615
Animation, 593–624. *See also* sprites
 bitmap, 103–134, 135–184
 cell, 594–602
 current technology, 674
 direction of movement, 618-619
 double buffering, 625
 flicker-free, 625
 masks, 618
 random movement, 649
ANSIChar type, 234
ANSIString type, 240, 567
API (Application Programming Interface)
 Application.ProcessMessages, 279
 BitBlt, 335
 bitmap constants, 362
 callbacks, 766
 color access, 299–319
  AnimatePalette, 317, 322
  PC_RESERVED flag, 318
  CreatePalette, 308
  CreateSolidBrush, 309
  GetSystemPalette Entries, 307, 310
  palette manipulation, 306
  SelectPalette, 308
  SetPaletteEntries, 311
  TLogPalette record, 299
  TPaletteEntry record, 299
 CreateDIBitmap, 359
 CreatePolygonRgn, 488
 CreatePolyPolygonRgn, 488
 CreateRectRgn, 403
 flag parameters, 226
 GetDC, 307
 GetPrivateProfileString, 765
 GetTickCount, 370
 LoadFromFile method, 330
 mciExecute, 10, 213, 215, 220
 midiIn functions, 768
 midiInClose, 771
 midiInGetDevCaps, 770
 midiInGetNumDevs, 770
 midiInOpen, 770
 midiInReset, 771
 midiInStart, 771
 midiInStop, 771
 Multimedia, 219–222
 PostMessage, 780
 RGB, 294
  return value, 295
 ROP code calculations, 362
 SetBkMode, 402
 SetTextAlign, 54
 StretchDIBits, 672
 VCL support, 10
 WaveFormatString, 694
 Windows 95, 788
 wrapper, 255
Application Programming Interface. *See* API
Application-Modal display, 431
Array, open, 137
Audio
 aliasing, 679
 CD. *See* redbook audio
 digital. *See* digital audio
 MIDI. *See* MIDI
 PCM format. *See* PCM
 redbook. *See* redbook audio

825

waveform. *See* waveform audio.
Automatic type conversion
   to **pchar**, 240
AVI files
   playing, 213, 219

B

Base class, 89
Baseline, digital audio, 700
BDE (Borland Database
      Engine), 460, 463, 467
   adding records, 470
   alias, 467
   database navigation, 470
   Edit method, 470
   field objects, 467
   First method, 470
   GotoKey method, 470, 473
   Insert method, 470
   Next method, 470
   Post method, 470
   Prior method, 470
   SetKey method, 470, 472
   table objects, 467
   table, creating, 467–469
   TBLObField, 463
   virtual record buffer, 470
Bit masks
   bitwise operations, 693
   waveform output device, 691
BitBlting ... (Project), 337–338
   event handling code, 338
BitBtn control
   caption, centering, 401
   Glyph bitmap, 400
   invisible hotspot, 398–402
Bitmap constants, API, 362
Bitmaps, 284. *See also* raster operations
   animation, 593–624, 616, 625–674.
       See also sprites
   BitBlt (API), 335
   block transfer function (**BitBlt**), 335
   combining, 360–363

   dimensions, 599
   displaying, 330
   dissolving, 374
   loading, 290
   masks, 614
      creating, 614, 624
      implementing, 615
   multiple, displaying, 290
   Pattern Brush, 346
   structure, 353
   TBitmapInfo record, **354**
   TBitmapInfoHeader record, **354**
   transparent, 614
   TRGBQuad record, **354**
Bitwise operations
   bit masks, 693
   comparison, 693
   flags, 246
   shift, 694
   pixels, 361
Blob. *see* **TBLObField**
Blt Animation (Project), 608–619
   Usprite2 unit, 610
Bounding rectangles, 54, 409
Browser I: Bringing Images ...
      (Project), 543–571
   <IMG> tag, 546
   DispBuf unit, **558**
   HTML unit, **547**
   images
      loading, 551
      storing, 551
   Main unit, **567**
   PicList unit, **551**
Browser II: Surf's Up! (Project),
      572–588
   DispBuf unit, **580**
   Internet file access, 573–580
   Internet unit, **574**
   Main unit, 585–588
Browsers, hypermedia, 29. *See also*
      web browser
Building a Bitmap (Project), 347–363
   urops2 unit, **349**

C

Callback functions, 766
  DLL, 777
  interrupt-driven processes, 777
  parameters, 780
  PostMessage (API), 780
  time-stamp, 766
Callbacks, Windows. *See* callback functions, window message callbacks
Canvas object, 80
  BitBlt (API), 336
  clipping rectangle, 401
  CopyRect method, 336, 401
  and device context, 54
  Draw method, 556
  ellipse method, 328
  PenPos method, 51
  SetTextAlign, 54
  StretchDraw method, 556
  TextHeight method, 52
  TextWidth method, 51
Captions, centering, 401
Carriage-return/linefeed, 155
Casting, multiple
  global memory, 780
  variant record, 780
cDIB unit
  TDIB class, **652**
Cel (celluloid) animation, 602
Cell animation, 594–602
Changing Colors ... (Project), 300–311
  upalexp2 unit, **302**
Character sets, 150
Characters
  formatting values, MS Windows, 75
  named, 151
  ordinal values, range checking, 152
Child controls, 20
Chunk IDs, 248
Chunks
  data chunk, finding, 266
  fccType data field, 263
  locating, in RIFF files, 250

parent and child, 262
reading with **mmioDescend**, 250
RIFF files, 248
structure, 262
WAV files, 251
Client rectangle, 54
Clipping rectangle, 401
Color
  API access functions, 299–319
  pen property, **pmNot** mode, 333
Color modes
  dissolve, 373
  palettized dissolve, 392
Color palette. *See* palette
Color property, 295
Color representation, 285
  black and white, 330
  byte order, 318
Color resolutions, 284–287
Color table, 354
Colors. *See also* palette
  changing, 329
    in palettized dissolve, 386
  complementary, 416
  inverted, **pmNot** pen, 415
  inverting, 335
  non-static, 289
  RGB components, 285
  static, 287, 294
Command-Message Interface
  flags, 246
  mciSendCommand, 212, 242–248
  Play message, MCI_PLAY, 244
Command-String Interface
  mciSendString, 212, 235–242
Compact disc, audio. *See* redbook audio
Compiler directives {$R}, 317
  {$C}, 777
Compiler options
  string data types, 241
Constants, declaration, 72
Control: Creating Hotspots ... (Project), 396–404
  Main unit, **398**

Controls, Delphi, 13. *See also* individual control names
  as hyperlinks, 38
  BitBtn, 398–402
  Button, 394
  DragMode property, 764
  Edit, 38
  hotkeys, 23
  Image, 39
  leap-frogging, 493
  MediaPlayer, 17, 22
  Memo, 38
  Paint Box, 39
  Panel, 20
  parent and child, 20
  Rich Edit, 38
  Status Bar, 544
  Timer, 20
Cross-casting, 53
cSprite unit, **634**
  ConvertBitmapToSprite, 662
  TPosition record, **638**
  TSprite class, **634**, **657**

D

Data chunk
  finding, 266
  WAV files, 251
Data structures, 84
Database
  basic functions, 469
  indices, 471
  navigating, 470
DC (device context), 284
  Canvas property, 54, 298
  font display, 80
DC (display context), 284
  logical palette, 286
DDB (device dependent bitmap), 285
  creating, 359
Delphi
  base class, 89
  BDE (Borland Database Engine), 464
  controls, 13. *See also* controls, Delphi

DirectX components, 728
equivalent classes, cross-casting, 53
event procedures, 14
events, 13
FastGraph libraries, 674
forms, 13
functions, 12, 14
Graphics unit, 295
hyperlinks, 38
MediaPlayer component, 17
methods, 15
MMSystem unit, 226
object, 63
pointer operations on **pchar**s, 48
procedures, 14
properties, 13
resource-protection block, 99
result identifier, 257
scoping rules, 16
ShowModal method, 431
SysUtils unit, 214
typecasting, 53
units, 15
Delphi MIDI Piano (Project), 754–766
  keyboard, 755
  Piano unit, **758**
Destinations, hypertext, 36
  labels, 218
  named anchors, 201
Device context. *See* DC
Device, multimedia, 231, 275
Device-dependent bitmap. *See* DDB
Device-independent bitmap. *See* DIB
Dialog box control, 428–432
DIB (Device Independent Bitmap), 356–360
  scanline, 354
  structure, 353. *See also* bitmaps, structure
  TBitmapInfo record, **354**
  TBitmapInfoHeader record, **354**
  TRGBQuad record, **354**
DIB (device-independent bitmap), 285
DIB32c unit, **387**
Digital audio, 678–680

Index

echo effect, 700–704
volume control, 696
DirectSound audio mixer, 704–728
    buffers, 727
    features, 705
    implementing, 713
    testing, 725
DirectX components, 728
Dirty rectangle, 626
    calculation, 645
    effect on draw time, 650
DispBuf unit, 90–124, 161–168, **161**, 185–201, **185**, **513**, **538**, **558**, **580**
    Break_into_lines, **109**, 112–118
    Image, **502**
    overview, 91
    Parse_HTML, 103, 104, 502
    Start_new_line, 118
    tDisplay_buffer class, 93–124
Display, true-color vs. palettized, 285, 334
    true-color vs. palettized, 285, 334
Display context. *See* DC
Dissolve, palettized. *See* palettized dissolve
Dissolving images, 363–392, 374
DlgLoad unit, **426**
    TList_select_dialog class, **426**, 428
DLL (Dynamic Link Library)
    callback functions, 777
    {$C} compiler directive, 777
Document
    displaying, 55, 59–62
    opening, 59
Double buffering, 644
DragOver event, 764
DSWrap unit, **713**
    TDSBuffer class, **713**
    TDSound class, **713**

E

Echo effect, 700–704
    8-bit vs. 16-bit, 704
    analog, 701
    memory requirements, 703
    stereo vs. mono, 704
    trailing echoes, 703
Edit control, 38
Editor, hotspot. *See* hotspot editor
Edstrom, Arthur
    (Artic Software, Inc), 755
EParseError exception, 138
ERangeError exception, 152
Error handling
    in **Parse_tag**, **156**
    Load_error_message, 574
    web browser, 574
Error trapping
    in **mciSendString**, 238
    mmio functions, 252
Event handlers
    components, 765
    windows messages, 771
Event procedures, 14
Events, 13
Execution control, 232, 247
Explore the Grand Canyon (multimedia adventure), 33
External routines, 229

F

FastGraph for Windows (Ted Gruber Software), 674
Field objects, 467
File I/O, 59
File pointer, positioning, 250, 261
File retrieval, Internet, 573–580
First Dissolve (Project), 363–374
    udslvexp unit, **366**
Flags
    API, 226
    bitwise operations, 246
    Command-Message Interface, 246
    mmio, 256, 263, 264, 268
    palette entry, 300, 316, 318
    SND values, 227
    system alert, 220
Flicker Free Sprite Animation ...

(Project), 627–650
   cSprite unit, **634**
   uSprite4 unit, **628**
Flip Book (Project), 594–602
   event handling code, 600
   ucellani unit, **595**
Fmt chunk, 251
FmtText unit, **82**, 85–88,
   tFormatted_text class, **82**, 86–87
   tFormatted_text_list class, **82**, 87
Font unit, 74–82, **76**, 174–175
   Measurement_of, **81**
   Set_font_from_spec, **78**
   tHTML_format record, **82**
   tText_measurement record, **80**
Fonts
   dimensions, 52
   characteristics, measuring, 79–82
   HTML, vs. Windows fonts, 78
Forms, resizing, 60–62, 505, 566
Format specification, HTML, 219
FOURCC substructure, 249
Functions, 14
   capping, 255
   declaration, 72

G

GDI (Graphic Device Interface), 283
   CreatePolygonRgn, 455
   DeleteObject, 422
   GDI32, 219
   GetTextExtentPoint, 79
   GetTextMetrics, 79–82
   PtInRegion, 458
   regions, 403, 412
   TTextMetric record, **80**
Global memory, casting, 780
Glyph bitmap, 400
Graphic Device Interface. *See* GDI
Graphics unit, 295

H

Handles, 54

Hardware palette
   changing colors, 329
   RGB values, changing, 322
High-resolution timer, multimedia, 766
History list, 583–585
Horizontal rules, displaying in HTML
   document, 165
Hotlinks, highlighting, 39
Hotspot editor. *See also Hotspot I,*
   Hotspot II, Hotspot III
   designing, 406
   rectangles, drawing, 415
   user interface, 417
Hotspot I: ... Basic Hotspot Editor
   (Project), 404–443, 404
   DlgLoad unit, **426**
   drawing hotspots, 414
   hotspot records
      retrieving, 425
      storing, 409
   Hotspots unit, **407**
   hotspots
      deleting, 436–437
      drawing, 414
      loading, 435
      outlining, 412–416
   image files, loading, 419
   Image_link_file, 411
   Main unit, **437**
   menu events, 417–437
      File | Delete Hotspot, 436–437
      File | Edit Saved Hotspot, 434–436
      File | New Hotspot, 421
      File | Save Hotspot, 423
      Mode | Define, 422
      Mode | Test, 422
   menu system, 416
   mouse event handlers, 413
Hotspot II: ... Irregularly-Shaped Images
   (Project), 446–459
   Main unit, **448**
   polygons. *See also* polygons
      drawing, 453–457
      redrawing, 457
      starting, 459

Index 831

Hotspot III: ... (Irregular) Hotspot Editor
　(Project), 460–488
　hotspot database, 467
　Hotspot unit, **464**
　loading hotspots, 472
　Main unit, **480**
　menu events
　　File | Delete, 478
　　File | Edit, 478
　　File | New, 477
　　Mode | Define, 477
　menu events, 477–480
　polygonal hotspots
　　drawing, 473–475
　　representing and storing, 462,
　　　470–471
　　TBLOBField, 468
　user interface, 476
Hotspots
　coordinates, document vs.
　　window, 168
　detection, 168
　drawing, 414
　in images, 393–444
　invisible
　　BitBtn control, 398–402
　　Image control, 398
　　Label control, 396
　　PaintBox control, 398
　loading, 525
　locating in database, 473
　polygonal, 462, 468, 470–471,
　　473–475
　storing in database, 470–471
　tRegion class, 529
Hotspots unit, **407**, **464**
　Clear_hotspot, **407**, 408
　Load_hotspot_record, **408**, 409
　Save_hotspot_record, **407**, 409
　tHotspot_record, **408**, **463**
HTML tags
　<> (comments), 796
　<A> 218, 810
　　arguments, 183
　　HREF= parameter, 810
　　structure, 158

<ADDRESS>, 815
<B>, 800
<BASE>, 813
<BLINK>, 800
<BLOCKQUOTE>, 815
<BODY>, 796

, 217, 798
<CENTER>, 800
<EM>, 799
<FONT>, 800
<FORM>, 818
<HEAD>, 795
<Hn>, 217, 801
<I>, 800
<IMG>, 498, 546, 806
　ALT= parameter, 807
　SRC= parameter, 807
<INPUT>, 819
<LI>, 801
<NOBR>, 799
<OL>, 802
<P>, 799
<PRE>, 815
<SELECT>, 821
<TABLE>, 816
<TEXTAREA>, 821
<TITLE>, 797
<UL>, 803
<WBR>, 799
HTML (Hypertext Markup Language),
　33, 66, 793–822
　character set, extended, 151
　document structure, 795
　documents. *See also*
　　HTML documents
　editors, 794
　fonts, 78
　horizontal rules, displaying, 165
　keywords, optional switches, 137
　language, 793–822
　paragraph tags, multiple, 105
　parsing, 94
　　case sensitivity, 137
　　expression, end of, 137
　　HREF tag, 158

Index

line breaks, multiple, 115
  single word, 106
  linefeed character, 155
special characters, processing,
  151–155
string, scanning, 104
tags, 66. *See also* HTML tags
  effect on formatting, 67
  formatting, 219
  identifying, 157
  parsing, 133
  processing, 104
  special characters, 144
  terminating tag, 217
text
  formatted, 108–120
  preformatted, 198, 199
whitespace, 106
HTML documents
  address block, 796
  author's information, 796
  blinking text, 800
  body, 796
  bold text, 800
  centered text, 800
  character attributes, 799
  comments, 796
  emphasized text, 799
  font size, 800
  formatting specs, 219
  forms, 817
  header, 795
  headings, 801
  images, borders, 809
  inline images, 806–810
  italic text, 800
  line breaks, 798
  links, 810–812
  lists, 801–806
  multiple images, 808
  paragraph, 796, 799
  special characters, 814
  structure, 795
  tables, 815
  title, 797

  URLs, 812
  widgets, 819
  word breaks, 799
HTML unit, **145**, **176**, **511**, **547**
  HTML tags, parsing, 155–160
  Parse_A_tag, 159, **179**, 183
  Parse_end_A_Tag, **184**
  Parse_IMG_tag, **501**, **547**, 549
  Parse_tag, 156, 501, 553, **178**
    error handling, 156
  Process_special_character,
    153, **177**
  Process_tag, 157, **181**
  special characters, interpreting, 151
  Special_character_from, **152**
  Special_character_of, **145**, 151
  tHTML record, **500**
  tHTML_format record, 155,
    547, 549
HTTP (HyperText Transport
  Protocol), 574
Hyper I: Basic Formatted Text …
  (Project), 67–129
  DispBuf unit, 90–124
  event handling code, 124–129
  FmtText unit, 82–88
  Font unit, 74–82, **76**
  Main unit, 124–129, **124**
  MiscLib unit, 71–74
  MiscLib unit, **71**
Hyper II: Bringing HTML … (Project),
  131–169
  DispBuf unit, 161–168, **161**
  HyperLnk unit, **140**
  HTML unit, **145**, 150–160
  Parser unit, 133–138
Hyper III: A finished Hypertext…
  (Project)
  DispBuf unit, 185–201, **185**
  font capabilities, 174
  Font unit, 174–175
  HTML tags, 171
  HTML unit, **176**
  Main unit, **202**, 206–209,
Hyper IV: Plugging in… (Project),
  213–219

Hyperlinks, 29–33. *See also* hotlinks
  anchors, 36
  associating mouse clicks with, 142
  data structures, 138–142
  to files, 202
  to named destinations, 201, 208, 218
  underlining, 159
  URLs, 206
  using **Button** controls, 394
HyperLnk unit
  tNamed_rectangle_list class, **140**, 138–144
Hypermedia, 28–29
Hypertext, 29
  links, types of, 36
  loading and displaying, 127–129
  scrolling, 208
Hypertext Markup Language. *See* HTML

I

Identity palette, 289, 383
IDirectSound class, **711**
IDirectSoundBuffer class, **712**
  Lock, 724
  Unlock, 724
Image control
  AutoSize property, 19
  hotlinks, highlighting, 39
  in hypertext system, 39–41
  Stretch property, 523
Images. *See also* bitmaps
  <IMG> tag, 498
  adding hotspots, 393–444
  dissolving, 346, 360, 363–392, 374. *See also* palettized dissolve
    color modes, 373
    mixing pixels, 361
  embedded in document, 499
  loading, 525, 532
  polygonal hotspots, 459
  Reference_anchors rectangle list, 498
  scaling, 523–525

  in web browser
    displaying, 555
    embedded, 546
    inserting, 554
    loading, 551, 580
    positioning, 556
    storing, 551
ImgPanel unit, 520–523
  Load_image, **525**
  Set_image_in_panel, 520, **521**
  Stretch_panel_on_image_in_rect, **522**, 523–525
Internet access. *See* HTTP
Internet file retrieval, 573–580
  HTTP, default file, 579
Internet unit, **574**
  Get_file, **576**, 579
Interrupt driven processes, 766
  callback functions, 777
ipp_HTTP constant, 579

L

Leading, internal, 52
Linked lists, 85
Links, mappable, 30
LIST chunks, 252
List_select_dialog control, 428-432
  DlgLoad unit, **426**
Logical palette, 286, 288

M

Magic I: Basic Image ... (Project), 492–517
  DispBuf unit, 502–504, **513**
  HTML unit, 500–502, **511**
  Main unit, 504
Magic II: Images with Hotspots ... (Project), 518–540
  DispBuf unit, **538**
  ImgPanel unit, 520–523
  Main unit, 535–538
  RgnList unit, **526**

Index

Main unit, **55**, 206–209, **202**, **448**, **480**, 504, 535–538, **567**, 585–588
Able_to_get_word_from, 46, 47–49
Clear_for_new_image, **410**, 412
Delete_region, 421, 422, **452**
Display, **50**
Dist, **452**
Have_new_poly, **474**
Init_for_new_poly, **458**, **475**
Jump_to, 207, 214, 496, 532, **535**, 566, **568**, 584, **586**
Load_HTML, 127, **579**
Load_new_HTML, 128
Set_scrollbar, 208
TForm1 class, **55**, 124–27, 398–400
Vertex_finishes_polygon, **455**
Marquee Lights ... (Project), 322–330
   event handling code, 322–330
Umarquee unit, **323**
Mask, bitmap, 614, 624
MCI (Media Control Interface), 211, 231–248. *See also* Command-Message Interface, Command-String Interface
   Delphi encapsulation, 17
   execution control, 232
   mciExecute, 213, 215
   mciGetErrorString, 242
   mciSendCommand. *See* **mciSendCommand**
   mciSendString. *See* **mciSendString**
   mciSetYieldProc, 232
   MessageBeep, 220, 224
   sndPlaySounds, 225–229
   MCI_WAIT flag, 232
MCI Play I: ...with MessageBeep (Project), 222– 224
   Message_beep_button_click, **223**
MCI Play I: ...with SndPlaySound (Project), 224–228
   Play_sound_buttonClick, **228**
MCI Play II: Playing ... with mciSendString (Project), 235–242
MCI Play II: Playing ...with mciSendCommand, 242–248
MCI Play III: Playing ... with Low-Level Functions, 253–281
   Adding Low-Level Playback, 279
   MMIOWrap unit, **257**
   WavePlay unit, **269**
   WaveWrap unit, **272**
mciExecute, 10, 213, 215, 220
MMSystem unit, **229**
mciSendCommand, 242–248
   device type parameters, 246
mciSendString, 233, 234, 240–242
   callback message, 242
   return string, 241
MCI_CLOSE message, 247
MCI_OPEN_ ELEMENT flag, 246
MCI_OPEN_TYPE flag, 246
MCI_PLAY message, 244
MCI_WAIT flag, 247
Media Control Interface. *See* MCI.
Media Player, Windows, 3
MediaPlayer control, 17, 22
Memo control, 38
Menu events. *See* Hotspot I, Hotspot II
Message handlers, 772
Messages. *See* events
Messages, MIDI
   channel mode messages, 739–740
   channel voice messages, 736–739
   chronological precision, 785
   receiving, 766
   structure, 736
   system messages, 740
Methods, 15
   declaration, 72
   overriding, 89, 90
   replacing, 89
   virtual, 90
Microsoft
   Games SDK, 674, 711
   MSCDEX.EXE CD driver, 677
   WaveMix, 705
   WinG technology, 674

Index

MIDI (Musical Instrument Digital Interface), 677, 732–786
  devices, 734
  hardware, 734, 743
  MCI Play II, 235–242
  messages, 677, 735–741. *See also* messages, MIDI
  multimedia functions, 744
  network, 734
  PC sound cards, 744
  ports, 734
  premature exit, 768
  sequence, 734
  standards, 741
  synthesizer modules, 735
  synthesizers, 734
  vs. waveform audio, 677
  Windows API functions, 743, 750
    midiOutClose, 751
    midiOutOpen, 751
    midiOutShortMsg, 751
  Windows 95, 747
    Base-Level synthesizers, 748
    Extended-Level synthesizers, 748
MIDI files, playing, 213, 219
MIDI Mapper, Windows,
  Key Maps dialog box, 744
  MIDI Setups dialog box, 746
  Patch Maps, 744
MidiCBU unit, **778**, 779
  MidiShortMessage record, **778**, 780
MidiInFm unit
  TMidiInForm class, **772**
MidInFm2 unit
  TMidiInForm class, **781**
MIDI_MAPPER constant, 751
MidOutFm unit, **752**, 754
  TMidiOutForm class, **752**
MIME encoding, 151
MiscLib unit, 71–74
  implementation, **73**
  interface, **73**
Mixing Audio ... (Project), 704–728
  DirectSound interface, 710
  DSCAPS record, 718

DSWrap unit, **713**
IDirectSound class, **711**
IDirectSoundBuffer class, **712**
udstest unit, 725
mmio functions, 250–269
  error checking, 252
  mmioDescend, 250, 262
  mmioRead, 264
  TMMCKInfo record, 250
MMIOWrap unit, **257**
  eMMIO_error class, **260**
MMIO_FINDCHUNK flag, 264, 268
MMIO_FINDRIFF flag, 263
MMIO_READ flag, 257
MMM files, playing, 213
mmsyst keyword, 229
MMSystem unit
  data structures, **243**
  mciSendString, 233, 234
  sndPlaySound, 226, 229
  TMCI_Open_Parms record, **244**
  TMCI_Wave_Open_Parms record, **243**
  TMMCKInfo record, **248**
  TPCMWaveFormat record, **265**
  TWaveFormat record, **265**
  TWaveFormatEx record, **265**
  TWaveHdr record, **269**
Modal display, 431
Moving Pictures (Project), 17–22
  Timer Event Procedures, **21**
Multimedia
  feedback, 475
  high-resolution timer, 766
  multithreading, 789
  system requirements, 35
  Windows API, 219–222
Multimedia chunk information. *See* **MMSystem** unit, **TMMCKInfo** record
Multimedia i/o functions. *See* **mmio** functions
Multimedia the Delphi Way (Project), 22–25
Multithreading, 14
  multimedia, 789

Windows 95, 789
Musical Instrument Digital Interface.
See MIDI

N

Name anchor, 36
Named characters, 151
Not raster operation, 361
Not pen, 333, 335
Null rectangles, 409

O

Object, 63
OCX (OLE controls)
    installing, 571
    magic numbers, 578
    TTC Socket custom control, 573
    wrappers, 578
    wrapping, 571
OLE controls. *See* OCX
OpenDialog1 control (Windows), 418
Or raster operation, 362, 614

P

Paint Box control
    document, displaying, 59–62
    hotlinks, highlighting, 39
    in hypertext system, 39–41
    text, positioning, 54
Palette
    changing entries, 311
    hardware
        changing colors, 329
        RGB values, 322
    identity, 289, 383
    loading, 295
    logical, 286, 288
    management, 283–319
    manipulation, 306
    realizing, 288
    shared, 288–289
    system, 287, 288
    non-static entries, 289
    static entries, 287
Palette Aware Dissolve (Project), 374–392
    DIB32c unit, **387**
    uDissolv unit, **376**
Palette Manager, Windows, 287–290
Palette property, 295
Palette shifting, 392
Palettized display, 285
Palettized dissolve, 374–392, 385
    color modes, 392
    palette shifting, 392
Panel control, 20, 493
    dimensions, 504
Parent chunk, 261
Parent controls, 20
Parser unit
    TParser class, 133–138, **134**
PATPAINT operation, 342
Pattern Brush bitmap, 346
pchar type, 47
    automatic type conversion, 240
    pointer operations, 48
PCM (Pulse Code Modulation)
    MMSystem unit, 265
    principles, 678
    waveform data storage formats, 697
PC_EXPLICIT flag, 300
PC_NOCOLLAPSE flag, 289
PC_RESERVED flag, 316, 318, 327, 383
PenPos method, 51
Piano unit, **758**
    TPianoForm class, **758**
PicList unit
    tPicture_list class, **551**
Pixels
    boolean operations, 361
    changing colors, 286
    color values, changing, 386
    coordinate system, 284
    mixing, 333, 361
Playing ... Wave Data (Project), 680–704
    TWaveOutCaps record, **690**

uWave2 unit, **683**
Playing Multimedia with a Few...
    (Project), 10–12
pmNot pen, 333, 335, 415
Pointers treated as integers, 114
Polygonal hotspots
    drawing, 473–475
    representing and storing, 462
Polygons
    closing, 454
    complex, 456
    drawing, 453–457
    redrawing, 457
    representation, 453, 465, 468
    starting, 459
Port, default (HTTP), 574
Preemptive multitasking,
    Windows 95, 789
Preformatted text, 185–201
Procedures, 14
    declaration, 72
Programming environment, visual, 7
Projects. *See also* individual project
        names
    A Palette Aware Dissolve, 374–392
    BitBlting—Delphi's simple solution,
        337–338
    Blt Animation, 608–619
    Browser I: Bringing Images Inside,
        543–571
    Browser II: Surf's Up!, 572–588
    Building a Bitmap, 347–363
    Changing Colors in the Logical
        Color Palette, 300–311
    Control: Creating Hotspots with
        Assorted Controls, 396–404
    Flicker Free Sprite Animation with
        Delphi Objects, 627–650
    Hotspot I: Creating a Basic Hotspot
        Editor in Delphi, 404–443
    Hotspot II: Drawing Irregularly-
        Shaped Images, 446–459
    Hotspot III: The Powerful (Irregular)
        Hotspot Editor, 460–488
    Hyper I: Basic Formatted Text
        Display, 67–129

Hyper II: Bringing HTML to Life,
    131–169
Hyper III: A finished Hypertext
    Engine, 169–209
Hyper IV: Plugging into the High-
    Level MCI, 213–219
Magic I: Basic Image Support,
    492–517
Magic II: Images with Hotspots—A
    Finished Presentation Engine,
    518–540
Marquee Lights with Palette
    Animation, 322–330
MCI Play I: Playing WAV Files with
    MessageBeep, 222–224
MCI Play I: Playing WAV Files with
    SndPlaySnd, 224–228
MCI Play II: Playing MIDI Files with
    mciSendString, 235–242
MCI Play II: Playing WAV Files with
    mciSendCommand, 242–248
MCI Play III: Playing WAV Files
    Using Low-Level Functions,
    253–281
Mixing Audio and Beyond, 704–728
Moving Pictures, 17–22
Multimedia the Delphi Way, 22–25
Playing and Modifying Wave Data,
    680–704
Playing Multimedia with a Few...,
    10–12
Receiving MIDI Messages, 767–775
Receiving Time-Stamped MIDI
    Messages, 775–785
Selecting Colors by Numbers,
    296–300
Sending MIDI Messages, 750–754
Sprite and Mask Maker, 620–624
Sprite Animation from the Ground
    Up, 651–673
Sprites Over Easy, 603–607
The Delphi MIDI Piano, 754–766
The First Dissolve, 363–374
The Flip Book, 594–602
The Standard Windows Raster

Operations, 338–343
Using AnimatePalette() to Edit the Palette, 300–311
Using the MCI to Record Wave Audio, 728–731
Using the RGB() Function, 291–296
When is a Pen a "Not Pen," 331–335
Word Wrap: Basic Text Handling..., 43–62
Properties, 13
    protected, 53
protected keyword, 53
Pulse Code Modulation. *See* PCM

R

Range checking, 358
    compiler directive, 317
Raster operations, 331, 333
    AND, 361, 615
    binary, 333–335, 614
    hexadecimal representation, calculating, 362
    OR, 362, 614
    PATPAINT, 342
    SRCAND, 615
    SRCPAINT, 614
    static colors, 335
    XOR, 362
    ternary, 340, 342–343
Receiving MIDI Messages (Project), 767–775
    event handlers, 771
    MidiInFm unit, **772**
    MidInFm2 unit, **781**
Recordings, embedded (Windows), 5
Rectangles
    drawing, 411
    erasing, 414
    storing, 408
Redbook audio, 676
    MSCDEX.EXE CD driver (Microsoft), 677
    Windows [MCI] CD Audio driver, 677

Reference anchor, hypertext, 36
Regions
    CreateRectRgn (GDI), 403
    PtInRegion (GDI), 403
Resource Interchange File Format. *See* RIFF
Resource management, 383
Resource-protection block, 99, 308
result identifier, 257
RGB components, 285
RgnList **unit**, **526**
    tRegion class, **529**
    tRegion_list class, **530**
RichEdit control, 38
RIFF chunk, 248
    form type, 261
    WAV file, 251
RIFF files
    file pointer, positioning, 250
    locating chunks, 250
    low-level MCI functions, 248
    mmio functions, 250
    navigating, 250
    parent chunk, 261
Routines
    declaration, 72
    external, 229

S

Sampling, digital, 679–680
Scanline, device independent bitmap, 354
Scoping rules, Delphi, 16
Scroll bar, managing, 208
SDK (Software Development Kit). *See* Microsoft, Games SDK
Selecting Colors ... (Project), 296–300
    upalexp1 unit, **297**
Sending MIDI Messages (Project), 750–754
    MidOutFm unit, **752**
SGML (Standard Generalized Markup Language, 794
ShortString type, 240

SND flag values, 227
Sockets, 573, 579
    ipp_HTTP constant, 579
    ports, 574
Sound Recorder, Windows, 5
sound, SystemDefault
Special characters, 151
Springing, 505
Sprite and Mask Maker (Project), 620–624
    Umakemsk unit, **621**
Sprite Animation ... (Project), 651–673
    cDIB unit, **652**
    cSprite unit, **657**
    uSprite5 unit, **663**
Sprites, 614
    animation, 607, 618, 625–674
        direction of movement, 641
        double buffering, 644
        random movement, 649
    moving, 606
Sprites Over Easy (Project), 603–607
    Usprite unit, **604**
Standard ... Raster Operations (Project), 338–343
Status Bar control, 544
    SimplePanel property, 546
stdcall keyword, 233
Stream objects
    TMemoryStream class, 59, 472
    TBLOBField, 472
String, null-terminated, 47
String data types, 240–241
    ANSIString, 501
    default type, 501
    compiler options, 241
Synthesizers, 734, 737, 738
System alert flags, 220
System palette, 287
    raster operations, 335
System sounds registry, 220
SystemDefault sound, playing, 221
System-Modal display, 431
Systems Advisory Group Enterprises (DirectX components), 728

SysUtils unit
    ExtractFileExt, 214
    StrLen, 47

T

Table objects, 467
Tags. *See* HTML tags
Target, hypertext, 36
tAudio_Waveform class
    Play, **275**, **277**, **279**
    Read, 724
TA_BASELINE constant, 54
TA_UPDATECP constant, 54
TBLObField, 463
    LoadFromStream, 472
    SaveToStream, 472
    storing polygonal hotspots, 468
    stream objects, 472
TColor type, 295, 299
tDIB class, **387**
    Create_IdentPal256, **391**
tDisplay_buffer class, 93–124
    Add_buffer_to_list, **102**, **198**
    Break_into_lines, **163**, 166, **191**, 200, 555, 557, **559**
    Buffer data structure, **101**
    Display, 120–124, **120**, 503, **516**, 555, **564**
    Emit, **103**
    Image, **554**
    interface, **94**, **553**, **556**
    Horizontal_rule, **165**
    Line_after, **124**
    Line_list record, 114
    Load_HTML_file, 95–100
    New_line, **103**, **198**
    Parse_HTML, **186**, 199–201, **561**
    Process_HTML_string, **101**
    Reset_buffer, **102**
    Set_format, **103**
    Start_new_line, **163**, 167
TDSBuffer class, **713**, 717
    InitFile, **723**
TDSound class, **713**, 717

Init, 715
Ted Gruber Software (FastGraph for Windows), 674
Text
   baseline, 54
   current pen position, tracking, 54
   formatted, 82
      tFormatted_text class, 86–87
      tFormatted_text_list class, 87
   line dimensions, 113
   measuring, 78–82
   parsing, 46–49
   preformatted
      destination anchors, named, 201
      lines, measuring, 200
   preformatted, support for, 185–201
   scrolling, 208
TextHeight method, 52
TextWidth method, 51
TForm1 class, **55**, **398**
   Back_buttonClick, **567**
   Button1Click, 11
   Button_OnClick, **395**
   FilenameKeyPress, **128**
   FormClose, **411**, **458**
   FormCreate, **60**, **129**, 400–402, **411**-412, **457**, 504, **509**, **533**
   FormDestroy, 534
   FormMouseDown, **413**-414, **454**, **474**
   FormMouseMove, 414, **456**, **473**
   FormMouseUp, **413**, 415
   FormPaint, **457**
   FormResize, **61**, 506, **510**, 534, **537**, **565**
   Image1MouseDown, **533**
   Line, **453**
   Open_buttonClick, **59**, **128**
   OptFile_DeleteClick, **478**
   OptFile_DeleteHotspotClick, **433**, 436–437
   OptFile_EditClick, **478**
   OptFile_EditHotspotClick, 433-434
   OptFile_LoadPicture, **418**, 419
   OptFile_NewClick, **459**, **477**
   OptFile_NewHotspotClick, **421**
   OptFile_QuitClick, **459**
   OptFile_SaveHotspotClick, **423**
   OptMode_DefineClick, **421**, **477**
   OptMode_TestClick, **421**-422
   PaintBox1MouseDown, **207**
   PaintBox1MouseMove, **566**
   PaintBox1Paint, **60**
   Scrollbar1Change, **209**
   SendCommand_buttonClick, 244–248
   SendString_buttonClick, 239
   SpeedButtonClick, **338**
   WaveOut_buttonClick, **280**
tFormatted_text class, **82**
   Create, 86
   Create_direct, **87**
   Destroy, 87
   interface, **86**
tFormatted_text_list class, **82**, 85
   Break_at, **87**
   Destroy, 88
TGraphicControl class, 53
tGraphicControlWithCanvas class, **53**
tHotspot_table class
   Establish, 468
   Load, **466**, 473
   Save, **465**
Timer control, 20
Time-Stamped MIDI Messages (Project), 775–785
   MidiCBU unit, **778**
TList class, 85
TListBox class
   Add, 430
   Sorted property, 430
Tlist_select_dialog class, **426**
   Add, 430
   Destroy, 430
   Execute, **431**
   FormCreate, 430
TMain class, 382–387, **628**, **663**, **683**, **729**

Index   841

btnOpenClick, 721
Button1Click, 600, **648**
CreateCheckBrush, **355**, 356–360
FormCreate, **323**, **352**, **382**, 598, 647, 717
FormDestroy, **353**
FormPaint, **327**
lstROPSClick, **341**
mnuEEchoClick, **701**, 703
mnuEVolClick, **698**-699
mnuFGetCapsClick, **692**
mnuFOpenClick, **695**
MoveSprite, 606
sbDissolveClick, **370**, **383**, 385
Timer1Timer, **323**, 600
TMemoryStream class, 59, 472
   Memory property, 60
   Seek, 472
   Size property, 60
   Write, 472
TMidiInForm class, **772**, **781**
   FormCreate, 769
   StartStopButtonClick, 770
TMidiOutForm class, **752**
   SendMessageButtonClick, 753
tMMIO_file class
   Ascend, 267
   Close, 260
   Descend, 261
   First_descend, 262
   Open, 256
   Read, 264
tNamed_rectangle_list class, **140**, 138–144
   First_rect_of_name, **143**
   Name_of_point, **142**
Tobject class, 89
   Free (assembler version), **89**
Toupin, Edward *(OCX developer)*, 571
TPalEdit class
   FormCreate, 306
   FormDestroy, 308
   MakePalette, 311
   PaletteFromDesktop, 307
   pbPaletteMouseDown, 309

pbPalettePaint, 308
pnlColorClick, 310
TrackBarChange, 311
TPalMain class
   FormActivate, **297**, 298
TParser class, 133–138, **134**, **136**, 156
   case sensitivity, 137
   Error, **137**, 138
   exception handling, 138
   Expect, **135**, 137
   Expect_one_of, **135**, 137
   Find, 138
   No_errors, **137**, 138
   Raise_errors, **137**, 138
   Remainder, **136**, 138
TPianoForm class, **758**
   Panel2DragDrop, **763**
   Panel2DragOver, **763**
   ReadPatch, **761**, 765
tPicture_list class, **551**
tRegion class
   Create, 529
   Destroy, 529
   interface, **529**
tRegion_list class, 526–529
   Add, 530
   Add_regions_for, **528**, 531
   interface, **530**
   Target_reference_of, **531**
TRGBMain class
   TrackbarChange, **294**
TRGBQuad record, 318
   multiple, 358
True-color display, 285
try...except statement, 152
try...finally statement, 99
try...finally...end statement, 308
TSprite class, **634**, 638–641, 662
   properties, 639
   ReadBitmapFile, **636**, 641
TTable object
   FieldDefs.Add, 467
   IndexDefs.Add, 467
   properties, 467
TTC Connectivity Custom Controls

package (Edward Toupin), 571
TTC Socket custom control (OCX), 573
TTextMetric record, **80**
tWave_device class, **272**, 275–279
    Open, **276**
    Prepare_header, **276**
    TWaveHdr record, **269**
    Unprepare_header, **277**
    Write, **278**
Type declaration, 72

U

ucellani unit, **595**
    ShowCell, **601**
    TCellAnim record, **597**
uDissolv unit, **376**
    AnimateInterPal, **386**
    CreateDeltaPaletteVals, **385**
    TMain class, **376**
udslvexp unit, **366**
    CreateDissolveBrush, 365, **371**, 372
    TMain Class, **366**
    waitmil, **370**
udstest unit, 725
    DisplayCaps, **718**
Umakemsk unit, **621**, **624**
    ConvertImageToMask, **623**
    ConvertImageToSprite, **623**
Umarquee unit, **323**
    DrawMarquee, **327**
    TMain class, **323**
Unicode characters, 234
Units, Delphi, 15, 72–74
    implementation section, 73–74
    initialization section, 72
    interface section, 72–73
Unotpen unit
    TMain class, **332**
Untyped **var** parameter, 455
upalexp1 unit
    TPalMain class, **297**
upalexp2 unit
    TPalEdit class, **302**

upalexp3 unit
    TPalEdit class, **311**
URL (Uniform Resource Locator), 206
    HTTP:// prefix, 591
    parsing, 591
    optional :*port* argument, 579
    web browser, 579
urops2 unit
    TMain class, **349**
uses clause, 72
Using AnimatePalette() ... (Project), 300–311
    upalexp3 unit, **311**
Using the MCI to Record ... (Project), 728–731
    uwavercd unit, **729**
Using the RGB() Function (Project), 291–296
    TrackbarChange event, **294**
    uTestRGB unit, **292**
Usprite unit, **604**
Usprite2 unit, **610**
    DrawMoth, **617**, 619
    MoveMoth, **616**
    TSprite record, **615**
uSprite4 unit, **628**
    DrawMoth, **641**, 644–646
    MoveMoth, **648**
    TMain class, **628**
uSprite5 unit
    DrawMoth, **669**, 671
    TMain class, **663**
uTestRGB unit
    TRGBMain class, **292**
Uudecode, 151
Uuencode, 150
uWave2 unit, 690–704
    TMain class, **683**
uwavercd unit
    TMain class, **729**

V

var parameter, untyped, 455
Variable, declaration, 72

Index   843

VCL (Visual Class Library), 73
    Windows API, support for, 10
Virtual methods, 90
Visual environment, 7

W

WAV files
    chunks, 248
    compressed, 281
    data chunk, 251
        reading, 266–269
    extended waveform format
            structure, 266
    fmt chunk, 251
        reading, 263–266
    formats, 266
    header management, 276
    LIST chunks, 252
    locating, 220
    playback, 213, 219, 220, 272–281
        synchronous vs.
                asynchronous, 227
        asynchronous, 247
        Command-Message Interface, 244
    reading and processing, 256–269
    RIFF chunk, 263
    size, 268
    structure, 248–253, 251
    system sounds, locating, 220
    TPCMWaveFormat vs.
            TWaveFormatEx, 266
Waveform audio, 675–731, 678. See
        also digital audio, DirectSound
        audio mixer, *MCI Play II*, *MCI
        Play III*
    aliasing, 679
    changing amplitude, 696, 699, 700
    data structure, 268
        data storage formats (PCM), 697
    digital representation, 679
    echo effect, 700–704
    file
        loading, 696, 722
        playing, 696
    output device bit masks, 691

    real-time effects, 704
    representation, 679. *See also* PCM
    sampling, 679–680
        baseline, 700
    sound buffer, creating, 722
    stereo sound, representation, 680
    volume control, 696
        16-bit, 700
        8-bit, 699
    vs. CD audio, 678
    wave headers, 269
    wave format constant notation,
            691, 694
waveOutOpen, 275
waveOutPrepareHeader, 276
waveOutUnprepareHeader, 276
WavePlay unit, **269**
WaveWrap unit,
    tWaveDevice class, **272**, 275–279
WAVE_FORMAT_QUERY flag, 275
WAVE_MAPPER constant, 276
Web browser
    back button, 567
    default port, 579
    design, 542
    embedded images, 546
    error handling, 574
    form, resizing, 566
    history list, 583–585
    HTTP, 574
    images
        displaying, 555
        inserting, 554
        loading, 551, 580
        positioning, 556
        storing, 551
    Internet access, 574
    Internet file retrieval, 573–580
    URLs, 579, 591
    user interface, 542
When is a Pen a "Not Pen" (Project),
        331–335
    Unotpen unit, **332**
WideChar type, 234
Window message callbacks, 766

Windows 95
   32-bit development environment, 787–792
      API calls, 788
   flat 32-bit addressing, 791
   MIDI, 747
   Multimedia System, 2, 211
   multiple input queues, 790
   multi-threading, 14, 789
   operating system, 219
   preemptive multitasking, 789
   text-based application support, 790
   virtual memory, 791
   WinG, 674
windows messages, event handlers, 771
Windows, Microsoft
   non-preemptive multihanging, 279
   API. *See* API (Application Programing Interface)
   bounding rectangle, 54
   callbacks. *See* callbacks, Windows
   character formatting values, 75
   client rectangle, 54
   Common Controls, 418
   GDI. *See* GDI (Graphics Device Interface)
   hypermedia, 394
   identity palette, 289, 383
   messages. *See* events
   [MCI] CD Audio driver, 677
   MIDI Mapper, 744
   multimedia API, 219–222. *See also* **mmio** functions
   Multimedia System, 2
   OpenDialog1 control, 418
   Palette Manager, 287–290
   resource allocation, 308
   Sound Recorder utility, 5
   system palette, 287
WinG (Microsoft), 674
WINMM.DLL services, 220
WinProc procedure, 6
Word Wrap: Basic Text Handling... (Project), 43–62
   Main unit, **55**

X

XOr raster operation, 362
XOr pen, 335

Z

Z-order, 288
Z-string, 47

JAVA • VB • VC++ • DELPHI • SOFTWARE COMPONENTS • OCX, DLL

VISUAL DEVELOPER
magazine

Give Yourself the Visual Edge

Don't Lose Your Competitve Edge Act Now!

1 Year $21.95
(6 issues)

2 Years $37.95
(12 issues)

($53.95 Canada; $73.95 Elsewhere)
Please allow 4-6 weeks for delivery
All disk orders must be pre-paid

Create OLE Clients and Servers in VB4!

VISUAL DEVELOPER magazine

3D Universes
Creating Software That Adds a Dimension

Animated Screen Savers in Delphi

The Windows 95 Taskbar Tray

http://www.coriolis.com

The first magazine dedicated to the Visual Revolution

Join Jeff Duntemann and his crew of master authors for a tour of the visual software development universe. Peter Aitken, Al Williams, Ray Konopka, David Gerrold, Michael Covington, Tom Campbell, and all your favorites share their insights into rapid application design and programming, software component development, and content creation for the desktop, client/server, and online worlds. The whole visual world will be yours, six times per year: Windows 95 and NT, Multimedia, VRML, Java, HTML, Delphi, VC++, VB, and more. *Seeing is succeeding!*

1-800-410-0192

See *Visual Developer* on the Web! http://www.coriolis.com

7339 East Acoma Dr. Suite 7 • Scottsdale, Arizona 85260

WEB • CGI • JAVA • VB • VC++ • DELPHI • SOFTWARE COMPONENTS

Developing Custom Delphi Components

Teaches you how to easily create components through subclassing, or create all-new components from scratch

Only $39.99

Call 800-410-0192

Fax (602) 483-0193

Outside U.S.: 602-483-0192

This book with CD-ROM gets you up to speed with Delphi's new Object Pascal object model, and takes you through the development process of many different kinds of components. You'll build, debug, and test components, and learn the skills you'll need to become a star Delphi component creator. Included in the book are Object Pascal example code, a full suite of ready-to-use components, and more.

CORIOLIS GROUP BOOKS

http://www.coriolis.com

Visual Basic 4 Programming EXplorer

Step-by-step instructions for creating commercial-quality applications

Only $39.99

Call 800-410-0192

Fax (602) 483-0193

Outside U.S.: 602-483-0192

This book takes you inside the powerful new features of VB 4 including the data object model, OLE objects and servers, OCX controls, 32-bit programming, and much more. You'll get up to speed quickly with VB 4, and learn about a number of useful VB and Windows programming techniques including text processing, graphics, file access and management, serial communications, and multimedia.

CORIOLIS GROUP BOOKS

http://www.coriolis.com

Coriolis Group World Wide Web Home page

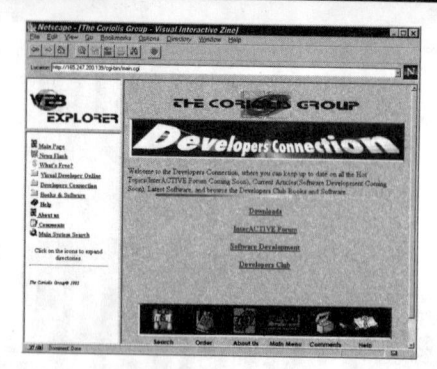

Delphi EXplorer—An incredible resource for Delphi programmers. Includes: commercial demos, dozens of shareware controls, sample code, articles, and two complete chapters from *Delphi Programming Explorer* by Jeff Duntemann, et al.

Explore the Grand Canyon—Take a Web wide view of this incredible new multimedia package produced by the Coriolis Group. Read the press releases, learn about amazing new NetSeeker technology, and view a few of the thousands of images from the software!

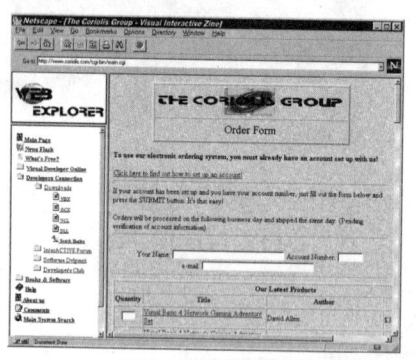

Online Ordering—Set up an account with the Coriolis Group and you can order all of your programming books over the Web. And not just Coriolis Group Books, you can order any of the books from our Developer's Club catalog!

Come visit us at:
http://www.coriolis.com